P9-COO-865

The 100 Most Popular Young Adult Authors

The 100 Most Popular Young Adult Authors

Biographical Sketches and Bibliographies

Revised First Edition

Bernard A. Drew

1997
Libraries Unlimited
A Division of Greenwood Publishing Group, Inc.
Englewood, Colorado

LIBRARIES UNLIMITED
A Division of Greenwood Publishing Group, Inc.
P.O. Box 6633
Englewood, CO 80155-6633
1-800-237-6124
www.lu.com

Production Editor: Kevin W. Perizzolo
Editorial Assistant: Shannon Graff
Proofreaders: Jason Cook and Judy Gay Matthews
Typesetter: Kay Minnis

Library of Congress Cataloging-in-Publication Data

Drew, Bernard A. (Bernard Alger), 1950-
The 100 most popular young adult authors : biographical sketches and bibliographies / by Bernard A. Drew. -- 1st ed. rev.
xxviii, 531 p. 19x26 cm.
Includes bibliographical references and indexes.
ISBN 1-56308-615-8
1. Young adult literature, American--Bio-bibliography. 2. Young adult literature, English--Bio-bibliography. 3. Authors, American--Biography--Dictionaries. 4. Authors, English--Biography--Dictionaries. I. Title.
PS490.D74 1997
810.9'9282--dc21
[B] 97-25882
CIP

To my sister, Marlene L. Drew,
a librarian who has learned
to shelve the discomfort,
file away the injustice,
catalogue the joys,
and keep on reading.

Contents

Introduction

The 100 Most Popular Young Adult Authors Revised First Edition is a ready reference source for teenagers looking for information about fiction writers for research papers or other reports. Those interested in learning about other titles by favorite writers or curious to find authors they may not be familiar with should also find this book handy. It may aid teachers in selecting authors for assignments or librarians in choosing titles for their shelves.

The compiler subscribes to the American Library Association designation of young adults as those in the age group twelve to eighteen, or attending junior high school and up. Publishers, bookstores, and librarians at times blur school grade and age lines in marketing or shelving young adult works. Readers, too, often ignore categories: After all, a good story is a good story, for any age.

Thus, a few of the authors presented in this book may hover at the sixth-grade end of the young adult range. Ann M. Martin and Betsy Byars, typically, write a lot for middle readers. This is balanced by the inclusion of a sampling of writers who intend their work for older readers but also are sought out by young adults. Among these are V. C. Andrews, Piers Anthony, Stephen King, and Anne McCaffrey.

The book could easily have included 200 authors. Selections were made with guidance from more than a dozen librarians, writers, and booksellers across the country, and with suggestions from the publisher. With a few exceptions, the emphasis is on authors who are very much active in the 1990s.

Louisa May Alcott, Jack London, Lucy Maud Montgomery, and Mark Twain are from an earlier generation of writers and are included because of the continued popularity of their books, the universality of their themes, and recent adaptations of some of their works into movies or television programs.

J. R. R. Tolkien, author of *The Hobbit*, inspired a generation of fantasy and young adult writers.

J. D. Salinger's *The Catcher in the Rye*, similarly, is a classic that struck a resounding note with a vast number of readers and influenced many young adult writers. The author is still living but no longer writing for publication.

Carolyn Keene and Franklin W. Dixon—who exist only as publishing house names created by Edward Stratemeyer—are listed because the Nancy Drew and Hardy Boys mysteries continue to appeal to a wide audience. The earliest staff writers behind these pseudonyms are included.

This reference also includes popular writers within categories such as ethnic (black, Native American, and Hispanic writers), geographic (Canadian, Australian, New Zealander, Irish, and British writers), and thematic (spiritual, humorous, and historical writers).

Since the 1970s, when young adult writers first ascended to create their own category of literature and began receiving critical attention, many novelists have concentrated on social, family, and coming-of-age themes. If there is a trend in the 1990s, it is, thanks to Stephen King, horror-suspense fiction. Thus such writers as Christopher Pike and R. L. Stine, warlocks of young adult chills, are included in this guide, as are spellbinders Caroline B. Cooney and Richie Tankersley Cusick.

Each entry begins with a few quick facts about the writer: name (or pen name); place of birth; date of birth; date of death (if no longer living); the author's main category (or categories) of fiction; and the title (or titles) of the author's best-known works or series.

Entries offer brief author biographies. They point out the important or better-known of the author's books and include critical commentary from a variety of sources. Where possible, they give comments by the writers themselves about the writing process. Bibliographies list all young adult fiction works by the authors, with title, year of issue, and (for novels) a brief plot encapsulation. These plot annotations are as complete as possible, given deadline constraints and resources available. Some of the authors' other fiction works, as well as dramas, screenplays, and poetry, are listed without annotations. Movies and television adaptations are noted, as are books edited by the author and books to which the author contributed. Also included are suggestions for further reading about the writers and their works. Complete and detailed indexes are included in this edition.

BERNARD A. DREW
Great Barrington, Massachusetts

Joan Aiken

Fantasy

Rye, Sussex, England
September 4, 1924
The Wolves of Willoughby Chase

Her father was a writer. A stepbrother and a sister became writers. So there was little doubt of Joan Aiken's future profession.

The third child of Pulitzer Prize–winning poet Conrad Aiken and his Canadian wife, Jessie McDonald Aiken, Joan Aiken saw little of her father when she was growing up. Her parents had divorced when she was young. In her twenties, she often fought with him, but she came to love him in her forties, before his death in 1973.

After the divorce, her mother remarried, and Aiken was taught at home until finances allowed her to attend boarding school. She went to Wynchwood School in Oxford at age twelve.

Aiken grew up with few people around. She was a loner at school. As a teen, she frequently disobeyed rules. In 1941, when she was still a teenager, one of her stories was broadcast on the British Broadcasting Corporation's (BBC) *Children's Hour.* As she attempted to publish more writing, however, more stories were returned with rejection letters.

Aiken worked as a clerk for the BBC from 1941 to 1943. She worked for St. Thomas' Hospital in London in 1943. She was secretary and librarian for the United Nations Information Office in London from 1943 to 1949. In 1945, she married Ronald George Brown, with whom she had two children. Brown died in 1955. Aiken married Julius Goldstein, an American painter, in 1976.

Aiken was features editor for *Argosy* magazine from 1955 to 1960. She was advertising copywriter for the J. Walter Thompson Advertising Agency in London in 1961. She left to become a full-time writer. In 1988, she was writer-in-residence at Lynchburg College.

Aiken wrote her first novel over a period of several years. "*The Wolves of Willoughby Chase* was one of those flashes," she told interviewer Catherine Courtney. "The book was based on exaggeration—the heroine didn't have one silk petticoat, she had twenty; the rich were terribly rich, and the misfortunes were dire, and so on. The book wrote itself really—that trite phrase!"

Of *The Wolves of Willoughby Chase*, said Mary Cadogan and Patricia Craig, "The Gothic mood predominates. . . . The principal girls in this story, Bonnie and Sylvia, are spirited but uninspired. . . . They lack the sheer perverse charm of the back-chatting urchin Dido Twite, whose appearance (in *Black Hearts in Battersea*) is unheralded by the conventional build-up for a heroine."

"These are stories of eye-defeating speed and complexity which carry the reader breathlessly onward from page to page," said John Rowe Townsend. "There is no time to stop and consider probabilities; and indeed any writer of a rapid-action adventure story, even without the open license which Joan Aiken has written for herself, faces less exacting standards of probability than does the realistic novelist."

"The main strength of *The Wolves of Willoughby Chase* sequence," observed David Rees, "is the breath-taking improbabilities of the plots. . . . As far as the heroes and heroines of these books are concerned, the girls are usually more convincing than the boys."

Wolves quickly grew into a series of books. In the second, *Black Hearts in Battersea*, the impish Dido Twite "nearly runs away with the story by sheer brash, scrawny vitality," said Michele Landsberg. She "speaks in a cheerfully invented version of cockney: 'Brush on, cullies,' she urges her comrades in derring-do on a listing ship, 'The ship's betwaddled . . . you *are* a loblolly.' Dido, with her rowdy appreciation of 'ripsmasher' and 'slumdigger' moments of excitement, is softened by the friendship offered by fifteen-year-old Simon, the sturdy, sensible, good-hearted sort of hero who is most at home in a fairy tale."

One sequel, *Nightbirds on Nantucket*, was inspired by Aiken's father's house on Cape Cod. She had planned to stop writing about Dido Twite after *Black Hearts* but was persuaded by a young letter writer's plea to continue writing about the character.

Of her writing, Aiken told Courtney, "I have to know the whole structure of a book before I begin. I like to start with a title because I find that if a whole book gets written and it still doesn't have a title, then you're really in trouble. My elder sister [Jane Aiken Hodge] writes serious historical novels for which she does an awful lot of research. She pretty well starts with a blank page, sits down at the typewriter and lets fly. I'd begun writing nonsense history novels for children, set in an imaginary period, and then became interested in writing *Midnight Is a Place* set in the Industrial Revolution."

"I make a chart of what's going to happen," Aiken explained to interviewer Stan Nicholls. "I don't necessarily follow it, but it relieves me to know it's there. I sometimes write the last page, or sentence, so I've a target to aim at. I like to write a short story in one session if I can. Finishing a piece in a single sitting gives it a sort of unity which otherwise it can never achieve."

Among her favorites are her Felix Brooke titles: *Go Saddle the Sea, Bridle the Wind*, and *The Teeth of the Gale*. Felix, she told Nicholls, "was to some extent taken from life. I saw a BBC-TV program called *Lifeline*, about a little boy who was a pyromaniac, and so dangerous he had to be shut up in an institution. It showed him at home with his family, and he was saying very stoically that, yes, he understood he would have to be put away for many years. Two tears stole down his cheeks. He seemed such a marvelous and interesting character I felt I must do something with him. So I wrote about a boy who's forced to be strait-laced by his family, because they don't understand him, and he has to get away from them. I was so fond of the character I went on to do two more books about him."

Writing for young readers is not easy, Aiken said to Nicholls. "You have to be much more careful and selective and put things across instantly, because children easily become bored. And humour is one of the most difficult things of all. People who can do it, like the late Roald Dahl, are worth their weight in gold."

"Really good writing for children should come out with the force of Niagara," Aiken said in Virginia Haviland's *Children and Literature*. "It ought to be concentrated; it needs to have everything that is in adult writing squeezed into a smaller compass. I mean that both literally and metaphorically: in a form adapted to children's capacities, and at shorter length, because of this shortage of reading-time. But the emotional range ought to be the same, if not greater; children's emotions are just as powerful as those of adults, and more compressed, since children have less means of expressing themselves, and less capacity for self-analysis."

Aiken has written in genres other than young adult fiction. She wrote *The Five-Minute Marriage* as a spoof of Georgette Heyer historical romances. She wrote pastiches of works by Jane Austen such as *Mansfield Revisited* (a sequel to Austen's *Mansfield Park*), and she wrote mysteries.

She cited many influences: "Victor Hugo impressed me as a child," she told Nicholls. "My mother read me *Les Miserables* in translation when I was seven or eight. Certain scenes from that, such as Jean Valjean's rescue of little Cosette from the evil Thenardiers and the sequences in the Paris sewers and in the galleys, were very impact-making. It's a book I've gone back to, over and over." Of contemporary writers, she said she enjoys Dick Francis mysteries. "I like them because he has such a strong sense of goodness and moral value."

YOUNG ADULT FICTION

All You've Ever Wanted, and Other Stories (1953)

More Than You Bargained For, and Other Stories (1955)

The Kingdom and the Cave (1960)
Mickle, the palace cat; Prince Michael; and Minewa, the wise old mare, search for the Underpeople.

A Necklace of Raindrops, and Other Stories (1968)

The Whispering Mountain (1968)
In the Welsh town of Pennygaff, many are interested in the Golden Harp of Teirtu.

Night Fall (1969)
Meg's dream—a horrible face swinging before her eyes—comes more and more often.

A Small Pinch of Weather, and Other Stories (1969)

Armitage, Armitage, Fly Away Home (1970)
This is the first zany adventure of Harriet and Mark, a unicorn and an evil lizard.

Smoke from Cromwell's Time, and Other Stories (1970)

All and More (1971)

The Kingdom Under the Sea, and Other Stories (1971)
Short stories of mermaids and witches.

A Harp of Fishbones, and Other Stories (1972)

The Escaped Black Mamba (1973)

All but a Few (1974)

The Bread Bin (1974)

Midnight Is a Place (1974)
Lucas hopes for a companion to share his adventures at Midnight Court, seat of the Grinsby family.

Not What You Expected: A Collection of Short Stories (1974)

A Bundle of Nerves: Stories of Horror, Suspense, and Fantasy (1976)

The Faithless Lolybird (1977)

The Far Forests: Tales of Romance, Fantasy, and Suspense (1977)

Mice and Mendelson (1978)
Short stories.

Tale of a One-Way Street, and Other Stories (1978)

A Touch of Chill: Tales for Sleepless Nights (1979)

The Shadow Guests (1980)
Haunted by the mysterious disappearance of his mother and older brother in Australia, Cosmo Curtoys is apprehensive about living in England with his cousin Ernie Doom, a scientist.

A Whisper in the Night: Stories of Horror, Suspense, and Fantasy (1982)

The Kitchen Warriors (1984)
Short stories.

Up the Chimney Down, and Other Stories (1984)

The Last Slice of Rainbow, and Other Stories (1985)

Past Eight O'clock: Goodnight Stories (1986)

A Goose on Your Grave (1987)

The Moon's Revenge (1988)
The seventh son of a seventh son, Seppy loves to play fiddle but is destined to be a coach maker.

Return to Harken House (1988); British title: *Voices* (1988)
Has Julie read too many horror novels, or is the house haunted?

The Erl King's Daughter (1989)

A Foot in the Grave (1989)
Ghost stories.

Give Yourself a Fright: Thirteen Tales of the Supernatural (1989)

A Fit of Shivers: Tales for Late at Night (1990)

A Cluster of Separate Sparks (1992)

The Haunting of Lamb House (1992)

The Embroidered Sunset (1993)

Morningquest (1993)

The Shoemaker's Boy (1993)

Simon and Dido Twite Series

The Wolves of Willoughby Chase (1963)
Bonnie, cousin Sylvia, and their friend, Simon, are distrustful of Miss Slighcarp.

Black Hearts in Battersea (1964)
Simon comes to nineteenth-century London to become an artist and meets Dido Twite, who drags him into wild adventures.

Nightbirds on Nantucket (1966)
Dido and Simon take part in Captain Casket's pursuit of the pink whale, Rosie.

The Cuckoo Tree (1971)
Dido Twite and Captain Hughes go to London to deliver a message for the admiralty.

The Stolen Lake (1981)
The ship on which Dido Twite is returning to England from Nantucket is summoned to help the queen of New Cambria.

Dido and Pa (1986)
Pa kidnaps Dido and takes her to London, where the evil Eisengrim is plotting to overthrow King Richard.

Is Underground (1993)
Dido's sister, Is, travels to London in search of their lost cousin, Arun.

Felix Brooke Series

Go Saddle the Sea (1977)
Felix Brooke, starving for affection in his grandfather's loveless household, decides to run away.

Bridle the Wind (1983)
Felix, thirteen, is rescued from a shipwreck off the coast of France, only to be pursued by a ghostly vision.

The Teeth of the Gale (1988)
In the 1820s, Felix de Cabezada y Brooke, eighteen and the only surviving heir to a Spanish count and an English duke, embarks on a rescue mission in war-torn Spain.

CONTRIBUTOR

Sixteen: Short Stories by Outstanding Writers for Young Adults, edited by Donald R. Gallo (1984)

Short Circuits: Thirteen Shocking Stories by Outstanding Writers for Young Adults, edited by Donald R. Gallo (1992)

FICTION FOR YOUNGER READERS

Fog Hounds, Wind Cat, Sea Mice (1984)
Short stories.

Past Eight O'clock: Goodnight Stories (1986)

The Shadow Guests (1980)

Mortimer Series

Arabel's Raven (1972)

Tales of Arabel's Raven (1974)

Mortimer's Tie (1976)

Mortimer and the Sword Excalibur (1979)

The Spiral Stair (1979)

Mortimer's Portrait on Glass (1982)

The Mystery of Mr. Jones's Disappearing Taxi (1982)

Mortimer's Cross (1984)

Mortimer Says Nothing (1985)

A Creepy Company: Ten Tales of Terror (1995)

DRAMA

Winterthing: A Play for Children (1972; first produced in 1970)

The Mooncusser's Daughter: A Play for Children (1973)

Street (1978; first produced in 1977)

Moon Mill (unpublished; first produced in 1982)

POETRY

The Skin Spinners: Poems (1976)

ADULT FICTION

The Silence of Herondale (1964)

The Fortune Hunters (1965)

Beware of the Bouquet (1966); alternate title: *The Trouble with Product X* (1966)

Dark Interval (1967); alternate title: *Hate Begins at Home* (1967)

The Ribs of Death (1967); alternate title: *The Crystal Crow* (1968)

The Windscreen Weepers, and Other Tales of Horror and Suspense (1969); alternate title: *Green Flash, and Other Tales of Horror, Suspense and Fantasy* (1971)

The Butterfly Picnic (1970); alternate title: *A Cluster of Separate Sparks* (1972)

The Embroidered Sunset (1970)

Nightly Deadshade (1971)

Died on a Rainy Sunday (1972)

Voices in an Empty House (1975)

Castle Barebane (1976)

The Five-Minute Marriage (1977)

Last Movement (1977)

The Smile of the Stranger (1978)

The Lightning Tree (1980); alternate title: *The Weeping Ash* (1980)

The Girl from Paris (1982); alternate title: *The Young Lady from Paris* (1982)

Foul Matter (1983)

Deception (1987)

If I Were You (1987)

Blackground (1989)

The Haunting of Lamb House (1991)

A Foot in the Grave (1992)

Sequels to Jane Austen Novels

Mansfield Revisited (1984)
Sequel to *Mansfield Park.*

Jane Fairfax: Jane Austen's Emma, Through Another's Eyes (1990)
Sequel to *Emma.*

Eliza's Daughter (1994)
Sequel to *Sense and Sensibility.*

TRANSLATION

The Angel Inn by Sophie De Segur (1976)

TELEPLAYS

The Dark Streets of Kimballs Green (1976)

The Apple of Trouble (1977)

Midnight Is a Place (1977)
A serial based on Aiken's story.

Armitage, Armitage, Fly Away Home (1978)
Based on Aiken's story.

The Rose of Puddle Fratrum (1978)

ADAPTATIONS IN OTHER MEDIA

Midnight Is a Place (1977)
British television.

The Wolves of Willoughby Chase (1988)
Film starring Stephanie Beacham, Mel Smith, and Geraldine James.

Apple of Discord
Teleplay for British television based on a short story.

The Rose of Puddle Fratrum
Teleplay for British television based on a short story.

FOR FURTHER READING

Aiken, Joan. *The Way to Write for Children.* New York: St. Martin's Press, 1982.

Cadogan, Mary, and Patricia Craig. *You're a Brick, Angela! A New Look at Girls' Fiction from 1839 to 1975.* London: Gollancz, 1976.

Courtney, Catherine. "Joan Aiken." In *Authors & Artists for Young Adults,* edited by Agnes Garrett and Helga P. McCue. Detroit: Gale Research, 1989.

Haviland, Virginia, ed. *Children and Literature: Views and Reviews.* Glenview, IL: Scott, Foresman, 1973.

Jones, Cornelia, and Olivia R. Way. *British Children's Authors: Interviews at Home.* Chicago: American Library Association, 1976.

Landsberg, Michele. *Reading for the Love of It: Best Books for Young Readers.* New York: Prentice Hall Press, 1987.

Nicholls, Stan. "Aiken to Write: The Extraordinary Joan Aiken Is Interviewed." *Million: The Magazine of Popular Fiction,* March–April 1991.

Rees, David. "The Virtues of Improbability: Joan Aiken." *Children's Literature in Education,* spring 1988.

Townsend, John Rowe. *A Sense of Story: Essays on Contemporary Writers for Children.* New York: J. B. Lippincott, 1971.

Louisa May Alcott

Family adventure

Philadelphia, Pennsylvania
November 29, 1832–March 6, 1888

Little Women

Louisa May Alcott was an early writer of realistic stories for young adults. She "attacks the false fronts and manners of people behaving conventionally and making a great show of politeness when they are actually backbiting," in the estimate of Emily Neville. "In Louisa May Alcott's books there is a variety of very short personal descriptions of people and very accurate conversations and detailed descriptions of people, mixed sometimes with very sentimental moralizing."

Alcott was the daughter of philosopher and educator Amos Bronson Alcott and his wife, Abigail. She grew up in Boston and Concord, Massachusetts. She received lessons at home from her father and from neighbors such as essayist Henry David Thoreau, poet and philosopher Ralph Waldo Emerson, and theologian Theodore Parker. The Alcotts had little money, and Louisa and her three sisters were accustomed to hard work around the home.

Alcott took jobs as a teacher, seamstress, and servant. She began to write for publication in 1848. Most of her stories were melodramatic tales that earned her five or ten dollars each. She also edited *Merry's Museum*, a children's magazine.

During the Civil War, she served as an army nurse in Washington, D.C. The experience marred her health, and she had to return home. Sketches written of the hospital in which she served were published and became well known.

Little Women is her best-remembered work. "She found all the material at hand in recollections of her own childhood," said Humphrey Carpenter and Mari Prichard. "Amy, Jo, Beth, and Meg are portraits of the four Alcott sisters, May, Louisa, Elizabeth, and Anna. 'Marmee,' the March children's mother, was copied from Mrs. Alcott, while the failure of Bronson Alcott to provide for his family was recast by Louisa into the March father's having lost all his money 'in trying to help an unfortunate friend.' Laurie, with whom Jo has a warm friendship but whose romantic advances she rejects, was partly suggested by a childhood friend and partly by a young Pole, Ladislas Wisniewski, with whom Louisa had a mild flirtation during her European trip of 1865."

The book's chief attraction, according to Elizabeth Janeway, is "its heroine, Jo, and Jo is a unique creation: the one young woman in nineteenth-century fiction who maintains her individual independence, who gives up no part of her autonomy as payment for being born a woman—and who gets away with it. . . . For this Victorian moral tract, sentimental and preachy, was written by a secret rebel against the order of the world and woman's place in it, and all the girls who ever read it know it."

The March sisters, said Constantine Georgiou, "come alive as nineteenth-century New England girls leading uneventful lives but with roots that run deep into American soil. The lifelike character studies of the March sisters mirror the dilemmas, fun, and pathos of family experience. Sentimentality runs high in this classic story of American girlhood, but it is in keeping with the emotional period when girls first come into contact with this book."

"Thanks to its psychological perceptions, its realistic characterizations, and its honest domesticity, *Little Women* has become an embodiment of the American home at its best," concluded Madeleine B. Stern. "Consciously or unconsciously all subsequent writers who have attempted the domestic novel for children have felt its influence, for in *Little Women* the local has been transmuted into the universal, and the incidents of family life have been translated to the domain of literature."

Despite her popularity as an author, Alcott's life was a sad one. Alcott was single and the sole income provider for her family. Her sister Elizabeth died in 1858. Her mother died in 1877, and her younger sister, May, died the same year, during childbirth.

Most of her later books (after *Little Women*) were intended for younger readers. *Little Men* was based on her nephews and continued the March family story.

An unknown Alcott manuscript titled *A Long Fatal Love Chase* was published in 1995. It was originally written for the magazine *The Flag of Our Union*, but was rejected by the editor. It is a story with a very current theme: Its heroine, eighteen-year-old Rosamund Vivian, is stalked by a former lover.

"Although regarded during much of the twentieth century only as the author of *Little Women*, [Alcott] had a many-faceted personality," said Alma J. Payne. Her "strength lay in her honesty, awareness of the danger of overmoralizing, and in her ability to present a story with a distinctive pattern and an atmosphere in which the common life, its joy or pain or despair, attains a true splendor."

FICTION

Flower Fables (1855)

The Rose Family (1864)

Morning-Glories, and Other Stories (1867)

Aunt Kipp (1868)

Kitty's Class Day (1868)

Psyche's Art (1868)

Three Proverb Stories (1868)

An Old-Fashioned Girl (1870)

Will's Wonder Book (1870)

Eight Cousins; or, The Aunt-Hill (1875)
This is the story of Rose and her seven cousins.

Rose in Bloom: A Sequel to Eight Cousins (1876)

A Modern Mephistopheles (1877)

Under the Lilacs (1877)
Ben and his performing dog, Sancho, along with Babs and Betty, have adventures on Miss Celie's estate.

Meadow Blossoms (1879)

Water Cresses (1879)

Jack and Jill: A Village Story (1880)

Proverb Stories (1882)

Spinning-Wheel Stories (1884)

Lulu's Library (1886)

A Garland for Girls (1888)

Behind a Mask: The Unknown Thrillers of Louisa May Alcott (1975)
Four stories, edited by Madeleine Stern. Reissued with a new afterword in 1995.

Louisa's Wonder Book (1975)

Plots and Counterplots (1976)

A Double Life (1988)

A Long Fatal Love Chase (1995)
Rosamund Vivian, raised by a reclusive grandfather on a remote island during Victorian times, is ensnared in handsome Philip Trent's world of deceit, treachery, and obsessive love.

Little Women Series

Little Women (1868–69)
Beautiful Amy, aspiring writer Jo, musical Beth, and ladylike Meg are the March sisters, growing up in New England.

Little Men (1871)
Jo and her husband, Fritz Bhaer, run the Plumfield School for boys.

My Boys: Aunt Jo's Scrap-Bag (1872)

Shawl Straps: Aunt Jo's Scrap-Bag II (1872)

Cupid and Chow-Chow: Aunt Jo's Scrap-Bag III (1874)

My Girls: Aunt Jo's Scrap-Bag IV (1878)

An Old-Fashioned Thanksgiving: Aunt Jo's Scrap-Bag V (1882)

Jo's Boys and How They Turned Out (1886)
Jo's husband is now president of a college in Plumfield.

Comic Tragedies Written by Jo and Meg and Acted by the Little Women (1893)

Little Women by Laurie Lawlor (1994)
Novelization of the screenplay by Robin Swicord.

ADAPTATIONS IN OTHER MEDIA

Little Women (1918)
Film with Lillian Hall, Dorothy Bernard, Florence Flimm, and Isabel Lamon.

Little Women (1933)
Film starring Katharine Hepburn, Joan Bennett, Jean Parker, and Frances Dee.

Little Men (1934)
Film with Ralph Morgan and Erin O'Brien-Moore.

Little Men (1941)
Film starring Kay Francis and Jack Oakie.

Little Women (1949)
Film featuring June Allyson, Margaret O'Brien, Janet Leigh, and Elizabeth Taylor.

An Old-Fashioned Girl (1949)
Film with Gloria Jean.

Little Women (1978)
NBC television movie with Dorothy McGuire.

Little Women (1979)
Television series sequel to the novel, featuring Dorothy McGuire.

Little Women (1994)
Film starring Winona Ryder, Trini Alvarado, Claire Danes, and Kirsten Dunst.

A Long Fatal Love Chase (1995)
ABC television mini-series.

FOR FURTHER READING

Carpenter, Humphrey, and Mari Prichard. *The Oxford Companion to Children's Literature.* New York: Oxford University Press, 1991.

Gadler, Enrica. "The Thrill of the Chase." *At Random,* fall 1995.

Georgiou, Constantine. *Children and Their Literature.* New York: Prentice Hall Press, 1969.

Janeway, Elizabeth. "Meg, Jo, Beth, Amy and Louisa." In *Only Connect: Readings on Children's Literature,* edited by Sheila Egoff, G. T. Stubbs, and L. F. Ashley. New York: Oxford University Press, 1969.

Johnston, Norma. *Louisa May: The World and Works of Louisa May Alcott.* New York: Four Winds Press, 1991.

King, Stephen. "Blood and Thunder in Concord" (review of *A Long Fatal Love Chase*). *The New York Times Book Review,* 10 September 1995.

Payne, Alma J. "Louisa May Alcott." In *American Women Writers from Colonial Times to the Present: A Critical Reference Guide,* edited by Lina Mainiero. Vol. 1. New York: Frederick Ungar, 1979.

Neville, Emily. "Social Values in Children's Literature." In *A Critical Approach to Children's Literature: The Thirty-first Annual Conference of the Graduate Library School, August 1–3, 1966,* edited by Sara Innis Fenwick. Chicago: University of Chicago Press, 1967.

Saxton, Martha. *Louisa May: A Modern Biography of Louisa May Alcott.* Boston: Houghton Mifflin, 1977.

Smith, Dinitia. "Of Faithful Friends and Alcott Experts." *The New York Times,* 29 August 1995.

Stern, Madeleine B. "Louisa May Alcott." In *Twentieth-Century Children's Writers,* edited by Tracy Chevalier. 3d ed. Chicago: St. James Press, 1989.

———. *Louisa May Alcott.* Norman: University of Oklahoma Press, 1950.

Van Gelder, Lawrence. "Random House to Issue Unpublished Alcott Novel." *The New York Times,* 1 January 1995.

Lloyd Alexander

Historical fantasy

Philadelphia, Pennsylvania
January 30, 1924

Chronicles of Prydain
Westmark Series

"Lloyd Alexander ranks as one of the best writers of high fantasy to emerge since Tolkien, and his five novels comprising the Chronicles of Prydain are true classics of the genre," Marshall B. Tymn has stated.

"Alexander's fantasy is based firmly upon legend, with a multitude of natural and supernatural characters, and some halfway between," explained reviewer Zena Sutherland.

The Chronicles of Prydain tell of Taran, a young hero who, in the course of five tales, rises from assistant pig-keeper to king. Along the way, he and his companions battle and outwit evil princes and enchantresses. Three related books for younger readers feature some of the minor characters from these young adult stories.

The son of a stockbroker and importer and a homemaker, Alexander became an avid reader as a child, though no others in his family were. Favorite books were *King Arthur and His Knights* by Sir Thomas Mallory, *The Wind in the Willows* by Kenneth Grahame, and *David Copperfield* by Charles Dickens.

As a youth, he was interested in music and proclaimed his intention to become a poet. He spent spare time writing stories and continued to write after leaving high school. He eventually attended West Chester State Teachers College, Lafayette College, and the Sorbonne, University of Paris.

Alexander entered the U.S. Army in 1942 and was assigned to an intelligence training center. He later sailed to Wales and France, where he served as a translator. There he met a French woman, Janine Denni, whom he married in 1946. They have a daughter.

After returning to the United States, Alexander worked as a cartoonist, advertising writer, layout artist, and associate editor for a trade magazine. He wrote in his spare moments and struggled to find publishers for his books. His first effort at fantasy, *Time Cat*, about a time-traveling feline, was published in 1963. Research for the book led to the writing of the Prydain Chronicles, which he loosely based on a collection of ancient Welsh myths and tales, *The Mabinogion*, and the Arthurian legends.

"Taran's quest is his [Taran's] theme, but Alexander's theme is Taran's growth into manhood," observed Donelson and Nilsen. "From a child who admires Prince Gwydion for his derring-do, Taran grows into a man who recognizes the Prince as a symbol of good, perhaps the power of good. From a child who idealizes Princess Eilonwy, he grows into a man who can woo and win her. . . . From a child who sees the quest as adventure leading to heroism, Taran grows into a man who recognizes that heroism requires making choices between good and evil and continuing the quest wherever it takes him."

Alexander said that he found creative freedom in writing for young adult readers. "In books for young people," he told Jill P. May, "I was able to express my own deepest feelings far more than I could ever do in writing for adults."

The Black Cauldron was named a Newbery Honor Book in 1966, and *The High King* won a Newbery Award in 1969. Alexander's Westmark trilogy received the American Book Award in Children's Literature in 1982.

"A superb craftsman, Alexander has concocted a marvelous tale of high adventure, replete with a lost princess, an engaging scoundrel, a modest orphan-hero, and an enjoyable hateful villain, and he makes them and their adventures wholly credible," said Zena Sutherland in a review of *Westmark*.

"The high adventure and picaresque comedy of Westmark . . . [evolves into] a more realistic and complex narrative form as the struggle for power in the kingdom erupts into betrayal, war and foreign invasion," observed Hazel Rochman in a review of *The Kestrel*. "The fast-paced plot, subtleties of character, ironic wit, quiet understatement, and pervasive animal imagery—all work with superb concentration to undercut the heroics of war, its slogans, uniforms, and myths of comradeship and glory."

Alexander sought a lighter tone in *The Illyrian Adventure*, which finds newly orphaned Vesper Holly dragging along her guardian, Brinnie, to the tiny country of Illyria to search for legendary treasure and an army of magical warriors—and to prove her father's theories correct.

Brinnie describes his sixteen-year-old charge this way: "Miss Vesper Holly has the digestive talents of a goat and the mind of a chess master. She is familiar with half a dozen languages and can swear fluently in all of them. She understands the use of a slide rule but prefers doing calculations in her head. She does not hesitate to risk life and limb—mine as well as her own. No doubt she has other qualities as yet undiscovered. I hope not."

In *Horn Book Magazine*, Alexander explained some of the difficulties in constructing fantasy characters and settings: "Once committed to his imaginary kingdom, the writer is not a monarch but a subject. Characters must appear plausible in their own setting, and the writer must go along with their inner logic. Happenings should have logical implications. Details should be tested for consistency. Shall animals speak? If so, do *all* animals speak? If not, then which—and how? Above all, why? Is it essential to the story, or lamely cute? Are there enchantments? How powerful? If an enchanter can perform such-and-such, can he not also do so-and-so?"

Alexander has also written several nonfiction works and has translated works by Jean-Paul Sartre and Paul Eluard into English.

YOUNG ADULT FICTION

The Cat Who Wished to Be a Man (1973)
Lionel, a wizard's cat, persuades his master to change him into a man. The wizard says he will find mankind greedy and corrupt. Lionel does find that but also discovers courage and determination in the young woman Gillian.

The Wizard in the Tree (1975)
Old enchanter Arbican rescues orphan girl Mallory from a life of drudgery.

The Town Cats, and Other Tales (1977)
Eight stories with cats as heroes.

The First Two Lives of Lukas-Kasha (1978)
Rascal Lukas accepts a challenge from a traveling magician, and before he knows it, he is declared king of Abadan.

The Remarkable Journey of Prince Jen (1991)
Jen sets off to find the legendary court of T'ien-Kuo.

The Arkadians (1995)
Lucien must complete a quest.

Chronicles of Prydain

The Book of Three (1964)
Taran, the assistant pig-keeper, longs to be a hero and sets out to help Prince Gwydion save the kingdom from the Horned King and the forces of evil.

The Black Cauldron (1965)
The cauldron, chief tool of villainy in Arawon, must be destroyed. Taran begins a second quest.

The Castle of Llyr (1966)
Princess Eilonwy is captured and bewitched by the wicked enchantress Achren. Taran and Prince Gwydion ride to save her.

Taran, Wanderer (1967)
Taran, now a teenager, hopes his quest will ennoble him in the eyes of Eilonwy, the princess with the red-gold hair.

The High King (1968)
When Arawon and the Death Lord obtain the powerful Sword of Dyrnwyn, Taran and Prince Gwydion raise an army of resistance. Answers are found about Taran's parentage.

Vesper Holly Series

The Illyrian Adventure (1986)
Vesper Holly searches for legendary treasure and an army of magical warriors belonging to King Vartan.

The El Dorado Adventure (1987)
Vesper and Professor Brinton Garret sail to El Dorado, where Vesper discovers that she owns a volcano.

The Drackenberg Adventure (1988)
Vesper Holly is involved in a revolution and the recovery of a priceless painting.

The Jedera Adventure (1989)
The return of a book to a library in Africa turns into wild adventure.

The Philadelphia Adventure (1990)
President Ulysses S. Grant asks Vesper's help against the scheming Dr. Helvitius.

Westmark Series

Westmark (1981)
With villainous Chief Minister Cabbarus in power, Westmark is a dangerous place. Apprentice Theo flees when his master, a printer, is killed by the king's chief minister. He roams the countryside in the company of an urchin called Mickle.

The Kestrel (1982)
Theo is attacked by an assassin and there is war. Mickle has taken her place at the palace.

The Beggar Queen (1984)
Mickle faces an old enemy when Cabbarus invades the country. Theo again must take up arms.

FICTION FOR YOUNGER READERS

Time Cat: The Remarkable Journeys of Jason and Gareth (1963); British title: *Nine Lives* (1963)

The Marvelous Misadventures of Sebastian (1970)

The King's Fountain (1971)

The Four Donkeys (1972)

The Fortune-Tellers (1992)

The Horse Gobbaleen (1995)

Prydain Series

Coll and His White Pig (1965)

The Truthful Harp (1967)

The Founding, and Other Tales of Prydain (1973)

ADULT FICTION

And Let the Credit Go (1955)

CONTRIBUTOR

Horn Book Reflections on Children's Books and Reading, edited by Elinor Whitney Field (1969)

Cricket's Choice (1974)

Celebrating Children's Books, edited by Betsy Hearne and Marilyn Kaye (1981)

Innocence and Experience, edited by Barbara Harrison and Gregory Macguire (1987)

The Voice of the Narrator in Children's Literature, edited by Charlotte F. Otten and Gary D. Schmidt (1989)

The Big Book for Peace, edited by Ann Durell and Margaret Sachs (1990)

ADAPTATIONS IN OTHER MEDIA

The Cat Who Wished to Be a Man
Produced onstage in Japan.

The Marvelous Misadventures of Sebastian
Produced as a television serial in Japan.

The Wizard in the Tree
Produced onstage in Japan.

The Black Cauldron (1985)
A Walt Disney animated film based on parts of the Prydain novels.

FOR FURTHER READING

Alexander, Lloyd. "The Flat-Heeled Muse." *Horn Book Magazine*, April 1965.

Donelson, Kenneth L., and Alleen Pace Nilsen. *Literature for Today's Young Adults*. Glenview, IL: Scott, Foresman, 1980.

Jacobs, James S. "Lloyd Alexander: A Critical Biography." Ph.D. diss., University of Georgia, 1978.

Livingston, Myra Cohn. *A Tribute to Lloyd Alexander*. Philadelphia: Drexel Institute, 1976.

May, Jill P. *Lloyd Alexander*. Boston: Twayne, 1991.

———. "Lloyd Alexander." In *Twentieth-Century Children's Writers*, edited by Tracy Chevalier. 3d ed. Chicago: St. James Press, 1989.

Rochman, Hazel. Review of *The Kestrel*. *School Library Journal*, April 1982.

Sutherland, Zena. Review of *Westmark*. *Bulletin of the Center for Children's Books*, June 1981.

Sutherland, Zena, Dianne L. Monson, and May Hill Arbuthnot. *Children and Books*. Glenview, IL: Scott, Foresman, 1981.

Tymn, Marshall B., Kenneth J. Zahorski, and Robert H. Boyer. *Fantasy Literature: A Core Collection and Reference Guide*. New York: R. R. Bowker, 1979.

Wintle, Justin, and Emma Fisher, eds. *The Pied Pipers: Interviews with the Influential Creators of Children's Literature*. New York: Paddington Press, 1975.

Zahorski, Kenneth J. *Lloyd Alexander, Evangeline Walton Ensley, Kenneth Morris: A Primary and Secondary Bibliography*. Boston: G. K. Hall, 1981.

V. C. Andrews

Gothic suspense

Portsmouth, Virginia
?–December 19, 1986

Flowers in the Attic

"In the early 1980s public libraries were swamped—and to some extent they still are—with teenage girls hunting for books by Virginia Andrews," observed Andy Sawyer. "Although by no means written for people of this age group (and a quick straw-poll in one particular library showed that Andrews' novels are equally popular among the over-60s) the sagas of the Dollangangers and Casteel/Tattertons turned out to be the female equivalent of stories about giant crabs and mutated slugs among their brothers. Perhaps it was the jewelry and the clothes. Perhaps it was the incest."

Virginia Cleo Andrews, whose peculiar style of Gothic horror stories has sold millions of copies worldwide, was the third child and first daughter of a tool and die maker and a telephone operator. She grew up in a working-class environment and was educated in Portsmouth. Later, she lived in Virginia Beach, Virginia. As a child, she read avidly, discovering a new world through the writings of Jules Verne, Edgar Allan Poe, Edgar Rice Burroughs, and the Brontë sisters. In her teen years, Andrews developed orthopedic problems and eventually had to use crutches and a wheelchair. After her father's death, when she was twenty, Andrews worked as a fashion illustrator and commercial artist to support herself. She also began writing, producing nine manuscripts in seven years. None was published. Finally, her 290,000-word manuscript, titled *The Obsessed*, brought some interest from publishers. So she revised it and retitled it *Flowers in the Attic*. A story of child abuse and incest, the novel was published in 1979 and became a best-seller. A sequel, *Petals on the*

Wind, also became a best-seller, as did the third in the series, *If There Be Thorns*.

Flowers in the Attic is about the four Dollanganger children, offspring of an incestuous union. They are locked in the attic of a hulking old mansion so their grandfather will not learn of their existence and disinherit their mother. Physically abused by their grandmother, they turn to each other for comfort and love.

In one scene, Cathy Dollanganger watches her brother Chris standing by the window: "My first impulse was to run to him, to put my arms around him, and lavish a million kisses on his face to make up for those he was missing from Momma. I'd draw his head down against my breast and cuddle it there as she used to do, and he'd go back to being the cheerful, sunny optimist who never had a sullen angry day like I used to. Even if I did all that Momma did once, I was wise enough to know it wouldn't be the same. It was *her* he wanted. He had all his hopes, dreams, and faith wrapped up in one single woman—Momma."

"Not long after my first novel, *Flowers in the Attic*, was published, many letters came to fill my mailbox, clearly indicating that most of my readers think I am writing about my own life," Andrews stated in *The Writer*. "Only in some ways is this true. Cathy Dollanganger's persona is not mine, but her way of responding to the traumatic events in her life reflects what mine would have been in the same situation. Her emotions are my emotions. Her dilemmas are somewhat similar to mine, but not precisely.

"It's difficult to say where a writer leaves off and the character takes over. One could hope to be as verbal as Cathy, and say all the right things at the right time, but in real life that seldom happens. Dialogue can move the action along speedily. When you construct a good strong character, often he or she will take off and lead the way, surprising you. Shout hooray when your characters do this for you."

"Why do I write about such oddball situations?" Andrews responded rhetorically to reporter Stephen Rubin. "Why have an imagination if you don't go that way? I guess I'm just drawn to that sort of thing. I don't like everything to be explained by scientists who say there are no little green men from Mars. I don't like that, I want them to be there." In another context, Andrews stated that she also believed in extrasensory perception and reincarnation.

In *The V. C. Andrews Trivia and Quiz Book*, Stephen J. Spignesi takes a superficial look at the Andrews literary legacy. He frequently emphasizes the prurient, asking, typically, of *Dark Angel*, "Which of Jillian's body parts first attracted Tony Tatterton to her? How many condoms did Fanny Casteel carry in her small red plastic purse?" (Her legs and five boxes, respectively.)

With tongue in cheek, he highlights certain philosophical statements made by various characters in Andrews's books, such as Billie in *My Sweet Audrina*: "A physical relationship is not everything, but it's very important as far as men are concerned. A good sex life makes the best cornerstone for a long and happy marriage." Or, as Cathy observes in *Petals on the Wind*, "Everything concerning human beings comes in shades of gray."

Andrews died in December 1986 of cancer. However, her family and publisher continued to bring out books under Andrews's name, at first claiming they were her work. Eventually they explained that the new books were by another writer: "Beginning with the final books in the Casteel series, we have been working closely with a carefully selected writer to expand upon her genius by creating new novels—like *Dawn*, *Secrets of the Morning*, *Twilight's Child*, *Midnight Whispers*, and now *Darkest Hour*—inspired by her wonderful storytelling talent," said the family in 1993.

The secret behind the new books was maintained by Spignesi "out of respect to the family." Sawyer, though, said they were being penned by horror writer Andrew Neiderman. The science fiction journal *Locus* in 1994 also mentioned "the uncredited author, Andrew Neiderman." The magazine reported that in 1990, the Internal Revenue Service assigned a value of $1.2 million to Andrews's name and billed the estate for nearly $1 million in back taxes and interest. After paying, the estate sued for a refund. A U.S. District Court judge found in favor of the estate, discounting the value of the name because the books were ghostwritten. Recent paperback versions of Neiderman's novels make no secret of his Andrews connection.

Neiderman was born October 26, 1940, in Brooklyn, New York. He attended Hunter College, Bronx Campus, and the State University of New York at Albany. He has been married to Diane Wilson since 1964. Neiderman has been a teacher of high school English as well as a writer.

Recent novels include *Angel of Mercy* (1994), which is about Faye Samuels, a nurse who cares for the terminally ill. Her twin sister, Susie, helps the survivors reunite with their loved ones. Neiderman told *Contemporary Authors* that he is fond of the theme of violence. "I am concerned with how we are driven to acts of violence by an imposing society and [an] entrapping environment," he said.

ADULT FICTION

My Sweet Audrina (1982)
The first Audrina was raped and killed by boys in the woods. Sixteen years later, the second Audrina is kept home from school, destined to become a living memorial to her namesake.

Casteel Family Series

Heaven (1985)
Heaven Leigh Casteel is a mountain girl born into a wretched existence: Her stepmother bears a stillborn child; her granny becomes sick; her father contracts syphilis. Heaven quits school to care for the rest of the family.

Dark Angel (1986)
Heaven goes to stay at her mother's parents' Farthinggale Manor and is offered an education and new start if she will forget her past.

Fallen Hearts (1990)
Two years later, Heaven is a teacher. She marries Logan Stonewall, and she learns certain secrets. There is terrible tragedy. Heaven becomes pregnant, but the child is not Logan's.

The Gates of Paradise (1990)
It has been seventeen years, and Heaven's daughter, Annie, is a painter. More family secrets are revealed.

Web of Dreams (1990)
Events in this book occur before those in *Heaven*. Leigh VanVoreen, Heaven's mother, among myriad other things, poses naked for Troy Tatterton for the design of his first Portrait Doll.

Cutler Family Series

Dawn (1990)
Dawn Longchamp moves with her family to Richmond, Virginia, where a new sister, Fern, is born. One of Dawn's classmates at Emerson Peabody School inexplicably hates her.

Secrets of the Morning (1991)
Dawn goes to New York to study singing. She and roommate Trisha Kramer become friends. Dawn becomes pregnant by a famous voice singer, Michael Sutton. There are surprising family revelations.

Twilight's Child (1992)
Dawn and her brother, Jimmy, search for Dawn's child, Christie, who was put up for adoption by her Cutler relatives.

Midnight Whispers (1992)
Dawn and Jimmy's son, Jefferson, is now nine, and Christie is sixteen. Dawn is still running Cutler's Cove Hotel. Tragedy strikes.

Darkest Hour (1993)
Events in this book occur before those in *Dawn*. Lillian Booth Cutler lives with her family at the Meadows, an old southern plantation.

Dollanganger Series

Flowers in the Attic (1979)
Four Dollanganger children, offspring of an incestuous relationship, are kept locked away in an attic so that a stern grandfather will not find out about them and disinherit their mother. The two older children begin to fall in love, and one of the younger ones dies.

Petals on the Wind (1980)
Escaping from Foxworth Hall, Cathy, Chris, and Carrie are taken in by and become legal wards of Dr. Paul Sheffield. Carrie is trapped in an attic by schoolmates; Cathy and Paul make love; Chris loves Cathy; Cathy goes to New York to dance (and that is only for starters).

If There Be Thorns (1981)
Cathy's son Bart is mesmerized by the Old Lady in Black, Corrine, who lives next door—unaware that she has just left a mental institution and is making evil plans with her strange, old butler.

Seeds of Yesterday (1984)
Fifteen years after Corrine's death, Cathy and Chris move into a rebuilt Foxworth Hall. Jory marries. Bart, a lawyer, cannot get along with adoptive stepsister Cindy.

Garden of Shadows (1987)
Events in this book precede those in *Flowers in the Attic*. The grandmother, Olivia Winfield, is twenty-four when she meets her future husband, Malcolm Foxworth, who, she soon learns, wants her only as a "breeder."

Landry Family Series

Ruby (1994)
Young, innocent Ruby Landry unearths a dark family secret that whisks her from her beloved Louisiana bayous to a privileged life in New Orleans.

Pearl in the Mist (1994)
Giving up boyfriend Beau, Ruby leaves for private school. Her stepmother is still cool to her, but her identical twin sister, Gisselle, is downright mean.

All That Glitters (1995)
Ruby has rediscovered Paul Tate, her first love, now a man of dazzling wealth. She is willing to forget the shocking reason that she and Paul remain husband and wife in name alone.

ADAPTATIONS IN OTHER MEDIA

Flowers in the Attic (1987)
Film starring Louise Fletcher, Victoria Tennant, Kristy Swanson, and Jeb Adams.

FOR FURTHER READING

Andrews, V. C. "Turning a Profit from Memories." *The Writer*, November 1982.

Metzger, Linda, ed. "Neiderman, Andrew." *Contemporary Authors New Revised Series.* Vol. 13. Detroit: Gale Research, 1984.

Rubin, Stephen. "Blooms of Darkness." *The Washington Post*, 20 September 1981.

Sawyer, Andy. "Fairy-Tale Horror." *Million*, July–August 1991.

Spignesi, Stephen J. *The V. C. Andrews Trivia and Quiz Book*. New York: Signet, 1994.

"V. C. Andrews® Gets Refund." *Locus*, July 1994.

Piers Anthony

Fantasy

Science fiction

Oxford, England
August 6, 1934

Xanth Series

"As a child I was fallible," said science fiction and fantasy writer Piers Anthony in his *Bio of an Ogre*, "and I went through the usual experiences of lying, cheating, and stealing. As an adult I detest those memories. The only thing I value more than integrity is life itself. I have had a horrendous history of conflict as a writer, because dishonesty is anathema to me, and I do constant battle against it, and no living person I know of matches my fanaticism about this. Many people don't even understand what motivates me, because integrity is only a word to them, not a principle to live by. Most people *say* they believe in honesty; I *mean* it." If this is an unusual statement, well, Anthony is an unusual writer.

Named Piers Anthony Dillingham Jacob at birth, Anthony has written under the names Piers A. D. Jacob and Robert Piers, as well as Piers Anthony. He became a science fiction fan by age thirteen. "Back when I was thirteen, perhaps fourteen," he related in *Bio of an Ogre*, "I had found an old magazine in my mother's office, *Astounding Science Fiction*. I had started reading it, to pass the time until my mother got out of work, and became entranced by the lead story, 'The Equalizer,' by Jack Williamson. I was allowed to keep the magazine, as it belonged to nobody, and that marked the onset of my lifetime's fascination with the genre. In fact, I credit science fiction with much of the emotional progress I made thereafter, because it provided me with an array of wonderful other worlds, each of which was better than my own. I lived for each new issue of the magazine. Thus I was conversant with the genre of science fiction, and I felt I could be original within it."

As a small child, Anthony moved with his family from England to Spain, then to the United States. A cousin died of cancer when Anthony was fifteen. His parents divorced when he was eighteen. These events were psychologically unsettling, and it shows up in his prose.

He explained in *Bio of an Ogre*: "My parents were doing relief work in Spain during the Spanish Civil War of 1936–39; since they did not want to take their children into war, my younger sister and I remained in England, cared for by a nanny. When that war ended, we joined our parents in Spain for a year, and I began to learn Spanish. Then my father was arrested, apparently by mistake; rather than admit error, the Franco government expelled him from Spain and took over the supplies of food intended for the hungry children there. In this manner we came to America, where my father's family lived. I had my sixth birthday on the ship, and got a cake made of sawdust, because of the limited wartime supplies."

Anthony came to the United States in 1940 and became a naturalized citizen eighteen years later. Though he had to repeat first grade twice because he had not learned to read, he eventually majored in creative writing at Goddard College. In 1956, he received his bachelor's degree and married Carol Ann Marble, with whom he has two daughters. The writer served in the U.S. Army from 1957 to 1959. He worked as a technical writer, teacher, and social worker. In 1966, he became a full-time writer.

Anthony's first published short story was "Possible to Rue" in *Fantastic* in 1962. He received several awards for his first novel, *Chthon*, which was published in 1967. Don D'Ammassa described the book as "an unusually powerful novel even for a more experienced writer. . . . He creates an entire society whose underlying psychological profile is so alien to the one with which we are familiar, it achieves an otherworldly quality that has rarely been equaled."

Many of Anthony's works are long novels broken into trilogies or series. The first was the Cluster tales, which eventually extended to five books. The Xanth titles began with *A Spell for Chameleon*. Don D'Ammassa said of the series, "Anthony creates an original, magical system, a convincing fantasy world, superimposes an intriguing plot with sympathetic characters, and enlivens the mixture with humor. It is unsurprising that sequels should follow."

"In the land of Xanth, everyone and everything—even a rock or tree—has a magical talent, except Bink," Deborah A. Stanley said. "*Chameleon* follows Bink on his quest to discover his talent or face exile to the boring, powerless land of Mundania. In the process, Bink gains not only knowledge of his talent but emotional maturity as well."

Anthony said of the series in *Bio*, "The name 'Xanth' was from my 'Names' book. I use these books not for the usual purpose of naming babies (though when we finally did have babies we could keep, I cheated and used the books for that) but for naming characters in my fiction. I am fascinated with unusual words and odd spellings, and Xanth appealed. I used it in a short story that never sold, so then I used it again as the name of my magic land, dropping the terminal e. It means blond, or yellow-haired, like my daughter Penny. It was an incidental use; neither the publisher nor I realized just how successful Xanth was going to be."

The Xanth stories are full of puns and other tricks of language. Less complex than some of Anthony's novels, they appeal more to young adult readers.

Anthony wrote one novel especially for and about teens, *Race Against Time*. It is about a future race and selective breeding of humans. The book came under some attack, as he described in *Bio*, "It was reviewed in *Locus* by Dave Hartwell, who claimed that its conclusion was racist because the white boy married the white girl, and the black boy married the black girl, and the yellow boy married the yellow girl despite having had some interest in those of the other colors. Now that novel was not racist; it showed that the cultures of the three couples were in the end the deciding factors in their relationships. Readers are welcome to verify this in that novel for themselves; it has been reprinted in paperback. I never took any guff from reviewers, and I did not this time."

Where does he get his ideas? "First, I happen to be blessed with an extremely active imagination; I couldn't turn it off if I wanted to," he stated in *Bio*. "As a child I did want to, and couldn't; my mind conjured monsters that pursued me by day, and horrors I witnessed by night, so that I couldn't sleep without a light. When I became a writer, I turned that imagination to positive things, and the monsters that had terrified me became friends, for they went into my fiction. Now I just love monsters!

"Second, I do a lot of adaptation. I turn mundane things into magic things, or symbolic things. I turned the state of Florida into the magic land of Xanth, with the details of the landscape assuming special properties."

To become a successful fiction writer, Anthony ventured, one needs imagination and desire; one needs to have certain basic skills and to work at the craft. Luck would not hurt, though originality and style are less critical.

YOUNG ADULT FICTION

Race Against Time (1973)
Teenagers of different nationalities are raised in a pseudo-1960s environment—but for what purpose?

ADULT FICTION

Chthon (1967)
The hero must escape a prison planet and search for his true nature.

The Ring (1968) with Robert E. Margroff
Jeff Font is convicted by a computerized court system and forced to wear a ring around his neck to keep him on the straight.

Macroscope (1969)
Messages come to the Macroscope of an advanced space civilization.

The E. S. P. Worm (1970) with Robert E. Margroff
Earth's first visitor is Qumax, a twelve-foot-long worm that delights in taking over human minds.

Prostho Plus (1971)
An Earth dentist is kidnapped and taken into space to fix teeth.

Rings of Ice (1974)
Two survivalists, a diabetic and a transvestite ex-cop, and a thirteen-year-old with cerebral palsy are the world's hope when the globe is flooded.

Triple Detente (1974)
Switching places, Earth's space fleet and alien forces conquer each other's planets.

Phthor (1975), sequel to *Chthon*
Hell is an underground prison planet populated by a race of minionettes who reverse their emotions.

But What of Earth? (1976 and 1989), revised by Robert Coulson
The 1989 edition, unedited, offers a long account of how the original publisher hired another writer to shorten and change the manuscript.

Steppe (1976)
A Turkish warrior from the past participates in a galactic game in the future.

Hasan (1977)
An Arabian Nights fantasy.

Pretender: Science Fiction (1979) with Frances Hall
A symbiotic alien crash-lands on Earth and finds himself in the body of a boy slave during the time of Babylon.

Mute (1981)
Knot is a mutant who works for the computer that rules the galaxy in the latter's fight against the enemy Piebald.

Anthonology (1985)
Short stories with notes by the author.

Ghost (1986)
Shetland, assigned to take his experimental spaceship beyond the universe to find a new energy source, finds a galaxy-wide black hole and, beyond, a ghost universe of incredible power.

Shade of the Tree (1986)
Josh Pinson is heir to his eccentric Uncle Elijah's Florida estate. The land is haunted by a giant oak tree.

Balook (1989)
Genetic engineering has brought back the hornless rhino of the Miocene Epoch. Called Balook, it makes friends with a junior game warden named Thor.

Pornucopia (1989)
The title suggests the subject matter.

Total Recall (1989)
Novelization of a movie based on the Philip K. Dick story "We Can Remember It for You Wholesale." Doug Quaid travels across the solar system to learn his true identity.

Hard Sell (1990)
Fisk Centers is a sharp, interplanetary salesman.

Dead Morn (1990) with Roberto Fuentes
A twenty-fifth-century rebel tries to change the future by traveling to the past.

Firefly (1990)
A terrifying creature preys on victims who die in a frenzied state of sexual ecstasy.

Through the Ice (1990) with Robert Kornwise
A young man falls through the ice into a dimension where magic works.

MerCycle (1991)
In a desperate attempt to save humanity, humans are given the ability to breathe underwater.

Tatham Mound (1991)
Fantasy novel about Native Americans before Columbus.

Alien Plot (1992)
A man ventures to the boundaries of an alien dimension.

The Caterpillar's Question (1992) with Philip Jose Farmer
Jack, a struggling art student, is hired to drive a mute, crippled girl cross-country. They enter the gateway to a world of strange creatures and pursuing agents.

If I Pay Thee Not in Gold (1993) with Mercedes Lackey
Women rule the Age of the Mazonians using magic. Xylina must defend against the queen her beliefs in her abilities.

Killobyte (1993)
Two physically challenged individuals forget their troubles playing a virtual reality computer game—a game that takes on a sinister reality.

Tales from the Great Turtle (1994) with Richard Gilliam

Apprentice Adept Series

Split Infinity (1980)
With the help of a werewolf and a unicorn, Stile must solve the riddle of his fate on two worlds.

Blue Adept (1981)
Stile battles enemies on the planet Proton, where science rules, and on Phaze, where magic works.

Juxtaposition (1982)
Stile begins to solve his problems on the two worlds.

Out of Phaze (1987)
Mach, the self-willed robot from Proton, and Bane, the apprentice wizard from Phaze, switch minds—and must link their respective scientific and magical worlds.

Robot Adept (1988)
Mach and Bane try to save their worlds from destruction.

Unicorn Point (1989)
Mach and Bane continue the fight.

Phaze Doubt (1991)
Can the two children Nepe and Flach save the world from the repulsive Hectare?

Battle Circle Series

Sos the Rope (1968)
Sos is an educated barbarian who controls a nomadic tribe in a post-nuclear holocaust world.

Var the Stick (1972)
A war pits primitive tribes against industrial centers.

Neq the Sword (1975)
Neq attempts to rebuild civilization.

Bio of a Space Tyrant Series

Refugee (1983)
Hope Hubris, fifteen, is converted from a quiet schoolboy to a skilled fighter when pirates blast his family from their home in Callisto.

Mercenary (1984)
Hubris, with the Navy of Jupiter, begins his crusade against the space pirates.

Politician (1985)
A military legend, Hubris becomes a candidate—and a prisoner of a nightmare that knows no past.

Executive (1985)
Hubris rules as absolute dictator of Jupiter—and also has a secret identity as a rebel.

Statesman (1986)
Hope Hubris's epic adventure concludes.

Cluster Series

Cluster (1977); British title: *Vicinity Cluster* (1979)
An uneducated tribesman is chosen as Earth's ambassador to the galaxy, because he is the only one able to withstand transmission into other bodies.

Chaining the Lady (1978)
Melody of Mintaka tries to prevent the Andromedons from controlling the minds of space fleet officers.

Kirlian Quest (1978)
Herald the Healer must go to distant Amoeba to counter an invasion.

Thousandstar (1980)
At the edge of the Milky Way, a race begins for the legacy of the Ancients.

Viscous Circle (1982)
An alien hero holds a strange secret that could change his race's relationship with humanity.

Geodyssey Series

Isle of Woman (1993)
The story of humanity begins with Blaze, the fireworker, and Ember, the green-eyed woman who haunts his dreams.

Shame of Man (1994)
Continuation of the story of humanity, as told through one family born again and again through the ages.

Incarnations of Immortality Series

On a Pale Horse (1983)
Zane accidentally kills Death personified and must take his place to face the Devil.

Bearing an Hourglass (1984)
A wanderer named Norton becomes Time and battles Satan.

With a Tangled Skein (1985)
A woman becomes Fate and fights Satan.

Wielding a Red Sword (1987)
Myron becomes the embodiment of War and goes head to head with Satan.

Being a Green Mother (1987)
Orb's mother, Niobe, relinquishes her role as Green Mother to bear children. Now Orb becomes Green Mother and is destined to marry Satan.

For Love of Evil (1988)
Parry is a gifted musician and an apprentice in the art of white magic. When his flame, Julie, dies, he turns to dark magic.

And Eternity (1990)
Orlene, daughter of Gaea, travels with Julie, consort of Satan, to try to understand the eternal question of good versus evil.

Jason Striker Series with Roberto Fuentes

Kiai! (1974)
Striker is a master of karate, kung fu, aikido, and judo.

Mistress of Death (1974)

The Bamboo Bloodbath (1975)

Ninja's Revenge (1975)

Amazon Slaughter (1976)

Kelvin Hackleberry Series with Robert E. Margroff

Dragon's Gold (1991)
An evil sorcerer rules the kingdom of Rud in the name of his evil daughter. Only Kelvin and Jon have other plans—when they find a dragon with scales of gold.

Orc's Opal (1991)
Witch Zady vows Kelvin will pay for the deaths of her children.

Serpent's Silver (1991)
Kelvin must save his father and renegade half brother from a dungeon.

Chimaera's Copper (1992)
Kelvin meets old enemies Zoanna, sadistic witch queen of Hud, and Rowforth, king of Hud.

Mouvar's Magic (1993)
The hero battles the evil wizards of the universe—Professor Devole and his servant, Zade.

Mode Series

Virtual Mode (1991)
Colene searches for her lover through a world of monsters, dragons, and impossible dreams.

Fractal Mode (1992)
Star-crossed lovers Colene and Darius encounter bizarre characters in their quest for happiness.

Chaos Mode (1994)
An unlikely band of heroes travels through multiple universes.

Of Man and Mantra Trilogy

Omnivore (1968)
On Tarot, where the Animation curtain moves across the world, fantasy turns into reality, and creatures from Tarot cards come to life.

Orn (1971)
The heroes are transported to a prehistoric world.

Ox (1976)
Cal, Veg, and Aquilon are trapped in an alternate dimension.

Tarot Trilogy

God of Tarot (1979)
Paul, a wandering monk, must go on a quest to save a star colony.

Vision of Tarot (1980)
Paul's adventures continue.

Faith of Tarot (1980)
Dragons and demons and unholy lusts abound.

Xanth Series

A Spell for Chameleon (1977)
Everyone in the magical world of Xanth has a spell—except the hero, Bink.

The Source of Magic (1979)
Bink must discover the source of all magic in Xanth.

Castle Roogna (1979)
Bink's son, Dor, goes on a magical quest into the past.

Centaur Aisle (1981)
Dor searches for King Trent in Mundania, along with a golem, an ogre, a centaur, and Trent's daughter.

Ogre, Ogre (1982)
Smash, a kindly ogre, escorts a motley collection of women on their various quests.

Night Mare (1983)
Mare Imbrium, the night mare who delivers bad dreams, is exiled to Xanth in the midst of a barbarian invasion.

Dragon on a Pedestal (1983)
The Gap Dragon escapes and ravishes the land. Good Magician Humphrey might have the solution.

Crewel Lye: A Caustic Yarn (1985)
Jordan is a ghost in the Castle Roogna. He spends time with a five-year-old named Ivy and watches his knightly past unfold on a tapestry.

Golem in the Gears (1986)
Grundy Golem travels to the Ivy Tower to find the lost dragon, Stanley Steamer.

Vale of the Vole (1987)
Esk, the ogre-nymph-human, tries to save the inhabitants of the Vale of the Vole from a demon horde.

Heaven Cent (1988)
Prince Dolph seeks a magic coin that will lead him to the missing sorcerer, Humphrey.

Man from Mundania (1989)
Bored with sitting around the castle in Xanth, Princess Ivy uses the Heaven Cent to travel to Uundania, where she meets a student who does not believe in magic.

Isle of View (1990)
Prince Dolph must choose between two women for his bride.

Question Quest (1991)
Lacuna, one of the twin children of the Zombie Monster, and Millie the Ghost hunt for the Elixir of Youth.

The Color of Her Panties (1992)
Gwenny Goblin and friends struggle to beat out her awful half brother for the chieftainship of the goblin horde.

Demons Don't Dream (1993)
Two Mundanian escapees are transported to a forest glade in Xanth.

Harpy Thyme (1994)
Gloha, the last of her species, searches for a mate.

Geis of the Gargoyle (1995)
A gargoyle in human form must save the river Swanknee before it dries up. He asks Magician Humphrey for assistance.

Roc and a Hard Place (1995)

EDITOR

Uncollected Stars (1986) with Martin H. Greenberg

CONTRIBUTOR

Nova One: An Anthology of Original Science Fiction, edited by Harry Harrison (1970)

Science Against Man, edited by Anthony Cheetham (1970)

Again, Dangerous Visions, edited by Harlan Ellison (1972)

Generations, edited by David Gerrold (1972)

The Berkley Showcase, edited by Victoria Schochet and John Silbersack (1981)

Uncollected Stars, edited with Barry Malzberg and Martin H. Greenberg (1986)

FOR FURTHER READING

Anthony, Piers. *Bio of an Ogre: The Autobiography of Piers Anthony to Age 50*. New York: Ace, 1988.

———. *Letters to Jenny*. New York: Tor, 1993.

Anthony, Piers, with Judy Lynn Nye. *Piers Anthony's Visual Guide to Xanth*. New York: Avon Books, 1989.

Clute, John, and Peter Nicholls. *The Encyclopedia of Science Fiction*. New York: St. Martin's Press, 1993.

Cowart, David, ed. *Dictionary of Literary Biography: Twentieth-Century American Science Fiction Writers*. Part 1: A–L. Detroit: Gale Research, 1981.

D'Ammassa, Don. "Piers Anthony." In *Twentieth-Century Science Fiction Writers*, edited by Noelle Watson and Paul E. Schellinger. 3d ed. Chicago: St. James Press, 1991.

Stanley, Deborah A. "Piers Anthony." In *Authors & Artists for Young Adults*, edited by Kevin S. Hile. Vol. 11. Detroit: Gale Research, 1993.

Avi

Historical fiction

Drama

New York City
December 23, 1937

The Man Who Was Poe

Avi is an award-winning writer of mystery, adventure, historical, supernatural, coming-of-age, and comic novels. "I try to write about complex issues—young people in an adult world—full of irony and contradiction, in a narrative style that relies heavily on suspense with a texture rich in emotion and imagery," Avi said in *Twentieth-Century Children's Writers*.

He continued, "I take a great deal of satisfaction in using popular forms—the adventure, the mystery, the thriller—so as to hold my reader with the sheer pleasure of a good story. At the same time I try to resolve my books with an ambiguity that compels engagement. In short, I want my readers to feel, to think, sometimes to laugh, but most of all I want them to enjoy a good read."

Born Avi Wortis, the son of a psychiatrist and a social worker, Avi attended Antioch University, the University of Wisconsin–Madison, and Columbia University. He married Joan Gabriner, a weaver, in 1963. After their divorce, he married Coppelia Kahn, an English professor. They have three children, one by Kahn's previous marriage.

"The first books I discovered on my own were the many volumes of Thornton W. Burgess: *Blackie the Crow*, *Sammy the Jay* and *Lightfoot the Deer*," said Avi in *Books I Read When I Was Young*. "They and many more became important friends of mine. Cheap, I saved my money and bought as many of these novels as I could and so acquired a library of my own. Perhaps the most important book I read when I was young was Kenneth Grahame's *The Wind in the Willows*. It had all I desired: deeply felt characters, wonderful adventures, rich comedy, stirring language. At the same time there was something mysterious about the book that moved me greatly. My boyhood copy still sits on my shelf."

Avi had grandparents and an aunt who were writers, uncles who were painters and composers. His parents both wrote, and his twin sister is a writer. Other family members are active in the arts. His family has also long supported human rights issues.

Avi failed in one school because a dysfunction called dysgraphia, which impeded his writing abilities, went undetected. This caused him to reverse letters in words or spell them wrong. Still, he wanted to write. He studied playwriting at Antioch University and later said he learned his sense of writing structure from a teacher there. A play of his, written while he was in college, won a contest and was published in a magazine.

Avi worked for the theater collection of the New York Public Library from 1962 to 1970. He also worked as a librarian in London for a year, and he was assistant professor and humanities librarian at Trenton State College, New Jersey, from 1970 to 1986.

Telling stories to his two sons inspired him to write for young readers. "Most of all I like to write the kinds of stories I enjoy reading—adventures, mysteries, suspense tales," he said in a promotional flyer. "I believe that we who presume to write for children have a number of obligations. The first is to write as well as we can. The second is to be honest. The third is that we hold out a vision of achievement. It does not matter if the vision is happy or tragic, witty or somber. What matters is that we proclaim that life is worth living, that the struggle we undertake together must be one that fulfills the promise of ourselves. I try to write from the heart. A good children's book is a book of promises. And promises are meant to be kept."

Things That Sometimes Happen, his first book, was published in 1970. He wrote several more children's books, then settled on young adult novels. The first several had historical settings. *Captain Grey* is about pirates. *The Fighting Ground* is set during the American Revolution. Avi gives a nod to S. E. Hinton's *The Outsiders* in *Nothing but the Truth*: the hero, Philip Malloy, reads Hinton's book, which is about teenage gangs.

Avi stated in *Something About the Author*, "It's not an accident that in the last decades the book most read by young people is *The Outsiders*. I wish Stephen King's novels were taught in the schools, so that kids could respond to them and talk about them."

In a piece for *The Writer*, Avi described how he crafts his books: "The key question for me has always been, not, how do I find ideas, but rather, how do I choose the ones I wish to work on? Not all ideas make good books for me.

"I do it by building a brief outline that consists, in the main, of a series of *events*, usually no more than twenty. Since my perception of plot has to do with interlocking events that have a culmination, in time these events become chapter concepts. . . . Usually, for a while, I don't go beyond the construction of an outline. I sit back and think and think, and having done that, think a while more. Occasionally I've jumped in quickly upon the page with a new idea, but more often than not, I'll think it over for a period of months, maybe a couple of years. I will fuss with that event-outline a good bit, adding, subtracting, but always keeping it brief, to the point, and focused on *events*. I make no notes about persons, places, characters. I think about it. Above all, I try hard not to think what I *mean*."

Susan Stan echoed, "Although his work has been described as innovative—especially *The Man Who Was Poe*—Avi has neither attempted to be innovative nor considered himself so." Of that book, she said: "Set in Rhode Island in 1848, a young boy runs headlong into Poe in a dark street. Poe agrees to help the boy find his lost sister, and as the complicated story progresses, Poe's motives slowly come to light. Avi explains the origin of the story in this way: 'Poe is an incredible and complex figure who's absolutely adored by many young people. What happens if you confront him—this crazy, alcoholic, weird, brilliant man—with a kid? That's a historical question, but after that, it's about the relationship, not about history or the moment in history. One could have written the story today about what it's like to depend on someone who's an alcoholic. You can tell that story in a hundred different ways.'"

Avi is as comfortable with young heroines as he is with young heroes, as in *The True Confessions of Charlotte Doyle.* "A breathtaking seafaring adventure, set in 1832, Charlotte Doyle, thirteen, returning from school in England to join her family in Rhode Island, is deposited on a seedy ship with a ruthless, mad captain and a mutinous crew," explained reviewer Trev Jones. "Refusing to heed warnings about Captain Jaggery's brutality, Charlotte seeks his guidance and approval only to become his victim, a pariah to the entire crew, and a convicted felon for the murder of the first mate. There is no doubt that she will survive, however, for the telling is all hers, masterfully related in a voice that perfectly suits the period and the heroine."

Avi used a historical setting for *The Barn*, in which three pioneer children struggle to keep the homestead going when their father is stricken. They set about building a barn, but their father dies before it is completed.

YOUNG ADULT FICTION

Captain Grey (1977)
Kevin Cartwright is a match for the wily Captain Grey, the pirate who forced the eleven-year-old to join his murdering band.

Emily Upham's Revenge; or, How Deadwood Dick Saved the Banker's Niece: A Massachusetts Adventure (1978)
In nineteenth-century Massachusetts, Emily Upham has been raised as a proper young lady. She must go to live with her well-to-do but nasty uncle.

Night Journeys (1979)
Orphan Peter York, sent to live with Quakers in colonial Pennsylvania, helps two indentured servants flee.

Encounter at Easton (1980), sequel to *Night Journeys*
Nathaniel Hill, a gambler and bully, is hired to track two young runaway indentured servants, Elizabeth Mawes and Robert Linnly.

Man from the Sky (1980)
A learning disability hampers Jamie's reading, so he makes up stories about images he sees in the clouds.

A Place Called Ugly (1981)
Despite all the other changes in fourteen-year-old Owen Coughlin's life, Grenlow's Island has been his summer haven for ten years. This may be the last year.

Sometimes I Think I Hear My Name (1982)
Thirteen-year-old Conrad Murray's parents are divorcing and sending him to England for the summer. He meets an enigmatic girl named Nancy.

Shadrach's Crossing (1983); alternate title: *Smuggler's Island* (1994)
In 1932, no one on Lucker's Island, where Shadrach Faherty lives, likes the liquor smugglers.

Devil's Race (1984), sequel to *Sometimes I Think I Hear My Name*
Conrad, thirteen, is determined to find the parents he has not seen for a year.

The Fighting Ground (1984)
Jonathan is a thirteen-year-old New Jersey boy caught up in the American Revolution.

S. O. R. Losers (1984)
Players on the South Orange River Middle School soccer team are accustomed to losing.

Bright Shadow (1985)
In a time of wizards and magic, Morwenna, twelve, accidentally becomes bearer of the last wishes of the land.

Wolf Rider: A Tale of Terror (1986)
Andy Zadinski, fifteen, receives a telephone call from a killer—but no one believes him.

Romeo and Juliet—Together (and Alive!)—at Last (1987), sequel to *S. O. R. Losers*
Now in the eighth grade, the S. O. R. gang puts on a greatly abridged and unintentionally riotous version of a Shakespeare play.

Something Upstairs: A Tale of Ghosts (1988)
A young man confronts the ghost of a murdered slave in his family's house in Providence.

The Man Who Was Poe (1989)
A dark, mysterious stranger follows Edmund through the shadowy city. Is it Edgar Allan Poe?

The True Confessions of Charlotte Doyle (1990)
In 1832, caught between the madness of a ruthless captain and the rage of a mutinous crew on the high seas, thirteen-year-old Charlotte Doyle is found guilty of murder.

Blue Heron (1992)
Why is Maggie's father making secret phone calls? And who is trying to kill the beautiful heron on the marsh?

Who Was That Masked Man, Anyway? (1992)
In the spring of 1945 in Brooklyn, New York, Franklin D. Wattleson and Mario Calvino, inspired by *The Lone Ranger* and *The Green Hornet* on radio, set out to right the world's wrongs.

City of Light, City of Dark: A Comic Book Novel (1993)
Carlos Juarez dreams of leaving the city and returning home.

Judy and Punch (1993)
A boy becomes Punch in Joe McSneed's traveling show, but only Judy, the owner's daughter, likes him.

Nothing but the Truth: A Documentary Novel (1993)
Ninth-grader Philip Malloy constantly hums the national anthem, annoying Miss Narwin so much she keeps him off the track team.

The Barn (1994)
In Oregon Territory, 1855, three children—Ben, nine; Nettie, fifteen; and Harrison, thirteen—struggle to maintain the family homestead after their pioneer father suffers a stroke.

Tom, Babette, and Simon: Three Tales of Transformation (1995)

FICTION FOR YOUNGER READERS

Things That Sometimes Happen (1970)
Short stories.

Snail Tale: The Adventures of a Rather Small Snail (1972)

No More Magic (1975)

The History of Helpless Harry: To Which Is Added a Variety of Amusing and Entertaining Adventures (1980)

Man from the Sky (1980)

Who Stole the Wizard of Oz? (1980)

Windcatcher (1991)

The Bird, the Frogs and the Light (1994)

Poppy (1995)

FOR FURTHER READING

Avi. New York: Avon Books, 1990.

Avi. New York: Orchard Books, 1992.

Avi. "Writing Books for Young People." *The Writer*, March 1982.

Banks, Ann. Review of *The Barn*. *The New York Times Book Review*, 1 January 1995.

Benson, Sonia. "Avi." In *Something About the Author*, edited by Diane Telgen. Vol. 71. Detroit: Gale Research, 1993.

Commire, Anne, ed. "Avi Wortis." In *Something About the Author*. Vol. 14. Detroit: Gale Research, 1978.

Cullinan, Bernice, and M. Jerry Weiss, eds. *Books I Read When I Was Young: The Favorite Books of Famous People*. New York: Avon Books, 1980.

Jones, Trev. Review of *The True Confessions of Charlotte Doyle*. *School Library Journal*, September 1990.

Moss, Anita. "Avi." In *Twentieth-Century Children's Writers*, edited by Tracy Chevalier. 3d ed. Chicago: St. James Press, 1989.

Stan, Susan. "Conversations: Avi." *Five Owls*, January–February 1990.

Jay Bennett

Suspense

New York City
December 24, 1912

The Hooded Man

"I went into the field [of writing young adult fiction] to try to reach the young with all the skill and thought I had learned in a lifetime of writing in many genres," Jay Bennett said in *Literature for Today's Young Adults*. "I felt that the young were alive, questioning, and in the main were far more decent human beings than were their elders."

"Readers suffer and triumph with Bennett's lonely heroes who pit themselves against organized crime, deadly racists, and—especially—sinister adults who seem harmless on the surface," Anne Janette Johnson said.

Bennett's fictional victims "have real blood, not catchup, and the screams aren't caused by the rocking chair coming down on the cat's tail," George A. Woods stated.

The son of a Jewish immigrant businessman, Bennett held a variety of jobs as an adult: on a farm, in a factory, and at a beach. He also was a mailman, a salesman, and an editor for an encyclopedia. During World War II, from 1942 to 1945, he wrote for the Office of War Information.

Besides writing fiction for young adults and adults, he has crafted two plays and several radio scripts, including *Miracle Before Christmas* and *The Wind and Stars Are Witness*. He has written television scripts for *Alfred Hitchcock Presents; Crime Syndicated; Wide, Wide World; Cameo Theater;* and *Monodrama Theatre*. Bennett, who looks to William Shakespeare as an influence, was the first to adapt *Hamlet* for television, winning an award from the Shakespeare Society for this.

"I always look for a central character and then let him find the story for me," Bennett said in *Contemporary Authors*. "In a way, I embark upon a voyage of discovery. I constantly find myself surprised at the revelations that come through the unconsciousness and onto the page. However, this must be kept in mind, I have spent many long years learning my craft of writing, particularly that of the suspense genre. So this knowledge always comes into play."

The author said that he respects his readers. "All through my years I have been intensely interested in the young and their problems and hopes. Their dreams and despairs," he said in *Authors & Artists for Young Adults*. "My wife still calls me a child who will never grow up and in one sense she's absolutely right. And that's why it's so easy for me to write my books for that readership. But there's more to it than that. I feel very strongly that it's up to the young to help turn things around. We can't go on much longer the way we are."

Bennett won the Mystery Writers of America's Edgar Allan Poe Award for best juvenile mystery in 1974 and 1975, for *The Dangling Witness* and *The Long Black Coat*, respectively. His mystery *The Skeleton Man* was nominated for an Edgar in 1987.

Bennett's young adult novels contain much anxiety as well as suspense. The hero of *The Dangling Witness* has seen a murder but cannot bring himself to tell the police. In *The Long Black Coat*, the main character has to elude murderous army veterans who are looking for stolen money. In *The Birthday Murderer*, a youth grapples with the fear that he caused a fatal accident when he was five years old.

In *The Hooded Man*, Cory Brenner blames himself for the fraternity prank that killed his good friend, Fred Harris. Cory and his buddies, Miles Kenton and Frank Shea, decide that Fred should help them swipe the bell from the tower of the abandoned old meeting house. Cory climbs the tower with Fred, but when he slips, he falls against Fred—and Fred plunges to his death.

Cory is agonized enough, but one of his professors and a coach will not let up in their accusations. A mysterious hooded man begins following them. Miles dies. Then Frank. Who is out to get revenge? The book is plot driven. There's little room for character development. It has short sentences, and it has one-sentence paragraphs. These techniques speed the reader suspensefully along.

YOUNG ADULT FICTION

Deathman, Do Not Follow Me, A Novel (1968)
Teen Danny Morgan has feared the Deathman ever since a van Gogh painting disappeared from the Brooklyn Museum.

The Deadly Gift; A Novel (1969)
A desperate stranger gives John-Tom Dawes a box full of money on a rainy night.

The Killing Tree; A Novel (1972)
The African tribal statue turns out to be more than a mere death link to Fred Willis's late anthropologist father.

Masks: A Love Story (1972)
Jennifer falls in love with Peter Chen—pushing her parents to the limits of their tolerance.

The Long Black Coat; A Mystery (1973)
With his mother dead and his father long gone, Phil Brant looks for guidance from his older brother, Vinnie. Then Vinnie dies in Vietnam.

The Dangling Witness (1974)
Matthew Garth witnesses a murder but is reluctant to go to the authorities.

Say Hello to the Hit Man; A Mystery (1976)
A New York City college student receives threatening phone calls.

The Birthday Murderer: A Mystery (1977)
Shan Rourke cannot remember the incident, but he believes he caused a fatal accident when he was younger.

The Pigeon (1980)
Brian Cowley, seventeen, is set up to take the blame for his girlfriend's death.

The Executioner (1982)
Indirectly responsible for a friend's death, Bruce feels guilty—and scared—when someone sets out to get him.

Slowly, Slowly, I Raise the Gun (1983)

I Never Said I Loved You (1984)

The Death Ticket (1985)
A lottery ticket is worth $6 million dollars—and a few lives.

To Be a Killer (1985)
Someone wants to crush Paul Moore's dream of becoming a great football player.

The Skeleton Man: A Novel (1986)
Ray Bond accepts $30,000 as a birthday gift from his mysterious Uncle Ed—who then leaps to his death from a twelfth-floor window.

The Haunted One (1989)
Champion swimmer Paul Barrett, working as a lifeguard at a resort, is haunted by the beautiful Jody, floundering beyond the breakers.

The Dark Corridor (1990)
Kerry loves Alicia, the richest girl in town. He cannot believe it when she apparently takes her own life, part of a shocking wave of teenage suicides.

Sing Me a Death Song: A Novel (1990)
Jason is the only one who believes his mother is innocent of a murder charge.

Coverup: A Novel (1991)
Waking up with a hangover, Brad has a feeling something terrible happened while he was riding home from a party.

Skinhead: A Novel (1991)
Jonathan Atwood faces a group of murderous neo-Nazi skinheads.

Death Grip (1993)
Someone has stolen Shane Lockwood's violin and threatened murder. Could beautiful Laurie Carson be the cause of his nightmare?

The Hooded Man (1993)
Cory and three friends once played a fraternity prank, and now a hooded man is stalking them.

ADULT FICTION

Catacombs (1959)

All Her Vices (1961) as Steve Rand

So Sweet, So Wicked (1961) as Steve Rand

Murder Money (1963); British title: *Murder for Money* (1963)

Death Is a Silent Room (1965)

Shadows Offstage: A Novel (1974)

DRAMA

No Hiding Place (first produced in 1949)

Lions After Slumber (first produced in 1951)

ADAPTATIONS IN OTHER MEDIA

The Woman Who Wouldn't Die (1965)
A film based on an unidentified Bennett novel.

FOR FURTHER READING

Donelson, Kenneth L., and Alleen Pace Nilsen, eds. "People Behind the Books: Jay Bennett." In *Literature for Today's Young Adults*. Glenview, IL: Scott, Foresman, 1980.

Evory, Ann, and Linda Metzger, eds. "Bennett, Jay." In *Contemporary Authors New Revision Series*. Vol. 11. Detroit: Gale Research, 1984.

Johnson, Anne Janette. "Jay Bennett." In *Authors & Artists for Young Adults*, edited by Kevin S. Hile. Vol. 10. Detroit: Gale Research, 1993.

Woods, George A. Review of *Deathman, Do Not Follow Me*. *The New York Times Book Review*, 7 July 1968.

Cynthia Blair

Humorous adventure

Long Island, New York
June 21, 1953

Bubble Gum Gang Mysteries

"In all my writings I strive to create strong, independent female characters who are involved in making emotional decisions and personal choices," said Cynthia Blair in *Contemporary Authors*. "I write for the same reason that I suspect a lot of other writers do—to validate my own perceptions and experiences and to appease the compulsion to write. Because of these two driving forces, my novels are a continuation of autobiography; they relate things I've done, or have fantasized about doing, and involve people I have known. Of course, all of this is vastly distorted by my own interpretations and creative embellishments, since real life, despite rumors to the contrary, is rarely as interesting as fiction."

The daughter of an English teacher and an artist, Blair attended Bryn Mawr College, earning a bachelor of arts degree in 1975. Two years later, she received a master's degree at the Massachusetts Institute of Technology.

Blair worked from 1977 to 1981 as a marketing manager for Avon Products, Standard Brands, and Nestlé. She became a full-time writer. In 1982, she married Richard Smith, an architect, with whom she has a son.

In *Contemporary Authors*, the writer said she believes that young adult readers are more idealistic than adult readers and perhaps not as ready to accept large doses of reality in what they read.

Her Bubble Gum Gang Mysteries feature Carla Farrell, Samantha Langtree, and Betsy Crane—pals who stick together like bubble gum. In *Buried Treasure . . . in My Own Attic?*, Carla is down in the dumps over her weight: "I'd 'plateau'd,' as they say. That means I'd reached a certain weight at which my body said, 'Okay. That's good enough.' The fat cells wouldn't budge, and neither would the scale. It was discouraging to be working so hard, eating right and exercising, while the scale thumbed its nose at me day after day. I'd tried not to think about it too much, but the fact remained that having stopped losing weight was getting me down, too."

Carla's friends talk her into becoming a volunteer sister to a girl who is having trouble in school. The girl turns out to be less than enthusiastic about the idea. Then one day, while helping clean the attic, Carla comes upon her great-grandaunt's diary with directions to a hidden treasure. As she pieces together the clues to the treasure, Carla comes to realize her many strengths: "I had come to understand that I mattered. There were people who cared about me, people who loved me. In turn, I cared about them, too. And that was the best 'treasure' anybody could ever hope for."

YOUNG ADULT FICTION

Starstruck (1987)

Freedom to Dream (1987)

Crazy in Love (1988)
Sallie meets Saul at a party but makes the mistake of introducing him to her best friend, Rachel.

Going Solo (1991)
Three very different roommates are thrown together at the Wildwood Summer Program.

A Summer in Paris (1992)
Nina, who has always dreamed of going to Paris; Kristy, who has nothing better to do; and Jennifer, who has no interest in Paris, embark on an adventure.

Molly and the Great American Family (1994)
Molly Witherspoon, fifteen, the middle of five sisters, must hold the family together. Dad is an absent-minded professor and Mom is going to Japan on a business trip.

Temptation (1994)

Bubble Gum Gang Mysteries

There's No Such Thing as a Haunted House (1991)
Betsy does not believe in haunted houses, until she looks out the window of her new bedroom and sees the creepy house next door.

Chocolate Is My Middle Name (1992)
Carla's sister is accused of stealing a bracelet from a new store at the mall. She enlists the Bubble Gum Gang to investigate.

Warning: Baby-Sitting May Be Hazardous to Your Health (1993)
Someone is selling secrets at Samantha's father's computer firm.

What Do Rock Stars Eat for Breakfast? (1993)
The Gang must help Betsy persuade rock star Johnny Rainbow to play at Hanover Junior High—and clear themselves of charges of vandalism at the school.

Buried Treasure . . . in My Own Attic? (1994)
Carla finds her great-grandaunt's eighty-year-old diary and clues to a hidden treasure.

Dark Moon Legacy

The Curse (1993)
Dangerously in love, a stranger watches Miranda from afar.

Seduction (1993)
Garth tempts Miranda with the promise of unlimited power.

The Rebellion (1993)
Featherwoman lures a determined Garth and a brave Miranda to their doom.

Susan and Christine Series

The Banana Split Affair (1985)
Fraternal twins Susan (straight-A student and artist) and Christine (fashionable and popular with boys) Pratt decide to switch places for a week.

The Hot Fudge Sunday Affair (1985)
Christine is honorary queen of Centennial Week but feels guilty because Susan helped write her winning research project.

Strawberry Summer (1986)
The twins use their "switching powers" to save their camp from a plague of accidents.

The Pumpkin Principle (1986)
The Pratts meet their match: twin brothers.

Marshmallow Masquerade (1987)

The Candy Cane Caper (1987)
At Christmas, the Pratt parents want to go to Mexico. The twins are glum, until they are invited to visit grandparents in Vermont.

The Pink Lemonade Charade (1988)
The twins and schoolmates are on a spring tour of Washington, D.C., eager to see Russian ballet dancers.

The Double Dip Disguise (1988)
The twins visit their grandparents on Seagull Island and take jobs to earn money for college.

The Popcorn Project (1989)
In Los Angeles to help an aunt who has injured her ankle, the Pratts become involved in a Hollywood studio mystery.

Apple Pie Adventure (1989)

The Jelly Bean Scheme (1990)
The twins' town history is being considered for a national prize, and they fly to New Orleans for the contest.

The Lollipop Plot (1990)
Christine and Susan look forward to leaving college in New York for homecoming weekend at their high school.

Coconut Connection (1991)
On an exciting vacation in Hawaii, Chris and Susan meet Steven, the nephew of powerful Charles Collier. When their photos of Collier's coconut plantation are stolen, they realize that something dangerous is happening.

ADULT FICTION

Once There Was a Fat Girl (1980)

Lover's Choice (1981)

Forever Rainbows (1982)

Beautiful Dreamer (1983)

Commitment (1983)

Battle Scars (1984)

Just Married (1984)

All Our Secrets (1985)

The Three of Us (1988)

Summer House (1989)

Close to Home (1990)

Temptation (1993)

FOR FURTHER READING

May, Hal, ed. "Cynthia Blair." In *Contemporary Authors*. Vol. 118. Detroit: Gale Research, 1986.

Francesca Lia Block

Urban drama

Hollywood, California
December 3, 1962

Weetzie Bat

Weetzie Bat, Francesca Lia Block's first novel, "burst on the young adult book scene like a rainbow bubble showering clouds of roses, feathers, tiny shells and a rubber chicken," said Patty Campbell.

The daughter of an artist and a poet, Block grew up in Los Angeles and the San Fernando Valley. She attended North Hollywood High School, living what she described as the "fairy-tale magic" of the city. She received a bachelor of arts degree from the University of California, Berkeley, in 1986.

Block first wrote poetry and short stories. Later, she began putting together the novel *Weetzie Bat*, strictly for pleasure. A friend mailed a copy to a publisher, who took an immediate interest.

Block "scares those who evaluate and buy young-adult materials," commented Patrick Jones. He noted that Block is frequently described as unconventional and controversial. "The controversy centers not so much around the usual suspects—sex, violence, or foul language—but rather the alternative lifestyles of Block's characters. The passion and division which Block creates in the YA world is not new: in fact, it is as old as contemporary young-adult literature itself." Comparing Block's effect on librarians and critics, as well as readers, to that of S. E. Hinton, Jones said the controversy centers on "tone and language; matter-of-fact attitude (in Block's case, about sex rather than violence); the lack of adults and conventional families; and the overriding concern about becoming a good person in a world filled with death and disaster."

Weetzie Bat, set in Los Angeles, is about a punk princess. Weetzie wears her bleached blond hair in a flattop and sews a fringe on her minis to show unity with the plight of Native Americans. Her one close (and gay) friend is Dirk, who drives a red '55 Pontiac. Weetzie falls in love with My Secret Agent Lover Man. Dirk finds companionship with Duck, another male. They move into a house that Dirk inherited from his grandmother. "They" have a baby, Cherokee Bat. Another child, Witch Baby, is left on their doorstep. They extend their household to include friends and pets. They listen to punk music. They eat good food. They lead artistic and extravagant lives.

Weetzie Bat "is a punk, young adult fairy tale, an ingeniously lyrical narrative of two friends, Weetzie and Dirk, who weave a nest of Hollywood illusions and hard-core loyalty," said Betsy Hearn. "Although each of the four main characters is shaken by a terrible loss, the group survives through the knowledge that they are all each one has."

Block's next book, *Witch Baby*, finds the title character looking for independence. "The novel is reminiscent of a music video," said Maeve Visser Knoth. "Scenes and sensory images flash across the page; characters speak in complicated slang and create a safe haven for themselves in the midst of a shifting, confusing world. An untraditional novel, *Witch Baby* is honest to the experience of many young adults, who use music, fads, and material possessions to try to understand the world."

In *Cherokee Bat and the Goat Guys*, Cherokee puts together a musical group with Raphael, Chong Jah-Love, and Angel Juan Perez. "Their band gains popularity, and the fans become demanding," said Knoth. "The four high-school students become heavily involved in sex, drugs, and alcohol to live up to their image and cope with the stress. Their lives spin out of control, and Cherokee Bat almost commits suicide. Coyote [a Native American friend] steps in and helps them remember that they are still children."

"All of these stories are told with wildly imaginative prose and dialogue loaded with L. A. 'slanguage,' " said Jones, "making Block, operating alone in her genre of fantastic realism, a unique voice in young-adult literature."

"Technicolor descriptions, fizzy juxtapositions and a bouncy, upbeat tone helped make Francesca Lia Block's first four young-adult novels . . . both irresistible and invaluable to canny adolescent readers," said Jim Gladstone. He said the funkiness of the characters and story may have deceived some readers who "soon found that Ms. Block's stories were not soda pop but complex, bittersweet concoctions in which the young characters had to deal with major problems. Her positive outlook did not lead her to ignore or sugar-coat the hard realities of modern teen-age life. Ms. Block's uncanned and unpreachy takes on pregnancy, sexual identity, broken families and drug use are what make her short, punchy novels invaluable."

The Hanged Man, a recent novel, is about Laurel, who struggles with the loss of her father—who had sexually abused her. "In its language, its acute observation of modern families and its portrayal of Laurel as a psychologically complex, very real character, the book is a significant step forward," said Gladstone. *Publishers Weekly* found the novel "disturbing but ultimately exhilarating."

YOUNG ADULT FICTION

The Hanged Man (1994)
Laurel still imagines the sound of shattering glass before her father died.

Primavera (1994)
Primavera refuses to believe she lives in Paradise. She tries to escape the city of Elysia before it claims her.

Weetzie Bat Series

Weetzie Bat (1989)
Weetzie and her companions have a baby and create an extended family in hip Los Angeles.

Witch Baby (1990)
Left as a foundling on Weetzie Bat's doorstep, Witch Baby strikes out on her own.

Cherokee Bat and the Goat Guys (1991)
Weetzie's child, Cherokee Bat, forms a band with her friends, but the stress soon wrenches their lives out of control.

Missing Angel Juan (1993)
Witch Baby leaves Los Angeles to search for Angel Juan Perez, who has moved to New York to play music on his own.

Baby Be-Bop (1995)

CONTRIBUTOR

Am I Blue? Coming Out from the Silence, edited by Marion Dane Bauer (1994)

FOR FURTHER READING

Block, Francesca Lia. "Punk Pixies in the Canyon." *The Los Angeles Times Book Review*, 26 July 1992.

Campbell, Patty. Review of *Cherokee Bat and the Goat Guys. The New York Times Book Review*, 20 September 1992.

Gladstone, Jim. Review of *The Hanged Man. The New York Times Book Review*, 26 February 1995.

Hearne, Betsy. "Pretty in Punk." Review of *Weetzie Bat. The New York Times Book Review*, 21 May 1989.

Jones, Patrick. "People Are Talking About Francesca Lia Block." *Horn Book Magazine*, November–December 1992.

Knoth, Maeve Visser. Review of *Cherokee Bat and the Goat Guys. Horn Book Magazine*, September–October 1992.

———. Review of *Witch Baby. Horn Book Magazine*, January–February 1992.

Review of *The Hanged Man. Publishers Weekly*, 18 July 1994.

Judy Blume

Suburban adolescence

Elizabeth, New Jersey
February 12, 1938

Tiger Eyes

Judy Blume is known for her frank books that deal with such topics as menstruation, obesity, and premarital sex. Her books have made her popular with many teens and controversial with some adults.

Judy Sussman Blume has described her mother as a shy individual who was fond of reading. Her father, a dentist, was outgoing and handy with tools. Blume has said she is more like her father, and her brother, David, four years older, is more like their mother.

Favorite books from her youth were *Madeline* by Ludwig Bemelmans and, when she was in fifth grade, the Betsy and Tacy books by Maud Hart Lovelace.

As a child, Blume said, she felt frustrated by the answers she received to questions about sex. She learned more through friends at school than at home.

Blume married John Blume, a young lawyer, in 1959; they have two children. In 1960, Blume received a bachelor of arts degree from New York University. At the same time that she was beginning her life as a wife and mother, she began writing. She signed up for a course in fiction for children and teens and wrote several stories for the class, including an early version of what would later be published as *The One in the Middle Is the Green Kangaroo.*

Taking the course a second time, Blume completed what became her first novel, *Iggie's House*. At the same time, she began selling stories to magazines.

Her third book, *Are You There, God? It's Me, Margaret*, was considered by some to be overly graphic in its descriptions of Margaret's body changes as she goes through puberty. Still, it was named an Outstanding Children's Book of 1970 by *The New York Times*.

Subsequent titles also ran into controversy. *Blubber* was decried for its realistic dialogue, *Deenie* for talking about masturbation, and *Forever* for its frank depiction of first-time physical love.

"If I were writing *Forever* [published in 1975] today, it would have to be published as an adult novel," Blume told Norma Klein in a 1983 interview. "And that's a sad twist. I don't feel I can write realistically about today's teenagers, in their own language, and publish it as a book for young people. Ten giant steps backward."

"I think that a lot of adults in our society are uncomfortable with their own sexuality, and therefore their children's sexuality is a threat to them," Blume told Justin Wintle and Emma Fisher. "That's not true of everyone of course. I have had some very negative responses from adults, but I've also had some very positive ones. The negative responses don't usually come to me directly, but through a librarian or some other intermediary who tells me about some parent who comes in carrying a book of mine demanding that it be removed."

"I think I write about sexuality because when I was young, that's what I most wanted to know about," Blume said in Diana Gleasner's *Breakthrough: Women in Writing*. "I identify very strongly with kids. Twelve- and thirteen-year-olds feel things very intensely. They need to know about what they are feeling, and more than anything else, they want reassurance that their feelings are normal. Besides, sex is very interesting."

"At an age when social acceptance by the peer group is the longed-for panacea, when prepubescent anxiety and narcissism are at their peak and when a restless curiosity about sex is linked with personal inadequacy, fear, and excitement, these books become classroom bibles, passed from hand to hand and giggled over at recess," in the view of Michele Landsberg. "They become almost a talisman of belonging, like the latest style of sneakers or gimmick pencils." The critic went on to call Blume "the poorest of all the problem novelists" and to charge that it is not Blume's frankness "but her bland and unquestioning acceptance of majority values, of conformity, consumerism, materialism, unbounded narcissism, and flat, sloppy, ungrammatical, inexpressive speech," that should be criticized.

Richard W. Jackson narrowed in on why Blume is so appealing: Her "books talk to kids. Hundreds of letters tell us so. For one thing, her stories sparkle with kids' talk. Her dialogue seems to be theirs, not so much written as overheard. But few people can know the part that talk plays while Judy is creating her book.

"Early in her career Judy Blume found a writing style exactly right for her stories (and her readers), and she's perfected it."

R. A. Siegel agreed that Blume's books are popular, but "for what they *are not* as much as for what *they are*. That is, her books are not very demanding and they make for the kind of easy, rapid reading that children like to relax with. Since all her books are told through the voice of a child narrator, the vocabulary is necessarily limited and the sentence construction basic and repetitious."

Judith M. Goldberger looked beyond this to observe, "Judy Blume was a pioneer, breaking barriers of silence with novels such as *Are You There, God? It's Me, Margaret*, which relates a young girl's most private thoughts about the onset of her sexual maturity. . . . Judy Blume writes for and about today's children. And, because she writes about children's feelings, the honesty of her books is a key factor to her. Her allies—millions of juvenile (and adult) fans—would probably agree that it is her honesty which is a large part of what makes her so good to read. But it is also her honesty that makes her opponents so angry with her."

In 1975, Blume's first marriage ended. A year later, she wed Thomas Kitchens, a physicist, and they moved to New Mexico. Blume continued to write fiction for young adults and younger readers, but she also produced *Wifey*, her first adult novel, in 1977. As she explained in *Literature for Today's Young Adults*, "I need the freedom, the challenge, of dealing with all age groups. I expect to write novels about young people as well as adults. I expect to write about those subjects that are important to me. And what is especially important are human relationships. I hope to deal with the realities of life, to present characters and situations that will cause readers to think."

Blume divorced a second time, and in 1987 she married George Cooper, a law professor and writer. A year later, she collaborated with her son, Larry, to adapt her book *Otherwise Known as Sheila the Great* as a film.

The Kids Fund, which Blume established in 1981, is financed with royalties from *The Judy Blume Diary: The Place to Put Your Own Feelings* (1981); *Letters to Judy: What Your Kids Wish They Could Tell You* (1986), and *The Judy Blume Memory Book* (1988). It contributes money each year to nonprofit organizations to help young people.

YOUNG ADULT FICTION

Are You There, God? It's Me, Margaret (1970)
Margaret Simon, twelve, struggling to grow up, has frequent conversations with God.

Then Again, Maybe I Won't (1971)
Tony daydreams of snitching on his shoplifter friend, Joel, or seeing Lisa undress at night. He is a thirteen-year-old, after all.

It's Not the End of the World (1972)
Karen cannot believe that her parents are divorcing.

Deenie (1973)
A thirteen-year-old must cope with curvature of the spine.

Forever . . . (1975)
A first sexual relationship does not mean a lasting relationship for Katherine and Michael.

Tiger Eyes (1981)
Davey Wexler and her family move to New Mexico and try to sort out their lives after her father is killed in a holdup at his 7-Eleven store.

Just As Long As We're Together (1987)
Stephanie, thirteen, is in seventh grade and enjoys her close friends, Rachel and Alison, but her father's continued absence begins to trouble her.

Here's to You, Rachel Robinson (1992), sequel to *Just As Long As We're Together*
Rachel has enjoyed the freedom of older brother Charles being away at boarding school. Then he is expelled.

FICTION FOR YOUNGER READERS

The One in the Middle Is the Green Kangaroo (1969, 1981, and 1991)

Iggie's House (1970)

Freckle Juice (1971)

Otherwise Known as Sheila the Great (1972)

Blubber (1974)

Starring Sally J. Freedman as Herself (1977)

The Pain and the Great One (1984)

Fudge Series

Tales of a Fourth Grade Nothing (1972)

Superfudge (1980)

Fudge-a-Mania (1990)

CONTRIBUTOR

Once upon a Time . . . (1986)

ADULT FICTION

Wifey (1977)

Smart Women (1984)

ADAPTATIONS IN OTHER MEDIA

Forever . . . (1978)
Television movie.

Freckle Juice (1987)
Animated film.

Otherwise Known as Sheila the Great (1988)
Screenplay by Judy Blume and Lawrence Blume.

Fudge (1995)
Television series based on the Fudge series.

Fudge-a-Mania (1995)
Television movie based on the Fudge series.

FOR FURTHER READING

The Judy Blume Diary: The Place to Put Your Own Feelings. New York: Dell, 1981.

Letters to Judy: What Your Kids Wish They Could Tell You. New York: Putnam, 1986.

The Judy Blume Memory Book: With Judy Blume's Own Personal Memories. New York: Dell, 1988.

Donelson, Kenneth L., and Alleen Pace Nilsen, eds. "The People Behind the Books: Judy Blume." In *Literature for Today's Young Adults*. Glenview, IL: Scott, Foresman, 1980.

Gleasner, Diana. *Breakthrough: Women in Writing*. New York: Walker, 1980.

Goldberger, Judith M. "Judy Blume: Target of the Censor." *Newsletter on Intellectual Freedom*, May 1981.

Jackson, Richard W. "Books That Blume: An Appreciation." *Elementary English*, September 1974.

Klein, Norma. "Some Thoughts on Censorship: An Author Symposium." *Top of the News*, winter 1983.

Landsberg, Michele. *Reading for the Love of It*. New York: Prentice Hall Press, 1987.

Siegel, R. A. "Are You There, God? It's Me, Me, ME! Judy Blume's Self-Absorbed Narrators." *The Lion and the Unicorn*, fall 1978.

Wintle, Justin, and Emma Fisher. *The Pied Pipers*. New York: Paddington Press, 1975.

Sue Ellen Bridgers

Rural drama

Greenville, South Carolina
September 20, 1942

Notes for Another Life: A Novel

"In books we can travel the road not taken; we can, for a little while, live another life, absorb the sights and sounds of another place," said Sue Ellen Bridgers in a publisher's promotional pamphlet. "We can know what it is like to be someone else. That private pleasure, that gift of knowing, is what I demand of everything I read and what I strive for in everything I write."

Sue Ellen Hunsucker, the daughter of a farmer, has been a writer since 1970. She attended East Carolina University from 1960 to 1963, and earned a bachelor of arts degree at Western Carolina University in 1976. She and her husband, attorney Ben Bridgers, married in 1963 and have three children.

"The longer I work with the characters who people my books," the author said in *ALAN Review*, "the less sure I am of where they come from and why. There are some like Maggie Grover in *Home Before Dark* who take on a life apart from my intention and thereby change the course of the story, and some like Mae Willis who are so unsure and desperate that they let me control their destinies. There is Hazard Whitaker in *All Together Now* who proposed to Pansy quite spontaneously and against my better judgment. There is Jane Flanagan who assumed with ease and validity the role I gave her. I give up trying to approach these people in an objective fashion. I will leave that to scholars and reviewers whose hapless job it is to study creative-after-the-fact."

Her first novel, *Home Before Dark,* is set in North Carolina, where the author grew up. It is about the Willises, traveling tobacco pickers who finally have a chance to settle down. "The author speaks with a voice that is intensely lyrical yet wholly un-self-conscious," in the view of Barbara Helfgott. "Character and theme have been developed with such painstaking attention that each episode seems inevitable and right."

The book looks "at the lives of migrant workers and at the need to settle and the need not to settle for failure and success," Linda Bachelder said. It is "flawlessly written and loaded, like the great Southern novels, with Gothic humor and with fascinating characters."

Bridgers's *All Together Now* looks at a special relationship that develops between a teenage girl and an older, mentally retarded man. "The thoughts and feelings of each character are revealed through shifting viewpoints as each in his own time learns that love must be based on truth and acceptance," Kate M. Flanagan noted. "And when Dwayne is threatened with institutionalization, Casey comes to understand that a commitment to another person cannot be passive."

Bridgers's "young protagonists enact their emotional dramas in the context of family and neighbors," said Anita Moss, "and are rooted in traditional southern life; home, land, church, and community remain abiding values to these rather unsophisticated but genuinely likable people. Her young characters are usually sensitive, and her adults are rounded, caring, and sometimes flawed, not the persecuting and abusive authority figures who inhabit the pages of so many young adult novels."

"I am not sure there needs to be a category of young adult literature at all," the author stated in *Literature for Today's Young Adults,* "and I don't understand the criteria for its classification. If it means that, because of their style or subject matter, beautifully written, accomplished stories that stretch the reader's understanding of life are eliminated, then I hope young adult literature as a category dies quickly. If it means that young people are given access to good books that might otherwise go unpublished for lack of a market, then I have warm wishes for its future."

YOUNG ADULT FICTION

Home Before Dark: A Novel (1976)
Stella Mae Willis, fourteen, is accustomed to wandering with her crop-picking family until Uncle Newt gives them a sharecropper's cabin.

All Together Now: A Novel (1979)
Twelve-year-old Casey Flanagan has no friends when she arrives to spend the summer in a small town with her grandparents. Then Dwayne Pickens, a retarded man, becomes a special friend.

Notes for Another Life: A Novel (1981)
Wren, thirteen, and her older brother, Kevin, live with their grandparents because their father is a patient in a mental hospital and their mother has gone to the city for a fashion career.

Sara Will (1985)
Trapped in her fifties, between youth and old age, Sara Will Burney lives in a world of order. Then Fate Jessup, his unwed teenage niece, and her baby arrive and turn things topsy-turvy.

Permanent Connections (1987)
Rob is secretive and sullen—he is fooling around with drugs. Sent to the country to live with relatives, he falls in love with Ellery and things begin to change.

Keeping Christina (1993)
A story of friendship and jealousy.

CONTRIBUTOR

Connections: Short Stories by Outstanding Writers for Young Adults, edited by Donald R. Gallo (1989)

FOR FURTHER READING

Bachelder, Linda. "Looking Backward: Trying to Find the Classic Young Adult Novel." *English Journal*, September 1980.

Bridgers, Sue Ellen. "Stories My Grandmother Told Me." Part 1. *ALAN Review*, fall 1985.

———. "Stories My Grandmother Told Me." Part 2. *ALAN Review*, winter 1986.

Carroll, Pamela, ed. *Teacher's Guide to the Novels of Sue Ellen Bridgers*. New York: Bantam Books, 1989.

Donelson, Kenneth L., and Alleen Pace Nilsen, eds. "The People Behind the Books: Sue Ellen Bridgers." In *Literature for Today's Young Adults*. Glenview, IL: Scott, Foresman, 1980.

Flanagan, Kate M. Review of *All Together Now. Horn Book Magazine*, April 1979.

Helfgott, Barbara. Review of *Home Before Dark. The New York Times Book Review*, 14 November 1976.

Moss, Anita. "Sue Ellen Bridgers." In *Twentieth-Century Children's Writers*, edited by Tracy Chevalier. 3d ed. Chicago: St. James Press, 1989.

Bruce Brooks

Coming-of-age stories

Richmond, Virginia
September 23, 1950

The Moves Make the Man: A Novel

"Talented, confident, independent, disciplined, excited by challenge: these characteristics describe Jerome Foxworthy, the smart, steady basketball player who narrates *The Moves Make the Man*, and Sib Spooner, the world-class cellist, daughter of former hippies, who describes a journey in *Midnight Hour Encores*. The description also fits Bruce Brooks, creator of both characters, who admits, 'I have an affinity for independence, for loners, for smart people who are watchers,' " Christine McDonnell said.

Distinguishing Brooks's prose, she added, are a "confident, intense first-person voice; the insightful probing into characters' complicated inner lives; the imaginative metaphors, often funny, always fresh. Like Jerome and Sib, Brooks's tough, cocky narrators, the author insists on independence, values honesty, and goes his own way. He does not accept any limits in the structure, style, or content of his books."

"Both *The Moves Make the Man* and *Everywhere* examine a relationship between two youngsters, one black, the other white," explained Leonard S. Marcus. "In certain scenes of the earlier book, especially, the day-to-day consequences of living in a prejudiced society are brought searingly to the fore. Nonetheless, Brooks noted, the racial differences in *The Moves Make the Man* 'turn out not to be nearly as strong as other differences, and certain similarities of circumstance and internal makeup' that ultimately define the complex relationship between Jerome and the elusive Bix Rivers."

"*The Moves Make the Man* is an excellent novel about values and the way people relate to one another," said Mel Watkins. "It is entertaining and accessible; the chapters in which Jerome teaches Bix how to play basketball could serve as a primer for any young athlete. Because Jerome is such an intelligent, streetwise narrator, it is a novel that adults will relish as well."

"I owe my characters a great deal for their collaborative influence," said Brooks in accepting the Boston Globe–Horn Book Award for *Moves*. "I first wrote the story of Bix and Jerome as fourteen pages of summary background in a mammoth, towering novel about certain other characters later on in their lives. I had grandiose designs for this sprawling castle of a story, and the tale of 'Jerome and Bix' served only as a fillip of crenellation in architecture.

"But the boys wouldn't shut up, once I had let them show their faces," he continued. "They kept nagging me as I forged pedantically ahead with my bigger plans."

Brooks earned a bachelor of arts degree at the University of North Carolina, Chapel Hill, in 1978. He received a master's degree in 1980 from the University of Iowa. In 1978, he married Penelope Winslow, with whom he has a son. Brooks has worked as a letterpress printer, a newspaper and magazine reporter, and a teacher.

His first four books had youthful protagonists, he once said, because he was curious about his own childhood. His parents divorced when he was six, and he split his time between two homes. His mother was an alcoholic and experienced nervous breakdowns. Brooks once ran away to live with a grandmother.

Marcus noted, "Brooks was not, he thinks, a 'great fantasizer' in the sense that he would lose himself in speculations about realities that were not his own—'the planet Znarg, say.' His curiosity tended instead to gravitate toward near-at-hand anomalies: the precise nature, for instance, of a certain activity observed in the street from a passing bus. Impulsively but deliberately, the boy would get off the bus and return to the scene. Brooks's novels are similarly grounded in realistic particulars and in a fascination with process—the way things work—whether in music-making or competitive sports or seventh-grade home economics class."

In Brooks's *Midnight Hour Encores,* Sib Spooner is a world-known prodigy cellist. "She's convinced she's done it all herself: Taxi [her father] 'stands behind me so quietly I don't even know he's there.' On their cross-country journey to meet her mother, Connie, who gave Sib up at birth, Taxi tries to explain the sixties so that Sib will understand her mother's desertion in the context of those times.

Sib responds harshly with sarcastic gibes at Connie's superficial hippie pursuits, until slowly Sib comes to see that it is Taxi who loves the sixties and remains committed to its ideals," Hazel Rochman noted. "Perhaps predictably, Connie turns out to be a cool, sophisticated real-estate whiz, contemptuous of her self-indulgent hippie past and of Taxi's lack of 'ego.' Yet, to her own surprise, Sib likes her mother, even understanding Connie's inability to nurture a baby."

Brooks also wrote the nonfiction books *On the Wing: The Life of Birds from Feathers to Flight* (1989), *Nature by Design* (1991), and *Predator* (1991).

YOUNG ADULT FICTION

The Moves Make the Man: A Novel (1985)
Jerome and Bix, a black athlete and a white athlete, though very different, share tips and become friends.

Midnight Hour Encores (1986)
Sib, musically talented, travels with her father to a distant audition and meets her ex-hippie mother, who moved out after she was born.

No Kidding (1989)
Sam, fourteen, worries about his alcoholic mother and younger brother.

Everywhere (1990)
Turley worries about his grandfather, who has suffered a heart attack.

What Hearts (1992)
Stories about Asa at different ages, confronting change at home, challenged by baseball, and learning about love.

Boys Will Be (1993)

FOR FURTHER READING

Brooks, Bruce. "In Collaboration with My Characters." *Horn Book Magazine*, January–February 1986.

Marcus, Leonard S. "Bruce Brooks. "*Publishers Weekly*, 27 July 1990.

McDonnell, Christine. "New Voices, New Visions: Bruce Brooks." *Horn Book Magazine*, March–April 1987.

Rochman, Hazel. Review of *Midnight Hour Encores. Booklist*, 15 September 1986.

Watkins, Mel. "A Trickster and His Upright Friend." *The New York Times Book Review*, 11 November 1984.

Betsy Byars

Family drama

Charlotte, North Carolina
August 7, 1928

The Summer of the Swans

Betsy Byars began writing in 1955. It took nine rejections before her first book was published, seven years later. Since then, she has won a Newbery Award, in 1971 for *The Summer of the Swans*, and has been a National Book Award finalist, in 1973 for *The House of Wings*.

"My one goal in writing . . . is to get my story down on paper, because until the story is on paper, I don't have anything to work with," Byars said in *School Librarian*. "And I rely totally on instinct. If my instinct tells me the story is not moving fast enough, I speed it up. If my instinct tells me I've told this too quickly, I divide the chapter and add some bull. And the difference between someone who has been writing for twenty-five years and someone who is just starting, is the quality of this instinct. When I first started, I agonized over everything—should I take this out? Should I change this? Is this funny? Is this stupid? And every time I changed something I had the feeling I was ruining a potential masterpiece. After twenty-five years I have learned to follow my instinct without question."

Born Betsy Cromer, daughter of a cotton mill executive and a homemaker, the writer told Bernice Cullinan and M. Jerry Weiss, "When I was a girl, the first book that I really loved was *The Adventures of Mabel*. It was the first book I ever wanted to own, and I read it again and again. Mabel's life was the way I wanted my own to be—safe and secure and yet filled with very imaginative adventures."

Byars attended Furman University and received a bachelor of arts degree from Queens College in Charlotte in 1950. In 1950, she married Edward Ford Byars, an engineering professor with whom she has four children. The writer holds a pilot's license.

"I find many of the ideas for my books in things that happen around me—in newspaper stories, in things my children tell me happen in their schools, in magazine articles," she said in the *Third Book of Junior Authors*. "The idea for *The Summer of the Swans* came from an article in my college alumni magazine telling about the swans on the university lake, which persisted in flying away to other, less desirable ponds."

"Reviewers have not always been . . . kind to Betsy Byars," Ina Robertson noted. "Her early books received little praise from critics, but fortunately for all who have been captivated by her later works, she did continue to write and has created outstanding modern, realistic stories enjoyed by children and adults." Robertson continued, "Many of Byars' books do not have the more traditionally-accepted happy endings. . . . [She] challenges children as readers and challenges the commonplace assumptions about children and childhood."

Lois R. Kuznets explained Byars the writer: "1) She often depicts 'the call of the wild,' the fascination that rural field, forest, stream, animal and bird exert on most Americans, even those from modern urban areas; 2) she expresses the fascination with mass-produced objects and entertainment that is similarly a part of our culture . . . ; 3) she is concerned with bringing to the attention of her readers the consciousness of creatures (both animal and human) that are inarticulate, naturally or unnaturally, and often maimed and vulnerable; 4) she is interested in the role that a combination of imaginative playfulness and self-deprecating . . . humor has in the growth and development of her typical young protagonists. These traits, combined with the contemporary American sensitivity to the breakdown of the nuclear family, seem to . . . be exhibited to a greater or lesser extent in most of Byars' novels."

"Although few of her books are humorous, there is in most of Betsy Byars' writing a quiet, understated sense of humor that children quickly recognize and enjoy," Zena Sutherland and May Hill Arbuthnot said. "More evident, and just as much appreciated, are her compassion and her understanding of the deepest emotions of children."

Byars's young adult books are noted for their depictions of troubled adolescents who feel lonely or isolated. "The protagonists of many of Byars' novels feel isolated," said Rosanne Fraine Donahue, mentioning *The Midnight Fox*, "and often unloved and abandoned by their parents. Sammy in *The House of Wings* wakes one morning to find his parents have left for Detroit and he has been left behind with a grandfather he does not know. Warren in *The Two-Thousand-Pound Goldfish* longs for his mother, who started out simply protesting government policy, but has now become involved in bombings and can't come home because she is wanted by the FBI.... Carlie, Harvey, and Thomas J. in *The Pinballs* are foster children, abandoned or abused by their parents. Carlie initially feels like a pinball: out of control, without rights, and pushed around by others. She, like most of Byars' characters, finds that she does have choices; she is not a pinball, she can make things better for herself."

Donahue added, "Byars shows that she is capable of being humorous even while writing about very difficult subjects. In *The Summer of the Swans* the frightening news that learning-disabled Charlie is missing impinges directly on the scene in which Sara, trying to dye her orange sneakers light blue, has just succeeded in turning them puce. Her distress and fear for Charlie is mixed with her comic embarrassment about the hideous color of her sneakers."

In a review of *The Dark Stairs, Publishers Weekly* noted the author's "eye for telling detail and her penchant for strong, quirky characters."

Byars resisted writing series books for many years, until *The Not-Just-Anybody Family,* when she discovered she had more to say about the southern clan. In these stories for middle readers, Vicki Blossom is a stunt rider on the rodeo circuit. Her husband, a steer roper, was killed by a steer. Pap, her father-in-law, cares for the children while she is at work. The kids include Maggie, Vern, and Junior, seven years old, an indefatigable inventor.

The Moon and I is Byars's autobiography.

YOUNG ADULT FICTION

Trouble River (1969)
Dewey, twelve, homesteading on the prairie, is alone with his grandma at their cabin when they are attacked.

The Summer of the Swans (1970)
Sara cannot account for her mood changes this summer, but when her mentally retarded younger brother, Charlie, disappears, all is forgotten.

After the Goat Man (1974)
Figgy's grandfather, nicknamed Goat Man, has barricaded himself in an old cabin and is holding off a wrecking crew that wants to build a new highway.

The TV Kid (1976)
Lennie is caught up in a video world.

The Pinballs (1977)
Three battered children from a dysfunctional family move into a foster home.

The Cartoonist (1978)
Evenings when he is supposed to be doing homework, Alfie Mason is in the attic, drawing cartoons.

Goodbye, Chicken Little (1979)
Jimmie Little blames himself for not stopping Uncle Pete from disappearing down the coal mine on Monday River.

The Night Swimmers (1980)
Retta, Johnny, and Roy are alone nights when their father performs as a country-western singer.

The Cybil War (1981)
Simon battles Tony for the affections of red-haired Cybil.

The Animal, the Vegetable, and John D. Jones (1982)
Clara and Deanie are upset when a woman and her son join them and their divorced father for vacation.

The Two-Thousand-Pound Goldfish (1982)
Warren Otis has not seen his mother for three years; then the FBI comes looking for her.

The Glory Girl (1983)
Why must Anna Glory—one of the Glory Gospel Singers—be the only one in her family who cannot carry a tune?

Cracker Jackson (1985)
Cracker discovers that his former babysitter has been beaten by her husband, and he and his friend, Goat, take her to a shelter.

Coast to Coast (1992)
Birch impulsively goes with her grandfather when he decides to fly cross-country in a Piper Cub airplane.

McMummy (1993)
No one believes that Mozie is scared out of his wits by "McMummy."

The Dark Stairs: A Herculeah Jones Mystery (1994)
Her dad is a policeman, her mom a private investigator. So, naturally, thirteen-year-old Herculeah Jones solves mysteries. This one is set at Dead Oaks estate.

Tarot Says Beware (1995), sequel to *The Dark Stairs*
Herculeah Jones solves another puzzle.

FICTION FOR YOUNGER READERS

Clementine (1962)

The Dancing Camel (1965)

Rama, the Gypsy Cat (1966)

The Groober (1967)

The Midnight Fox (1968)

Go and Hush the Baby (1971)

The House of Wings (1972)

The 18th Emergency (1973)

The Winged Colt of Casa Mia (1973)

The Lace Snail (1975)

The Computer Nut (1984)

Beans on the Roof (1988)

Seven Treasure Hunts (1991)

Bingo Brown Series

The Burning Questions of Bingo Brown (1988)

Bingo Brown and the Language of Love (1989)

Bingo Brown, Gypsy Lover (1990)

Blossom Family Series

The Not-Just-Anybody Family (1986)

The Blossoms Meet the Vulture Lady (1986)

A Blossom Promise (1987)

The Blossoms and the Green Phantom (1987)

Wanted . . . Mud Blossom (1991)

Golly Sisters Series

The Golly Sisters Go West (1986)

Hooray for the Golly Sisters (1990)

The Golly Sisters Ride Again (1994)

ADAPTATIONS IN OTHER MEDIA

Pssst! Hammerman's After You (1973)
ABC *Afterschool Special* adapting *The 18th Emergency.*

Sara's Summer of the Swans (1974)
ABC *Afterschool Special* adapting *The Summer of the Swans.*

Trouble River (1975)
ABC *Afterschool Special* based on the novel of the same title.

The Winged Colt (1976)
ABC *Afterschool Special* based on *The Winged Colt of Casa Mia.*

The Pinballs (1977)
ABC *Afterschool Special* based on the novel of the same title.

Daddy, I'm Their Momma Now (1981)
ABC *Afterschool Special* adapting *The Night Swimmers.*

FOR FURTHER READING

Byars, Betsy. *The Moon and I.* New York: Messner, 1992.

———. "Spinning Straw into Gold." *School Librarian,* March 1986.

Cullinan, Bernice, and M. Jerry Weiss, eds. *Books I Read When I Was Young: The Favorite Books of Famous People.* New York: Avon Books, 1980.

DeMontreville, Doris, and Donna Hill, eds. *Third Book of Junior Authors.* New York: H. W. Wilson, 1972.

Donahue, Rosanne Fraine. "Betsy Byars." In *Twentieth-Century Children's Writers,* edited by Tracy Chevalier. 3d ed. Chicago: St. James Press, 1989.

Kuznets, Lois R. "Betsy Byars' Slice of 'American Pie.' " *Children's Literature Association Quarterly,* winter 1981.

Meet Betsy Byars. New York: Dell, circa 1987.

Mercer, Sandy. *A Teacher's Guide to the Novels of Betsy Byars: The Blossom Family Quartet.* New York: Dell, circa 1987.

Presenting Betsy Byars. New York: Dell, circa 1991.

Review of *The Dark Stairs. Publishers Weekly,* 18 July 1994.

Robertson, Ina. "Betsy Byars—Writer for Today's Child." *Language Arts,* March 1980.

Sutherland, Zena, and May Hill Arbuthnot. *Children and Books.* 7th ed. Glenview, IL: Scott, Foresman, 1986.

Alice Childress

Urban drama

Charleston, South Carolina
October 12, 1920–August 14, 1994

A Hero Ain't Nothin' But a Sandwich

"When the social agitation of the 1960s brought about the development of a new genre of hard-hitting problem novels aimed specifically at teenage readers, editor F. N. Monjo challenged playwright Alice Childress to devote her writing skills to a book for young readers. The result was *A Hero Ain't Nothin' But a Sandwich,* which is such a powerful book that it helped shape the new genre as well as bring it respect," according to Alleen Pace Nilsen.

Sandwich tells the story of Benjie, an inner-city boy on the brink of becoming a heroin addict. He says, "Now I am thirteen, but when I was a chile, it was hard to be a chile because my block is a tough block and my school is a tough school. I'm not trying to cop out on what I do or don't do cause man is man and chile is chile, but I ain't a chile no more. Don't nobody wanta be no chile cause, for some reason, it just hold you back in a lotta ways. . . .

"My block ain't no place to be a chile in peace. Somebody gonna cop your money and might knowk you don cause you walkin with short bread and didn't even make it worth their while to stop and frisk you over. Ain't no letrit light bulb in my hallway for two three floors and we livin up next to the top floor. You best get over bein seven or eight, right soon, cause seven and eight is too big for relatives to be holdin your hand like when you was three, four, and five. No, Jack, you on your own and they got they thing to do, like workin, or goin to court, or seein after they gas and letrit bills, and they dispossess—or final notice, bout on-time payments—and like that, you dig?"

Benjie's mother, Rose, is so busy working to support her son and his grandmother that she has no time to give him moral guidance. Benjie is reluctant to trust his mother's new boyfriend, Butler Craig, who makes an attempt to reach out to the boy. He experiments with heroin, is sent to a rehabilitation program, and, when he returns, steals from his family to buy more heroin. There is uncertainty in the ending, when Butler meets him at a rehab center. Will he be sent away again, or will he be released to Butler's care?

The story is alternately told by Benjie and other characters, including his mother, friends, teachers, a pusher, and Butler, whom some reviewers have described as one of the more noble individuals in young adult fiction.

Sandwich was controversial because of its stark depiction of ghetto life. It "created a fiery dialogue, pro and con, between librarians, teachers, parents and students, on the subject of drug abuse and the written word," Childress said in *Literature for Today's Young Adults*. "The book is startling because I wanted the attention of the reader, without glossing over the subject matter to make it other than what it has proven to be . . . a tragic destruction, particularly of the young, by adults who profiteer from misery." She said children must be encouraged to seek answers.

Sandwich is "a compelling and timely commentary on society and personal values," according to Denise Perry Donavin. "It remains one of the best of the socially aware young adult novels of the 1970s," Eden Ross Lipson said.

The book won a number of awards, including Best Young Adult Book of 1975 from the American Library Association. It was also banned by several school libraries. It took an order of the U.S. Supreme Court in 1983 before the book was returned to the shelf at one library in Long Island, New York.

In *Children's Literature Review*, Childress said she herself had some second thoughts about including the character of the pusher. "The villain was too persuasive, too good at self-defense, too winning in his sinning; however, he is the toughest form of street temptation, so I let him live," she said. "There's more than a single villain in the book; the environment around Benjie conspires against him."

Rainbow Jordan, the writer's second young adult novel, is about a girl whose mother, a go-go dancer, periodically skips town with passing boyfriends. Rainbow takes refuge with Josephine, a middle-aged dressmaker. "Miss Josie, who has humiliations of her own to hide, treats Rainbow with tact and grace," said Anne Tyler. "Gradually, she and Rainbow come to care for each other—not in any instantaneous Hollywood style but with exactly the mixture of caution, hope and suspicion that you would expect from two such battle-weary people."

Childress has stated that she refuses to write about individuals who have triumphed over their harsh surroundings, whether it be poverty, racism, or sexism. She said, though, that she hopes to inspire readers to strive to win.

The descendant of slaves, Childress lived in Harlem after the age of five and attended public schools. She credits her grandmother with inspiring her as a storyteller. In 1940, she first appeared as an actress in *On Strivers Row*. She worked until 1952 as an actress and director with the American Negro Theater in New York and appeared in stage plays such as *Natural Man* (1941) and *Anna Lucasta* (1944).

In 1949, she directed and performed in her own play, *Florence*. It is about a black woman and a white woman conversing at a segregated train station. Mama is on her way to New York to bring home her daughter, Florence. Florence has failed in her attempt to become a professional actress. Mrs. Carter, a bigot, condescendingly offers to find Florence a job as a domestic when she returns. At the play's end, Mama decides not to go to New York after all and wires her train fare to Florence, telling her to "keep trying."

Childress performed on Broadway and in television. Her play *The Wedding Band* was presented by Joseph Papp's Public Theatre in 1972 and 1973. She lectured and taught at Fisk University and the Radcliffe Institute for Independent Study. She won numerous awards for her dramatic works and traveled to the former Soviet Union, Europe, and China. Twice married, she was the mother of one child.

Childress also wrote, edited, and contributed to nonfiction works, including *Black Women Writers (1950–1980): A Critical Evaluation*, edited by Mari Evans (1984).

"At the time of her death [in 1994], she was working on a novel for young adults about her African great-grandmother and her Scotch-Irish great-grandmother," *The New York Times* said.

YOUNG ADULT FICTION

A Hero Ain't Nothin' But a Sandwich (1973)
Young, black Benjie Johnson is well on his way to being hooked on heroin.

When the Rattlesnake Sounds: A Play (1975)
Harriet Tubman and two younger women work as laundresses at a summer hotel in New Jersey.

Let's Hear It for the Queen: A Play (1976)
This is based on the nursery-rhyme lyric "The Queen of Hearts made some tarts."

Rainbow Jordan (1981)
Josephine, a dressmaker, offers fourteen-year-old Rainbow a home when Rainbow's mother, Katie, periodically abandons her.

Those Other People (1989)
Jonathan, a gay seventeen-year-old, struggles to come to terms with his homosexuality in an unsympathetic world.

ADULT FICTION

A Short Walk (1979)
Cora James is the daughter of a wealthy white boy she never met and a poor black girl who died in childbirth.

DRAMA

Florence (first produced in 1949)

Just a Little Simple (first produced in 1950)
Based on the Langston Hughes short story collection *Simple Speaks His Mind.*

Gold Through the Trees (first produced in 1952)

Trouble in Mind (first produced in 1955; revised and published in 1971)

The Wedding Band: A Love/Hate Story in Black and White (first produced in 1966; published in 1973)

The World on a Hill (1968)

The Freedom Drum (first produced 1969–71), also known as *Young Martin Luther King*

A Man Bearing a Pitcher (1969)

Martin Luther King at Montgomery, Alabama (1969)

String (first produced in 1969)
Based on Guy de Maupassant's story "A Piece of String."

Mojo: A Black Love Story (first produced in 1970)

The African Garden (1971)

Sea Island Song (first produced in 1977; published in 1984)

Gullah (first produced in 1984)

Moms: A Praise Play for a Black Comedienne (first produced in 1986)

Vashti's Magic Mirror

SCREENPLAYS

Wine in the Wilderness: A Comedy-Drama (1969)
Public television production.

The Wedding Band (1973)
Television program based on the play of the same name.

A Hero Ain't Nothin' But a Sandwich (1978)
Film starring Cicely Tyson and Paul Winfield.

String (1979)
Public television program based on the play of the same name.

EDITOR

Black Scenes (1971)
Collection of scenes from plays.

CONTRIBUTOR

The Best Short Stories by Negro Writers: An Anthology from 1899 to the Present, edited by Langston Hughes (1967)

Plays to Remember (1968)

The Best Short Plays of 1972, edited by Stanley Richards (1972)

Success in Reading (1972)

The Young American Basic Reading Program (1972)

Best Short Plays of the World Theatre, 1968–1973, edited by Stanley Richards (1973)

FOR FURTHER READING

"Alice Childress, 77, a Novelist; Drew Themes from Black Life." *The New York Times*, 19 August 1994.

Donavin, Denise Perry, ed. *American Library Association Best of the Best for Children.* New York: Random House, 1992.

Donelson, Kenneth L., and Alleen Pace Nilsen, eds. "The People Behind the Books: Alice Childress." In *Literature for Today's Young Adults*. Glenview, IL: Scott, Foresman, 1980.

Lipson, Eden Ross. *The New York Times Parent's Guide to the Best Books for Children*. New York: Times Books, 1991.

Nilsen, Alleen Pace. "Alice Childress." In *Twentieth-Century Children's Writers*, edited by Tracy Chevalier. 3d ed. Chicago: St. James Press, 1989.

Tyler, Anne. "Looking for Mom." *The New York Times Book Review*, 26 April 1981.

James L. Collier
Christopher Collier

Historical drama

James L. Collier
New York City
June 27, 1928

Christopher Collier
New York City
January 29, 1930

My Brother Sam Is Dead

Brothers James L. Collier and Christopher Collier have written several young adult books with historical and political themes. They try to encourage their readers to think about important moral issues. The Collier brothers' father was editor, fiction writer, and biographer Edmund Collier.

James Collier received a degree from Hamilton College in 1950. Twice married, he has two children. He is a professional writer. Besides young adult fiction, James writes frequently on jazz and other musical themes. His nonfiction books include *Battleground: The United States Army in World War II* (1965), *A Visit to the Firehouse* (1967), and *Which Musical Instrument Shall I Play?* (1969).

Christopher Collier received a Ph.D. from Columbia University in 1964. He has been twice married and has three children. He taught in public schools in Connecticut and has been a professor of history as well as chairman of the department at the University of Bridgeport, Connecticut. Christopher served in the U.S. Army from 1952 to

1954. He edited *Public Records of the State of Connecticut, 1965–1967* (1967).

James had written fifteen books and Christopher four when they decided to collaborate on *My Brother Sam Is Dead*. This 1975 Newbery Honor book "represents a breakthrough in historical novels for children," Linda S. Levstik said. "Its graphic depiction of the brutality of both sides during the American Revolution, and the protagonist's ability to see the good and evil on both sides marks it as a real departure from such nationalistic novels as Esther Forbes's *Johnny Tremain*. . . . [*My Brother*] is a post-Vietnam approach to America's involvement in wars, and to what children should learn about war and history. It is also moving, thought-provoking and fast-paced—a rare combination in historical fiction."

"With its sharp revelation of the human aspects of Revolutionary War life and its probing of political views and divided loyalties, this stirring and authoritative novel earns a place beside our best historical fiction," said Virginia Haviland.

The Bloody Country, also a Collier collaboration, is about settlers migrating to the Wyoming Valley of Pennsylvania. *Booklist* stated that it offers "smooth storytelling in modern speech patterns [and] is sharp and speedy."

A trio of books produced by the brothers, also set at the time of the American Revolution, spotlights black characters. In *Jump Ship to Freedom*, Daniel Arabus and his mother are indentured to a Connecticut sea captain, even though Daniel's father fought against the British and earned his freedom. But his father is dead, the captain holds his notes, and Daniel is put on a ship for the West Indies to be sold. Daniel's cousin, in *War Comes to Willy Freeman*, loses her father when British soldiers kill him and kidnap her mother. She dresses as a boy and sets out to find her mother.

The Civil War is the backdrop for *With Every Drop of Blood*. "Although there is action aplenty, the strength of the book lies in Johnny's introspection," reviewer Elizabeth S. Watson said. "His widening experiences lead him to question assumptions regarding African Americans that he's always been told were true."

On his own, James Collier has written children's, young adult, and adult fiction on a variety of themes, including depictions of abusive parents. "Writing is not fun, but you can make yourself do it," the writer told Hughes Moir. "I find improvising jazz and writing fiction are very much the same. Both require me to perform," he said in *Speaking for Ourselves*.

YOUNG ADULT FICTION

The Teddy Bear Habit; or How I Became Rich and Famous . . . , by James L. Collier (1967)
George Stable, a Greenwich Village thirteen-year-old, is groomed as the "Boy Next Door" singing sensation. Then he becomes involved in a jewel theft.

Rock Star by James L. Collier (1970)
His dad wants him to become a doctor, but Tim Anderson would rather be a musician.

Why Does Everyone Think I'm Nutty? by James L. Collier (1971)
Even Harold Leroy doubts his adventures in a medieval town could have been real.

It's Murder at St. Basket's by James L. Collier (1972)
An American boy helps a Pakistani abused by English schoolmasters.

My Brother Sam Is Dead by James L. Collier and Christopher Collier (1974)
Tim Meeker is an anxious observer as his Loyalist father and rebellious older brother, Sam, face each other during the American Revolution.

Rich and Famous: The Further Adventures of George Stable by James L. Collier (1975), sequel to *The Teddy Bear Habit*
The hero discovers that a recording company big shot is a cocaine dealer.

The Bloody Country by James L. Collier and Christopher Collier (1976)
Young Ben Buck and his family migrate from Connecticut to Pennsylvania during the American Revolution, but the Pennonites already there do not want them.

Give Dad My Best by James L. Collier (1976)
Jack, fourteen, struggles to hold his motherless household together.

The Winter Hero by James L. Collier and Christopher Collier (1978)
Massachusetts farmers rebel at unfair taxation in the years after the Revolution.

Planet out of the Past by James L. Collier (1983)
Char, Weddy, and Nuell are excited that their expedition has discovered the strange planet Pleisto but terrified that their leader has disappeared.

When the Stars Begin to Fall by James L. Collier (1986)
Harry White hopes that exposing a polluting carpet factory will bring his family respectability.

Outside Looking In by James L. Collier (1987)
Fergie, fourteen, is ashamed of his parents' vagabond lifestyle. They live in a van, sell quack medicine, and "reclaim" things they need from others.

The Winchesters by James L. Collier (1989)
Chris Winchester must choose between his well-to-do family and the striking workers at Winchester Mills.

The Clock by James L. Collier and Christopher Collier (1991)
In 1810, Annie, fifteen, works as a spinner in a textile mill to pay her father's debt in purchasing a clock.

My Crooked Family by James L. Collier (1991)
Roger and his little sister Lulu live in a slum in 1910. Their parents drink, and the children are drawn to gangs and thievery.

The Jazz Kid by James L. Collier (1994)
Paulie Horvath knows that jazz is his life, but it is not easy for a twelve-year-old in gangland Chicago to see the big shows or learn to play.

Promises to Keep by James L. Collier and Christopher Collier (1994)

With Every Drop of Blood by James L. Collier and Christopher Collier (1994)
In 1865, before Pa died of his war wounds, Johnny, fourteen, promised to protect his family and not join the fighting.

Arabus Family Saga by James L. Collier and Christopher Collier

Jump Ship to Freedom (1981)
At the time of the American Revolution, Daniel Arabus, a slave in Connecticut, should be free, but Captain Ivers holds his father's papers. Soon Daniel is on a ship, bound for auction in the West Indies.

War Comes to Willy Freeman (1982)
Fearing for her freedom, Willy disguises herself as a boy and sets out to find her mother, who may have been taken captive by the British.

Who Is Carrie? (1984)
Carrie, a young black girl who knows Daniel and his cousin, Willy, becomes a slave in the home of President George Washington in New York.

ADULT FICTION BY JAMES L. COLLIER

Cheers (1960)

Somebody Up There Hates Me (1962)

Fires of Youth (1968)

FOR FURTHER READING

Collier, Christopher. "Johnny and Sam: Old and New Approaches to the American Revolution." *Horn Book Magazine,* April 1976.

Gallo, Donald R., ed. *Speaking for Ourselves.* Urbana, IL: National Council for Teachers of English, 1990.

Haviland, Virginia. Review of *My Brother Sam Is Dead. Horn Book Magazine,* April 1975.

Levstik, Linda S. "James Lincoln Collier." In *Twentieth-Century Children's Writers,* edited by Tracy Chevalier. 3d ed. Chicago: St. James Press, 1989.

Moir, Hughes. "Profile: James and Christopher Collier—More Than Just a Good Read." *Language Arts,* March 1978.

Ratner, Megan. "Christopher and James Collier." In *Authors & Artists for Young Adults,* edited by Kevin S. Hile and E. A. DesChenes. Vol. 13. Detroit: Gale Research, 1994.

Review of *The Bloody Country. Booklist,* 1 June 1976.

Caroline B. Cooney

Family drama

Old Greenwich, Connecticut
May 10, 1947

The Face on the Milk Carton

Caroline Bruce Cooney, the daughter of a purchasing agent and a teacher, grew up in Old Greenwich, Connecticut. There she led what she has described as a happy, suburban childhood. She studied and played piano and organ, and she read widely, preferring children's books, for their happy endings, over adult books. She has one brother.

She attended Indiana University, Massachusetts General Hospital School of Nursing, and the University of Connecticut. A music major, she struggled at college and never finished. Though she stood out in high school, in college she was only average. This, she said, was a severe blow to her ego.

At age twenty, Cooney married, eventually having three children. She is now divorced. After her marriage, she began writing, and at age twenty-four she completed her first novel. She wrote seven more, none of which found publishers. The magazine *Seventeen*, however, accepted one of her humorous stories, and her first young adult book, *Safe as the Grave*, a mystery, was published in 1979. The next year, her first adult novel, *Rear-View Mirror*, was published. From 1981 on, she concentrated on young adult books.

There's "no question that many of today's teenagers must contend with drug abuse, alcohol abuse, and widespread sexual activity which often begins frighteningly early," she told Deborah Klezmer. "Though it's ridiculous to suggest that these problems don't exist, I have the impression that kids still yearn for absolutely wholesome childhoods. They want hope, want things to work out, want reassurance that even were they to do something rotten, they and the people around them would still be all right."

Cooney writes five days a week. She works out most of her plots before putting words to paper. About half of Caroline B. Cooney's young adult novels are romances; the rest deal with realistic and suspense themes.

Typical of her suspense novels is *The Face on the Milk Carton*. The main character, Janie Johnson, fifteen, is leading a happy, normal life. Then one day in the high school cafeteria, she sees a milk carton bearing the face of a three-year-old girl in tight pigtails, wearing a dress with a narrow white collar. The girl was said to have been kidnapped from a New Jersey shopping mall twelve years before.

Janie is haunted by the picture. With the help of her boyfriend, Reeve, she eventually learns that her parents are really her grandparents. Her mother, Hannah, joined a religious cult and abandoned Janie years before. Janie finally musters the courage to call her real mother.

In the companion book *Whatever Happened to Janie?*, Janie goes to live with her parents, the Springs—she is really Jennie Spring—but does not find it easy to change her lifestyle or fit in with her three newfound brothers and a sister.

YOUNG ADULT FICTION

Safe as the Grave (1979)
An eleven-year-old girl works secretly at the family cemetery.

An April Love Story (1981)

The Paper Caper (1981)
Lynn has a knack for getting into trouble, often with her twin, Victoria.

He Loves Me Not (1982)

Nancy and Nick (1982)
Nancy has lots of dream dates, but no real ones. She never knows what to say or how to act around boys—but things are different with Nick.

Holly in Love (1983)

A Stage Set for Love: A Follow Your Heart Romance (1983)

I'm Not Your Other Half (1984)
When Fraser and Annie find boyfriends, their longtime friendship is strained.

Nice Girls Don't (1984)

Sun, Sea, and Boys (1984)

The Morning After (1985)

Racing to Love (1985)

Suntanned Days (1985)

Don't Blame the Music (1986)
When her sister, Ashley, a rock and roll singer, returns home after three years' absence, Susan's family life falls apart.

Saturday Night (1986)
Anne and her boyfriend, Con, have moved too fast, gone too far, and now it is too late to hide the truth.

Last Dance (1987)
Eight months have passed since that unforgettable dance, and Anne has kept herself hidden away. Mike insists he and Kip are "just friends," and Molly has stolen Anne's sexy boyfriend.

Among Friends (1987)
Inseparable high school girls, the "Awesome Threesome," begin to draw apart.

The Rah Rah Girl (1987)

Camp Girl-Meets-Boy (1988)

Camp Reunion (1988), sequel to *Camp Girl-Meets-Boy*

New Year's Eve (1988)

The Girl Who Invented Romance (1988)
Kelly has to study romance in sociology class.

Summer Nights (1988), sequel to *Saturday Night*
Anne hopes for one more perfect night with Con before she goes off to begin a glamorous new job.

Family Reunion (1989)
Looked down on by her relatives because her mother left and her father remarried, Shelley is not eager to attend a family reunion.

The Face on the Milk Carton (1990)
Janie Johnson, fifteen, is leading a happy, normal life until she sees a milk carton listing her as a missing child.

The Cheerleader (1991)
"Suppose," he says with an evil smile, "that I could make you popular?" All Althea has to do is agree to a simple bargain.

The Party's Over (1991)
Hallie Revness, a senior at Waverly High, is prom queen and captain of the cheerleaders, but she is not going to college, and she is not sure what to do with herself.

Flight # 116 Is Down (1992)
Heidi Landseth, sixteen, struggles out of the 747 jetliner's wreckage and works to save other victims.

Freeze Tag (1992)
When Meghan and West fall in love, Lannie is jealous and ready to play freeze tag—for real.

Operation: Homefront (1992)
During the Persian Gulf War, Laura's mother is called to serve in Operation Desert Shield. She and her siblings must help her father run the household.

The Perfume (1992)
Something forces Dove to buy the perfume, and it unlocks hidden aspects of her personality.

The Return of the Vampire (1992)
Devnee, tired of feeling plain and dull, has her wishes answered when her family moves into a strange, dark house with a circular tower.

Forbidden (1993)
Annabel Jayquith, eighteen-year-old daughter of a billionaire, falls for Daniel Ransom, son of an assassinated senator.

Twenty Pageants Later (1993)
Scottie-Anne is disgusted that her older sister has become a professional participant in beauty pageants. She is even more shocked when she decides she wants to win one herself.

The Vampire's Promise (1993)
A vampire takes Lacey and the others prisoner in a strange, dark house. It is a night they will never forget.

Whatever Happened to Janie? (1993), sequel to *The Face on the Milk Carton*
Janie goes to live with the Springs—she is really Jennie Spring—but does not find it easy to change her lifestyle or fit in with three brothers and a sister.

Driver's Ed (1994)
Remy Marland prayed to the God of Driver Education that she would get behind the wheel today.

Emergency Room (1994)
Volunteers Diana and Seth arrive at the ER eager to help save lives—completely unprepared for what lies ahead.

Twins (1994)
When Mary Lee and her sister, Madrigal, are separated, Mary Lee feels lost and alone and wishes she could be as popular and outgoing as her sister. When her wish comes true, Mary Lee learns that Madrigal is not the person she seemed to be.

Unforgettable (1994)
After witnessing a shocking crime, Hope cannot remember anything about her life. Mitch helps her work to regain her memory.

Both Sides of Time (1995)

Flash Fire (1995)
A California wildfire threatens a community.

Night School (1995)
A mysterious teacher casts a spell over Mariah and the class.

Cheerleaders Series

Titles listed are by Cooney. Other authors wrote the other books in the series.

Trying Out (1985)
Mary Ellen, Pres, Nancy, Olivia, Walt, Vanessa, and Susan vie to become cheerleaders.

Rumors (1985)

All the Way (1985)

Saying Yes (1987)

Chrystal Falls Series

Titles listed are by Cooney. Other authors wrote the other books in the series.

The Bad and the Beautiful (1985)

A Stranger in Town (annotated but unpublished)

Horror Trilogy

The Fog (1989)
Christina leaves her island home in Maine to attend school—and deal with the Evil.

The Snow (1990)
In a high-stakes game, the evil principal, Mr. Shevington, and his cruel wife have set out to destroy Christina's dearest friend.

The Fire (1990)
The Evil is taking over and threatens Christina with fire.

ADULT FICTION

Rear-View Mirror (1980)
A woman must chauffeur two killers.

ADAPTATIONS IN OTHER MEDIA

Rear-View Mirror (1984)
Television movie starring Lee Remick.

FOR FURTHER READING

Klezmer, Deborah. "Caroline B. Cooney." In *Authors & Artists for Young Adults*, edited by Agnes Garrett and Helga P. McCue. Vol. 5. Detroit: Gale Research, 1990.

Review of *The Face on the Milk Carton. Bulletin of the Center for Children's Books*, February 1990.

Susan Cooper

Historical fantasy

Burnham, Buckinghamshire, England
May 23, 1935
The Dark Is Rising

"I simply write whatever my imagination happens at any given moment to offer me," fantasy writer Susan Cooper said in *Literature for Today's Young Adults*. She added that she has no particular preference for young adult novels but writes in the form when the story seems most appropriate there. Cooper broke into fiction writing when she entered a writing contest in 1965, resulting in the publication of her first book of fiction.

Susan Mary Cooper, the daughter of a railroad employee and a teacher, received a master's degree from Somerville College, Oxford, in 1956. Cooper joined the *Sunday Times* in London that year as a reporter and feature writer. In 1963, she moved to the United States. She married Nicholas J. Grant, a college professor, and they divorced two years later. Cooper has two children and three stepchildren.

"The age-old myths of Britain and Wales that she heard as a child in wartime England have found their way into her stories, along with a strong conviction that good can prevail over evil," *Authors & Artists for Young Adults* stated.

"I'm really one of those authors who belong back in an age before labels," Cooper said in *Speaking for Ourselves*, "when all storytellers produced folktales—for folk, which meant everyone. I love being able to try to make magic: to make you laugh, or cry, or experience what Aristotle called a catharsis—which means, in effect, feeling better even though a story has slugged you on the back of the head."

Noting the powerful effect of World War II on writers who grew up during the time, Anne Wood observed that Cooper's book *Dawn of Fear* "is a largely autobiographical account of life for a child in Buckinghamshire during the war—the disturbing nights crowded in air raid shelters during the worst of the Blitz, the stunned effect of the loss in a bombing raid of a real friend with whom one had played war games."

Added *The Times Literary Supplement*, "Susan Cooper really makes her young readers face the facts. War is not just a matter of battlefield heroics, of life-sized Action men. It is a matter of innocent ordinary people dying. Peter, Derek's best friend, is killed in an air-raid. It is unusual these days to find death in a children's book—though not as startling as it would have been a few years ago."

"Susan Cooper is one of the small and very select company of writers who—somehow, somewhere—have been touched by magic; the gift of creation is theirs, the power to bring to life for ordinary mortals 'the best of symbolic high fantasy,' " in the view of Margaret K. McElderry. "Music and song, old tales and legends, prose and poetry, theater and reality, imagination and intellect, power and control, a strong sense of place and people both past and present—all are part of the magic that has touched Susan Cooper. She is undismayed by the challenge of crossing borders old and new, physical and metaphysical. Her journeys add great luster to the world of literature."

Cooper's well-known series The Dark Is Rising is about the conflict of good and evil, of the Servants of Light and the Powers of Dark. The writer weaves ancient lore and mythology into a modern setting. The three Drew children, vacationing in Cornwall, find an old map. With the help of their uncle, they search for a treasure. "The children are credible and their adventures shift so cunningly from the plausible to the legendary as to be totally absorbing," said C. E. J. Smith of the first book in the series, *Over Sea, Under Stone*. "There is pace, suspense and mystery, and the final scene on the jagged rocks amid an incoming tide is a feast for any imaginative twelve- or thirteen-year-old."

"Cooper's most recent full-length work to date is *Seaward*, which is perhaps the most complex and least clear-cut of all of her works," said Karen Patricia Smith in 1989. "Here she appears purposely to avoid explanations and instead chooses to offer the reader a world of possibilities, so many in fact that they create an extremely ambiguous text. This is a challenging novel, with subtleties which may perhaps be best appreciated by an adult audience. The protagonists, Cally and West, are adolescents caught up in the drama of having to cope with the deaths of their parents, events around which swirl mystery and innuendo. At the height of their personal tragedy they are transported to a Celtic world ruled by the old gods who would use the children should they be unable to resist the temptations placed before them. This is an allegorical tale about coming of age in a hostile world."

YOUNG ADULT FICTION

Dawn of Fear (1970)
A gang of neighborhood boys tries to save treasures from destruction by Nazi bombs in war-torn England during World War II.

Seaward (1983)
Cally and Westerly, who have lost their parents, are thrown into a haunted "other world."

The Boggart (1992)
The Volnik family inherits a remote castle in Scotland. A mischievous spirit lives there and likes to play jokes.

The Dark Is Rising Series

Over Sea, Under Stone (1965)
Barney, Simon, and Jane Drew find a map with a clue to the legendary Grail. They begin a quest, protected from forces of evil by Great-Uncle Merry.

The Dark Is Rising (1973)
Will Stanton, the seventh son of a seventh son, is the last of the Old Ones, who must gather six magical Signs to fight the evil of Dark. Uncle Merry helps Will in his quest.

Greenwitch (1974)
At Uncle Merry's urging, the Drew children help Will Stanton recover the priceless golden Grail.

The Grey King (1975)
Convalescing in Wales, Will meets Bran, son of King Arthur. Together, they organize the forces of good for a major battle with evil.

Silver on the Tree (1977)
Will, Bran, and the Drews, along with Uncle Merry, travel through time and space searching for a crystal sword.

FICTION FOR YOUNGER READERS

Jethro and the Jumbie (1979)

The Silver Cow: A Welsh Tale (1983)
Retelling.

The Selkie Girl (1986)
Retelling.

Matthew's Dragon (1991)

Tam Lin (1991)

Danny and the Kings (1993)

ADULT FICTION

Mandrake (1964)

DRAMA

Foxfire (first produced in 1980), with Hume Cronyn

TELEPLAYS AND SCREENPLAYS

Dark Encounter (1976)

The Dollmaker (1983), with Hume Cronyn
Based on a novel by Hariette Arnow.

The Cloud People

Dinner at the Homesick Restaurant (n.d.)
Based on a novel by Anne Tyler.

FOR FURTHER READING

Donelson, Kenneth L., and Alleen Pace Nilsen, eds. "The People Behind the Books: Susan Cooper." In *Literature for Today's Young Adults*. Glenview, IL: Scott, Foresman, 1980.

Johnson, Janette. "Susan Cooper." In *Authors & Artists for Young Adults*, edited by Kevin S. Hile and E. A. DesChenes. Vol. 13. Detroit: Gale Research, 1994.

McElderry, Margaret K. "Susan Cooper." *Horn Book Magazine*, August 1976.

Review of *Dawn of Fear. The Times Literary Supplement*, 14 July 1972.

Smith, C. E. J. Review of *Over Sea, Under Stone. School Librarian and School Library Review*, December 1965.

Smith, Karen Patricia. "Susan Cooper." In *Twentieth-Century Children's Writers*, edited by Tracy Chevalier. 3d ed. Chicago: St. James Press, 1989.

Wood, Anne. "Adventure." *Books for Your Children*, spring 1976.

Robert Cormier

Contemporary drama

Leominster, Massachusetts
January 17, 1925

The Chocolate War

If young adult fiction "has one best-selling heavyweight writer . . . he is Robert Cormier," *Newsweek* said in 1979. The magazine compared Cormier with such writers of serious adult fiction as Saul Bellow and William Styron. The compliment was based on Cormier's first three novels for young adults. He has written another eight books since.

Robert Cormier's books have unusual plots. They are suspenseful, and they make readers think. "I have always been interested in the plight of the individual versus the system, whether the system is the family, the school, the government or society in general," Cormier said in *Literature for Today's Young Adults*. He said he is interested in creating characters that are credible as individuals and in developing situations that can bring shocks of recognition to readers. "And I'm willing to let these characters take me where they will, even if I have to abandon preconceived notions about a particular theme. What's beautiful about this is that I can deal with character and theme in a manner that satisfies me as an author and have my work accepted in the field of adolescent literature."

It is Cormier's "hard-hitting unsentimentality that most sets him apart from other writers in his field, and some critics complain that he goes too far," said *Newsweek*. For example, *Booklist*, a journal for librarians and bookstore buyers, put a black border around its review of *The Chocolate War* because it found the novel too violent and its ending too downbeat. Cormier responded in the *Newsweek* story, "As long as what I write is true and believable, why should I have to create happy endings? My books are an antidote to the TV view of life."

The son of a factory worker, Cormier preferred reading over sports as a youth. Three books that particularly influenced him were Mark Twain's *The Adventures of Tom Sawyer*, Thomas Wolfe's *The Web and the Rock*, and William Saroyan's *The Daring Young Man on the Flying Trapeze*. "Each of these books affected me in a different way," he said in *Books I Read When I Was Young*. "But they pointed me in the same direction, toward my eventual destination: becoming a writer. Without these books, my life might have been entirely different from what it is and has been." Specifically, he noted the drama of life in Twain; the hunger for knowledge, love, and fame found in Wolfe; and Saroyan's simplicity of style.

His prose, Cormier has said, is also influenced by Ernest Hemingway's crisp, simple style. In the works of William Saroyan, he came to recognize that an ethnic neighborhood—in Cormier's case his French-Canadian family and their friends—was an acceptable background for writing.

While Cormier was attending Fitchburg State College, a teacher found a publisher for one of his first stories (without his knowledge). Cormier received a check for seventy-five dollars—early proof of Cormier's talent.

Before becoming a full-time writer, Cormier worked for a radio station, then for newspapers, moving gradually from reporter to an editorial position. In 1948, he and Constance B. Senay were married; they have four children.

Two human interest stories that Cormier wrote while on the staff of the *Fitchburg Sentinel* were selected as best of the year by the Associated Press in New England (in 1959 and 1973). He received an honorary Doctor of Letters degree from Fitchburg State College in 1977. In 1978, Cormier decided to leave journalism to devote his full energies to freelance writing and fiction writing, though he continued to write a newspaper column. By that time, he had published five novels, including *The Chocolate War*, one of his most controversial.

Cormier based *The Chocolate War* on an incident at his teenage son's school. The book's hero, Jerry Renault, is a high school student who recently lost his mother. He ponders a poster in his locker: "Do I dare disturb the universe?" Dare he does. When a secret school society, the Vigils, decide to sell chocolate as a fund-raiser, Jerry refuses to participate. Archie Costello, the Vigils leader, himself, has been intimidated into spearheading the candy sale by an ambitious teacher. With increasing violence, Archie bullies Jerry, turning him into a lone, vulnerable outcast. The novel examines the ability of power to corrupt and the price of passiveness and resistance.

Kenneth L. Donelson and Alleen Pace Nilsen described *The Chocolate War* as "an example of the best of modern realism for young adults. . . . It contains the kind of realism that many other books had been just leading up to. Its message about conformity and human manipulation is all the more powerful because the young protagonist is so vulnerable. The religious symbolism that pervades the book serves as a contrasting backdrop to the terrible evil that pervades Trinity High School where the protagonist is a freshman."

The Chocolate War "is, on the surface, a political book," said David Rees. "It is about power, power structures, corruption—about how absolute power corrupts absolutely. But, more subtly, beneath the surface, it is about compromise and the choice between hunting with the pack or searching for strength as an individual: about the toughness needed in the struggle to be a successful outsider. Jerry Renault, the central character, is a fascinating and complex creation, considerably more ambiguous than he initially appears to be."

The New York Times selected *The Chocolate War* as the Outstanding Book of the Year in 1974. It later gave the same honor to Cormier's next two young adult novels, *I Am the Cheese* and *After the First Death*. The American Library Association, Media & Methods Maxi Awards, Lewis Carroll Shelf Award, and *School Library Journal* also singled out *The Chocolate War* for recognition.

Still, the book had its detractors, particularly for its ending. "People don't ride off into the sunset in my books, they walk off hobbled and crippled maybe, into the dark night," Cormier told an interviewer for *Something About the Author.*

The Chocolate War troubled many librarians. Herbert N. Foerstel said that allegations were made at a Maine middle school library that the book had "a lack of positive role models, a negative view of the Catholic church, and an unhappy ending. The teacher requested that the book be removed from the middle school and placed instead in the high school. The district superintendent upheld a review committee's recommendation to retain the book in the middle school library."

Cormier, challenged for the views expressed in *The Chocolate War*, wrote the sequel, *Beyond the Chocolate War*, to let readers know how incidents in the first book might have changed the characters years later. *Horn Book Magazine* gave the novel an Honor List citation in 1986.

Cormier's second young adult book, *I Am the Cheese*, was no less driving in its tension nor less troubling in the questions it posed. The plot weaves together a description of the frantic bicycle pedaling of a boy on his way to meet his father with a series of clinical interviews of an institutionalized youth struggling to remember his family's secrets. There's an underlying, ominous political theme. Young Adam Farmer's family is living a sham life. His father testified against several important people and is now in a witness protection program. They have moved far from home, and they have different names, but just how protective is the program? Who is to be trusted?

Emotionally, the book is autobiographical, Cormier said in a publisher's promotional pamphlet, *Presenting Robert Cormier*. "If I'm the good guy in my book, I'm also the bad guy: we're sums of what we write about."

"It is a terribly bleak story, without an escape route for its protagonist," Anne Scott MacLeod commented. "The point made—among others—is that size alone is fearsome: losing human scale, organizations also lose human meaning."

Rebecca Lukens drew a comparison with J. D. Salinger's *The Catcher in the Rye*: Cormier "begins from quite another premise [than Salinger's, that the world cannot be all bad]. The world is rotten; the honest people flee; those who remain are corrupt; the government is ineffectual but controlling; organized violence is ubiquitous. There is no hope. Between 1951 and 1974 the world-view in popular literature flipped."

Cormier's *After the First Death* describes the hijacking of a busload of children for political blackmail. It is "written in crackling prose that weaves together the stories of the pretty teen-age girl bus driver, a teen-age terrorist who is attracted to her and another teenager who becomes the crucial messenger in the negotiations. It deals thoughtfully with not only the topical issue of terrorism but power and its abuses, loyalty and betrayal, courage and fear," said *Newsweek*.

"I didn't start writing specifically for adolescents," Cormier told Geraldine DeLuca. "I was surrounded by my kids and their friends who were teenagers, and I realized that they were really leading a life that was more exciting than mine. I was going to work every day and coming back home, but for them the emotional pendulum was swinging back and forth all the time. They were getting invited to the prom, falling in love—you know those things—and even though the experiences might have been transient, they were really lacerating for them. So I began to write short stories about young people."

Cormier has explored new, yet dark, themes of psychological complexity. Barney, the main character in *The Bumblebee Flies Anyway*, considers himself healthy and does not know why he is a patient at an experimental facility for the terminally ill. The book "moves with relentless inevitability . . . to the requiem of hopeless despair that, for each patient, still holds some passion for an affirmative act of life," Zena Sutherland noted. The book received a citation from *School Library Journal* in 1983.

Cormier told Anita Silvey, "There is very little that is accidental in my work. I believe in serendipity for developments of plot, but the actual writing is arrived at by very hard work."

YOUNG ADULT FICTION

The Chocolate War (1974)
Jerry Renault boycotts a private school fund-raiser—and suffers severe cruelty from members of a secret society.

I Am the Cheese: A Novel (1977)
Adam Farmer struggles to understand his family's secrets—but must not.

After the First Death (1979)
The lives of Miro, a terrorist hijacker; Kate, a bus driver; and Ben, the son of a general, are forcefully intertwined.

Eight Plus One: Stories (1980)
Short stories about friendships, first love, first mustache, fathers, and daughters.

The Bumblebee Flies Anyway (1983)
At an experimental hospital for terminally ill young people, Barney Snow, sixteen, falls in love, overcomes dislikes, and takes the ride of his life.

Beyond the Chocolate War: A Novel (1985), sequel to *The Chocolate War*
Jerry Renault is still haunted by the cruel events he suffered, but Archie Costello, head of the Vigils, is unchanged.

Fade (1988)
Paul Moreaux discovers he has the power to "fade," but when he becomes invisible, he sees secrets he should not see.

Other Bells for Us to Ring (1990)
Darcy's father is transferred to an army camp in Massachusetts, and she feels isolated in her French-Canadian neighborhood until she meets Kathleen and learns about Catholicism.

We All Fall Down (1991)
When Jane Jerome's house is vandalized and her sister assaulted by four kids from a neighboring town, a silent avenger seeks payback.

Tunes for Bears to Dance To (1992)
Henry befriends a victim of the Holocaust and is put to the test.

In the Middle of the Night (1995)
A boy is haunted by an accident that involved his father and claimed the lives of twenty-two children.

ADULT FICTION

Now and at the Hour (1960)
A New England mill worker, Alph LeBlanc, is dying of cancer but will not tell his family.

A Little Raw on Monday Mornings (1963)
A widowed mother of three becomes pregnant, in conflict with her Catholic beliefs.

Take Me Where the Good Times Are: A Novel (1965)
Oldster Tommy Bartin takes a brief, violent excursion out of the city infirmary.

ADAPTATIONS IN OTHER MEDIA

I Am the Cheese (1983)
Film starring Robert Wagner, Hope Lange, Don Murray, Robert MacNaughton, Cynthia Nixon, Sudie Bond, and Robert Cormier.

The Chocolate War (1988)
Film starring John Glover, Ian Mitchell-Smith, Wally Ward, and Bud Cort.

FOR FURTHER READING

Campbell, Patricia J. *Presenting Robert Cormier*. Boston: Twayne, 1985.

Commire, Anne, ed. "Robert (Edmund) Cormier." In *Something About the Author*. Vol. 45. Detroit: Gale Research, 1985.

Cullinan, Bernice, and M. Jerry Weiss, eds. *Books I Read When I Was Young: The Favorite Books of Famous People*. New York: Avon Books, 1980.

DeLuca, Geraldine, with Roni Natov. Interview with Robert Cormier. *The Lion and the Unicorn*, fall 1978.

Donelson, Kenneth L., and Alleen Pace Nilsen, eds. "The People Behind the Books: Robert Cormier." In *Literature for Today's Young Adults*. Glenview, IL: Scott, Foresman, 1980.

Foerstel, Herbert N. *Banned in the USA: A Reference Guide to Book Censorship in Schools and Public Libraries*. Westport, CT: Greenwood, 1994.

Foster, Stephen, ed. *Teacher's Guide: 8 Plus 1 Stories by Robert Cormier*. New York: Dell, 1991.

Lukens, Rebecca. "From Salinger to Cormier: Disillusionment to Despair in Thirty Years." *ALAN Review*, fall 1981.

MacLeod, Anne Scott. "Robert (Edmund) Cormier." In *Twentieth-Century Children's Writers*, edited by Tracy Chevalier. 3d ed. Chicago: St. James Press, 1989.

Presenting Robert Cormier. New York: Dell, 1991.

Rees, David. *Marble in the Water: Essays on Contemporary Writers of Fiction for Children and Young Adults*. Boston: Horn Book Magazine, 1980.

Schwartz, Tony. "Teen-Agers' Laureate." *Newsweek*, 16 July 1979.

Silvey, Anita. Interview with Robert Cormier. *Horn Book Magazine*, May–June 1985.

Sutherland, Zena. Review of *The Bumblebee Flies Anyway*. *Bulletin of the Center for Children's Books*, September 1983.

Chris Crutcher

Contemporary drama

Dayton, Ohio
July 17, 1946

Running Loose

Chris Crutcher "possesses a novelist's greatest asset: an ability to create people who are real and believable and about whom the reader can care deeply," reviewer Nancy Vasilakis said.

Christopher C. Crutcher, the son of a county clerk, received a bachelor of arts degree from Eastern Washington State College (now University) in 1968. Crutcher has taught high school, directed a community mental health center, and worked as a mental health therapist. He also directed Lakeside, an alternative school in Oakland, California, an area that has a high crime rate.

Crutcher said his experiences with young people, many of them suffering from stress and emotional problems, prompted him to begin writing fiction. His protagonists face physical and sexual abuse and the loss of family members. Crutcher is an avid athlete, and his heroes often find an outlet in sports.

"Crutcher's background as a family therapist comes out on nearly every page here," *Kirkus Reviews* stated of *Iron Man.*

"People always want us to be adults rather than become adults," Crutcher told Thomas Kozikowski. "Everybody wants the finished product, and nobody wants to look at how it's made."

That is the problem facing Louie Banks, the hero of *Running Loose,* who gets along well with his parents, has a girlfriend named Becky, and is on the starting squad for the school football team. When he refuses the coach's order to try to injure a black quarterback on a rival team, he is thrown off the squad. Schoolmates and townspeople do not understand his situation—or they believe the coach's version.

His life is complicated further when Becky is involved in a car accident.

Critic Christine McDonnell credits the vitality of Crutcher's books to "the characterization, the physical action, and quick dialogue. Crutcher gives us believable glimpses of locker rooms and practice sessions, spiced with irreverent, sometimes coarse, male humor. He shows brief awkward moments of romance in contrast with the honesty, ease, and trust of male friendships. These books are overwhelmingly male, peopled with teammates, coaches, bosses, fathers, and father figures. Women do appear as mothers, girlfriends, even as a coach, and issues of sex and love surface. In *Running Loose* the death of Louie's girlfriend is a central crisis in the book. But for the most part although women are attractive, strong, and smart, they are peripheral to the action, relegated more to fantasy than to day-to-day life."

Crutcher explained to Dave Jenkinson how he writes: "I'll get a core idea or a core set of characters, and I start off. I usually have to do a lot of editing on my first chapter when I get to the end. My first few chapters take some work because I haven't gotten the direction, but I get my direction by telling the story. I like the idea that the story can tell itself and that I don't know what's going to happen. Nortie Wheeler's taking over *Stotan!* was one of the magic things in my life. I had no idea of what was going to happen to *Crazy Horse*'s Willie Weaver. I didn't know whether he was going to go back home and stay or leave or what. I like the magical part, the part that says maybe I'm not in control."

"Crutcher's work is marked by his willingness to go toe-to-toe with the many pitfalls of adolescence: relationships, divorce fall-out, and parent/child power struggles," said Heather Vogel Frederick. "He has also tackled grittier issues like child abuse and abortion (*Staying Fat for Sarah Byrnes*, 1993); racism and accidental death (*Running Loose*, 1983); and suicide, teen pregnancy and sexual molestation (*Chinese Handcuffs*, 1989)."

Critic Jerry Flack found the boys in *Stotan!* "typical of many teenagers; they think a lot about sex; their language isn't always clean. They face difficult, adult situations—violence, racial prejudice, Jeff's impending death. Crutcher's novel more than moves and entertains; it teaches. It teaches young people about responsibility, about courage and heroism, and ultimately about life itself."

Reviewer Anita Silvey found *The Crazy Horse Electric Game* marred by plot problems but said, "The book magnificently portrays the thoughts and feelings of a crippled athlete and is a testimony to the indomitability of the human spirit."

"Crutcher often writes in the first person, partly due to the influence of that one novel he read in high school, Harper Lee's *To Kill a Mockingbird,*" said Frederick. "He recalls scanning the flap to see if he could weasel out of actually reading the book for an exam. After a peek at the first page, however, he got 'swept away,' finishing it, he notes dryly, 'about three weeks after the test.' Years later when he sat down to write, he couldn't get the book out of his head. And indeed, just as the voice of Scout Finch is synonymous with *To Kill a Mockingbird*, so is Louie Banks with *Running Loose*."

YOUNG ADULT FICTION

Running Loose (1983)
Senior Louie Banks has a terrific girlfriend, Becky, and a starting spot on the football team—until he is tossed out for refusing the coach's order to take an illegal hit.

Stotan! (1986)
The coach provides a grueling week for four members of the Frost High swim team.

The Crazy Horse Electric Game (1987)
Star athlete Willie Weaver is sidelined by a crippling accident.

Chinese Handcuffs (1989)
After Dillon Hemingway witnesses his brother's suicide, his life falls apart.

Athletic Shorts: Six Short Stories (1991)

Staying Fat for Sarah Byrnes (1993)
Burn-scarred Sarah and overweight Eric Calhoune are "terminal uglies"—and friends.

Iron Man: A Novel (1995)
Bo Brewster was bullied by his father for years. When his football coach tries the same, he quits.

CONTRIBUTOR

Connections: Short Stories by Outstanding Writers for Young Adults, edited by Donald R. Gallo (1989)

ADULT FICTION

The Deep End: A Novel of Suspense (1991)

FOR FURTHER READING

Flack, Jerry. Review of *Stotan! School Library Journal*, May 1986.

Frederick, Heather Vogel. "Chris Crutcher: 'What's Known Can't Be Unknown.' " *Publishers Weekly*, 20 February 1995.

Jenkinson, Dave. "Portraits: Chris Crutcher." *Emergency Librarian*, January–February 1991.

Kozikowski, Thomas. "Chris Crutcher." In *Authors & Artists for Young Adults*, edited by Laurie Collier. Vol. 9. Detroit: Gale Research, 1992.

McDonnell, Christine. "New Voices, New Visions: Chris Crutcher." *Horn Book Magazine*, May–June 1988.

Review of *Iron Man: A Novel. Kirkus Reviews*, 15 March 1995.

Silvey, Anita. Review of *The Crazy Horse Electric Game. Horn Book Magazine*, November–December 1987.

Vasilakis, Nancy. Review of *Staying Fat for Sarah Byrnes. Horn Book Magazine*, May–June 1993.

Richie Tankersley Cusick

Suspense

New Orleans, Louisiana
April 1, 1952
The Lifeguard

"I've always believed in the supernatural," Richie Tankersley Cusick told *Contemporary Authors*, "and I grew up with a ghost in my house. I've always loved scary books and movies—even though my parents didn't want me to watch horror films. I'd sometimes manage to sneak in and turn on the television when my folks weren't in the room. In Girl Scouts I was the troop storyteller and would make up tales of haunted houses and murderers."

Richie Tankersley, the daughter of a petroleum engineer and a homemaker, worked summers as a ward clerk at Oschsner Foundation Hospital in New Orleans. She received a degree from the University of Southwestern Louisiana in 1975. She worked for Hallmark Cards as a writer for nine years before becoming a freelance writer. She married Rick Cusick, a book designer and graphic artist, in 1980.

"Richie enjoys writing when it is rainy and gloomy outside," an endnote in a 1994 edition of *April Fools* stated, "and likes to have a spooky soundtrack playing in the background. She writes at a desk that originally belonged to a funeral director in the 1800s and that she believes is haunted.

"Halloween is one of her favorite holidays. She and her husband decorate the entire house, which includes having a body laid out in state in the parlor, life-size models of Frankenstein's monster, the figure of Death to keep watch, and scary costumes for Hannah and Meg, their dogs."

"Writing is very important to me—being about creating people, adventures, and worlds where readers can lose themselves for a little while," said the writer in a publisher's guide for teachers. "It's very hard work, but very rewarding. I hate it when a book ends and I have to tell my characters good-bye! I get so close to them, that they linger in my own personality for days . . . and I guess when it comes right down to it, I never really lose them. They just become another part of me . . . or perhaps they were all along!"

Cusick described her writing process to Barbara Kramer: "I can't write from an outline. I don't like to do outlines or synopses—they make me feel like my imagination is all tied up. When I start a book I don't have any idea who the bad guy is, any idea what's going to happen.

"I always start with characters and a lot of times I don't know what they're going to be like, they'll just kind of take off and do what they want. I usually don't know until I'm about three-fourths the way through who the villain is and then it's always a surprise to me."

At times she gets so wrapped up in her writing, she told Sarah Verney, "I lose all track of where I am and what hour of the day or night it is."

Typical of Cusick's work is *The Locker*, in which Marlee Fleming, recovering from the nightmarish death of her parents, hopes to settle down at a new school. New friends Tyler and Noreen have an odd reaction when they see the locker she has been assigned. They tell her it once was Suellen's, and Suellen disappeared. When she opens the locker, Marlee sees a horrifying vision—she has been chosen to find Suellen, even if it costs her her life.

In *Help Wanted*, Robin Bailey takes a job cataloging books in a private library. She makes friends with the family's teenage step-daughter, Claudia, who says she is being haunted by her dead mother.

April Fools finds Belinda, Frank, and Hildy driving home from a party. They are involved in a gruesome accident. Frank insists on leaving the scene, saying the people in the other car could not have survived. Two weeks later, the deadly pranks begin; someone wants revenge.

YOUNG ADULT FICTION

Evil on the Bayou (1984)
Meg Daton finds the old lady she is caring for nice enough, but her tight-lipped son is scary, and Dr. Lavane is downright menacing.

The Lifeguard (1988)
Could the apparent drowning have been . . . murder?

Trick or Treat (1989)
With Halloween approaching, Martha knows there is something evil about the house into which she is moving.

April Fools (1990)
On April 1, three teens are driving home from a party when they get involved in a gruesome accident and leave the scene. Soon, vengeful pranks begin.

Teacher's Pet (1990)
Kate is thrilled to attend a week-long writing conference with the famous master of horror himself, but with a teacher like that, you practically have to kill for attention.

Fatal Secrets (1991)
Ryan must discover the deadly secret of what her sister, Marissa, was trying to say before she fell through the ice and drowned.

Vampire (1991)
Gory fun turns to real terror when bodies are found with teeth marks on their throats at the Dungeon of Horrors, owned by Darcy Thomas's uncle.

Buffy, the Vampire Slayer (1992)
Novelization of the movie of the same name: A high school cheerleader drops her pom-poms and takes up a stake to pursue vampires.

The Mall (1992)
The creepy customer hanging around Muffin Mania, where Trish works, knows her secrets.

Help Wanted (1993)
Robin is plunged into the dark and twisted family saga of Parker Swanson, the gorgeous new guy at school.

Silent Stalker (1993)
Summer vacation becomes a nightmare when Jenny and her father are invited to stay at a forbidding castle.

The Drifter (1994)
Carolyn offers room and board to Joss in exchange for work on the island retreat, but the house becomes a trap of sinister secrets.

The Locker (1994)
After the death of her parents, Marlee Fleming starts over at a new school. Her friends act strangely, though, when they see which locker she has been assigned.

Someone at the Door (1994)
Hannah, her younger sister, Meg, and their deaf dog are snowbound at their farmhouse, with no electricity or telephone, when they hear a radio warning of an escaped convict.

Overdue (1995)
Kathleen is about to close the library when somebody returns four overdue books—grisly books about death.

ADULT FICTION

Scarecrow (1990)

Blood Roots (1992)

FOR FURTHER READING

Cusick, Richie Tankersley. *April Fools*. New York: Archway Paperbacks, 1994.

Kramer, Barbara. "Interview: Richie Tankersley Cusick." *Mystery Scene*, April 1991.

Teacher's Guide to Young Adult Mystery/Horror Bestsellers. New York: Archway Paperbacks, 1991.

Trosky, Susan M., ed. "Richie Tankersley Cusick." In *Contemporary Authors*. Vol. 134. Detroit: Gale Research, 1992.

Verney, Sarah. "Richie Tankersley Cusick." In *Authors & Artists for Young Adults*, edited by E. A. DesChenes. Vol. 14. Detroit: Gale Research, 1994.

Paula Danziger

Humorous drama

Washington, D.C.
August 18, 1944

The Cat Ate My Gymsuit: A Novel

Mixing equal doses of realism and humor in her depictions of teenagers in the process of growing up, Paula Danziger has found a wide audience.

The daughter of a garment district worker and a nurse, Danziger read Nancy Drew, Sue Barton, Cherry Ames, and other series books when young. In high school, she was particularly inspired by J. D. Salinger's *The Catcher in the Rye*. Most of the heroines of her books show some of the same outlaw tendencies as Holden Caulfield in *The Catcher in the Rye*. Other books she enjoyed while growing up were Jane Austen's *Pride and Prejudice* and John Knowles's *A Separate Peace*.

Danziger received a master's degree from Montclair State College, and she taught school from 1967 to 1978. During one year teaching in a junior high school, her "slip fell down in class and two students crazy-glued desks to the floor. The realization came that it was incredibly hard to be a good creative writer and a good creative teacher. Each was a full-time job," the writer recalled in *English Journal*. So she took up writing full time. A friendship with poet John Ciardi broadened her literary awareness.

The Cat Ate My Gymsuit, written while she was undergoing physical therapy after two car accidents, is autobiographical, Danziger told interviewers. She remembered herself as a fat kid, frustrated with her mother and disliking her father—just like the book's heroine, Marcy Lewis, who ultimately comes to grips with her problem.

Gymsuit's "fresh and funny fiction grabbed teenagers' attention because it was so different from the serious realistic novels that adult critics were raving over," noted Alleen Pace Nilsen. "Danziger's plots center around young teenage girls faced with the problems of establishing a grownup identity, separate from their parents and different from what they were as children yet pleasing to all concerned. She treats this basically serious theme with enough humor that teenagers begin to smile at themselves and come away from her books a little more confident that they too will make it."

Reviewer Perry Nodelman chided the author, saying that her writing in this book lacked "subtlety for a specific reason: no distinctive detail, apparently on the assumption that readers dislike such detail. . . . In *The Cat Ate My Gymsuit,* readers find out many things about Marcy Lewis, her family, her appearance, and her attitudes. But interestingly enough, not one of these details is unusual or surprising; none of them separates Marcy from the vast sea of theoretically typical teenage girls we all assume exist somewhere outside our immediate acquaintance in towns we have never visited. It seems that readers who like these books prefer clichés to carefully described experience."

Danziger brought Marcy back in *There's a Bat in Bunk Five*. This time, Marcy is looking forward to getting away from home for the summer. It takes a long time to convince her father, however. "He's always afraid I'm going to be too radical or something." As a junior camp counselor, she is soon enjoying a first love with another counselor, Ted. She becomes anxious that she is not doing enough to help some of the campers, such as Ginger Simon, a girl from a broken home whom no one likes and who will not open up to express her real feelings.

This book, too, brought mixed views, with Natalie Babbitt saying that "by romanticizing the distortions that complicate the healing of family rifts, [*Bunk Five*] may be perpetuating some of the very miseries for which she shows much sympathy." Conversely, Harriet McClain said that Danziger "skillfully balanced her insight into the daily trauma of the young adult years with liberal doses of humor."

"Amanda, the sister from Hell," is how sixth-grader Matthew Martin describes his older sister in *Not for a Billion, Gazillion Dollars,* the latest in another series. "Life isn't fair. Amanda got born first and then she acted like a little angel for years so that he got into trouble for being the bad little brother. Then zap, one day she stopped being a little angel and Mr. and Mrs. Martin decided to become much stricter parents. And now, Matthew is stuck trying to deal with all their new techniques."

Matthew is anxious for his parents to buy him an expensive computer program, but they insist he earn at least half the money. His first idea is to rent out his sister's room when she leaves for summer arts camp. When that does not work, he teams up with friends Jil! Hudson and Joshua Jackson in a sign-making business. Matthew learns a lesson in the end, when he finally purchases the computer program.

Danziger has said that her experiences in teaching have helped her storytelling. She uses real experiences; she creates characters based on real students; and she relies on the school for a "cool sense of place for my readers."

"If Ms. Danziger's characters speak and act like real kids, her adults are better than the real thing, especially when it comes to providing understanding and support," observed Kathleen Leverich. "These grown-ups may divorce. They may separate from their families or haul them cross-country on job-related moves. But they are always ready to order the celebratory pizza, to share a bowl of double-fudge brownie batter, uncooked, along with a heart-to-heart, or simply to allow a child the space and time to think things through."

When not writing, Danziger travels around the country speaking to parents, children, teachers, and librarians. She logs about 30,000 miles a year, according to her publisher.

YOUNG ADULT FICTION

The Cat Ate My Gymsuit: A Novel (1974)
Overweight Marcy Lewis offers a creative excuse for not participating in gym class.

The Pistachio Prescription: A Novel (1978)
Cassie Stephen, twelve, a mousy brunette in a family of blonds and redheads, pigs out on pistachio nuts to get over her feelings of insecurity.

Can You Sue Your Parents for Malpractice? A Novel (1979)
Lauren Allen, fourteen, thinks life is the pits. Bobby Tayler has jilted her; her ninth-grade teachers are giving out demerits like crazy; and she must share her bedroom with a messy younger sister.

There's a Bat in Bunk Five (1980), sequel to *The Cat Ate My Gymsuit*
Marcy, junior counselor at a creative arts camp, now turning fifteen, is eager to be away from her parents for the summer but must cope with all sorts of problems in Bunk Five.

The Divorce Express (1982)
Rosie rides the bus—which she calls the "Divorce Express"—back and forth on weekends between her father's Greenwich Village apartment and her mother's Woodstock home.

It's an Aardvark-Eat-Turtle World (1985), sequel to *The Divorce Express*
Best friends Rosie and Phoebe are not so sure they want their respective single parents to fall in love.

This Place Has No Atmosphere (1986)
In the year 2057, students take classes in ESP and people live in malls, but fourteen-year-old Aurora hates life on the moon.

Remember Me to Harold Square (1987)
Kendra Kaye, fourteen, dreads the long, hot summer ahead, stuck in New York City with her bratty brother and her parents—until Frank Lee comes from Wisconsin.

Thames Doesn't Rhyme with James (1994), sequel to *Remember Me to Harold Square*
Kendra Kaye gets to spend two weeks in London with heartthrob Frank Lee. Oh, and her folks come along, and so do his parents.

Matthew Martin Series

Everyone Else's Parents Said Yes (1989)
Matthew Martin is planning a big sleep-over party—but it is the same weekend his thirteen-year-old sister, Amanda, is going on her first date.

Make Like a Tree and Leave (1990)
Matthew is in charge of the Mummy Committee for the Egypt Unit Project at school.

Earth to Matthew (1992)
Matthew and his classmates study ecology—with an interesting recycling project.

Not for a Billion, Gazillion Dollars (1992)
Matthew is afraid he will not see his girlfriend Jil! all summer.

FICTION FOR MIDDLE READERS

Amber Brown Series

Amber Brown Is Not a Crayon (1994)

You Can't Eat Your Chicken Pox, Amber Brown (1995)

Amber Brown Wants Extra Credit (1995)

FOR FURTHER READING

Babbitt, Natalie. Review of *There's a Bat in Bunk Five. The New York Times Book Review*, 23 November 1980.

Danziger, Paula, et al. "Facets: Successful Authors Talk About Connections Between Teaching and Writing." *English Journal*, November 1984.

Leverich, Kathleen. Review of *You Can't Eat Your Chicken Pox, Amber Brown. The New York Times Book Review*, 21 May 1995.

McClain, Harriet. Review of *There's a Bat in Bunk Five. School Library Journal*, January 1981.

Nilsen, Alleen Pace. "Paula Danziger." In *Twentieth-Century Children's Writers*, edited by Tracy Chevalier. 3d ed. Chicago: St. James Press, 1989.

Nodelman, Perry. "How Typical Children Read Typical Books." *Children's Literature in Education*, winter 1981.

Paula Danziger: Author. New York: Dell, 1988.

Peter Dickinson

Contemporary drama

Livingstone, Northern Rhodesia
December 16, 1927

Changes Trilogy

"Peter Dickinson arrived on the children's book scene in 1969, and by spring of the following year could be regarded as established and successful," John Rowe Townsend said. Dickinson is noted for his strong storytelling, unusual plot elements, fast action, and broad interest in ideas.

The writer's first seven years were spent in Northern Rhodesia, where his father was a British civil servant and his mother a tomb restorer. Upon their return to England, his father died.

After attending Eton College on a scholarship, Dickinson entered the military. He served as a district signals officer during World War II. He later attended King's College, Cambridge, where he earned a degree in English literature in 1951. He then went to work for *Punch*, a humor magazine, where his duties included reviewing crime novels.

With a knowledge of what worked and what did not work in mysteries, Dickinson wrote his first novel, *The Glass-sided Ants' Nest*. It incorporated elements of anthropology and a tribe of aborigines living in London. His police inspector hero, Jimmy Pibble, was an older, bland individual without the detective skills of a Sherlock Holmes.

The author's "gift to the crime story has been an imagination of unusual, even extraordinary, forcefulness," H. R. F. Keating said, adding that Dickinson's mysteries follow classical patterns, but that each "has had its extraordinary 'background,' its small odd world."

Further, "Dickinson writes extremely well. Not only are those characters wonderfully vivid and his settings such that you remember them for years afterwards, but the actual prose is excellent. Phrases leap out, sending sharp images into the distant reader's mind."

Dickinson's *The Weathermonger*, his first novel for young adult readers, and the first book in the Changes Trilogy, is set in present-day England—but an England where people are mysteriously afraid of technology. Geoffrey, who has an unusual ability to alter the weather, sets out with his sister, Sally, to find out what has caused the Changes. They discover the source: King Arthur's wizard, Merlin, has been revived from centuries of sleep. Now a morphine addict, he is being manipulated by a chemist named Furbelow. Subsequent books in the trilogy tell earlier stories of the Changes.

"Peter Dickinson made a startling debut last year with *The Weathermonger*, surely one of the most original of first novels. Mr. Dickinson showed an England which, not far in the future, had turned against the machine. The situation was highly intriguing: the explanation just a little hard to follow. . . . Mr. Dickinson's imaginative control is absolute. He makes the reader feel the weight of the spirit of this strange age, so that the children's success in resisting it is the more impressive," *The Times Literary Supplement* stated in 1969.

In later works, Dickinson explores a range of topics. In *Healer*, he looks at a cult that grows around Pinkie, a girl who has the ability to heal people. *Tulku* takes a boy on an adventure into Tibet with a lama who is questing for the child reincarnate of a holy man named Siddha Asara. *The Blue Hawk* depicts an imaginary country with a rigid society, and a boy, Tron, whose interference with rituals results in the king's death.

"The crucial thing about any act of the imagination is its self-coherence, the way in which each part of it fits with all the other parts and by doing so authenticates them," Dickinson said in *Children's Literature in Education*. "This is the way in which we know and authenticate our real world."

"Peter Dickinson remains the most fascinating, unpredictable of contemporary writers for the young," *The Times Literary Supplement* said. "Each book, while containing the common qualities of unobtrusively excellent writing and sound psychology, turns in a new direction."

In books such as *AK* and *Shadow of a Hero*, Dickinson examines recent world events. Margery Fisher said, "As a subject, international politics has been largely untouched or skirted round in junior novels, at least until recent years. During the 1970s two writers [Dickinson and Robert Cormier (see p. 77)] challenged this particular omission and in doing so they took the thriller to extreme limits—extreme, especially, in the sense that the subject of terrorism in the context of today might even be considered inadmissible in the genre of the adventure story."

"This may be fiction, but it has all the marks of reality. As comment on the sufferings of the Third World the book has much relevance," suggested reviewer M. Crouch.

"As he did in his acclaimed novel *Eva*, Dickinson uses other primate life forms to shed light on our humanity, in this case going back rather than forward in time," Nancy Vasilakis said in reviewing *A Bone from a Dry Sea*. "Vinny is spending the summer with her archaeologist father on a dig in Africa. As she is drawn into his work, analyzing fossils that reveal the mysteries of our prehuman ancestors, she is also making sense of her own life by delving into the nature of the relationship between her divorced parents and herself."

The writer's first wife was Mary Rose Barnard, an artist. They had four children. After her death, he wed Robin McKinley, a writer (see p. 277)

YOUNG ADULT FICTION

Emma Tupper's Diary (1971)
A girl summers with cousins near a Scottish loch. They decide to make a fake monster.

The Dancing Bear (1972)
In Byzantium in the sixth century, Silvester, a young slave, sets out with Holy John and Bubba the bear on a dangerous mission to Hannish lands.

Gift (1973)
Young Davy Price, whose father, at times, is foolish, and whose mother, at times, goes off with another man, has the gift of seeing pictures of people's thoughts.

Chance, Luck and Destiny (1975)
This is a different telling of the story of Oedipus.

The Blue Hawk (1976)
Tron, a boy priest of the god Gdu, is involved in a powerful struggle in a country that resembles ancient Egypt.

Annerton Pit (1977)
When the postcards stop coming from his ghost-hunting dad, blind Jake Bertold worries. He and his brother, Martin, ride off on a motorcycle in search.

The Flight of Dragons (1979)
This is a "scientific" study of dragons and their flight characteristics.

Tulku (1979)
In China at the time of the Boxer Rebellion, Theodore Tewker is orphaned after dissidents destroy his missionary father's home. He joins a flower collector and a lama on a quest in Tibet.

City of Gold, and Other Stories from the Old Testament (1980)
Retellings of stories from the Bible.

Giant Cold (1981)
A family vacationing on an island explores a volcano—and a series of mysterious events begins.

The Seventh Raven (1981)
Doll Jacobs must keep her cool when she and other children are held hostage by revolutionaries.

Healer (1983)
Is Pinkie Proudfoot being exploited by the Foundation because of her healing powers?

A Box of Nothing (1985)
The box of nothing that young James purchases, for nought, from the odd proprietor of a derelict shop, turns into a vast landscape of lakes and mountains.

Merlin Dreams (1987)
Knights, damsels in distress, and other familiar elements stalk the old magician's reveries.

Eva (1989)
Eva, thirteen, wakes up in a hospital, unable to remember anything since the picnic at the beach. She has been in an accident. What have they done, with their amazing medical techniques, to save her?

AK (1990)
Paul Kagomi, a youth guerrilla, buries his trusted AK weapon with the promise of peace. He leaves school to recover it when disruption returns.

A Bone from a Dry Sea (1992)
On a dig searching for fossils, Vinny, a Thinker, links with Li, another Thinker from the past.

Shadow of a Hero (1994)
Can an old man named Restaur Vax and his granddaughter, Letta, make a difference as the tiny East European country of Varina struggles for independence?

Changes Trilogy

The Weathermonger (1968)
In the near future, Geoffrey and his sister, Sally, are sent to find out what has caused the Changes, making people fearful of technology and giving some the power to alter the weather.

Heartsease (1969)
Before the events in *The Weathermonger*, Margaret and Jonathan help an American flee; he is thought to be a witch.

The Devil's Children (1970)
Nicola, twelve, who is repulsed by machinery, is taken in by a group of Sikhs, who have no fear of technology and are being persecuted.

FICTION FOR YOUNGER READERS

The Iron Lion (1972)

Hepzibah (1980)

Mole Hole (1987)

Time and the Clock Mice, Etc. (1994)

EDITOR

Presto! Humorous Bits and Pieces (1975)

Hundreds and Hundreds (1984)

ADULT FICTION

The Green Gene (1973)

The Poison Oracle (1974)

The Lively Dead (1975)

King and Joker (1976)

Walking Dead (1977)

A Summer in the Twenties (1981)

The Last House-Party (1982)

Hindsight (1983)

Death of a Unicorn (1984)

Tefuga: A Novel of Suspense (1985)

Perfect Gallows: A Novel of Suspense (1987)

Skeleton-in-Waiting (1989)

Play Dead (1992)

A Pride of Heroes (1993)

The Yellow Room Conspiracy (1994)

Inspector Pibble Series

The Glass-sided Ants' Nest (1968); British title: *Skin Deep* (1968)

The Old English Peep Show (1969); British title: *A Pride of Heroes* (1969)

The Sinful Stones (1970); British title: *The Seals* (1970)

Sleep and His Brother (1971)

The Lizard in the Cup (1972)

One Foot in the Grave (1979)

CONTRIBUTOR

Verdict of Thirteen, edited by Julian Symons (1979)

Guardian Angels, edited by Stephanie Nettell (1986)

Imaginary Lands, edited by Robin McKinley (1985)

Beware! Beware!, edited by Jean Richardson (1987)

SCREENPLAYS

Mandog (1972)

The Flight of Dragons (1982)

FOR FURTHER READING

"After the Machine Age." *The Times Literary Supplement*, 26 June 1969.

Crouch, M. Review of *AK*. *Junior Bookshelf*, December 1990.

Dickinson, Peter. "Fantasy: The Need for Realism." *Children's Literature in Education*, spring 1986.

Fisher, Margery. *The Bright Face of Danger*. Boston: Horn Book Magazine, 1986.

Keating, H. R. F. "Peter Dickinson." In *Twentieth-Century Crime and Mystery Writers*, edited by Lesley Henderson. 3d ed. Chicago: St. James Press, 1991.

Townsend, John Rowe. "Peter Dickinson." In *Twentieth-Century Children's Writers*, edited by Tracy Chevalier. 3d ed. Chicago: St. James Press, 1989.

"Unquiet Spirits." *The Times Literary Supplement*, 6 April 1973.

Vasilakis, Nancy. Review of *A Bone from a Dry Sea*. *Horn Book Magazine*, July–August 1993.

Franklin W. Dixon

Mystery

Bayport
1927

The Hardy Boys Series

Franklin W. Dixon has been writing young adult adventure novels about Frank and Joe Hardy since 1927 without any visible loss of energy. That's because there is no real "Dixon." A dozen or more individuals have written under the name over the decades.

Edward Stratemeyer (1862–1930) created Dixon and the Hardy Boys. "Stratemeyer started writing when he worked in his brother's tobacco store," Clarence T. Hubbard said. "He wrote dime novels which preceded his cloth-covered library-type books. He was once associated with Street and Smith, publishers in this field. But he finally emerged with an updated remodeled 'hero' for boys, a sort of middle class youngster who was a cut above [Horatio] Alger's bootblacks and much more dignified than Nick Carter or Deadwood Dick." (Stratemeyer also created the pen name Carolyn Keene, "author" of the Nancy Drew series. For more about Stratemeyer's background, see the Carolyn Keene entry on page 174.)

Besides the Hardy Boys books, Dixon's byline appeared on twenty books in the Ted Scott Flying Stories series from 1927 to 1943.

Stratemeyer was a wizard at developing series books. His first successful novel, *Dewey at Manila*, "would have sold for a dime in paperback, [but] made a fortune as a hardcover book at a dollar," Leslie McFarlane said. "Obviously, Stratemeyer decided, the real money was in hardcover juveniles. So he conjured up 'The Rover Boys' in 1899 and introduced a couple of new ideas. Normally a juvenile series was content with one hero; but if one hero was good, wouldn't *two* heroes be twice as good? . . .

"He had learned from the 'Old Glory' books that a series didn't pick up momentum until several volumes were on the market. This took time. He solved the problem ingeniously. He launched 'The Rover Boys' by publishing three books simultaneously: *The Rover Boys at School, The Rover Boys at Sea,* and *The Rover Boys in the Jungle.* Each book contained a few judicious paragraphs plugging the other two books and each book ended by announcing the title of the book to follow with a hint of the goodies in store."

Kenneth L. Donelson and Alleen Pace Nilsen observed, "Stratemeyer was aware that he could create plots and series faster than he could possibly write them. Details of how the Stratemeyer Syndicate operated are fuzzy, but the general outline is clear. Stratemeyer advertised for writers who needed money, and then sent them sketches of settings and characters along with a chapter-by-chapter outline of the plot. Writers had a few weeks to fill in the outlines, and when the copy arrived, Stratemeyer tightened the prose and checked for discrepancies with earlier volumes of the series. Then the manuscript was off to the printer and checks went out to the writers, from fifty to one hundred dollars depending upon the writer and the importance of the series."

He "planned and wrote the series until his death in 1930, but a number of others have necessarily contributed to this long-running success story—among them, Leslie McFarlane, Harriet Stratemeyer Adams, and Andrew E. Svenson. The series is now carried on by a determinedly inconspicuous Syndicate staff," Carol Billman said.

Characters in the Hardy Boys series include Frank and Joe, detective brothers; their parents, Fenton and Laura Hardy; Aunt Gertrude; and friends Chet Morton, Tony Prito, Biff Hooper, Phil Cohen, Callie Shaw, and Iola Morton. Many of the adventures take place in a fictional town called Bayport.

Leslie McFarlane

Leslie McFarlane (1902–1977) wrote the first eleven and eventually ten additional Hardy Boys Mysteries. Born in Carleton Place, Ontario, Canada, he was the son of an elementary school principal. He worked as a writer, screenwriter, producer, and director. In the 1910s and 1920s, he was a newspaper reporter in Ontario and, later, in Springfield, Massachusetts. He was twice married and had three children.

McFarlane signed a contract with Stratemeyer in 1926 and began writing Hardys. He also wrote four Dana Girls books from 1934 to 1935 as Carolyn Keene and seven Dave Fearless books from 1926 to 1927 as Roy Rockwood. He wrote one X Bar X Boys book as James Cody Ferris.

In his autobiography, *Ghost of the Hardy Boys*, McFarlane explained how the first Hardys were written. He received a letter from Stratemeyer in 1926 describing plans for a new series. "He had observed, Stratemeyer wrote, that detective stories had become very popular in the world of adult fiction. . . .

"It had recently occurred to him, Stratemeyer continued, that the growing boys of America might welcome similar fare. . . . What [he] had in mind was a series of detective stories on the juvenile level, involving two brothers of high-school age who would solve such mysteries as came their way. To lend credibility to their talents, they would be the sons of a professional private investigator, so big in his field that he had become a sleuth of international fame. His name—Fenton Hardy. His sons, Frank and Joe, would therefore be known as . . . 'The Hardy Boys'!

"This would be the title of the series. My pseudonym would be Franklin W. Dixon. (I never did learn what the 'W' represented. Certainly not Wealthy.)"

McFarlane received $125 per book, and although common sense said he should churn out the books as quickly as possible, "I opted for Quality," he said. For example, McFarlane's outline told him simply that the heroes were invited to dinner. McFarlane decided, "Why skimp? What Franklin W. Dixon provided was a banquet, a feast. He saw to it that young readers savored the sight, smell and taste of roast chicken 'crisp and brown' with huge helpings of mashed potatoes and gravy. He served them pickles, vegetables and salads. He encouraged seconds. And when it came to dessert, he didn't take the easy way out and settle for a couple of cartons of ice cream. He whomped up half a dozen kinds of pie *with* ice cream."

Obviously, McFarlane relished what artistic freedom he had within the confines of the outline. "Millions of dismayed mothers probably wondered about the national decline in juvenile table manners which swept the nation in 1927 and subsequent years," he added. "Now they know."

Andrew E. Svenson

Andrew E. Svenson (1910–1975) was a newspaper reporter in New Jersey for several years. He worked for the Stratemeyer Literary Syndicate as a writer and editor from 1948 to 1975 and was a partner from 1961 to 1975. He plotted and edited the Tom Swift Jr., Bobbsey Twins, Bret King, Linda Craig, Honey Bunch and Norman, and Hardy Boys series books.

"Andy Svenson loves getting people into trouble," said James V. O'Connor, "but only for the fun of getting them out of it."

"The trick in writing children's books is to set up danger, mystery, and excitement on page one," Svenson told Roger B. May. "Force the kid to turn the page. I've written page one as many as 20 times. Then in the middle of each chapter there's a dramatic point of excitement, and at chapter's end, a cliffhanger."

Svenson himself created and wrote the Happy Hollister series and the Tolliver Adventure series, featuring a black family.

James Duncan Lawrence

Another Hardy Boys author who has been identified is James Duncan Lawrence, born in 1918. Lawrence wrote scripts for the radio shows *The Lone Ranger*, *Sky King*, *Sergeant Preston of the Yukon*, and *The Green Hornet* in the 1940s. He also wrote for newspaper comic strips such as *Buck Rogers*, *Friday Foster*, and *Captain Easy*; and he wrote under the pseudonyms Victor Appleton II (for books about Tom Swift Jr.), Dixon (for the Hardy Boys), Carolyn Keene (for Nancy Drew), and Laura Lee Hope (for the Bobbsey Twins).

He worked for the Stratemeyer Literary Syndicate from the mid-1950s until 1967.

YOUNG ADULT FICTION

Hardy Boys Case Files

All books appear under the Franklin W. Dixon house name. The syndicate keeps the names of the authors secret.

1. *Dead on Target* (1987)
   Joe Hardy's girlfriend, Iola Morton, is blown to bits by a bomb meant for the brothers.
2. *Evil, Inc.* (1987)
   In France, Frank and Joe penetrate the shadowy world of Reynard and company.
3. *Cult of Crime* (1987)
   The Hardys rescue friend Holly from a cult in the Adirondacks.
4. *The Lazarus Plot* (1987)
   Camping in the Maine woods, the Hardys are surprised to see . . . Iola Morton!
5. *Edge of Destruction* (1987)
   Fenton Hardy is kidnapped in the middle of a political banquet.
6. *The Crowning Terror* (1987)
   Frank and Joe are in trouble with an American espionage unit when their Uncle Hugh is kidnapped.
7. *Deathgame* (1987)
   Biff Hooper goes off to a survival game camp in Georgia—and never comes back.
8. *See No Evil* (1987)
   Callie Shaw believes a top-secret code book will be the perfect case to begin her crime-fighting career with boyfriend Frank Hardy.
9. *The Genius Thieves* (1987)
   A daring million-dollar bank robbery leads Frank and Joe to Chartwell Academy.
10. *Hostage to Hate* (1987)
    Callie is among hostages taken in a hijacking in Washington, D.C.
11. *Brother Against Brother* (1988)
    After losing his memory, Joe thinks Frank is an enemy.
12. *Perfect Getaway* (1988)
    The Hardys pose as crooks to expose Perfect Getaway Travel Ltd.
13. *The Borgia Dagger* (1988)
    Fearing the ancient curse on the jeweled dagger, Tessa Carpenter asks the Hardys to help recover it.
14. *Too Many Traitors* (1988)
    Frank and Joe end up running from the law when they take a vacation on Spain's Costa del Sol.
15. *Blood Relations* (1988)
    Greg and Mike Rawley suspect their stepfather of plotting to kill their mother.
16. *Line of Fire* (1988)
    Denny Payson believes his father was murdered in a chemical plant fire five years ago.
17. *The Number File* (1988)
    The Hardys check out a credit card scam in Bermuda.
18. *A Killing in the Market* (1988)
    The brothers investigate the disappearance of Cyril Bayard, a shady investment counselor who has been dating Aunt Gertrude.
19. *Nightmare in Angel City* (1988)
    Callie disappears while shooting a video for her summer class at UCLA.
20. *Witness to Murder* (1988)
    Phil is a prime suspect in a million-dollar diamond robbery, and old girlfriend Annie may be involved.
21. *Street Spies* (1988)
    Frank and Joe go undercover as city bicycle messengers to crack a gang of high-tech thieves.
22. *Double Exposure* (1988)
    When Frank and Joe decide to meet their father's contact on their own, they find long-lost brother Chris Hardy, who may be a hired triggerman.
23. *Disaster for Hire* (1989)
    Frank and Joe race to Seattle to help their father, who has been accused of murder.
24. *Scene of the Crime* (1989)
    The Hardys go undercover as stuntmen on a major movie.
25. *The Borderline Case* (1989)
    In Greece on a student exchange program, the Hardys land in trouble.

26. *Trouble in the Pipeline* (1989)
In Alaska, the detectives trace Scott Sanders, who is working a top-secret project for a mining firm.

27. *Nowhere to Run* (1989)
"Biker" Bob Conway roars into town, looking for Frank and Joe to clear him of hijacking charges.

28. *Countdown to Terror* (1989)
In Halifax, Nova Scotia, the Hardys investigate an insurance scam.

29. *Thick as Thieves* (1989)
During a daring gem robbery, Joe and Frank spot the thief: their old enemy Charity.

30. *The Deadliest Dare* (1989)
Bayport is hit by a rash of vicious pranks.

31. *Without a Trace* (1989)
Frank and Joe look for the cowboy missing from Roy Carlson's New Mexico ranch.

32. *Blood Money* (1989)
Crime lord Josh Moran leaves a will dividing $10 million among his enemies—or those who are surviving in three months.

33. *Collision Course* (1989)
The Hardys investigate the mysterious death of a world-champion Grand Prix racer.

34. *Final Cut* (1989)
Working as gofers at the new Bayport movie studios, Frank and Joe solve the murder of Bennett Fairburn.

35. *The Dead Season* (1990)
Callie Shaw invites Frank and Joe to Runner's Harbor Hotel—which has a skeleton in every closet.

36. *Running on Empty* (1990)
The brothers go undercover to get the drop on a chop-shop ring.

37. *Danger Zone* (1990)
The Hardy Boys and their father launch an all-out mission to rescue Laura Hardy and foil a devious plan of the top-secret Prometheus Computer Corporation.

38. *Diplomatic Deceit* (1990)
Callie finally meets her French pen pal, Madeleine, who acts rude and nasty and does not look like her photograph. Frank and Joe discover she is an impostor, and the real Berots are being held hostage.

39. *Flesh and Blood* (1990)
Is Hardy friend Chet Morton really the son of a murderer seeking revenge on Fenton Hardy?

40. *Fright Wave* (1990)
Someone is trying to kill champion surfer Jade Roberts in Hawaii, and the Hardy Boys decide to keep an eye on her.

41. *Highway Robbery* (1990)
The detectives set out to crack a truck-hijacking scheme.

42. *Last Laugh* (1990)
The legendary publisher of Zenith Comics is kidnapped by the Human Dreadnought and the Flame Fiend at a comic book convention.

43. *Strategic Moves* (1990)
Frank's Russian roommate at summer school at England's Oxford University becomes a pawn in an international power play.

44. *Castle Fear* (1990)
The Hardy Boys are hired to protect Jed Shanon, a young American movie star on location in England.

45. *In Self-Defense* (1990)
The Scorpions want to run Bayport's newest martial arts school off their turf.

46. *Foul Play* (1990)
Someone is embezzling money from the minor league Bayport Blues, and retired baseball great Stuart Murphy is the prime suspect.

47. *Flight into Danger* (1991)
Frank's friend Ray, a former navy ace, disappears along with the state-of-the-art jet he has been hired to test.

48. *Rock 'n' Revenge* (1991)
Danger takes center stage when Buddy Death's heavy metal band comes to Bayport. The Hardys have been hired as bodyguards.

49. *Dirty Deeds* (1991)
Kerry Prescott's father discovers a method for extracting new gold from old Nevada mines.

50. *Power Play* (1991)
The detectives protect a powerful, new solar energy cell from industrial spies.

51. *Choke Hold* (1991)
Pro wrestler Sammy "The Kung Fu King" Rand, is in trouble up to his triceps.

52. *Uncivil War* (1991)
Historian Andrew Donnell invites Frank and Joe to Tennessee for a reenactment of the battle of Shiloh—but Donnell dies from a real bullet.

53. *Web of Horror* (1991)
The producer dies on the set of the latest cult classic, *Horror House V*, where the Hardys are working security.

54. *Deep Trouble* (1991)
Frank and Joe search for lost treasure in the Bahamas and become the targets of saboteurs.

55. *Beyond the Law* (1991)
Scandal rocks the Bayport police force when the new commissioner suspends Chief Ezra Collig.

56. *Height of Danger* (1991)
Frank and Joe, providing security at the World Snowboarding Championships in Austria, face the Network.

57. *Terror on Track* (1991)
Frank and Joe act as decoys on a cross-country train ride to uncover a top-secret plan to transport a deadly virus.

58. *Spiked!* (1991)
The brothers are vacationing in Laguna Beach when a big-time volleyball contest turns into a tournament of terror.

59. *Open Season* (1992)
On a cross-country skiing trip in the Colorado Rockies, Frank and Joe befriend K. D. Becker, a woman dedicated to saving the endangered mountain lion—and a woman with violent enemies.

60. *Deadfall* (1992)
An explosion claims the life of a mill owner, and police accuse environmentalist Stan Shaw.

61. *Grave Danger* (1992)
The Hardys are in the Yucatan to stop robbers stealing Mexican artifacts.

62. *Final Gambit* (1992)
Frank, in Las Vegas to compete in a chess tournament, is a suspect in a kidnapping.

63. *Cold Sweat* (1992)
Chet joins a new health club, but he is more interested in aerobics instructor Dawn Reynolds than in losing weight.

64. *Endangered Species* (Operation Phoenix Trilogy) (1992)
The Hardys are on the trail of a multimillion-dollar smuggling operation in the African wild.

65. *No Mercy* (Operation Phoenix Trilogy) (1992)
A mission of revenge leads Frank and Joe from Kenya to Stockholm on the deadly trail of Phoenix Enterprises.

66. *The Phoenix Equation* (Operation Phoenix Trilogy) (1992)
The Hardys have come thousands of miles in search of their father's killer. Now they are shocked to learn Fenton Hardy may still be alive.

67. *Lethal Cargo* (1992)
While sailing a friend's yacht from St. Martin to the coast of Florida, Frank and Joe find a freighter with a missing crew and a secret cargo.

68. *Rough Riding* (1992)
The Hardys are staying at a Texas ranch when a rodeo star named Buck is set up for something he did not do.

69. *Mayhem in Motion* (1992)
It is a rude welcome to Bayport High when someone slashes Vanessa Bender's tires.

70. *Rigged for Revenge* (1992)
The Hardys are on a floating oil rig in the Gulf of Mexico to find the terrorists trying to sabotage the operation.

71. *Real Horror* (1993)
Someone is trying to dethrone Mark Stevens, king of horror writers.

72. *Screamers* (1993)
At a convention, gunmen kidnap the daughter of the owner of a computer company.

73. *Bad Rap* (1993)
Someone is counterfeiting copies of rap artist Randy Rand's hottest tunes.

74. *Road Pirates* (1993)
Frank and Joe trail a car-jacking gang from New York to the Caribbean.

75. *No Way Out* (1993)
Frank and Joe are learning orienteering from Rob Niles in the Idaho mountains—but someone sets a deadly trap.

76. *Tagged for Terror* (The Ring of Evil Trilogy) (1993)
A luggage theft ring chokes the resources of Eddings Airline.

77. *Survival Run* (The Ring of Evil Trilogy) (1993)
The Hardys discover an international terrorist ring—the Assassins—that deals in smuggling and murder.

78. *The Pacific Conspiracy* (The Ring of Evil Trilogy) (1993)
Frank and Joe penetrate the headquarters of a worldwide terrorist network in Indonesia.

79. *Danger Unlimited* (1993)
Pilot Brett Cooper hopes to compete in the air races and set a speed record, but someone has targeted him for terror.

80. *Dead of Night* (1993)
Frank and Joe are the only witnesses to three shocking murders on Halloween night.

81. *Sheer Terror* (1993)
Chemist Sam Gentle's body lies at the bottom of Wolf's Tooth Canyon, leaving behind a deadly hidden legacy.

82. *Poisoned Paradise* (1993)
Ed Yanomanma, son of a Venezuelan tribal chief, is attending an environmental conference in New York when he is accused of kidnapping.

83. *Toxic Revenge* (1994)
Sabotage threatens a new recycling campaign at Bayport High.

84. *False Alarm* (1994)
Frank and Joe face a criminal mastermind.

85. *Winner Take All* (1994)
Hardy friend Ben wins $5 million in the state lottery, but his sister is kidnapped for a huge ransom.

86. *Virtual Villainy* (1994)
The detectives uncover high-tech industrial espionage while attending a video game convention in San Francisco.

87. *Dead Man in Deadwood* (1994)
The Hardys land in the middle of a feud between Sioux and a local developer when they attend the annual Wild West Week in Deadwood.

88. *Inferno of Fear* (1994)
Who is setting forest fires in Alaska's Denali National Park?

89. *Darkness Falls* (1994)
The expedition leader is murdered at a scientific research project at the Mauna Kea Observatory in Hawaii.

90. *Deadly Engagement* (1994)
Frank and Joe are in New York to help jeweler Biju Kimar find his missing son, Sanjay.

91. *Hot Wheels* (1994)
Temperatures soar as the Hardys compete in the Suntex Solar challenge in the Arizona desert.

92. *Sabotage at Sea* (1994)
The boys sign on with the *Sea Spirit*, a replica of a century-old schooner, but the voyage turns into terror.

93. *Mission: Mayhem* (1994)
Frank and Joe join an astronaut pretraining program, but someone on the team wants to scuttle the mission.

94. *A Taste for Terror* (1994)
A killer is on the loose at the 100th anniversary meeting of the International Explorer's Guild.

95. *Illegal Procedure* (1995)
Crime infiltrates the San Diego Sharks football team.

96. *Against All Odds* (1995)
Against All Odds, the racehorse, is missing from the Bayport fairgrounds.

97. *Pure Evil* (1995)
Someone sours the maple sugar harvest of Callie's Uncle Adam in New Hampshire.

98. *Murder by Magic* (1995)
The brothers are stagehands at the show "Legerdemain" when someone kills Gideon the Great's assistant, Miranda.

99. *Frame-Up* (1995)
The annual Computer Horizons convention brings the Hardys to New Orleans—and trouble.

100. *True Thriller* (1995)
Oliver Richards, a writer, wants to feature Frank and Joe in his next novel, but thanks to him, an international gang called the Assassins is back.

101. *Peak of Danger* (1995)
Bayport High soccer player Carlos Capac is nearly killed by saboteurs.

102. *Wrong Side of the Law* (1995)
Masked gunmen hit local banks.

103. *Campaign of Crime* (1995)
A computer whiz is candidate for president.

Nancy Drew–Hardy Boys Super Sleuth Mysteries

See page 184, under Carolyn Keene.

Hardy Boys and Tom Swift Ultra Thriller

All books appear under the Franklin W. Dixon house name. The syndicate keeps the names of the authors secret.

Time Bomb (1992)
Tom Swift and the Hardys try to stop the evil Black Dragon before he turns a time machine into the ultimate doomsday device.

FICTION FOR MIDDLE READERS

Hardy Boys Mysteries

All books appear under the Franklin W. Dixon house name. The syndicate keeps the names of the authors secret. Older titles can still be found in libraries.

1. *Tower Treasure* (1927, 1959)
2. *The House on the Cliff* (1927, 1959)
3. *The Secret of the Old Mill* (1927, 1962)
4. *The Missing Chums* (1928, 1962)
5. *Hunting for Hidden Gold* (1928, 1963)
6. *The Shore Road Mystery* (1928, 1964)
7. *The Secret of the Caves* (1929, 1964)
8. *The Mystery of Cabin Islands* (1929, 1966)
9. *The Great Airport Mystery* (1930, 1965)
10. *What Happened at Midnight* (1931, 1967)
11. *While the Clock Ticked* (1932, 1962)
12. *Footprints Under the Window* (1933, 1965)
13. *The Mark on the Door* (1934, 1967)
14. *The Hidden Harbor Mystery* (1935, 1961)
15. *The Sinister Sign Post* (1936, 1968)
16. *A Figure in Hiding* (1937, 1965)
17. *The Secret Warning* (1938, 1966)
18. *The Twisted Claw* (1939, 1969)
19. *The Disappearing Floor* (1940, 1964)
20. *The Mystery of the Flying Express* (1941, 1970)
21. *The Clue of the Broken Blade* (1942, 1970)
22. *The Flickering Torch Mystery* (1943, 1971)
23. *Melted Coins* (1944, 1970)
24. *The Short-Wave Mystery* (1945, 1966)
25. *The Secret Panel* (1946, 1969)
26. *The Phantom Freighter* (1947, 1970)
27. *The Secret of Skull Mountain* (1948, 1966)
28. *The Sign of the Crooked Arrow* (1949, 1960)
29. *The Secret of the Lost Tunnel* (1950, 1968)
30. *The Wailing Siren Mystery* (1951, 1968)
31. *The Secret of Wildcat Swamp* (1952, 1969)
32. *The Crisscross Shadow* (1953, 1969)
33. *The Yellow Feather Mystery* (1953, 1971)
34. *The Hooded Hawk Mystery* (1954, 1971)
35. *The Clue in the Embers* (1955, 1972)
36. *The Secret of Pirates Hill* (1956, 1972)
37. *The Ghost of Skeleton Rock* (1957, 1966)
38. *The Mystery at Devil's Paw* (1959, 1973)
39. *The Mystery of the Chinese Junk* (1960)
40. *The Mystery of the Desert Giant* (1961)
41. *The Clue of the Screeching Owl* (1962)
42. *The Viking Symbol Mystery* (1963)
43. *The Mystery of the Aztec Warrior* (1964)
44. *The Haunted Fort* (1965)
45. *The Mystery of the Spiral Bridge* (1966)
46. *The Secret Agent on Flight 101* (1967)
47. *The Mystery of the Whale Tattoo* (1968)
48. *The Arctic Patrol Mystery* (1969)
49. *The Bombay Boomerang* (1970)
50. *Danger on Vampire Trail* (1971)
51. *The Masked Monkey* (1972)
52. *The Shattered Helmet* (1973)
53. *The Clue of the Hissing Serpent* (1974)
54. *The Mysterious Caravan* (1975)
55. *The Witch-Masters Key* (1976)
56. *Jungle Pyramid* (1977)
57. *Mystery of the Firebird Rocket* (1978)
58. *Sting of the Scorpion* (1979)
59. *Night of the Werewolf* (1979)
60. *Mystery of the Samurai Sword* (1979)
61. *The Pentagon Spy* (1980)

62. *The Apeman's Secret* (1980)
63. *The Mummy Case* (1980)
64. *The Mystery of Smuggler's Cave* (1980)
65. *The Stone Idol* (1981)
66. *The Vanishing Thieves* (1981)
67. *The Outlaw's Silver* (1981)
68. *The Submarine Caper* (1981)
69. *The Four-Headed Dragon* (1981)
70. *The Infinity Clue* (1981)
71. *Track of the Zombie* (1982)
72. *Voodoo Plot* (1982)
73. *The Billion Dollar Plot* (1982)
74. *Tic-Tac-Terror* (1982)
75. *Trapped at Sea* (1982)
76. *Gameplan for Disaster* (1982)
77. *The Crimson Flame* (1983)
78. *Cave-In* (1983)
79. *The Roaring River Mystery* (1984)
80. *Sky Sabotage* (1984)
81. *Demon's Den* (1984)
82. *The Blackwing Puzzle* (1984)
83. *The Swamp Monster* (1985)
84. *The Skyfire Puzzle* (1985)
85. *Revenge of the Desert Phantom* (1986)
86. *Mystery of the Space Shuttle* (1986)
87. *Program for Destruction* (1987)
88. *Tricky Business* (1988)
89. *The Sky Blue Frame* (1988)
90. *Danger on the Diamond* (1988)
91. *Shield of Fear* (1988)
92. *The Shadow Killers* (1988)
93. *The Serpent's Tooth Mystery* (1988)
94. *Breakdown in Axleblade* (1989)
95. *Danger on the Air* (1989)
96. *Wipeout* (1989)
97. *Cast of Criminals* (1989)
98. *Spark of Suspicion* (1989)
99. *Dungeon of Doom* (1989)
100. *The Secret of the Island Treasure* (1990)
101. *The Money Hunt* (1990)
102. *Terminal Shock* (1990)
103. *The Million Dollar Nightmare* (1990)
104. *Tricks of the Trade* (1990)
105. *The Smoke Screen Mystery* (1990)
106. *Attack of the Video Villains* (1991)
107. *Panic on Gull Island* (1991)
108. *Fear on Wheels* (1991)
109. *The Prime-Time Crime* (1991)
110. *The Secret of Sigma Seven* (1991)
111. *Three-Ring Terror* (1991)
112. *The Demolition Mission* (1992)
113. *Radical Moves* (1992)
114. *Case of the Counterfeit Criminals* (1992)
115. *Sabotage at Sports City* (1992)
116. *Rock 'n' Roll Renegades* (1992)
117. *The Baseball Card Conspiracy* (1992)
118. *Danger in the Fourth Dimension* (1993)
119. *Trouble at Coyote Canyon* (1993)
120. *The Case of the Cosmic Kidnapping* (1993)
121. *The Mystery in the Old Mine* (1993)
122. *Carnival of Crime* (1993)
123. *The Robot's Revenge* (1993)
124. *Mystery with a Dangerous Beat* (1994)
125. *Mystery on Makatunk Island* (1994)
126. *Racing with Disaster* (1994)
127. *Reel Thrills* (1994)
128. *Day of the Dinosaurs* (1994)
129. *The Treasure at Dolphin Bay* (1994)
130. *Sidetracked to Danger* (1995)
131. *Crusade of the Flaming Sword* (1995)
132. *Maximum Challenge* (1995)
133. *Crime in the Kennel* (1995)

Hardy Boys Detective Handbook (1959)

Hardy Boys Handbook: Seven Stories of Survival (1980)

Hardy Boys Ghost Stories, edited by Ann Greenberg (1993)

Nancy Drew and Hardy Boys Be a Detective Mystery Stories

See page 189, under Carolyn Keene.

ADAPTATIONS IN OTHER MEDIA

The Hardy Boys (circa 1956)
Television serials on *The Mickey Mouse Club*: "The Mystery of the Applegate Treasure" and "The Mystery of Ghost Farm," both starring Tim Considine and Tommy Kirk.

The Hardy Boys (1969–70)
Animated television series, with voices of Dallas McKennon, Jane Webb, and Byron Kane.

The Hardy Boys Mysteries (1977–79)
ABC television series starring Shaun Cassidy and Parker Stevenson.

FOR FURTHER READING

Billman, Carol. *The Secret of the Stratemeyer Syndicate: Nancy Drew, the Hardy Boys, and the Million Dollar Fiction Factory*. New York: Frederick Ungar, 1986.

Bishop, Barbara A., ed. *American Boys' Series Books 1900 to 1980*. Tampa: University of South Florida Library Associates, 1987.

Donelson, Kenneth L., and Alleen Pace Nilsen, eds. Article in *Literature for Today's Young Adults*. Glenview, IL: Scott, Foresman, 1980.

Enright, John M. "Alias: Franklin W. Dixon." *The Mystery & Adventure Series Review*, summer 1989.

———. "Hardy Boys Tie-Ins." *The Mystery & Adventure Series Review*, spring 1981.

———. "Mr. McFarlane's Magic." *The Mystery & Adventure Series Review*, spring 1981.

Erickson, Cliff. "The Complete Collector's Hardy Boys Formats." *The Mystery & Adventure Series Review*, summer 1984.

Hand, Judson. "Frank, Joe & Nancy Still Wow the Kids." *The New York Sunday News*, 23 January 1977.

Hudson, Harry K. *A Bibliography of Hard-Cover Boys' Books*. Tampa, FL: Hudson, 1977.

Jordan, Charles J. "Tom Swift and the Hardcover Heroes." *Collectibles Illustrated*, May–June 1982.

May, Roger B. "Andrew E. Svenson." *The Wall Street Journal*, 15 January 1975.

McFarlane, Leslie. *Ghost of the Hardy Boys*. New York: Methuen/Two Continents, 1976.

O'Connor, James V. "Andrew E. Svenson." *Rotary International Magazine*, September 1973.

Praeger, Arthur. "Edward Stratemeyer and His Book Machine." *Saturday Review*, 10 July 1971.

———. *Rascals at Large; or, The Clue in the Old Nostalgia*. New York: Doubleday, 1971.

Soderbergh, Peter A. "Your Favorite (Unknown) Author." *Modern Maturity*, June–July 1975.

Zuckerman, Ed. "The Great Hardy Boys' Whodunit: The Strange Tale of the Stratemeyer Syndicate and . . . Look Out! . . . Groupies!" *Rolling Stone*, 9 September 1976.

Lois Duncan

Suspense

Philadelphia, Pennsylvania
April 28, 1934

Killing Mr. Griffin

"A writer 'gets started' the day he is born," Lois Duncan wrote in her autobiography, *Chapters: My Growth As a Writer*. "The mind he brings into the world with him is the amazing machine his stories will come out of, and the more he feeds into it the richer those stories will be.

"I cannot remember a time when I did not consider myself a writer. When I was three years old I was dictating stories to my parents, and as soon as I learned to print, I was writing them down myself. I shared a room with my younger brother, and at night I would lie in bed inventing tales to give him nightmares."

Born Lois Duncan Steinmetz, the writer described her childhood in *Chapters*: "Aside from tormenting Billy, I had few hobbies. A fat, shy little girl, I was a bookworm and a dreamer. I grew up in Sarasota, Florida, and spent a lot of time playing alone in the woods and on the beaches." Both her parents were magazine photographers.

"The books I loved most as a child," Duncan said in *Books I Read When I Was Young*, "were those that contained elements of magic—the whole series of Oz books, *Mary Poppins*, *The Princess and the Goblin*—I could name them indefinitely. When I grew up and became a writer, I was told by my editors, 'Children today are too sophisticated for books like those, they want to read about real people involved in real situations.'

"Which was fine, to a point," continued Duncan. "I did write a number of such books. But the thought kept nagging at me that it would be fun to try to combine both elements, realism and fantasy, and write about forms of magic which might actually exist in today's world. My first attempt at this was *A Gift of Magic*, about a girl with ESP. When that proved successful, I went a bit further and tried a supernatural Gothic, *Down a Dark Hall*, and a book about Ozark witchcraft, *Summer of Fear*. With each of these books, it was like reaching back into my own youth to please the child I used to be."

She published her first story at age thirteen in the magazine *Calling All Girls*. She struggled with her writing and won a *Seventeen* magazine prize for a story about a Korean War soldier returning home. Most of the main characters in her early stories were boys.

"I had always wanted to be a boy," Duncan admitted in *Chapters*. "Boys didn't have to be pretty. An overweight boy was 'husky,' while an overweight girl was 'fat.' I dressed like a boy as often as my mother would let me and almost pulled my arm out of the socket trying to kiss my elbow, which I'd heard was the magic formula for changing sex. Needless to say, I was unsuccessful."

By her early thirties, Duncan had dropped out of college as well as her first marriage. "I had married anticipating the same sort of easy companionship my parents enjoyed, but I did not find it," she said in *Chapters*. Raising three children, she wrote twelve hours a day and did not earn a lot of money. She sold several novels and turned out stories for confession magazines such as *True Story*. Eventually a breakthrough came, and she began selling to the best-known magazines, such as *Ladies' Home Journal* and *Redbook*. Editors called her with story ideas. When she later returned to writing young adult novels with *Ransom*, she found that sex, divorce, mental illness, and other themes had appeared in the genre.

Duncan attended Duke University and received a bachelor of arts degree from the University of New Mexico in 1977. Remarried, she has four surviving children and one deceased child (whose death inspired Duncan's 1992 nonfiction book *Who Killed My Daughter?*). Duncan's career includes writing young adult and adult novels; magazine articles, and short stories; magazine photographer; journalism instructor at the University of New Mexico; and writers' conferences lecturer.

She gravitates to young adult writing, she said in a publisher's promotional piece, "because I love the sensitivity, vulnerability and responsiveness of that age reader."

She explained that her books usually begin with a concept or situation. "The idea for *Locked in Time*, for example, originated when the youngest of my five children turned thirteen. Overnight my darling Kate changed from an adorable cherub who thought her mother was perfect into a hostile teenager who thought everything about Mother, from her hairstyle to her 'dumb jokes,' was 'utterly gross.' My husband tried to comfort me by saying, 'It's just a phase all adolescents go through. Our other kids outgrew it, and so will Kate.'

"The Mother part of me knew that he was right.

"The Writer part of me whispered—'What if she *doesn't*?'

"What if a mother and her adolescent daughter were locked in time? What would it be like to live for all eternity with a hostile, rebellious thirteen-year-old who never outgrew her training bra—who never got rid of her acne—and who knew that I, her mother, was responsible for that situation?

"Once I'd gotten that far in my thinking, I was racing for the typewriter."

She said that her books, especially the suspense novels, are "tightly plotted and carefully constructed; every sentence in them is there for a reason. Personally, I can't imagine writing a book without knowing exactly how it's going to end. It would be like setting out on a cross-country trip without a roadmap."

Typical of her thrillers is *I Know What You Did Last Summer*. Teens Julie James, Barry Cox, Helen Rivers, and Raymond Bronson share a dark secret: They were all riding in a car when it struck a young boy on a bicycle. Although guilty about their knowledge and deed, they are hoping to get on with their lives. Julie has just been accepted at college. Barry, who was dating Helen and driving the car that night, is now thinking of other girls, although Helen is still hopelessly in love with Barry.

All are having second thoughts about their pact. " 'You phoned for the ambulance,' " Julie tells Barry. " 'You wanted to go back.' " 'But I didn't insist on it. You wanted to go back too, but we didn't. We let Barry talk us into the pact. I could have held out, but I didn't. I must have wanted to be talked into it. I'm no better than Barry, Ju.' "

Now someone is sending them notes and trying to kill them. The suspense builds as the unknown stalker strikes his goals.

Duncan bases many of her fictional characters on real ones. "I fashioned the girl [in *Debutante Hill*] after myself, named her Lynn, and placed her in the familiar setting of my own high school years," she explained in *Chapters*. "The town was Sarasota, renamed Rivertown. Although I myself had never experienced the mad whirl of the debutante social season, my brother had. Bill had been a senior the year the deb program had been established and had been drafted as escort for one of the girls. Because of this, and because they had been chaperones at some of the parties, my parents were able to give me a detailed description of what they had been like."

As her children grew older, Duncan tapped their experiences. "The character of Mark in *Killing Mr. Griffin* is based on Robin's horrible first boyfriend," the author said. "Kit, in *Down a Dark Hall,* is Kerry, and the mischievous Brendon in *A Gift of Magic* is Brett. Young Don and Kate are Neal and Megan in *Stranger with My Face.*"

Killing Mr. Griffin is one of Duncan's more controversial books. "Lois Duncan breaks some new ground in a novel without sex, drugs or black leather jackets," said reviewer Richard Peck. "But the taboo she tampers with is far more potent and pervasive: the unleashed fury of the permissively reared against any assault on their egos and authority. A group of high-school seniors kill an English teacher who dares trouble them with grades, homework and standards."

"The author is unreserved in the way she explores the consequences of the kidnapping—a crude burial, the intimidation of Susan, a younger and unwilling accomplice, the hasty switching of cars and inevitable discovery, are described with harsh, literal detail of event and talk," critic Margery Fisher said.

Duncan told Roger Sutton that the story grew from a single character, Mark, based on her oldest daughter's first real boyfriend. "He was a very sick young man, and he was the most charming young man you could ever meet. It wasn't until things got very bad that we discovered he was the kind of guy who would swerve in the road to run over a dog. . . . Teenagers are so easily influenced, so easily led by charismatic people, that I started thinking about what could happen with a teenage psychopath of that type in a high school setting and what type of young people he would attract as followers. . . . Then I thought 'What could he make them do?' The book moved from there."

"The style Duncan has used is a simple one," Audrey Eaglen observed. "She places an individual or a group of normal, believable young people in what appears to be a prosaic setting such as a suburban neighborhood or an American high school; on the surface everything is as it should be, until Duncan introduces an element of surprise that gives the story an entirely new twist."

Duncan noted in *Literature for Today's Young Adults* that the genre has changed considerably since she first began writing. "The subject matter of today's youth novels has no boundaries. The only taboo seems to be sex discrimination. . . . I can only guess about where we're going, but I think we have come about as far as we can in the direction of 'let-it-all-hang-out' realism. My reader-mail indicates that kids are beginning to feel bogged down with so much depressing slice-of-life. My own most successful books have been those that were high in entertainment value, especially those touching on the supernatural."

If there is an underlying theme to Duncan's books, beyond entertainment, it is "the importance of taking responsibility for one's own actions," she said in a publisher's flyer. "My surface goal in writing *The Twisted Window*, for example, was to produce a fast-paced page-turner, exciting enough to lure teenagers away from TV screens. The story has a second level, however. My heroine, Tracy, does something she senses is wrong and is caught in a current of events that sweeps her toward disaster. The subliminal message in this book is, 'Don't give in to peer pressure. Stand firm for what you feel at gut level is right.' "

Duncan has written two nonfiction books for young adults, *Major Andre: Brave Enemy* (1969) and *Peggy* (1970), and one for adults, *How to Write and Sell Your Personal Experiences* (1979).

YOUNG ADULT FICTION

Debutante Hill (1958)
What about the small-town girl, such as Lynn Chambers, who is not chosen to be a deb?

Love Song for Joyce (1958) as Lois Kerry
Joyce Reynolds is a freshman at college.

A Promise for Joyce (1959) as Lois Kerry, sequel to *Love Song for Joyce*
As a sophomore, Joyce is troubled by boyfriend Jeff's rigid program of pre-med studies.

The Middle Sister (1961)
Ruth Audrey Porter gradually blossoms from a tall, shy girl into a confident, lovable personality.

Game of Danger (1962)
Anne and Rob are bewildered by their mother's instructions to take an important letter to an old friend in Maine.

Season of Two-Heart (1964)
A young Pueblo Indian girl, Martha Weekoty, moves in with a prosperous Albuquerque family to attend public high school and tend the family's two boys during the evenings.

Ransom (1966); paperback title: *Five Were Missing* (1972)
Teenagers are kidnapped by their school bus driver.

They Never Came Home (1969)
After Joan gets a mysterious call, she and Frank go looking for her brother, Dan, and his buddy, Larry, who have not returned from a camping weekend.

Peggy (1970)
Peggy Shippen is a vixen from Philadelphia who becomes Mrs. Benedict Arnold.

I Know What You Did Last Summer (1973)
Four terrified friends make a pact to conceal a shocking secret—but now, someone has learned the truth.

Down a Dark Hall (1974)
Kit goes off to boarding school and discovers that the headmistress is a medium who brings back malevolent ghosts of dead artists and writers.

Summer of Fear (1976)
A young witch charms herself into an unsuspecting family.

Killing Mr. Griffin (1978)
A group of high school students kidnap their strict English teacher in an attempt to force him to give less homework. The plan is only to scare him, but things get out of hand.

Daughters of Eve (1979)
A high school girls' club adviser leads her charges into ever more violent acts in the name of feminism.

Stranger with My Face (1981)
Who, or what, is trying to take over seventeen-year-old Laurie's life?

The Third Eye (1984); British title: *The Eyes of Karen Connors* (1985)
Karen Connors, eighteen, uses her unusual powers to lead police to a missing boy and to where a child was drowned.

Locked in Time (1985)
Nora Robbins does not look forward to summer at a Louisiana plantation with her new stepfamily.

The Twisted Window (1987)
Tracy Lloyd *feels* Brad Johnson watching her.

Don't Look Behind You (1989)
April Corrigan's father has been working undercover for the FBI, and the family now must relocate under the federal Witness Security Program.

FICTION FOR YOUNGER READERS

The Littlest One in the Family (1960)

Silly Mother (1962)

Giving Away Suzanne (1963)

A Gift of Magic (1971)

Hotel for Dogs (1971)

Horses of Dreamland (1985)

Wonder Kid Meets the Evil Lunch Snatcher (1988)

The Birthday Moon (1989)

Songs from Dreamland: Original Lullabies (1989)

The Circus Comes Home: When the Greatest Show on Earth Rode the Rails (1992)

POETRY FOR YOUNGER READERS

From Spring to Spring: Poems and Photographs (1982)

The Terrible Tales of Happy Days School (1983)

ADULT FICTION

Point of Violence (1966)

When the Bough Breaks (1974)

ADAPTATIONS IN OTHER MEDIA

Strangers in Our House (1978)
Television movie adapted from *Summer of Fear.*

FOR FURTHER READING

Conversation with Lois Duncan. New York: Dell, circa 1988.

Cullinan, Bernice, and M. Jerry Weiss, eds. *Books I Read When I Was Young: The Favorite Books of Famous People*. New York: Avon Books, 1980.

Donelson, Kenneth L., and Alleen Pace Nilsen, eds. "The People Behind the Books: Lois Duncan." In *Literature for Today's Young Adults*. Glenview, IL: Scott, Foresman, 1980.

Duncan, Lois. *Chapters: My Growth As a Writer*. Boston: Little, Brown, 1982.

Eaglen, Audrey. "Lois Duncan." In *Twentieth-Century Children's Writers*, edited by Tracy Chevalier. 3d ed. Chicago: St. James Press, 1989.

Fisher, Margery. Review of *Killing Mr. Griffin*. *Growing Point*, November 1980.

Peck, Richard. "Teaching Teacher a Lesson." *The New York Times Book Review*, 30 April 1978.

Sutton, Roger. *A Conversation with Lois Duncan*. *School Library Journal*, June 1992.

Paula Fox

Historical drama

Contemporary drama

New York City
April 22, 1923
The Slave Dancer: A Novel

Paula Fox "is conscious that in a complicated and changing society it is hard for the generations to live together satisfactorily," John Rowe Townsend wrote. "In her books the 'good' grown-ups are the flexible ones who appreciate the variousness of things and people."

She "is an unusually perceptive writer who has a remarkable ability to portray a world as it exclusively appears through the eyes of a youthful protagonist," Marilyn Kaye asserted. "She captures the intensity of young emotions through carefully crafted stories which unravel with a quiet precision, and ultimately culminate in some newfound wisdom."

Fox's father, a writer, worked in the 1920s as a "play fixer." He traveled with road shows to try to improve scripts as programs were ready to open. He also wrote plays of his own, eventually joining a group of writers and actors who started the Provincetown Theater in Massachusetts. Later, he and his wife, Elsie (de Sola) Fox, went to Hollywood to work for MGM. Then they moved to England to work for Gaumont Studios.

Paula Fox did not see much of her parents. She was raised until age six by a Congregational minister who lived with his invalid mother near the Hudson River. Fox later lived in California and on a sugar plantation in Cuba. By age twelve, she had attended nine schools.

After World War II, living in New York, she married Richard Sigerson. They had two sons and later divorced. She is now married to Martin Greenburg, a professor. She attended Columbia University.

"I always wanted to write," Fox said in a publisher's pamphlet, "ever since childhood. But I didn't start writing until I started a job teaching troubled children. Before teaching, I worked in a wide variety of jobs. At sixteen, I was reading books for Warner Brothers, including Spanish novels. I also was a salesgirl, a model, a worker in a rivet-sorting shop, and lastly a lathe operator at Bethlehem Steel. I wrote my first adult novel, entitled *Poor George*, while I was living in Greece with my family. My first children's book, *Maurice's Room*, quickly followed."

Fox's books have been praised for their craftsmanship, sharp observation, and integrity. *The Slave Dancer*, one of her best-known books, was both hailed and derided. It tells the story of ninety-eight Ashantis (natives of Ghana, Africa) illegally captured in 1840 and transported by sea to enslavement.

C. S. Hannabuss, in *Children's Book Review*, called Fox "one of the most exciting writers practicing for children and young people today," while Albert Schwartz, in *Interracial Books for Children*, said *The Slave Dancer* was racist and depicted blacks as "pathetic sufferers."

"Each of the sailors is sharply individualized, the inhuman treatment of the captives is conveyed straight to the nose and stomach rather than the bleeding heart, and the scenes in which Jessie is forced to play his fife to 'dance the slave' for their morning exercise become a haunting, focusing image for the whole bizarre undertaking," *Kirkus Reviews* wrote.

Yet to Julius Lester, "None of the characters . . . are much more than devices. The slave ship captain is a second-rate Wolf Larsen and the crew only a little less villainous. The Africans are depicted as rather pathetic and dumb creatures, so much so in fact that it is difficult to have sympathy for them."

Uncomfortable with the mixed reception, Fox gave an eloquent speech in accepting the Newbery Medal in 1974 for *The Slave Dancer*. She told interviewer Marguerite Feitlowitz, "There are those who feel that slavery debased the enslaved. It is not so. Slavery engulfed whole peoples, swallowed up their lives, committed such offenses that in considering them, the heart falters, the mind recoils. Slavery debased the enslavers. . . .

"There are others who feel that black people can only be humiliated by being reminded that once they were brought to this country as slaves. But it is not the victim who is shamed. It is the persecutor, who has refused the shame of what he has done and, as the last turn of the screw, would burden the victim with the ultimate responsibility of the crime itself.

"I wrote *The Slave Dancer* as a never-quite-to-be-freed captive of a white childhood in a dark condition. . . . Writing *The Slave Dancer* was the closest I could get to events of spirit and flesh which cannot help but elude in their reality all who did not experience them."

Fox does not outline her books ahead of time but compiles notebooks as she goes. She works at least four hours and often longer each day a book is in progress. She said in a publisher's pamphlet, "As I sit at my typewriter, working, there are moments when I feel I cannot write another word, when the sheer difficulty of discovering what I mean to say and how to say it is so daunting that I want to stop forever. I haven't yet stopped. I stay in my chair, pen in hand, yellow-lined pad on the desk next to the machine, doodling or writing down fragments of sentences, hoping some unified principle will, like a net, draw them together. On the whole, most writing is the questions one asks oneself. What has happened to me? Does it have meaning? It's a peculiar process. One of the nicest things about writing is that you make yourself laugh. You don't have to wait for a comedian to come along!"

One-Eyed Cat, which won a Newbery Honor Book designation in 1986, is about eleven-year-old Ned Wallis. He lives with his family on their old homestead outside Tyler, New York. Ned's mother is bedridden. His father, a Congregational minister, forbids him to fire the air rifle, a gift from an uncle. Ned takes the gun one night and disobeys. He shoots at a shadow. He feels guilty when he believes he has put out the eye of a cat belonging to a neighbor, Mr. Scully. The two nurture the cat back to health, then Mr. Scully falls ill and has to go into a nursing home. Ned's life begins to change. He matures.

Western Wind is about Elizabeth Benedict, a girl sent to live with her artist grandmother while her parents bring home a new baby. "Unsentimental, proud and opinionated, Gran is a stickler for proper English usage, honesty and clean living," Cyrisse Jaffee said. "So Elizabeth must grapple not only with the lack of electricity and indoor plumbing and with Gran's silences, but also with loneliness and boredom, fueled by the anger she feels about being abandoned by her parents."

"For me, stories begin with character," Fox said in *Horn Book Magazine* in 1991. "And character shows itself not only in the high drama of crisis but in small daily gestures. The way a passer-by pauses to stroke the muzzle of a horse that stands patiently in its traces, attached to one of those cabriolets that take people for rides in Central Park; the way a woman, bending over her child to take her hand before crossing a street, suddenly smiles at no one in particular but rather as though at some inner revelation of the perfection of that moment when she is both protector and companion of the child; the way people look in a hospital corridor just before the moment they must enter the room where someone they care about is lying in an iron bed, desperately ill.

"There are thousands of fleeting glimpses, if we pay attention, if we notice, into what is individual yet ordinary, secret yet transparent—seconds of vision that can quicken one's imagination with their sudden illumination of other lives, other ways of seeing and feeling."

YOUNG ADULT FICTION

How Many Miles to Babylon? A Novel (1967)
Jimmy leads a lonely and frightening existence as a black youth in Brooklyn.

The King's Falcon (1969)
The monarch does not want to reign.

Portrait of Ivan (1969)
Ivan is a lonely, motherless boy whose father travels a lot.

Blowfish Live in the Sea (1970)
Through the eyes of twelve-year-old Carrie Felix, her brother, Ben, eighteen, tries to come to terms with himself and his real father.

The Slave Dancer: A Novel (1973)
In 1840, Jessie, a thirteen-year-old street musician, is kidnapped and forced to work on a slave ship.

A Place Apart (1980)
After Victoria Finch's father dies, she and her mother move from Boston to a small town. She is unhappy until she meets Hugh Todd.

One-Eyed Cat: A Novel (1984)
Ned Wallis, eleven, is forbidden by his father from firing an air rifle, but he does anyway.

The Moonlight Man (1986)
Teenager Catherine lives with her divorced father for the summer.

The Village by the Sea (1988)
Emma, ten, dreads being sent to her aunt and uncle's home on Long Island as her father undergoes heart surgery.

In a Place of Danger (1989)

The God of Nightmares (1990)

Monkey Island (1991)
Abandoned Clay, eleven, wanders the streets of New York and takes refuge with two homeless men.

Western Wind: A Novel (1993)
Elizabeth Benedict, eleven, goes to spend a month with Gran while her parents bring home the new baby.

The Eagle Kite: A Novel (1995)
A boy learns that his father has AIDS.

FICTION FOR YOUNGER READERS

Maurice's Room (1966)

A Likely Place (1967)

The Stone-Faced Boy (1968)

Hungry Fred (1969)

Good Ethan (1973)

The Little Swineherd, and Other Tales (1978)

Lily and the Lost Boy (1987); British title: *The Lost Boy* (1988)

Amzat and His Brothers: Three Italian Tales (1993)

ADULT FICTION

Poor George (1967)

Dear Prosper (1968)

Desperate Characters (1970)

The Western Coast (1972)

The Widow's Children (1976)

A Servant's Tale (1984)

INTRODUCTORY READING

Tell Me That You Love Me, Junie Moon by Marjorie Kellogg (1984)

FOR FURTHER READING

Feitlowitz, Marguerite. "Paula Fox." In *Authors & Artists for Young Adults*, edited by Agnes Garrett and Helga P. McCue. Vol. 3. Detroit: Gale Research, 1989.

Fox, Paula. "To Write Simply." *Horn Book Magazine*, September–October 1991.

———. "The Village by the Sea." *Horn Book Magazine*, January–February 1990.

Hannabuss, C. S. Review of *The Slave Dancer. Children's Book Review*, winter 1974–75.

Interracial Books for Children. London: Writers and Readers Publishing Cooperative, 1975.

Jaffee, Cyrisse. Review of *Western Wind. The New York Times Book Review*, 10 April 1994.

Kaye, Marilyn. "Paula Fox." In *Twentieth-Century Children's Writers*, edited by Tracy Chevalier. 3d ed. Chicago: St. James Press, 1989.

Lester, Julius. Review of *The Slave Dancer. The New York Times Book Review*, 20 January 1974.

Paula Fox. New York: Orchard Books, 1993.

Review of *The Slave Dancer. Kirkus Reviews*, 1 October 1973.

Townsend, John Rowe. *A Sense of Story: Essays on Contemporary Writings for Children*. New York: J. B. Lippincott, 1971.

Jean Craighead George

Outdoor drama

Washington, D.C.
July 2, 1919
My Side of the Mountain

Jean Craighead George, a naturalist and natural history writer, writes books about animals. She also writes books about young people surviving in the wilderness, such as *Julie of the Wolves*, which won a Newbery Medal in 1976.

"Though diverse in setting, characterization, and plot, her books have many themes in common," Mary J. Lickteig noted. "Her characters observe the mysteries of nature and seek answers that help them understand these mysteries. As they seek answers, they reflect on the secrets that nature holds."

George's family had a great love for the outdoors. Her ancestors settled in southern Pennsylvania in the mid-1700s in an area that became known as Craigheads. Her father studied forestry and entomology. As youths, she and her brothers, who were twins, spent summers on the ancestral land, where they caught fish and frogs, swam in ponds, played softball, and rode on farm wagons.

The author received a degree from Pennsylvania State University. She also attended Louisiana State University, Baton Rouge, and the University of Michigan. She married John Lothar George in 1944; they later divorced. They have four children.

She worked as a reporter for International News Service and later for *The Washington Post* and *Times-Herald* in Washington, D.C. She was an artist for *Pageant* magazine, an artist and reporter for the Newspaper Enterprise Association, and a teacher in Chappaqua,

New York. She was a staff writer for *Reader's Digest* from 1969 to 1974 and a roving reporter through 1980.

George has written many nonfiction books, including the Thirteen Moons series (1967–1969) and *How to Talk to Your Animals* (1985).

One of the author's best-known fiction books is *My Side of the Mountain*. It is a survival story about a teenage boy, Sam, who flees New York City for the forest. He lives there for a year. Reviewer Zena Sutherland called it an "amazing and unusual book," describing it as "a first-person report by an adolescent boy who has decided to try his luck living off the land." Its "vivid descriptions of animal life, and mouth-watering recipes dictated by necessity make Sam's record more real. The thoughts and attitudes he quotes from his diary indicate his maturation and deepening self-perception in a wholly convincing manner."

The writer said in her autobiography, *Journey Inward*, that she struggled with the mechanics of placing her young hero in the wilderness. Then one day, in her own family circumstances, she thought, " 'If I could just run away for a few hours.' . . . I closed my eyes and went back to my childhood. I could see the falcons shooting across the sky like crossbows, could smell the wild garlic in the pot of mussel soup dad was serving in a turtle shell. I could feel the crisp snap of a sagittaria tuber between my teeth and hear John and Frank [her brothers] call from the river that they had a mess of catfish for dinner. That's how I get Sam Gribley into the woods, I thought. He runs away as I am doing now. He even tells his father he is going to go, as I had told my mother when I was a kid and marched off into the night—only to turn around and come back. His father will expect him back . . . but Sam Gribley won't turn around. He'll make it."

George's *Julie of the Wolves* is about a young Eskimo woman who is adopted by relatives and marries at age thirteen so she can leave her foster home. Unhappy in marriage, she takes off to find a pen pal in California. She becomes lost in the tundra and has to fight to survive by joining a wolf pack.

"Her patient, intelligent courting of the animals—observing their signs of leadership, submission, etc., and aping the appropriate ones—and her resourcefulness in keeping herself alive . . . are meticulously observed," *Kirkus Reviews* stated.

Alice Miller Bregman called it a "compelling story." She added, "George has captured the subtle nuances of Eskimo life, animal habits, the pain of growing up, and combines these elements into a thrilling adventure which is, at the same time, a poignant love story."

Brian W. Alderson noted the book's unusual heroine: "a girl—and a girl from a 'racial minority' at that—acting resourcefully in adverse circumstances." The book, he continued, "sustains a powerful case not only for conservation but also for the preservation of man's natural skills. It will appeal to the less rigid among us because of its integrity and its wholly convincing portrayal of its setting."

"George has provided readers an opportunity to experience nature with a guide who understands its workings and appreciates its ways," Lickteig concluded. "Only occasionally do literary critics question some element of the human characterization or the story structure. The fact that she weaves good stories while describing nature in an accurate, detailed, and exciting fashion is never challenged."

YOUNG ADULT FICTION

My Side of the Mountain (1959)
Sam takes a penknife, a ball of string, an ax, flint and steel, and $40 and goes to live at the old Gribley place in the Catskills for a year.

The Summer of the Falcon (1962)
June Pritchard trains a sparrowhawk, Zander.

Gull Number 737 (1963) as Jean George
A doctor and his sixteen-year-old son clash over the value of pure research while studying gulls at Block Island.

Red Robin, Fly Up! (1963) as Jean George

Hold Zero! (1966) as Jean George
Four high school boys build and prepare to launch a three-stage rocket.

Coyote in Manhattan (1968)
Tenny Harkness, a black girl in Harlem, releases a wild coyote in New York City.

Julie of the Wolves (1972)
Miyax, or Julie, thirteen, rebels against her Eskimo home and strikes off for San Francisco, becoming lost in the tundra.

All upon a Sidewalk (1974)

Hook a Fish, Catch a Mountain (1975)
Spinner is surprised to catch the whopper that makes her champion fisher of three generations of Shafters.

Going to the Sun (1976)
Melissa and Marcus, secretly wed, set up camp in the high mountains of Montana so Marcus can study wild goats—which his father wants to hunt.

The Wentletrap Trap (1978)

The Wounded Wolf (1978)

River Rats, Inc. (1979)
Joe and Crowbar take the job of transporting a mysterious urn down the Colorado River rapids at night.

The Cry of the Crow (1980)
The story of a girl and a crow that mimics hunters.

The Talking Earth (1983)
Billie Wind, thirteen and a Florida Seminole, questions her tribe's legends about animals that talk.

Water Sky (1987)
Lincoln searches in Alaska for his Uncle Jack, but Eskimo Vincent Olugak is not helpful.

Shark Beneath the Reef (1989)
Tomas Torres is determined to catch the shark—the greatest prize for a fisherman of the Sea of Cortez.

On the Far Side of the Mountain (1990), sequel to *My Side of the Mountain*
Sam follows the trail of his sister, Alice, on the Gribley land.

DRAMA

Tree House (produced in 1962)

FICTION FOR YOUNGER READERS

Vulpes, the Red Fox (1948) as Jean George, with John Lothar George

Vison, the Mink (1949) as Jean George, with John Lothar George

Masked Prowler: The Story of a Raccoon (1950) as Jean George, with John Lothar George

Meph, the Pet Skunk (1952) as Jean George, with John Lothar George

Bubo, the Great Horned Owl (1954) as Jean George, with John Lothar George

Dipper of Copper Creek (1956) as Jean George, with John Lothar George

The Hole in the Tree (1957) as Jean George

Snow Tracks (1958) as Jean George

All upon a Stone (1971)

Who Really Killed Cock Robin? An Ecological Mystery (1971)

The Grizzly Bear with the Golden Ears (1982)

Missing 'Gator of Gumbo Limbo: An Ecological Mystery (1992)

Dear Rebecca, Winter Is Here (1993)

The Firebug Connection: An Ecological Mystery (1993)

Animals Who Have Won Our Hearts (1994)

Everglades (1995)

There's an Owl in the Shower (1995)

To Climb a Waterfall (1995)

FOR FURTHER READING

Alderson, Brian W. Review of *Julie of the Wolves. Children's Book Review,* spring 1974.

Bregman, Alice Miller. Review of *Julie of the Wolves. School Library Journal,* January 1973.

George, Jean Craighead. *Journey Inward.* New York: E. P. Dutton, 1982.

Lickteig, Mary J. "Jean Craighead George." In *Twentieth-Century Children's Writers,* edited by Tracy Chevalier. 3d ed. Chicago: St. James Press, 1989.

Review of *Julie of the Wolves. Kirkus Reviews,* 15 November 1972.

Ruchman, Hazel. Review of *Julie of the Wolves. The New York Times Book Review,* 13 November 1994.

Sutherland, Zena. Review of *My Side of the Mountain. Bulletin of the Center for Children's Books,* June 1960.

Yglesias, Rafael. "Meanwhile, Back in the Catskills." *The New York Times Book Review,* 20 May 1990.

Eileen Goudge

Romance

San Mateo, California
July 4, 1950

Seniors Series
Swept Away Series

Eileen Goudge said she uses her memories of high school for ideas for her various young adult series.

She was not part of the in-crowd at school. "A lot of the kids who read my books are also in the same predicament," she told Marc Caplan. "Most of them aren't in the cool crowd, and the novels give them a chance to live that life vicariously. The crucial difference is my characters' sense of compassion—the cool crowd at my school weren't particularly sympathetic people. They weren't very open to society at large, nor did they care about the rest of us in school. My characters have a more understanding view of mankind, and in this respect I've succeeded as a writer because many of the kids who've written me say that these characters are their best friends. And that feels nice."

The daughter of an insurance executive and a homemaker, Goudge was the second of six children. She grew up in suburban San Francisco, in what she has described as an unremarkable childhood. She was a "shy bookworm."

In 1968, during the Vietnam War, Goudge left San Diego College to marry. She and her husband moved to Canada so he could avoid the draft. They had one child and eventually divorced. She then returned to California, for a time living on welfare—an experience she said she found demeaning. She was trapped, however; to work for low wages was to earn less than the monthly welfare check.

The author began to rebuild her life with a second marriage in 1974 to a Navy veteran and gardener. Because of health problems, he was chronically unemployed.

Goudge began to write and sold a piece to *National Star* for twenty dollars. She wrote more, took a night-school-writing course, and was encouraged to try a Gothic romance. She attended San Diego State College, where she earned a vocational degree and soon began teaching writing. Still, the family struggled with financial and personal problems. She and her second husband had one child but eventually divorced. Her third husband is Albert J. Zuckerman, a literary agent.

When she separated from her second husband in 1982, Goudge had begun writing young adult fiction. The first were novels for the Sweet Dreams series. With the proceeds, she moved to New York, where she wrote— using a pseudonym—five of the first twelve Sweet Valley High novels (created by Francine Pascal).

The author worked with a book packager on her own series, Seniors, about four girls in their last year of high school. Sexy Kit McCoy, athletic Alex Eromoto, brainy Elaine Gregory, and beautiful Lori Woodhouse are students at Glenwood High School in California. Goudge wrote the first eight of the twenty-four-book series and outlined plots for the rest.

"Writing for children has been the greatest 'university' for me in terms of seasoning my craft. I never write down to my teen audience, because they are the most discriminating of all readers," she told *Contemporary Authors*. "If a book doesn't grab their interest by page three, they'll put it down (unless it is assigned reading in school, in which case they'll either suffer through till the end or try to sneak by on Cliff Notes). But if the magic clicks, they'll devour the book, and everything else the author has written, inside a matter of weeks—sometimes days. Teens are passionate in their appetites. An author must be unstinting when it comes to filling their hunger for pathos, romance, fun."

Though it meant a change in writing approach, Goudge switched to adult fiction with *Garden of Lies*. The book sold for $900,000 (along with rights to her next novel) to Viking Penguin. It is about an exchange of babies by a socialite during a hospital fire in 1943. The two children grow up, one in upper-class Manhattan, the other in lower-class Brooklyn. When they become involved with the same Vietnam veteran, one as an attorney, the other as a doctor, their secret unravels.

YOUNG ADULT FICTION

It Must Be Magic (1982) as Marian Woodruff

Dial L for Love (1983) as Marian Woodruff

Forbidden Love (1983) as Marian Woodruff

The Perfect Match (1983) as Marian Woodruff

Kiss Me Creep (1984) as Marian Woodruff

'Till We Meet Again (1984) as Elizabeth Merrit

Eileen Goudge's Seniors Created by Goudge

Too Much Too Soon (1984)
Kit falls in love with Justin Kennerly.

Smart Enough to Know (1984)
Only her close friends know Elaine is also the school's rowdy mascot, Wilbur the Wildcat.

Winner All the Way (1984)

Afraid to Love (1984)
A high school senior is afraid others will find out she was once overweight.

Before It's Too Late (1985)

Too Hot to Handle (1985)

Hands Off, He's Mine (1985)
Elaine's boyfriend suggests they date other people.

Forbidden Kisses (1985)

A Touch of Ginger (1985)
Kit's cousin, Ginger, visits from New York, and things change with boyfriend Craig.

Presenting Superhunk (1985)

Bad Girl (1985)

Don't Say Goodbye (1985)
Roseanne's boyfriend is severely injured in an accident, straining their relationship.

Kiss and Make Up (1986)

Looking for Love (1986)

Sweet Talk (1986)
Elaine is now more attracted to Zack than to Carl.

Heart for Sale (1986)

Life of the Party (1986)
Sueanne Carpenter is the funniest girl at Glenwood High, but her parents are getting a divorce, and she is desperate for someone in whom she can confide. Will Eric Woolery be sensitive enough to listen?

Night After Night (1986)
Marcia's boyfriend shows his true colors after a plane crash.

Treat Me Right (1986)

Against the Rules (1986)
Alex's former boyfriend comes to work at her school.

Super Seniors 1. *Old Enough* (1986)

Super Seniors 2. *Hawaiian Christmas* (1986)

Super Seniors 3. *Something Borrowed, Something Blue* (1988)

Super Seniors 4. *Deep-Sea Summer* (1988)

Eileen Goudge's Swept Away Series Created by Goudge

Gone with the Wish (1986) by Eileen Goudge

Woodstock Magic (1986) by Fran Lantz
Louise travels back in time to the Woodstock music festival.

Love on the Range (1986) by Louise E. Powers

Star Struck (1986) by Fran Lantz

Spell Bound (1986) by Jennifer Rabin

Once upon a Kiss (1986) by Mar Garrido
Miranda uses Ashley's computer to visit the days of King Arthur, and she finds a boyfriend who is not so chivalrous when he visits the 1980s.

Pirate Moon (1987) by Merrilee Steiner

All Shook Up (1987) by Fran Lantz
Louise Greenspan needs her friend Ashley's computer to visit the rock and roll fifties in an elaborate plan to keep her boyfriend, Ethan, from moving away.

Who Killed Peggy Sue Series Created by Goudge

1. *Dying to Win* (1991)
   Hope Hubbard is desperate to find the person who murdered her cousin April.
2. *Cross Your Heart, Hope to Die* (1991)
3. *If Looks Could Kill* (1991)
4. *Jailbird* (1991)

ADULT FICTION

Garden of Lies (1989)
Girls are switched at birth and later face each other in a courtroom battle—one is a lawyer and the other, a doctor.

Such Devoted Sisters (1992)

Blessing in Disguise (1994)
Three women, at crossroads in their lives, struggle with conscience and heartache over second-time loves.

FOR FURTHER READING

Caplan, Marc. "Eileen Goudge." In *Authors & Artists for Young Adults,* edited by Agnes Garrett and Helga P. McCue. Vol. 6. Detroit: Gale Research, 1991.

"Eileen Goudge." *Publishers Weekly,* 23 September 1988.

Goudge, Eileen. "Creating Villians You Hate to Like." *The Writer,* October 1995.

———. "From Welfare Mom to Millionaire." *Ladies' Home Journal,* August 1989.

Trosky, Susan, ed. "Eileen Goudge." In *Contemporary Authors.* Vol. 126. Detroit: Gale Research, 1989.

Bette Greene

Family drama

Memphis, Tennessee
June 28, 1934

Summer of My German Soldier

Bette Greene's young adult novel *Summer of My German Soldier* was published in 1973, to wide acclaim. The book took the writer several years to complete. A writing professor at Harvard dismissed the manuscript, but Greene showed it to publishers, finally finding one who would print it.

Set in a small Arkansas town after the end of World War II, it is about the friendship between a lonely Jewish girl and a soft-spoken German soldier. She helps him escape a prisoner-of-war camp and hides him, but he is discovered and killed. The girl is chastised by parents and townspeople.

The book's issues of prejudice, violence, and the Holocaust were considered intense by some critics, who questioned its appropriateness for a young adult readership. It was nevertheless nominated for a National Book Award in 1974.

Although suggesting that the characters—a loving black maid, a nasty clergyman's wife, a determined girl reporter, a bigoted businessman, a town gossip, a spoiled-brat younger sister—are melodramatic, on the surface, the book succeeds, in the opinion of reviewer Peter Sourian, because of its freshness and "its fineness, in the literal sense. The stuff of it is fine, like the texture of Patty herself. The detail is too meaningfully specific, too highly selective to be trite."

"The growth of World War Two stories for young people reflects today's concern for the problems spinning off from Vietnam, the Middle East, racism and so on," C. S. Hannabuss said. "*Summer of My*

German Soldier is a courageous but patchy example of how things like this have influenced writing for young people. . . . The issues raised, and the characters who raise them, are proof of the book's integrity."

Born Bette Evensky, the daughter of merchants, Greene grew up in Arkansas. Hers was a Jewish family in a largely Christian town. Her parents were busy running a store, so she spent a lot of time with a black housekeeper. She experienced great cultural diversity in her youth, she told Chris Hunter. "Growing up Jewish in the middle of the Bible Belt. Being white but having, for all practical purposes, a black mother. And not really fitting into the black culture fully because of my skin, but understanding a lot more than most because, in a way, I was part of it."

Greene struggled through elementary and high school. She attended the University of Alabama, Memphis State University, Alliance Française in Paris, Columbia University, and Harvard University. In 1959, she married Donald S. Greene, a physician. They have two children.

Greene worked as a writer and reporter for *Hebrew Watchman*, *Commercial Appeal*, and United Press International. She was an information officer for Boston State Psychiatric Hospital and the American Red Cross.

Philip Hall Likes Me. I Reckon Maybe won a Newbery Award in 1975. The book is about a black student whose crush on a high-achieving boy holds her back from becoming the top student in class herself. "The relaxed, humorous story tells of a year in the life of a bright and lively black girl whose only real problems resulted from her infatuation with the boy from the next farm," Ethel L. Heins said. "The writing style is deceptively casual," Zena Sutherland stated, "characterization and dialogue are sound, and the protagonist (who tells the story) a resourceful, lively girl whose charm and vitality come through clearly."

YOUNG ADULT FICTION

Summer of My German Soldier (1973)
A Jewish girl, Patty Bergen, twelve, befriends a German prisoner of war, Anton Reiker.

Philip Hall Likes Me. I Reckon Maybe (1974)
A black girl, Beth Lambert, develops a crush on her high school rival.

Morning Is a Long Time Coming (1978), sequel to *Summer of My German Soldier*
Patty, alienated from her parents, travels to Europe and tries to find Anton's mother.

Get on out of Here, Philip Hall (1981), sequel to *Philip Hall Likes Me. I Reckon Maybe*
Philip, not Beth, receives the school leadership award and is forced to cope with failure.

Them That Glitter and Them That Don't (1983)
Carol Ann Delaney, a high school senior, is musically talented but has an unhappy home life. She decides to move to Nashville to become a country singer.

The Drowning of Stephen Jones (1991)
A young gay man drowns after three youths throw him off a bridge.

ADAPTATIONS IN OTHER MEDIA

Summer of My German Soldier (1978)
Television movie with Kristy McNichol, Bruce Davison, and Esther Rolle.

FOR FURTHER READING

Bridgers, Sue Ellen. "Stories of Rural Childhoods." *The Washington Post Book World*, 10 May 1981.

Burns, Mary M. Review of *Summer of My German Soldier. Horn Book Magazine*, February 1974.

Hannabuss, C. S. Review of *Summer of My German Soldier. Children's Book Review*, spring 1975.

Heins, Ethel L. Review of *Philip Hall Likes Me. I Reckon Maybe. Horn Book Magazine*, April 1975.

Hunter, Chris. "Bette Greene." In *Authors & Artists for Young Adults*, edited by Laurie Collier. Vol. 7. Detroit: Gale Research, 1991.

Roginski, Jim. *Behind the Covers*. Englewood, CO: Libraries Unlimited, 1985.

Sourian, Peter. Review of *Summer of My German Soldier. The New York Times Book Review*, 4 November 1973.

Sutherland, Zena. Review of *Philip Hall Likes Me. I Reckon Maybe. Bulletin of the Center for Children's Books*, April 1975.

Rosa Guy

Urban drama

Diego Martin, Trinidad, West Indies
September 1, 1928

Imamu Jones Series

Rosa Cuthbert Guy describes herself as primarily a storyteller. "I hope that young people of today are like I was yesterday in reading tastes," she said in *Horn Book Magazine*. "I have always liked interesting books with exciting characters, held together by invisible but well-conceived plots. And I always wanted to believe, when putting down a book, that my time had not been wasted in pure enjoyment and that I had learned something more than I knew before I picked it up. I wanted to know about people, places, and those things that had not drawn my attention before."

"Rosa Guy is a Black American writer who has been described as 'the creator of some of the most memorable adolescent characters in modern literature,' " *Books for Keeps* stated. "Her stories are hard-hitting and compellingly realistic, with a powerful message for young people. She demonstrates a deep understanding and sympathy for young people and the many difficulties they face growing up or purely surviving today."

The strong storytelling tradition of Trinidad, West Indies, the British colony where Guy was born, greatly influenced her writings. She came to the United States in 1932 when her parents settled in Harlem. When their mother became ill, Guy and her older sister, Ameze, went to live with cousins who were followers of Marcus Garvey, leader of a back-to-Africa movement. Their influence, she later said, is seen in her human rights activism and her love of language.

After Guy and her sister were orphaned, Guy quit school to work in a garment factory and care for Ameze, who had become ill.

Later she married Warner Guy, and they had a son. Rosa Guy attended New York University and studied with the American Negro Theater. She also joined the Harlem Writers Guild and tried writing short stories. Her first book, *Bird at My Window,* dedicated to Malcolm X, was not published until 1966. By then, she had moved to Haiti, after her ex-husband (Warner) was murdered.

When Dr. Martin Luther King, Jr. was assassinated, Guy went to the South. She edited a nonfiction anthology, *Children of Longing* (1971). After traveling in the Caribbean, she wrote her second novel and second young adult book, *The Friends*. It was named one of the best of the year by the American Library Association in 1973.

"Rosa Guy's trilogy, *The Friends*, *Ruby*, and *Edith Jackson*, exemplifies one of these alternative explorations that would not have been presented to young readers a generation ago," Kenneth L. Donelson and Alleen Pace Nilsen wrote. "The first book in the group treats an unlikely but believable friendship between Phyllisia and Edith, who are both rejects in the social structure of their Harlem neighborhood. Phyllisia is too good for the neighborhood. Her family has immigrated from the West Indies and her overly strict restaurant-owner father constantly instills in her a feeling of superiority. He is horrified when Phyllisia brings home poor 'ragamuffin' Edith with her ragged coat, holey socks, turned-over shoes, and matted hair. Edith's mother is dead and her father has disappeared. She is trying to hold together her family of four little sisters and two brothers. One unusual thing about the book is that it treats the friendship of two girls with the same kind of serious respect with which boys' friendships have traditionally been written about. In most earlier books, girls' friendships always broke up as soon as boys appeared on the scene.

"The second book in Guy's trilogy, *Ruby*, focuses on Phyllisia's sister, who is two years older than Edith and Phyll. It includes the story of a lesbian relationship between Ruby and a beautiful classmate. *Publishers Weekly* described the book as 'a sensitive novel in which adolescent homosexuality is viewed as nothing so frightening, but perhaps just a way-step toward maturity.' In *Edith Jackson,* the protagonist is looking forward to her eighteenth birthday, when she hopes to be free of foster homes and the Institution so that she can try again to set up a home for her sisters. But, by the end of the book, the girls are scattered, and Edith realizes that it is her own life she must plan. She has had a brief love affair with a handsome Harlem playboy almost twice her age and is excited at finding herself pregnant. But in the end of the book, she has decided that the mature thing to do is to have an abortion."

"The trilogy makes a powerful statement about the failure of adults to meet the complex needs of young people," *Authors & Artists for Young Adults* stated.

The Disappearance was the first in Guy's series of young adult novels about streetwise Imamu Jones. He is implicated in a holdup, but the court frees him while convicting his mates. Ann Aimsley takes an interest in Imamu, and rather than see him move back to his Harlem flat (his father is gone, his mother drinks), she offers to take him into her family. He agrees, though quickly bangs heads with Peter Aimsley. Imamu is the first accused when young Perk Aimsley disappears. When there is no proof against him, he agrees to help Gail Aimsley look for her sister. Once she is found, he is out of their lives. The solution is not a pleasant one.

"In *The Disappearance* and also its sequel, *New Guys Around the Block*, the challenge to the reader is two-fold," Guy said in a 1983 promotional piece, "solving a mind-boggling whodunit on the one hand, and on the other, attempting to unlock secret passages of minds that have been closed to us—minds developed in the so-called underbelly of our society, where wits are sharpened by the constant struggle for survival—from criminal elements and from daily confrontation with the law.

"Thus Imamu Jones—poor, orphaned by the death of his father and chronic alcoholism of his mother—rises above the ugliness of his environment to shoulder the burden of *my* imposed responsibility. A shrewd observer of people, sensitive, with a natural intelligence, a boy who accepts as normal the fragility of his friends' morals, a high school dropout, Imamu with his street wisdom can solve crimes that baffle the police."

Harlem is a strong setting in the books. "This background is unsparingly painted in her novels," observed Beverly Anderson. "There is no attempt to glamorize the characters or setting, but her message to the young is an optimistic one. Many of her main characters come to feel that they can take control of their lives and climb out of the destructive environment in which they are placed."

In Guy's *The Music of Summer*, a girl is asked to spend two weeks with a lighter-skinned girl and her family on Cape Cod. The novel is "a look at middle-class black culture that's rare in YA books, and, equally rare, Guy confronts the painful discrimination sometimes visited upon darker-skinned blacks," said the *Bulletin of the Center for Children's Books*.

YOUNG ADULT FICTION

Bird at My Window (1966)

Mirror of Her Own (1981)
Mary, seventeen, finds romance—and more conflict with her beautiful older sister.

A Measure of Time (1983)

My Love, My Love; or, The Peasant Girl (1985)
Desiree Dieu-Donne, a young Creole peasant, falls in love with the son of a rich landowning family on a Caribbean island.

The Music of Summer (1991)
Sara, a talented pianist, feels left out by Cathy and her light-skinned friends on Cape Cod, but a new love helps her overcome the racism.

Imamu Jones Series

The Disappearance (1979)
Imamu Jones, whose father is dead and whose mother drinks, agrees to move from Harlem into the Aimsley home in Brooklyn. When the Aimsley's daughter disappears, he is the first accused.

New Guys Around the Block (1983)
Joining Jones in solving a mystery about a burglar is Olivette, who has lived in several inner cities and is more widely experienced than Jones.

And I Heard a Bird Sing (1986)
Working as a delivery boy, Jones meets a physically disabled heiress, Margaret Maldroon.

Trilogy

The Friends (1973)
Though of vastly different backgrounds, Phyllisia Cathy, from the West Indies, becomes an unlikely friend of Edith Jackson in Harlem.

Ruby: A Novel (1976)
Phyllisia's older sister, Ruby, has a secret homosexual relationship with Daphne, a beautiful classmate.

Edith Jackson (1976)
Seventeen-year-old Edith struggles with a pregnancy.

FICTION FOR YOUNGER READERS

Mother Crocodile: An Uncle Amadou Tale from Senegal (1982)

Paris, Pee Wee, and Big Dog (1984)

The Ups and Downs of Carl Davis III (1989)

Billy the Great (1992)

DRAMA

Venetian Blind (1954)

SCREENPLAYS

British television documentary about Guy's novel *The Friends*

ADAPTATIONS IN OTHER MEDIA

There Is an Island (first produced in 1990)
Musical based on *My Love, My Love; or, The Peasant Girl*

FOR FURTHER READING

Anderson, Beverly. "The Orphan Factor." *The Times Educational Supplement*, 3 June 1983.

"Authorgraph No. 30: Rosa Guy." *Books for Keeps*, January 1985.

Donelson, Kenneth L., and Alleen Pace Nilsen, eds. Article in *Literature for Today's Young Adults*. Glenview, IL: Scott, Foresman, 1980.

Garrett, Agnes, and Helga P. McCue, eds. "Rosa Guy." In *Authors & Artists for Young Adults*. Vol. 4. Detroit: Gale Research, 1990.

Guy, Rosa. "Young Adults Books: I Am a Storyteller." *Horn Book Magazine*, March–April 1985.

Review of *The Music of Summer*. *Bulletin of the Center for Children's Books*, March 1992.

Lynn Hall

Animal stories

Lombard, Illinois
November 9, 1937

A Horse Called Dragon

Lynn Hall's love of animals permeates her many young adult books. "From earliest memory I had been yearning toward the country, toward animals, specifically toward horses and dogs," she said in *Something About the Author Autobiography Series*. "All of my clearest childhood memories center around animals."

"My family couldn't afford a horse, didn't really want a dog, and assumed that I was going through a stage. Wrong," she said in the *Fifth Book of Junior Authors*. "My hunger for these animals went unfed except for the nourishment of *The Black Stallion* and *Misty of Chincoteaque* and *Lad: A Dog*. I was a voracious reader, but only in these areas, and had to be forced to read other kinds of books."

The daughter of a Standard Oil executive and a high school teacher, Hall attended schools in Iowa. She married Dean W. Green in 1960 and divorced a year later. Hall has worked as a secretary and a veterinarian's assistant. She has been a full-time writer since 1968.

Reading what she considered to be a poorly written horse book one day, Hall decided she could do better. She researched how well-written books are crafted, and produced her first story about a dog show. However, her second manuscript, *The Shy Ones* was the first to be accepted by a publisher, and was released in 1967.

"The loves of my life, horses and dogs, provide the impetus for my writing," Hall said in *Contemporary Authors*. "The truth is that I write not so much to provide books for children as to relish the sheer fun of a good horse story or a good dog story. When I've read all the horse stories I can find, then there's nothing to do but make up some new ones."

Hall uses events from her past in her books. *The Stray*, for example, incorporates her childhood interest in being adopted by a farmer so she could be close to animals. Each tale in *Lynn Hall's Dog Stories* is about a dog she owned at one time or another. *The Horse Trader* reflects her first experience buying a horse.

Hall also focuses on human topics. In *Sticks and Stones*, for instance, the hero, Tom, befriends a young man who is a homosexual. This prompts rumors at school that Tom, too, is homosexual. Reviewer Judy Blume said, "Hall has handled a difficult subject with intelligence and understanding."

The Boy in the Off-White Hat is about a baby-sitter who realizes that one of her charges has been sexually molested by the mother's boyfriend. In *Dagmar Schultz and the Green-Eyed Monster*, the heroine is jealous when a new girl at school seems to be winning away her friends.

YOUNG ADULT FICTION

The Shy Ones (1967)
A girl is as shy as her pet dog.

The Secret of Stonehouse (1968)

Ride a Wild Dream (1969)

Gently Touch the Milkweed (1970)
Janet was the only boy her father had for years.

Too Near the Sun (1970)

The Famous Battle of Bravery Creek (1972)

The Siege of Silent Henry (1972)

Sticks and Stones (1972)
Tom makes friends with a young man who has been dismissed from the military for being homosexual.

Troublemaker (1974)
Willis Crosley takes his sister deer hunting.

Shadows (1977)

The Mystery of Pony Hollow (1978)

Dog of the Bondi Castle (1979)

The Mystery of the Lost and Found Hound (1979)

The Mystery of the Schoolhouse Dog (1979)

The Whispered Horse (1979)

The Leaving (1980)
Fresh out of high school, Roxanne has to leave the farm to find a job in Des Moines.

Danza! (1981)
This is the story of a sensitive Puerto Rican boy, his powerful grandfather, and a Paso Fino stallion named Danza.

The Horse Trader (1981)
Lady Bay is the horse Harley Williams promised Karen on her fifteenth birthday.

Half the Battle (1982)
A blind boy and his brother go on a 100-mile endurance ride on horseback.

Tin Can Tucker (1982)
State ward Ann Tucker's only link to the parents she never knew is a trophy buckle won in a rodeo competition.

Denison's Daughter (1983)
Sandy loves living on the farm and taking care of her imperfect horse, Charlie, but she feels that her father does not love her.

Megan's Mare (1983)

The Mystery of the Pony Hollow Panda (1983)

The Boy in the Off-White Hat (1984)
A baby-sitter discovers that a child has been sexually molested.

Nobody's Dog (1984)

Uphill All the Way (1984)
Callie Kiffin, seventeen, is determined to become the best farrier in Liberty, Oklahoma.

The Giver (1985)
Mary, fifteen, falls in love with her middle-aged teacher, Mr. Flicker.

Just One Friend (1985)
Dori's mother is so dependent on alcohol that she no longer attends to her children's needs.

Tazo and Me (1985)

Danger Dog (1986)
A boy tries to retrain an attack dog so it will not be put to sleep.

If Winter Comes (1986)
Two teens spend what they believe will be their last weekend on earth—under nuclear threat.

The Solitary (1986)
Jane, seventeen, goes to live in the woods to get away from family troubles.

Flyaway (1987)
Ariel Brecht, seventeen, needs to break away from her rigid father.

Letting Go (1987)
Pat Cruise shares her mother's interest in dog breeding—but needs to get out on her own.

Ride a Dark Horse (1987)
Seventeen-year-old Gusty McCaw's father is found dead. It is obvious something dangerous is happening at their horse farm.

A Killing Freeze (1988)
Claire Forrester finds her next-door neighbor, Mrs. Amling, dead in the snow, and her small, happy town becomes the center of a murder investigation.

Murder at the Spaniel Show (1988)
Tabby lands a summer job at Quintessence, a first-class kennel for springer spaniels.

Murder in a Pig's Eye (1989)
A teen, Bodie Tureon, sets out to find the body of a woman he believes has been murdered.

Where Have All the Tigers Gone? (1989)

Fair Maiden (1990)
Jennifer works weekends at the town's Renaissance Fair, a place where she can escape reality and fall in love.

Halsey's Pride (1990)
March Halsey, thirteen, wants to keep her epilepsy a secret from the kids at her new school. She helps her father with his dog kennel.

The Tormentors (1990)
Someone steals Cesare's dog, Heidi.

Flying Changes (1991)
Denny, seventeen, lives with his grandmother while his father goes on the rodeo circuit.

The Soul of the Silver Dog (1992)
Cory, adjusting to the death of her little sister and the divorce of her parents, is given a newly blind show dog, Sterling.

Windsong (1992)

The Mystery of the Phantom Pony (1993)

Zelda Series

In Trouble Again, Zelda Hammersmith? (1987)

Zelda Strikes Again! (1988)

Here Comes Zelda Claus: And Other Holiday Disasters (1989)

FICTION FOR YOUNGER READERS

Lynn Hall's Dog Stories (1972)

Barry, the Bravest St. Bernard (1973)

Flash, Dog of Old Egypt (1973)

Riff, Remember (1973)

To Catch a Tartar (1973)

Bob, Watchdog of the River (1974)

The Stray (1974)

Kids and Dog Shows (1975)

Captain: Canada's Flying Pony (1976)

Flowers of Anger (1976)

Owney, the Traveling Dog (1977)

The Disappearing Grandad (1980)

The Haunting of the Green Bird (1980)

The Mysterious Moortown Bridge (1980)

The Mystery of Plum Park Pony (1980)

The Mystery of the Stubborn Old Man (1980)

The Ghost of the Great River Inn (1981)

The Mystery of the Caramel Cat (1981)

The Something-Special Horse (1985)

Mrs. Portree's Pony (1986)

Dagmar Schultz Series

The Secret Life of Dagmar Schultz (1988)

Dagmar Schultz and the Powers of Darkness (1988)

Dagmar Schultz and the Angel Edna (1989)

Dagmar Schultz and the Green-Eyed Monster (1991)

Dragon Series

A Horse Called Dragon (Follett, 1971); *Wild Mustang* (Scholastic, 1976)

New Day for Dragon (1975), sequel to *A Horse Called Dragon.*

Dragon Defiant (1977)

Dragon's Delight (1980)

FOR FURTHER READING

Blume, Judy. Review of *Sticks and Stones. The New York Times Book Review,* 28 May 1972.

"Hall, Lynn." *Something About the Author Autobiography Series.* Vol. 4. Detroit: Gale Research, 1987.

Holtze, Sally Holmes. *Fifth Book of Junior Authors & Illustrators.* New York: H. W. Wilson, 1983.

Nasso, Christine, ed. "Lynn Hall." In *Contemporary Authors.* First Revision. Vol. 21-24. Detroit: Gale Research, 1977.

Virginia Hamilton

Family drama

Yellow Springs, Ohio
March 12, 1936

M. C. Higgins, the Great

Virginia Hamilton was the first author to win both the National Book Award and the Newbery Medal, in 1975, for the young adult novel *M. C. Higgins, the Great.*

"Few writers of fiction for young people are as daring, inventive, and challenging to read—or to review—as Virginia Hamilton," Ethel L. Heins said. "Frankly making demands on her readers, she nevertheless expresses herself in a style essentially simple and concise."

Hamilton frequently writes of African American life. For example, *M. C. Higgins* is about a country-born hero who toils hard on his ancestral home, first farmed by a former slave. "M. C. has passed all the land's tests of toughness but must face the outside threat of intruders upon the land—a stripminer's spoil heap that could bury his cabin any time, a music collector who takes his mother's voice on tapes in exchange for empty hints of help, a young stranger who tempts M. C.'s heart to follow her," Betsy Hearne said. "The pictures and the relationships and the sounds that fit together here deepen in perspective with each reading. There is a sure direction that never slips into contrivance, an opening and closure of another world that one wants to visit—a unique place where six-fingered, red-haired blacks have made a vegetable farming commune stretched over with a robe web where children can climb and play. And they are as believable as the strength M. C. finds in himself, his family, his friends, his mountain."

"All of the characters [in *M. C. Higgins*] have vitality and credibility as well as a unique quality that makes them unforgettable," Beryl Robinson added. "Visual images are strong and vivid; and many passages are poetic in their beauty."

Another of the writer's novels is *Zeely*, which John Rowe Townsend described as "a book without bitterness or paranoia. . . . It is deeply concerned with black dignity: the splendor of Zeely in contrast with her humble occupation, the associations of night traveling with escape from slavery. It is easy to read a message into the book—walk tall—but this does not detract from its merit."

Hamilton's father was a musician and her mother was descended from a fugitive slave who settled in Ohio. The author grew up in a close family of farmers and storytellers. She married Arnold Adoff, an anthropologist and poet, in 1960. She is a Distinguished Visiting Professor at Queens College and Ohio State University.

"Family is an important theme in all of Hamilton's books," *Contemporary Authors* said, "and her strong faith and love of family, along with the fact that she has always considered herself to be a loner, has influenced the characterization in her novels."

"Virginia Hamilton has heightened the standards for children's literature as few other authors have," said Hearne. "She does not address children so much as she explores with them, sometimes ahead of them, the full possibilities of imagination. Even her farthest flung thoughts, however, are leashed to the craft of writing."

"I've written things down since the time I could put words together to make sentences," Hamilton stated in a brochure issued by Harcourt Brace Jovanovich. "I suspect I was in second or third grade. But I remember *really* writing more than a page or two by the age of nine. I grew up reading as well. I don't remember the moment I knew what words meant, but, one day, I could read—that's what I remember clearly. And a whole world seemed to open before me. It was as if I were sucking life in through my eyes. . . .

"It was later, when I started college, that writing seemed to shake down as more important than anything else. I majored in writing at Antioch College in Ohio. I went on to Ohio State University, majoring in literature, and then to the New School for Social Research in New York, where I took courses in novel writing. I think you can learn a lot about the technique of writing in college literature and writing courses. By this time, I thought of myself as a writer, and I was seriously attempting to be a published author. That took a while to accomplish. . . .

"I concentrate totally when I am writing books," she continued. "I do a great amount of research, and I need large blocks of time, sometimes a year or two, to complete a project. I usually work on two books at the same time, and I work on a word processor."

Hamilton also wrote about her writing process in *Horn Book Magazine*: "A novelist can do about anything she wishes with the novel form, save stand still within it. She must grow and change and become better at revealing what is important. What's important is expressed by a kind of illumination at the core; better, at the mind's eye of the self. It is like a brief foresight of the all-important source: the experience of living and partly living, to use a T. S. Eliot phrase, that each novelist has and which is unique to each."

Dorothy Sterling noted Hamilton's careful prose: "*The House of Dies Drear* is written with poetic precision. Miss Hamilton polishes her sentences with care, develops her characters with imagination and love. Thomas is a sensitive boy, self-sufficient, sometimes lonely."

Hamilton has written several books of Jahdu tales, in the style of the traditional folktale and incorporating elements of fantasy. "The Jahdu stories are told with consummate skill," in the view of Zena Sutherland, "and the framing narrative has a warmth and substance that are a firm base for the tales." Conversely, critic Sidney D. Long found the stories "superficial and unsatisfying . . . stark and sometimes distorted."

YOUNG ADULT FICTION

Zeely (1967)
Geeder imagines the tall woman she sees on a farm as a Watusi queen.

The House of Dies Drear (1968)
A mystery involves the Underground Railroad.

The Planet of Junior Brown (1971)
Chubby Junior, weird Mr. Pool, and streetwise Buddy meet secretly in a room in the school basement.

M. C. Higgins, the Great (1974)
The Higgins family's ancestral home in Ohio is threatened by a nearby strip mine.

Arilla Sun Down (1976)
Arilla, in admiration of her handsome, self-assured brother, Jack, seeks her identity.

Sweet Whispers, Brother Rush (1982)
Tree, fourteen, learns of her family from Brother Rush, her uncle's ghost.

The Magical Adventures of Pretty Pearl (1983)
During Reconstruction, Pretty Pearl joins a hidden community of blacks.

Willie Bea and the Time the Martians Landed (1983)
Willie Bea is a believer when Orson Welles makes his famous 1938 radio broadcast that Martians have invaded America.

A Little Love (1984)
Insecure Sheema, supported by her boyfriend and grandparents, searches for her father.

Junius over Far (1985)
Grandfather Jackabo is lonesome when he leaves his son and grandson in the United States and returns to the Caribbean island of his youth.

The People Could Fly: American Black Folktales (1985)

The Mystery of Drear House: The Conclusion of the Dies Drear Chronicle (1987), sequel to *The House of Dies Drear*

A White Romance (1987)
Talley Barbour, a black student, comes of age in a newly integrated high school.

Anthony Burns: The Defeat and Triumph of a Fugitive Slave (1988)
In 1854, an escaped slave is returned to the South under the Fugitive Slave Law.

In the Beginning: Creation Stories from Around the World (1988)

Bells of Christmas (1989)
Jason looks forward to the arrival of the Bells at Yule: Uncle Levi Bell, Aunt Ella, and Cousin Tisha—his best friend.

Cousins (1990)
Patricia Ann is good at everything, thinks her eleven-year-old cousin, Cammy, who feels overwhelmed. Then comes the day of the flood and a call for great courage.

The Dark Way: Stories from the Spirit World (1990)

Drylongso (1992)
Lindy's midwestern farm family struggles through a drought.

Many Thousand Gone: African Americans from Slavery to Freedom (1992)

Plain City (1993)
Buhlaire must deal with the new realization that she is of mixed racial heritage.

Jahdu Tales

The Time-Ago Tales of Jahdu (1969)
In the style of the African folktale, Jahdu has adventures with such allegorical figures as Sweetdream, Nightmare, Trouble, and Chameleon.

Time-Ago Lost: More Tales of Jahdu (1973)

Jahdu (1980)

The All Jahdu Storybook (1991)

Justice Trilogy

Justice and Her Brothers (1978)
Tice (Justice) Douglass, eleven, is afraid of her brother Thomas but feels comfortable with his twin, Lee.

Dustland (1980)
The children enter a future, imaginary world.

The Gathering (1981)
The time travelers Justice, the twins, and friend Dorian must merge their parapsychological powers to fight their final battle with Mal.

FICTION FOR YOUNGER READERS

Jaguarundi (1994)

When Birds Could Talk and Bats Could Sing: The Adventures of Bruh Sparrow, Sis Wren, and Their Friends (1995)

ADAPTATIONS IN OTHER MEDIA

The House of Dies Drear (1984)
For public television's *Wonderworks* series.

FOR FURTHER READING

Hamilton, Virginia. "Writing the Source: In Other Words." *Horn Book Magazine*, December 1978.

Hearne, Betsy. "Virginia Hamilton." In *Twentieth-Century Children's Writers*, edited by Tracy Chevalier. 3d ed. Chicago: St. James Press, 1989.

Lesniak, James G., ed. "Virginia Hamilton." In *Contemporary Authors*. Rev. ed. Vol. 37. Detroit: Gale Research, 1992.

Long, Sidney D. Review of *Time-Ago Lost: More Tales of Jahdu*. *Horn Book Magazine*, June 1973.

Robinson, Beryl. Review of *M. C. Higgins, the Great*. *Horn Book Magazine*, October 1974.

Sterling, Dorothy. Review of *The House of Dies Drear*. *The New York Times Book Review*, 13 October 1968.

Sutherland, Zena. Review of *Time-Ago Lost: More Tales of Jahdu*. *Bulletin of the Center for Children's Books*, April 1973.

Townsend, John Rowe. *Written for Children: An Outline of English Language Children's Literature*. Philadelphia: J. B. Lippincott, 1974.

Virginia Hamilton: HBJ Profiles. New York: Harcourt Brace Jovanovich, circa 1988.

Jamake Highwater

Outdoor adventure

Mythic adventure

Glacier County, Montana
February 14, 1942

Ghost Horse Cycle

In his fiction, Jamake Highwater incorporates many stories from the Native American oral tradition. *Anpao: An American Indian Odeyssey*, his first novel, relates the journey of a Native American boy who wants to find the sun. Traveling with him is his brother, Oapna, who says everything backward. After Oapna dies, Anpao realizes that Oapna was actually his contrary self. The book was a Newbery Honor book in 1978.

"I created Anpao out of many stories of the boyhood of early Indians," Highwater said in "The Storyteller's Farewell," "and from my own experience as well, in order to make an Indian 'Ulysses' who could become the central dramatic character in the saga of Indian life in North America.

"North American Indians did not evolve a written language, at least not the kind of language familiar to the peoples of Europe. This book is my personal effort to use the vast facilities of the tradition of written literature to convey the energy, uniqueness, and imagery of Indian oral tradition. I have approached it, however, not as a stenographer or as an ethnologist, who would tend to value verbatim transcriptions. I have written these stories as a writer. But I have been careful to preserve the qualities unique to non-written folk history."

Descended from Blackfeet and Cherokee Indians, Jamake Mamake Highwater's father was a rodeo clown and movie stuntman.

Because of their poverty, his parents put him up for adoption at about age seven. He was taken in by a white couple living in California.

Highwater's youth was not a comfortable one, because of his own belligerence and because of resentment by white children. He developed a strong attachment to the youngest of his sisters in his adoptive family. Her departure for married life left a void in his own life. From neighbor friends, he came to enjoy classical music, novels, and dance. A sympathetic teacher helped him through school and dreamed he would become a writer.

He attended colleges in California and worked as a dance choreographer, founding a modern dance troupe. He has lectured at universities in the United States and Canada and taught at several universities. From 1971 to 1975, he was a senior editor of Fodor's travel guides. He has hosted public television programs on Native American topics and has organized and directed Native American arts festivals.

A member of former President Jimmy Carter's art task force, Highwater also was the founding president of the Native Lands Foundation and a member of the National Support Committee of the Native American Rights Fund.

"In his work Highwater tries to impart not only a strong sense of Indian heritage but also 'a purely Indian concept of reality and identity,' " according to Myra Immell. " 'To the Indian mentality,' he notes, 'dead people walk and things go backward and forward in time, and these are absolutely real and vivid ideas to my head.' This mystical strain, combined with Highwater's storytelling skills, makes his writing exceptionally moving and powerful."

"Highwater has created an exceptional book of rare beauty and insight," reviewer James Norsworthy said of *Anpao*. "To say that Highwater did for American Indian culture what Homer did for the people of Ancient Greece may seem astonishing or perhaps overstated, but it is true. Using traditional tales from many North American Indian tribes, Highwater has skillfully woven them until they form the odyssey of Anpao, who, because of his love for the beautiful Ko-ko-mik-e-is, must undertake the dangerous quest of finding the house of the sun so that he can ask the sun to remove the scar from his face as proof that these two young people may marry."

"For so long there was no expressive outlet, no recognition," Highwater said of Native American literature in an interview with Sarah Crichton. "Now people are saying, 'Wow, we want a book from you; we want this, we want that!' It's marvelous. It's super. I can finally write what I want to write about: Native America. Because, this is really what I know about; this is what I feel; this is what I'm at home with; this is what I'm best at."

The Sun, He Dies, set in the world of the Aztec, won Highwater critical acclaim. "The destruction of the powerful Aztec culture in the 16th Century by a handful of Spanish adventurers has been chronicled before, but never has it been told with the eloquent, progressively angry Indian voice Highwater has created," John Adams said of *The Sun, He Dies*.

Highwater's four-novel Ghost Horse cycle also won him critical acclaim. The cycle centers on Amana, who, as an eleven-year-old, loses her parents to smallpox in the first book. "Highwater's theme is the end of legend days—Indian culture—at the hands of the encroaching white race's civilization; however, there is a spiritual progression to the story, as well as an historical one," Dorcas Hand said of *Legend Days*, the first book in the Ghost Horse cycle. "Highwater's writing is poetic; his use of mythic symbolism does not interfere with the telling of the story. While there are episodes of violence and gore, they stem from the survival aspects of the tale and are crucial to the story."

Eyes of Darkness is a fictionalized account of the life of Dr. Charles Alexander Eastman, a Sioux Indian who grew up in the white world. Noted *Kirkus Reviews*, the story is one "of desperation and hope, capturing the spirit of these tribes that perished without mercy."

Before turning to fiction, Highwater wrote nonfiction on such popular culture subjects as *Mick Jagger: The Singer Not the Song* (1973, using the pen name J. Marks) and *Fodor's Indian America* (1975). He also created a niche for himself as a critic of Native American topics with such books as *Song from the Earth: American Indian Painting* (1976) and *The Primal Mind: Vision and Reality in Indian America* (1981). He wrote screenplays for *The Primal Mind* (PBS, 1985) and *Native Land* (PBS, 1986), and he contributed introductions to several books, including *Indian Boyhood* (1976) by Charles Eastman. He edited *Europe Under Twenty-Five: A Young Person's Guide* (1971) as J. Marks-Highwater.

YOUNG ADULT FICTION

Anpao: An American Indian Odyssey (1977)
A Native American boy emerges from childhood into adulthood. Ko-ko-mik-e-is agrees to marriage if Anpao can secure the permission of the sun.

Journey to the Sky: A Novel About the True Adventures of Two Men in Search of the Lost Maya Kingdom (1978)

The Sun, He Dies: A Novel About the End of the Aztec World (1980)
Nanautzin, an Aztec Indian, becomes spokesman of Montezuma.

Eyes of Darkness: A Novel (1983)
Yesa, raised as a warrior and a deeply spiritual young man, is forced into another world by the unexpected return of his father, who has been converted to Christianity by white settlers.

Dark Legend: A Novel (1994)

Rama: A Legend (1994)
This fantasy is based on the epics of India and Southeast Asia.

Ghost Horse Cycle

Legend Days (1984)
After the loss of her parents, Amana learns the ways of the warrior from her Grandfather Fox.

The Ceremony of Innocence (1984)
There is a struggle between Amana, a mother with too many memories, and Jemina, a daughter with too few.

I Wear the Morning Star (1986)
The old woman of the tribe, Amana, hopes her grandson, Sitko, will bring the legend back to life.

Kill Hole (1988)

POETRY

Moonsong Lullaby (1981)

Songs for the Seasons (1991)

FOR FURTHER READING

Adams, John. Review of *The Sun, He Dies. School Library Journal*, October 1980.

Crichton, Sarah. "P W Interviews: Jamake Highwater." *Publishers Weekly*, 6 November 1978.

Hand, Dorcas. Review of *Legend Days. School Library Journal*, August 1984.

Highwater, Jamake. "The Storyteller's Farewell." In *Anpao: An American Indian Odyssey*. New York: J. B. Lippincott, 1977.

Immell, Myra, ed. *The Young Adult Reader's Advisory*. The Best in Literature and Language Arts, Mathematics & Computer Science. Vol. 1. New Providence, NJ: R. R. Bowker, 1989.

Norsworthy, James. Review of *Anpao: An American Indian Odyssey. Catholic Library World*, December 1977.

Review of *Eyes of Darkness. Kirkus Reviews*, 15 September 1985.

Stott, Jon C. "Narrative Expectations and Textual Misreadings: Jamake Highwater's 'Anpao' Analyzed and Reanalyzed." *Studies in the Literary Imagination*, fall 1985.

S. E. Hinton

Social drama

Tulsa, Oklahoma
1950

The Outsiders

"S. E. Hinton wrote *The Outsiders* when she was sixteen years old, and adolescent literature will never be quite the same," Lou Willett Stanek said. "The success of a book about gangs, violence, and teen-age have-nots gave courage or motivation to a herd of writers to take on a host of previously taboo subjects. Few of them drew the real outsiders in, as Hinton did. Boys read *The Outsiders* as well as girls, most of them more than once, and the majority vowed to write something just like it."

Novels by writers such as S. E. Hinton in the late 1960s "had a new candor to them. Hinton wrote about the Socs and the Greasers, and it was the Greasers whose story she told. Prior to this, it had nearly always been stories about the society kids in their white middle-class neighborhoods that found their way into adolescent fiction," Kenneth L. Donelson and Alleen Pace Nilsen amplified.

Susan Eloise Hinton received a bachelor of science degree from the University of Tulsa in 1970. That year, she married David E. Inhofe, a businessman. They have one son.

Hinton credits reading as the greatest influence on her writing. In her early school years, she wrote about horses and cowboys. When she was attending Will Rogers High School in Tulsa in 1967, her novel *The Outsiders* was published and revolutionized the young adult fiction field.

"The reason I wrote *The Outsiders* was that I had read all the horse stories and there wasn't anything else to read because I didn't want to read *Jeannie Goes to the Prom*. With the new trends in adolescent literature, I don't think kids will ever again have that experience. More and more good writers are realizing that teenagers make up a reading audience that in many ways is preferable to the adult audience," she said in *Literature for Today's Young Adults*.

"This probably sounds funny coming from me, but I think for a while the profession went out on a limb with stark realism," she continued. "Writers were so relieved to be able to tackle any subject that they overdid it. To write a good book—a book that will last beyond its topic—an author has to start with people rather than problems."

"Hinton's teenage groups grow up too fast, leading grim lives on the wrong side of the law; they carry knives and guns and are no strangers to violence or murder," Susan Thompson said. "The main character in *The Outsiders*, Ponyboy, is a member of a 'greaser' gang. The events of the novel develop out of the rivalry between the working-class greasers and the 'socs' or 'socials' who live on the better side of town."

It took Hinton a year and a half to write *The Outsiders*. She began the first of four drafts when she was fifteen. She was seventeen when it was published. She used her initials for the byline, because it is written from a boy's point of view.

"I can't write from a female point of view," Hinton said in *From Writers to Students*. "I've tried it, but I can't do it. It's just that when I was growing up, all my close friends were guys. I identified with the male culture; I was a tomboy; and, while I realize now I used to think I had a male mind, I think I just had a female mind that didn't conform to the female culture at that time. It's just a thing I feel very comfortable with, and I realize I reach all my audience that way. While girls will read boys' books, boys very often will not read girls' books; so one can appeal to both of them that way."

Alethea K. Helbig and Agnes Regan Perkins hailed *The Outsiders* as "a groundbreaking book in the New Realism for adolescent readers. . . . The formulaic plot is occasionally melodramatic, and some incidents seem very unlikely. They are also implausible as to be almost ludicrous, upon reflection, but, interestingly, they hold up well during reading, probably because the author makes Pony's concerns and the warm relationship between the brothers seem very real."

With the book's success—selling 4 million copies initially—Hinton was able to attend college. Her fame, however, also brought writer's block, and she was unable to write another book for four years. Her husband encouraged her to write *That Was Then, This Is Now,* and she did, at a slow, deliberate pace. The book portrays a boy's seeming betrayal of a friend who has become a drug pusher.

She continued to write about delinquent or borderline-delinquent boys with *Rumble Fish,* about a youth who wants to act tough.

Tex is likely her most popular book. "In *Tex,* the raw energy for which Hinton has justifiably reaped praise has not been tamed—it's been cultivated, and the result is a fine, solidly constructed, and well-paced story," Marilyn Kaye said. "Fourteen-year-old Tex lives with his 17-year-old brother, Mason, in a rural area. Their father hasn't been home in five months, and the relationship between the two boys is tense. Each has his own problems, fears, and growing pains which keep him alienated from his brother, until a dramatic and terrifying experience forces them to seek comfort and support from each other."

Critics hailed the book and teenagers devoured it for its realism; but parents found the characters violent and uncontrolled. Hinton said the characters were all real, based on people she knew, though she herself was not a member of a gang.

"In all Hinton's novels, 'appearance' takes the venerated form of an illusory group identity—the gang—while 'reality' is the lonelier pursuit of self-realization," commented Cynthia Rose. "It's a realization which always leads the heroes to oppose the kind of mindlessness and impulse towards self-destruction which perpetuate the gangs. The protagonists are 'heroic' by inherited teenage standards."

Critic Michael Malone said a librarian told him, "Hinton and Judy Blume have long been the most popular authors of 'reluctant readers' in the junior-high age group, youngsters who generally 'wouldn't be caught dead in a library.' "

YOUNG ADULT FICTION

The Outsiders (1967)
Ponyboy Curtis is a member of a "greasers" gang, whose rivals are the upper-middle-class "socs."

That Was Then, This Is Now (1971)
They are closer than brothers, until Bryon discovers that Mark deals drugs.

Rumble Fish (1975)
Rusty James wants to be just like his brother, Motorcycle Boy, the most respected hood in town.

Tex (1979)
Tex thinks he has a fine life, living with his older brother; then he learns a secret about their rodeo-rider father that changes his life.

Taming the Star Runner (1988)
Travis and the horse Star Runner are untamable free spirits.

FICTION FOR YOUNGER READERS

Big David, Little David (1995)

The Puppy Sister (1995)

ADAPTATIONS IN OTHER MEDIA

Tex (1982)
Film, based on the novel of the same name, starring Matt Dillon, Jim Metzler, and Meg Tilly. Hinton appears briefly as a teacher.

The Outsiders (1983)
Film, based on the novel of the same name, starring C. Thomas Howell, Matt Dillon, and Ralph Macchio.

Rumble Fish (1983)
Film, based on the novel of the same name, starring Matt Dillon, Mickey Rourke, and Diane Lane.

That Was Then, This Is Now (1985)
Film, based on the novel of the same name, starring Emilio Estevez, Craig Sheffer, and Kim Delaney.

The Outsiders (1990)
Television series, based on the novel of the same name, starring Jay Ferguson, Rodney Harvey, and Boyd Kestner.

FOR FURTHER READING

Donelson, Kenneth L., and Alleen Pace Nilsen, eds. Article in *Literature for Today's Young Adults*. Glenview, IL: Scott, Foresman, 1980.

Helbig, Alethea K., and Agnes Regan Perkins. *Dictionary of American Children's Fiction, 1960–84: Recent Books of Recognized Merit*. New York: Greenwood, 1986.

Kaye, Marilyn. Review of *Tex*. *School Library Journal*, November 1979.

Malone, Michael. "Tough Puppies." *The Nation*, 8 March 1986.

Rose, Cynthia. "Rebels Redux: The Fiction of S. E. Hinton." *Monthly Film Bulletin*, September 1983.

Stanek, Lou Willett. *Teacher's Guide to the Paperback Editions of the Novels of S. E. Hinton*. New York: Dell, 1980.

Thompson, Susan. "Images of Adolescence: Part II." *Signal*, May 1981.

Weiss, M. Jerry, ed. *From Writers to Students: The Pleasures and Pains of Writing*. Newark, DE: International Reading Association, 1979.

Isabelle Holland

Family drama

Basel, Switzerland
June 16, 1920
The Man Without a Face

"My books have always dealt with the relationship between the child or adolescent and the adult or adults who live in and dominate the young person's portrait of self," Isabelle Holland said in *Literature for Today's Young Adults*. "In later years that child, become an adult, may be able to see that the first portrait was as much created by the prejudices, fears, anxieties and desires within the adult as within the child."

Born in Basel, Switzerland, Holland is the daughter of a U.S. Foreign Service officer. She grew up in Guatemala and later lived in England, where she attended the University of Liverpool. She later went to Tulane University, Louisiana.

On the eve of World War II, her father sent Holland and her mother to the United States to live. In their new home, the author said, mother told her stories to amuse her, and this inspired her own interest in storytelling. Among her favorite books as a child were *Little Women* by Louisa May Alcott, *Alice in Wonderland* by Lewis Carroll, *Anne of Green Gables* by Lucy Maud Montgomery, the Winnie the Pooh books by A. A. Milne, the William books by Richard Crompton, and the David books by E. F. Benson.

Holland is noted for her Gothic mysteries and realistic young adult books, which at times have stirred controversy. Her books' characters are social outcasts—often young Americans abroad—and also neglected children and sexually curious children.

Holland was thirteen when she sold a story, "Naughty Betty," to *Tiger Tim*, a children's magazine in England. She based the heroine on real-life experience—she does not like to take her piano lessons.

Holland's first young adult novel, *Cecily*, was published in 1967, before most publishers considered young adult fiction a distinct category. Her third book, *The Man Without a Face*, is one of her best known. It drew attention because of the hero Charles's hatred for women (his mother has married and divorced four times). He is afraid of close relationships with anyone. He seeks out Justin McLeod, a recluse said to have been responsible for the accidental death of a young boy. The two develop a friendship. Charles begins to learn about his feelings and needs. Their relationship culminates in an implied homosexual encounter one night. Justin dies and leaves all his possessions to Charles. Some found the homosexual encounter key to the book's story, as an emotional release for Charles. Others viewed it as an unnecessarily corrupting influence on young readers.

"*The Man Without a Face* . . . was widely discussed because of the controversial element of homosexuality," the *Fifth Book of Junior Authors & Illustrators* stated. "But the attention drawn by the book was largely in praise of the sensitive, perceptive treatment of the relation between McLeod, an island recluse whose face has been badly scarred, and Charles, a fourteen-year-old boy who seeks out the man's help as a summer tutor. The book presents several themes that recur in Holland's work: among them, the complexity of relationships between individuals of different generations and the difficulty of making one's way through the grey areas of life and mortality."

Holland told *Horn Book Magazine*, "I started this book with only the idea of a fatherless boy who experiences with a man some of the forms of companionship and love that have been nonexistent in his life." She said that Justin's qualities of strength and kindness are more important "than the almost incidental fact that the book is about love between two people of the same sex."

"A great many of Holland's protagonists are lonely, isolated children or young adults," noted Anita Moss. "Often these characters are struggling to survive in a painful family situation. In *Amanda's Choice* the central character is the daughter of a loving father and his selfish second wife. Amanda herself belongs to a tradition of obnoxious, misunderstood children in children's literature. When her conflicts become unbearable, she runs away and seeks her friend Manuel in New York City. Without family, friends, or resources, Amanda at last begins to accept her father's love."

"The main lessons I have learned about writing," Holland said in a publisher's pamphlet, "are 1) to keep writing no matter what, even when I'm discouraged, and 2) to write every day, if possible—even a small amount. I write in the morning. I've never been able to understand writers who say they sit at their desks and work all day. All I can do is four hours. Then I have to bounce out of the house looking for company to play with.

"I try to write four pages a day. Sometimes I can do this in an hour and a half, and then I can write more; sometimes I write myself out after four pages and have to stop; sometimes it takes four hours to write four pages. When I'm at the end of a book—when I know where I am and I understand my characters—I can write more than four pages, but not much more. Once a book is written, I can revise all day.

"What I am most interested in is the relationship between the generations, between a younger person and an older one. I am much more interested in that than I am in the relationship between two young people or between two adults."

YOUNG ADULT FICTION

Cecily: The Novel (1967)
The setting is Langley School, an English boarding school. Cecily, thirteen, is awkward, overweight, and miserable, and she imbalances Elizabeth, a young teacher.

The Man Without a Face (1972)
Charles does not know much about love—little of it has come his way until the summer he turns fourteen and he meets a man who becomes his teacher and friend.

Heads You Win, Tails I Lose: A Novel (1973)
As her parents have marital problems, an overweight girl is anxious to diet.

Of Love and Death and Other Journeys (1975); British title: *Ask No Questions* (1978)
Meg Grant's mother dies of cancer, and Meg must come to grips with adulthood.

Hitchhike (1977)
Pud, sixteen and in boarding school, wants to get even with her father for breaking his promise to take her camping.

Dinah and the Green Fat Kingdom (1978)
Dinah, who is overweight, comes to appreciate her personal worth.

Now Is Not Too Late (1980)
A motherless eleven-year-old turns to her grandmother.

Summer of My First Love (1981)
Sarah—known to her family as Sam—falls in love with Steve and becomes pregnant.

Abbie's God Book (1982)
A girl records thoughts and questions about God in a journal.

After the First Love (1983), sequel to *Summer of My First Love*
Sarah wants to go to art school and get over Steve. She meets two interesting men at school—maybe one will be the right one.

The Empty House (1983)
Betsy Smith's father is in jail for tax fraud, and she is afraid friends at the beach club will find out.

God, Mrs. Muskrat and Aunt Dot (1983)
Eleven-year-old orphan Rebecca Smith finds comfort in an imaginary friend.

Perdita (1983)
She does not know her name, where she came from, or how old she is. The nurses name her Perdita.

The Island (1984)
Hilda is invited to visit an aunt and uncle on the island of Maenad—but she finds something ominous there.

Jennie Kiss'd Me (1985)
Jill Hamilton is surprised and afraid when Nathan Vandermark, who attends an exclusive prep school, begins paying attention to her.

Henry and Grudge (1986)

Love and the Genetic Factor (1987)

Toby the Splendid (1987)
Janet West has trouble making friends in school, unless you count Morris "Meow" Blair. She buys a dapple-gray horse.

Thief (1988)
Cressida, an orphan, tries to find out about her past and if she is responsible for her parents' deaths.

The Journey Home (1990)
Parentless girls, seeking a new home, board an orphan train headed to the frontier.

The Unfrightened Dark: A Novel (1990)
A deranged person kidnaps a blind girl's Seeing Eye dog.

The House in the Woods: A Novel (1991)
Five years after her adoptive mother's death, Bridget, fourteen, believes that her father is only interested in his biological children.

Search (1991)
Claudia Ransom, sixteen, put her baby up for adoption. Yet she could not forget, and she must now find the baby to get her life in order.

Behind the Lines (1994)

Family Trust (1994)

FICTION FOR YOUNGER READERS

Amanda's Choice (1970)

The Mystery of Castle Rinaldi (1972)

Journey for Three (1974)

Alan and the Animal Kingdom (1977)

A Horse Named Peaceable (1982)

Green Andrew Green (1984)

Kevin's Hat: Story (1984)

The Christmas Cat (1987)

The Easter Donkey (1989)

ADULT FICTION

Kilgaren (1974)

Trelawny (1974)

Moncrieff: A Novel (1975)

Darcourt: A Novel (1976)

Gernelle: A Novel of Suspense (1976)

The de Maury Papers (1977)

Tower Abbey: A Novel of Suspense (1978)

Counterpoint (1980)

The Marchington Papers (1980)

The Lost Madonna (1981)

A Death at St. Anselm's (1984)

Flight of the Archangel (1985)

A Lover Scorned (1986)

Bump in the Night (1988)

A Fatal Advent: A St. Anselm's Mystery (1989)

The Long Search (1990)

Love and Inheritance (1991)

ADAPTATIONS IN OTHER MEDIA

The Man Without a Face (1994)
Film, based on the novel of the same name, starring Mel Gibson.

FOR FURTHER READING

Donelson, Kenneth L., and Alleen Pace Nilsen, eds. "The People Behind the Books: Isabelle Holland." In *Literature for Today's Young Adults*. Glenview, IL: Scott, Foresman, 1980.

Holland, Isabelle. "Tilting at Taboos." *Horn Book Magazine*, June 1973.

Holtze, Sally Holmes, ed. *Fifth Book of Junior Authors & Illustrators*. New York: H. W. Wilson, 1983.

Moss, Anita. "Isabelle Holland." In *Twentieth-Century Children's Writers*, edited by Tracy Chevalier. 3d ed. Chicago: St. James Press, 1989.

Personal Glimpse: Isabelle Holland. New York: Fawcett Juniper, n.d.

H. M. Hoover

Science fiction

Stark County, Ohio
April 5, 1935

The Shepherd Moon: A Novel of the Future

"H. M. Hoover consistently produces youth science fiction of very high quality," Thomas P. Dunn said, "finding in SF a congenial and fertile ground for exploring those problems young people may face in less exotic environments: alienation from parents, feelings of isolation, feelings of being trapped or of being an anomalous creature out of sync with the Universe. Often Hoover's young people have special talents and sensitivities unappreciated by the adults around them."

Helen Mary Hoover, the daughter of teachers, said in the *Fifth Book of Junior Authors & Illustrators*, "My parents were great readers. So were their four children, either by choice or in self-defense. I don't really remember a time when I couldn't read or was not read to. I do recall that the reading texts in school came as a distinct shock. I couldn't believe I was being asked to waste my time with Dick and Jane after reading 'The Relief of Lucknow' in the McGuffey's *Fifth* in our attic."

The author attended Mount Union College and the Los Angeles County School of Nursing. She worked at various clerical jobs in New York before beginning to write.

"Writing is a matter of discipline," Hoover continued in the *Fifth Book of Junior Authors & Illustrators*, "of working at it each day, of thinking about it in the bathtub, or while reading or watching TV—but never when driving or cooking. . . . Some days it's fun to write; other days it's not."

She described in *Top of the News* the difficulty of writing science fiction: "In some respects fantastic worlds must be more real, more logically detailed and specific than straight fiction. When one writes about an alien world, it is just that to the reader. He or she must be told how and why it functions, and the telling must have consistency or all is lost. It also must be part of the story and not an inventory of facts."

Typical of her work is *The Shepherd Moon*, set centuries in the future, when culture and technology are in decline. The well-born Meredith Ambrose encounters Mikel, who has traveled from a habitat created long ago and forgotten. Mikel "makes her aware of the inequity of her life of freedom and affluence compared to that of the rest of society," said *Authors & Artists for Young Adults*. "As her warnings of Mikel's evil intentions continue to fall on deaf ears, Meredith also recognizes that although she is ignored and considered troublesome by her frivolous parents, her thoughtfulness and intelligence are not the negative qualities she once believed."

Hoover contributed to *Literature for Today's Young Adults* (1985), edited by Alleen Pace Nilsen and Kenneth L. Donelson, and *Innocence and Experience: Essays and Conversations on Children's Literature* (1987).

YOUNG ADULT FICTION

Children of Morrow (1973)
In the future, telepathic Tia and Rabbit cope with ecological disaster.

The Lion's Cub (1974)
In nineteenth-century Russia, a boy is captured by the enemy during a holy war.

Treasures of Morrow (1976), sequel to *Children of Morrow*

The Delikon (1977)
Once Varina saw the starship, she knew it was time to leave the students she had instructed so long on Earth.

The Rains of Eridan (1977)
Theo and Karen team up to survive and explore their planet's life-forms.

The Lost Star (1979)
Lian Webster is drawn to a puzzling excavation on Balthor, a Class Five planet.

The Return to Earth (1980)
Galen is governor-general of the colony of Marsat. He returns to Earth to search for a successor.

This Time of Darkness (1980)
Amy and Axel live isolated in an underground hive.

Another Heaven, Another Earth (1981)
An Earth expedition visits a neglected space colony.

The Bell Tree (1982)
Jenny, fifteen, and her father, vacationing on the planet Tanin, discover that nothing is what it seems in the country of Bell Tree.

The Shepherd Moon: A Novel of the Future (1984)
Meredith Ambrose, thirteen, one of the elite ruling class on forty-third-century Earth, meets Mikel, a troubling youth from a long-forgotten space habitat.

Orvis (1987)
Toby and Thaddeus find an old robot, Orvis, who is destined for the scrap heap.

The Dawn Palace: The Story of Medea (1988)
Medea aids Jason and the Argonauts in their quest for the Golden Fleece.

Away Is a Strange Place to Be (1990)
In the year 2349, Abby, twelve, wakes from drugged sleep to find she has been kidnapped and taken to a new space habitat.

Only Child (1991)
Cody, twelve, has only known life onboard a spaceship. When it lands on the planet Patma, his secluded existence ends.

The Winds of Mars (1995)
A young Martian uncovers family secrets.

FOR FURTHER READING

Dunn, Thomas P. "H. M. Hoover." In *Science Fiction Writers*, edited by Noell Watson and Paul E. Schellinger. 3d ed. Chicago: St. James Press, 1991.

Hile, Kevin S., ed. "H. M. Hoover." In *Authors & Artists for Young Adults*. Vol. 11. Detroit: Gale Research, 1993.

Holtze, Sally Holmes, ed. "Helen M. Hoover." In *Fifth Book of Junior Authors & Illustrators*. New York: H. W. Wilson, 1983.

Hoover, H. M. "Where Do You Get Your Ideas?" *Top of the News*, fall 1982.

Monica Hughes

Science fiction

Liverpool, England
November 3, 1925

Isis Trilogy

"I find writing is a very lonely business," Monica Hughes said in *Canadian Children's Literature*, "even writing for children, which should be, of course, and is, at the same time very joyful. . . .

"I've always known . . . that magic lay between the covers of books, and all that was necessary to do to partake of the treasures was to open the covers and plunge in. All the time I was growing up I was reading: *The Wind in the Willows, Black Beauty, Coral Island, The Children of the New Forest,* Arthur Ransome, all the books of E. Nesbit."

Monica Ince, whose father was a mathematician and amateur astronomer, grew up in Egypt and was educated privately in England and Scotland. In 1957, she married Glen Hughes, with whom she has two children.

She served with the Women's Royal Naval Service from 1943 to 1946. She worked as a dress designer in England and Rhodesia. From 1952 to 1957, she was a laboratory technician for the National Research Council in Ottawa, Ontario, Canada.

A resident of Alberta, Canada, she has been a full-time writer since 1975. Most of her books are set in Canada or—as she specializes in science fiction—in an alien world resembling Canada.

The author's Isis Trilogy is an ambitious work. Set on an isolated planet, it looks at social evolution over three generations. The main character is Olwen Pendennis, sixteen, an orphan raised in isolation by a kind-hearted robot.

The Keeper of the Isis Light is the first of the trilogy. "Sixteen-year-old Olwen has been brought up on the planet Isis in complete solitude except for her guardian, an anthropomorphic robot," Norman Culpan said. "Life is idyllic until a party of Earth settlers arrives, when she learns to love and finds she is hated. SF elements abound, are of interest in themselves, and are basic to the plot; but it is Olwen's discovery of her own nature and her own values that is of paramount importance."

Although some reviewers were disappointed in *The Guardian of Isis*, the next book, M. Crouch said, "Monica Hughes brings before us the strange world of Isis in all its beauty, and integrates setting and action and character in exemplary fashion. Her book is an excellent 'read,' a tract on society and a relevant commentary on the history of our own times."

Hughes herself noted in *Language Arts* the dangers of writing multiple volumes. "There are dangers in writing sequels—some of these I had run into in *Guardian*—and the biggest challenge was to plot the story without introducing any new parameters into Isis, which had been a closed society since its beginning."

Gerald Rubio said *The Isis Pedlar* "completes and unifies a trilogy which is surely the most impressive achievement in young adult literature to appear in a very long time. Moreover, it is a radical departure from her earlier works; to her usual ingredients of heroic adventure, truth of character, and mythic implications, she here adds broad comedy, romantic love, and even self-parody."

In *Canadian Children's Literature,* Hughes described the writing life as being lonely yet vastly rewarding. "Even now when I'm writing I look at the page and I think, 'It's still magic, isn't it?' These scrawls on paper—and you don't have to think about it as your hand actually puts it down—are an incarnation of one's deepest thoughts and emotions solidified into two dimensions right there. I would so much like to see reading and writing brought back into schools with this sense of magic: vibrant, instead of a physiological and psychological exercise which is painful for teachers and students."

"Curiously, few are aware of how essentially Canadian a writer Monica Hughes is," Gerald Rubio stated in *Canadian Children's Literature,* noting that not only "are many of her locales and subjects explicitly Canadian, but even the works set in new and distant worlds are permeated by uniquely Canadian themes. Are there, for example, more relevant 'Canadian' themes than those central to her novels: the exploitation of natural resources by multi-national conglomerates? or the varieties of alienation experienced by immigrants to 'new worlds'? or the importance of adaptation to hostile environments for survival?"

"Hughes has been rightly recognized as 'one of the best Canadian, perhaps world, authors of juvenile fiction at work today,' " noted Irma McDonough. "She brings reason and intellect to bear on all of her work. She recognizes three levels of communication in writing fiction: the straight adventure happening to the hero/heroine; the universal that brings the work into commonality with world literature; and the myth level that involves the author's intuitive knowledge about her country's past which is 'carried in the genes' from generation to generation."

"There is a gentleness to her books that is rare in science fiction," said Sarah Ellis. "The hairsbreadth escape, the exotic flora and fauna, the humanoids, the vast intergalactic reaches, the villains and the heroes—all are enclosed in one overriding concern, subtle but ever-present; the value of kindness. This theme seems a rather nonrobust one for science fiction. But Monica Hughes manages to clothe the homey quality in flesh and blood (or in pink blob-tissue or high-technology robot metal) to give it strength and resilience. Hers is a major contribution to the fields of Canadian writing for children and of juvenile science fiction."

"Monica Hughes writes carefully and scrupulously," Mike Hayhoe observed. "She also raises serious moral issues in her novels, here [*Devil on My Back*] about the nature of wisdom as opposed to factual knowledge; about the consequences of selfishness and generosity; about the choices which affect the nature and purpose of a community."

YOUNG ADULT FICTION

Gold-Fever Trail: A Klondike Adventure (1974)
Harry, thirteen, and his sister, Sarah, eleven, may be separated when their mother dies—if their father does not return from gold prospecting in the Yukon.

Crisis on Conshelf Ten (1975)
Kepler, born on a Moon colony, travels with his father to Earth on a diplomatic mission. He stays in an underwater community and meets the Gillmen.

Earthdark (1977)
The story of a lunar colonial mission in the year 2005.

Ghost Dance Caper (1978)
Tom, part Native American, is desperate to "find his Spirit."

The Tomorrow City (1978)
Caro and her friend, David, thwart a machine's plans to run the city.

Beyond the Dark River (1979)
In the post-nuclear-holocaust year 2026, Benjamin Gross is looking for a cure to a mysterious illness.

Beckoning Lights (1982)

Hunter in the Dark (1982)
Sixteen-year-old Mike learns he has leukemia.

Ring-Rise, Ring-Set (1982)
In the near future, civilization's technology has gone underground. Liza, uncomfortable with her situation, ends up being adopted into a tribe of nomads.

The Treasure of the Long Sault (1982)
Two brothers search for Native American treasure.

My Name Is Paula Popowich (1983)
Paula, twelve, seeks her birth father, who she was told had died.

Space Trap (1983)
Valerie, Frank, and Susan are captured by aliens as specimens for study.

Devil on My Back (1984)
Knowledge is preserved underground at Arc One in the early twenty-first century. Tomi, son of Lord Bentt, is caught in a revolt of slaves.

Sand Writer (1985)
A spoiled young princess expects to marry when she visits a desertlike kingdom.

Blaine's Way (1986)

Dream Catcher (1986), companion to *Devil on My Back*
Ruth, a misfit who lives in a dome city, sets out on a journey.

Log Jam (1987)

Invitation to the Game (1992)
In the future, Lisse and friends are assigned to a bleak neighborhood for the permanently unemployed. They are invited to the Game, which transports them to paradise.

The Promise (1992)

The Crystal Drop (1993)

The Golden Aquarians (1995)
A science fiction story about a boy and his father.

Isis Trilogy

The Keeper of the Isis Light (1980)
Olwen, sixteen, reared on the planet Isis by a robot guardian, faces considerable change when a party of Earth settlers arrives.

The Guardian of Isis (1981)
The colonists on Isis, going through a primitive agricultural stage, resort to a taboo-riddled religion.

The Isis Pedlar (1982)
The Guardian has protected the settlers with a quarantine, but an unscrupulous space trader decides to exploit them.

FOR FURTHER READING

Crouch, M. Review of *The Guardian of Isis*. *Junior Bookshelf*, October 1981.

Culpan, Norman. Review of *The Keeper of the Isis Light*. *School Librarian*, September 1980.

Ellis, Sarah. "News from the North." *Horn Book Magazine*, September–October 1984.

Hayhoe, Mike. Review of *Devil on My Back*. *School Librarian*, September 1984.

Hughes, Monica. "On the Writing of *The Isis Pedlar*." *Language Arts*, January 1984.

———. "The Writer's Quest." *Canadian Children's Literature: A Journal of Criticism and Review*, 1982, Annual.

McDonough, Irma. "Profile: Monica Hughes." *In Review: Canadian Books for Children*, February 1981.

Rubio, Gerald. "Monica Hughes: An Overview." *Canadian Children's Literature: A Journal of Criticism and Review*, 1980, Annual.

———. Review of *The Isis Pedlar*. *Quill and Quire*, March 1983.

Hadley Irwin

Family drama

Lee Hadley
Earlham, Iowa
October 10, 1934–August 22, 1995

Annabelle Bowen Irwin
Peterson, Iowa
October 8, 1915

What About Grandma?

"We have spent most of our lives working with people younger than ourselves," writers Lee Hadley and Ann Irwin stated in a brief afterword to *So Long at the Fair*, "and if we've learned anything it is that the concerns, problems, and emotions of the young are basically the same as those of the adult. We respect this audience of young adults and try to write with honesty, humor, and understanding. Ann says it helps to have raised four children. Lee says it helps to have survived one's own adolescence. What is certain is that Hadley Irwin has become very real to us. We hope she's just as real to the readers of her books."

Hadley and Irwin wrote young adult books under the joint pen name Hadley Irwin. The two met while teaching at Iowa State University in Ames and began writing together in 1979. They first collaborated on professional writing for the university and later moved to fiction.

Lee Hadley, the daughter of farmers, attended Drake University and the University of Wisconsin–Madison. She worked as a copywriter for a department store, taught high school English, and lectured as a college English professor.

Annabelle Bowen Irwin, the daughter of a farmer and a teacher, attended Morningside College and the University of Iowa. She has worked as a writer and a high school and college English instructor.

"How do we write with each other? Very easily," the writers said in a publisher's promotional pamphlet. "Writing together is a fascinating experience and we've often discussed why it works so well for us. Both of our lives are filled with words, whether it's teaching composition courses, doing crossword puzzles, or fighting our ongoing Scrabble battle. Probably more important, we genuinely like and respect each other; there has never been a sense of competition in our relationship. In each other we have an instant editor; if we disagree, which is seldom, there's a standard response: 'Put it in parentheses with a question mark.' Best of all, when one of us would rather do almost anything—make coffee, water plants, fix lunch—but confront the blank page in the typewriter, the other flicks the whip and the writing goes on."

The writers said that they focused on young adults because they respect them. "Their triumphs, their defeats, their joys, their sorrows, their frustrations, their accomplishments have intrinsic worth and extraordinary meaning, for they mirror the past, the present, and the future of us all. They are a wonderful mixture of the individual and universal experience.

"The questions that young-adult readers confront, the range (right or wrong) of their solutions, the result of their choices—all of these are the raw materials from which Hadley Irwin's stories come."

The writers said that they strive to convey beauty and meaning in worlds other than those best known to the readers, as well as a respect for ethnic groups. "Nothing is more constricting than being locked into one's own experience when there is a universe of differences to explore."

Hadley Irwin has addressed the subjects of incest, divorce, and prejudice. In *The Original Freddie Ackerman*, for example, the main character refuses to make life easy for his new stepmother. *Bring to a Boil and Separate* depicts Katie Wagner's difficulty in understanding why her veterinarian parents have separated.

Sixteen-year-old Rhys, in *What About Grandma?*, passes up summer vacation to help care for her grandmother, Wyn, who is no longer able to live alone. "This novel is wonderful," reviewer Sari Feldman said. "The authors . . . have done a superb job portraying Wyn's last days at home."

Abby, My Love tells of Chip Martin's attempts to learn why his friend Abigail is so remote and quiet. Her secret is sexual abuse by her father. "This is an important book that adults and young adults should be aware of in terms of subject matter and quality," Maria B. Salvadore said.

In the historical novel *Jim-Dandy*, Caleb loves the horse that his stepfather sells to the Seventh Cavalry. He goes to Fort Hays and gets a job caring for the animal, which General George Custer wants to turn into a war horse. "The complicated relationship between Caleb and his stepfather and Caleb's growing disgust at Custer's senselessly brutal campaign against the Cheyenne add depth and texture to the story," reviewer Elizabeth S. Watson stated. "Historical details are accurate; the horse scenes, realistic; and emotions, believably portrayed."

YOUNG ADULT FICTION

The Lilith Summer (1979)
A twelve-year-old girl and a seventy-seven-year-old woman cross paths.

Bring to a Boil and Separate (1980)
Thirteen-year-old Katie learns that her parents are divorcing and needs to become more independent.

We Are Mesquakie, We Are One (1980)
Mesquakie Native Americans resist pressure from the federal government to give up their land.

Moon and Me (1981)
Fourteen-year-old E. J. hates to give up Paris for six months to live on a farm, but she soon makes friends with Moon, a twelve-year-old whiz kid.

What About Grandma? (1982)
After Rhys's grandmother breaks a hip, Rhys and her mother go to spend a month at the older woman's house. Grandma stubbornly resists being told what to do, and the summer turns into one of discovery for three generations of women.

I Be Somebody (1984)
Anson J. Davis, ten, tries to understand why people in his black community in Oklahoma are treated the way they are.

Abby, My Love (1985)
Abigail is keeping a secret about her father that she should not. Friend Chip helps her come out of her shell and become class valedictorian.

Kim, Kimi (1987)
Japanese American Kim Anderson is uncomfortable when the subject of World War II comes up at her midwestern school.

So Long at the Fair (1988)
Joel Logan thinks he has it all until childhood friend Ashley calls it quits, leaving him crushed, betrayed, and alone.

I Can't Hear You Listening (1990)
Tracy Spencer, sixteen, tries to help her friend Stanley, who is dependent on alcohol and drugs.

The Original Freddie Ackerman (1992)
When his mother and newest stepfather leave on a honeymoon, Freddie refuses to stay with his father, stepmother, and their scrambled family.

Jim-Dandy (1994)
In post–Civil War Kansas, a bond grows between twelve-year-old Caleb and the foal Dandy.

FICTION FOR YOUNGER READERS

Hawkeye Adventure (1966) by Ann Irwin, with Bernice Reida

Hawkeye Lore (1968) by Ann Irwin, with Bernice Reida

One Bite at a Time (1973) by Ann Irwin

Moon of the Strawberry (1977) by Ann Irwin, with Bernice Reida

Until We Reach the Valley (1979) by Ann Irwin, with Bernice Reida

DRAMA

And the Fullness Thereof (1962)
One-act play by Ann Irwin.

Pieces of Silver (1963)
One-act play by Ann Irwin.

FOR FURTHER READING

"Children's Writer Hadley Dead at 60." *Berkshire Eagle*, 26 August 1995.

Feldman, Sari. Review of *What About Grandma? Voice of Youth Advocates*, August 1982.

Hadley Irwin. New York: Margaret K. McElderry Books, 1992.

Irwin, Hadley. "Dialogue Between Ann Irwin and Lee Hadley." *ALAN Review*, fall 1992.

———. *Writing Young Adult Novels*. Cincinnati, OH: Writer's Digest, 1988

Salvadore, Maria B. Review of *Abby, My Love. School Library Journal*, May 1985.

Watson, Elizabeth S. Review of *Jim-Dandy. Horn Book Magazine*, July–August 1994.

Brian Jacques

Fantasy

Liverpool, England
June 15, 1939

Redwall Series

"I sometimes think it ironic for a 49-year-old ex-sea-man, longshoreman, truck driver, policeman, bus driver, etc., to find success writing children's novels," Brian Jacques stated in a publisher's promotional piece.

The son of a truck driver and a homemaker, Jacques attended a Roman Catholic school in Liverpool. He worked several jobs—besides those already mentioned, he was a railway fireman, a docks representative, and a freelance radio broadcaster. His music programs included "Jakestown" on British Broadcasting Corporation and "Saturday with Brian Jacques." He wrote several documentaries and plays for television, radio, and the stage.

A patron of the Royal Wavertree School for the Blind, he wrote his first novel, *Redwall*, intending it to be read at this children's home. A publisher took an interest in the book, and the story stretched into a trilogy and then beyond. Teenagers as well as adults are fans of Jacques's Redwall series, books about animal characters in medieval times.

"What on the surface appears to be just another medieval fantasy peopled with animals enacting the fight to the death between good and evil is actually a rich and thought-provoking novel on the nature of good and evil," reviewer Susan M. Harding commented on Jacques's *Redwall*. "The peaceful life of the mice of Redwall Abbey is shattered by the onslaught of the fierce rat, Cluny the Scourge, and his army of rats, weasels and other vermin. . . . Cluny cannot be completely defeated, however, until the sword of Martin, the legendary warrior who founded Redwall Abbey, can be found. A young novice, Matthias, embarks on a quest and ultimately finds it, but a wise cat reminds him that it is just a sword."

The Redwall books are works of epic fantasy, featuring characters such as Cluny the Scourge, Slager the Fox, and Martin the Warrior—humanlike animals. Jacques said that he believes in telling a good story and in putting forth a strong moral sense for his readers. Not surprisingly, his books have been praised for their narrative strengths and characterization. The novels offer a mixture of humor, warmth, and romance with a dose of rough-and-tumble battles and death.

"All the Tolkien essentials are here: magic swords, long journeys, skirmishes and set-piece battles, wild creatures who speak in distinctive Gollum-style languages, quaint dialect-speaking little animals who burst into song and a hero who humbly accepts the mantle of destined greatness," wrote reviewer Michele Landsberg.

Ann A. Flowers, though, suggested the characters may be too black-and-white: "The lines drawn between good and evil are never ambiguous, not allowing for that shiver of doubt and wonder about the outcome." Reviewer M. Crouch said the books are overlong, as "Mr. Jacques' trouble is that he cannot bear to leave anything out. Every detail of every operation is faithfully reported, not to mention every bit of tedious backchat between the characters."

Still, Jane Inglis found *Redwall* "impossible to put down and wonderful to read aloud. It's a fast-moving saga of siege and struggle. . . . The story is packed with dramatic incident, the climax satisfying—victory snatched in the nick of time from the very jaws of defeat—the narrative style forceful and flowing. Dialogue is superb, each character finding a distinctive voice. Brian Jacques has a tremendous sense of fun, but does not spare his readers the inevitable tragedies of violent conflict. His creatures are true first and foremost to their animal natures."

"Jacques has perfected his formula in this long-awaited book about the legendary warrior-mouse, Martin," said Kathryn Pierson Jennings in a review of *Martin the Warrior*. The reviewer was disappointed, however, that the hero does not rise above formula. "The moral here: Martin's just another hero who puts his pants on one leg at a time like the rest of them. Burr, hurr."

In *Waldenbooks Hailing Frequencies*, Jacques said: "The figure of Martin intrigued me. He is the ultimate warrior, the spirit of the abbey, and the mouse that all the creatures of Redwall look up to for his spiritual guidance when he appears in dreams. To me, a warrior is somebody you always can trust, somebody who will defend the weak and who's not a bully. A warrior is somebody all of us can look up to, and say, 'You can go anywhere with that person. You can trust that person's word.' They're very good to the family, and always true to their friends. I always say to a kid, 'Now that's what a warrior is, and you ought to be a proper warrior, if you want to be a warrior.' "

YOUNG ADULT FICTION

Redwall Series

Redwall (1987)
At the ancient stone abbey of Redwall, the gentle mice of Mossflower Wood gather to celebrate a year of peace and abundance—and to ready for an assault by Cluny, the terrible one-eyed cat, and his horde.

Mossflower (1988)
Prior to the events in *Redwall*, Martin the Warrior, a mouse, battles the wildcat ruler of Mossflower Wood.

Mattimeo (1990)
Slager the Fox, a cunning fox, and his evil henchmen kidnap the woodland children, including Mattimeo, son of the warrior mouse Matthias. Matthias plans a bold rescue—in which Mattimeo becomes, unexpectedly, a hero.

Mariel of Redwall (1992)
Cast adrift at sea by Gabool the Wild, a wicked rat pirate king, Mariel has only her trusty Gullwhacker to protect her. Found and brought to Redwall Abbey, she vows to avenge her father; with three Mossflower companions, she sets off in search of her enemy.

Salamandastron: A Tale from Redwall (1993)
A weasel assassin, Ferhago, comes to change the peaceful world around the abbey forever.

Martin the Warrior (1994)
As a child, Martin is brought to the stronghold of Badrang the Tyrant and enslaved. Escape is not his only goal.

The Bellmaker (1995)
Joseph the Bellmaker steals a pirate ship and sets off to find his daughter, Mariel.

FICTION FOR YOUNGER READERS

Seven Strange & Ghostly Tales (1991)

The Great Redwall Feast (1995)

FOR FURTHER READING

Brian Jacques. New York: Philomel Books, 1989.

"Brian Jacques: The Master of Redwall." *Waldenbooks Hailing Frequencies*, March–April 1995.

Crouch, M. Review of *Mossflower. Junior Bookshelf*, December 1988.

Flowers, Ann A. Review of *Redwall. Horn Book Magazine*, January–February 1988.

Harding, Susan M. Review of *Redwall. School Library Journal*, August 1987.

Inglis, Jane. Review of *Redwall. Books for Your Children*, spring 1988.

Jennings, Kathryn Pierson. Review of *Mariel of Redwall. Bulletin of the Center for Children's Books*, March 1992.

———. Review of *Martin the Warrior. Bulletin of the Center for Children's Books*, January 1994.

Landsberg, Michele. "Robin Hood Rides Again." *The Washington Post Book World*, 6 November 1988.

Diana Wynne Jones

Fantasy

London, England
August 16, 1934
Dalemark Cycle

"Diana Wynne Jones's books overflow with magic, mystery and suspense," Fiona Lafferty said. "They tell of fantastic adventures in this world and in parallel fantasy worlds and portray events in the past, present and future—often simultaneously. Her stories feature witches, wizards and warlocks, ghosts, space-age time travelers, mythological characters and, just very occasionally, ordinary people." "Diana Wynne Jones is a British fantasist of astonishing originality and power," in the estimate of Michele Landsberg.

The daughter of educators, Jones grew up during World War II with relatives in Wales and learned to speak Welsh. She received a bachelor of arts degree in 1956 from St. Anne's College, Oxford. That same year, she married John A. Burrow, a university professor. They have three sons.

Jones decided to write fantasy, Lafferty said, "firstly because she had been starved of it as a child and, secondly, because she feels books should provide something other than reality. This is not to suggest that her books aren't firmly rooted in reality, albeit a rather distorted reality. She creates fantastic worlds and situations, but her characters are very real and the ways they behave are entirely plausible."

Her first book was *Wilkin's Tooth*. "Frank and Jess find themselves without pocket money because they have broken a chair," J. Murphy explained, "so they set up an 'Own Back' Agency Ltd. in their back shed. Their first customer is the local bully and gang leader,

Buster, who asks them to get him one of Vernon Wilkin's teeth in revenge. They oblige, but use a milk tooth belonging to Vernon's young brother. Imagine their consternation when the child's face begins to swell at an alarming rate and they discover that Buster is involved with Biddy, the local witch. The plot concerns their breaking of her power and settling various scores as they go."

Cart and Cwidder was the first of four related books set in an imaginary, medieval-like kingdom. "A fantasy adventure, especially one that culminates in the gathering of armies, epic fashion, invites comparison with *The Hobbit*," Jill Paton Walsh noted, "but this is not another derivative book, for Diana Wynne Jones has a subject of her own to involve us in. Not the eternal war of good and evil, as in Tolkien, but the mysterious power of song is at the heart of her story. For one of the instruments in Clennan's cart is a huge old cwidder, that once belonged to one of the heroes of his songs, and if played with passion enough this instrument does strange things."

Jones uses Dalemark to do more than just tell a story. Jessica Yates suggested, "Here is scope for serious political commentary relevant to our times, and Clennan spies for the North in *Cart and Cwidder*, and Mitt joins the underground revolutionaries in *Drowned Ammet*. The supernatural element in Dalemark is derived not so much from magical talent as from the gods of Dalemark, who bestow their favours on our heroes and heroines when they decide, however uncertain and ignorant of their potential, to dare their utmost in the service of Good against Evil."

In *Books for Your Children*, Jones described a book as a form of enchanted circle. "Any book, whether realistic or fantasy, is a self-contained world with the reader in control (if you do not like the game the writer is playing, you can always stop reading). My feeling is that children get most from books which work along the same lines as they do—in other words, by *'Let's Pretend.'* I am not saying that a fantasy needs to ape children's games, but I do think it should be like them in a number of important respects. Above all, it should be as exciting and engrossing as the games in the wood. I aim to be as gripped by the book I am writing as I hope any reader will be. I want to know what happens next. If it bores me, I stop. But a book has an additional asset: it seems to be real. If you say a thing is real in a book, then in that book it *is* real."

YOUNG ADULT FICTION

Wilkin's Tooth (1973); British title: *Witch's Business* (1974)
Needing money, Frank and Jess start a business—selling revenge to other kids. Their first customer, the bully Buster, wants them to get him one of Vernon Wilkin's teeth. Then a local witch becomes involved.

Eight Days of Luke (1974)
David has to spend his school holidays with frightful relatives. He calls up a spirit, Luke, who needs help escaping pursuers.

Dogsbody (1975)
Sirius, the hot-tempered star, is framed for murder and banished.

Power of Three (1976)
Three children of the Mound People bring their tribe together with the Dorig and the Giants, traditional enemies.

Who Got Rid of Angus Flint? (1978)
Flint, leaving his wife, comes to visit and disrupts the family's life.

The Four Grannies (1980)
Emily and Erg's parents were previously wed to other people. As a result, they have four grandmothers who come to care for them.

The Homeward Bounders (1981)
This fantasy novel begins in 1879 when Jamie, thirteen, witnesses faceless, cloaked figures playing a mysterious game.

The Time of the Ghost (1981)
A ghost plagues the three Melford sisters.

Archer's Goon (1984)
Quentin Sykes defies the magicians and refuses to write his quota of words for the mysterious Mountjoy.

The Skiver's Guide (1984)

Warlock at the Wheel, and Other Stories (1984)

Howl's Moving Castle (1986)
In the land of Ingary, a witch turns Sophie, seventeen, into an old woman, and she becomes enmeshed in bizarre doings at the wizard Howl's castle.

A Tale of Time City (1987)
Vivian Smith, eleven, is kidnapped in 1939 by two young time travelers who mistakenly think she is the "Time Lady."

Castle in the Air (1990)
Abdullah, a poor young rug dealer, one day buys a magic carpet.

Hidden Turnings (1990)

Aunt Maria (1991)
Could civilized Aunt Maria have anything to do with what happened to Mig's brother, Chris?

Wild Robert (1992)

Yes, Dear (1992)

A Sudden Wild Magic (1993)
Witches band to defeat the magicians of Arth, who want to misuse Earth's technology.

Hexwood (1994)

Chrestomanci Cycle

Charmed Life (1977)
In a world of magic, Cat Chant uses up several of his nine lives obeying the directives of his bossy witch sister, Gwendolen.

The Magicians of Caprona (1980)
Tonino Montana, who is slow to learn his spells, believes that the words to an angelic old tune will bring peace.

Witch Week (1982)
Only the headmistress of Larwood House knows which children are witch orphans.

The Lives of Christopher Chant (1988)
In events prior to *Charmed Life*, Christopher's dreams send him to strange worlds that he calls "the Anywheres."

Dalemark Cycle

Cart and Cwidder (1975)
In an imaginary world, Dalemark, singer Clennan journeys between North and South, playing his cwidder, an instrument of legend.

Drowned Ammet (1977)
Sea god Ammet and Libby Beer must save Hildy and Mitt.

The Spellcoats (1979)
A father and son must go off to war, leaving behind four children to face a hostile community.

The Crown of Dalemark (1995)
The Countess and Lord send Mitt to kill a young woman who claims to know where the lost crown is hidden.

FICTION FOR YOUNGER READERS

The Ogre Downstairs (1974)

Fire and Hemlock (1985)

Chair Person (1989)

DRAMA

The Batterpool Business (first produced in 1968)

The King's Things (first produced in 1970)

The Terrible Fisk Machine (first produced in 1971)

CONTRIBUTOR

The Cat-Flap and the Apple Pie (1979)

Hecate's Cauldron (1981)

Hundreds and Hundreds (1984)

Dragons and Dreams (1986)

Guardian Angels (1987)

ADULT FICTION

Changeover (1970)

EDITOR

Fantasy Stories (1994)

FOR FURTHER READING

Jones, Diana Wynne. "Far Out Fantasy." *Books for Your Children*, autumn–winter 1981.

Lafferty, Fiona. "Realms of Fantasy: An Interview with Diana Wynne Jones." *British Book News Children's Books*, winter 1987.

Landsberg, Michele. *Reading for the Love of It: Best Books for Young Readers*. New York: Prentice Hall Press, 1987.

Murphy, J. Review of *Wilkin's Tooth*. *Junior Bookshelf*, August 1973.

Walsh, Jill Paton. "Epic Ventures." *The Times Literary Supplement*, 11 July 1975.

Yates, Jessica. "Diana Wynne Jones." In *Twentieth-Century Children's Writers*, edited by Tracy Chevalier. 3d ed. Chicago: St. James Press, 1989.

Carolyn Keene

Mystery

River Heights
1930

Nancy Drew Series

Carolyn Keene does not exist. Along with Franklin W. Dixon she links this generation's popular young adult fiction with that of previous generations. Her fictional heroine Nancy Drew has solved hundreds of crime cases since she first appeared in 1930.

"I think it is not overstating the case to maintain that the original Nancy Drew is a mythic character in the psyches of the American women who followed her adventures as they were growing up. She may have been Superman, Batman, and Green Hornet, all wrapped up in a pretty girl in a blue convertible," mystery writer Nancy Picard stated in the introduction to a recent hardcover reprint of *The Hidden Staircase*.

Keene is a name made up by Edward L. Stratemeyer, an industrious fiction syndicator. Stratemeyer invented interesting characters for several series of books and hired writers to flesh out his story outlines. (Stratemeyer also created the pen name Franklin W. Dixon. For more information, see the Dixon entry, page 98.)

Stratemeyer was born in Elizabeth, New Jersey, in 1862; his father was a dry goods dealer. He married Magdalene Baker Van Camp in 1891, and they had two daughters: Harriet Stratemeyer Adams, who took over his syndicate after his death in 1930, and Edna Camilla Stratemeyer Squier.

After completing local school, Stratemeyer worked in the family store until 1889. He managed his own stationery store for a brief time before becoming a writer. His first book was *The Minute Boys of Lexington* (1898). He worked for Street and Smith, a publisher of magazines and dime novels by such popular writers as William T. Adams ("Oliver Optic") and Horatio Alger, Jr.

Stratemeyer wrote books under his own name as well as pseudonyms such as Optic and Captain Ralph Bonehill. He wrote books in partnership, such as with his brother, Louis. These novels were intended for juvenile readers and bore such titles as *Three Young Ranchmen; or, Daring Adventures in the Great West* (1901), using the Bonehill byline, and *Bob the Photographer; or, A Hero in Spite of Himself* (1902), as Arthur M. Winfield.

Stratemeyer soon had a best-seller. "War was glamour in those days," Arthur Praeger stated in *Saturday Review*. "Uniforms were splendid, and battles were glorious. . . . He turned out a book about two boys on a battleship and mailed it off to Lothrop, Lee & Shepard, a Boston publishing house. There was an interval of waiting, during which the newspapers announced the glad tidings of Admiral Dewey's victory at Manila bay. The next mail brought an acceptance letter from Boston. Could the author revise his manuscript so that it would parallel the great event of the day? He certainly could. Teenage hero Larry Russell and his pals were promptly transferred to the Pacific Fleet, and the result was called *Under Dewey at Manila*. It was the financial hit of the juvenile publishing industry in 1899."

Tiring of working for others, in 1906 Stratemeyer established his Stratemeyer Literary Syndicate in New York. He plotted the books, hired writers for as little as $100 a book, and edited their manuscripts. He had the stories set in type and rented the printing plates to publishers. It could take as little as six weeks from plot to print.

His first series featured the Bobbsey Twins. Stratemeyer wrote or had others write books in such series as Ship and Shore, Bound to Succeed, Old Glory, Rover Boys, Flag and Frontier, Motor Boys, Baseball Joe, and Ruth Fielding. His most enduring series were begun toward the end of his career: the Tom Swift science fiction books, the Happy Hollisters juvenile books, and the Nancy Drew and Hardy Boys series, which are still appearing today.

"Stratemeyer's life, like many of his books, followed the rise-to-respectability pattern set forth in Horatio Alger's novels he so admired as a child. Alger's heroes are forthright, confident, and—above all—industrious and lucky. Stratemeyer, clearly, was composed of goodly measures of these attributes," Carol Billman said.

"Stratemeyer's series books depend on action galore," Billman added, "most of it more or less loosely plotted around a conflict between good and bad characters: traps are set, assaults are made on enemy quarters, and chases (in every mode of transportation imaginable) are conducted by the heroes. Their opponents, in turn, spy on, harass, trick, and sometimes kidnap . . . them."

Harriet Stratemeyer Adams

Harriet Stratemeyer Adams (1892–1982) served as senior partner in the fiction syndicate started by her father. Born in Newark, New Jersey, she graduated from Wellesley College in 1914. She apprenticed for a year, then joined the syndicate full-time. In 1915, she married Russell Vroom Adams, an investment banker, with whom she had four children. He died in 1966.

Adams worked as a plot writer and editor. She typically claimed to have written at least the early books, as in an article by Judson Hand for the *New York Sunday News*: "Generally, she writes a 60-page outline of a new Nancy Drew mystery in pencil, then dictates the book in from two weeks to two months. She always uses the pen name, Carolyn Keene, for the Nancy Drew books.

" 'The books do have some educational value and we go to great lengths to make them authentic,' said Mrs. Adams recently in her office. 'From one book they may learn about archaeology and from another they may get a lesson in conserving natural resources, but they always learn something.' "

In a 1977 article for *TV Guide*, Adams said, "Being an author is my main consideration as well as my preference, and nothing pleases me more than to be starting a new Nancy Drew or Dana Girls mystery story."

In the 1980s, Adams's claim to Nancy Drew authorship began to unravel. "It took half a century, a major court case, and tireless investigating by avid book collectors to discover the truth about Nancy Drew's author," Karen Plunkett-Powell wrote. Nancy's first, real author kept the secret because that's what her contract insisted she do. Even Library of Congress records hid the real identity of Carolyn Keene. There was a court case, however, in 1979–80 when Adams decided to change publishers. In the course of the lawsuit, Mildred Wirt Benson, in a letter to *Publishers Weekly* in 1986, emerged to claim authorship of the first books.

Benson's authorship of the Nancy Drews was suspected as early as 1940 but was not confirmed until the 1980 court case involving the publisher, Grosset & Dunlap. Still, the Adams myth persisted. In her 1986 article in *Publishers Weekly*, Benson wrote to set the record straight: "I turned out 50,000 word volumes that became instant best sellers. In 1930, without writing experience, Adams took over the business. But at the request of the publisher, I was kept on for many years as the sole writer of the Nancy Drews."

Mildred Augustine Wirt Benson

Mildred Augustine Wirt Benson, born July 10, 1905, in Ladora, Iowa, was the daughter of a doctor. She was the first woman to receive a master's degree from the University of Iowa's school of journalism. She graduated from journalism school and went to work in 1925 for the *Clinton Herald* in Iowa. She married Asa Alvin Wirt, who worked for the Associated Press. They had one child. Wirt died in 1947, and in 1950, Mildred married George A. Benson, a newspaper editor. He died in 1959. Her avocations include an interest in pre-Columbian archaeology and flying.

Benson became a newspaper columnist and court reporter, writing for many years her "On the Go" column for the *Toledo Blade* (Ohio), a paper she joined in 1944.

A year after Benson started her first newspaper job at the *Clinton Herald*, Christina Mierau wrote in *Mystery Scene*, "A newspaper advertisement offering the opportunity to write children's books led her to New York City, where she would meet a man who would dramatically alter her life."

In 1926, Benson signed on to ghostwrite a Ruth Fielding book for Edward Stratemeyer. She was paid $125. The book appeared under the pseudonym Alice B. Emerson. Sent an outline for the first Nancy Drew (the series that became Nancy Drew Mysteries), Benson said she changed the "namby-pamby, Pollyanna-type" heroine into a more athletic and independent girl detective. Stratemeyer thought Nancy was overly flip and bossy, but the publisher (Grosset & Dunlap) was delighted with the character and ordered more.

"America's blond-haired, blue-eyed, lock-picking dynamo instantly captured readers' hearts when the first title in the series, *The Secret of the Old Clock*, was released in 1930," Plunkett-Powell said. "And why not? Unlike the majority of her rather prim, Victorian predecessors, Nancy burst onto the scene early in the Great Depression as a courageous, intelligent, and inspiring heroine. With an unlimited supply of luck, this Gothic Girl Scout could do anything, while her father, the illustrious Carson Drew, provided a steady stream of emotional support (and spending money) to aid her noble pursuits."

After writing the first seven Nancy Drew books, Benson left Stratemeyer when the syndicate attempted to reduce her payment to $75 per book. She began her own series books, producing seventeen Penny Parker mysteries. Eventually she returned to the syndicate to write sixteen more Nancy Drews.

"Mildred Wirt Benson's career as a writer of juvenile fiction spanned thirty-two years and produced a body of work in excess of 120 complete novels for young readers," said Mierau.

Nancy Drew books written in the 1930s and 1940s eventually became dated. As Adams said in *TV Guide*, "Over a period of years it has been necessary for me to revise and even completely rewrite the early volumes. In 1930 and for several years thereafter, I was kept busy acceding to the wishes of many ethnic groups who requested the removal of their own dialects from these stories.

"Then there have been changes in customs and laws that require a new *modus operandi* in the stories. There are no more running boards on cars. . . . Gone are Nancy Drew's little blue roadster and the Hardy Boys' sports cars and convertibles. For today's readers, they must drive a closed 1977 model with perhaps a sunroof."

All the early novels have been rewritten to update the details, but Nancy's spunk remains unchanged. For example, the 1931 version of *The Secret at Shadow Ranch* finds Nancy and her chums Bess Martin and George Fayne summering at Bess's uncle's Shadow Ranch in Arizona. There are a number of adventures, and Nancy, carrying a pistol, uses the weapon to discourage a large lynx that menaces the young women.

"Nancy caught a glimpse of the prowling lynx. Taking aim, she fired.

"The bullet struck the animal in the shoulder. It snarled and turned, ready to spring.

"Her heart in her throat, for she realized that she must not fail, Nancy fired once more.

"As the bullet found its mark, there was a terrible crashing and smashing in the underbrush, and then all was quiet."

The chief mystery is the identity of the young girl in the care of the gruff Martha Shaw at a neighboring ranch. Martha's brother, Zany, has been in and out of trouble. Through Nancy's investigation, it is learned the girl was kidnapped from her home back East.

The Secret at Shadow Ranch, as substantially revised in 1965, still finds the three young women vacationing at an Arizona Ranch, but the mystery this time concerns a phantom horse and malicious damage by persons unknown. Local legend has it the ghost animal belonged to the romantic outlaw Dirk Valentine, killed many years ago at Shadow Ranch. Nancy suspects Valentine's treasure is hidden somewhere on the property. Their adventures include being trapped in a building toppled by a rock slide. Modern arms regulations preclude Nancy carrying a loaded firearm, this time out.

The Nancy Drew Files have a slightly older reader in mind than the original books; however, they still rely on plot formulas. Typically, in Casefile 95: *An Instinct for Trouble*, Nancy travels to Yellowstone National Park to help her boyfriend, Ned Nickerson. He is working with a college professor on marmot research. The puzzle: Who is sabotaging the expedition and trapping the marmots, which are valuable for sale as pets? Nancy's suspects include Professor Dan Trainey, whose project is running out of money; Ranger Jack Billings, who flirts with Nancy; and Gerald and Edith Turkower, who do not seem to be the tourists they claim to be.

What makes Nancy so popular? Plunkett-Powell suggested, "Unlike many other children's book heroines, whose personalities often border on the cartoonish, Nancy Drew is not a black-and-white character. . . . [Her] image has changed quite a bit through the decades. When fans describe what they remember most about Nancy, they are remembering a Nancy Drew of a particular era. Do you recall the sophisticated, golden-haired Nancy, age sixteen, who coolly raced about town in a snappy roadster protecting the interests of the idle rich? Or the eighteen-year-old sleuth of the 1950s, her hair slightly darkened and her convertible in fourth gear, venturing out into the world of international intrigue? Or the Nancy Drew of the 1980s, with reddish blond hair, behind the wheel of her Mustang, somewhat less spirited but more physically active?"

"Imitative authors saw the outlines of the pattern clearly enough: the one parent, two chums, one boyfriend, and comfortable middle-class girl sleuth soon became a standard figure in series fiction," said Anne Scott MacLeod. "Some authors stressed their heroines' independence, as Adams did, and most supplied the admiration that surrounds Nancy Drew like a cloud of sweet scent. Yet all of them overlooked or weakened important parts of the formula. The autonomy that was Nancy's without question, for example, and the single focus of the narratives were blurred in other series, though in retrospect, at least, both look like key elements in the Nancy Drew success."

In other words, Nancy Drew was an early feminist in young adult literature.

YOUNG ADULT FICTION

Nancy Drew Files

All books appear under the Carolyn Keene house name. The syndicate keeps the names of the authors secret.

1. *Secrets Can Kill* (1986)
A nighttime thief stalks the halls at Bedford High.

2. *Deadly Intent* (1986)
The lead guitarist of the hot group Bent Fender disappears just before a concert at Radio City Music Hall.

3. *Murder on Ice* (1986)
Nancy and Ned hope to rekindle their romance on the slopes—but run into deadly peril.

4. *Smile and Say Murder* (1986)
Nancy goes undercover at *Flash*, the country's top teen magazine.

5. *Hit and Run Holiday* (1986)
Nancy, Bess, and George go to Fort Lauderdale for a weekend of fun—and end up searching for a hit-and-run driver.

6. *White Water Terror* (1986)
Nancy, Ned, and George raft a wild Montana river.

7. *Deadly Doubles* (1987)
Nancy, George, and Bess, in Washington, D.C., get tangled in a case of mistaken identity at a tennis tournament.

8. *Two Points to Murder* (1987)
A practical joker terrorizes the Emerson College basketball team.

9. *False Moves* (1987)
A thief snatches the famous Raja diamond from a dancer's costume—on live national television.

10. *Buried Secrets* (1987)
Nancy saves young candidate Todd Harrington from a sniper's bullet.

11. *Heart of Danger* (1987)
Nancy helps Texas rancher Robert Reigert find his missing daughter, Catarina.

12. *Fatal Ransom* (1987)
Teen heir Hal Colson is kidnapped.

13. *Wings of Fear* (1987)
Nancy investigates a possible murder in Seattle.

14. *This Side of Evil* (1987)
In Montreal, Nancy matches wits with a master criminal.

15. *Trial by Fire* (1987)
Carson Drew is arrested on bribery charges.

16. *Never Say Die* (1987)
George Fayne may be in danger in an international bicycle race.

17. *Stay Tuned for Danger* (1987)
Nancy and Bess are extras on a popular television soap opera when the star receives nasty threats.

18. *Circle of Evil* (1988)
Nancy investigates a major jewel theft, but rookie cop John Ryan wants to get the credit.

19. *Sisters in Crime* (1988)
Susan Victors doubts that her sorority sister, Rina Charles, drowned accidentally.

20. *Very Deadly Years* (1988)
Bess ignores Nancy's advice and answers a romantic personals ad in the newspaper.

21. *Recipe for Murder* (1988)
Nancy and Ned enroll in an international cooking school to settle a bet. They find a body in the freezer.

22. *Fatal Attraction* (1988)
Newspaper publisher Frazier Carlton asks Nancy to check out his daughter's new boyfriend.

23. *Sinister Paradise* (1988)
Nancy looks for a millionaire's runaway daughter in Hawaii.

24. *'Til Death Do Us Part* (1988)
Turned down by Nancy, Ned asks Jessica Thorne to marry him.

25. *Rich and Dangerous* (1988)
Is someone out to poison Sarah Amberly for her money?

26. *Playing with Fire* (1988)
A priceless miniature portrait of Napoleon mysteriously explodes in Victory Airlines President Preston Talbot's vault.

27. *Most Likely to Die* (1988)
Cheerleader Wendy Harriman is not as popular as she thinks.

28. *The Black Widow* (1988)
Carson Drew takes Nancy on a cruise to Rio de Janeiro. A widow, Nina da Silva, becomes top suspect as a diamond thief.

29. *Pure Poison* (1988)
Gossip columnist Beverly Bishop is after Nancy's friend, Senator Marilyn Kilpatrick.

30. *Death by Design* (1988)
Nancy and Bess help a Chicago fashion designer who has been receiving death threats.

31. *Trouble in Tahiti* (1989)
Bree Gordon, in Tahiti, receives disturbing letters saying her movie-star mother's death was no accident.

32. *High Marks for Malice* (1989)
Nancy and Ned find skeletons in the closets at exclusive Basson College.

33. *Danger in Disguise* (1989)
Nancy helps Michael Mulvaney, a young builder who has broken the law.

34. *Vanishing Act* (1989)
Superstar Jesse Slade has been missing for three years—until Nancy spots a clue on a videotape of his last concert.

35. *Bad Medicine* (1989)
Nancy goes undercover at River Heights Hospital to help a young doctor blamed for a death.

36. *Over the Edge* (1989)
Nancy checks out a series of threats at Marva Phillips's Club High Adventure.

37. *Last Dance* (1989)
Nancy does some dangerous dancing when she meets a super-smooth deejay.

38. *The Final Scene* (1989)
Film star Brady Armstrong is in River Heights for the premiere of his new movie—and someone kidnaps Bess in his stead.

39. *The Suspect Next Door* (1989)
Nancy's neighbor, Nikki Masters, is a prime suspect when her boyfriend turns up dead.

40. *Shadow of a Doubt* (1989)
An anonymous letter sent to lawyer Carson Drew threatens to destroy his career.

41. *Something to Hide* (1989)
Nancy and Bess help Ned with a college marketing project, but someone laces their Spotless beauty cream with deadly poison.

42. *The Wrong Chemistry* (1989)
Someone is stealing from a top-secret experiment conducted by a visiting scientist at Emerson College.

43. *False Impressions* (1990)
An impostor uses Nancy's name to con wealthy townspeople out of thousands of dollars.

44. *Scent of Danger* (1990)
Nancy sets out to find who stole two civets from the River Heights Zoo, to use their musk to re-create a famous perfume.

45. *Out of Bounds* (1990)
Money is missing from the Touchdown restaurant, and blackmail may be involved.

46. *Win, Place or Die* (1990)
Nancy is in Louisville for the Kentucky Derby. Her job is to keep an eye on Pied Piper, a horse in which her father owns part interest.

47. *Flirting with Danger* (1990)
Ned and Nancy, in Southern California for friend Rachel's graduation, investigate when she is taken by a bizarre secret society.

48. *A Date with Deception* (1990)
Nancy's Aunt Eloise sponsors Soviet dancer Sasha Petrov at an international workshop in town. He takes an interest in Nancy. Then allegations of espionage begin.

49. *Portrait in Crime* (1990)
Bess's new friend, water-skiing instructor Tommy Gray, draws her into a sinister mystery. Who stole a painting from his mother's gallery?

50. *Deep Secrets* (1990)
Nancy searches for a wealthy executive's daughter missing at sea—sidetracking her from having to decide between new and old boyfriends, Sasha and Ned.

51. *A Model Crime* (1990)
Bess is a finalist in a popular teen magazine's Face of the Year contest, but someone begins a campaign of dirty tricks.

52. *Danger for Hire* (1990)
Who is setting up Hayward Security Company to take a fall?

53. *Trail of Lies* (1990)
Nancy and George join Carson Drew on a visit to Anchorage, Alaska, and uncover an ivory smuggling scheme.

54. *Cold as Ice* (1991)
Nancy, Bess, and George join Ned for a winter weekend of skiing, skating, sleigh riding—and a jewelry heist.

55. *Don't Look Twice* (1991)
The heroine is shocked to see Ned make a pass at Denise Mason, a cheerleader who bears a striking resemblance to Nancy. Then a kidnapper takes Denise—thinking she is Nancy.

56. *Make No Mistake* (1991)
Carson Drew's client Clayton Glover is killed. Nancy is resolute to find the truth.

57. *Into Thin Air* (1991)
With Nancy's help, private detective Mark Rubin hopes to solve a disappearance.

58. *Hot Pursuit* (1991)
Someone tries to murder rock and roller Ricky Angeles at the Virgin Islands resort where Nancy, Bess, and George are vacationing.

59. *High Risk* (1991)
Ned, an investigator for an insurance company, is convinced that Toby Foyle has filed a false injury claim. When Foyle turns up dead, Ned is a suspect.

60. *Poison Pen* (1991)
An unsigned letter to an advice column claims the writer is going to be murdered by her husband.

61. *Sweet Revenge* (1991)
Brock Sawyer, a television celebrity at the chocolate festival at Oakwood Inn, is poisoned.

62. *Easy Marks* (1991)
There is grade-changing computer fraud at Brewster Academy.

63. *Mixed Signals* (1991)
Anonymous threats have quarterback Randy Simpson running scared. Nancy has to solve the crime before the big homecoming game.

64. *The Wrong Track* (1991)
Posing as a reporter for a ski magazine, Nancy uncovers the clever culprit behind a cross-country double cross at a resort.

65. *Final Notes* (1991)
Nancy looks for country-western entertainer Curtis Taylor, who supposedly died in a car crash five years earlier.

66. *Tall, Dark and Deadly* (1992)
Freshman Ava Woods turns up missing after a date arranged by Campus Connections. Nancy and Bess go undercover to solve the case.

67. *Nobody's Business* (1992)
Ned's pal Andrew wants to turn Lakeside Inn into a hot rock club, but a series of sinister accidents may cancel the plan.

68. *Crosscurrents* (1992)
Threats are made against the staff of the National Aquarium in Baltimore.

69. *Running Scared* (1992)
George plans to run in a Chicago marathon against some of the country's best female athletes. When top runner Annette Lang receives death threats, Nancy steps in.

70. *Cutting Edge* (1992)
Nancy suspects sabotage when a top female skater takes a terrible fall at the National Figure Skating Championships in Chicago.

71. *Hot Tracks* (1992)
Bess's yellow Camaro is stolen. Nancy sniffs a conspiracy.

72. *Swiss Secrets* (Passport to Romance Trilogy) (1992)
Nancy, Bess, and George get caught up in a storm of romantic intrigue, family scandal, and blackmail in Switzerland.

73. *Rendezvous in Rome* (Passport to Romance Trilogy) (1992)
On a shopping spree in Rome, the three girls become the targets of cunning criminals.

74. *Greek Odyssey* (Passport to Romance Trilogy) (1992)
Nancy finds a testing ground for terrorists in Greece.

75. *A Talent for Murder* (1992)
A talent agency's top model is found dead.

76. *The Perfect Plot* (1992)
The former home of author Dorothea Burden is now a meeting place and museum for mystery buffs—and a crime scene when the writer's longtime editor is killed.

77. *Danger on Parade* (1992)
Nancy and Bess follow clues when a string of crimes threatens Mitchell's Department Store's star-studded Thanksgiving Day parade.

78. *Update on Crime* (1992)
Someone has it in for WRVH-TV anchorman Hal Taylor.

79. *No Laughing Matter* (1993)
The new comedy club's accountant has been jailed for embezzlement. Nancy wants to prove his innocence.

80. *Power of Suggestion* (1993)
Nancy and Bess visit Nick at college and help clear a fraternity brother who has been accused of murdering a research assistant.

81. *Making Waves* (1993)
Nancy is sure her friend Andy Devereux's boat will win the sailing regatta—but he is arrested for murder. Nancy has a case of missing money, missing boats, and missing bodies on her hands.

82. *Dangerous Relations* (1993)
Looking into the heritage of adopted trapeze artist Natalia Petronov, Nancy is convinced her life is in danger.

83. *Diamond Deceit* (1993)
Fading movie star Joanna Burton accuses a jeweler of replacing the diamonds in her necklace with fakes.

84. *Choosing Sides* (1993)
Small-time hood Bobby Rouse implicates mayoral candidate Caroline Hill. Nancy works to save her candidate's reputation.

85. *Sea of Suspicion* (1993)
Nancy suspects a setup when police charge Sean Mahoney, captain of the *Lady Jane*, in the death of a crew member.

86. *Let's Talk Terror* (1993)
Teen talk show host Marcy Robbins receives death threats.

87. *Moving Target* (1993)
A series of accidents plagues a three-day bike ride for Nancy and friends.

88. *False Pretenses* (1993)
Carson Drew is a suspect when a blackmailing member of his law firm is killed.

89. *Designs in Crime* (1993)
Nancy visits Beau Winston's New York fashion studio to figure out who is stealing his designs.

90. *Stage Fright* (1993)
A firebug threatens actress Evelyn Caldwell's attempts to transform a Connecticut barn into a big-time theater.

91. *If Looks Could Kill* (1994)
Crime strikes the Caribbean resort where supermodel Martika has opened Cloud Nine, her new health spa.

92. *My Deadly Valentine* (1994)
Someone is threatening Valentine's Day activities at Emerson College.

93. *Hotline to Danger* (1994)
Answering a call for a teen hotline, Nancy discovers the body of fellow volunteer Paul Remer.

94. *Illusions of Evil* (1994)
Someone is sabotaging Riverfront Amusement Park, which illusionist Adriana Plidori inherited after her uncle's tragic death.

95. *An Instinct for Trouble* (1994)
In Yellowstone National Park, Nancy helps Ned find out who has been stealing prized marmots to sell on the black market.

96. *The Runaway Bride* (1994)
Nancy is in Tokyo to attend the wedding of former exchange student Midori Kato—but the bride disappears!

97. *Squeeze Play* (1994)
Threats against his daughter hamper the playing abilities of Sean Reeves, a member of the River Heights Falcons.

98. *Isle of Secrets* (1994)
Nancy and friend Barb discover the body of fisherman Tom Haines off Block Island.

99. *The Cheating Heart* (1994)
Nancy's reunion with Ned at Emerson College turns sour when campus scandal erupts.

100. *Dance Till You Die* (1994)
Nancy dances with danger when Bess mysteriously disappears at the hottest club in town.

101. *The Picture of Guilt* (1994)
In Paris for Thanksgiving, Nancy investigates the death of an art researcher.

102. *Counterfeit Christmas* (1994)
Nancy traces funny money. A prime suspect is handsome Stuart Teal.

103. *Heart of Ice* (1995)
There is a campaign of terror against the Alpine Adventures guide service. Nancy must find the answer—at the top of Mount Rainier.

104. *Kiss and Tell* (1995)
Rumors swirl when best-selling romance author Esme Moore comes to River Heights.

105. *Stolen Affections* (1995)
Nancy and detective Sam Farelli investigate the kidnapping of an eight-year-old.

106. *Flying High* (1995)
Naval flight trainee Jill Perker dies in a fiery crash at Florida's Davis Field. Evidence points to sabotage.

107. *Anything for Love* (1995)
Off-camera action heats up on the set of a top-rated soap opera, *Love and Loss*.

108. *Captive Heart* (1995)
Nancy goes to Belize on holiday to visit Ned, but tensions arise between them—and hijackers appear.

109. *Love Notes* (1995)
Competitors are dropping out of a classical music festival in the Berkshires.

110. *Hidden Meaning* (1995)
There's sabotage at the Great Lakes High School Press Association convention.

111. *The Stolen Kiss* (1995)
A painting disappears from a museum.

Nancy Drew–Hardy Boys Super Sleuth Mysteries

All books appear under the Carolyn Keene and Franklin W. Dixon house names. The syndicate keeps the names of the authors secret.

1. *Double Crossing* (1988)
On a cruise ship, the Hardys are undercover, tracking thieves. Nancy, also on board, overhears a plot to sell CIA secrets.

2. *A Crime for Christmas* (1988)
The trio teams to pursue a pair of big-time cat burglars.

3. *Shock Waves* (1990)
A body is found in a sunken wreck off Padre Island, on the Gulf Coast.

4. *Dangerous Games* (1990)
Black Knight wants to disrupt the International Championship Games in California.

5. *The Last Resort: A Nancy Drew and Hardy Boys Supermystery* (1990)
The heroes work security at a posh winter paradise where a rock star is shooting a video. A music mogul is found murdered.

6. *The Paris Connection* (1990)
The investigators cross paths in Paris and find that their cases are connected.

7. *Buried in Time* (1991)
Frank and Joe trace a hijacked Air Force shipment. Nancy investigates a series of thefts at an archaeological dig. Both puzzles lead to an old Indian grave.

8. *Mystery Train* (1991)
The Drew-Hardy team cracks the mystery of the stolen Comstock diamond.

9. *Best of Enemies* (1991)
The Hardys are on a top-secret mission involving an American spy. Nancy Drew assists Beau Davis, the prime suspect in the murder of the Hardys' contact man.

10. *High Survival* (1991)
Nancy suspects that accidents on a survival trek in Wyoming are not accidents. The Hardys help investigate.

11. *New Year's Evil* (1991)
Frank and Joe are attending a winter carnival to see the auto ice racing. Nancy is looking into sabotage on a Quebec television location. All three join to find a killer.

12. *Tour of Danger* (1992)
Frank and Joe work undercover for an electronics conglomerate. Nancy's Japanese vacation is disrupted when she sees a woman falsely accused of smuggling.

13. *Spies and Lies* (1992)
The Hardys pose as trainees to expose a corrupt FBI agent. Nancy works undercover to protect Judy Noll, FBI trainee and daughter of a senator.

14. *Tropic of Fear* (1992)
Frank and Joe infiltrate a gang of art thieves. Vacationing in Hawaii, Nancy finds a murdered man.

15. *Courting Disaster* (1993)
Frank and Joe protect tennis superstar Pat Flynn from an unknown assailant. Nancy is backstage when television veejay Terry Alford's life is jeopardized.

16. *Hits and Misses* (1993)
Frank and Joe dig into dirty business to help hot new singer Angelique. Bess has a chance at a nationally televised talent show, creating a big mystery for Nancy.

17. *Evil in Amsterdam* (1993)
The Hardys search for a cache of gold bullion. Nancy and George try to find their missing friend, Merissa, in Holland.

18. *Desperate Measures* (1994)
Nancy helps friend Molly Keegan look for her missing father, a scientist for Tercon Industries. The Hardys are also investigating the company.

19. *Passport to Danger* (1994)
The Hardys track down a stolen Maya jade mask. Nancy is in Mexico to help Helen and David Oberman avert a counterfeiting scandal at their art school.

20. *Hollywood Horror* (1994)
Frank and Joe check out sabotage at a high-tech theme park. Danger steals the show when Nancy is on the set of the sitcom *Sunny-Side Up*.

21. *Copper Canyon Conspiracy* (1994)
The detectives investigate death threats against marathon runners.

22. *Danger Down Under* (1995)
Nellie Mabo, an Australian aborigine, discovers that a tribal artifact is missing.

23. *Dead on Arrival* (1995)
The three check out illegal body-parts trafficking in River Heights.

24. *Target for Terror* (1995)
A terrorist lures the trio to a San Francisco college campus.

25. *Secrets of the Nile* (1995)

Nancy Drew on Campus Series

All books appear under the Carolyn Keene house name. The syndicate keeps the names of the authors secret.

1. *New Lives, New Loves* (1995)
There's a series of thefts at the co-ed dorm where Nancy, Bess, and George live at Wilder University.

2. *On Her Own* (1995)
Nancy calls it quits with longtime boyfriend Ned Nickerson.

3. *Don't Look Back* (1995)
Television star Casey Fontaine has enrolled at Wilder University.

4. *Tell Me the Truth* (1995)

5. *Secret Rules* (1996)

River Heights Series

All books appear under the Carolyn Keene house name. The syndicate keeps the names of the authors secret.

1. *Love Times Three* (1989)
Nikki Masters has beauty, brains, and talent—and a murder charge against her—until her River Heights neighbor and amateur detective Nancy Drew clears it up.

2. *Guilty Secrets* (1989)
Will Tim's hidden past come between him and Nikki? What will Brittany Tate's next move be?

3. *Going Too Far* (1990)
Dark-haired Brittany cannot believe she is dating college man Jack Reilly.

4. *Stolen Kisses* (1990)
Brittany's romance with Jack is getting too hot to handle, so she decides to date another boy.

5. *Between the Lines* (1990)
   Nikki and Tim are romantic leads in the school production of *Our Town*. Are they a case of life imitating art?

6. *Lessons in Love* (1990)
   Samantha Daley is bored silly by all the guys at River Heights High—except Monsieur le Blanc, the substitute French teacher.

7. *Cheating Hearts* (1990)
   If Karen Jacobs breaks the story about a cheating ring at River Heights High, she is sure to be picked as editor-in-chief the next year; but if she covers it up, she might win the heart of junior class president Ben Newhouse.

8. *The Trouble with Love* (1990)
   Dating Ben is a dream come true for Karen—but is he still dreaming of his old girlfriend?

9. *Lies and Whispers* (1991)
   Brittany plans to snare the perfect boyfriend, Chip Worthington, a senior at Talbot School.

10. *Mixed Emotions* (1991)
    Nikki learns that Niles's British girlfriend is coming to America, and Karen contends with Ben's ex, model Emily Van Patten.

11. *Broken Hearts* (1991)
    Niles's girlfriend, Gillian, a classical violinist, is cool, classy, and sophisticated, and Nikki is tired of playing second fiddle.

12. *Hard to Handle* (1991)
    Rich is coming back to school. But he is not coming back to Lacey.

(unnumbered).
River Heights Super Sizzler: Junior Class Trip (1991)
The junior class trip to Washington, D.C., means Nikki can spend time alone with Tim. Brittany, however, is looking for exciting new guys such as Tom Connors, the mysterious college student.

13. *A Mind of Her Own* (1991)
    Lacey has not told her old boyfriend, Rick, that she is seeing his brother, Tom.

14. *Love and Games* (1992)
    The junior class agrees to let Kyle Kirkwood and his computer mix and match couples for the class luau, but Kyle's girlfriend, Samantha, is determined to be his partner—no matter what it takes.

15. *Friends and Rivals* (1992)
    Brittany and Samantha vie for the last spot on the new school television show.

16. *The Jealousy Trap* (1992)
    With Lacey spending all her time with Tom, Robin starts hanging out with Katie Fox—who becomes her top rival in a swim meet.

FICTION FOR MIDDLE READERS

Dana Girls Series

All books appear under the Carolyn Keene house name. The syndicate keeps the names of the authors secret. Older titles can still be found in libraries.

By the Light of the Study Lamp (1934)

The Secret at Lone Tree Cottage (1934)

In the Shadow of the Tower (1934)

A Three-Cornered Mystery (1935)

The Secret at the Hermitage (1936)

The Circle of Footprints (1937)

The Mystery of the Locked Room (1938)

The Clue in the Cobweb (1939)

The Secret at the Gatehouse (1940)

The Mysterious Fireplace (1941)

The Clue of the Rusty Key (1942)

The Portrait in the Sand (1943)

The Secret in the Old Well (1944)

The Clue in the Ivy (1952)

The Secret of the Jade Ring (1953)

The Mystery at the Crossroads (1954)

The Ghost in the Gallery (1955)

The Clue of the Black Flower (1956)

The Winking Ruby Mystery (1957, 1974)

The Secret of the Swiss Chalet (1958, 1973)

The Haunted Lagoon (1959, 1973)

The Mystery of the Bamboo Bird (1960, 1973)

The Sierra Gold Mystery (1961, 1973)

The Secret of Lost Lake (1963, 1973)

The Mystery of the Stone Tiger (1963, 1972)

The Riddle of the Frozen Fountain (1964, 1972)

The Secret of the Silver Dolphin (1965, 1972)

The Mystery of the Wax Queen (1966, 1972)

The Secret of the Minstrel's Guitar (1967, 1972)

The Phantom Surfer (1968, 1972)

The Curious Coronation (1976)

The Hundred-Year Mystery (1977)

The Mountain Peak Mystery (1978)

The Witch's Omen (1979)

Original Nancy Drew Mysteries

All books appear under the Carolyn Keene house name. The syndicate keeps the names of the authors secret. Older titles can still be found in libraries.

1. *The Secret of the Old Clock* (1930, 1959)
2. *The Hidden Staircase* (1930, 1959)
3. *The Bungalow Mystery* (1930, 1960)
4. *The Mystery at Lilac Inn* (1930, 1961)
5. *The Secret of Shadow Ranch* (1931, 1965)
6. *The Secret of Red Gate Farm* (1931, 1961)
7. *The Clue in the Diary* (1932, 1962)
8. *Nancy's Mysterious Letter* (1932, 1968)
9. *The Sign of the Twisted Candles* (1933, 1968)
10. *The Password to Larkspur Lane* (1933, 1966)
11. *The Clue of the Broken Locket* (1934, 1965)
12. *The Message in the Hollow Oak* (1935, 1972)
13. *The Mystery of the Ivory Charm* (1936, 1974)
14. *The Whispering Statue* (1937, 1970)
15. *The Haunted Bridge* (1937, 1972)
16. *The Clue of the Tapping Heels* (1939, 1969)
17. *The Mystery of the Brass-Bound Trunk* (1940, 1976)
18. *The Mystery at the Moss-Covered Mansion* (1941, 1971)
19. *The Quest of the Missing Map* (1942, 1969)
20. *The Clue in the Jewel Box* (1943, 1972)
21. *The Secret in the Old Attic* (1944, 1970)
22. *The Clue in the Crumbling Wall* (1945, 1973)
23. *The Mystery of the Tolling Bell* (1946, 1973)
24. *The Clue in the Old Album* (1947, 1977)
25. *The Ghost of Blackwood Hall* (1948, 1967)
26. *The Clue of the Leaning Chimney* (1949, 1967)
27. *The Secret of the Wooden Lady* (1950, 1967)
28. *The Clue of the Black Keys* (1951, 1968)
29. *The Mystery at the Ski Jump* (1952, 1968)
30. *The Clue of the Velvet Mask* (1953, 1969)
31. *The Ringmaster's Secret* (1953, 1974)
32. *The Scarlet Slipper Mystery* (1954, 1974)
33. *The Witch Tree Symbol* (1955, 1975)
34. *The Hidden Window Mystery* (1957, 1975)
35. *The Haunted Showboat* (1958, 1975)
36. *The Secret of the Golden Pavilion* (1959)
37. *The Clue in the Old Stagecoach* (1960)
38. *The Mystery of the Fire Dragon* (1961)
39. *The Clue of the Dancing Puppet* (1962)
40. *The Moonstone Castle Mystery* (1963)
41. *The Clue of the Whistling Bagpipes* (1964)
42. *The Phantom of Pine Hill* (1965)
43. *The Mystery of the Ninety-Nine Steps* (1967)
44. *The Clue in the Crossword Cipher* (1968)
45. *The Spider Sapphire Mystery* (1969)
46. *The Invisible Intruder* (1970)
47. *The Mysterious Mannequin* (1971)
48. *The Crooked Banister* (1972)
49. *The Secret of Mirror Bay* (1973)
50. *The Double Jinx Mystery* (1974)
51. *The Mystery of the Glowing Eye* (1975)
52. *The Secret of the Forgotten City* (1975)

53. *The Sky Phantom* (1976)
54. *The Strange Message in the Parchment* (1977)
55. *The Mystery of Crocodile Island* (1978)
56. *The Thirteenth Pearl* (1979)
57. *The Triple Hoax* (1979)
58. *The Flying Saucer Mystery* (1980)
59. *The Secret in the Old Lace* (1980)
60. *The Greek Symbol Mystery* (1981)
61. *The Swami's Ring* (1981)
62. *The Kachina Doll Mystery* (1981)
63. *The Twin Dilemma* (1981)
64. *The Captive Witness* (1981)
65. *Mystery of the Winged Lion* (1982)
66. *Race Against Time* (1982)
67. *The Sinister Omen* (1982)
68. *The Elusive Heiress* (1982)
69. *The Clue in the Ancient Disguise* (1982)
70. *The Broken Anchor* (1983)
71. *The Silver Cobweb* (1983)
72. *The Haunted Carousel* (1983)
73. *Enemy Match* (1984)
74. *The Mysterious Image* (1984)
75. *The Emerald-Eyed Cat* (1984)
76. *The Eskimo's Secret* (1985)
77. *The Bluebeard Room* (1985)
78. *The Ghost in the Gondola* (1985)
79. *The Double Horror of Fenley Place* (1987)
80. *The Case of the Disappearing Diamonds* (1987)
81. *The Mardi Gras Mystery* (1988)
82. *The Clue in the Camera* (1988)
83. *The Case of the Vanishing Veil* (1988)
84. *The Joker's Revenge* (1988)
85. *The Secret of the Shady Glen* (1988)
86. *The Mystery of Misty Canyon* (1988)
87. *The Case of the Rising Stars* (1988)
88. *The Search for Cindy Austin* (1988)
89. *The Case of the Disappearing Deejay* (1989)
90. *The Puzzle at Pineview School* (1989)
91. *The Girl Who Couldn't Remember* (1989)
92. *The Ghost of Craven Cove* (1989)
93. *The Case of the Safecracker's Secret* (1990)
94. *The Picture-Perfect Mystery* (1990)
95. *The Silent Suspect* (1990)
96. *The Case of the Photo Finish* (1990)
97. *The Mystery at Magnolia Mansion* (1990)
98. *The Haunting of Horse Island* (1990)
99. *The Secret of Seven Rocks* (1991)
100. *A Secret in Time: Nancy Drew's 100th Anniversary Edition* (1991)
101. *The Mystery of the Missing Millionairess* (1991)
102. *A Secret in the Dark* (1991)
103. *The Stranger in the Shadows* (1991)
104. *The Mystery of the Jade Tiger* (1991)
105. *The Clue in the Antique Trunk* (1992)
106. *The Case of the Artful Crime* (1992)
107. *The Legend of Miner's Creek* (1992)
108. *The Secret of the Tibetan Treasure* (1992)
109. *The Mystery of the Masked Rider* (1992)
110. *The Nutcracker Ballet Mystery* (1992)
111. *The Secret at Solaire* (1993)
112. *Crime in the Queen's Court* (1993)
113. *The Secret Lost at Sea* (1993)
114. *The Search for the Silver Persian* (1993)
115. *The Suspect in the Smoke* (1993)
116. *The Case of the Twin Teddy Bears* (1993)
117. *Mystery on the Menu* (1994)
118. *Trouble at Lake Tahoe* (1994)
119. *The Mystery of the Missing Mascot* (1994)
120. *The Case of the Floating Crime* (1994)
121. *The Fortune Teller's Secret* (1994)
122. *The Message from the Haunted Mansion* (1994)
123. *The Clue on the Silver Screen* (1995)
124. *The Secret of the Scarlet Hand* (1995)

125. *The Teen Model Mystery* (1995)
126. *The Riddle in the Rare Book* (1995)

The Nancy Drew Sleuth Book: Clues to Good Sleuthing (1969)

The Nancy Drew Cookbook (1973)

Nancy Drew Secret Codes by Evan Morley (1977)

Nancy Drew & Hardy Boys Super Sleuths 1 (1982)

The Nancy Drew Ghost Stories, edited by Meg Schneider (1983)

Nancy Drew & Hardy Boys Super Sleuths 2 (1984)

The Nancy Drew Ghost Stories II, edited by Diane Arico (1985)

Nancy Drew & Hardy Boys Camp Fire Stories (1984)

Nancy Drew and Hardy Boys Be a Detective Mystery Stories

All books appear under the Carolyn Keene and Franklin W. Dixon house names. The syndicate keeps the names of the authors secret.

1. *The Secret of the Knight's Sword* (1984)
2. *Danger on Ice* (1984)
3. *The Feathered Serpent* (1984)
4. *Secret Cargo* (1984)
5. *The Alaskan Mystery* (1985)
6. *The Missing Money Mystery* (1985)
7. *Jungle of Evil* (1985)
8. *Ticket to Intrigue* (1985)

Nancy Drew Notebooks

All books appear under the Carolyn Keene house name. The syndicate keeps the names of the authors secret.

1. *The Slumber Party Secret* (1994)
2. *The Lost Locket* (1994)
3. *The Secret Santa* (1994)
4. *Bad Days for Ballet* (1995)
5. *The Soccer Shoe Clue* (1995)
6. *The Ice Cream Scoop* (1995)
7. *Trouble at Camp Treehouse* (1995)
8. *The Best Detective* (1995)
9. *The Thanksgiving Surprise* (1995)

ADAPTATIONS IN OTHER MEDIA

Nancy Drew, Detective (1938)
Film with Bonita Granville.

Nancy Drew—Reporter (1939)
Film with Bonita Granville.

Nancy Drew—Trouble Shooter (1939)
Film with Bonita Granville.

Nancy Drew and the Hidden Staircase (1939)
Film with Bonita Granville, based on the book *The Hidden Staircase*.

The Hardy Boys/Nancy Drew Mysteries (1977–79)
Television series starring Pamela Sue Martin and, later, Janet Louise Johnson as Nancy Drew.

Nancy Drew (1995)
Television series starring Tracy Ryan and Scott Speedman.

FOR FURTHER READING

Adams, Harriet. "Their Success Is No Mystery." *TV Guide*, 25 June 1977.

"Author Harriet Adams Dies at 89; Wrote Nancy Drew, Other Stories." *The Berkshire Eagle*, 29 March 1982.

Basler, Barbara. "A Sleuth's Newest Venture: Romance Edges Out Mystery As Simon & Schuster Woos Young Adults." *The New York Times*, 26 October 1986.

Bendor, Karen. "Looking Out for Nancy Drew." *Country Accents Collectibles*, fall 1995.

Benson, Mildred Wirt. Letter to the editor. *Publishers Weekly*, 26 September 1986.

Billman, Carol. *The Secret of the Stratemeyer Syndicate: Nancy Drew, the Hardy Boys, and the Million-Dollar Fiction Factory*. New York: Frederick Ungar, 1986.

Conklin, Doris. "A Critical Glance at Nancy Drew." *The Match*, July–August 1972.

Dyer, Carolyn Stewart, and Nancy Tillman Romatov, eds. *Rediscovering Nancy Drew.* Iowa City: University of Iowa Press, 1995.

Enright, John M. "Nancy Drew in Review." *Mystery & Adventure Series Review*, winter 1981.

———. "Series Subjects" (Dana Girls). *Mystery & Adventure Series Review*, spring 1991.

———. "TV's Nancy Drew." *Mystery & Adventure Series Review*, winter 1981.

Girls Series Books: A Checklist of Hardback Books Published 1900–1975. Minneapolis: Children's Literature Research Collections, University of Minnesota Libraries, 1978.

Hand, Judson. "Frank, Joe & Nancy Still Wow the Kids." *New York Sunday News*, 23 January 1977.

Hellmich, Nanci. "The Case of the Updated Detective." *USA Today*, 24 July 1986.

———. "Will Ned Fit in College Life of Nancy Drew?" *USA Today*, 11 August 1995.

Johnson, Mary Ellen, and Bernadine Chapman. "Nancy Drew Collectibles." *Antiques Journal*, July 1975.

Jordan, Charles J. "Tom Swift and the Hardcover Heroes." *Collectibles Illustrated*, May–June 1982.

Kovanis, Georgea. "Nancy Drew Stories Get Update as Sleuth Heads Off to College." *Hartford Courant*, 24 September 1995.

Lapin, Geoffrey S. "Carolyn Keene, Pseud." *Yellowback Library*, March–April 1984.

MacLeod, Anne Scott. "Nancy Drew and Her Rivals: No Contest." Part 1. *Horn Book Magazine*, May–June 1987.

———. "Nancy Drew and Her Rivals: No Contest." Part 2. *Horn Book Magazine*, July–August 1987.

Mierau, Christina. "Much Ado About Nancy Drew." *Mystery Scene*, July 1993.

"Nancy Drew: The Eternal Teen-ager." *Newsweek*, 26 March 1984.

Plunkett-Powell, Karen. *The Nancy Drew Scrapbook: 60 Years of America's Favorite Teenage Sleuth.* New York: St. Martin's Press, 1993.

Praeger, Arthur. "Edward Stratemeyer and His Book Machine." *Saturday Review*, 10 July 1971.

———. *Rascals at Large; or, The Clue in the Old Nostalgia*. New York: Doubleday, 1971.

Soderbergh, Peter A. "Your Favorite (Unknown) Author." *Modern Maturity*, June–July 1975.

Williams, Donna Kay. "That Drew Girl! Gumshoes in Bobby Socks." *Boston Phoenix*, 2 December 1980.

Winslow, Kent. "The Critic's Clew . . . to Miss Drew." *Mystery & Adventure Series Review*, winter 1981.

Woods, Brenda. "Goody Goody Gumshoe: Kids Still Find Nancy Drew 'Tough to Put Down.' " *New York Daily News*, 13 April 1980.

"Writer Says She Created Nancy Drew." *Mystery & Adventure Series Review*, summer 1982.

M. E. Kerr

Teenage drama

Auburn, New York
May 27, 1927

Dinky Hocker Shoots Smack!

Kids have written M. E. Kerr to tell her what they think of her work. One said that her name on a book means that "half the time they're good." Another said his English class was forced to read her books.

"What more could a writer ask for than a captive audience?" Kerr asked, relating the anecdote in her autobiography, *Me, Me, Me, Me, Me*.

Kerr, whose real name is Marijane Agnes Meaker, was inspired to become a writer by both her parents. Her father, Ellis R. Meaker, who owned Ivanhoe Foods, a major producer of mayonnaise, was an avid reader of the classics. As a teenager, Kerr wrote stories using the pen name Eric Ranthram McKay, which had the same initials as her father's name. Her mother, who came from a German immigrant background, gave the budding writer a sense of drama in storytelling and an appreciation of ethnic and economic differences in people.

Kerr attended Vermont Junior College, where she edited the school newspaper. Her first short story was published there: "The Air and I," about flying lessons. She later transferred to the University of Missouri and received a bachelor of arts degree there in 1949. Moving to New York City, she landed a job as an assistant with E. P. Dutton Publishing and continued writing in her spare time. She held several other jobs, including one with Fawcett Publications. When *Ladies' Home Journal* paid her $750 for a story she submitted under the name Laura Winston, Kerr was more determined than ever to become a full-time writer.

Fawcett published several novels by Kerr, issuing them under its Gold Medal imprint, beginning in 1952, under the name Vin

Packer. The name, of indistinguishable gender, was considered an advantage to a woman writer because men were not seen as likely to buy books by women. "Even in the '60's, when I did a nonfiction book on suicide for Doubleday, called *Sudden Endings*, my editor suggested that I call myself M. J. Meaker, instead of Marijane Meaker. 'Marijane,' she said, 'isn't right for a book on suicide.' While I did do a few novels under my real name, I always felt better when I 'named my pen,' " Kerr stated in *Me, Me, Me, Me, Me*.

"Gold Medal was in fact the first paperback series to release really important original work," Piet Schreuders said, and Vin Packer was among its first writers. Lee Server wrote that the Packer book *Spring Fire* "was erotic fiction with a new twist for the mass market: a relatively sincere, realistic account of a lesbian relationship." The book sold several million copies and enabled Kerr to become a full-time writer. The unexpected popularity of the book with lesbian readers prompted a second line of books under the Ann Aldrich name and featuring lesbian characters.

The writer explained how she switched to writing for younger readers. "Long before I ever wrote books for young adults, I wrote suspense and murder novels," Kerr said in *Me, Me, Me, Me, Me*. "I was friends with the writer Louise Fitzhugh, who longed to write murder and suspense novels. She thought I ought to write for young adults as she did. We used to laugh about it, and wonder if we traded typewriters we could perhaps each do the kind of books the other was doing.

"We used to swap stories and discuss ideas, and when she wrote her first book for young people, called *Harriet the Spy*, I said, 'Hey, wait a minute! That's my story! I told you I was Marijane the Spy, and you stole that idea from me!' Louise said all kids are spies when they're little. She was and I was . . . and she just beat me to the punch and told the story first.

" 'You'd better get going on a YA book before I beat you to the punch again,' she said.

"I think she's definitely one of the reasons I got going."

Kerr's experiences as a volunteer at a high school in New York City provided the background for her first young adult effort. It was *Dinky Hocker Shoots Smack!* and it came out under yet another pen name, M. E. Kerr. (If you say it fast enough, it gives away the writer's real last name.)

"In my books for young adults," she explained in *Me, Me, Me, Me, Me*, "I updated everything that happened to me in my teens, to make my stories more contemporary, probably not trusting the idea I could interest today's kids in yesterday's happenings. . . .

"I think that whenever you find a little smart-mouth, tomboy kid in any of my books, you have found me from long ago, but Dinky Hocker and Brenda Belle Blossom, in particular, were so me I hardly had to think up their lines."

"This novel from the wave of provocative young adult titles of the 1970s holds up very well," in the view of Eden Ross Lipson. "The adolescent issues are timeless, and the dialogue remains sharp and funny."

"Kerr thinks funny, sees funny, hears funny, and writes funny, but the concerns of her characters are real enough to most teenagers—how to break free from parental guidance and misguidance," reviewer Janet P. Benestad observed.

The success of the book decided a new writing direction for Kerr. About this time, in 1972, she moved to East Hampton, Long Island, which soon became Seaview, the setting for several of her novels, including *Gentlehands*.

Gentlehands, Kerr said, was one of the easiest books for her to write. It is about teenager Buddy Boyle, a resident of the unfashionable town of Seaview. He lives in a cramped house on the bay with his father, a policeman, his mother, and his young brother, Streaker. Buddy's dad opposes his going out with Skye Pennington, whose wealthy family is spending the summer at a nearby estate, but Buddy has fallen in love. As he falls under Skye's spell, he grows disobedient and irresponsible at home and at his job. Then he finds refuge with his Grandpa Trenker, who treats the couple in a sophisticated fashion, talking about wines and opera.

Buddy learns things he is unable to learn from his parents. " 'Confidence isn't something you're born with, Buddy,' " his grandfather tells him, " 'and it isn't something that comes down on you one day like the rain. You get it for yourself, gradually, willfully, and it's the best gift you can give yourself.' "

Buddy's mother is estranged from Grandpa Trenker, her father, who never took part in her rearing. A German, he has come to this country to retire. Grandpa falls under suspicion when a Nazi-hunting Jewish journalist discovers where he is living. Buddy does not want to believe that his grandfather could have been a war criminal called Gentlehands. The unraveling of his belief in his grandfather, of his loyalty, and of his desire to be something he is not intertwine and change Buddy's life.

"I was interested in the idea that as Pogo used to say, 'the enemy is us.' I was interested that the Nazis, our great enemies in World War II, were probably not a great deal different from some of us in Vietnam," Kerr told interviewer Jim Roginski. "We know the soldiers as family men and the enemy knows them in quite a different way. I got caught up in the idea of what is evil. I wanted to provoke the idea of what if you meet a nice guy, a really nice man, and what if you find out that in his past he wasn't such a nice man? How would you feel? How would you feel about him in your family? That was how it started."

"I hope I can woo young adults away from the boob tube, not just with entertaining stories, but also with subject matter which will provoke concern and a questioning about this complicated and often unfair world we live in," Kerr said in *Literature for Today's Young Adults*.

"Kerr is an excellent contemporary writer with an ear for dialogue that makes all the characters of every age and social class thoroughly believable," said Michele Landsberg.

Is That You, Miss Blue? is about a religious mystic who teaches at a private girls' school. She gradually loses her sanity but makes a new friend in young Flanders, fifteen. "This is a sophisticated book," said Zena Sutherland, "one that demands understanding from its readers and can, at the same time, lead them toward understanding. There are some acid portraits: the arrogant head of the school, the lesbian teachers who bicker with each other, and some scheming classmates, but they are shrewd and convincing portraits, and the book evokes with remarkable conviction the closed world of a private girls' school."

Kerr has often written about the children of religious leaders. She noted in *Me, Me, Me, Me, Me,* "My interest in preachers' kids probably started when I roomed with Kay Walters, the first P. K. I ever really knew.

"Preachers' kids figure in *Is That You, Miss Blue?* and are the main characters in *What I Really Think of You.*

"In my book *Little Little,* a young evangelist preacher is featured who is also a dwarf, and the grandfather of the main character is a preacher.

"While I came from a religious background (with one aunt who was a Roman Catholic nun) and attended an Episcopal boarding school, I always seemed to have a quarrel with organized religion.

"I suppose the reason was simply that I always had a quarrel with authority of any kind."

YOUNG ADULT FICTION

Dinky Hocker Shoots Smack! (1972)
An overweight girl goes to extremes to win her parents' attention.

If I Love You, Am I Trapped Forever? (1973)
How could cool Alan Bennett lose his girl to balding, antisocial, anti-sports Duncan Stein?

The Son of Someone Famous (1974)
Adam Blessing, son of a diplomat, goes to live with his Uncle Charlie in Vermont and befriends a local girl who feels as much an outcast as he does.

Is That You, Miss Blue? (1975)
Deeply religious Miss Blue is nudged toward insanity by her students at a boarding school.

Love Is a Missing Person (1975)
Suzy, fifteen, observes that love has its effect on everyone else: her father, who ran off with a chorus girl; her sister, Chicago, who rides a motorcycle; the librarian who pines for the lover who left her during World War II; and her friend, Nan, whose boyfriend, Roger, has taken up with Chicago.

I'll Love You When You're More Like Me (1977)
Wally Witherspoon does not want to be an undertaker like his father. He meets Sabra St. Amour, who does not want to be written out of the television soap opera in which she appears.

Gentlehands (1978)
Buddy Boyle's infatuation with well-to-do Skye Pennington is jarred by his grandfather's exposure as a Nazi war criminal.

Little Little (1981)
Little Little and Sydney Cinnamon are teenage dwarfs.

What I Really Think of You (1982)
Opal is ashamed of her parents: her father, who preaches the Rapture, and her mother, who speaks in tongues.

Him She Loves? (1984)
Henry Schiller, seventeen, has the misfortune to fall in love with Valerie Kissenwise, the beautiful but spoiled daughter of a famous comedian.

I Stay Near You (1985)
A ring bearing these four words has a powerful effect on several generations.

Night Kites (1986)
Erick Rudd, who is falling in love with his best friend's girl, is shattered by the discovery that his older brother has AIDS.

Linger (1993)
What is the secret of Linger, the restaurant in which Gary Peel's brother, Bobby, now a soldier in the Gulf War, swore he would never again set foot?

Deliver Us from Evie (1994)
Farm boy Parr Burrman is used to hearing jokes about Evie, his strong, masculine older sister, but is she a lesbian?

John Fell Series

Fell (1987)
John Fell is offered money to pretend to be Woodrow Pingree's son.

Fell Back (1989)
One of Fell's classmates commits suicide.

Fell Down (1991)
Fell inherits a ventriloquist's dummy from his best friend, who died in a car accident.

CONTRIBUTOR

Sixteen: Short Stories by Outstanding Writers for Young Adults, edited by Donald R. Gallo (1984)

Connections: Short Stories by Outstanding Writers for Young Adults, edited by Donald R. Gallo (1989)

Am I Blue? Coming Out from the Silence, edited by Marion Dane Bauer (1994)

FICTION FOR YOUNGER READERS

Shoebag (1990) as Mary James

ADULT FICTION

Dark Intruder (1952) as Vin Packer

Spring Fire (1952) as Vin Packer

Look Back to Love (1953) as Vin Packer

Come Destroy Me (1954) as Vin Packer

Whisper His Sin (1954) as Vin Packer

The Thrill Kids (1955) as Vin Packer

We Walk Alone (1955) as Ann Aldrich

Dark Don't Catch Me (1956) as Vin Packer

The Young and Violent (1956) as Vin Packer

Three Day Terror (1957) as Vin Packer

The Evil Friendship (1958) as Vin Packer

5:45 to Suburbia (1958) as Vin Packer

The Twisted Ones (1959) as Vin Packer

We Too Must Love (1958) as Ann Aldrich

Carol, in a Thousand Cities (1960) as Ann Aldrich

The Damnation of Adam Blessing (1961) as Vin Packer

The Girl on the Best Seller List (1961) as Vin Packer

Something in the Shadows (1961) as Vin Packer

Intimate Victims (1962) as Vin Packer

Alone at Night (1963) as Vin Packer

We Two Won't Last (1963) as Ann Aldrich

The Hare in March (1967) as Vin Packer

Hometown (1967) as M. J. Meaker

Game of Survival (1968) as M. J. Meaker

Don't Rely on Gemini (1969) as Vin Packer

Shockproof Sydney Skate (1972) as M. J. Meaker

ADAPTATIONS IN OTHER MEDIA

Dinky Hocker Shoots Smack! (1978)
Afternoon television special starring Wendie Jo Sperba.

FOR FURTHER READING

Benestad, Janet P. Review of *I'll Love You When You're More Like Me. Best Sellers*, December 1977.

Donelson, Kenneth L., and Alleen Pace Nilsen, eds. "The People Behind the Books: M. E. Kerr." In *Literature for Today's Young Adults*. Glenview, IL: Scott, Foresman, 1980.

Kerr, M. E. *Me, Me, Me, Me, Me: Not a Novel*. New York: Harper, 1983.

Landsberg, Michele. *Reading for the Love of It: Best Books for Young Readers*. New York: Prentice Hall Press, 1987.

Lipson, Eden Ross. *The New York Times Parent's Guide to the Best Books for Children*. New York: Times Books, 1991.

Roginski, Jim. *Behind the Covers*. Vol. 2. Englewood, CO: Libraries Unlimited, 1989.

Schreuders, Piet. *Paperbacks, U.S.A.: A Graphic History, 1939–1959*. San Diego, CA: Blue Dolphin, 1981.

Server, Lee. *Over My Dead Body: The Sensational Age of the American Paperback: 1945–1955*. San Francisco: Chronicle Books, 1994.

Sutherland, Zena. Review of *Is That You, Miss Blue? Bulletin of the Center for Children's Books*, July–August 1975.

Stephen King

Horror

Suspense

Portland, Maine
September 21, 1947

Carrie

Stephen King has forgotten where he got the idea for his first novel, *Carrie,* he told interviewer Charles L. Grant. At the time, about 1970, he was writing short stories for a men's magazine called *Cavalier*.

"Then, as I started to publish more, some woman said, 'You write all those macho things, but you can't write about women. You're scared of women.' I said, 'I'm not scared of women. I could write about them if I wanted to.'

"So I got an idea for a short story about this incident in a girls' shower room, and the girl would be telekinetic. The other girls would pelt her with sanitary napkins when she got her period. The period would release the right hormones, and she would rain down destruction on them. (I have to admit, though, that this hormone thing wasn't very clear in my mind.) Anyway, I did the shower scene, but I hated it and threw it away. My wife fished it out of the wastebasket and read it. She said, 'I think this is pretty good. Would you go on with it?' So I did. And I really got sadistic about it. I said, 'I can't have her rain destruction on them yet; they've got to *do* more to her.' So they did more, and they did more—and finally it wasn't a short story, it was a novel. But I can't remember the real kernel, where the idea came from."

King, America's preeminent horror and suspense writer, was the second son of a merchant seaman who abandoned the family when King was two. King's mother struggled to keep the family together. King, who felt overweight and uncoordinated as a youngster, said he would dream of his inadequacies. He had an active imagination and became preoccupied at times with death. For example, he kept a scrapbook of the 1950s mass murderer Charlie Starkweather, and he liked horror and science fiction movies. After an incident in high school—he wrote a not-well-received satiric newspaper called *The Village Vomit*—he took a part-time sportswriting job with the *Lisbon Enterprise*. "This editor was the man who taught me everything I know about writing in ten minutes. His name was John Gould," King said in *The Writer.*

King received a bachelor of science degree from the University of Maine at Orono in 1970. A year later he married Tabitha Jane Spruce, a poet and novelist. They have three children. King worked variously as a janitor, laundry man, and knitting-mill hand. He taught English in Hampden, Maine from 1971 to 1973, and from 1978 to 1979 he was a writer-in-residence at the university in Orono.

King began writing short stories and had completed four other unpublished novels by the time he finished *Carrie*, which he submitted to the publisher Doubleday. It was accepted with a $2,500 advance payment. King said some of the novel's characters were based on people he went to school with.

"Carrie . . . lives out a nightmare that all teen-agers go through," the author said in *Down East*. "Not being accepted by peers. And all high school kids are full of suppressed violence. Remember how you used to go home and throw your books across a room if you'd flunked a quiz? Carrie lets people relive that violent urge of adolescence."

King's second book was *Salem's Lot*, which he said owes as much to the movie *Invasion of the Body Snatchers* as it does to *Dracula*. The writer told Stefan Kanfer, only half seriously, "I've had about three original ideas in my life. The rest of them were bounces. I sense the limitation of where my talents are."

King, a busy writer, sometimes produces more prose than his publisher wants to bring out in a year's time. Thus, his novel *Rage* was issued in 1977 under the name Richard Bachman. There have been four more Bachman books.

In 1978 King's long novel *The Stand* appeared, which starts with a plague that has wiped out much of civilization. It was difficult to write, he said, and was cut by the publisher. Years later, a full version was reissued. In 1980, when *Firestarter* was published, King became the first author to have three books simultaneously on *The New York Times* best-seller list: *Firestarter, The Dead Zone,* and *The Shining.*

"Grimmer stories that strike deep into the core fears of the human unconscious—*Aliens* and *Psycho,* Blatty's *The Exorcist* and Stephen King's *The Shining*—may be beneficial because they purge us of the psychological muck that is a residue of getting through life's bad moments," suggested Dean R. Koontz, another popular suspense writer. "And if the lead characters of such stories have honor and courage—and are portrayed with depth—the tales may also serve as examples of how one can face death, loss, loneliness, and other real-life tragedies with dignity. In other words, suspense fiction can provide both thrills and subtle—heed that word '*subtle*'—moral lessons."

King began using a word processor when collaborating on *The Talisman* with Peter Straub, and his output of horror prose increased.

King has felt censorship over the years. Some people, for example, wanted *The Shining* and *Cujo* removed from library shelves. Profanity in *Christine,* according to Herbert N. Foerstel, prompted parents in a Michigan community to ask that the book be removed from a high school curriculum. It was.

"Stephen King is the most remarkable publishing phenomenon in modern literature," summed up S. T. Joshi. "To say this, however, is not to say that he is the most remarkable literary phenomenon even in the narrow confines of weird fiction. King is remarkable principally in the quantity of books he has sold over the past 15 years. . . . It seems as if King has consciously gone into the business of writing not out of a need for abstract self-expression but out of a desire to appeal to as wide a public as he can."

King, Joshi continued, is a "writer who has purportedly 'humanized' the weird tale by enmeshing it in the everyday lives of ordinary people."

"After twenty years of writing popular fiction and being dismissed by the more intellectual critics as a hack (the intellectual's definition of a hack seems to be 'an artist whose work is appreciated by too many people')," King said in *Nightmares & Dreamscapes,* "I will gladly testify that craft is terribly important, that the often tiresome process of draft, redraft, and then draft again is necessary to produce good work, and that hard work is the only acceptable practice for those of us who have some talent but little or no genius.

"Still, there *is* magic in this job, and it comes most frequently at that instant when a story pops into a writer's head, usually as a fragment but sometimes as a complete thing (and having that happen is a little like being hit by a tactical nuke). The writer can later relate where he was when that happened, and what the elements were that combined to give him his idea, but the idea itself is a new thing, a sum greater than its parts, something that is created from nothing. It is, to paraphrase Marianne Moore, a real toad in an imaginary garden. So you need not fear to read the notes that follow on the grounds that I will spoil the magic by telling you how the tricks work. There are no tricks to real magic; when it comes to real magic, there is only history."

Brian DePalma's film version of *Carrie* was one of the top money-earners of 1976. More than two dozen films of King stories have followed, making him one of the most frequently adapted writers in film and television.

"Maybe there's no accounting for it, other than the fact that audiences have an almost limitless appetite for things that go bump in the night," John Clark said, "and King has an almost limitless capacity to serve them up."

King also wrote the nonfiction *Danse Macabre* (1981). " 'Ever Et Raw Meat?' and Other Weird Questions" was a humorous essay in *The New York Times Book Review* about typical bizarre questions the writer fields from readers and fans.

ADULT FICTION

Carrie (1974)
High school misfit Carietta White uses her telekinetic abilities to get revenge on those who torment her.

Salem's Lot (1975)
Vampires take over a New England town.

Rage (1977) as Richard Bachman
Charles Dexter's twisted mind turns a quiet classroom into a world of terror.

The Shining (1977)
A resort hotel in Colorado has an evil history.

Night Shift (1978)
Short stories.

The Stand (1978 [original edition], 1990 [complete and uncut edition])
There is no defense against a strain of super flu. Battle begins among the survivors, between good and evil.

The Dead Zone (1979)
Coming out of a coma after five years, Johnny Smith has the knack of prescience—and encounters a dark vision of the future.

The Long Walk (1979) as Richard Bachman
The marathon is a contest to the death.

Firestarter (1980)
Charlene McGee's pyrokinetic abilities interest the government.

Cujo (1981)
In Castle Rock, Maine, the Chamberses' huge St. Bernard, Cujo, is bitten on the nose by a bat and goes on a rampage.

Roadwork (1981) as Richard Bachman
A man's life is threatened by a wrecking ball and he fights back.

Creepshow (1982)
Short stories in the grisly vein of the old EC horror comics of the 1950s.

Different Seasons (1982)
Four novellas.

The Running Man (1982) as Richard Bachman
America in 2025—and the game show is for real.

Christine (1983)
Arnie Cunningham buys an old Plymouth that is haunted.

Cycle of the Werewolf (1983)
A werewolf stalks victims in rural Tarker's Mills, Maine.

Pet Sematary (1983)
Dr. Louis Cred's daughter's cat comes back to life—but it is not the same.

The Eyes of the Dragon: A Story (1984)
"Once, in a Kingdom called Delain, there was a King with two sons" begins the tale of dragons and evil wizards and adventure.

The Talisman (1984) with Peter Straub
A young boy goes looking for a mystical talisman in a parallel world that resembles the Middle Ages.

Thinner (1984) as Richard Bachman
Billy Halleck sideswipes an old Gypsy woman as she crosses the street, and her father passes a bizarre and terrible judgment on him.

Skeleton Crew (1985)
Short stories.

It (1986)
Seven people who met It as children return as adults to fight It.

Maximum Overdrive (1986)
Short stories.

Misery (1987)
Former nurse Annie Wilkes is a psychotic who nurses writer Paul Sheldon after he has been in a car accident. She forces him to bring her favorite fictional character, Misery, back to life in print.

The Tommyknockers (1987)
Inhabitants of Haven, Maine, are absorbed by the wreckage of an old spaceship.

The Dark Half (1989)
Thad Beaumont for years has published novels under the pen name "George Stark." When he tries to abandon his alter ego, he is suddenly thrust into a nightmarish dream in which Stark is his darker half.

Dolan's Cadillac (1989)
Short story (later included in *Nightmares & Dreamscapes*).

My Pretty Pony (1989)
Non-horror short story, limited edition.

Four Past Midnight (1990)
Four stories.

Needful Things: The Last Castle Rock Story (1991)
Leland Gaunt's new store in Castle Rock sells anything—for a price.

Night Shift: Excursions into Horror (1991)
Short stories.

Dolores Claiborne (1992)
Inhabitants of Little Tall Island have waited three decades to find out what happened the day Dolores Claiborne's husband died.

Gerald's Game (1992)
A young woman, Jessie, is stranded in a remote cabin, handcuffed nude to a bed as part of a sex game with her husband—who has just died of a heart attack.

Nightmares & Dreamscapes (1993)
Short stories.

Insomnia (1994)
When the hero's wife dies, he develops insomnia—and a strange power to see otherworldly beings who have malevolent plans for humanity.

Rose Madder (1995)
Rose Daniels is pursued by an obtrusive, obsessive husband.

The Dark Tower Trilogy

The Gunslinger (1982)
The hero pursues "the man in black" in a world of slow mutants, nameless vampires, and speaking demons.

The Drawing of the Three (1987)
Roland, the Last Gunfighter in a world that eerily reflects ours, quests for the Dark Tower.

The Waste Lands (1992)
Roland continues his quest for the Dark Tower, traveling across the Desert of Damnation.

ADAPTATIONS IN OTHER MEDIA

Carrie (1976)
Film based on the novel of the same name, starring Sissy Spacek, William Katt, and John Travolta.

Salem's Lot (1979)
Television miniseries based on the novel of the same name, starring David Soul, Lane Kerwin, James Mason, and Bonnie Bedelia.

The Shining (1980)
Film based on the novel of the same name, starring Jack Nicholson and Shelley Duvall.

Creepshow (1982)
Film from a King screenplay.

Christine (1983)
Film based on the novel of the same name, starring Keith Gordon and John Stockwell.

Cujo (1983)
Film based on the novel of the same name, starring Dee Wallace and Daniel Hugh-Kelly.

The Dead Zone (1983)
Film based on the novel of the same name, starring Christopher Walken and Brooke Adams.

Firestarter (1984)
Film based on the novel of the same name, directed by King and starring David Keith, George C. Scott, Martin Sheen, and Drew Barrymore.

Stephen King's Children of the Corn (1984)
Film starring John Franklin and Peter Horton, based on a short story from *Night Shift*.

Cat's Eye (1985)
Film scripted by King and based on his stories "The General," a new story, and "Quitters, Inc." and "The Ledge" from *Night Shift*.

Stephen King's Night Shift Collection (1985)
Film including adaptations of "The Boogeyman" and "The Woman in the Room" from *Night Shift*.

Stephen King's Silver Bullet (1985)
Film starring Gary Busey, from the novelette *Cycle of the Werewolf*.

Tales from the Darkside (1985)
Television episode "Word Processor of the Gods," based on the story in *Skeleton Crew*.

Maximum Overdrive (1986)
Film written and directed by King and starring Emilio Estevez and Pat Hingle.

Stand by Me (1986)
Film, based on "The Body" from *Different Seasons*, starring Wil Wheaton, River Phoenix, Kiefer Sutherland, and Richard Dreyfuss.

The Twilight Zone (1986)
Television episode "Gramma," based on the story from *Skeleton Crew*.

Creepshow II (1987), sequel
Film starring Dorothy Lamour and George Kennedy.

Return to Salem's Lot (1987), sequel
Film.

The Running Man (1987)
Film based on the novel of the same name, starring Arnold Schwarzenegger.

Tales from the Darkside (1987)
Television episode "Sorry, Right Number," from a King teleplay.

Pet Sematary (1989)
Film based on the novel of the same name, starring Dale Midkiff, Denise Crosby, and Fred Gwynne.

Graveyard Shift (1990)
Film starring David Andrews and Kelly Wolf, based on the short story from *Night Shift*.

It (1990)
Television miniseries based on the novel of the same name.

Misery (1990)
Film based on the novel of the same name, starring James Caan and Kathy Bates.

Stephen King's Golden Years (1991)
Seven-episode television miniseries with Keith Szarabajka and Felicity Huffman.

Stephen King's Sometimes They Come Back (1991)
Television film with Tim Matheson, based on a short story.

The Lawnmower Man (1992)
Film starring Jeff Fahey, Pierce Brosnan, and Jenny Wright, based on a short story.

Pet Sematary II (1992), sequel
Film starring Edward Furlong and Anthony Edwards.

Stephen King's Sleepwalkers (1992)
Film starring Brian Krause, Madchen Amick, and Alice Krige, from a King script.

Children of the Corn II—The Final Sacrifice (1993), sequel
Film starring Terence Knox and Paul Scherrer.

Needful Things (1993)
Film based on the novel of the same name, starring Max von Sydow, Ed Harris, and Bonnie Bedelia.

The Shawshank Redemption (1994)
Film based on the story "Rita Hayworth and the Shawshank Redemption," from *Different Seasons.*

The Stand (1994)
Television miniseries based on the novel of the same name.

Dolores Claiborne (1995)
Film based on the novel of the same name, starring Kathy Bates and Jennifer Jason Leigh.

Mangler (1995)
Film based on the story from *Night Shift.*

Stephen King's The Langoliers (1995)
Television miniseries starring Bronson Pinchot, Patricia Wettig, and Dean Stockwell.

The Shining (1996)
Television miniseries.

FOR FURTHER READING

Beahm, George, ed. *The Stephen King Companion.* Kansas City, MO: Andrews & McMeel, 1989.

———. *The Stephen King Story—A Literary Profile.* Kansas City, MO: Andrews & McMeel, 1991.

Clark, John. Review of *The Films of Stephen King. Premiere,* January 1995.

Collings, Michael R. *The Annotated Guide to Stephen King: A Primary & Secondary Bibliography of the Works of America's Premier Horror Writer.* San Bernardino, CA: Borgo Press, 1986.

———. *The Films of Stephen King.* San Bernardino, CA: Borgo Press, 1986.

———. *The Many Facets of Stephen King.* San Bernardino, CA: Borgo Press, 1985.

———. *Stephen King as Richard Bachman.* San Bernardino, CA: Borgo Press, 1985.

———. *The Work of Stephen King: An Annotated Bibliography and Guide.* San Bernardino, CA: Borgo Press, 1994.

Collings, Michael R., and David Engebretson. *The Shorter Works of Stephen King.* San Bernardino, CA: Borgo Press, 1985.

Docherty, Brian, ed. *American Horror Fiction: From Brockden Brown to Stephen King.* New York: St. Martin's Press, 1990.

Foerstel, Herbert N. *Banned in the USA: A Reference Guide to Book Censorship in Schools and Public Libraries.* Westport, CT: Greenwood, 1994.

Grant, Charles L. "Stephen King: 'I Like to Go for the Jugular.' " *Rod Serling's The Twilight Zone Magazine,* April 1981.

Herron, Don, ed. *Reign of Fear: The Fiction and the Films of Stephen King.* Novato, CA: Underwood-Miller, 1992.

Hoppenstand, Gary, and Ray B. Browne, eds. *The Gothic World of Stephen King: Landscape of Nightmare.* Bowling Green, OH: Bowling Green University Press, 1987.

Immell, Myra, ed. *The Young Adult Reader's Advisory: The Best in Literature and Language Arts, Mathematics and Computer Science.* New Providence, NJ: R. R. Bowker, 1989.

Joshi, S. T. "The King's New Clothes." *Million,* January–February 1993.

Kanfer, Stefan. "King of Horror." *Time,* 6 October 1986.

King, Stephen. " 'Ever Et Raw Meat?' and Other Weird Questions." *The New York Times Book Review,* 6 December 1987.

———. Introduction to *Nightmares & Dreamscapes.* New York: Viking, 1993.

———. *The Writer,* June 1975.

King, Tyson. *The Unseen King.* West Linn, OR: Starmont House, 1989.

Koontz, Dean R. "Keeping the Reader on the Edge of His Seat." In *How to Write Tales of Horror, Fantasy & Science Fiction*, edited by J. N. Williamson. Cincinnati, OH: Writer's Digest Books, 1987.

Lloyd, Ann. *The Films of Stephen King*. New York: St. Martin's Press, 1994.

Lowry, Lois. "King of the Occult." *Down East* (1978).

Magistrale, Anthony. *Landscape of Fear: Stephen King's American Gothic*. Bowling Green, OH: Bowling Green University Press, 1988.

———. *Moral Voyages of Stephen King*. San Bernardino, CA: Borgo Press, 1989.

———. *Stephen King: The Second Decade: Danse Macabre to the Dark Half*. New York: Macmillan, 1992.

———, ed. *Casebook on "The Stand."* San Bernardino, CA: Borgo Press, 1992.

———, ed. *The Dark Descent: Essays Defining Stephen King's Horrorscape*. Westport, CT: Greenwood, 1992.

Reino, Joseph. *A to Z: A Dictionary of People, Places and Things in the Works of the King of Horror*. Ann Arbor, MI: Popular Culture, 1994.

———. *The First Decade, Carrie to Pet Sematary*. New York: Macmillan, 1988.

———. *Stephen King Quiz Book*. New York: New American Library, 1990.

Saidman, Anne. *Stephen King: Master of Horror*. Minneapolis, MN: Lerner, 1992.

Schweitzer, Darrell, ed. *Discovering Stephen King*. San Bernardino, CA: Borgo Press, 1985.

Spignesi, Stephen J. *The Complete Stephen King Encyclopedia: The Definitive Guide to the Works of America's Master of Horror*. Chicago: Contemporary Books, 1993.

———. *Second Stephen King Quiz Book*. New York: New American Library, 1992.

Terrell, Caroll F. *Stephen King: Man and Artist*. Cincinnati, OH: North Lights, 1991.

Tychimba, Cheo. "An Eye for Talent." *Writer's Yearbook '96*, January 1996.

Underwood, Tim, and Chuck Miller, eds. *Feast of Fear: Conversations with Stephen King*. New York: McGraw-Hill, 1989.

———. *Kingdom of Fear: The World of Stephen King*. New York: New American Library, 1987.

Van Hise, James. *More Stephen King and Clive Barker: The Illustrated Guide to the Masters of the Macabre*. Las Vegas, NV: Movie Publications Services, 1992.

———. *Stephen King and Clive Barker, Illustrated Guide*. Las Vegas, NV: Movie Publications Services, 1990.

Winter, Douglas E. *Stephen King: The Art of Darkness*. New York: New American Library, 1986.

Norma Klein

Social drama

New York City
May 13, 1938–April 25, 1989
Mom, the Wolf Man and Me

Norma Klein tackles often controversial topics in her young adult novels. A perceptive writer, she describes what it is like to share close friendships and face the problems of growing up. Many of her main characters come from liberal, upper-class, urban backgrounds.

Klein grew up in Manhattan. She attended Cornell University, Barnard College, and Columbia University. She married Erwin Fleissner, a biochemist, in 1963. They have two children.

The daughter of a psychoanalyst, Klein was raised under her parents' liberal political beliefs, their love of literature and music, and their preference for Freud over God. She and her younger brother underwent psychoanalysis involuntarily as children, then voluntarily as adults. After her father died, Klein said she came to reject much of the theory and practice of psychoanalysis.

Klein's first short story was accepted for publication when she was nineteen. She devoted her full energies to writing, though she took time off to earn a master's degree in Slavic languages and to give birth to a daughter in 1967.

She initially wrote children's books, but her agent urged her to try young adult novels. *Mom, the Wolf Man and Me* was her first effort. She said she has often been compared with writer Judy Blume.

"I feel my own YA novels are much more akin to Salinger's *The Catcher in the Rye*," she said in *Authors & Artists for Young Adults*. "They are about the last two years of high school or, increasingly, college, and the anxieties are about what profession one will enter, how to evaluate one's parents as one approaches adulthood, what direction one's burgeoning sexuality will take. . . .

"I also feel the world in which Judy's characters live is unlike the world of my heroes and heroines," Klein continued. "Judy's characters usually grow up in the suburbs where a great effort is made to conform and fit in, to do what everyone else is doing when they are doing it. My heroes and heroines tend to grow up as I did, in Manhattan, in a world which cherishes and encourages individuality. My characters are usually intellectual, thoughtful, responsible and, occasionally, sexually active."

"In the fifties, I remember my brother (who was a year and a half younger) and me reading sections from *Catcher in the Rye* aloud and literally breaking down in helpless laughter," Klein said in *School Media Quarterly*. "I remember our response to one of the early scenes in the book in which the hero, expelled from boarding school, goes to see one of his professors, who hands him back his final exam. What amazed us was that an author could use real language, colloquial language, in a book. Here were our friends, here were unidealized young people, doing badly in school, cursing, at odds with the world, described in the very words we would have used to describe them. And this was in a book; it was literature.

"Today Salinger is a classic, so one would think that some of the things he taught us would have become accepted in the world of teenage literature—for one, just the realization that a novel told in colloquial language can be just as 'literary' as one told in fancy, stiff, enigmatic prose. Not so, alas. Critics still cling to the idea that the more accessible and down-to-earth a book is, the less 'good' it must be for the reader. If it goes down like bad medicine, with difficulty and pain, then it's 'literature.' "

"In all her books for young adults Klein seems to strike a note with her readers that few other authors for this age group do consistently," Audrey Eaglen observed. "This is obvious because she writes about the things that concern young people, both boys and girls: sexuality, sex roles and sexual behavior, peer relations, and family ties. She is both frank and honest in her portrayals of teenage angst, and, like her friend Judy Blume, both respects and cares for her readers. Like Blume also, she leavens her message with wit and humor."

"I've sometimes been asked why I write so frequently about children of divorced or single parents, given that my own parents were married exclusively to each other for nearly fifty years and that my husband and I are creeping toward the twenty-year mark in a quite amiable fashion," Klein said in a speech delivered in Albany, New York (reprinted in *A Study Guide to the Novels of Norma Klein*). "One reason for this is that I am not primarily an autobiographical writer. Many writers experience something and then rush to their typewriters. My own life has never seemed to me sufficiently exciting or symbolic to warrant literary exposure. I also tend to feel few people have the detachment to write about their own experiences very well. For me writing, like reading, is in part a fantasy escape into the lives of other people, occasionally people with whom in 'real life' I might have little in common. . . .

"I write about single parents and divorced families not only because I read about them in the paper, but because the lives of my friends have always seemed to me an extension of my own life, and I observed their experiences and found material which both interested and touched me. I did, indeed, know a young woman who decided to raise her own daughter, as in *Mom, the Wolf Man and Me*, and only later got married to a man who was not the father of that born-out-of-wedlock child, but who welcomed and nurtured the child as though it had been his own."

The advent of AIDS, Klein said, may well mean a retreat from the attention sex has received in young adult fiction. She said she believes the Sweet Valley High and similar series books are dishonest in their centering on sexy white heroines and fluffing over sexuality.

Her book *Snapshots*, for example, finds Sean and Marc quizzed about sexual matters they never even considered after they shoot a roll of film of Marc's eight-year-old sister. Marc thinks she would make a good professional model, but she needs some sample photos to prove it. They pose her in a bikini and have her kiss a balloon for fun.

The fun ends when the police question Marc's father on a possible child pornography charge. A kids'-eye view of what child molesters are interested in, the novel is a tense drama as the boys fret through a police interview and the parents defend their sons and question authorities who see what is not there in a set of photos.

Some of Klein's depictions of sex have drawn criticism, however. *Domestic Arrangements*, in the view of Deborah Hollander, has a "seeming lack of concrete values toward sexuality and life in general presented by the parents of two teenage daughters, Tatiana and Cordelia. The sophistication level of the mother, Samantha, is indistinguishable from that of her daughters. For example, when 14-year-old Tatiana asks if her boyfriend can sleep overnight with her, Mom replies, 'Sure, for how long?' with little concern. . . . When Tatiana asks her father for a diaphragm for a Christmas present (her 16-year-old sister had received one the year before), Dad's response is, 'I don't feel comfortable with the idea, you're fourteen, sweetheart. That's still extremely young.' As a reader this was quite disturbing; after all, Dad has been very much aware of Tatiana's intimate relationship with her boyfriend for several months."

Klein said she has published with several companies because she prefers to submit completed works. If one editor does not like it, another likely will. She disdains many of the rules associated with young adult novels, such as length, the use of a single narrator, downplaying of adult characters, and avoiding sexual feelings.

"Many of these rules are carryovers from an earlier time," she told *Authors & Artists for Young Adults*. "I think I write well about sex, but my sex scenes are, as often as not, humorous and awkward. I don't incline toward the lyrical or the pornographic, but I try to show what sex is like between two often inexperienced, nervous teenagers. I have no fear that if I portray sex as an occasionally enjoyable activity, my readers, be they fourteen, twelve or eight, will instantly rush out and 'do it,' thereby neglecting their piano lessons or hockey practice. Many of my readers are the way I was at their age, intellectually far ahead of their social development. These are the teenagers who can recite chapter and verse from *Lady Chatterley's Lover*, but are still waiting for someone to ask them out."

YOUNG ADULT FICTION

Mom, the Wolf Man and Me (1972)
A girl's life with her unwed mother is not easy.

It's Not What You Expect (1973)
Kids help raise money for an abortion for Sara Lee.

Coming to Life (1974)

Confessions of an Only Child (1974)
Antonia narrates episodes about growing up.

Taking Sides (1974)
Twelve-year-old Nell's parents are divorced. Her grandmother drinks too much, her father is having an affair, and her mother lives with another woman.

What It's All About (1975)
Bernie is surprised at her new Vietnamese foster sister Suzu's attachment.

Girls Turn Wives (1976)

Hiding (1976)
Krii Halliday, eighteen and introverted, trains in ballet in London rather than go to college.

It's Okay If You Don't Love Me (1977)
Jody, from a liberal New York background, is surprised that midwesterner Lyle looks for love as part of a relationship.

Love Is One of the Choices: A Novel (1978)
Caroline marries her high school science teacher.

Tomboy (1978), sequel to *Confessions of an Only Child*
Toe, ten, is not sure she wants to grow up and have her body spurt in funny directions.

French Postcards (1979), based on a screenplay
American teenagers spend their junior year of college in Paris, including voluptuous Melanie, naive Joel, obsessed Alex, and faithful Laura.

Breaking Up: A Novel (1980)
Ali's father seeks her custody after he learns that her mother has a lesbian friend.

A Honey of a Chimp: A Novel (1980)
Emily and her family find a home for a pygmy chimpanzee.

Domestic Arrangements: A Novel (1981)
Tatiana is caught having sex with her boyfriend in the family bathroom.

Robbie and the Leap Year Blues (1981)
Eleven-year-old Robbie has to split his time between his divorced parents.

Beginner's Love (1982)
Joel is shy with girls; he never knows what to say. Then Leda calls. She is experienced, she went pretty far with a boyfriend, and Joel will not be a beginner for long.

The Queen of the What Ifs (1982)
Her father is leaving, her mother is feeling inadequate, her sister is seeing an "older" man—it is not the greatest time for Robin to experience first love.

Bizou: A Novel (1983)
A spunky French teenager uncovers surprises in her family on an adventurous trip to the United States.

Angel Face (1984)
Jason's father has moved out, his sisters are away at school, his brother lives with his girlfriend, and his mother cannot find a job. Now Jason is falling in love—and hopes it will not bother Mom.

Snapshots (1984)
Sean does not imagine the trouble he will start when he takes pictures of friend Marc's eight-year-old sister, Tiffany, and his father is charged with child pornography.

The Cheerleader (1985)
Evan Siegal, a ninth-grader, organizes his buddies as cheerleaders for the girls' teams.

Family Secrets (1985)
Leslie and Peter, childhood friends, become lovers in their last year of high school. Their relationship is stretched when Peter's divorced father marries Leslie's divorced mother.

Give and Take (1985)
Athletic, good-natured high school senior Spence meets an older woman and has to help a pregnant young friend.

Going Backwards (1986)
Charles Goldberg thinks of himself as a fat social bungler with no chance of finding romance.

My Life as a Body (1987)
When shy Augie agrees to tutor Sam, a new boy at school, she never dreams they will fall in love.

Older Men (1987)
Elise, sixteen, is troubled that she may be too close to her father.

No More Saturday Nights (1988)
Tim Weber does not realize how difficult it will be to keep and raise Cheryl's baby by himself.

Now That I Know (1988)
Nina spends half of each week with each of her divorced parents. She has a chance at becoming editor of the school paper, but she is not prepared for the news her parents are about to spring—her father is gay.

That's My Baby (1988)
Seventeen-year-old Paul Gold has a lot going for him, but women do not swoon at his feet—until he answers an ad for a dog walker.

Learning How to Fall (1989)
Dustin is released from a mental hospital after having a psychotic episode.

Just Friends (1990)
Isabel and Stuart have been "just friends" for years, but when Ketti sets her sights on Stuart, Iz makes a play for Gregory to make Stuart jealous.

Sunshine Series

Sunshine: A Novel (1974), based on a television special by Carol Sobieski
Katherine Haydon marries at sixteen, divorces at nineteen, settles down to raise her daughter alone, and discovers she has cancer.

The Sunshine Years (1975), based on a television series; sequel to *Sunshine*
Sam, twenty-six, an unemployed musician, is raising his late wife's five-year-old daughter.

Sunshine Christmas (1977), based on a teleplay by Carol Sobieski
Sam brings daughter Jill back to his family in Texas at holiday time.

FICTION FOR YOUNGER READERS

Girls Can Be Anything (1973)

Dinosaur's Housewarming Party (1974)

If I Had It My Way (1974)

Naomi in the Middle (1974)

A Train for Jane (1974)

Red Sky, Blue Trees (1975)

Baryshnikov's Nutcracker (1979)

Visiting Pamela (1979)

ADULT FICTION

Love and Other Euphemisms (1972)

Give Me One Good Reason (1973)

Domestic Arrangements: A Novel (1981)

Wives and Other Women (1982)

Sextet in a Minor: A Novella and Thirteen Short Stories (1983)

The Swap (1983)

Lovers (1984)

American Dreams (1987)

The World As It Is (1989)

CONTRIBUTOR

Prize Stories: The O. Henry Awards (1963)

Prize Stories: The O. Henry Awards (1968)

The Best American Short Stories of 1969 (1969)

ADAPTATIONS IN OTHER MEDIA

Mom, the Wolf Man and Me (1979)
Television movie starring Patty Duke Astin and David Birney.

FOR FURTHER READING

Eaglen, Audrey. "Norma Klein." In *Twentieth-Century Children's Writers*, edited by Tracy Chevalier. 3d ed. Chicago: St. James Press, 1989.

Garrett, Agnes, and Helga P. McCue, eds. "Norma Klein." In *Authors & Artists for Young Adults*. Vol. 2. Detroit: Gale Research, 1989.

Hollander, Deborah. Review of *Domestic Arrangements*. *Voice of Youth Advocates*, October 1981.

Klein, Norma. "Books to Help Kids Deal with Difficult Times, I." *School Media Quarterly*, spring 1987.

———. "Fictional Portrayals of the American Family in My Own Work and Others: A Speech Delivered by Norma Klein in October 1980, in Albany, New York." In *A Study Guide to the Novels of Norma Klein* by Lou Willett Stanek. New York: Avon Books, 1980.

Ronald Koertge

Family drama

Olney, Illinois
April 22, 1940

The Harmony Arms

"As a poet and a fiction writer I have worked and reworked my childhood to such an extent that a reality shortage set in long ago," Ronald Koertge told *Authors & Artists for Young Adults*. "I would much rather have an interesting childhood than a so-called true one, anyway."

The son of a farmer who went into the military during World War II, the writer grew up surrounded by his mother and two aunts in what he has described as a happy childhood. His parents later opened an ice cream business. Koertge began writing while in high school.

In 1962, he received a bachelor of arts degree from the University of Illinois. He received a master's from the University of Arizona in 1965. After that, he began seeking publication of his writing. A poet as well as a prose writer, he is concerned about language and the sound of his writing.

Finding much of young adult fiction dull, he spiced his first effort in that field, *Where the Kissing Never Stops*, with a hero who craves junk food, whose mother works at a burlesque parlor, and whose girlfriend is a mall lover. Within all this, he created compelling, earnest characters. Betty Carter described *Where the Kissing Never Stops*: "In a warmly humorous first-person narrative, seventeen-year-old

Walker deals with his father's death, his mother's new job as a stripper, and his attraction to Rachel."

Koertge's reputation is for young adult books about realistically depicted characters coming to grips with a range of problems, from acne to divorce to AIDS.

The Harmony Arms is about a divorced father, Sumner McKay, and his son, Gabriel. They move temporarily to Los Angeles, where Sumner takes a job as a screenwriter. Until now, Gabriel had always thought that his father was odd. "This sojourn in L. A. opens Gabriel up to the possibility that his father is *not* the weirdest guy around," Nancy Vasilakis said. "More to the point, neither is he. The inhabitants of their temporary residence, the Harmony Arms apartment complex, are responsible for this enlightenment. Gabriel's companion in this journey to self-discovery is wise-cracking Tess, a fourteen-year-old aspiring filmmaker who carries a camcorder around with her everywhere in order to film the story of her life as it is taking place. . . . Koertge's brash, outrageous characters give new meaning to the word *diversity*. He offers a lively defense of the West Coast's let-it-all-hang-out spirit in his funniest novel to date."

YOUNG ADULT FICTION

Where the Kissing Never Stops (1987)
Seventeen-year-old Walker decides it is more important to farm a piece of land than sell it to a developer.

The Arizona Kid (1988)
Billy Kennedy, sixteen, away from home for the first time, is put to work by his uncle shoveling horse manure at the Tucson racetrack with a pretty, blonde horse trainer.

The Boy in the Moon (1990)
A shy boy finds the courage to date his best friend.

Mariposa Blues (1991)
Graham grapples with his feelings about his friend, Leslie.

The Harmony Arms (1992)
Gabriel meets a wonderfully eccentric collection of characters when he and his father move from a small town to a Los Angeles condominium.

Tiger, Tiger, Burning Bright: A Novel (1994)
Jesse is sure his grandfather has gone nuts. He keeps talking about seeing tiger tracks in California.

ADULT FICTION

The Boogeyman (1980)

POETRY

The Father-Poems (1973)

Meat: Cherry's Market Diary (1973)

The Hired Nose (1974)

My Summer Vacation (1975)

Sex Object (1975, revised 1979)

Tarzan and Shane Meet the Toad, with Charles Stetler and Gerald Locklin (1975)
Poetry and prose.

Cheap Thrills (1976)

Men Under Fire (1976)

Twelve Photographs of Yellowstone (1976)

How to Live on Five Dollars a Week, Etc. (1977)

The Jockey Poems (1980)

Dairy Cows (1982)

Life on the Edge of the Continent: Selected Poems of Ronald Koertge (1982)

High School Dirty Poems: Poems (1992)

FOR FURTHER READING

Carter, Betty. *Best Books for Young Adults: The Selections, the History, the Romance.* Chicago: American Library Association, 1994.

Johnson, Janette. "Ron Koertge." In *Authors & Artists for Young Adults,* edited by Kevin S. Hile. Vol. 11. Detroit: Gale Research, 1993.

Vasilakis, Nancy. Review of *The Harmony Arms. Horn Book Magazine,* November–December 1992.

E. L. Konigsburg

Family drama

New York City
February 10, 1930

From the Mixed-Up Files of Mrs. Basil E. Frankweiler

In 1968, E. L. Konigsburg's *From the Mixed-Up Files of Mrs. Basil E. Frankweiler* won the Newbery Medal and her *Jennifer, Hecate, Macbeth, William McKinley, and Me, Elizabeth* was runner-up.

Describing *Frankweiler* as appealing to sophisticated preteens, Elva Harmon said that it "has almost all they hope for in a book: humor, suspense, intrigue, and their problems acknowledged seriously but not somberly."

The book takes place in the Metropolitan Museum of Art, where Claudia and Jamie are living. "It's part of Claudia's scheme to escape from the suburbs," Eden Ross Lipson wrote. "The children are smart, but Mrs. Frankweiler, the rich old lady whose files reveal all, is the really clever one. A prized comic novel."

Praising an original plot and natural characters, Elinor Cullen said that *Jennifer* "is a funny and distinctively unpatronizing presentation of the relationship between a white girl and a Negro. . . . Despite the girls' careful preparations, Elizabeth flunks the witch test, and her failure culminates in a very satisfying way, allowing both girls to relax into a comfortable friendship, the strength of which is developed without moralizing by contemporary characters in an entertaining tale that has staying power."

Both books, Ruth Hill Viguers said, "are in tune with the personalities and imaginations of the children involved. The style in

Jennifer . . . maintains the flavor of an articulate fifth-grader. . . . *From the Mixed-Up Files* . . . has the dignity and wry humor of a well-educated, literate woman, enlivened by her enjoyment of the discoveries she has made about the children's characters and personalities. The books are very much alive."

Born Elaine Lobl, the daughter of a businessman, she grew up in a small town in Pennsylvania. As a girl she read everything from *The Secret Garden* to *Gone with the Wind*.

She attended the Carnegie Institute of Technology, the University of Pittsburgh, and the Art Students' League. In 1952, she married David Konigsburg, an industrial psychologist. They have three children.

Konigsburg has worked as a bookkeeper, a science teacher, and, since 1967, a writer. She has illustrated several of her books.

"E. L. Konigsburg is a patchy, unpredictable, and fascinating writer," Joan McGrath observed. "Her contribution to children's literature can be conservatively assessed as superior, and since she is amazingly inventive and prolific, it is happily permissible to assume that there will be more very good things to come."

YOUNG ADULT FICTION

From the Mixed-Up Files of Mrs. Basil E. Frankweiler (1967)
A well-to-do art-collecting woman describes an unusual adventure involving children who live at the Metropolitan Museum of Art in New York.

Jennifer, Hecate, Macbeth, William McKinley, and Me, Elizabeth (1967); British title: *Jennifer, Hecate, Macbeth and Me* (1968)
Elizabeth apprentices to Jennifer, a master witch.

About the B'nai Bagels (1969)
Twelve-year-old Mark's very Jewish mother mismanages the Little League B'nai Bagels team.

Altogether, One at a Time (1971)
Short stories.

(George) (1970); British title: *Benjamin Dickenson Carr and His (George)* (1974)
(George) is the little man-conscience living inside Benjamin.

A Proud Taste for Scarlet and Miniver (1973)
The historical figure Eleanor of Aquitaine is featured.

The Dragon in the Ghetto Caper (1974)
Andrew J. Chronister ventures into the ghetto and becomes involved with a local numbers runner.

The Second Mrs. Giaconda (1975)
The real story of the *Mona Lisa* is related by Leonardo da Vinci's apprentice, Salai.

Father's Arcane Daughter (1976)
A mysterious half sister helps overprotected children grow up normally.

Throwing Shadows (1979)
Short stories.

Journey to an 800 Number (1982); British title: *Journey by First Class Camel* (1983)
When his mother goes on honeymoon with her new husband, spoiled Bo must live with his father, an itinerant camel-keeper on the convention circuit.

Up from Jericho Tel (1986)
Left to their own devices, Jeanmarie Troxell and Malcom Soo meet the spirit of a dead actress named Tallulah.

T-Backs, T-Shirts, Coat and Suit (1993)
Spending summer in Peco, Florida, with Bernadette is not Chloe's first choice, nor her second nor third, but she must because of the "hair contract."

FICTION FOR YOUNGER READERS

Samuel Todd's Book of Great Colors (1990)

Samuel Todd's Book of Great Inventions (1991)

Amy Elizabeth Explores Bloomingdale's (1992)

CONTRIBUTOR

Expectations 1980, produced by Braille Institute of America (1980, 32d ed.)

DRAMA

The Second Mrs. Giaconda (first produced in 1976)

ADAPTATIONS IN OTHER MEDIA

Jennifer and Me (1973)
Television movie based on *Jennifer, Hecate, Macbeth, William McKinley, and Me, Elizabeth.*

The Hideaways (1974)
Film based on *From the Mixed-Up Files of Mrs. Basil E. Frankweiler.*

Caroline? (1990)
Television movie based on *Father's Arcane Daughter.*

From the Secret Mixed-Up Files of Mrs. Basil E. Frankweiler (1995)
Television movie starring Jean Marie Barnwell and Lauren Bacall.

FOR FURTHER READING

Cullen, Elinor. Review of *Jennifer, Hecate, Macbeth, William McKinley, and Me, Elizabeth. School Library Journal,* May 1967.

Harmon, Elva. Review of *From the Mixed-Up Files of Mrs. Basil E. Frankweiler. School Library Journal,* October 1967.

Lipson, Eden Ross. *The New York Times Parent's Guide to the Best Books for Children.* Rev. ed., updated. New York: Times Books, 1991.

McGrath, Joan. "E. L. Konigsburg." In *Twentieth-Century Children's Writers,* edited by Tracy Chevalier. 3d ed. Chicago: St. James Press, 1989.

Viguers, Ruth Hill. *A Critical History of Children's Literature,* edited by Cornelia Meigs. Rev. ed. New York: Macmillan, 1969.

Gordon Korman

Humor

Montreal, Quebec, Canada
October 23, 1963

Macdonald Hall Series

Gordon Korman's books "are notable for their slapstick humor, one-line jokes, zany settings . . . spree-filled escapades, highly energetic characters who seem to be refugees from Mack Sennett movies, and always an adult authority figure forever poised to break up the fun going on," Patrick Hynan said in an article in Toronto's *Globe & Mail*.

The son of a chartered accountant and a journalist, Korman wrote his first book at age twelve as an assignment for an English class. It was *This Can't Be Happening at Macdonald Hall*. The writer received a degree in 1985 from New York University.

"They're not super-realistic," Korman said of his books, in a promotional piece from his publisher, "but the dialogue is true-to-life. I think I have a pretty good sense of how kids think." He observed, "In my own education, I found that many of the books we read in school had no relation to what we liked to read on our own. I write my books to be enjoyed." Korman said of his audience, "One thing about fourth to tenth graders—they're a very honest bunch. If they like what you're saying, you know it; if they don't you know it even better. . . . And the next time I'm at my desk writing, I'll have a real feeling for the people at the other end."

Korman's books about Macdonald Hall, a private boarding school for boys, feature Bruno, Boots, and friends. Reviewer S. J. Freisen found them "stereotypes. They, like the plot, are merely a frame on which to hang a series of funny incidents and running gags. . . . Korman's characters and events are bent to the purpose of his books—making people laugh."

Korman told interviewer Chris Ferns that his writing has evolved. "First of all, I got older—and my characters got a little older. I tend to write about stages which I've just been through, meaning that when I was in high school I wrote about 13-year-olds, and now that I'm in University, the last couple of books are about high school students. My writing's changed in a number of ways: when I was writing the first couple of books I sincerely believed that my strength was not so much as a writer, but more as an idea person: I came up with ideas, and I communicated them the best way I knew how—meaning that a pencil and paper were a lot more accessible to me than two million dollars worth of film production equipment, or video, or something. So I did what I could. . . . But somewhere around the sixth book I began to get the impression that there was something more to writing: that I actually was a writer, rather than someone who just managed to express himself through prose because that was the only way, and I think that now I'm very much a prose writer."

He told Ferns that he sees himself somewhat as a Canadian writer: "I have a lot of trouble with what the Canadian identity is. Reading all the trade publications, I sometimes believe that in order to achieve the Canadian identity, tragedies have to befall everybody. Or you have to write about native peoples, or something like that. I don't. . . . I've got nothing against the notion that I'm a Canadian author, but I definitely don't think that where you're an author from is based on a heart affiliation. Does it make me a New York author, because I live in New York?"

YOUNG ADULT FICTION

Who Is Bugs Potter? (1980)
Bugs Potter is crazy about heavy-metal music.

I Want to Go Home (1981)
Rudy Miller is sick of Camp Algonquin Island, also known as Alcatraz.

Our Man Weston (1982)
Sidney West cannot convince officials that someone is out to steal a high-tech airplane from Trilliam Air Base.

Bugs Potter: Live at Nickaninny (1983), sequel to *Who Is Bugs Potter?*
Bugs has to spend two weeks with his family in the remote northern wilderness—without his music.

No Coins, Please (1984)
Two counselors and six boys are on a Junior Tour of America—full of mishaps.

Don't Care High (1985)
Characters include the "Locker Baron," who accepts junk food in payment for lockers in prime locations.

Son of Interflux (1986)
Simon Irving, settling into a new school, is disturbed to learn that his father's company, Interflux, plans to build on a vacant lot next door.

A Semester in the Life of a Garbage Bag (1987)
Sean Delancey clings to his school popularity. His partner in an English assignment yearns to win a trip to a Greek island.

Radio Fifth Grade (1989)
Fifth-graders Benjy, Mark, and Ellen-Louise produce "Kidsview" for a local FM radio station.

Losing Joe's Place (1990)
Jason, sixteen, and two buddies spend the summer, without adult supervision, at brother Joe's bachelor pad.

The Twinkie Squad (1992)
Douglas Fairchild, son of diplomats, a visionary and dreamer, leads Thaddeus G. Little Middle School's Special Discussion Group, also known as the Twinkie Squad.

The Toilet Paper Tigers (1993)
Corey Johnson never dreamed Little League could be so humiliating—that was before he joined the Feather-Soft Tigers.

The Three Z's (1994)

Bruno & Boots Series

This Can't Be Happening at Macdonald Hall (1977)
At a South Ontario boarding school, Bruno Walton and Boots O'Neal are roommates—and constant practical jokers.

Go Jump in the Pool! (1979)
Bruno and Boots again terrorize headmaster Sturgeon and raise $25,000 for a pool.

Beware the Fish! (1980)
Mysterious messages disrupt television broadcasts in the Macdonald Hall neighborhood.

The War with Mr. Wizzle (1982)
The roommates try to rid the school of computer whiz Walter C. Wizzle and his Magnetronic 515.

The Zucchini Warriors (1988)
Macdonald Hall has a lackluster football team—until Cathy Burton of Miss Scrimmage's Finishing School for Young Ladies becomes quarterback.

Macdonald Hall Goes Hollywood (1991)

Something Fishy at Macdonald Hall (1995)

POETRY

The D-Poems of Jeremy Bloom: A Collection of Poems About School, Homework, and Life (Sort Of) (1992) with Bernice Korman

CONTRIBUTOR

Connections: Short Stories by Outstanding Writers for Young Adults, edited by Donald R. Gallo (1989)

FOR FURTHER READING

Ferns, Chris. Interview with Gordon Korman. *Canadian Children's Literature*, 1985.

Freisen, S. J. "Literacy: The Case for Light Reading." *Canadian Children's Literature*, 1980.

Gordon Korman. New York: Scholastic Books, n.d.

Madeleine L'Engle

Fantasy

New York City
November 29, 1918
A Wrinkle in Time

"As a lonely only child growing up in New York City, I read a great deal," Madeleine L'Engle said in *Books I Read When I Was Young*. She cited Lucy Maud Montgomery's *Emily of New Moon* and its sequels as particular favorites. "While I enjoyed the 'Anne' books, Emily meant a great deal more to me because she, too, wanted to be a writer. She also had gifts in what we would now call parapsychology, and her ability to break through the limited barriers of ordinary living also appealed to me and helped me to widen my own horizons."

Born Madeleine L'Engle Camp, L'Engle said that her parents, a foreign correspondent and writer and a pianist, were overprotective, not even allowing her to go to the library. After she had read everything on hand, she began to write her own stories. She wrote her first novel at age twelve. In school, she won a poetry contest.

The family moved to Europe in 1930 because of her father's health—he had been gassed during World War I. Her parents stayed in the French Alps while Madeleine went to boarding school, first in England and later near Lake Geneva in Switzerland. From her experiences came material for *The Small Rain* and *And Both Were Young*. The family later returned to the United States, and she attended a school in South Carolina. Her father's death in 1936 prompted her to return to writing.

In 1941, L'Engle graduated from Smith College. She was active in the theater in the early 1940s, touring with a drama company. During World War II, she taught with the Committee for Refugee Education. In 1945, she found a publisher for *The Small Rain*. The next year, she married Hugh Franklin, an actor. They had three children, and Franklin died in 1986.

After her marriage, L'Engle continued to write, though some books found publishers more quickly than others. The family settled in Connecticut, where her husband bought a country store. "A lot of what I learned in our store was of immense value to a writer," L'Engle said in a publisher's pamphlet. "Our customers included Gypsies, carnival men, farmers, factory workers, artists, and philosophers. I have already published one book written directly out of our life there. It's called *Meet the Austins*, but it could easily be called 'Meet the Franklins.' "

Meet the Austins was controversial because it begins with a death—a no-no in children's literature at the time. "They talk it out quietly in between long healing silences, and then they go home. Life goes on, but changed. . . . The children's ups and downs, a serious brother-sister conflict, some funny and some grave situations—all develop against a background of family love," according to May Hill Arbuthnot. "This is a fine family story, as unusual and provocative throughout as is its first chapter."

One of L'Engle's best-known novels, *A Wrinkle in Time*, was rejected by twenty-six publishers, for various reasons. It was not easily categorized as science fiction, fantasy, or mainstream. "It was written in the terms of a modern world in which children know about brainwashing and the corruption of evil," she said in *National Catholic Reporter*. "It's based on Einstein's theory of relativity and Planck's quantum theory. It's good, solid science, but also it's good, solid theology."

The heroine Meg Murry sets out to find her scientist father, who has disappeared. Her brother, Charles Wallace, and his friend, Calvin, both of whom have ESP, journey with her. Mrs. Whatsit, Mrs. Who, and Mrs. Which help them travel across "a wrinkle in time" to the planet Camazotz, which is in evil hands.

The novel "rises above most children's science fiction in its portrayal of the children and their odd helpers," Humphrey Carpenter and Mari Prichard stated, "though the chapters set on Camazotz fall into many of the clichés of the genre."

The book was challenged for its content. In Alabama, for instance, it was said to send "a mixed signal to children about good and evil, since witches are among the fantasy creatures that help a child," Herbert N. Foerstel said.

"Very few children have any problem with the world of the imagination," L'Engle said when accepting the Newbery Award for *Wrinkle* in 1963, "it's their own world, the world of their daily life, and it's our loss that so many of us grow out of it."

"Miss L'Engle's main themes are the clash of good and evil, the difficulty and necessity of deciding which is which and of committing oneself, the search for fulfillment and self-knowledge," John Rowe Townsend summarized. These themes are determined by what the author *is*; and she is a practising and active Christian."

"Books of fantasy and science fiction, in particular, are books in which the writer can express a vision, in most cases a vision of hope," L'Engle said in *Through the Eyes of a Child*. "A writer of fantasy usually looks at the seeming meaninglessness in what is happening on this planet, and says, 'No, I won't accept that. There has got to be some meaning, some shape and pattern in all of this,' and then looks to story for the discovery of that shape and pattern. . . .

"Concepts which are too difficult for adults are open to children, who are not yet afraid of new ideas, who don't mind having the boat rocked, or new doors opened, or mixing metaphors! That is one very solid reason my science fiction/fantasy books are marketed for children; only children are open enough to understand them. Let's never underestimate the capacity of the child for a wide and glorious imagination, an ability to accept what is going on in our troubled world, and the courage to endure it with courage, and respond to it with a realistic hope."

L'Engle has written several volumes of essays and nonfiction. She contributed to *The Language of the Night: Essays on Fantasy and Science Fiction* (1978), edited by Susan Wood.

YOUNG ADULT FICTION

The Small Rain (1945); first half reissued as *Prelude* (1968)
Katherine Forrester is a promising but precocious pianist whose mother was injured in an accident.

And Both Were Young (1949)
Flip does not think she will ever fit in at a Swiss boarding school.

Camilla Dickinson, A Novel (Simon & Schuster, 1951); alternate title: *Camilla* (Thomas Y. Crowell, 1965)
Camilla's parents vie for her allegiance, and she is torn between them.

Dragons in the Waters (1976), sequel to *The Arm of the Starfish* (See the Austin Family Series, below)
The O'Keefes join Simon Bolivar Renier and his weird Cousin Phair on a voyage to Venezuela.

The Sphinx at Dawn: Two Stories (1982)

A House Like a Lotus (1984)
Polly, sixteen, on her way to a job on Cyprus, tries to figure out what went wrong in her friendship with Max.

An Acceptable Time (1989)
A flash of lightning sends Polly back in time 3,000 years.

Austin Family Series

Meet the Austins (1960)
Vicky Austin feels guilty and resentful when the orphan Maggy Hamilton joins the Austin family and turns things upside down.

The Moon by Night (1963)
The Austins camp out in California, and Vicky, fourteen, meets a troubled boy named Zachary.

The Arm of the Starfish (1965)
Marine biology student Adam Eddington—Vicky's friend—becomes involved in a mystery while working with the renowned Dr. O'Keefe.

The Young Unicorns (1968)
Emily Gregory, a gifted musician, copes with her blindness with the help of Dave Davison, a former gang member. Members of the Austin family appear.

A Ring of Endless Light (1980)
Vicky is stretched by the dreams of three young men and the needs of a dying grandfather.

The Anti-Muffins (1980)
Vicky tells how she, her brother, and their friends come to accept the orphan Maggy.

The Twenty-Four Days Before Christmas: An Austin Family Story (1984)
For younger readers, seven-year-old Vicky's adventures are recounted.

Troubling a Star (1994)
Adam Eddington's Great-Aunt Serena takes Vicky on a trip to Antarctica—but fellow travelers are not what they seem.

The Time Trilogy

A Wrinkle in Time (1962)
Meg Murry and her brother, Charles Wallace, search for their missing father on the dark planet Camazotz.

A Wind in the Door (1973)
Meg is concerned for Charles's welfare in school—and is soon propelled into galactic space.

A Swiftly Tilting Planet (1978)
Now grown, Charles Wallace undertakes a perilous journey with the unicorn Gaudior.

FICTION FOR YOUNGER READERS

Dance in the Desert (1969)

Many Waters (1986)

The Glorious Impossible (1990)

POETRY FOR YOUNGER READERS

Lines Scribbled on an Envelope, and Other Poems (1969)

DRAMA

18 Washington Square, South (first produced in 1940)

How Now Brown Cow, with Robert Hartung (first produced in 1949)

The Journey with Jonah (first produced in 1970)

ADULT FICTION

Ilsa (1946)

A Winter's Love (1957)

The Love Letters (1966)

The Other Side of the Sun: A Novel (1971)

A Severed Wasp (1982)

Certain Women (1992)

POETRY FOR ADULTS

The Weather of the Heart (1978)

FOR FURTHER READING

Arbuthnot, May Hill. *Children and Books.* Glenview, IL: Scott, Foresman, 1964.

Cullinan, Bernice, and M. Jerry Weiss, eds. *Books I Read When I Was Young: The Favorite Books of Famous People.* New York: Avon Books, 1980.

Farrell, Michael J. "Madeleine L'Engle: In Search of Where Lion and Lamb Abide." *National Catholic Reporter,* 20 June 1986.

Foerstel, Herbert N. *Banned in the USA: A Reference Guide to Book Censorship in Schools and Public Libraries.* Westport, CT: Greenwood, 1994.

Kingman, Lee, ed. *Newbery and Caldecott Medal Books: 1956–1965.* Boston: Horn Book, 1965.

L'Engle, Madeleine. "Through the Eyes of an Author: The Search for Truth." In *Through the Eyes of a Child: An Introduction to Children's Literature,* edited by Donna E. Norton. 2d ed. Columbus, OH: Merrill, 1987.

L'Engle, Madeleine, and Avery Brooke. *Trailing Clouds of Glory: Spiritual Values in Children's Books.* Westminster, CO: Westminster, 1985.

L'Engle, Madeleine, and William B. Green, eds. *Spirit and Light: Essays in Historical Theology.* New York: Harper, 1976.

Madeleine L'Engle. New York: Farrar, Straus & Giroux, 1989.

Townsend, John Rowe. *A Sense of Story: Essays on Contemporary Writers for Children.* Philadelphia: J. B. Lippincott, 1971.

C. S. Lewis

Fantasy

Belfast, Northern Ireland
November 29, 1898–November 22, 1963

Chronicles of Narnia

"[C. S.] Lewis's Narnian tales have always dauntlessly cut across contemporary fashion; a great part of their strength derives from this, and from their author's readiness to break into such emotional fields as chivalry, pain, power, fear, worship, Homeric wrath," *The Times Literary Supplement* stated.

M. S. Crouch explained that Lewis is "a Christian apologist. Whether writing of the nature of sin, of an imaginary world, of Milton's Satan, or of the mediaeval romances of the Grail, he is working out his conception of the Christian myth and the Christian philosophy. In the 'Narnia' stories, he expounds the same theme in terms of allegory. Sometimes, as in *The Lion, the Witch and the Wardrobe*, the allegory follows closely the pattern of the Gospel story; sometimes, as in *The Horse and His Boy*, its lessons are of a more general character; but the books are all part of a general pattern. One may prefer one book to another; one cannot dispense with any."

Clive Staples "Jack" Lewis was the son of a solicitor who also enjoyed oration and storytelling. There were many books in the home, and Lewis's mother, the daughter of a clergyman, had her younger son tutored in French and Latin. He and his older brother, Warren, were strong allies, despite differences in their personalities. When Warren was sent off to boarding school, life became more isolated for Clive.

The death of his mother was a wrenching experience for young Lewis. In 1908, he was sent to boarding school in England with his brother. Later, Lewis went to Oxford on a scholarship, but World War I cut his studies short. He joined the Somerset Light Infantry and ended up in France. Wounded in 1918, he was sent to London to recover.

He attended Malvern College for a year, then returned to Oxford, where he graduated with three firsts in his class and the Chancellor's Prize for an English Essay. During his academic career, Lewis lectured at Oxford University, Magdalene College, Cambridge University, the University of Wales, Cardiff, the University of Durham, and Trinity College. A Christian essayist and scholar as well as a critic of English literature, he was a fellow with the British Academy and the Royal Society of Literature and served as a president of the Sir Walter Scott Society. In 1925, Lewis became a fellow at Magdalene College, Oxford.

Lewis wrote books on theological topics and literary criticism, including *Studies in Medieval and Renaissance Literature* (1967). He contributed to other works on similar topics. In 1954, he accepted a professorship at Cambridge.

Raised a Protestant, Lewis became an atheist in his teens. By the 1930s, he had renewed his belief in Christianity, largely through the influence of Oxford colleague J. R. R. Tolkien. Lewis worked out religious themes in a trio of science fiction novels, beginning with *Out of the Silent Planet* (1938).

In 1940, Lewis had an idea for an adult novel and wrote *The Screwtape Letters*. In the 1950s, he wrote seven volumes of fantasy for young adults, the Chronicles of Narnia. Inspired by a series of nightmares he had, Lewis's books reimagine the Christian story in a new setting. Children venturing through the wardrobe to Narnia meet the main events in the Christian story, only skewed to another world. The stories are not allegories but direct tellings. Narnia can only be entered by children, and only at certain times.

"Each story has its own landscape—or seascape. For C. S. Lewis, the face of nature, its changing moods and seasons, whether seen in windswept wastes or in a small mossy glade where hawthorn is in bloom, has its part in his developing theme, in shaping the sequence of events and in giving reality to the reader's imaginings as he accompanies the characters of the story on their adventures in the magical land of Narnia," Lillian H. Smith observed.

"I did not say to myself 'Let us represent Jesus as He really is in our world by a Lion in Narnia': I said 'Let us *suppose* that there were a land like Narnia and that the son of God, as He became a Man in our world, became a Lion there, and then imagine what would happen.' If you think about it, you will see that it is quite a different thing," Lewis said in *Letters to Children*, one of several collections of his missives.

Not all critics were thrilled by Narnia. "There is much that is distasteful, or merely absurd, in the content of the books," Penelope Lively said. "The very dubious Utopia of Narnia, where the children rule by some kind of Divine Right . . . and their subjects, dwarfs, badgers, moles, etc., are 'decent little chaps' who speak ungrammatically but are unfailingly loyal, have all the coziness of old family retainers, and make useful cannon-fodder when the time comes for the inevitable battle."

Lewis offered these rules for writing: Write what you mean clearly; use plain, direct words; use concrete nouns whenever possible; do not use adjectives; do not use words that are too big for the subject. Further, he offered these suggestions to a schoolgirl in the 1950s:

1. Turn off the radio.
2. Read all the good books you can, and avoid nearly all magazines.
3. Always write (and read) with the ear, not the eye. You should hear every sentence you write as if it was being read aloud or spoken. If it does not sound nice, try again.
4. Write about what really interests you, whether it is real things or imaginary things, and nothing else. (Notice this means that if you are interested *only* in writing you will never be a writer, because you will have nothing to write about. . . .)
5. Take great pains to be *clear*. Remember that though you start by knowing what you mean, the reader doesn't, and a single ill-chosen word may lead to a total misunderstanding. In a story it is terribly easy just to forget that you have not told the reader something that he wants to know—the whole picture is so clear in your own mind that you forget that it isn't the same in his.
6. When you give up a bit of work, don't (unless it is hopelessly bad) throw it away. Put it in a drawer. It may come in useful later. Much of my best work, or what I think my best, is the rewriting of things begun and abandoned years earlier.

7. Don't use a typewriter. The noise will destroy your sense of rhythm, which still needs years of training.
8. Be sure you know the meaning (or meanings) of every word you use.

Lewis wed Joy Davidman Gresham, a poet and novelist, in 1956. She had cancer when they married, and she died in 1960. Their romance was depicted in a public television special, *Shadowlands*, in 1986, with Joss Ackland playing Lewis, and in a motion picture of the same name in 1993, featuring Anthony Hopkins as Lewis.

YOUNG ADULT FICTION

Chronicles of Narnia

The Lion, the Witch and the Wardrobe (1950)
Narnia is a magical land where talking animals, fauns, dwarfs, centaurs, and friendly giants live in peace, but when English schoolchildren Peter, Susan, Edmund, and Lucy arrive, the wicked White Witch casts a spell. The children help the lion king Aslan defeat the witch.

Prince Caspian: The Return to Narnia (1951)
Peter, Susan, Edmund, and Lucy return to Narnia and find that an evil king from Telmarine has taken power.

The Voyage of the "Dawn Treader" (1952)
Lucy and Edmund find Narnian adventure aboard the ship *Dawn Treader* and soon reunite with Prince Caspian.

The Silver Chair (1953)
Aslan calls Eustace and Jill to Narnia to follow four clues and find Prince Rilian.

The Horse and His Boy (1954)
In a country south of Narnia, Bree, a talking horse, and Shasta, a boy, plan their escape from bondage with the help of the runaway girl Aravist and her horse, Hwin.

The Magician's Nephew (1955)
At the dawn of Narnia, a scheming old magician sends nephew Digony and his friend, Polly, to the world between the worlds.

The Last Battle: A Story for Children (1956)
Short stories. Aslan eventually leads his people to a new paradise.

ADULT FICTION

The Pilgrim's Regress: An Allegorical Apology for Christianity, Reason, and Romanticism (1933, 1977)

The Screwtape Letters (1942); revised editions: *The Screwtape Letters and Screwtape Proposes a Toast* (1961); *The Screwtape Letters; with, Screwtape Proposes a Toast* (1982)

The Great Divorce: A Dream (1945)

Till We Have Faces: A Myth Retold (1956)

Space Trilogy

Out of the Silent Planet (1938)

Perelandra: A Novel (1944); British title: *Voyage to Venus* (1960)

That Hideous Strength: A Modern Fairy-Tale for Grownups (Macmillan, 1945); alternate title: *The Tortured Planet* (Avon, 1958)

POETRY

Spirits in Bondage (1917) as Clive Hamilton; reissued under the title *Spirits in Bondage: A Cycle of Lyrics* (1984) as C. S. Lewis

Dymer (1926) as Clive Hamilton

Poems, edited by Walter Hooper (1964)

Narrative Poems, edited by Walter Hooper (1969)

ADAPTATIONS IN OTHER MEDIA

The Lion, the Witch and the Wardrobe (1979)
Television movie.

The Chronicles of Narnia (1989)
Series for public television.

FOR FURTHER READING

Crouch, M. S. "Chronicles of Narnia." *Junior Bookshelf* (November 1956).

Dorsett, Lyle W., and Marjorie Lamp Mead, eds. *C. S. Lewis: Letters to Children*. New York: Macmillan, 1985.

"End of a Saga." *The Times Literary Supplement*, 11 May 1956.

Ford, Paul E. *Companion to Narnia: A Complete Guide to the Enchanting World of C. S. Lewis's The Chronicles of Narnia*. San Francisco: HarperCollins, 1994.

Lewis, W. H., ed. *Letters of C. S. Lewis*. New York: Harcourt, 1966.

Lively, Penelope. "The Wrath of God: An Opinion of the 'Narnia' Books." *Use of English*, winter 1968.

Smith, Lillian H. "News from Narnia." *Horn Book Magazine*, October 1963.

Robert Lipsyte

Sports drama

New York City
January 16, 1938
The Contender

"If YA literature is to be worthwhile, to be *necessary*, it must go beyond to expose more questions (young people often need the right questions more than answers) about relationships between girls and boys, about the possibility of relationships that don't put sexual pressure on boys and girls, about ways of diffusing the terrible pressures of 'scoring' for boys, of losing or keeping virginity for girls, honest ways of looking at sex, through characters we can identify with and who entertain us, and perhaps coming to the radical conclusion that sex is at once less important than the deodorant makers would have us believe, yet more intrinsic a part of our lives than books up to now have told us," Robert Lipsyte stated in *Literature for Today's Young Adults*.

Lipsyte, the son of a school principal and a teacher, said in *Books I Read When I Was Young* that *The Catcher in the Rye* by J. D. Salinger was one of the books that made a difference in his life. "I read this book when I was fourteen. It was a portable support group. Here was a character, intelligent, sensitive, real, who was crazier than I was. But only by degree. And he was speaking directly to me."

He graduated from Columbia University with a bachelor's degree in 1957 and earned a master's two years later. From 1957 to 1959, he worked at *The New York Times* as a copyboy. After a stint in the U.S. Army in 1961, he gained a wide audience as a sportswriter from 1967 to 1971. He also worked for *The New York Post*, CBS-TV, NBC-TV, and PBS. He returned to *The New York Times* as a columnist in 1991. Lipsyte's fiction writing was interrupted by his own health problems—he overcame testicular cancer—and a second career as a television broadcaster.

Lipsyte's young adult fiction frequently depicts realistic sports settings. *The Contender*, for example, is about a scared seventeen-year-old, Alfred Brooks, with a dead-end job at a grocery store. His best friend is sinking into drug addiction. Street kids are after him for something he did not do. He begins going to a boxing club in Harlem. There he learns self-discipline and optimism as he trains. His trainer, though, does not think he has the killer instinct. Brooks insists on one more bout to find out.

The Contender "is considered a classic of the genre," *Children's Literature Review* stated. "As a white author writing about the black experience during a time when the subject was only beginning to be explored in young adult literature, Lipsyte is credited with vividly and authentically describing the worlds of boxing and ghetto life; during the course of the novel, he also addresses such issues as black militancy and the concerns of white merchants in black communities."

Lipsyte knew his subject well; he covered boxing for *The Times*. He told interviewer Betty Miles, "Sports is, or should be, just one of the things people do—an integral part of life, but only one aspect of it. Sport's is a good experience. It's fun. It ought to be inexpensive and accessible to everybody. Kids should go out and play, test and extend their bodies, feel good about what they can achieve on their own or with a team. And children's books about sports should encourage that approach.

"Instead, adults try to make sports into a metaphor—a preparation for life. We endow sports with mystical qualities that don't exist and raise unreal expectations about what it can do. At the same time, by making sports into a metaphor, we devalue it for itself. It's no wonder that the kids who read sports books are confused by them."

The writer's Bobby Marks series, set in the 1950s, is about an adolescent who struggles with a weight problem. The setting for *One Fat Summer* is Rumson Lake, an upstate New York resort town where Bobby's family spends each summer. To overcome his problems, Bobby is determined, hardworking, and optimistic. Equally determined is Jack Ryder, the high school pitcher who uses prescription drugs to overcome arm pain. The book was praised for its look at drug use.

Suggesting that Bobby is the only fully realized character in the book, reviewer Stephen Krensky said, "The dramatic movement of Bobby's metamorphosis is effectively rendered. As the summer progresses, he sheds pounds and illusions in equal measure, and in the process, both his mind and body begin to shape up. His long struggle culminates in the realization that he has the independence to meet life on his terms—and that's a weighty enough idea for anyone."

A sequel, *Summer Rules*, finds Bobby working as a counselor at Happy Valley Day Camp. "My enthusiasm for this book is boundless," Gail Tansill Lambert said. "Robert Lipsyte is the adolescent male's answer to Judy Blume, universally loved by young girls.

"He is a heavyweight in the field of children's literature. Nevertheless, he writes for kids, not for prestigious awards. His dialogue is earthy and humorous in a kid-smart vein, his characters are recognizable, and his plots compelling."

Lipsyte's first book was *Nigger* (1964), written with Dick Gregory. His nonfiction books for young adults are *Assignment: Sports* (1970), with Steve Cady, and *Free to Be Muhammed Ali* (1978). He also wrote *Jim Thorpe: 20th-Century Jock* and *Arnold Schwarzenegger: Hercules in America* (both 1995). Adult nonfiction titles include *The Masculine Mystique* (1966) and *SportsWorld: An American Dreamland* (1975). His two screenplays are *That's the Way of the World* (1975) and *The Act* (1982).

YOUNG ADULT FICTION

Jock and Jill: A Novel (1982)
Jack Ryder, ace high school hurler, needs a sports scholarship but interrupts a key game to take a stand against the false arrest of a Hispanic gang leader.

The Chemo Kid (1992)
Fred Bauer, a high school wimp, discovers a cancerous growth on his neck—and it changes his life.

Boxing Trilogy

The Contender (1967)
High school dropout Alfred Brooks learns that sometimes you can be a winner as a boxer even when you think you are down.

The Brave (1991)
Sonny Bear, seventeen, runs away from the reservation and meets Alfred Brooks, now a police officer in New York City.

The Chief (1993)
An incapacitated Alfred Brooks continues to train Sonny Bear, a fighter going nowhere.

Bobby Marks Trilogy

One Fat Summer (1977)
Fourteen-year-old Bobby "Crisco Kid" Marks has to overcome a weight problem and deal with the town bully, Willie Rumson.

Summer Rules: A Novel (1981)
Bobby, now sixteen, is a counselor at Happy Valley Day Camp.

The Summerboy: A Novel (1982)
Though eighteen and a college student, Bobby is taunted by his coworkers at the Lenape Laundry in their resort town.

ADULT FICTION

Something Going (1973)

Liberty Two (1974)

FOR FURTHER READING

Cullinan, Bernice, and M. Jerry Weiss, eds. *Books I Read When I Was Young: The Favorite Books of Famous People*. New York: Avon Books, 1980.

Donelson, Kenneth L., and Alleen Pace Nilsen, eds. "The People Behind the Books: Robert Lipsyte." *Literature for Today's Young Adults*. Glenview, IL: Scott, Foresman, 1980.

Lambert, Gail Tansill. Review of *Summer Rules. Best Sellers,* May 1981.

Krensky, Stephen. Review of *One Fat Summer. The New York Times Book Review,* 10 July 1977.

Miles, Betty. "Robert Lipsyte on Kids/Sports/Books." *Children's Literature in Education,* spring 1980.

"Robert Lipsyte." In *Children's Literature Review,* edited by Gerard J. Senick. Vol. 23. Detroit: Gale Research, 1991.

Scales, Pat. *A Teacher's Resource to Robert Lipsyte.* New York: HarperCollins Children's Books, 1992.

Jack London

Outdoor adventure

San Francisco
January 12, 1876–November 22, 1916
The Call of the Wild

John Griffith Chaney "Jack" London, the illegitimate son of an itinerant astrologer, grew up in a family that moved frequently. He attended school only occasionally, and he and other youths sometimes raided oyster beds in the San Francisco bay. In 1893, the teenage Jack London boarded a ship and sailed to Japan.

He tramped through the United States and Canada, briefly attended the University of California, returned to the waterfront, developed an interest in the Socialist Party, and, in 1897, joined the gold rush to the Klondike. There he got to know the rugged individuals who would become characters in his books. *Smoke Bellew*, typically, describes the hero's adventures, both hair-raising (struggling up an icy escarpment) and humorous (trying to corner the market on fresh eggs), in frontier Alaska.

"His experience in the Klondike was the turning point in his career," the *Dictionary of Literary Biography* stated, quoting London: " 'It was in the Klondike that I found myself,' he confessed. 'There you get your perspective. I got mine.' Forced by an attack of scurvy to return home the next summer, he took back no gold, but a wealth of experiences—not only his own but also those of the argonauts and sourdoughs with whom he had spent the richest winter of his life, experiences which his artistic genius could then transmute into marketable fictions."

London began writing in 1898, his stories appearing in such publications as *Overland Monthly* and *Atlantic Monthly*. *The Son of the Wolf*, his first collection, was published in 1900. He soon achieved considerable popularity and success.

"London's Klondike stories brought strong praise; he was called the successor to Poe, the equal of Kipling, a new voice rising above the prissy sentiment of the genteel tradition," Leonard Unger explained in *American Writers*. "The best of his stories have extraordinary power, which is generated by bold ideas, vigor and concreteness of language, and that combination of mystery and suspense that is the mark of the born storyteller. London jumps into the middle of his situation; he keeps the reader on tenterhooks by withholding facts in a way that makes him participate in the action."

London earned $75,000 some years, though he spent more than that. He became a war reporter for the Hearst papers during the Russo-Japanese War. He lectured, sailed to the Caribbean and South Seas, and served as a correspondent in Mexico. He built a $100,000 estate in California, Wolf House, which burned before he could move in.

London wed Bessie Mae ("Bess") Maddern in 1900. She retained custody of their two daughters when they divorced five years later. The writer saw little of his daughters after that. He married Clara Charmian Kittredge in 1905. They had one daughter, who died shortly after birth in 1910.

In 1914, at a relatively young age, London suffered deteriorating health, including kidney problems and acute rheumatism. His ability to write good fiction declined. He moved to Hawaii for his health and resorted to morphine to relieve pain. He died of apparent gastro-intestinal uremia in 1916, though an overdose of morphine suggested that he may have comitted suicide. He was forty.

"London's special genius appears in his command of detail and pace," said Unger. "He knows how to produce realism and suspense by giving the minutest factual items of a situation—and how on the other hand to jump over large areas of fact and make the reader supply the information or the meaning. He can bring the most seasoned sophisticate to the edge of his chair and have him fidgeting with anxiety as a story builds toward its climax."

Irving Stone described how London came to write perhaps his best-known book, *The Call of the Wild*. It began with a short story that grew out of hand. "He decided that he would name it *The Call of the Wild*, and let it grow however it willed, for the story was master now and he the servant writing it; it had taken hold of his imagination and fired him as no other yarn he had ever tackled. For thirty glorious, labor-laden days he wrote with his thick pencil on the rough scratch paper, made his few word corrections, and transferred the material to the typewriter. He neglected everything else—friends, family, debts, the new baby, galley proofs arriving in daily batches from Macmillan; living only with his dog Buck, half Saint Bernard and half Scotch shepherd, who had been living with a country gentleman on a ranch in the Santa Clara Valley until he was kidnapped and shipped into the primitive wilds of the Klondike."

A Darwinian theme of survival by adapting to the environment is at the heart of the book. Buck must adapt to both cruel men and cruel climate. Escaping a vicious master, Buck later finds then loses a kind one and ultimately must link with a wolf pack to survive.

White Fang is the reverse, the story of a dog who leaves the wild to live with people. Stone said, "It is a beautiful and moving dog story, carrying with it the thrill of first-rate literature."

The Sea-Wolf is about the strong, amoral captain of the *Ghost*, a tramp steamer. He rescues from the sea Humphrey Van Weyden, a wealthy and delicate individual. Captain Larsen puts him to work as a cabin boy, his harsh treatment forcing Van Weyden to shape up as a man. The ship picks up survivors of a wreck, among them Maude Brewster, a poet. Humphrey falls in love with Maude, but Larsen also lusts for her. The lovers escape in a boat to a small island and later care for Larsen when, mortally ill, he is deserted by his crew.

The book was a big hit. It "shot onto the market like a thunderbolt, became the rage overnight, was on everybody's lips to be praised or cursed," Stone said. "Many readers were insulted and offended by its attitudes; others valiantly took up the cudgels in its defense. Part of the press called it cruel, brutal, and revolting, but the greater part agreed that it was 'rare and original genius.' "

The writer was capable of Poe-esque tales such as "Moon-Face" (in *Moon-Face and Other Stories*), about a hateful man who seeks vengeance on a neighbor, and of Twain-like humor such as "The Leopard Man's Story," in which a circus knife-thrower gets revenge on the lion tamer for looking at his wife. He drops snuff on the lion tamer's hair, and when the tamer places his head in the lion's mouth during the performance, the animal sneezes and bites off his head.

London thrived on writing. "To Jack, one of the greatest things in the world was words," Stone said, "beautiful words, musical words, strong and sharp and incisive words. He read the heavy and learned tomes always with a dictionary at hand, wrote down words on sheets of paper, and stuck the sheets into the crack between the wood and mirror of his bureau, where he could memorize them while he shaved and dressed; he strung lists of them on a clothesline with clothespins so that every time he looked up or crossed the room he could see the new words and their meanings. He carried lists of them in every pocket, read them while he walked to the library or to Mabel's, mumbled them as he sat over his food or prepared for sleep. When the need came in a story for a precise word, and out of the hundreds of lists sprang the one with the exact shade of meaning, he was thrilled to the core of his being."

YOUNG ADULT FICTION

The Cruise of the Dazzler (1902)

Tales of the Fish Patrol (1915)

Jerry of the Islands (1917)

Michael, Brother of Jerry (1917)

FICTION

The Son of the Wolf (1900); alternate titles: *An Odyssey of the North* (1915); *The Son of the Wolf, Tales of the Far North* (1930); *The Son of the Wolf: Stories of the Northland* (1981)

The God of His Fathers, and Other Stories (1901); British title: *The God of His Fathers: Tales of the Klondyke* (1902); British revised edition: *The Man with the Gash, and Other Stories* (1981)

A Daughter of the Snows (1902)

Children of the Frost (1902)

The Call of the Wild (1903)
Buck, half Scotch shepherd, half Saint Bernard, is stolen, sold, and put into dogsled service in the Klondike. He eventually is rescued and cared for by John Thornton.

The Faith of Men, and Other Stories (1904)

The Sea-Wolf (1904)
Wolf Larsen is the ruthless captain of the tramp steamer *Ghost*.

The Game (1905)
Boxer Joe Fleming tries to explain the fascination of prize fighting to his fiancée, Genevieve.

Before Adam (1906)
Big Tooth and his mate, Swift One, are Fire People in prehistoric times.

Love of Life, and Other Stories (1906)

Moon-Face, and Other Stories (1906)

White Fang (1906)
Three-quarters wolf, White Fang, ill-treated by Beauty Smith, is tortured into fighting other dogs. Weedon Scott saves the dog and eventually tames it with love.

The Iron Heel (1907)
Ernest Everhard is a socialist revolutionary in this "prophetic" novel.

Martin Eden (1909)
Eden, becoming successful as a writer, attempts to revive romance with Ruth Morse.

Burning Daylight (1910)

Lost Face (1910)

Adventure (1911)

South Sea Tales (Macmillan, 1911); paperback title: *The Seed of McCoy, and Other Stories: South Sea Tales* (Pyramid, 1925)

When God Laughs, and Other Stories (1911)

The House of Pride, and Other Tales of Hawaii (1912)

Smoke Bellew (1912); British title: *Smoke and Shorty* (1920)
Kit Bellew and his friend, Shorty, head for the northern gold fields in search of riches and adventure.

A Son of the Sun (1912); revised edition: *The Adventures of Captain Grief* (1954); retitled, revised edition: *Captain David Grief* (1987)

The Abysmal Brute (1913)

John Barleycorn (1913); British title: *John Barleycorn; or, Alcoholic Memoirs* (1914)

The Night-Born (1913)

The Valley of the Moon (1913)

The Mutiny of the Elsinore (1914); retitled edition: *Mutiny of the Elsinore: A Novel of Seagoing Gangsters* (1987)

Strength of the Strong (1914)

The Scarlet Plague (1915)

The Star Rover (1915)

The Little Lady of the Big House (1916)

The Turtles of Tasman (1916)

The Human Drift (1917)

The Red One (1918)

On the Makaloa Mat (1919); British title: *Island Tales* (1923)

Hearts of Three (1920)

Dutch Courage, and Other Stories (1922)

The Assassination Bureau, Ltd., completed by Robert L. Fish (1963)

DRAMA

The Great Interrogation (first produced in 1905)

Scorn of Women (1906)

Theft: A Play in Four Acts (1910)

The Acorn-Planter: A California Forest Play (1916)

Daughters of the Rich: A Play (1971), edited by James E. Sisson

Gold: A Play (1972) with Herbert Heron, edited by James E. Sisson

ADAPTATIONS IN OTHER MEDIA

A Piece of Steak (1913)
Film based on the story "A Piece of Steak."

To Kill a Man (1913)
Film based on the story "To Kill a Man."

John Barleycorn (1914)
Film.

The Mutiny (1920)
Film based on *The Mutiny of the Elsinore.*

The Star Rover (1920)
Film.

The Abysmal Brute (1923)
Film.

Adventure (1925)
Film.

Burning Daylight (1928)
Film.

Devil's Skipper (1928)
Film based on the story "Demetrios Contos."

Son of the Wolf (1928)
Film.

Stormy Waters (1928)
Film based on the story "Yellow Handkerchief."

Wife of the King (1928)
Film based on the story "Wife of the King."

Smoke Bellew (1929)
Film.

The Sea-Wolf (1930)
Film.

The Call of the Wild (1935)
Film starring Clark Gable and Loretta Young.

Conflict (1936)
Film based on *The Abysmal Brute.*

White Fang (1936)
Film.

The Mutiny of the Elsinore (1939)
Film.

Romance of the Redwoods (1939)
Film based on the story "The White Silence."

Torture Ship (1939)
Film based on the story "A Thousand Deaths."

Wolf Call (1939)
Film.

Queen of the Yukon (1940)
Film based on the story "Queen of the Yukon."

North to the Klondike (1941)
Film based on the story "Gold Hunters of the North."

The Sea-Wolf (1941)
Film starring Edward G. Robinson and John Garfield.

Sign of the Wolf (1941)
Film based on the story "That Spot."

The Adventures of Martin Eden (1942)
Film based on *Martin Eden*, starring Glenn Ford and Evelyn Keyes.

Jack London (1943)
Film based on the author's life, as described in *The Book of Jack London* by Charmian London (1921).

Alaska (1944)
Film based on the story "Flush of Gold."

The Fighter (1951)
Film based on the story "The Mexican," starring Richard Conte.

Wolf Larsen (1958)
Film based on *The Sea-Wolf*, starring Barry Sullivan.

The Assassination Bureau (1969)
Film starring Oliver Reed and Diana Rigg.

White Fang (1972)
Film starring Franco Nero and Virna Lisi.

Challenge to White Fang (1975)
Film starring Franco Nero and Virna Lisi.

The Call of the Wild (1976)
Television movie starring John Beck.

The Legend of Sea Wolf (1978)
Film based on *The Sea-Wolf*.

White Fang and the Hunter (1985)
Film starring Robert Wood.

White Fang (1991)
Film starring Ethan Hawke.

White Fang II: Myth of the White Wolf (1994), sequel
Film starring Scott Bairstow.

Legends of the North (1995)
Television movie based on *Smoke Bellew*, starring Randy Quaid.

FOR FURTHER READING

Labor, Earle. "Jack London." In *Dictionary of Literary Biography*, edited by Donald Pizer and Earll N. Harbert. *American Realists and Naturalists*. vol. 12, Detroit: Gale Research, 1982.

London, Joan. *Jack London: An Unconventional Biography*. New York: Doubleday, 1939.

O'Connor, Richard. *Jack London: A Biography*. Boston: Little, Brown, 1964.

Stone, Irving. *Sailor on Horseback: The Biography of Jack London*. Boston: Houghton Mifflin, 1938.

Unger, Leonard, ed. *American Writers: A Collection of Literary Biographies*. Vol. 2. New York: Charles Scribner's Sons, 1974.

Walker, Franklin. *Jack London and the Klondike: The Genesis of an American Writer*. San Marino, CA: Huntington Library, 1966.

Lois Lowry

Family drama

Honolulu, Hawaii
March 20, 1937

The Giver

Gut-wrenching is the only way to describe Lois Lowry's first young adult book, *A Summer to Die*. It is a story of birth and death. Fifteen-year-old Molly Chalmers, who has leukemia, latches onto the young neighbors who are soon expecting the home-birth of their baby. The story is told by younger sister Meg, who feels she is an ugly duckling compared with Molly. Meg's life is both shattered and reaffirmed.

"Her story captures the mysteries of living and dying without manipulating the readers' emotions," Linda R. Silver said, "providing understanding and a comforting sense of completion."

The daughter of a dentist who was a career military officer, Lois Hammersberg Lowry spent her childhood mostly with her mother, a teacher. During World War II, her mother took the family to live with her parents in Pennsylvania while her husband served with the U.S. Army Dental Corps in the Pacific. Lowry once observed that her father's absence led her to write strong father figures into her books—she was acting out a fantasy.

By age three, Lowry could read and write, which set her apart from her mates when she began school. A shy child with an active imagination, she was pushed ahead several grades but struggled with arithmetic and other subjects.

In 1948, the family moved to Japan to join their father, who was with the occupation forces there. Lowry spent two years in Tokyo, attending an English-language school with her sister, Helen. She later attended Brown University and the University of Maine but left in 1956, at the end of her sophomore year, to marry. She and her husband, Donald G. Lowry, an attorney, moved frequently. They had four children and divorced in 1977.

Lowry wrote two textbooks, *Black American Literature* (1973) and *Literature of the American Revolution* (1974). After that, she began her first novel, *A Summer to Die*, basing it on her experiences when her sister, Helen, died.

Lowry's second book, *Find a Stranger, Say Goodbye*, is about a girl seeking her "real" mother. "No sharp edges snag the fluent storytelling; everything has been neatly rounded off, and there is even one wonderfully funny episode. But the very attractiveness of the characters and the tidiness of the plot constitute the weakness of the book; for it is the kind of novel that reminds the reader that realism can often be less of an honest revelation of life than fantasy," reviewer Ethel L. Heins wrote.

Lowry's popular series featuring Anastasia Krupnik is for middle readers. The spunky, rebellious, and funny heroine is a composite of the writer's two daughters and Amy Carter, then-President Jimmy Carter's daughter. Two books also feature Anastasia's younger brother, Sam.

"Lowry's fictional families are not perfect—they would not be realistic if they were—but they provide unconditional love and support when calamity strikes," said Laura M. Zaidman. "While avoiding shocking 'problem novels,' Lowry does not shelter her adolescent readers from the real world. They can identify, laugh, and cry with these believable characters who grow wiser with each problem resolved. Thus, Lowry helps children answer their own baffling questions about self-identity and human relationships."

Lowry's young adult book *Number the Stars* won the Newbery Medal, in 1990, as did *The Giver*. In her acceptance speech for the second award, in 1993, Lowry said the first medal "freed me to risk failure" in attempting *The Giver*.

The Giver, a science fiction novel, "takes place in a nameless community, at an unidentified future time," Ann A. Flowers explained. "The life is utopian: there is no hunger, no disease, no pollution, no fear; old age is tenderly cared for; every child has concerned and attentive parents. Each aspect of life has a prescribed rule: one-year-olds—'Ones'—are Named and given to their chosen family; 'Nines' get their first bicycles; Birthmothers give birth to three children and then become Laborers; 'family units' get two children, one male, one female.

"In Jonas's family, his father is a Nurturer, one who cares for the 'new children' before they go to a family unit; his mother is in the Department of Justice; and he has a younger sister, Lily. But although their life seems perfect, the reader somehow becomes uneasily aware that all is not well. Young Jonas is eagerly awaiting his Ceremony of Twelve, the time when all the twelve-year-olds in the community receive their Assignments for their lifelong professions."

Jonas is to become a Receiver of Memories, one of the most respected of Elders. As he learns his task from The Giver, he discovers that the community knows no memories of pain or grief; only the Giver knows these, and he is to pass them along to Jonas.

Lowry "is a risk taker," Walter Lorraine observed, "and a just plain good guy in an often cynical world. She has always taken chances. *Rabble Starkey* and *Autumn Street* are powerful and individual statements. The Anastasia stories are very funny, but woven into that humor is far more worldly insight than is usual for such popular fiction. In an age of conformity, Lois is a unique and important voice. She is an author who truly has something to say and is willing to risk saying it."

Lowry "invites each reader to bring his or her personal experience to the story," Lorraine said. "In one sense her writing becomes more complete with the reader's participation—a true Gestalt in which the whole is greater than the sum of its parts. Often provocative contradictions result, sometimes to the extent that the protagonist dies or lives happily ever, each reader being convinced of a different interpretation."

YOUNG ADULT FICTION

A Summer to Die (1977)
Thirteen-year-old Meg's older sister, Molly, who is terminally ill, takes deep and poignant interest in the neighbor's new baby.

Find a Stranger, Say Goodbye (1978)
Seventeen-year-old Natalie Armstrong, pretty and intelligent, with a loving family and a great boyfriend, is missing something: Who is her biological mother?

Autumn Street (1980); British title: *The Woods at the End of Autumn Street* (1987)
Elizabeth Lorimer is just a child during World War II, when she becomes best friends with Charles, the son of the family's black cook.

Us and Uncle Fraud (1984)
Uncle Claude visits Louise Cunningham's home, then departs abruptly, leaving a strange clue.

Rabble Starkey (1987); British title: *The Road Ahead* (1988)
Her family life disrupted, Rabble yearns for stability. The twelve-year-old and her twenty-six-year-old mother move in with a family whose mother has been institutionalized.

Number the Stars (1989)
In 1943, Annemarie Johansen's family takes in her Jewish friend, Ellen Rosen, to hide her from the Nazis occupying Copenhagen.

The Giver (1993)
Jonas inhabits a seemingly ideal world without conflict, poverty, injustice, or inequity. It is December, and he is about to receive his life assignment.

CONTRIBUTOR

Am I Blue? Coming Out from the Silence, edited by Marion Dane Bauer (1994)

FICTION FOR MIDDLE READERS

Taking Care of Terrific (1983)

Anastasia Series

Anastasia Krupnik (1979)

Anastasia Again! (1981)

Anastasia at Your Service (1982)

Anastasia, Ask Your Analyst (1984)

Anastasia on Her Own (1985)

Anastasia's Chosen Career (1987)

Anastasia Has the Answers (1987)

All About Sam (1988)
Features Anastasia's little brother.

Anastasia at This Address (1991)

Attaboy Sam (1993), sequel to *All About Sam*

Anastasia, Absolutely (1995)

Caroline Tate Series

The One Hundredth Thing About Caroline (1983)

Switcharound (1985)

Your Move, J. P. (1990)

ADAPTATIONS IN OTHER MEDIA

I Don't Know Who I Am (1980)
ABC *Afterschool Special* based on *Find a Stranger, Say Goodbye.*

FOR FURTHER READING

Flowers, Ann A. Review of *The Giver. Horn Book Magazine*, July–August 1993.

Heins, Ethel L. Review of *Find a Stranger, Say Goodbye. Horn Book Magazine*, June 1978.

Lois Lowry and Anastasia Krupnik: The Whole Truth! New York: Dell, n.d.

Lorraine, Walter. "Lois Lowry." *Horn Book Magazine*, July–August 1994.

Silver, Linda R. Review of *A Summer to Die. School Library Journal*, May 1977.

Zaidman, Laura M. "Lois Lowry." In *Twentieth-Century Children's Writers*, edited by Tracy Chevalier. 3d ed. Chicago: St. James Press, 1989.

Margaret Mahy

Fantasy and family drama

Whakatane, New Zealand
March 21, 1936
The Haunting

"I write the kind of book that reflects the European middle-class family I came from," Margaret Mahy said in *Books for Keeps*.

Mahy, the daughter of a builder and a teacher, began writing "from the time I was seven onwards . . . in a spirit of implacable plagiarism because, reading widely as I did, I rapidly came to feel that everything worthwhile had already been written. I do believe now that the games I acted out, talking aloud as I did, were the *real* stories I was inventing."

Mahy said that she shies away from trying to make a moral point. She noted that she is still fond of Mark Twain's *The Adventures of Tom Sawyer* and Robert Louis Stevenson's *Treasure Island*. "I try to tell an exciting story, something which children enjoy reading. For older children I try to suggest the world is not a rigidly defined place, that they can allow their imaginations to move and have a lot of freedom."

Mahy received a bachelor of arts degree from the University of New Zealand in 1958 and worked as a librarian from 1958 to 1980. She has published a steady stream of books for young adults and younger readers since 1969.

"I decided in childhood that I wanted to be a writer," Mahy said in a publisher's pamphlet, "and I used to write in little notebooks, which I also illustrated. When I got to the middle of the notebook, I always celebrated by drawing a picture, and if I got tired of the story, I would draw many more pictures, for they took up room. I always thought the stories I wrote should be exactly the same length as the notebook. . . .

"All the time I was trying to be a nurse or going to college, I was writing, and I had found what I enjoyed writing most was children's stories. I think this is because in the 1950s there was not a great deal of fantasy for adults published, and I enjoyed writing and reading fantasy stories. I began to have stories published in the New Zealand school journal in 1961 and in due course began to have books published, too. It was quite hard to get stories published in New Zealand in those days, and my first stories were published in the United States and in the United Kingdom."

A frequent theme in Mahy's books is a fantastical adventure that tells about people getting along together. *A Lion in the Meadow,* for example, tells of a mother who does not believe her son's bizarre stories. She thinks he is just playing a game when he says there is a lion in the meadow. She offers him a small box containing matches and tells him a dragon inside will scare away the beast. He believes her, and she soon regrets having made up the lie.

Underrunners is about a boy who plays in tunnels behind his home. "Seeking escape underground are Tris, a boy still troubled by his mother's long-ago desertion, and Winola, a girl hiding from her abusive father," the *Bulletin of the Center for Children's Books* commented. "The children's friendship is based partly on a shared fantasy game and partly on what turns out to be, for Tris, a very real memory." The reviewer also remarked on Mahy's "uncanny sense of metaphor and experienced capability for supporting images with ordinary detail."

A young man finds he is to inherit psychic powers in Mahy's *The Haunting,* and he believes it is more a curse than blessing. "Here is an absolutely first-rate contemporary novel of the supernatural," Michael Cart said. "The compelling story involves the 'haunting' of eight-year-old Barney Palmer and the discovery of both a long lost great-uncle with psychic powers and a family curse—or is it?"

"*The Haunting* manages to combine a realistic approach to family life—in which how you feel about your parents and yourself is actually important—with a strong and terrifying line in fantasy," Sarah Hayes said. "The story is built round conversations over family meals which are linked by graphic descriptions of what is going on inside the head of Barney Palmer."

Noting Mahy's use of New Zealand settings in her young adult novels, Paul Heins said, "They evoke, on the whole, an international 20th century ambiance in which divorced parents, single-parent families, and even Alzheimer's disease are part of the social fabric, along with shopping malls, television, portable radios, and wrecked cars."

As well as writing a screenplay based on *The Haunting*, Mahy has written several scripts for New Zealand television productions.

YOUNG ADULT FICTION

The Haunting (1982)
Barney Palmer is not sure he wants to become a psychic.

The Changeover: A Supernatural Romance (1984)
Fourteen-year-old Laura enters the world of witchcraft and the supernatural to save her young brother's life.

The Catalogue of the Universe (1985)
High school friends work out their problems, such as living without a father and looking for a meaning to life.

Aliens in the Family (1986)
Twelve-year-old Jake has trouble fitting in with her new stepfamily.

The Tricksters (1987)
The Hamiltons of New Zealand celebrate Christmas with their British friend, Anthony, and take turns telling him the story of the beach house and a boy who drowned.

Memory (1988)
Jonny Dart blames himself for the accidental death of his sister.

Underrunners (1992)
Tris flees to a fantasy world in tunnels near his home, joining an escapee from a children's home.

The Pirates' Mixed-Up Voyage: Dark Doings in the Thousand Islands (1993)

FICTION FOR YOUNGER READERS

The Dragon of an Ordinary Family (1969)

A Lion in the Meadow (1969); expanded edition: *A Lion in the Meadow, and Five Other Favourites* (1976)

Mrs. Discombobulous (1969)

Pilycock's Shop (1969)

The Procession (1969)

The Little Witch (1970)

Sailor Jack and the 20 Orphans (1970)

The Princess and the Clown (1971)

The Boy with Two Shadows (1972)

The First Margaret Mahy Story Book: Stories and Poems (1972)

The Man Whose Mother Was a Pirate (1972)

The Railway Engine and the Hairy Brigands (1972)

The Second Margaret Mahy Story Book: Stories and Poems (1973)

The Bus Under the Leaves (1974)

Clancy's Cabin (1974)

The Rare Spotted Birthday Party (1974)

Rooms for Rent (1974); British title: *Rooms to Let* (1974)

Stepmother (1974)

The Witch in the Cherry Tree (1974)

The Great Millionaire Kidnap (1975)

The Third Margaret Mahy Story Book: Stories and Poems (1975)

Ultra-Violet Catastrophe! Or, the Unexpected Walk with Great-Uncle Mangus Pringle (1975)

The Boy Who Was Followed Home (1976)

David's Witch Doctor (1976)

Leaf Magic (1976)

The Wind Between the Stars (1976)

Look Under V (1977)

The Nonstop Nonsense Book (1977)

The Pirate Uncle (1977)

The Great Piratical Rumbustification, and the Librarian and the Robbers (1978)

Raging Robots and Unruly Uncles (1981)

The Crocodile's Christmas Sandals (1982), Australian edition; 2d Australian edition: *The Crocodile's Christmas Thongs* (1985)

The Great Chewing-Gum Rescue, and Other Stories (1982)

Story Chest Books (5 vols., 1982) with Joy Cowley and June Melser

The Bubbling Crocodile (1983)

A Crocodile in the Library (1983)

Mrs. Bubble's Baby (1983)

Shopping with a Crocodile (1983)

The Birthday Burglar, and a Very Wicked Headmistress (1984)

The Dragon's Birthday (1984)

Fantail, Fantail (1984)

Going to the Beach (1984)

The Great Grumbler and the Wonder Tree (1984)

Leaf Magic, and Five Other Favourites (1984)

The Spider in the Shower (1984)

Ups and Downs, and Other Stories (1984)

The Adventures of a Kite (1985)

The Cake (1985)

The Catten (1985)

Clever Hamburger (1985)

A Crocodile in the Garden (1985)

The Earthquake (1985)

Jam: A True Story (1985)

Out in the Big Wide World (1985)

Rain (1985)

Sophie's Singing Mother (1985)

A Vary Happy Bathday (1985)

Arguments (1986)

Baby's Breakfast (1986)

Beautiful Pig (1986)

The Downhill Crocodile Whizz, and Other Stories (1986)

An Elephant in the House (1986)

Feeling Funny (1986)

The Fight on the Hill (1986)

The Funny Funny Clown Face (1986)

The Garden Party (1986)

Jacko, the Junk Shop Man (1986)

The Long Grass of Tumbledown Road (1986)

Mahy Magic (3 vols., 1986)
Short stories.

The Man Who Enjoyed Grumbling (1986)

The Mouse Wedding (1986)

Mr. Rooster's Dilemma (1986), Australian title; British title: *How Mr. Rooster Didn't Get Married* (1986)

Muppy's Ball (1986)

My Wonderful Aunt (4 vols., 1986)

The New House Villain (1986)

A Pet to the Vet (1986)

The Pop Group (1986)

The Robber Pig and the Ginger Beer (1986)

The Robber Pig and the Green Eggs (1986)

Squeak in the Gate (1986)

Tai Taylor and His Education (1986)

Tai Taylor and the Sweet Annie (1986)

The Three Wishes (1986)

Tinny Tiny Tinker (1986)

The Tree Doctor (1986)

Trouble on the Bus (1986)

The Girl Who Washed in Moonlight (1987)

Guinea Pig Grass (1987)

The Haunting of Miss Cardamon (1987)

The Horrible Story and Others (1987)

Iris La Bonga and the Helpful Taxi Driver (1987)

The Mad Puppet (1987)

The Man Who Walked on His Hands (1987)

Mr. Rumfitt (1987)

No Dinner for Sally (1987)

Tai Taylor Goes to School (1987)

As Luck Would Have It (1988)

The Door in the Air, and Other Stories (1988)

A Not-So-Quiet Evening (1988)

Sarah, the Bear and the Kangaroo (1988)

When the King Rides By (1988)

The Blood-and-Thunder Adventure on Hurricane Peak (1989)

Chocolate Porridge, and Other Stories (1989)

Making Friends (1990)

Seven Chinese Brothers (1990)

Dangerous Spaces (1991)

The Horrendous Hullabaloo (1991)

Keeping House (1991)

Pumpkin Man and the Crafty Creeper (1991)

The Queen's Goat (1991)

The Girl with the Green Ear: Stories About Magic in Nature (1992)

A Tall Story, and Other Tales (1992)

A Busy Day for a Good Grandmother (1993)

The Three-Legged Cat (1993)

The Christmas Tree Tangle (1994)

The Greatest Show off Earth (1994)

The Pirate Uncle (1994)

The Rattlebang Picnic (1994)

Tick-Tock Tale: Stories to Read Around the Clock (1994)

Cousins Quartet

The Good Fortunes Gang (1993)

A Fortunate Name (1993)

A Fortune Branches Out (1994)

Tangled Fortunes (1994)

POETRY

Seventeen Kings and Forty-Two Elephants (1972)

The Tin Can Band, and Other Poems (1989)

Bubble Trouble, and Other Poems and Stories (1992)

ADAPTATIONS IN OTHER MEDIA

The Haunting of Barney Palmer (1987) Screenplay by Mahy, based on *The Haunting*.

FOR FURTHER READING

"Authorgraph No. 24: Margaret Mahy." *Books for Keeps*, January 1984.

Flowers, Ann A. Review of *The Good Fortunes Gang*. *Horn Book Magazine*, July–August 1993.

Hayes, Sarah. "Unearthing the Family Ghosts." *The Times Literary Supplement*, 17 September 1982.

Heins, Paul. "Margaret Mahy." In *Twentieth-Century Children's Writers*, edited by Tracy Chevalier. 3d ed. Chicago: St. James Press, 1989.

Margaret Mahy. New York: Margaret K. McElderry Books, 1986.

Review of *Underrunners*. *Bulletin of the Center for Children's Books*, March 1992.

Ann M. Martin

Family drama

Princeton, New Jersey
August 12, 1955
The Baby-Sitters Club Series

Ann M. Martin, the daughter of an illustrator and a teacher, wrote more than a dozen books for young adults before beginning the popular Baby-Sitters Club series. She began writing her first young adult novel, *Bummer Summer*, in 1980. It was not finished for three years, because Martin could only find time to write early in the morning.

The story is about twelve-year-old Kammy Whitlock, whose widower father remarries. Suddenly, she has a new three-year-old stepsister, Muffin, and a baby stepbrother, Baby Boy. Kammy's paints are flushed down the toilet and her cat is tormented. She never has a private moment with her father. She is exasperated. Spending the summer away at Camp Arrowhead does not excite her—at first—but being at camp helps her sort out her family situation.

"As a child," biographer Margot Becker "R." (Rubin) said, "Ann read many classic children's books such as Frances Hodgson Burnett's *The Secret Garden*, L. Frank Baum's Wizard of Oz series, Lewis Carroll's *Alice in Wonderland* and Hugh Lofting's *Doctor Dolittle*." She also delved into the works of Roald Dahl, Marguerite Henry's horse stories, Astrid Lindgren's Pippi Longstocking books, and Betty MacDonald's Mrs. Piggle Wiggle books. In her teen years, Martin read a lot of fantasy and science fiction. As an adult she gravitates toward writers who "write stories about things that could really happen," according to Becker.

Graduating from Smith College in 1977, Martin taught elementary school in Connecticut for a year before joining Pocket Books in New York City as an editorial assistant for Archway Paperbacks. In 1980, she moved to Scholastic Book Services as a copywriter for the Teen Age Book Club. She later became an associate editor, then an editor. From 1983 to 1985, she was senior editor for Bantam's Books for Young Readers, then she left to devote full time to writing and editing.

Of the craft of writing, Martin told Becker, "When you're making up a story, you're in charge. You can solve problems the way you wish they could be solved in real life. It's a way to work out the 'if onlys' and the 'what ifs.' The 'if onlys' are all the things you think about, all the solutions to problems in your own life that you didn't come up with fast enough."

The author has worked many youthful concerns into her Baby-Sitters Club series, which began in 1986. "Into each story are integrated situations that reflect life as it really is lived across America, and that includes elements such as stepfamilies, working mothers, death, adoption and friends or relatives with disabilities," Leslie Dreyfous said. "The girls also encounter all sorts of smaller prepubescent woes in each monthly addition to the . . . series.

"More kids today have been exposed to divorce . . . or moved around a lot," Martin told Dreyfous. "They start watching television at an earlier age and watch things that are more sophisticated than what we watched at an early age."

Martin looks at coping with dyslexia in *Yours Turly, Shirley*, autism in *Inside Out*, and the death of a family member in *With You and Without You*.

In this last title, Liza O'Hara's father is dying of heart disease. The family accepts his gradual decline—not willingly but with courage. When he dies, Liza, her brother, and her two sisters react in different ways. Little sister Hope finds it hardest to realize that Daddy will not be coming back. Martin presents death matter-of-factly, recognizing that it is an emotional drain but also affirming the human spirit.

"Life would go on. Not the same as usual, but it would go on," Liza says bravely when first learning of her father's illness. Still, his death is a shock. "Sometimes I fantasized that dad hadn't really died," she later says. "It had all been an elaborate government plan for him to escape from our family and his own past and to assume a new identity. Everyone had been in on it—the doctors, the private nurse, the men who took him away. It all made sense, really . . . I could convince myself that this was true."

Liza finds that it is most difficult to deal with the loss around the Christmas holiday; she declares that no one should have a good time because her father is not there to enjoy it. Drawing Liza out of her shell is a boy, Marc Radlay, who invites her on a date. She makes excuses and jeopardizes their relationship. He is patient, though, and her mother and friends are supportive, allowing Liza to overcome her reluctance.

Martin told interviewer Jean W. Ross, "Quite a bit of the dialogue results just from remembering what it was like to be a kid talking with my friends. I go on a lot of school visits and autographings now. And I'm connected with a school in New York, P. S. 2, so I see the kids down there a lot."

Martin's Baby-Sitters Club books "are uncommonly well written for a paperback children's series," N. R. Kleinfield stated. "They sometimes incline toward soap-opera-style plots, but the twists and turns are less formulaic than the genre usually offers."

In the first few years of the series, Martin wrote all the books, which are intended for eight- to thirteen-year-olds. When Baby-Sitters' Little Sister and various special books were added to the schedule, ghostwriters were brought in.

The idea for the series originated with a book publisher. "In 1983," according to Kleinfield, "Jean Feiwel, a Scholastic editor, noticed that a book about a young girl's baby-sitting job had sold well for the company, and she thought there might be something in a series revolving around a group of baby-sitters. This was about the time that Bantam's 'Sweet Valley High' titles had captivated young hearts and books about groups of girls were selling briskly."

The editor recruited Martin to write the series, which is still going strong. "I'm a very disciplined person, a trait I picked up from my father, a self-employed cartoonist," the writer said in a publisher's pamphlet. "I usually work on two or three books at a time. If I get stuck—which does happen—I try to force myself to write. If I'm *really* stuck, I put it away and go back to it the next day. I never stop at the end of a chapter—it's always easier for me to begin in the middle of something."

YOUNG ADULT FICTION

Bummer Summer (1983)
When her widowed father remarries, Kammy, twelve, is saddled with an unwanted three-year-old stepsister, Muffin, and a baby stepbrother.

Just You and Me (1983)

Inside Out (1984)
Autistic James Peterson holds back his brother, Jonno, from joining the "in crowd."

Me and Katie (the Pest) (1985)
Against a background of horseback riding, a ten-year-old girl copes with her older sister's greater success.

Missing Since Monday (1986)
When little sister Courtenay does not return from preschool, tenth-grader Maggie and her older brother, Mike, do not know what to do. Their father and stepmother are off on a long-delayed honeymoon.

With You and Without You (1986)
Twelve-year-old Liza O'Hara's father has only a few months to live, and she and other family members have a hard time coping.

Just a Summer Romance (1987)
Melanie Braderman, fourteen, meets the boy of her dreams, Justin Hurt. When summer is over and they part, she sees his face on the cover of *People Weekly*.

Slam Book (1987)
Anna and her ninth-grade friends write comments about each other in the "slam book." Then it becomes a tool of cruelty.

Ten Kids, No Pets (1988)
The Rosso family of ten children ranges from Abbie to Woody.

Yours Turly, Shirley (1988)
A girl with dyslexia has to accept that her adoptive Vietnamese sister is doing better in school than she is.

Eleven Kids, One Summer (1991), sequel to *Ten Kids, No Pets*
The thoroughly organized Mrs. Rosso, the absent-minded Mr. Rosso, and their brood return.

The Million Dollar Kid (1991)
A girl wins the lottery.

FICTION FOR YOUNGER READERS

My Puppy Scrapbook (1983) with Betsy Ryan

Stage Fright (1984)

Fancy Dance in Feather Town (1988)

Ma and Pa Dracula (1989)

Moving Day in Feather Town (1989), sequel to *Fancy Dance in Feather Town*

Rachel Parker, Kindergarten Show-Off (1992)

The Baby-Sitters Club Series

1. *Kristy's Great Idea* (1986)
2. *Claudia and the Phantom Phone Calls* (1986)
3. *The Truth About Stacey* (1986)
4. *Mary Anne Saves the Day* (1987)
5. *Dawn and the Impossible Three* (1987)
6. *Kristy's Big Day* (1987)
7. *Claudia and Mean Janine* (1987)
8. *Boy-Crazy Stacey* (1987)
9. *The Ghost at Dawn's House* (1988)
10. *Logan Likes Mary Anne!* (1988)
11. *Kristy and the Snobs* (1988)
12. *Claudia and the New Girl* (1988)
13. *Good-bye Stacey, Good-bye* (1988)
14. *Hello, Mallory* (1988)
15. *Little Miss Stoneybrook . . . and Dawn* (1988)
16. *Jessi's Secret Language* (1988)
17. *Mary Anne's Bad-Luck Mystery* (1988)
18. *Stacey's Mistake* (1988)
19. *Claudia and the Bad Joke* (1988)
20. *Kristy and the Walking Disaster* (1989)
21. *Mallory and the Trouble with Twins* (1989)
22. *Jessi Ramsey, Pet-Sitter* (1989)
23. *Dawn on the Coast* (1989)
24. *Kristy and the Mother's Day Surprise* (1989)

25. *Mary Anne and the Search for Tigger* (1989)
26. *Claudia and the Sad Good-bye* (1989)
27. *Jessi and the Superbrat* (1989)
28. *Welcome Back, Stacey!* (1989)
29. *Mallory and the Mystery Diary* (1989)
30. *Mary Anne and the Great Romance* (1990)
31. *Dawn's Wicked Stepsister* (1990)
32. *Kristy and the Secret of Susan* (1990)
33. *Claudia and the Great Search* (1990)
34. *Mary Anne and Too Many Boys* (1990)
35. *Stacey and the Mystery of Stoneybrook* (1990)
36. *Jessi's Baby-Sitter* (1990)
37. *Dawn and the Older Boy* (1990)
38. *Kristy's Mystery Admirer* (1990)
39. *Poor Mallory* (1990)
40. *Claudia and Middle School* (1991)
41. *Mary Anne vs. Logan* (1991)
42. *Jessi and the Dance School Phantom* (1991)
43. *Stacey's Emergency* (1991)
44. *Dawn and the Big Sleepover* (1991)
45. *Kristy and the Baby Parade* (1991)
46. *Mary Anne Misses Logan* (1991)
47. *Mallory on Strike* (1991)
48. *Jessi's Wish* (1991)
49. *Claudia and the Genius of Elm Street* (1991)
50. *Dawn's Big Date* (1992)
51. *Stacey's Ex-Best Friend* (1992)
52. *Mary Anne and Too Many Babies* (1992)
53. *Kristy for President* (1992)
54. *Mallory's Dream House* (1992)
55. *Jessi's Gold Medal* (1992)
56. *Keep Out, Claudia!* (1992)
57. *Dawn Saves the Planet* (1992)
58. *Stacey's Choice* (1992)
59. *Mallory Hates Boys (and Gym)* (1992)
60. *Mary Anne's Makeover* (1993)
61. *Jessi and the Awful Secret* (1993)
62. *Kristy and the Worst Kid Ever* (1993)
63. *Claudia's Friend* (1993)
64. *Dawn's Family Feud* (1993)
65. *Stacey's Big Crush* (1993)
66. *Maid Mary Anne* (1993)
67. *Dawn's Big Move* (1993)
68. *Jessi and the Bad Baby-Sitter* (1993)
69. *Get Well Soon, Mallory* (1994)
70. *Stacey and the Cheerleaders* (1994)
71. *Claudia and the Perfect Boy* (1994)
72. *Dawn and the We Love Kids Club* (1994)
73. *Mary Anne and Miss Priss* (1994)
74. *Kristy and the Copy Cat* (1994)
75. *Jessi's Horrible Prank* (1994)
76. *Stacey's Lie* (1994)
77. *Dawn and Whitney: Friends Forever* (1994)
78. *Mary Anne Breaks the Rules* (1994)
79. *Claudia and Crazy Peaches* (1994)
80. *Mallory Pike, No. 1 Fan* (1994)
81. *Kristy and Mr. Mom* (1995)
82. *Jessi and the Troublemaker* (1995)
83. *Stacey vs. the BSC* (1995)
84. *Dawn and the School Spirit War* (1995)
85. *Claudia Kishi, Live from WSTO!* (1995)
86. *Mary Anne and Camp BSC* (1995)
87. *Stacey & the Bad Girls* (1995)
88. *Farewell, Dawn* (1995)
89. *Kristy and the Dirty Diapers* (1995)
90. *Welcome to the BSC, Abby* (1995)
91. *Claudia and the First Thanksgiving* (1995)

Baby-Sitters Club Planner and Date Book (1991)

Baby-Sitters Club Postcard Book (1991)

Baby-Sitters Club Trivia and Puzzle Fun Book (1992)

The BSC Guide to Baby-Sitting (1993)

Baby-Sitters Club Secret Santa (1994)

The Baby-Sitters Club (1995) by A. L. Singer
Based on a screenplay by Dalene Young, Jane Startz, Eileen Cowel, Maria Gillen, Melanie Mayron, Cynthia Mort, and Caitlin Adams.

The Baby-Sitters Club (1995) By Kathryn Christoldi
Based on the screenplay.

Baby-Sitters Club Mysteries

1. *Stacey and the Missing Ring* (1991)
2. *Beware Dawn!* (1991)
3. *Mallory and the Ghost Cat* (1992)
4. *Kristy and the Missing Child* (1992)
5. *Mary Anne and the Secret in the Attic* (1992)
6. *The Mystery at Claudia's House* (1992)
7. *Dawn and the Disappearing Dogs* (1993)
8. *Jessi and the Jewel Thieves* (1993)
9. *Kristy and the Haunted Mansion* (1993)
10. *Stacey and the Mystery Money* (1993)
11. *Claudia and the Mystery at the Museum* (1994)
12. *Dawn and the Surfer Ghost* (1994)
13. *Mary Anne and the Library Mystery* (1994)
14. *Stacey and the Mystery at the Mall* (1994)
15. *Kristy and the Vampires* (1994)
16. *Claudia and the Clue in the Photograph* (1994)
17. *Dawn and the Halloween Mystery* (1994)
18. *Stacey and the Mystery at the Empty House* (1994)
19. *Kristy and the Missing Fortune* (1995)
20. *Mary Anne and the Mystery at the Zoo* (1995)
21. *Claudia and the Recipe for Danger* (1995)
22. *Stacey and the Haunted Masquerade* (1995)

Baby-Sitters Club Portrait Collection

1. *Stacey's Book* (1994)
2. *Claudia's Book* (1995)
3. *Dawn's Book* (1995)

Baby-Sitters Club Special Edition Readers' Request

Logan's Story (1992)

Logan Bruno, Boy Baby-Sitter (1993)

Baby-Sitters Club Super Mystery

The Baby-Sitters' Haunted House (1995)

Baby-Sitters Club Super-Specials

1. *Baby-Sitters on Board!* (1988)
2. *Baby-Sitters' Summer Vacation* (1989)
3. *Baby-Sitters' Winter Vacation* (1989)
4. *Baby-Sitters' Island Adventure* (1990)
5. *California Girls!* (1990)
6. *New York, New York!* (1991)
7. *Snowbound* (1991)
8. *Baby-Sitters at Shadow Lake* (1992)
9. *Starring the Baby-Sitters Club* (1992)
10. *Sea City, Here We Come!* (1993)
11. *The Baby-Sitters Remember* (1994)
12. *Here Come the Bridesmaids* (1994)

Baby-Sitters' Little Sister

1. *Karen's Witch* (1988)
2. *Karen's Roller Skates* (1988)
3. *Karen's Worst Day* (1989)
4. *Karen's Kittycat Club* (1989)
5. *Karen's School Picture* (1989)
6. *Karen's Little Sister* (1989)
7. *Karen's Birthday* (1989)
8. *Karen's Haircut* (1990)
9. *Karen's Sleepover* (1990)
10. *Karen's Grandmothers* (1990)
11. *Karen's Prize* (1990)
12. *Karen's Ghost* (1990)

13. *Karen's Surprise* (1991)
14. *Karen's New Year* (1991)
15. *Karen's in Love* (1991)
16. *Karen's Goldfish* (1991)
17. *Karen's Brother* (1991)
18. *Karen's Home Run* (1991)
19. *Karen's Good-bye* (1991)
20. *Karen's Carnival* (1991)
21. *Karen's New Teacher* (1991)
22. *Karen's Little Witch* (1991)
23. *Karen's Doll* (1991)
24. *Karen's School Trip* (1991)
25. *Karen's Pen Pal* (1992)
26. *Karen's Ducklings* (1992)
27. *Karen's Big Joke* (1992)
28. *Karen's Tea Party* (1992)
29. *Karen's Cartwheel* (1992)
30. *Karen's Kittens* (1992)
31. *Karen's Bully* (1992)
32. *Karen's Pumpkin Patch* (1992)
33. *Karen's Secret* (1992)
34. *Karen's Snowy Day* (1993)
35. *Karen's Doll House* (1993)
36. *Karen's New Friend* (1993)
37. *Karen's Tuba* (1993)
38. *Karen's Big Lie* (1993)
39. *Karen's Wedding* (1993)
40. *Karen's Newspaper* (1993)
41. *Karen's School* (1993)
42. *Karen's Pizza Party* (1993)
43. *Karen's Toothache* (1993)
44. *Karen's Big Weekend* (1993)
45. *Karen's Twin* (1994)
46. *Karen's Baby-Sitter* (1994)
47. *Karen's Kite* (1994)
48. *Karen's Two Families* (1994)
49. *Karen's Stepmother* (1994)
50. *Karen's Lucky Penny* (1994)
51. *Karen's Big Top* (1994)
52. *Karen's Mermaid* (1994)
53. *Karen's School Bus* (1994)
54. *Karen's Candy* (1994)
55. *Karen's Magician* (1994)
56. *Karen's Ice Skates* (1994)
57. *Karen's School Mystery* (1995)
58. *Karen's Ski Trip* (1995)
59. *Karen's Leprechaun* (1995)
60. *Karen's Pony* (1995)
61. *Karen's Tattletale* (1995)
62. *Karen's New Bike* (1995)
63. *Karen's Movie* (1995)
64. *Karen's Lemonade Stand* (1995)
65. *Karen's Toys* (1995)
66. *Karen's Monsters* (1995)

Baby-Sitters' Little Sister Super Specials

1. *Karen's Wish* (1990)
2. *Karen's Plane Trip* (1991)
3. *Karen's Mystery* (1991)
4. *Karen, Hannie, and Nancy: The Three Musketeers* (1992)
5. *Karen's Baby* (1992)
6. *Karen's Campout* (1993)

Baby-Sitters' Little Sister Jump Rope Rhymes Pack (1995)

Baby-Sitters' Little Sister Summer Fill-In Book (1995)

The Kids in Ms. Coleman's Class Series

1. *Teacher's Pet* (1995)
2. *Author's Day* (1995)

ADAPTATIONS IN OTHER MEDIA

Mary Anne and the Brunettes, Dawn and the Haunted Horse, and *Stacey's Big Break* are among stories issued on video.

The Baby-Sitters Club (1994)
Television series, Disney Channel.

The Baby-Sitters Club (1995)
Film starring Schuyler Fisk, Peter Horton, Zelda Harris, Austin O'Brien, Larisa Oleynik, Christina Oliver, and Bridget Geraghty.

FOR FURTHER READING

Ann M. Martin. New York: Scholastic, n.d.

"Ann M. Martin." *Publisher's Weekly,* 15 July 1988.

Baby-Sitters Club Newsletter. New York: Scholastic, 1994–95.

Dreyfous, Leslie. "Aura of Reality Is Appeal of Martin Books." *The Berkshire Eagle,* 20 January 1991.

Kleinfield, N. R. "Children's Books: Inside the Baby-Sitters Club." *The New York Times Book Review,* 30 April 1989.

Ross, Jean W. "Ann M. Martin." In *Contemporary Authors New Revised Series,* edited by James G. Lesniak. Vol. 32. Detroit: Gale Research, 1991.

R(ubin), Margot Becker. *Ann M. Martin: The Story of the Author of The Baby-Sitters Club.* New York: Scholastic, 1993.

Span, Paula. "Celebrity Status Surprises 'Baby-Sitters Club' Author." *The Berkshire Eagle* (syndicated from *The Washington Post*), 27 August 1995.

"Who's That Girl? She's Ann M. Martin!" *American Girl,* May–June 1995.

Harry Mazer

Family drama

Adventure

New York City
May 31, 1925

Snowbound

"When I was a boy I read with a passion," Harry Mazer said in *Books I Read When I Was Young*, "the same passion I had for food and games. Reading, I would say, came after food, and before games. I loved reading. I loved books and libraries, and the feel and smell of books. I still love to sniff new books. . . . When I came from the library, my arms bulged with books. I read whole shelves of books, or so it seemed to me: the entire Rover Boys series, then the Tom Swifts, then Jules Verne's books, and all of Mark Twain, in green bindings, and Charles Dickens in maroon. I liked authors who had written a lot of books. If possible I read them in order from the first book to the last. . . .

"It's only as I grew older that I became interested in meaning and symbolism and the realistic treatment of character," he continued.

Mazer made sporadic attempts to write during his adolescence. "I didn't know what the world of writing was like," he said in a pamphlet from Scholastic. "All I had were the classics and they just told me I was hopeless. So it took me many years before I began to write."

"I've always liked the idea of writing, but it's never been easy," he said in an interview published by Bantam. "Writing is hard work for me. I've resisted writing all my life. Put it off. Procrastinated.

Waited until the last minute. And yet I've always felt that writing was the way I would know what I thought, what I felt, and how I would reach other people."

To aspiring writers, Mazer suggested, "Believe in yourself. Which is the hardest thing that I've found to do. I sometimes feel that belief comes before writing. That is, you need to play at being a writer. It's a little bit of a performance. Reality is yet to come. Pose as a writer. Say it not only to yourself but to the world. *I am a writer*. Even if you haven't written a word. If it's there, if you have it, it'll come. The words will come."

Mazer's parents were Polish-Jewish immigrants who worked in factories as dressmakers. Mazer served in the U.S. Air Force during World War II and later attended Union College. After graduating in 1950, he married Norma Fox (see p. 261). They have four children. He later attended Syracuse University and received his master's degree in 1960. About that time, both Mazers began to write.

Mazer's first effort was based on a memory from the sixth grade, the impression made on him by a tall, thin girl with long hair at P. S. 96 in the Bronx.

His first book was published in 1971. His second, two years later, was a survival story called *Snowbound* that was later adapted for television.

"*Snowbound* . . . is a story of raw survival," Tom Heffernan said. "The two teenagers who are stranded in a blizzard in the most desolate part of New York State contend with the familiar perils from cold, near-starvation, inability to signal rescuers, and despair. These are expertly described, but the real merit of the book is in the representation of the psychology of the two young people. Both are independent and, in different ways, defiant. The boy is bold and impulsive, the girl is intelligent and vexed by what she sees as her stiffness in relating to others. She is the more mature of the two, and her eventual responsibility for their rescue alters the thinking of both of them."

Tony, the boy in *Snowbound*, asks: " 'I wonder what happens when you die.'

" 'We're not going to die,' Cindy said sharply. 'We're too young to die. We're getting out of this place. We'll find a way. We have to. It would be too stupid to die here because I stuck out my thumb, and you took a wrong turn.' "

"I'm primarily interested in my characters' inner life," Mazer said. "Not the trappings of character but their feelings. . . . Very often in my books the character becomes disillusioned . . . and realizes that he must and can face the world on his own strength."

The Solid Gold Kid was the first of Mazer's occasional collaborations with his wife, Norma Fox Mazer. Though they usually write separately, they discuss everything in their respective books, Mazer said.

Some have complained of Mazer's use of strong language and occasional descriptions of premarital sex. He responds that the absence of these elements could lead to a sugar-coated, bland literature.

"Harry Mazer writes about young people caught in the midst of moral crises, often of their own making," Kenneth Donelson observed. "Searching for a way out, they discover themselves, or rather they learn that the first step in extricating themselves from their physical or moral dilemmas is self-discovery. Intensely moral as Mazer's books are, they present young people thinking and talking and acting believably, and for that reason, some parents and teachers may object, particularly to the language in *The Last Mission*" (*The Last Mission* is about a boy who joins the military).

Mazer stated in *Literature for Today's Young Adults* that he is increasingly drawn to historical fiction. "Perhaps the trend has started in my work already with *The Last Mission*, which is set in the Second World War. More and more, I find myself thinking back to those years, and the years earlier, to the years of my childhood. There is an aura, a glow to those years, a sense that those were better times; simpler, realer, families closer, friendships truer, the air purer, the world less complicated."

YOUNG ADULT FICTION

Guy Lenny (1971)
Twelve-year-old Guy has a choice: stay with his divorced father, who has a new girlfriend, or go to live with his remarried mother.

Snowbound (1973)
Tony Laport is fifteen and spoiled. When his parents refuse to let him keep a stray dog, he runs off in his mother's old Plymouth in the middle of a severe snowstorm. He picks up a hitchhiker, Cindy Reichert, and they end up stranded.

The Dollar Man (1974)
Marcus Aurelius Rosenbloom, fourteen, overweight and shy, takes the rap for others who smoked pot in school.

The Solid Gold Kid: A Novel (1977) with Norma Fox Mazer
The teenage son of a millionaire is kidnapped with four companions and has to fight to survive.

The War on Villa Street: A Novel (1978), featuring characters from *The Dollar Man*
Willis Pierce runs to vent his daily frustrations and coaches retarded Richard Hayfoot for an upcoming athletic event.

The Last Mission (1979)
In 1943, Jack Raab, fifteen, uses his older brother's identification to join the army. He trains as a gunner on a fighter plane.

I Love You, Stupid! (1981), sequel to *The Dollar Man*
Marcus is a high school senior and a virgin, but his relationship with dynamic Wendy Barrett proves that neither sex, friendship, nor love is ever simple.

The Island Keeper (1981)
In Canada, Cleo Murphy discovers a tiny island and claims it for herself.

Hey, Kid! Does She Love Me? (1984)
Jeff Orloff drops plans for college to hang around Mary Silver, who is back in town. Jeff had a crush on her years ago, but she has a new baby and no romantic interest in Jeff.

When the Phone Rang (1985)
Sixteen-year-old Billy Keller and his siblings lose their parents in a plane crash. Now they must struggle to make it alone.

Cave Under the City (1986)
Brothers Tolley and Bubber stick together during the Great Depression.

The Girl of His Dreams (1987), sequel to *The War on Villa Street*
Willis, a dedicated runner, is working in a factory. He meets another loner, Sophie.

City Light (1988)
George Farina, seventeen, is crushed when his girlfriend breaks up with him. After a while, he begins to see that the changes in his life might be positive.

Heartbeat (1989) with Norma Fox Mazer
Tod Ellerbee introduces Hilary Goodman to his friend, Amos, then falls in love with her himself.

Someone's Mother Is Missing: A Novel (1990)
Sam's wealthy uncle dies, and his aunt walks out on his cousins, Lisa and Robyn, forcing them to move in with Sam's family. Soon, Sam and Lisa work together to find the missing woman.

Bright Days, Stupid Nights (1992) with Norma Fox Mazer
Four teenagers are thrown together for eight weeks when they land summer internships on a Pulitzer Prize–winning newspaper.

Who Is Eddie Leonard? A Novel (1993)
One day when he is almost fifteen, Eddie sees his face on a poster for missing children.

CONTRIBUTOR

Sixteen: Short Stories by Outstanding Writers for Young Adults, edited by Donald R. Gallo (1984)
Mazer's story "Furlough—1944" features characters from *The Last Mission*.

ADAPTATIONS IN OTHER MEDIA

Snowbound (1978)
Television movie.

FOR FURTHER READING

Cullinan, Bernice, and M. Jerry Weiss, eds. *Books I Read When I Was Young: The Favorite Books of Famous People*. New York: Avon Books, 1980.

Donelson, Kenneth L., and Alleen Pace Nilsen, eds. "The People Behind the Books: Harry Mazer." In *Literature for Today's Young Adults*. Glenview, IL: Scott, Foresman, 1980.

———. "Searchers and Doers: Heroes in Five Harry Mazer Novels." *Voice of Youth Advocates*, February 1983.

Harry Mazer. New York: Scholastic, n.d.

Harry Mazer & Norma Fox Mazer. New York: Bantam Books, 1990.

Heffernan, Tom. Review of *Snowbound*. *Children's Literature: Annual of the Modern Language Association Seminar on Children's Literature and the Children's Literature Association*, 1975.

Norma Fox Mazer

Social drama

Suspense

New York City
May 15, 1931

Taking Terri Mueller

High school football player Rollo and his best buddies, Brig and Candy, the "Lethal Threesome," are surprised when sensitive outsider Valerie stands up to their taunts. Then one afternoon the situation gets *Out of Control*. This suspenseful story line is typical of the young adult novels of Norma Fox Mazer.

The daughter of a Ukrainian-Jewish truck driver and a sales clerk, Norma Fox was the middle of three sisters. She grew up in Glenns Falls, New York. She attended Antioch College and Syracuse University. In 1950, she married Harry Mazer, also a young adult novelist, with whom she has four children.

As a youngster she avidly read such books as the Nancy Drew mysteries, *Gulliver's Travels*, and *The Diary of Anne Frank*. "I love stories," Mazer said in *Top of the News*. "I'm convinced that everyone does, and whether we recognize it or not, each of us tells stories. A day doesn't pass when we don't put our lives into story."

"When I first began writing, I wrote blindly, wanting only to put down words on paper," Mazer continued. "The first real lesson I learned about writing was that I needed to—and did—have something to say. That something was there, inside me, waiting to be called out. That struggle, I think—not only for the writer, but just for living in this world with self-respect—is to find what's uniquely one's own:

the real, the true things one thinks, which reflect one's own view of the world, one's own experiences, one's own perceptions and visions."

Her first writing sale was a short item to *Parents* magazine. She often wrote at night, after rising to tend one of their children. Her husband soon joined her to write in the late hours. Using the proceeds from an insurance settlement for an earlier car accident, the couple decided to devote full time to freelance writing. In 1970, she wrote her first book, *I, Trissy,* which was published in 1971. Since then, Mazer has written steadily. Several of her books have won awards: *A Figure of Speech,* National Book Award Finalist, 1974; *Up in Seth's Room,* American Library Association Best of the Best Books, 1970–1983; *Taking Terri Mueller,* Mystery Writers of America, Edgar Allan Poe Award for Best Juvenile Mystery, 1982.

"All through my adolescence, I had an acute sense of being different, an outsider," Mazer said in a pamphlet issued by Avon Books. "I was never 'cool,' either in its literal meaning (I blushed often and hotly) or its symbolic meaning. I was never 'in' (another word which teenagers use so well); I was always on the periphery, on the edge, on the outside, peering in. This was, in fact, the way I saw my Junior Prom, standing at a window with a girlfriend, both of us on tiptoes, looking into the gym, which was decorated with long loops of green and yellow crepe paper.

"So perhaps that's why I write. To stand again and again on tiptoes, peering into that window, trying to understand why some people dance and some people watch."

"Mazer's descriptive ability is excellent," Mary Lystad observed. "The reader is able to see vividly what her characters look like, what their physical environment consists of, and most importantly, how they feel about themselves and others."

"Books for the young are, I hope, getting tougher, realer, and truer," Mazer said in *Literature for Today's Young Adults*. "The world is big, bigger, bigger than ever; hard, confusing, difficult, demanding. Lies won't do. The truth will help. I don't mean political truths, but the truth about people, human beings, how they live, what they feel, how they love, what they want—the truth about the human condition, if you will. It's the news of this truth which fiction has the power to bring us most accurately."

"At her best, Mazer can cut right to the bone of teenage troubles and then show us how the wounds will heal," Suzanne Freeman commented. "She can set down the everyday scenes of her characters' lives in images that are scalpel-sharp. In Mazer's books, we find lovers who cheat and fathers who cry. We find elephant jokes and pink champagne. We find college students who live in apartments which smell of cats, and we find high school kids who walk through corridors which smell of 'Lysol, oregano (pizza for lunch again) and cigarette smoke.' What's apparent throughout all of this is that Mazer has taken great care to get to know the world she writes about."

The Solid Gold Kid is about Derek Chapman, sixteen, the only son of millionaire Jimmy Neal Chapman. He attends Payne Boarding School. With four other teens he does not know, he accepts a ride into town with a couple in a van. It turns out they are kidnappers, and they are holding him for ransom. The group struggles with captivity. Members are eventually separated and hurt. Derek begins to understand his own resourcefulness, as well as friendship, responsibilities, and even love.

Mazer collaborated on the book with her husband. Reviews were mixed. Joyce Milton said that the writers "gum up the works trying to make serious statements." *Kirkus Reviews* called their second collaboration, *Heartbeat*, "a perfect example of a well-worn plot made new by its fully realized characters."

Another of Mazer's suspenseful solo books is *Taking Terri Mueller*. Terri is troubled that her father does not want to talk about her late mother: "He didn't answer. His silence meant, I don't want to talk about this. She hesitated. Should she stop before she made a fool of herself? Or before they arrived at that point of stubborn silence where she would have to challenge him to get what she wanted? She had questions. She needed answers. She wanted answers. Only the worst part was, she didn't know exactly what it was she wanted—or what she might find out."

"Considering all the recent publicity about divorced parents who kidnap their own children, there was certain to be a juvenile novel on the subject sooner or later," said Karen Ritter of *Taking Terri Mueller*. "And this is a good one, not just capitalizing on that gimmick—in fact, readers don't learn until halfway through the book what has actually happened—but developing strong characters and a plot that involves the kidnapping angle as a basic element. . . . All the characters are very human. Both parents are portrayed sympathetically; while the author does not excuse or approve of the father's actions, it is clear that he acted out of love."

YOUNG ADULT FICTION

I, Trissy (1971)
Some problems Trissy will only discuss with her diary.

A Figure of Speech (1973)
Jenny Pennoyer, thirteen, loves her grandpa and stands up for him when her brother and his bride want to move into the elder's apartment in the basement.

Saturday, the Twelfth of October (1975)
Zan Ford, fourteen, is whisked by a time warp from a New York park back to the Stone Age.

Dear Bill, Remember Me? and Other Stories (1976)

The Solid Gold Kid: A Novel (1977) with Harry Mazer
Kidnappers take Derek Chapman, sixteen, son of a self-made millionaire. Four other youths, in the wrong place at the wrong time, are also kidnapped.

Up in Seth's Room: A Love Story (1979)
Fifteen-year-old Finn does not go quite all the way with Seth, who is four years older.

Mrs. Fish, Ape, and Me, the Dump Queen (1980)
A teenager struggles for acceptance by her peers—and herself.

Taking Terri Mueller (1981)
Why are Terri and her father always moving? What is the truth he keeps from her? Is it possible her mother is not dead after all?

Summer Girls, Love Boys, and Other Short Stories (1982)

When We First Met (1982), sequel to *A Figure of Speech*
Jenny Pennoyer and Rob Montana fall in love and share everything—then discover that Rob's mother is the drunken driver who killed Jenny's sister, Gail, two years earlier.

Someone to Love (1983)
Meeting Mitch cures Nina's college blues. She moves in with him. But when their spats escalate, she realizes they are both changing.

Downtown (1984)
Eight years ago, Pete's parents blew up a laboratory in an antiwar protest. He has not seen them since.

Supergirl (1984), based on the motion picture
Superman's cousin must retrieve an omegahedron for the survival of her planet.

Three Sisters (1986)
Oldest sister Liz is a poet, and pretty. Middle sister Tobi is smart and outgoing. Youngest sister Karen, fifteen, feels she is a loser.

After the Rain (1987)
Rachel, fifteen, is a little afraid of sharp-tongued Grandpa Izzy, but she comes to know him better when the family learns he has cancer.

B, My Name Is Bunny (1987); British title: *A Name Like Bunny* (1988)
Bunny meets James, who is eighteen and thinks she is older than her thirteen years.

A, My Name Is Ami (1988); British title: *A for Ami* (1988)
There are ups and downs in twelve-year-old Ami's relationship with her best friend Mia.

Silver (1988)
A girl is attending a junior high for rich kids—kids from homes where her mother works as a cleaning woman.

Heartbeat (1989) with Harry Mazer
Tod Ellerbee's relationship with his father, a Vietnam vet, is strained. At the same time, he and his friend, Amos, vie for the attentions of Hilary.

Babyface (1990)
Toni Chessmore, fifteen, has a perfect life until her best friend leaves for California and she learns a long-buried family secret.

C, My Name Is Cal (1990)
Cal Miller's mother is a housekeeper. His long-gone father may be coming back.

D, My Name Is Danita (1991)
Dani Merritt, thirteen, was a premature baby. She wishes that her parents would not still fuss over her so much.

E, My Name Is Emily (1991)
Emily is mad at her mother, at her mother's new boyfriend, and at her best friend, Bunny.

Bright Days, Stupid Nights (1992) with Harry Mazer
Four teenagers are thrown together for eight weeks when they land summer internships on a Pulitzer Prize–winning newspaper.

Out of Control (1993)
Valerie, a sensitive outsider, stands up to the taunts of tough Brig, who is buddies with Rollo and Candy. When she does not back down, the situation gets out of control.

Missing Pieces (1994)
Jessie sets out to find her father.

EDITOR

Waltzing on Water: Poetry by Women (1989) with Marjorie Lewis

CONTRIBUTOR

Sixteen: Short Stories by Outstanding Writers for Young Adults, edited by Donald R. Gallo (1984)

Visions: Nineteen Short Stories by Outstanding Writers for Young Adults, edited by Donald R. Gallo (1987)

TELEPLAYS

When We First Met (1984), co-author

FOR FURTHER READING

Donelson, Kenneth L., and Alleen Pace Nilsen, eds. "The People Behind the Books: Norma Fox Mazer." In *Literature for Today's Young Adults*. Glenview, IL: Scott, Foresman, 1980.

Freeman, Suzanne. "The Truth About the Teens." *The Washington Post Book World*, 10 April 1983.

Harry Mazer & Norma Fox Mazer. New York: Bantam Books, 1990.

Lystad, Mary. "Norma Fox Mazer." In *Twentieth-Century Children's Writers*, edited by Tracy Chevalier. 3d ed. Chicago: St. James Press, 1989.

Mazer, Norma Fox. "Breathing Life into a Story." *The Writer*, September 1995.

———. "Growing Up with Stories." *Top of the News*, winter 1985.

Milton, Joyce. "A Kid's Ransom." *The Washington Post Book World*, 10 July 1977.

Norma Fox Mazer. New York: Avon Books, 1990.

Norma Fox Mazer. New York: Scholastic, n.d.

Review of *Heartbeat*. *Kirkus Reviews*, 15 May 1989.

Ritter, Karen. Review of *Taking Terri Mueller*. *School Library Journal*, December 1981.

Anne McCaffrey

Fantasy

Cambridge, Massachusetts
April 1, 1926

Harper Hall of Pern Series

"I'm never sure what image readers construct of me from reading my books," McCaffrey said in the introduction to *The Girl Who Heard Dragons*. "But, generally, when I get a response of 'You're Anne McCaffrey?' I haven't had the nerve to ask what they were expecting. Tones range from skepticism to deep disappointment and incredulity. Yet I do describe myself: 'My hair is silver, my eyes are green, and I freckle. The rest is subject to change without notice'—the 'rest' being the unrepentant bulk of me."

"I'm a story teller, basically," she expanded in *Literature for Today's Young Adults*, "and unconsciously reflect in my stories the pressures, the problems, and the ambiance which beset me and our world while I am writing a story. . . . I say I write love stories, and that is the truth. I also write xenophilic stories, rather than xenophobic since I do feel that we shall, one day or another, encounter other sentient beings. I can devoutly hope that our species will greet them with tolerance and an overwhelming desire to understand alien minds and mores."

McCaffrey's father was a city administrator and U.S. Army colonel and her mother was a real estate agent. She earned a degree from Radcliffe College in 1947 and did graduate study in meteorology at the University of the City of Dublin. She also studied voice for nine years. Divorced, she has three children.

McCaffrey is best known for her fantasy novels featuring the dragonriders of the planet Pern. In *Dragonsong*, she provides a background to the series: The small planet Pern had an erratic neighboring Red Star that spun off spore life "which proliferated at an incredible rate on the Red Star's wild surface, spun off into space and bridged the gap to Pern. The spores fell as thin threads on the temperate, hospitable planet, and devoured anything organic in their way, seeking to establish burrows in Pern's warm earth from which to set out more voracious Threads."

The Thread took a toll on crops and vegetation, and on people. Fire killed the Thread on land, water on sea, and only stone or metal could hinder its rampant invasion. Adapting, the inhabitants began to breed a specialized "dragon" that moved by teleportation and, after consuming phosphine-bearing rock, emitted a flaming gas. "Thus the flying dragons could char Thread to ash midair and escape its ravages themselves."

McCaffrey continued, "The dragons and their riders in their Weyrs, and the people in the cave holdings, went about their separate tasks and each developed habits that became custom, which solidified into tradition as incontrovertible as law." Six Weyrs developed for the protection of Pern. The rest of the population lived in cavernous Holds and tithed to support the Weyrs and the dragon fighters, as the latter had no tillable land on which to produce food.

All became complacent, until a quirk of the planet and its satellites meant Thread did not arrive any longer. "And the Pernese forgot about the danger. The people prospered, spreading out across the rich land, carving more Holds out of solid rock and becoming so busy with their pursuits, that they did not realize that there were only a few dragons in the skies, and only one Weyr of dragonriders left on Pern."

When the Red Star once again spun close enough to send its Thread to Pern, F'lar, rider of the bronze dragon Mnementh, and his half brother, F'nor, rider of brown Canth, retrieved the last golden egg of a dying queen dragon. They found Lessa, "the only surviving member of the proud bloodline of Ruatha Hold." The three rode to defend the planet against Thread, rallying their scant and long-forgotten resources.

McCaffrey's "concern with women's roles and struggles in Pern's society is most vividly realized in *Dragonsong* (1976) and *Dragonsinger* (1977), both of which center upon Menolly, a young woman whose ambition to be a harper runs counter to Pern's social norm for women," said Lina Mainero. "Menolly achieves her goals through perseverance, courage and quick wit."

McCaffrey loved the Rudyard Kipling Mowgli stories that her mother read to her. When she was about ten, her mother suggested that she read A. Merritt's *The Ship of Ishtar*, which was then a serial in *Argosy* magazine. McCaffrey said in *Books I Read When I Was Young:* "I devoured any of Mr. Merritt's books I could find. You might say that between Kipling and Merritt the groundwork was laid for my fascination with science fiction and science fantasy.

"Of even more lasting significance was my discovery of Austin Tappan Wright's *Islandia*, which I read at fourteen. This meticulously developed 'other continent on our planet' influenced me more than any other single book. It was, alas, his only published work."

Before her success as a writer, McCaffrey worked as a writer and layout designer for Liberty Music Shops in New York City and as a copywriter and secretary for Helena Rubinstein. Inspired to try writing science fiction after reading Edmund Hamilton's *Star Kings*, she submitted a short story, "Freedom of the Race," to Sam Moskowitz's anthology *Science Fiction Plus*. It was published in 1953, her first story in print.

McCaffrey kept writing but did not sell another story for five years. In 1959, her "Lady in the Tower" appeared in *Magazine of Fantasy and Science Fiction*. The story and a sequel, "A Meeting of Minds," involve parapsychology and romance.

McCaffrey is adept at shorter fiction forms, in the view of Mary Turzillo Brizzi. "In all, her style has a neo-classic flavor in wit, sarcasm, and clarity. She is at her strongest depicting love and bonding, between lovers, family members, humans and animals, humans and aliens. Her flight imagery—dragons, Pegasus, spaceship—is compelling. With these, her characterization and world-building make her a significant science-fiction writer."

McCaffrey met other science fiction writers such as James Blish and Robert Silverberg, who gave her writing tips. Through the English Milford writer conferences, she received useful criticism and direction for several of her early works. In the mid-1960s, she was able to devote more time to writing. After her divorce in 1970, she moved to Ireland.

McCaffrey now lives in Ireland in a home she calls Dragonhold. "Ireland is a relaxed country," McCaffrey told interviewer Jessica Palmer. "It's a peaceful place and quiet. I'm allowed my own space. If a fan wants to come visit me, he's got to travel thousands of miles to do it."

"I've accomplished a few firsts in my life," she said. "I was the first in my field, a bona fide science-fiction writer, to get on *The New York Times* best-seller list."

YOUNG ADULT FICTION

Harper Hall of Pern Series

Dragonsong (1976)
Teenage Menolly wants to become a harper on Pern, against the wishes of her father. Chronologically, this and the next two titles follow *The White Dragon* (see "Adult Fiction," below).

Dragonsinger (1977)
Menolly runs away from home and lives in a cave. Robinton, the master harper of Pern, likes her songs.

Dragondrums (1978)
Pienur is chosen for a leading role at the Harperhall of Pern; then his voice begins to change.

ADULT FICTION

Restoree (1967)
A New York woman awakens in a new body on a new and strange planet.

The Mark of Merlin (1971)

Ring of Fear (1971)

To Ride Pegasus (1973)
Telepaths and psis band together for their own protection.

The Kilternan Legacy (1975)

A Time When: Being a Tale of Young Lord Jaxom, His White Dragon, Ruth, and Various Fire-Lizards (1975)
Short stories.

Get Off the Unicorn (1977)
Short stories, including the first Rowan story, "The Lady in the Tower," and a Pern tale, "The Smallest Dragon Boy."

Dinosaur Planet (1978)
Lightweights Varian and Kai, Disciples of Discipline, suspect the Heavy Worlders are reverting to their hunting, killing ways.

The Worlds of Anne McCaffrey (1981)
Short stories.

The Coelura (1983)
The Lady Caissa flees to the forbidden zone rather than marry a man she despises.

The Dinosaur Planet Survivors (1984), sequel to *Dinosaur Planet*

Stitch in Snow (1984)
A children's book writer is stranded in a snowstorm with a riveting, attractive man.

Habit Is an Old Horse (1986)
This contains the title story and "Fallen Angel." Limited edition.

To Ride Pegasus (1986)
They could read minds, heal bodies, divert disasters—they were pariahs among their own kind.

The Year of the Lucy (1986)

The Lady (1987)

The Carradyne Touch (1988)

Pegasus in Flight (1990)
Rhysa Owen coordinates jobs for psychically gifted Talents, who are building a space station. She encounters an extraordinary man with no measurable talent at all and two children with very odd talents.

Three Gothic Novels: Ring of Fear, Mark of Merlin, The Kilternan Legacy (1990)

Generation Warriors (1991) with Elizabeth Moon
Ordered to report to FedCentral for the trial of a mutineer named Tanegli, Sassinak decides not to follow the rules.

Three Women (1992)

The City Who Fought (1993) with S. M. Stirling
Simon, a brain in charge of a mining colony, must transmute his wargame hobby into the real thing to fend off attacking space barbarians.

Freedom's Landing (1995)
An incredible experiment takes place on a planet where colonists have the chance to build a free life—or die trying.

Crystal Singer Series

Crystal Singer (1981)
Killashandra Ree, after training for ten years, aspires to one of the most dangerous and skilled jobs in the universe—joining the Heptite Guild on Planet Ballybran, where the fabled Black Crystal was found.

Killashandra (1985)
In Optheria to tune the crystals of a famous organ, Killashandra is abducted by subversives and uncovers a mass brainwashing plot.

Crystal Line (1992)
When Killashandra joined the mysterious Heptite Guild as a crystal singer, she knew that, little by little, her memories would be destroyed forever. Will she risk the pain of a restoration technique?

Doona Series

Decision at Doona (1969)
The planet Doona is colonized by humans and catlike Hrrubans.

Crisis on Doona (1992) with Jody Lynn Nye
A prominent citizen of the Hrrubans is framed for a crime—and peace may be destroyed.

Treaty at Doona (1994) with Jody Lynn Nye
The Humans and Hrrubans encounter a new threat to their peaceful coexistence: the Gringgs.

Dragonriders of Pern Series

Dragonflight (1968)
The telepathic Dragons of Pern soar the skies, protecting their planet from the deadly silver Threads that fall from the wandering Red Star. Lessa is ready to claim her birthright as a rider.

Dragonquest: Being the Further Adventures of the Dragonriders of Pern (1971)
The old-time Dragonriders of Pern, brought by Lessa from the past to help, now expect to be taken care of.

The White Dragon (1978)
Lord Jaxon's dragon, Ruth, has many talents; they train in secret to destroy the deadly silver Threads.

Moreta: Dragonlady of Pern (1983)
The Weyrwoman of Fort Weyr has to fight a mysterious and rampant ailment as well as the ever-present Threads.

The Girl Who Heard Dragons (1985); with other short stories (1994)
In the title story, Aramina and her family roam the land, hiding from bandits.

Nerilka's Story: A Pern Adventure (1986)
Ashamed of her father's refusal to share, Nerilka carries medicine and supplies to help her people against a deadly epidemic on Pern.

Dragonsdawn (1988)
Geneticists work to develop dragonlike lizards to fight the Threads. Chronologically, this is the first in the Pern series and provides background.

The People of Pern (1988) with Robin Wood

The Dragonlover's Guide to Pern (1989) with Jody Lynn Nye

The Renegades of Pern (1989)
The traders prefer freedom to life in the Holds, which are protected by the Weyrs and their Dragonriders. Lady Thella leads a band of renegades—her quarry is Aramina, who can hear the dragons.

Rescue Run (1991)
Novella.

All the Weyrs of Pern (1991)
The Dragonriders hope to eradicate the Thread entirely.

The Chronicles of Pern: First Fall (1992)
Short stories from Pernese history, including one telling how Ruatha Hold was founded.

The Dolphins of Pern (1994)
When the Threads came, intelligence-enhanced dolphins who settled on Pern with the humans were forgotten. T'lion, a young bronze rider relegated to delivering messages, renews contact with the legendary "ship fish."

Planet Pirate Series

Sassinak (1990) with Elizabeth Moon
Sassinak, twelve, is just old enough to be used by the raiders, but she turns out to be more than the typical slave girl.

The Death of Sleep (1990) with Jody Lynn Nye
Lunzie Mespil is a Healer plagued by a curse.

Generation Warriors (1991) with Elizabeth Moon
Sassinak and Lunzie join to defeat the planet pirates.

Power Series

Powers That Be (1993) with Elizabeth Ann Scarborough
Major Yanaba Maddock is retired to the icy planet Petaybee to become a spy. She finds something strange and wonderful there.

Power Lines (1994) with Elizabeth Ann Scarborough
Officials of Intergal plan to strip Petaybee of its minerals. Maddock and her Selkie lover must prove that the planet is worth more to humankind alive than dead.

Power Play (1995) with Elizabeth Ann Scarborough

The Rowan Series

The Rowan (1990)
One of the strongest Talents ever born, the Rowan may have met his power match in an unknown named Jeff Raven.

Damia (1991)
The Rowan's daughter, Damia, is a Talent of great power. In a universe under siege, only the power of love can defeat fear.

Damia's Children (1993)
It is up to Damia's offspring to defeat the alien attackers that she deflected.

Lyon's Pride (1994)
The Hivers threaten the peace that has been passed along to the children of Damia and Afra Lyon.

The Ship Who Sang Series

The Ship Who Sang (1969)
Helva, a deformed woman, is engineered into a starship's brain, bringing her freedom and happiness.

PartnerShip (1992) with Margaret Ball
Nancia, the brain for a new ship, joins the elite Courier Service of the Central Worlds. She is partnered with a brawn, Forister; together, they might be able to save the galaxy.

The Ship Who Searched (1992) with Mercedes Lackey
Tia, a shellperson, searches for the EsKays, a star-faring race whose fate is a mystery.

The Ship Who Won (1994) with Jody Lynn Nye
Carialle, a spaceship, and her brawn, Keff, search the galaxy for intelligent beings.

EDITOR

Alchemy and Academe (1970)

Cooking out of This World (1973)

CONTRIBUTOR

Crime Prevention in the 30th Century, compiled by Hans Stefan Santesson (1969)

The Disappearing Future (London: Panther Books, 1970)

Infinity One: A Magazine of Speculative Fiction in Book Form, edited by R. A. Hoskins (1970)

The Many Worlds of Science Fiction, edited by Ben Bova (1971)

Demon Kind: Eleven New Stories of Children with Strange and Supernatural Powers (New York: Avon, 1973)

Future Quest, edited by Roger Elwood (1973)

Omega (1973)

Science Fiction Tales, compiled by Roger Elwood (1973)

Ten Tomorrows, edited by Roger Elwood (1973)

Continuum, edited by Roger Elwood (1974)

Future Love: A Science Fiction Triad (Indianapolis, IN: Bobbs-Merrill, 1977)

Cassandra Rising, edited by Alice Laurance (1978)

Visitors' Book (Poolbeg Press, 1979)

The Great Science Fiction Series, edited by Frederick Pohl, Martin Harry Greenberg, and Joseph Olander (1980)

The Best of Randall Garrett, edited by Randall Garrett (1982)

A Dragon-Lover's Treasury of the Fantastic, edited by Margaret Weis (1994)

Women of Wonder: The Classic Years—Science Fiction by Women from the 1940s to the 1970s (1995), edited by Pamela Sargent

FOR FURTHER READING

Brizzi, Mary Turzillo. "Anne McCaffrey." In *Twentieth-Century Science-Fiction Writers*, edited by Noelle Watson and Paul E. Schellinger. 3d ed. Chicago: St. James Press, 1991.

Cullinan, Bernice, and M. Jerry Weiss, eds. *Books I Read When I Was Young: The Favorite Books of Famous People*. New York: Avon Books, 1980.

Donelson, Kenneth L., and Alleen Pace Nilsen, eds. "The People Behind the Books: Anne McCaffrey." In *Literature for Today's Young Adults*. Glenview, IL: Scott, Foresman, 1980.

Mainiero, Lina, ed. *American Women Writers from Colonial Times to the Present: A Critical Reference Guide*. Vol. 3. New York: Frederick Ungar, 1981.

Palmer, Jessica. "Dragons and Beyond." *Million*, May–June 1991.

Lurlene McDaniel

Inspirational

Philadelphia, Pennsylvania
April 5, 1944

Too Young to Die

Lurlene McDaniel's young heroes and heroines lose family members to death or face life-threatening illnesses themselves.

Typically, Lacey Duval in *All the Days of Her Life* has accepted her parents' divorce and spends a summer at Jenny House, learning to deal with her diabetes. Now she wants to start a new life. She is determined to fit in with the best crowd at school and gain the eye of handsome Todd Larson, but she tries to lose weight by skipping meals and experimenting with her medication—ingredients for disaster.

" 'You know, Lacey, you're the person who won't accept that you have a disease. Why is that?' " a friend, Jeff, asks.

"She whirled on him. 'How can you ask me that when you've just admitted that girls drop you once they discover you're a bleeder? You of all people should understand why I keep my little secret.'

" 'I don't like being a hemophiliac, but it's what I am. I can't be responsible for girls who can't handle it. Who can't see past the illness and accept *me*. I do know that I have some pretty incredible friends who know about my problem and who care in spite of it. Give people a chance, Lacey. They just might pleasantly surprise you.' "

Lurlene Gallagher McDaniel, the daughter of a career naval officer and a homemaker, attended the University of Florida. In 1966, she married Joseph McDaniel. They have two sons.

As a child, McDaniel loved hearing stories. She began writing prose and verse in the first grade. Two years later, she wrote a play that her classmates performed. In high school, she edited the student newspaper and yearbook. She majored in English in college and minored in advertising and public relations. Later, she worked for television stations in Florida and Michigan. She also was fiction editor of *Faith 'n' Stuff, the Magazine for Kids.*

In 1973, her son Sean, diagnosed with juvenile diabetes, nearly died. His illness changed the family routines, and McDaniel curtailed her writing for a time. After her divorce in 1987, she devoted her full energies to writing. One of her first books was about a thirteen-year-old ballet dancer who becomes diabetic. She wrote other books about young people overcoming major medical challenges. *Six Months to Live* sold half a million copies through book fairs and clubs and was placed in a literary time capsule in the Library of Congress in 1990. *Too Young to Die* and *Goodbye Doesn't Mean Forever* were Children's Choice books of the International Readers Association in 1989.

"My novels deal with characters facing, through no fault of their own, a life-altering event—usually medical in nature—and overcoming the event," she said in *Something About the Author.* "Sometimes my characters actually die in the book, but this leads readers to tell me, 'It was like real life.' "

In 1992, the publisher Bantam began to issue the One Last Wish series. A book came out every other month, centering on "terminally ill teenagers who have 'one last wish' granted by an anonymous benefactor," Sally Lodge said. McDaniel is the only author for the series, and titles are still being published. "McDaniel has become identified with a genre sometimes called '10-hankie novels' or 'tear-jerkers,' labels she finds somewhat misleading. 'I've heard people say my books are about death and dying, and this is not true,' she asserts. 'I write about life. But in today's culture kids come upon many harsh realities, and learn early that nobody has control of all that happens to them in life. But what we *do* have control of is how we respond to what happens. And that is the positive message of my books.' "

McDaniel, according to Lodge, has a strong following that she calls "my girls." "She notes that 'they are an incredibly loyal group of kids, and each letter I receive renews my desire to write more and more stories. Life can be so funny. When I think back on how I began writing—what could be more horrible than having your perfect three-year-old almost die in your arms? But out of that came my whole life's work. Life works out if you don't give up on it."

YOUNG ADULT FICTION

Goodbye Doesn't Mean Forever (1989)
Jory Delaney's money can buy anything but the life of her leukemia-stricken best friend, Melissa.

Too Young to Die (1989)
Melissa Austin, sixteen, is devastated to learn she has leukemia. With the support of family and friends, she finds the courage to face an uncertain future.

Now I Lay Me Down to Sleep (1991)
Carrie Blake, fifteen, has leukemia but is in remission. Her parents are divorced. She meets Keith Gardner at a cancer support group.

Time to Let Go (1991)
Erin has to deal with the death of her younger sister, unexplained headaches, and an annoying young man.

When Happily Ever After Ends (1992)
Shannon Campbell's father, a Vietnam vet, commits suicide, and she and her mother have to cope.

Baby Alicia Is Dying (1993)
Desi thinks it is unfair that innocent baby Alicia is born HIV positive.

Don't Die My Love (1995)
Julie and Luke, friends since sixth grade, learn the shattering news that what was thought to be only a virus is actually something else.

Saving Jessica (1996)

Dawn Rochelle Series

Six Months to Live (1995)
Dawn, thirteen, cannot believe the doctor's diagnosis: leukemia.

I Want to Live (1995)
Dawn is frightened that her remissions won't last.

So Much to Live For (1996)

No Time to Cry (1996)

One Last Wish Series

A Time to Die (1992)
Kara Fischer, sixteen, born with cystic fibrosis, develops a close bond with Eric and Vince.

All the Days of Her Life (1992)
Lacey Duval, a diabetic, goes to Jenny House, where she will get one last wish.

Mother, Help Me Live (1992)
Sarah MacGregor needs a bone marrow transplant to live.

Someone Dies, Someone Lives (1992)
After having a heart transplant, Katie O'Roark meets Josh Martel.

Sixteen and Dying (1992)
Anne is diagnosed HIV positive after a tainted blood transfusion. She spends the summer on a ranch and meets Morgan but cannot confide in him about her condition.

Let Him Live (1992)
Megan Carneli is a candy striper who helps grant one last wish to Donovan Jacoby, seventeen.

Mourning Song (1992)
Dani Vanoy's older sister, Cassie, has a brain tumor.

The Legacy: Making Wishes Come True (1993)
Who is J W C, and how was the One Last Wish Foundation created?

She Died Too Young (1994)
Chelsea James and Katie O'Roark, who met at Jenny House, befriend a new girl, Jillian.

A Season for Goodbyes (1995)
A year after they met at Jenny House, Katie, Chelsea, and Lacey are Big Sisters to a new group of girls facing life-threatening illnesses.

FICTION FOR YOUNGER READERS

I'm a Cover Girl Now (1982)

The Pony That Nobody Wanted (1982)

What's It Like to Be a Star? (1982)

The Battle of Zorn (1983)

Head over Heels (1983)

If I Should Die Before I Wake (1983)

Sometimes Love Just Isn't Enough (1984)

Three's a Crowd (1984)

Peanut Butter for Supper Again (1985)

The Secret Life of Steffie Martin (1985)

Six Months to Live (1985)

Why Did She Have to Die? (1986)

I Want to Live (1987)

More Than Just a Smart Girl (1987)

Mother, Please Don't Die (1988)

My Secret Boyfriend (1988)

A Horse for Mandy (1991)

So Much to Live For (1991)

Somewhere Between Life and Death (1991)

FOR FURTHER READING

Lodge, Sally. "Lurlene McDaniel." *Publishers Weekly*, 6 April 1992.

Telgen, Diane, ed. "Lurlene McDaniel." In *Something About the Author.* Vol. 71. Detroit: Gale Research, 1993.

Verney, Sarah. "Lurlene McDaniel." In *Authors & Artists for Young Adults*, edited by E. A. DesChenes. Vol. 15. Detroit: Gale Research, 1995.

Robin McKinley

Fantasy

Warren, Ohio
November 16, 1952
The Blue Sword

"I can't remember a time when the stories I told myself weren't about shy, bumbling girls who turned out to be heroes," fantasy writer Robin McKinley said in accepting the Newbery Medal in 1985 for *The Hero and the Crown*.

Typical of McKinley's fantasy books is *The Blue Sword*, which in the view of Sally Estes "is a zesty, romantic heroic fantasy with an appealing, stalwart heroine, a finely realized mythical kingdom, and a grounding in reality that enhances the tale's verve as a fantasy. Kidnapped from a remote Homelander outpost by Corlath, king of the old Damarians . . . Harry Crewe soon learns that, possessed of untrained power herself, she is destined to follow in the footsteps and under the protection of a legendary female warrior who, generations before, had led the Damarians into battle against their enemy. McKinley sparks her narrative with marvelous portrayals of Narknon, a hunting cat that adopts Harry, becoming a true companion, and of the magnificent native horses—particularly in scenes of Harry's warrior training as well as those of her riding, first for the sheer joy of it and finally riding into bloody battle against an evil, powerful nonhuman force."

That book won an American Library Association Newbery Honor in 1983. McKinley's next book, *The Hero and the Crown*, received the medal two years later. Of the second book, Merri Rosenberg commented, "In this haunting fantasy of spells and sorcerers, long-lost amulets and primeval struggles between good and evil, Miss McKinley borrows liberally from J. R. R. Tolkien, the Arthurian legends, Celtic and Norse mythology—and even 'Star Wars' symbolism" and has "created an utterly engrossing fantasy, replete with a fairly mature romantic subplot as well as adventure. She transports the reader into a beguiling realm of pseudomedieval pageantry and ritual, where the supernatural is never far below the surface of the ordinary."

The daughter of a sailor and a teacher, McKinley recalls being read aloud to as a youngster. Her father was in the U.S. Navy, later the Merchant Marines, and often returned home loaded with books. Her mother brought home books from the library.

The family moved frequently, living in Virginia, California, New York, and Japan. Her final year of high school was in Maine. McKinley attended Dickinson College. She worked as a motorcycle messenger and a stenographic transcriber. When she married, she and her husband entered Bowdoin College. McKinley majored in English. After graduation, her husband became a police officer, and she began to write.

McKinley's first completed work was *Beauty*. "Robin McKinley's *Beauty* [is] a retelling of the old legend of Beauty and the Beast. Differing from the older version in a few details here and there, none significant, McKinley's Beauty is strong and unafraid and loving. When her father tells her that he has been condemned to death by the Beast for stealing a rose, Beauty gladly agrees to go in place of her father. . . . It is a fine fantasy about reality," Donelson and Nilsen said in *Literature for Today's Young Adults*.

"Writing has always been the other side of reading for me," McKinley stated in *Authors & Artists for Young Adults*: "It never occurred to me not to make up stories. Once I became old enough to realize that authorship existed as a thing one might aspire to, I knew it was for me. But I was also secretly determined to follow in seven-league-boot-sized footsteps like Dickens' and George Eliot's and Hardy's and Conrad's and Kipling's—and J. R. R. Tolkien's. I never will resign myself to the fact that I am not going to write *Tess of the D'Urbervilles* or *Rewards and Fairies*. I don't entirely blame my younger self for spending a lot of time sharpening pencils. I still sharpen a lot of pencils."

Beauty found a publisher in 1978. At the same time, McKinley left her husband and Maine, going to work for a small prep school in

Massachusetts. She joined Little, Brown, a Boston publisher, but managed to write only sporadically. A change of publishers and an opportunity to live as a caretaker on a horse farm provided impetus to go more strongly into writing. She later moved to New York, where she still lives with her second husband, writer Peter Dickinson.

McKinley has retold a number of classic tales. "In *The Outlaws of Sherwood*," Hilary S. Crew noted, "McKinley's Robin Hood is an anxious, cautious, and somewhat enigmatic character, whose necessary escape after killing a fellow forester is seen by Lady Marian and the philosophizing Much as an opportunity to establish a rebel Saxon band deep within Sherwood Forest. A spirit of humorous 'derring-do,' romance, and high adventure is carried, rather, by other members of his band, while Lady Marian dons his mantle of decisive leadership. The disguised boy outlaw, Lady Cecily, is another of McKinley's spirited and courageous heroines—whose love for Little John adds a tender note. The story has both traditional and unique elements, and life in Sherwood Forest for the 'green young outlaws' is vividly presented in a version which McKinley hopes is 'historically unembarrassing.' "

Ann A. Flowers described *A Knot in the Grain* as "a superb collection of five stories . . . by a master storyteller [that] deals mainly with love: true, enduring love between apparently ill-matched lovers. . . . Robin McKinley is deservedly acclaimed for her works of fantasy. She has at her command a clear, apparently effortless style; fresh, original ideas; a romantic outlook; and a remarkable ability to evoke wonder and belief, especially evident in these stories."

"My books are also about hope—I hope," McKinley said in *Authors & Artists for Young Adults*. "Much of modern literature has given up hope and deals with anti-heroes and despair. It seems to me that human beings by their very natures need heroes, real heroes, and are happier with them."

McKinley said she writes her first drafts in longhand. She said she is sensitive to the rhythms in telling a story, the rhythms of characters talking, the pace and movement of plot. She said she does not do well at rewriting; thus, the first draft has to be close to a finished draft.

YOUNG ADULT FICTION

Beauty: A Retelling of the Story of Beauty and the Beast (1978)
Honour is a beauty who encounters a beast.

The Door in the Hedge (1981)
Short stories, including "The Stolen Princess," about a girl whose twin sister is kidnapped, and "The Princess and the Frog," about a kindly maiden who finds her true love when she helps an enchanted frog.

The Outlaws of Sherwood (1988)
A retelling of the story of Robin Hood and his Merry Men.

The Damarian Cycle

The Blue Sword (1982)
A girl, Harry Crewe, wants to cross the desert and climb the mountains to where no Homelander has ever set foot.

The Hero and the Crown (1984)
Aerin, only child of Damar the King, is also the daughter of a witch woman of the North. The Damarians do not trust her enough to allow her to become heir to the throne.

A Knot in the Grain, and Other Stories (1994)
Short stories, including four set in Damar.

ADULT FICTION

Deerskin (1993)
Princess Lissar is the very image of her mother, the queen, and the target of her father's wrath. She flees the kingdom with her loyal dog, Ash, and in the wilderness finds a new identity as Deerskin.

FICTION FOR YOUNGER READERS

My Father Is in the Navy (1992)

Rowan (1992)

CONTRIBUTOR

Elsewhere, vol. II, edited by Terri Windling and Mark Alan Arnold (1982)

Elsewhere, vol. III, edited by Terri Windling and Mark Alan Arnold (1984)

Faery, edited by Terri Windling (1985)

Imaginary Lands, edited by Robin McKinley (1985)

Writers for Children, edited by Jane M. Bingham (1988)

ADAPTATIONS IN OTHER MEDIA

Jungle Book Tales by Rudyard Kipling (1985)

Black Beauty by Anna Sewell (1986)

The Light Princess by George MacDonald (1988)

FOR FURTHER READING

Campbell, Patty. Review of *Beauty. Wilson Library Bulletin*, November 1978.

Crew, Hilary S. "Robin McKinley." In *Twentieth-Century Children's Writers*, edited by Tracy Chevalier. 3d ed. Chicago: St. James Press, 1989.

Donelson, Kenneth L., and Alleen Pace Nilsen, eds. Article in *Literature for Today's Young Adults*. Glenview, IL: Scott, Foresman, 1980.

Estes, Sally. Review of *The Blue Sword. Booklist*, October 1982.

Flowers, Ann A. Review of *A Knot in the Grain, and Other Stories. Horn Book Magazine*, July–August 1994.

Garrett, Agnes, and Helga P. McCue, eds. "Robin McKinley." In *Authors & Artists for Young Adults*. Vol. 4. Detroit: Gale Research, 1990.

Rosenberg, Merri. Review of *The Hero and the Crown. The New York Times Book Review*, 27 January 1985.

Nicholasa Mohr

Urban drama

New York City
November 1, 1935

Felita

One of Mohr's favorite writers when she was a young teen, she said in *Books I Read When I Was Young*, was Mark Twain: "Exciting characterizations. Wonderful humor and touching relationships between the people he wrote about," she said. She also liked Jack London: "High adventure and drama. Stories about people and parts of the world I had never read about before"; and Agatha Christie: "Lots of fun trying to solve the mystery before the end of the book."

Nicholasa Golpe attended the Art Students' League and later the Taller de Grafica in Mexico City, the New School for Social Research, the Brooklyn Museum of Art School, and the Pratt Center for Contemporary Printmaking. She married Irwin Mohr, a clinical child psychologist, in 1957. He later died. She has two sons.

Mohr has worked as a fine arts painter and printmaker. She also has taught and worked as an artist and writer in residence. She was head creative writer and co-producer of the video series *Aqui y Ahora* (*Here and Now*).

Mohr's young adult books are based on the Puerto Rican experience. She "is recognized for accurately representing the hardships and struggles of her people in the El Barrio section of New York City while celebrating their resilience, solidarity, pride, and variety of life," according to *Children's Literature Review*.

Although she spent much of her life as an artist, Mohr told Paul Janeczko that writing affords opportunity to "be very specific; I could tell a story, really tell a story, and I could make people laugh. I could make people aware of what it was like for myself at the time. It was almost like a catharsis, the first book. I was even thinking of going into sculpture, but all of a sudden I found a medium where I was really comfortable. I could draw a picture with words, and it was extremely stimulating and eye-opening to realize what one could do with words."

Nilda, her first book, is about a girl living in the Puerto Rican neighborhood during World War II. "The main story line concerns Mama's efforts to take care of her large family—five children, sick husband, crazy aunt, and pregnant girlfriend of one son," Marilyn Sachs noted. "But what makes the book remarkable is the richness of detail and the aching sense of a child's feelings. When Nilda is sent to a Catholic charity camp and forced along with other girls to take nightly doses of milk of magnesia by a terrifying, smiling nun, it is hard not to feel her humiliation. It is equally hard not to rejoice with Nilda and her friends when they get their revenge on Miss Reilly, a language teacher who is trying to teach Castilian Spanish to her class of Puerto Rican students."

Mohr continued to explore the barrio in collections of stories and in *Felita* and *Going Home. Felita* "has strong characters and is significant for its honest, realistic view of an important aspect of contemporary American life," Virginia Haviland said. *Going Home* "is bright and honest, and the story line is well developed through Felita's relationships—both positive and negative. There are few stories of Puerto Rican children, and this is deftly written and lively—an enjoyable story for any reader."

YOUNG ADULT FICTION

Nilda: A Novel (1973)
In a story set in the early 1940s, Nilda and her family struggle to survive in the Puerto Rican ghetto of New York City.

El Bronx Remembered: A Novella and Stories (1975)

In Nueva York (1977)
Short stories.

Felita (1979)
Felita misses her friends when her family moves to a "better" neighborhood.

Going Home (1986), sequel to *Felita*
Felita, now eleven, is thrilled to go on a trip to Puerto Rico.

Jaime and the Conch Shell (1995)

FICTION FOR YOUNGER READERS

The Magic Shell (1995)

ADULT FICTION

Rituals of Survival: A Women's Portfolio (1985)

SCREENPLAYS

The Artist, with Ray Blanco

FOR FURTHER READING

Cullinan, Bernice, and M. Jerry Weiss, eds. *Books I Read When I Was Young: The Favorite Books of Famous People*. New York: Avon Books, 1980.

Greenlaw, M. Jean. *A Teacher's Guide to* Felita *and* Going Home *by Nicholasa Mohr*. New York: Bantam Doubleday Dell, n.d.

Haviland, Virginia. Review of *Felita. Horn Book Magazine*, February 1980.

Janeczko, Paul. Interview with Nicholasa Mohr. In *From Writers to Students: The Pleasures and Pains of Writing*, edited by M. Jerry Weiss. Newark, DE: International Reading Association, 1979.

"Nicholasa Mohr." In *Children's Literature Review*, edited by Gerard J. Senick. Vol. 22. Detroit: Gale Research, 1991.

Sachs, Marilyn. Review of *Nilda. The New York Times Book Review*, 4 November 1973.

Wilms, Denise M. Review of *Going Home. Booklist*, July 1986.

Lucy Maud Montgomery

Family drama

Clifton, Prince Edward Island, Canada
November 30, 1874–April 24, 1942

Anne of Green Gables

Lucy Maud Montgomery's impetuous, red-headed orphan, Anne Shirley, was not the boy expected by the Prince Edward Island couple who adopted her. Nevertheless, the fictional heroine worked her way into their hearts and into the hearts of several generations of young adult and adult readers.

Montgomery, whose mother died when she was two years old, was raised by her strict, Presbyterian maternal grandparents. Kept away from other children, she wrote detailed journals of her thoughts. Her isolation, she wrote in a journal, "drove me in on myself and early forced me to construct for myself a world of fancy and imagination very different indeed from the world in which I lived."

In 1887, her father remarried and settled in Saskatchewan. Montgomery joined him but could not get along with her stepmother. At fifteen, she was kept home from school to help care for her stepbrother and stepsister. In 1891, she returned east to live with her grandparents. Three years later, she earned her teaching certificate and taught until 1898. When her grandfather died, she returned to live with and care for her grandmother. For a time, she worked for a newspaper in Nova Scotia. She also began writing; her novel *Anne of Green Gables* was published in 1908.

In 1911, Montgomery married the Reverend Ewan Macdonald after a secret, five-year engagement. They moved to Ontario, where she gave birth to three sons. Though her life was difficult—one of their sons was stillborn, her husband suffered a mental breakdown, and she sued her first publisher, L. C. Page, over royalties in 1919—she continued to produce popular novels. Montgomery herself suffered nervous and physical collapses in 1938 and 1940. She never recovered. Lucy Montgomery died in 1942.

Montgomery's most popular works were *Anne of Green Gables* and its sequels. Anne and the writer's other heroines were children who never quite grew up. They continued to display a rebellious streak—a key to their appeal. *Anne* went through several printings the first year.

In the beginning of the series, Anne is eleven, red-haired, freckle-faced, willowy, and prone to pranks. She arrives at Green Gables from an orphanage in Nova Scotia. Anne encounters Gilbert Blythe, a boy she at first dislikes for pulling her braids and calling her "carrot-top." Later in the series she comes to like and marry him. Anne is sensitive, an eternal optimist.

Jane Spence Southron commented in *The New York Times Book Review*: "Mark Twain, had he been alive, would have approved of the later Anne. She has worn well; or rather, there is no sign of wear about her. Natural wit, a fine constitution and a zest for living nothing could dampen, plus the inherent capacity for doing the decent thing in a crisis (as when she gave up ambition for the sake of the aging woman who had mothered her), have kept her sweet as a sound-cored apple with a good sharp bite to it."

Lesley Willis's view was not so rosy: "Anne of Green Gables is unquestionably one of the best-known examples of Canadian children's fiction," she wrote. "But much of the book's appeal consists in its catering to a desire for wish-fulfillment and, on the part of the older reader, nostalgia for a sentimentally-envisioned past; and these desires are catered to largely through the use, or misuse, of myth and fairy tale, which are so distorted that only their pleasant associations remain."

"*Anne of Avonlea* contains much the same gentle charm that made *Anne of Green Gables* so delectable a book," Margaret Merwin said, adding that the characters "continue their hushed, secluded, leisurely lives in a way calculated to yield the reader weary of the steam riveter and the automobile, the career and the fad, a refreshing sense of peace. None of the problems of modern life enter the quiet page. But there is plenty of sunshine and green shadow, of the timid and yet serene faith of untried youth, and not a little blue and silver love making."

"L. M. Montgomery was a highly disciplined and efficient writer, who was, in some of her other novels, too aware of her reading public, and too willing to conform to their taste so as to sell," Mary

Rubio wrote in *L. M. Montgomery: An Assessment*. "She turned out a great amount of material which she herself seems to consider 'hack' work in her letters."

A second series heroine, Emily, is highly autobiographical. Emily Byrd Starr, aspiring writer, is followed from her preteen years through adulthood.

"In spite of the likeness between the two heroines, Emily has the distinction of being closer to her creator," said Margery Fisher. "There is much of the young Lucy Maud in this first book of the 'New Moon' trilogy—with the 'flashes' of perception that drive Emily to write poetry and the sense of justice which is so easily hurt by her disciplinarian aunt. The 'Anne' books are perhaps richer in pen portraits of village worthies and have a fuller social scope, but Emily's story offers a sharper picture of a child fighting for her identity in a world of adult values.

"Some of the scenes in *Emily of New Moon*—confrontations at school with insensitive Miss Brownell, Aunt Elizabeth's decree about the stray kitten, a punitive session in the dark spare room 'where a stuffed, white Arctic owl' stared at her 'with uncanny eyes'—have a marked intensity that lifts them from the particular to the world of childhood as a whole; though sentiments are often expressed in a way that now seems mawkish and embarrassing, the real crises of the book ring true."

FICTION

Kilmeny of the Orchard (1910)
A young schoolteacher finds romance on Prince Edward Island.

The Story Girl (1911)
Sara Stanley, one of the merry children of the island, has a knack for preserving and relating fairy tales and legends.

The Golden Road (1913), sequel to *The Story Girl*
Sara Stanley continues to weave her dream stories.

The Blue Castle (1926)
Valancy Stirling, twenty-nine and single, is the only plain woman in a family of beauties.

Magic for Marigold (1927)
Little Marigold is an imaginative child growing up in a household of old people.

A Tangled Web (1931); British title: *Aunt Becky Began It* (1931)
Acid-tongued Aunt Becky will name the recipient of the treasured Dark family jug.

Pat of Silver Bush (1933)
Patricia Gardiner grows to womanhood on the farm Silver Bush.

Mistress Pat: A Novel of Silver Bush (1935), sequel to *Pat of Silver Bush*
Pat is so enamored of the old farm that she refuses to leave or to entertain suitors.

Jane of Lantern Hill (1937)
Jane Victoria Stuart lives in Toronto with her beautiful but ineffectual mother and domineering grandmother.

The Road to Yesterday (1974)
Short stories.

The Doctor's Sweetheart, and Other Stories, edited by Catherine McLay (1979)

Akin to Anne: Tales of Other Orphans, edited by Rea Wilmhurst (1988)

Along the Shore: Tales by the Sea, edited by Rea Wilmhurst (1989)

Against the Odds: Tales of Achievement (1994)
Short stories.

At the Altar: Matrimonial Tales, edited by Rea Wilmhurst (1995)

Anne Shirley Series

Anne of Green Gables (1908)
A Prince Edward Island farmer and his sister expect a boy from the orphanage—but it is a girl, and a red-haired, impetuous one at that.

Anne of Avonlea (1909)
Anne is a little older but no less imaginative or prone to predicaments.

Chronicles of Avonlea, in Which Anne Shirley of Green Gables and Avonlea Plays Some Part (1912)
Short stories in which Anne appears only incidentally.

Anne of the Island (1915)
During her years at the university in Kingsport, Anne stays in touch with friends in Avonlea. Gilbert is destined to marry Anne—or is he?

Anne's House of Dreams (1917)
Anne's romantic fantasy comes true with an orchard wedding to Gilbert Blythe.

Rainbow Valley (1919)
Mrs. Anne Blythe has six children—and they have adventures of their own.

Further Chronicles of Avonlea: Which Have to Do with Many Personalities and Events in and About Avonlea (1920)
Short stories.

Rilla of Ingleside (1921)
Anne's daughter Rilla is a spirited girl.

Anne of Windy Poplars (1936); British title: *Anne of Windy Willows* (1936)
Anne has graduated from the university and is principal of a high school in Summerside. Gilbert is attending medical school.

Anne of Ingleside (1939)
After Anne and Gilbert move to Ingleside, they raise five more children.

Emily Byrd Starr Series

Emily of New Moon (1923)
After the death of her parents, Emily Starr goes to live with two maiden aunts. She clashes with stern Aunt Elizabeth.

Emily Climbs (1924)
Emily joins friends Ilse, Teddy, and Perry at Shrewsbury High School.

Emily's Quest (1927)
Now an adult, Emily yearns to become a successful writer.

Road to Avonlea Series Based on the Montgomery Books

The Journey Begins by Dennis Adair and Janet Rosenstock (1991)

The Story Girl Earns Her Name by Gail Hamilton (1991)

Song of the Night by Fiona McHugh (1991)

The Materializing of Duncan McTavish by Heather Conkie (1991)

Quarantine at Alexander Abraham's by Fiona McHugh (1991)

Conversions (1992)

Aunt Abigail's Beau by Amy J. Cooper (1992)

Malcolm and the Baby by Heather Conkie (1992)

Felicity's Challenge by Gail Hamilton (1992)

The Hope Chest of Arabella King by Linda Zwicker (1993)

Nothing Endures but Change by Gail Hamilton (1993)

Sara's Homecoming by Heather Conkie (1993)

Aunt Hetty's Ordeal by Gail Hamilton (1993)

Of Corsets and Secrets and True, True Love by Fiona McHugh (1993)

Old Quarrels, Old Love by Heather Conkie (1993)

Family Rivalry by Gail Hamilton (1993)

May the Best Man Win by Gail Hamilton (1993)

Dreamer of Dreams by Heather Conkie (1993)

It's Just a Stage (1993)

Misfits and Miracles by Rosenstock (1994)

The Ties That Bind by Heather Conkie (1994)

Felix and Blackie by Rosenstock (1994)

But When She Was Bad . . . by Marlene Matthew (1994)

Double Trouble by Marlene Matthew (1994)

A Dark and Stormy Night by Gail Hamilton (1994)

Friends and Relations by Heather Conkie (1995)

Vows of Silence by Gail Hamilton (1995)

ADAPTATIONS IN OTHER MEDIA

Anne of Green Gables (1919)
Film starring Mary Miles Minter and Paul Kelly.

Anne of Green Gables (1934)
Film starring Anne Shirley and Tom Brown.

Anne of Windy Poplars (1940)
Film starring Anne Shirley and James Ellison.

Anne of Green Gables (1972)
British television movie and sequel.

Anne of Green Gables (1985)
Canadian television movie starring Megan Follows, Richard Farnsworth, Colleen Dewhurst, and Jonathan Crombie.

Anne of Avonlea (1987)
Canadian television movie starring Megan Follows, Colleen Dewhurst, Frank Converse, and Jonathan Crombie.

The Road to Avonlea (1990–)
Disney Channel television series.

POETRY

The Poetry of Lucy Maud Montgomery, edited by John Ferns and Kevin McCabe (1987)

DRAMA

Anne of Green Gables (1937)
Play.

Anne of Green Gables (1953)
Musical drama.

FOR FURTHER READING

Andronik, Catherine M. *Kindred Spirit: A Biography of Lucy Maud Montgomery, Creator of Anne of Green Gables*. New York: Atheneum, 1993.

Bolger, Francis W. P., and Elizabeth R. Epperly, eds. *My Dear Mr. M.: Letters to G. B. MacMillan from L. M. Montgomery*. Toronto: McGraw-Hill/Ryerson, 1980.

Bruce, Harry. *Maud: The Life of L. M. Montgomery, the Creator of the World of Anne of Green Gables*. New York: Bantam Books, 1994.

Eggleston, Wilfrid, ed. *The Green Gables Letters, from L. M. Montgomery to Ephraim Weber, 1905–1909*. Toronto: Ryerson, 1960.

Fisher, Margery. Review of *Emily of New Moon*. *Growing Point*, January 1978.

Merwin, Margaret. "L. M. Montgomery's 'Anne of Avonlea.'" *Bookman*, October 1909.

Montgomery, Lucy Maud. *The Alpine Path: The Story of My Career*. Markham, Ontario: Fitzhenry & Whiteside, 1974.

O'Reilly, Gabrielle. *The World of Lucy Maud Montgomery: A Teacher's Guide to the Bantam and Seal Works of L. M. Montgomery*. New York: Bantam Books, 1990.

Rubio, Mary. "Satire, Realism & Imagination in 'Anne of Green Gables.'" In *L. M. Montgomery: An Assessment*, edited by John Robert Sorfleet. Toronto: Canadian Children's Press, 1976.

Rubio, Mary, and Elizabeth Waterston, eds. *Selected Journals of L. M. Montgomery*. Vol. 1, 1889–1910; vol. 2, 1910–1921. Toronto: Oxford University Press, 1985–87.

Southron, Jane Spence. "After Green Gables." *The New York Times Book Review*, 30 July 1939.

Willis, Lesley. "The Bogus Ugly Duckling: Anne Shirley Unmasked." *Dalhousie Review*, summer 1976.

Walter Dean Myers

Urban drama

Martinsburg, West Virginia
August 12, 1937

Scorpions

"Harlem permeates Walter Dean Myers's novels for children and teenagers, even the stories set in places very remote from New York," Jack Forman observed. "Myers remembers from his own childhood many positive experience (such as reading from the newspaper to his mother while she did housework and getting his first typewriter from his father), but he doesn't look through rose-colored glasses when he writes about the dangerous and deadend reality of Harlem—the gangs (such as he depicts in *Scorpions*), drugs, school dropouts, broken families, crime, and pervasive hopelessness."

"Myers is recognized as a versatile author whose works, often set in Harlem, stress the positive attributes of the experiences and environment of his characters without shunning the negative elements," *Children's Literature Review* stated. "Considered an important black writer, he is often praised for his appealing characterizations, natural dialogue, exciting plots, successful integration of topics, and superior use of details."

"I am a product of Harlem and of the values, color, toughness, and caring that I found there as a child," Myers said in a publisher's flyer. "I learned my flat jump shot in the church basement and got my first kiss during recess at Bible school. I played the endless street games kids played in the pre-television days and paid enough attention to candy and junk food to dutifully alarm my mother. . . .

"The George Bruce Branch of the public library was my most treasured place. I couldn't believe my luck in discovering that what I enjoyed most, reading, was free. And I was tough enough to carry the books home through the streets without too many incidents. . . .

"Writing for me has been many things. It was a way to overcome the hindrance of speech problems as I tried to reach out to the world. It was a way of establishing my humanity in a world that often ignores the humanity of those in less favored positions. It was a way to make a few extra dollars when they were badly needed."

Born Walter Milton Myers, the author was descended from southern slaves. His mother died when he was three. He and two of seven siblings went to live with a foster family named Dean; all moved to Harlem. His foster father, he recalled, loved to tell ghost stories and stories of creatures from the sea, stories that at times scared the youngster.

"Books have always played a central role in my life," Myers said in *Books I Read When I Was Young*. "I came across *Laughing to Keep from Crying* by Langston Hughes at a point in my life when I thought all writers were white, and the subject of any book had to be far removed from my own experiences. The stories of Langston Hughes put this myth aside and introduced me to a joyous style of writing which I have loved since first reading the book. Hughes had treated the black experience with a style and dignity which I had felt, and he had done so without resorting to a literature of rage."

Myers began writing in school, composing read-aloud poems that avoided certain sounds that, because of his speech difficulty, prompted laughs from schoolmates. The writer was keenly sensitive about his race, however, and feared that there was no future for a black writer.

"When I began writing for young people, I was only vaguely aware of the problem with children's books as far as blacks were concerned," he said in *The New York Times Book Review*. "My own encounters with black symbols and black characters were no less painful than those of the generations that followed me. There was the first mention of blacks in history. There were 'slaves' being led from ships. Not captives, slaves. In truth, I don't remember Little Black Sambo, the large red lips pouting from the page, the wide eyes, the kinky hair going off in all directions, as being particularly bothersome. I'm not sure if it was the awe in which I held the tiger, or if I had just separated myself from this image. But later I do remember suffering through the Tom Swift books, and the demeaning portrait of Eradicate, the major black character in the series.

"The pain was not so much that the images of my people were poor, but that the poor images were being made public. There they were in books for all of my white classmates to see. I had already internalized the negative images, had taken them for truth. No matter that my mother said that I was as good as anyone. She had also told me, in words and in her obvious pride in my reading, that books were important, and yet it was in books that I found Eradicate Sampson and the other blacks who were lazy, dirty and, above all, comical."

Still, Myers wrote short stories and verse. He joined the army at seventeen and learned radio repair. He returned to New York and a succession of jobs. He married, worked for the post office, raised two children, and began to sell to black magazines such as *Liberator* and *Negro Digest* and to men's and adventure magazines. His marriage ended in divorce, and he wed a second time.

His young adult novel *Fast Sam, Cool Clyde, and Stuff* found a receptive publisher in 1975. Myers himself became a book editor. Seven years later, out of work, he decided to write full time.

"I enjoy writing for young people because the forms are less constricting, more forgiving to the stretched imagination," he stated in *Authors & Artists for Young Adults*. "I particularly enjoy writing about the city life I know best. Ultimately what I want to do with my writing is make the connection—reach out and touch the lives of my characters and share them with a reader."

Myers's novel *It Ain't All for Nothin'* describes Tippy's problems when his grandmother, suffering from arthritis and old age, moves into a nursing home and he goes to live with Lonnie, his ex-convict father, who survives by stealing. Thanks to Tippy, Lonnie gets on welfare. Lonnie briefly gets a job, then is fired. He forces Tippy to help pull off a robbery, and one of Lonnie's friends, Bubba, is shot. Another gang member, Stone, says to let him die, but Tippy knows he must go for help.

Scorpions, a Newbery Honor Book in 1989, is a portrait of Jamal Hicks, a twelve-year-old in Harlem struggling with his family's poverty and with crime. *Somewhere in the Darkness* tells of fifteen-year-old Jimmy, who has not seen his father since he was a baby. Then he meets a man who claims to be his father. "This is one of Myers's most memorable pieces of writing: there is not an unnecessary word or phrase; the scenes are vivid and emotionally powerful; and the characters are heartbreakingly realistic," critic Ellen Fader said. "A page-turner elevated to a higher plane by its theme of the universal quest of a son for his father."

The Glory Field follows the life of a black family over several generations. "Opening this episodic historical novel effectively with a scene of 11-year-old Muhammad Bilal bound in chains on a slave ship, Walter Dean Myers has set an ambitious course," reviewer Kenneth C. Davis said. "Mr. Myers attempts to consolidate nearly 200 years of history into one family's story."

Fallen Angels, a stark novel about soldiers trying to survive the Vietnam War, enraged parents in Ohio, Iowa, Georgia, and New Hampshire, who sought to ban Myers's novel from bookshelves because of its profane language, according to Herbert N. Foerstel.

Myers created the 18 Pine St. series, which is written by Stacie Johnson. The address is the name of a pizzeria that is a hangout for some kids who attend Murphy High.

YOUNG ADULT FICTION

Fast Sam, Cool Clyde, and Stuff (1975)
A group of 116th Street kids are mistakenly arrested, encounter drugs and violence, and lose family members as they grow up together.

Mojo and the Russians (1977)
Dean accidentally knocks down the West Indian mojo lady while riding his bicycle. Fearing he has been "fixed," he and his friends try to undo the hex.

Victory for Jamie (1977)

It Ain't All for Nothin' (1978)
When his aged grandmother must go into a nursing home, Tippy returns to live with his father, Lonnie, an ex-con.

The Young Landlords (1979)
Paul Williams and his Action Group friends buy an old slum for one dollar and try to fix it up.

Hoops: A Novel (1981)
Lonnie Jackson, eighteen, who has grown up in a fatherless home, develops a tentative friendship with former pro player Cal Jones, now coach of the basketball team.

The Legend of Tarik (1981)
In medieval North Africa, Tarik undergoes rigorous training to get revenge on El Muerte for his father's death.

Won't Know Till I Get There (1982)
Steve tries to prove himself tough when his family takes in Earl, a thirteen-year-old ex-delinquent. He ends up in juvenile court, ordered to work the summer in an old folks' home.

The Nicholas Factor: A Novel (1983)
Gerard is suspicious of the activities of the Crusader Society, especially when he and friend Jennifer come upon a Peruvian village full of sick and dying Indians.

Tales of a Dead King (1983)
John Robie and Karen Lacey, on an archaeological dig in Egypt, look for the missing Dr. Erich Leonhardt.

Motown and Didi: A Love Story (1984), featuring minor characters from *It Ain't All for Nothin'*
Didi desperately wants to attend college but feels trapped by her mother's deteriorating mental and physical health and her brother's worsening drug habit.

The Outside Shot (1984), sequel to *Hoops*
Lonnie Jackson leaves Harlem for a basketball scholarship at a midwestern college. If he can keep his head straight, he may have a chance at the pros, but he does not anticipate the pressure.

Sweet Illusions (1986)
In separate chapters, five unwed mothers and fathers, four family friends, and others tell their stories.

Crystal (1987)
Crystal Brown, sixteen, launches a modeling career based on a commercial made at her church, not expecting the sexual and other pressures.

Fallen Angels (1988)
Richie Perry, Lobel, Johnson, Brunner, and Peewee are in Vietnam for different reasons, but they share a common goal: getting out alive.

Scorpions (1988)
With older brother Randy in jail, Mama and Sissy worried all the time, and with the school principal on his back, Jamal is looking for a way out. He joins a gang.

Mouse Rap (1991)
Mouse, a fourteen-year-old rapper, and his friends search for money hidden by a gang in the 1930s.

The Righteous Revenge of Artemis Bonner (1992)
Artemis tracks a lost fortune through the Old West, hoping to recover it for his widowed aunt.

Somewhere in the Darkness (1992)
Crab knows that this is his last chance to break through to his son, Jimmy, so he takes the boy on a cross-country trip to visit old haunts.

Darnell Rock Reporting (1994)
Rock, thirteen, is given an ultimatum by the principal at South Oakdale Middle School, so he gets a job with the local newspaper.

The Glory Field (1994)
In five segments, the 200-year history of a black family is recounted, from Africa to a South Carolina plantation.

Arrow Series

Adventure in Granada (1985)
Two teenage brothers in Spain, Chris and Ken, clear a friend of theft charges.

The Hidden Shrine (1985)
Three teens expose thieves who are stealing artifacts from Hong Kong temples.

Duel in the Desert (1986)

Ambush in the Amazon (1986)

18 Pine St. Series Created by Myers, Written by Stacie Johnson

Sort of Sisters (1992)
Murphy High kids include Sarah Gordon, Tasha Gordon, Cindy Phillips, and Kwame Brown.

The Party (1992)
Jennifer Wilson plans a big party for the juniors.

The Prince (1992)
Sarah persuades the gang to do a rap version of *Romeo and Juliet*.

The Test (1993)
Tasha hopes to take top honors in the annual math contest.

Skyman (1993)
The new student, "Skyman" Hodges, is destined to be a basketball star.

Fashion by Tasha (1993)
Tasha's clothes are the hit of Madison's charity fashion show.

Intensive Care (1993)
Jennifer takes her mother's car without permission.

Dangerous Games (1993)
Sarah objects to the new student assassination game, KAOS.

Cindy's Baby (1994)
Cindy's friend Karin is in over her head as a single mom.

Kwame's Girl (1994)
Kwame Brown is in love with the new girl at Murphy High—but she sure does like to shop at the mall a lot.

The Diary (1994)
Sarah is shocked at what she reads in Julie's diary.

Taking Sides (1994)
Tasha finds an off-color joke an insult to African Americans and challenges the student who told it to a debate.

FICTION FOR YOUNGER READERS

Where Does the Day Go? (1969) as Walter M. Myers

The Dancers (1972)

The Dragon Takes a Wife (1972)

Fly, Jimmy, Fly! (1974)

Brainstorm (1977)

The Black Pearl and the Ghost; or, One Mystery After Another (1980)

The Golden Serpent (1980)

Mr. Monkey and the Gotcha Bird: An Original Tale (1984)

Me, Mop, and the Moondance Kid (1988)

Mop, Moondance and the Nagasaki Knights (1992)

Brown Angels: An Album of Pictures and Verse (1993)

Glorious Angels: A Celebration of Children (1995) Companion to *Brown Angels*.

How Mrs. Monkey Saw the Whole World (1995)

Shadow of the Red Moon (1995)

The Story of the Three Kingdoms (1995)

CONTRIBUTOR

What We Must See: Young Black Storytellers, edited by Orde Coombs (1971)

We Be Word Sorcerers: Twenty-Five Stories by Black Americans, edited by Sonia Sanchez (1973)

FOR FURTHER READING

Cullinan, Bernice, and M. Jerry Weiss, eds. *Books I Read When I Was Young: The Favorite Books of Famous People*. New York: Avon Books, 1980.

Davis, Kenneth C. Review of *The Glory Field*. *The New York Times Book Review*, 13 November 1994.

Fader, Ellen. Review of *Somewhere in the Darkness*. *Horn Book Magazine*, May–June 1992.

Foerstel, Herbert N. *Banned in the USA: A Reference Guide to Book Censorship in Schools and Public Libraries*. Westport, CT: Greenwood, 1994.

Forman, Jack. "Walter Dean Myers." In *Twentieth-Century Children's Writers*, edited by Tracy Chevalier. 3d ed. Chicago: St. James Press, 1989.

Garrett, Agnes, and Helga P. McCue, eds. "Walter Dean Myers." In *Authors & Artists for Young Adults*. Vol. 4. Detroit: Gale Research, 1990.

Holtze, Sally Holmes, ed. *Fifth Book of Junior Authors & Illustrators*. New York: H. W. Wilson, 1983.

Myers, Walter Dean. "I Actually Thought We Would Revolutionize the Industry." *The New York Times Book Review*, 9 November 1986.

"Walter Dean Myers." In *Children's Literature Review*, edited by Gerard J. Senick. Vol. 16. Detroit: Gale Research, 1989.

Walter Dean Myers: Author of the 1989 Newbery Honor Book Scorpions. New York: Harper Junior Books, 1989.

Phyllis Reynolds Naylor

Family drama

Anderson, Indiana
January 4, 1933

The Keeper

Phyllis Reynolds Naylor is a versatile writer. Her likable characters struggle toward maturity, often with the help of caring families. Her topics range from crib death to mental illness, from war to divorce.

"Perhaps I will work on a very serious book in the morning and a funny one in the afternoon," Naylor told Sally Holmes Holtze. "I particularly like writing books about realistic problems, books that are both sad and funny, but I have also done two trilogies of a different sort—a terrifying one about witchcraft . . . and a trilogy about ghosts and Gypsies."

The Witch books are about Lynn Morley's battle with good and evil; she tries to convince her parents that her older sister and a neighbor woman are really witches. The York trilogy is about Dan Roberts, a teenager who may have inherited the illness Huntington's chorea, as he travels through time to help a Gypsy family at the time of the plague.

"She writes well in a variety of forms and styles," John D. Stahl observed, "including comic adventure stories, philosophical time-travel fantasies, realistic novels about adolescents maturing, dark problem novels, and various kinds of nonfiction."

The daughter of a salesman and a teacher, Naylor grew up in what she has described as an ordinary, fairly religious midwestern family. "When I was growing up," she said in a publisher's pamphlet, "I hadn't the slightest curiosity about the authors of books I read; it was the *story* that was important. My mother, and sometimes my father, read aloud to us every night. They sang to us, too, and many of their songs were really stories. I could hardly wait until I could read and write my own books."

Naylor attended Joliet Junior College and the American University. She worked as a clinical secretary, elementary schoolteacher, assistant executive secretary, and editorial assistant. She has been active in civil rights and peace organizations. In 1960, she became a full-time writer. That same year she married her second husband, Dr. Rex V. Naylor, a speech pathologist. She has three children.

Naylor published her first story at age sixteen. For twenty-five years, she wrote a humorous church newspaper column for teenagers. She wrote a similar one for adult readers for ten years. She has produced more than 2,000 short stories and articles.

Naylor has written for all ages: children's picture books, young adult, and adult novels. The switch from stories to books was difficult at first, she said, for she expected books would take so long to write that she would become bored with them. Her first books were collections of stories. *What the Gulls Were Singing* in 1967 was her first full-length novel, and from then on she wrote one or two novels a year.

"I'm not happy unless I spend some time every day writing," Naylor said in a pamphlet. "It's as though pressure builds up inside me, and writing even a little helps to release it. Usually I write about six hours each day. Tending to other writing business, answering mail, and just thinking about a book takes another four hours. I spend from three months to a year on a children's book, depending on how well I know the characters before I begin and how much research I need to do. A novel for adults, because it is longer, takes a year or two. When my work is going well, I wake early in the mornings, hoping it is time to get up. When the writing is difficult and the words are flat, I am grouchy and not very pleasant to be around."

"She needs much of her time alone, relatively uninterrupted, for writing," her husband said in *Horn Book Magazine*. "But if the material is lighter, she can take a clipboard with her to the hairdresser or on a train and write in the middle of a hubbub. I once left her in the lobby of a hotel while I returned our rented car and came back to find her standing beside our luggage cart, writing away on top of a suitcase, oblivious to the racket around her. . . .

"Events from her life as family member, neighbor, concerned citizen, and passing stranger feed into the writing, but usually indirectly. Life-affirming and positive, Phyllis has nevertheless used writing to work through all manner of vexing concerns about herself, her work, family, friends, and the lives of those who spring from the pages of the newspapers—not to mention the creatures of her thriving imagination. One of her fears is that she will die with characters still trapped inside her. Some of her vivid, detailed, and often hilarious dreams betray how easily she worries."

Naylor has written an autobiography, *Crazy Love* (1977), describing her first marriage to a man who was institutionalized as a paranoid schizophrenic. She also wrote a fiction book on the subject of having a loved one with mental illness, *The Keeper*. A second autobiography, *How I Came to Be a Writer* (1978), tells how her career as a writer developed.

Controversy occasionally surrounds Naylor's books. One parent complained about *A String of Chances*. The young protagonist, Evie Hutchins, questions her parents' religion and does not come around to their way of thinking. This was exposing Christian children to ridicule, the parent said. Reviewers saw more depth to the story.

"Various people and experiences awaken a questioning in Evie, but the shattering impact of the tragic crib death of the Rawleys' beloved baby [Evie has been spending the summer with her Rawley cousins] pushes her first into a denial of faith and then into a search for a God in whom she can believe. Though the story centers on Evie's emotions and experiences, making her a fully realized character, it also gives other characters enough depth and emotional play to make them both viable and essential to the plot," said Sally Estes.

"What might have become trite and stereotypical is not at all so," Stahl stated. "Evie's father is loving and genuine and has a sense of humor; the baby's death and the consequent grief of all involved are presented with truthfulness and depth; and Evie emerges stronger and wiser but without easy resolutions to her religious questions or to her difficulties in romance."

"Writing is very definitely an addiction," Naylor said in *How I Came to Be a Writer*. "Once the thrill of putting words on paper had a hold on me, the magic of it never left. Though this is certainly not true for all writers, ideas now come faster than I can handle them. By the time I am halfway through one book, a new plot is already forming in my mind, distracting me and making me miserable until I can end the first manuscript and start the second. I already know what my next five books will be, and this is probably the way it will be for the rest of my life."

YOUNG ADULT FICTION

The Galloping Goat, and Other Stories (1965)

Grasshoppers in the Soup: Short Stories for Teenagers (1965)

Jennifer Jean, the Cross-Eyed Queen (1967)
Jennifer Jean is accustomed to her vision problems and to the teasing.

Knee Deep in Ice Cream, and Other Stories (1967)

The New Schoolmaster (1967)

A New Year's Surprise (1967)

To Shake a Shadow (1967)

What the Gulls Were Singing (1967)
The Buckleys are at the shore for the summer, and Marilyn resents it when older brother Peter gets a new bike and a new roommate, Nico, the Greek boy.

When Rivers Meet (1968)

The Dark Side of the Moon (1969)
Short stories.

Meet Murdock (1969)
A retired sailor named Murdock, with a pet parrot named Sir Walter, becomes an apartment house custodian and has to put up with kids from upstairs.

The Private I, and Other Stories (1969)

To Make a Wee Moon (1969)
Jean and Brian come from West Virginia to visit Grandmother's farm in rural Wisconsin.

Making It Happen (1970)

Ships in the Night (1970)

Wrestle the Mountain (1971)
Jed Jefferson Tate, eleven, does not want to work in the coal mines like his father.

No Easy Circle (1972)
Shelley is fifteen and physically immature; her parents are divorced, and her friend, Pogo, is pregnant.

To Walk the Sky Path (1973)
Billie Tommie, a Seminole, is the first of his family to go to the white man's school.

An Amish Family (1974)
Manners and customs of the Amish are depicted through Benjamin and Rebecca Stoltzfus and their children.

Walking Through the Dark (1976)
Ruth Wheeler is starting high school in Chicago in 1932 when the Depression leaves her father jobless and the family struggling.

How Lazy Can You Get? (1979)
Humorless Miss Brasscoat spends a week with the three Megglethorp children while their parents are away.

A Change in the Wind (1980)

Never Born a Hero (1982)
Short stories.

A String of Chances (1982)
The world turns upside-down for a girl who is away from home for the first time.

The Mad Gasser of Besseldorf Street (1983)

The Solomon System (1983)
At summer camp, Ted Solomon relies on his brother, Nory, to help him cope with their parents' pending divorce.

Night Cry (1984)
Her mother dead and her father a traveling salesman, Ellen is often alone at the Mississippi farm.

A Triangle Has Four Sides (1984)

The Dark of the Tunnel (1985)
Craig Sheldon is losing his mother to cancer.

The Keeper (1986)
A young boy's father is diagnosed as paranoid schizophrenic.

Unexpected Pleasures (1987)
A girl escaping her shiftless family finds romance with a bridge worker.

The Year of the Gopher (1987)
Refusing to go to college until he knows what he wants to do, George works as a gofer.

Send No Blessings (1991)
Marriage to Harless Prather is not the escape from her family's cramped trailer that Beth envisioned.

Shiloh (1991)
Marty Preston, eleven, loves to spend time in the hills behind his home in West Virginia. One day he comes across a beagle—and trouble begins.

The Grand Escape (1993)
House cats Marco and Polo sneak off, looking for a ranch to live on.

The Fear Place (1994)
Nothing can make fearful Doug go back to the ridge—unless it is to save his brother's life.

Alice Series

The Agony of Alice (1985)
Without a mother, Alice struggles through sixth grade, seeking guidance in female matters.

Alice in Rapture, Sort Of (1989)

Alice in April (1993)

Alice the Brave (1995)
Alice tries to overcome her eighth-grade troubles and her fear of swimming in deep water.

Witch Trilogy

Witch Sister (1975)
Lynn Morley suspects that her older sister, Judith, is a witch.

Witch Water (1977)
Lynn and her friend, "Mouse" Beasley, fear that old Mrs. Tuggle is a witch about to bring them under her power.

The Witch Herself (1978)
The continued struggle with Mrs. Tuggle ends in a scary midnight confrontation.

Second Witch Trilogy

Witch's Eye (1991)

Witch Weed (1992)

Witch Returns (1993)

York Trilogy

Shadows on the Wall (1980)
Dan Roberts, fifteen, traveling to England with his parents, is troubled by their secrecy. It turns out they are researching the family tree for clues to a hereditary disease.

Faces in the Water (1981)
During a summer visit to his grandmother's farm in Pennsylvania, Dan again becomes involved with the Gypsy family of Ambrose Faw and his daughter, Orlenda.

Footprints at the Window (1981)
In a time-trip to York, Dan accomplishes his mission of rescuing a girl from a plague threat.

FICTION FOR YOUNGER READERS

Eddie, Incorporated (1980)

All Because I'm Older (1981)

The Boy with the Helium Head (1982)

Old Sadie and the Christmas Bear (1984)

The Bodies in the Besseldorf Hotel (1986)

The Baby, the Bed, and the Rose (1987)

Beetles, Lightly Toasted (1987)

Maudie in the Middle (1988) with Lura Shield Reynolds

One of the Third Grade Thonkers (1988)

Keeping a Christmas Secret (1989)

Bernie and the Besseldorf Ghost (1990)

Josie's Troubles (1992)

Being Danny's Dog (1995)

Boys/Girls Series

The Boys Start the War (1993)

The Girls Get Even (1993)

Boys Against Girls (1994)

ADULT FICTION

In Small Doses (1979)

Revelations: A Novel (1979)

Unexpected Pleasures (1986)

The Christmas Surprise (1989)

Body Parts (announced)

Carrying On (announced)

ADAPTATIONS IN OTHER MEDIA

My Dad Can't Be Crazy . . . Can He? (1989) Television drama based on *The Keeper* and starring Loretta Swit, Don Murray, and Wil Wheaton.

FOR FURTHER READING

Estes, Sally. Review of *A String of Chances. Booklist*, August 1982.

Holtze, Sally Holmes, ed. "Phyllis Reynolds Naylor." In *Fifth Book of Junior Authors & Illustrators.* New York: H. W. Wilson, 1983.

Naylor, Phyllis Reynolds. *The Craft of Writing the Novel*. Boston: Writer, 1989.

———. *Crazy Love: An Autobiographical Account of Marriage and Madness*. New York: William Morrow, 1977.

———. *How I Came to Be a Writer*. New York: Atheneum, 1978.

Naylor, Rex. "Phyllis Reynolds Naylor." *Horn Book Magazine*, July–August 1992.

Phyllis Reynolds Naylor. New York: Atheneum, 1992.

Stahl, John D. "Phyllis Reynolds Naylor." In *Twentieth-Century Children's Writers*, edited by Tracy Chevalier. 3d ed. Chicago: St. James Press, 1989.

Joan Lowery Nixon

Contemporary drama

Historical drama

Los Angeles, California
February 3, 1927

Orphan Train Quartet
Orphan Train Adventures

Joan Lowery Nixon writes realistic contemporary and historical fiction for young adults. Among her series are the Orphan Train and Ellis Island books.

"Her mysteries for older children are psychological thrillers, involving complicated characterizations and plots and demanding the reader's participation in solving the crimes," Mary Lystad noted. "Two of these books, *The Kidnapping of Christina Lattimore* and *The Seance*, won the coveted Edgar Allan Poe award. In the former, Christina and a young reporter set out to prove her innocence when kidnappers claim that she was an accomplice to their crime. In the latter, what begins as a game, with Lauren and five other girls gathered in a candlelight circle, develops into murder of the participants; soon it will be Lauren's turn."

The writer frequently uses western settings. Ernestine Linck explained that Nixon "likes to show that children had a part in the development of the West and helped make its history more than a collection of dates and places where battles were fought. With the publication of her books about the Orphan Train Children, her popularity is reaching an ever-widening audience."

Nixon, the daughter of an accountant and a teacher, attended the University of Southern California and California State College. In 1949, she married Hershell H. Nixon, a petroleum geologist, with whom she has three children. She has worked as an elementary schoolteacher in Los Angeles and taught creative writing at Midland (Texas) College and the University of Houston.

Nixon won the Mystery Writers of America's Edgar Award for best juvenile mystery in 1980, 1981, and 1987. She won the Western Writers of America Golden Spur in 1988 and 1989 for books in her Orphan Train series.

At age three, Nixon taught herself to read by memorizing words in favorite books. She created verses for holidays and family occasions. Her first published poem appeared in *Children's Playmate* when she was ten.

After her family moved to East Hollywood, she had several well-known neighbors, among them film director and producer Cecil B. De Mille, comic actor W. C. Fields, and professional boxer Jack Dempsey. A high school teacher encouraged her to write, and she decided to study journalism in college.

After marriage and several job-related moves for her husband, they settled in Texas. Nixon wrote a mystery for young adults that was accepted by the thirteenth publisher to read it. Published in 1964, *The Mystery of Hurricane Castle* was based on a family incident, she said.

"Most young adults—those who love to read and those who read only school assignments, choose fiction that immediately grabs their attention and holds it to THE END. They're particularly fond of mystery novels, because good ones do this at the very beginning," Nixon observed in *The Writer*. "The opening sentences and paragraphs of a mystery must hook readers. While a story is growing and developing in my mind, I give a great deal of thought to how I will begin it. Each of the mysteries I've written opens with intrigue, action, or suspense and with a hint of the mystery to come. This usually means that any really necessary background information is woven in through short flashbacks as the story progresses."

In offering hints to budding writers, Nixon explained how her own prose works: "The plot of a story should have two levels: the main character's personal problem, which she must solve; and the mystery, which she must also solve. Both of these elements use suspense to keep readers in doubt, but it's the mystery itself in which writers can pull out all stops and create scenes so nerve-wracking and compelling that teenagers *must* keep reading to find out what happens next."

Some reviewers complained that Nixon's books, although appealing to readers, are also sometimes shallow. Leila Christenbury said of *The Specter*, "Nothing or no one is sufficiently developed to grip a reader's imagination and, by the end of the novel, the surprise ending is really not much of a surprise." Myra Seab observed of *Days of Fear*, "The theme of being courageous is obvious and heavy-handed, and both plot and characters are poorly developed."

Many of Nixon's books feature elements of mystery, and many are set a hundred years ago. Her Orphan Train books, for example, are based on the Children's Aid Society, which, between 1854 and 1929, placed children in foster homes in the West. In the books, the orphaned Kelly children struggle to stick together. Nixon explained in a teacher's guide to the Orphan Train Quartet, "At a time in which Charles Dickens was writing about the plight of street children in London, the same miserable situation existed in New York City. In the early eighteen hundreds, when the total population of New York City was about five hundred thousand, the police estimated that there were ten thousand homeless children wandering the streets."

Reviewer Dorothy M. Broderick praised *A Family Apart*, the first book in the series, stating: "This is as close to a perfect book as you'll buy this year. The plot is rational and well paced; the characters are real and believable; the time setting important to U.S. history; and the values all that anyone could ask for."

Teenage girls in a rugged western locale are featured in *High Trail to Danger* and its sequel, *A Deadly Promise*. In the first, Sarah Lindley travels from Chicago to the lawless mining town of Leadville, searching for her father. She finds him accused of murder and dying. With his last breath, he whispers a cryptic message. In the sequel, Sarah tries to solve the message. Meanwhile, she brings her younger sister, Susannah, to join her; relatives have taken over the family home, making it undesirable for Susannah to stay behind.

Liz Rafferty is the sixteen-year-old detective in *The Weekend Was Murder!* A summer employee of a hotel health club, she discovers a body. "Nixon keeps the diverse plot ingredients fizzing while adding a generous helping of farce," the *Bulletin of the Center for Children's Books* stated.

"The West to me is a state of mind," Nixon said in *The Writer*. "While immersed in stories set west of the Mississippi in the last half of the eighteen-hundreds, modern readers are discovering concepts like *sacrifice* and *self-denial* and *unwavering commitment to an ideal*—concepts that are not too common in today's very different world."

She said further, "Writing Western historical novels for young adults is immensely satisfying. It gives me the opportunity to show that history isn't simply a collection of dates and wars and kings and presidents, but that *children* have always helped make history, that *children* are not only important to the past but are helping to shape history being made today."

Nixon's Hollywood Daughters series is based on real life as Nixon observed it in the 1940s, particularly child film stars who were has-beens by the time they were teenagers.

Nixon told Sally Holmes Holtze, "I try to write every weekday morning from about 8:30 until noon. . . . I used to compose my stories on a typewriter, but as I write I rewrite, making many changes; and the pages were so scribbled over by the time they came out of the typewriter, sometimes it was hard for me to figure out what I had written. Now I use a word processor, where I can see what I'm writing on a screen and make changes on that screen. While it prints what I have written I can be doing something else."

YOUNG ADULT FICTION

The Mystery of Hurricane Castle (1964)
Kathy and Maureen Nickson and their younger brother, Danny, are left behind when a hurricane threatens their home.

The Mystery of the Grinning Idol (1965)
Eileen Harrigan, thirteen, learns that someone is smuggling artifacts out of Mexico.

The Mystery of the Hidden Cockatoo (1966)
A jeweled pin is lost in a house in New Orleans. The detective is thirteen-year-old Pam.

The Mystery of the Haunted Woods (1967), sequel to *The Mystery of Hurricane Castle*
The Nicksons are staying at Aunt Julia's ranch in New Mexico. They notice mysterious comings and goings in the woods.

The Kidnapping of Christina Lattimore (1979)
Christina is kidnapped and held for ransom, then suspected of engineering the whole thing.

The Seance (1980)
A girl disappears from a seance, and her body turns up days later. Lauren fears she will be the next victim.

The Specter (1982); British title: *The Spectre* (1983)
Dina, seventeen, is angry at the world because she has Hodgkin's disease. She becomes protector to a fellow patient, Jake, nine, who fears a killer is after him.

The Trouble with Charlie (1982) as Jaye Ellen
Charlie's older twin brothers, Rick and Adam, appoint themselves supervisors as the young teen begins dating.

Days of Fear (1983)
Eddie fears retribution if he tells on the neighborhood teenager who has been robbing people.

A Deadly Game of Magic (1983)
It is storming. Their car breaks down. Lisa and her three classmates find refuge at a secluded house where creepy things begin to happen.

The Gift (1983)
Salmon fishing, farm animals, and his grandfather's stories of the "little people" make up for eleven-year-old American Brian's disappointment at having to spend the summer in Ireland.

The Ghosts of Now (1984)
Angie's brother was struck by a hit-and-run driver and lies in a coma. She tries to unravel the events of that night.

The House on Hackman's Hill (1985)
Jeff and Debbie, hearing hair-raising stories about an old house, decide to check it out.

The Stalker (1985)
The police think Jennifer Lee Wilcox's best friend, Bobbie Trax, is a killer.

The Other Side of Dark (1986)
Seventeen-year-old Stacy awakens to find she has been in a coma for four years. An intruder shot her and killed her mother.

The Dark and Deadly Pool (1987)
When a shadowy figure emerges from the pool at the Ridley Hotel, Mary Elizabeth Rafferty has to solve a mystery.

Haunted Island (1987)
Chris Holt, thirteen, and his family fix up an island inn said to be haunted by the ghost of Amos Corley, who died 175 years earlier.

Secret, Silent Screams (1988)
There is a string of suicides at Farrington Park High School, but Marti suspects that Barry's death is not one of them.

The Island of Dangerous Dreams (1989)
Andrea, seventeen, helps track the killers of a judge in the Bahamas.

Whispers from the Dead (1989)
The minute Sarah enters her family's new home, she feels a smothering cold mist and hears the echo of a scream.

A Candidate for Murder (1991)
Someone is stalking Carry.

High Trail to Danger (1991)
Sarah Lindley travels from Chicago to Leadville in the Old West to find her missing father, only to discover he is a fugitive accused of murder.

Honeycutt Street Celebrities (1991)

The Haunted House on Honeycutt Street (1991), sequel to *Honeycutt Street Celebrities*

Mystery Box (1991)

A Deadly Promise (1992), sequel to *High Trail to Danger*
Sarah brings her younger sister, Susannah, to Leadville. She wants to figure out the cryptic message left by her dying father and perhaps clear his name.

The Weekend Was Murder! (1992), sequel to *The Dark and Deadly Pool*
It is murder mystery weekend at the plush Ridley Hotel, but Liz Rafferty would be happier if she had not met a ghost in her suite.

The Name of the Game Was Murder (1993)
Fifteen-year-old Samantha's great-uncle Augustus Trevor, a famous novelist, blackmails a group of celebrities to come to his island mansion to play a game.

Shadowmaker (1994)
A series of murders rocks the sleepy Texas town where Katie Gillian and her mother have moved.

Spirit Seeker (1995)
A boy is suspected in the murder of his parents.

Hollywood Daughters Trilogy

Star Baby (1989)
It is 1942. Can Abby "Cookie" Baynes, a former child star, create a fresh new image for herself despite her overbearing mother?

Overnight Sensation (1990)
Cassie Martin, the daughter of superstar comedienne Abby Grant, is furious when her mother refuses to help finance a handsome film student's production.

Encore (1990)
Erin Jenkins, teenage star of the popular sitcom *The Family Next Door*, feels closer to her television family than her real one. When her show is canceled, she turns to her grandmother, Hollywood legend Abby Grant.

Ellis Island or Land of Hope Series

Land of Hope (1992)
Youthful immigrants arrive at New York City's Ellis Island, among them Rebekah Levinsky and her Jewish family, who have fled the pogroms in Russia.

Land of Promise (1993)
Rose Carney, fifteen, comes from Ireland to Chicago. Her father has a drinking problem. Her sister and mother are back home. She works for money to bring them to America.

Land of Dreams (1994)
Kristen Swenson and her family cling to their Swedish roots at their new home, a farm in Minnesota, though Kristen yearns to adopt new ways.

Maggie Series

Maggie, Too (1985)
Maggie Ledoux's mother died years before. She is resentful when her father, a famous film director, wants to remarry.

And Maggie Makes Three (1986)
Maggie, now in seventh grade, spends the school year with her grandmother in Houston and dreads meeting her future stepmother, a young actress.

Maggie Forevermore (1987)
Maggie does not want to leave her grandmother to spend Christmas with her father and his new wife.

Orphan Train Quartet

A Family Apart (1987)
Orphans Frances Mary Kelly and her younger sister, Megan, are sent to live with the Swensons in Kansas.

Caught in the Act (1988)
Mike Kelly, twelve, has been adopted by the Friedrichs, a German immigrant family living in Missouri.

In the Face of Danger (1988)
Megan Kelly learns to overcome her grief at being separated from her siblings.

A Place to Belong (1989)
Danny and his younger sister, Peg, feel lucky to be adopted by kind Alfrid and Olga Swenson in St. Joseph, Missouri, but when Olga dies suddenly, they fear they will lose their wonderful new family.

Orphan Train Adventures

A Dangerous Promise (1994)
Mike Kelly, underage, joins the Union Army in 1861.

Keeping Secrets (1995)

CONTRIBUTOR

Short Circuits: Thirteen Shocking Stories by Outstanding Writers for Young Adults, edited by Donald R. Gallo (1992)

FICTION FOR YOUNGER READERS

The Mystery of the Secret Stowaway (1968)

Delbert, the Plainclothes Detective (1971)

The Alligator Under the Bed (1974)

The Mysterious Red Tape Gang (Putnam, 1974); alternate title: *The Adventures of the Red Tape Gang* (Scholastic, 1983)

The Secret Box Mystery (1974)

The Mysterious Prowler (1976)

The Boy Who Could Find Anything (1978)

Danger in Dinosaur Valley (1978)

Muffie Mouse and the Busy Birthday (Seabury, 1978); alternate title: *Muffy and the Birthday Party* (Scholastic, 1979)

Bigfoot Makes a Movie (1979)

Casey and the Great Idea (1980)

Gloria Chipmunk, Star! (1980)

The Spotlight Gang and the Backstage Ghost (1981)

Magnolia's Mixed-Up Magic (1983)

If You Were a Writer (1988)

Watch Out for Dinosaurs (1991)

When I Am Eight (1994)

Will You Give Me a Dream? (1994)

Claude and Shirley Series

If You Say So, Claude (1980)

Beats Me, Claude (1986)

Fat Chance, Claude (1987)

You Bet Your Britches, Claude (1989)

That's the Spirit, Claude (1990)

First Read-Alone Mysteries

The New Year's Mystery (1979)

The Halloween Mystery (1979)

The Valentine Mystery (1979)

The Happy Birthday Mystery (1979)

The Thanksgiving Mystery (1980)

The April Fool Mystery (1980)

The Easter Mystery (1981)

The Christmas Eve Mystery (1981)

Kleep: Space Detective Series

Kidnapped on Astarr (1981)

Mysterious Queen of Magic (1981)

Mystery Dolls from Planet Urd (1981)

FOR FURTHER READING

Abrahamson, Richard F. *A Teacher's Guide to the Orphan Train Quartet by Joan Lowery Nixon.* New York: Bantam Books, n.d.

Broderick, Dorothy M. Review of *A Family Apart. Voice of Youth Advocates,* October 1987.

Christenbury, Leila. Review of *The Specter. ALAN Review,* spring 1983.

Holtze, Sally Holmes, ed. "Joan Lowery Nixon." In *Fifth Book of Junior Authors & Illustrators.* New York: H. W. Wilson, 1983.

Linck, Ernestine. "Joan Lowery Nixon." *Roundup Magazine,* March–April 1995.

Lystad, Mary. "Joan Lowery Nixon." In *Twentieth-Century Children's Writers,* edited by Tracy Chevalier. 3d ed. Chicago: St. James Press, 1989.

Nixon, Joan Lowery. "Clues to the Juvenile Mystery." *The Writer,* February 1977.

———. "Creating Suspense in the Young Adult Mystery." *The Writer,* October 1987.

———. "Writing Mysteries Young Adults Want to Read." *The Writer,* July 1991.

———. *Writing Mysteries for Young People.* Boston: Writer, 1977.

Review of *The Weekend Was Murder! Bulletin of the Center for Children's Books,* March 1992.

Seab, Myra. Review of *Days of Fear. School Library Journal,* September 1983.

Andre Norton

Science fiction

Fantasy

Cleveland, Ohio
February 17, 1912

Witch World Series

"As a child I was an avid reader and went through any book which came to hand," Andre Norton recalled in *Books I Read When I Was Young*. "I went to the library once a week and, since we were limited to only two books at a time then, I chanced upon—to my great joy—shelves of the bound copies of the *St. Nicholas* magazine, which were the answer to my problem as two of such gave me a number of serials as well as short stories. . . .

"However, my greatest love—and I still often reread them to-day—were the Oz books. . . . They are the only truly American fairy tales. . . . When I reached high school the John Carter stories by [Edgar Rice] Burroughs (I never did like Tarzan very much) opened a whole new world of imagination for me—I had not been aware that that existed before, though I had always longed to find such tales."

Alice Mary Norton attended Western Reserve (now Case Western Reserve) University from 1930 to 1932. She worked as a children's librarian in Cleveland from 1930 to 1941 and from 1942 to 1951. During the year between, she managed a bookstore and lending library. Also in 1941, she worked as a special librarian for a citizenship project in Washington, D.C., and at the Library of Congress. She became a freelance writer in 1950. She was an editor with Gnome Press from 1950 to 1958.

Though Norton has written mystery and historical fiction, she is best known for her fantasy and science fiction. In fact, she was one of the first women to break into the science fiction genre. Her books are acknowledged as well researched and strong on characters with internal struggles. Norton won the Gandalf Master of Fantasy Award, World Science Fiction Convention, in 1977, for lifetime achievement. She was nominated for the Hugo Award, World Science Fiction Convention: in 1962, for *Star Hunter*; in 1964, for *Witch World*; and in 1968, for a story titled "Wizard's World."

Norton is "probably the leading writer of juvenile science fantasy since Edgar Rice Burroughs," James Gunn suggested. "Norton's work blurs the border between SF and fantasy. Her novels describe fascinating alternate worlds, parallel universes, and provocative futures in thoughtful, consistent detail, but they also offer myths, legends and magic."

"My involvement with the future began when I was still in high school, but then it was a reader's interest rather than a writer's preoccupation," she told Muriel Fuller. "Though, at that time, I had every intention of becoming a history teacher rather than a professional writer. However, I wrote my first book, an adventure-mystery, the year I graduated from high school. Some four years later, having learned a little more of my craft, I rewrote that same manuscript and sold it. But in the meantime I had already marketed my first book, a Graustarkian romance for teen-agers. . . .

"In 1952, I had published my first science-fiction adventure—*Star Man's Son*. Having long collected and read science fiction for my own pleasure, I had a liking for what is termed 'space opera,' the science-fiction adventure story, which is the type I wanted to write."

Norton's "early intention was to write fiction for boys, and she changed her name to enter this male-dominated market," Roger C. Schlobin said. "Fortunately for the millions of readers who have made her one of the best selling of contemporary fantasy and science-fiction authors, she turned to these two forms in 1947."

Schlobin added, "Technology and science are incidental to plot and character [in Norton's prose]. These major concerns reflect the influences of Edgar Rice Burroughs, H. Rider Haggard, A. Merritt and Talbot Mundy, and demonstrate also Norton's respect for their fast-moving plots and memorable characters."

Her most popular series is the Witch World. C. J. Cherryh wrote in an introduction to *Lore of the Witch World*: "For all of us who've ever created a world to dream about, for those of us who write and for those who keep theirs in their hearts . . . the Witch World stories hold a special place. It's a land, a world, a place of dark shadows and alien powers and human beings touched with strangeness, a place where men and women find extraordinary things within them and match themselves against an environment at once marvelously detailed and full of mysteries. The Witch World is never explored. The smallest valley holds strange happenings and a past which reaches into things stranger still. The traveler finds the unexpected, the ancient, the bizarre at every turn. Nature is powerful here, and those who open their hearts to it and to living things find themselves capable of marvels and involved in an old, old warfare."

"The Witch World stories are richly told with verve and color," Lin Carter said, "and the element of the supernatural, of fantasy and magic and the gods, is handled with a lively inventiveness, tempered and disciplined by a firm grounding in anthropology. Perhaps Miss Norton writes so convincingly about magical talismans and enchanted swords because she has a scholar's insight into how primitive peoples regarded such artifacts and knows the premises that evolved to account for their presumed powers."

"A look at Norton's formula makes it easy to see why her books have always appealed to teenage readers," Sarah Verney said in describing the frequent theme of rite of passage. She added, "Norton's achievement as a storyteller is remarkable. Her swiftly moving plots, engaging protagonists, and vividly described exotic settings have earned Norton a reputation as an author who consistently provides high-quality entertainment. Perhaps the most noteworthy of Norton's accomplishments is the depth of her imaginative vision."

YOUNG ADULT FICTION

The Prince Commands (1934)
A young American inherits a mythical kingdom beset with revolution and a menace known as the Werewolf.

Ralestone Luck (1938)
A mystery on a rundown Louisiana plantation including: a sword, a missing fortune, and the true identity of the heir.

Follow the Drum (1942)

Scarface (1948)
A boy is enslaved by bloodthirsty pirates in the West Indies.

Huon of the Horn (1951)
The legend of Charlemagne is retold.

Star Man's Son, 2250 A.D. (1952); paperback title: *Daybreak, 2250 A.D.* (1954)
Fors is a mutant driven to explore the empty northlands.

Star Rangers (1953); paperback title: *The Last Planet* (1955)
It's A.D. 8054, and the First Galactic Empire is crumbling.

The Stars Are Ours! (1954)
After the Burn-Out on Earth, two groups remain: Peacemen and Free Scientists.

Star Guard (1955), sequel to *Star Rangers*

Yankee Privateer (1955)
In Baltimore in 1779, Fitzhugh Lyon is shanghaied aboard the *Retallation*.

The Crossroads of Time (1956)

Stand to Horse (1956)

Sea Siege (1957)

Star Born (1957), sequel to *The Stars Are Ours!*

Star Gate (1958)
Space travelers colonize a primitive world.

The Beast Master (1959)
Navajo Hosteen Storm survives a major disaster and ends up on another planet, Arzor.

Shadow Hawk (1960)

The Sioux Spaceman (1960)
Kade Whitehawk uses his Sioux heritage to help others.

Storm over Warlock (1960)

Catseye (1961)

Ride Proud, Rebel! (1961)
Drew Rennie, fifteen, is an enthusiastic supporter of the Confederate cause during the Civil War.

Lord of Thunder (1962), sequel to *The Beast Master*

Rebel Spurs (1962)

Judgment on Janus (1963)
Naill Renfo escapes slave owners and flees into the forbidden forest.

Night of Masks (1964)

Ordeal in Otherwhere (1964), sequel to *Storm over Warlock*

Quest Crosstime (1965), sequel to *The Crossroads of Time;* British title: *Crosstime Agent* (1975)
Blake Walker must save the planet Vroom.

The X Factor (1965)
On the wild planet Mimir, a space traveler encounters unusual beings.

Victory on Janus (1966), sequel to *Judgment on Janus*

Operation Time Search (1967)
Ray Osborne goes back in time and is captured by a band of primitive hunters.

Dark Piper (1968)
Returning home after ten years at war, Griss Lugard finds Beltane relatively untouched.

The Zero Stone (1968)
Murdoc Zern, a gem trader on the run, seeks a mysterious ring stone of phenomenal power.

Uncharted Stars (1969), sequel to *The Zero Stone*
The stone may have caused the death of Zern's father. To find out, Murdoc partners with a catlike alien, Ect.

Dread Companion (1970)
A woman's only chance to leave a magical, alternate world rests with a human changeling.

Ice Crown (1970)
Offlas Keil and his niece, Roane, search for legendary treasure on Clio.

Android at Arms (1971)

Breed to Come (1972)

Here Abide Monsters (1973)
Nick and Linda travel in time to Arthurian England.

Iron Cage (1974)
Snatched by aliens, Jony has never known the outside.

The Jargoon Pard (1974)
There is unrest in the land of Arvon. Ketran is heir to the House of Cor Do Prawn and all its holdings.

The Day of the Ness (1975) with Michael Gilbert

Knave of Dreams (1975)

No Night Without Stars (1975)
Denied his rightful succession as a metalsmith, Sandor and his friend, Rhin, strike off and meet Fanyi, a shaman.

Outside (1975)
Sealed off from the outside world by a huge dome, Kristie and her brother, Len, are the last survivors of a polluted world.

Wraiths of Time (1976)
Young archaeologist Tallahassee Mifford is hurled back in time.

The Opal-Eyed Fan (1977)
Persis Roshe and her uncle are shipwrecked at Lost Lady Key, off the Florida coast.

Trey of Swords (1977)
Short stories.

Quag Keep (1978)
Forces of evil from another sphere try to use the roll of dice to conquer the world.

Seven Spells to Sunday (1979) with Phyllis Miller

Voorloper (1980)
A wanderer, his son, and his daughter, victims of the Shadow on Voor, set out to discover the secret behind the strange planet's horror.

Forerunner (1981)

Several Spells to Sunday (1981) with Phyllis Miller
Extraordinary answers appear when orphan Monnie, nine, puts a letter in a derelict mailbox.

Ten Mile Treasure (1981)

House of Shadows (1984) with Phyllis Miller
Children encounter ghosts in their great-aunt's house.

Ride the Green Dragon (1985)

Forerunner: The Second Venture (1985), sequel to *Forerunner*
Some are willing to kill for the knowledge of Simson, who was raised in the Burrows and has within her the spirit of the Elder One.

Dare to Go A-Hunting (1990)
What if the Little People of legend really exist? Faree, orphaned and a near slave, must find out.

The Mark of the Cat (1992)
Hyn Kliel, on a survival test, ventures into the secret world of cats.

Uncharted Stars (1993)

Magic Series

Steel Magic (World, 1967); alternate title: *Gray Magic* (Scholastic, 1967)
On a picnic, three Lowry children discover a miniature castle.

Octagon Magic (1967)
The children have more adventures in the ruined Castle of Avalon.

Fur Magic (1968)
Indian magic transforms a boy into an unusual animal.

Dragon Magic (1972)
Each of four boys trying to discover the magic of a dust-covered puzzle in an old house is caught in a spell that takes him back in time.

Lavender-Green Magic (1974)

Red Hart Magic (1976)
A model of an old inn triggers three strange and exciting adventures in earlier times.

Moon in Three Rings Series

Moon of Three Rings (1966)
Kip Vorland, a Free Trader, is on the planet Yiktor at the time of the Moon of Three Rings.

Exiles of the Stars (1971)
The crew of the Free Trader ship *Lydia* is caught in a civil war.

Flight in Yiktor (1986)
Maclen, the exiled Thassa sorceress, returns to her forbidden home to battle an intergalactic Thieves Guild with the help of Kip Vorland, a telepathic ex–Free Trader.

Ross Murdock/Time Trader Series

The Time Traders (1958)
Ross Murdock is a criminal turned Time Agent.

Galactic Derelict (1959)
Three adventurers encounter unusual civilizations.

The Defiant Agents (1962)

Key out of Time (1963)

Firehand (1994) with P. M. Griffin
Murdock is finally rescued from his involuntary exile on a colony world. He is recruited to help avert conquest of a humanoid race by the alien Baldies.

Solar Queen Series

Sargasso of Space (1955) as Andrew North; (1970) as Andre Norton

Plague Ship (1956) as Andrew North; (1971) as Andre Norton

Voodoo Planet (1959) as Andrew North

Postmarked the Stars (1969)

Redline the Stars (1993) with P. M. Griffin
A female physician joins the company of the Free Trader starship *Solar Queen*, bringing plenty of trouble.

Star Ka'at Series with Dorothy Madlee

Star Ka'at (1976)
After an exciting rescue mission from outer space, two supercats and two courageous children become friends.

Star Ka'at World (1978)
Jim and Elly Mae travel to a distant planet as guests of Tiro and Mer, members of a superintelligent race of Ka'ats.

Star Ka'at and the Planet People (1979)

Star Ka'ats and the Winged Warriors (1981)

Swords Trilogy

The Sword Is Drawn (1944)
Lorenz Van Norreys faces danger when the Nazis invade Holland in 1940.

Sword in Sheath (1949); British title: *Island of the Lost* (1953)

At Swords' Point (1954)

EDITOR, YOUNG ADULT FICTION

Gates to Tomorrow: An Introduction to Science Fiction (1973) with Ernestine Donaldy

Small Shadows Creep: Ghost Children (1974)

FICTION FOR YOUNGER READERS

Rogue Reynard (1947)

ADULT FICTION

Murder for Sale (1954) as Allen Weston, with Grace Hogarth (a joint pseudonym)

Secret of the Lost Race (1959); British title: *Wolfshead* (1977)

Star Hunter (1961)

Eye of the Monster (1962)

High Sorcery (1970)
Short stories.

Garan the Eternal (1972)
Short stories.

The Many Worlds of Andre Norton, edited by Roger Elwood (1974)

The Book of Andre Norton (1975)
Short stories.

Merlin's Mirror (1975)
King Arthur and Merlin the Magician are descended from space travelers.

The White Jade Fox (1975)

Perilous Dreams (1976)
Short stories.

Velvet Shadows (1977)

Snow Shadow (1979)

Iron Butterflies (1980)

Caroline (1982) with Enid Cushing

Moon Called (1982)
Thora, the Chosen One, and Makil, user of the magical Sword of Lur, descend into the underground world of machinery to battle the Dark Lord.

Wheel of Stars (1983)
Gwennan Daggert enters an underworld of hellish nightmares and beautiful dreams.

Stand and Deliver (1984)

Were-Wrath (1984)

Yurth Burden (1987)

Serpent's Tooth (1988)

Imperial Lady: A Fantasy of Han China (1989)
Adventures of a princess during the Han dynasty.

Moon Mirror (1989)
Short stories.

Wizard's World (1989)
Short stories.

Jekyll Legacy (1990) with Robert Bloch, sequel to Robert Louis Stevenson's *Dr. Jekyll and Mr. Hyde.*

The Empire of the Eagle (1991) with Susan Schwartz
Roman soldiers enslaved in China are caught in a battle between their captors and ancient sorcerers.

Brother to Shadows (1993)
Jufre, a young Shadow, is cast out of the brotherhood of spies and assassins and becomes guardian of a reptilian knowledge seeker.

Tiger Burning Bright (1995) with Marion Zimmer Bradley and Mercedes Lackey

World of the Three Moons Series

Black Trillium (1990) with Marion Zimmer Bradley and Julian May
Three of the king's daughters must go on quests to save the land.

Golden Trillium (1993)
Princess Kadiya, the headstrong Seeker-Warrior, encounters a timeless evil in the swamp of Rowenda that threatens the kingdom.

Mirror of Destiny (1995)
Tarilla is an orphaned apprentice to a well-known wise woman. She must wed to safely enter the primeval forest—her talisman is not enough.

Witch World Series

Witch World (1963)

Web of the Witch World (1964)

Three Against the Witch World (1965)
The offspring of Simon Tregarth, half earthling, half witch-brood, realize they alone can perceive the four directions and defy the sorcery that is secretly molding their destiny.

Year of the Unicorn (1965)
Were Riders come out of the Waste to help men of the High Hallock beat the Hounds of Aliza from their border. Gillian is one of thirteen brides of those Were Riders.

Warlock of the Witch World (1967)

Sorceress of the Witch World (1968)

The Spell of the Witch World (1972)
Short stories.

The Gate of the Cat (1987)
An Earthwoman, Kelsie McBlair, is trapped in the Witch World and faces the Lord of the Dark.

Witch World: Gryphon Trilogy

The Crystal Gryphon (1972)

Zarsthor's Bane (1978)

Gryphon in Glory (1981)
Kerovan and Joisan try to understand the mystery of Kerovan's birth and ties with the Old Ones.

Gryphon's Eyrie (1984) with A. C. Crispin
Kerovan and Joisan journey to the mountains to face those who walk the dark path.

Lore of the Witch World (1980)
Short stories, including "The Changeling."

Horn Crown (1981)
Humans first come to Witch World.

Ware Hawk (1983)
Tirtha of Hawkholme returns to her ancestral home in the hills of Estcarp with Falconer as her guide. In their path is a Dark One.

The Elvenbane: An Epic High Fantasy of the Halfblood Chronicles (1991) with Mercedes Lackey
The world is run by powerful elvenlords. Serina Daeth, formerly favored human concubine of elven overlord Dyren, is about to change things.

Sneeze on Sunday (1991) with Grace A. Hogarth

Witch World Chronicles 1: Storms of Victory (1992) with P. M. Griffin
Two short novels set after the Turning, when the witches defeat the invasion of Karsten.

Elvenblood: Book Two of the Halfblood Chronicles (1995), sequel to *The Elvenbane*
Shanna meets the Iron People, human nomads in the world ruled by elvenlords.

Witch World: The Turning Series

Flight of Vengeance (1992) with P. M. Griffin and Mary Schaub
Two stories from the time the Witches of Estcarp defeat the Pagin of Karsten by causing the Turning.

Storms of Victory (1992)
The chronicler of Lorm tells two more stories.

Songsmith: A Witch World Novel (1993) with A. C. Crispin

Flight of Vengeance (1993) with P. M. Griffin

The Hands of Lyr (1994)
A girl with psychic powers combats an ancient evil with the assistance of an embittered young noble.

On Wings of Magic (1994) with Patricia Mathews and Sasha Miller

EDITOR, ADULT FICTION

Bullard of the Space Patrol (1951) by Malcolm Jameson

Space Service (1953)

Space Pioneers (1954)

Space Police (1956)

Baleful Beasts and Eerie Creatures (1976)

Magic in Ithkar (1985) with Robert Adams

Magic in Ithkar 2 (1985) with Robert Adams

Magic in Ithkar 3 (1986) with Robert Adams

Magic in Ithkar 4 (1987) with Robert Adams

Tales of Witch World (1987–91)
Three volumes of short stories.

Catfantastic (1989) with Martin H. Greenberg

Catfantastic II (1989) with Martin H. Greenberg

Four from the Witch World (1989)

Grand Master's Choice (1991)

Catfantastic III (1994) with Martin H. Greenberg

FOR FURTHER READING

Carter, Lin. *Imaginary Worlds: The Art of Fantasy*. New York: Ballantine Books, 1973.

Cherryh, C. J. Introduction to *Lore of the Witch World* by Andre Norton. New York: Daw, 1980.

Clute, John. "Andre Norton." In *The Encyclopedia of Science Fiction*, edited by Peter Nicholls. London: Granada, 1979.

Cullinan, Bernice, and M. Jerry Weiss, eds. *Books I Read When I Was Young: The Favorite Books of Famous People*. New York: Avon Books, 1980.

Fuller, Muriel, ed. *More Junior Authors*. New York: H. W. Wilson, 1963.

Gillespie, John T. *Best Books for Junior High Readers*. New Providence, NJ: R. R. Bowker, 1991.

Gunn, James, ed. *The New Encyclopedia of Science Fiction*. New York: Viking, 1988.

Norton, Andre, with Bertha Stremm Norton. *Bertie and May*. New York: World, 1969.

Schlobin, Roger C. "Andre Norton." In *Twentieth-Century Science-Fiction Writers*, edited by Noelle Watson and Paul E. Schellinger. 3d ed. Chicago: St. James Press, 1991.

———. *Andre Norton: A Primary and Secondary Bibliography*. Boston: G. K. Hall, 1980.

Schlobin, Roger C., and Irene R. Harrison, eds. *Andre Norton: A Primary and Secondary Bibliography*. Framingham, MA: NESFA Press, 1995.

Verney, Sarah. "Andre Norton." In *Authors & Artists for Young Adults*, edited by E. A. DesChenes. Vol. 14. Detroit: Gale Research, 1995.

Scott O'Dell

Family drama

Historical drama

Los Angeles, California
May 23, 1903–October 15, 1989
Island of the Blue Dolphins

"History has a very valid connection with what we are now," Scott O'Dell said in talking with Peter Roop. "Many of my books are set in the past, but the problems of isolation, moral decisions, greed, need for love and affection are problems of today as well. I am didactic; I do want to teach through books. Not heavy-handedly but to provide a moral backdrop for readers to make their own decisions."

O'Dell worked as a cameraman and technical director in Hollywood before becoming a full-time writer in 1934. His credits include two dozen juvenile books, among them *Island of the Blue Dolphins* (1960) and *Streams to the River, River to the Sea: A Novel of Sacagawea* (1986). O'Dell won four Newbery Medals for his books: the John Newbery Medal from the American Library Association, in 1962, for *Island of the Blue Dolphins*; and three Newbery Honor Book awards—for *The King's Fifth*, in 1968; for *The Black Pearl*, in 1968; and for *Sing Down the Moon*, in 1971.

"O'Dell is, in a very real way, a different person each time he tells a story. This gives each of his books an individual quality that is uniquely suited for its natural and cultural setting," James E. Higgins observed.

The writer's first young adult book, *Island of the Blue Dolphins*, was inspired by strong emotion. He told Roop that the book "began in anger, anger at the hunters who invade the mountains where I live and who slaughter everything that creeps or walks or flies. This anger was also directed at myself, at the young man of many years ago, who thoughtlessly committed the same crimes against nature."

In the book, the protagonist at first kills animals, then learns a reverence for all life. It "was based on the true story of a girl who was left upon an island near the coast of Southern California and lived there alone for eighteen years," O'Dell said in Lee Bennett Hopkins's *Pauses*. "The novel was written without any thought of who might read it. In fact, I didn't know what young people were reading and I didn't consider it a children's book."

"Scott O'Dell's *Island of the Blue Dolphins* is a survival tale, an animal story, and a feminist parable," Ellen E. Seiter noted. "It is the account of a girl's passage into adulthood and her achievement of a rare maturity and wisdom. The author based this children's novel on an historical figure, 'The Lost Woman of San Nicolas,' who was left behind by her tribe on an island off the coast of Santa Barbara and lived alone there between 1835 and 1853. The heroine, Karana, narrates this simple, Robinson Crusoe–like tale of her adjustment to a solitary existence on the island."

"The fact that there is only one central character, in this remote and isolated setting . . . makes identification total," John Rowe Townsend said. "The reader must *be* Karana or the book is meaningless. The telling of the story has a memorable purity to which its fresh, direct concreteness contributes as much as the author's excellent ear. And the long, continuous time dimension allows the story to take itself outside our clock-and-calendar system altogether, to complete the islanding of a human being's experience."

In an overview of O'Dell's writing, Sally Anne Thompson commented, "One discovers several qualities ever present. The quality woven into the grain of his rich tapestry is his own personal philosophy. Nowhere does he overtly share innermost feelings or beliefs. These are felt or witnessed but not verbalized. From his writings though, we appreciate the fact that O'Dell is an individual with a strong moral sense. He has spent his life intricately meshing bits of his own moral fiber into his books, and ultimately into the minds of his readers. His style is perceptive, complete with insights, as he skillfully creates depths of texture and fiber within his characters. O'Dell expresses his point of view discretely through means of symbols and imagery, as manifested in Tyndale's not allowing his life to be saved by the killing of another human being in *The Hawk That Dare Not Hunt by Day*."

Thunder Rolling in the Mountains (1992) was completed following the author's death by his wife, Elizabeth Hall. Born in 1929 in California, she was a longtime research collaborator as well as librarian, writer, and editor of fiction and nonfiction. Told through the eyes of Sound of Running Feet, a Nez Perce girl, the story is about Chief Joseph and the tragic defeat of his tribe and its retreat to Canada.

"Their story of courage and determination in the face of cruelty, betrayal and bureaucratic ignorance" moved O'Dell deeply, Hall stated in a foreword. "So deeply that he continued to work on the manuscript in the hospital until two days before he died."

YOUNG ADULT FICTION

Island of the Blue Dolphins (1960)
In the early 1800s, an Indian girl lives alone for eighteen years on harsh San Nicolas Island off California.

The King's Fifth (1966)
In the seventeenth century, a young mapmaker, Esteban, is charged with murder.

The Black Pearl (1967)
Ramon Salazar, sixteen, learns about pearling off Baja California and about traditions and the quest for the magnificent Pearl of Heaven.

The Dark Canoe (1968)
Nathan Clegg is a cabin boy aboard a Nantucket whaler. His older brother, part-owner of the ship, has lost his captain's license under unusual circumstances.

Sing Down the Moon (1970)
Bright Morning, fourteen, enjoys a happy life taking sheep to pasture. Then one morning, the Spanish slavers ride down upon the Navajos.

Child of Fire (1974)
To prove himself, sixteen-year-old Manuel Castillo jumps into a bullring.

The Hawk That Dare Not Hunt by Day (1975)
Tom Barton and his Uncle Jack smuggle Tyndale's new English translation of the Bible into England.

Zia (1976), sequel to *Island of the Blue Dolphins*
Zia and her brother strike off by boat to find their aunt, who is on an island and has not been seen for nearly two decades.

The 290 (1976)
Jim Lynne, apprentice at Laird Brothers' shipyard in Liverpool, learns that the vessel they are working on, *The Alabama*, is intended for the Confederate Navy in America.

Carlota (1977); British title: *The Daughter of Don Saturnino* (1977)
On the American frontier, Carlota is like a son to her father. Her feelings change after riding to ambush Kit Carson.

Kathleen, Please Come Home (1978)
New at school, Kathleen gradually falls under the spell of rebellious, worldly Sybil.

Sarah Bishop (1980)
Life is hard for Sandy and her family on Long Island even before Birdsall's Raiders swoop down during the American Revolution.

The Spanish Smile (1982)
Lucinda de Cabrillo y Benvides, the only daughter of the descendant of a Spanish conquistador, is cloistered in a dark castle. Her father plans to restore Spanish rule to California.

The Castle in the Sea (1983), sequel to *The Spanish Smile*
Lucinda finds that her guardian, Ricardo Villaverde, still wants to carry out her late father's scheme.

Alexandra (1984)
Tragedy forces Alexandra Papadimitrius to join her family as sponge fishers in Florida.

The Road to Damietta (1985)
As told by Ricca di Montanaro, a willful young woman madly in love with Francis Bernardone, Francis becomes the famous Saint Francis of Assisi.

Streams to the River, River to the Sea: A Novel of Sacagawea (1986)
Sacagawea joins the Lewis and Clark expedition to the Pacific.

The Serpent Never Sleeps: A Novel of Jamestown and Pocahontas (1987)
Serena Lynn ships to the New World, wearing a serpent ring given to her by King James for protection.

Black Star, Bright Dawn (1988)
An Eskimo teenager, Bright Dawn, cannot believe that her father is asking her to take his place in the thousand-mile race.

My Name Is Not Angelica (1989)
Raisha is snatched from her home, transported across the sea, and put on the slave market in the West Indies.

Thunder Rolling in the Mountains (1992), completed by Elizabeth Hall
The tragic defeat of Chief Joseph of the Nez Perce is seen through a daughter's eyes.

Julian Escobar Series

The Captive (1979)
Julian Escobar is a young Jesuit seminarian devoted to fighting the Spanish conquerors' enslavement of Indians in sixteenth-century Mexico. He is cast away among the Maya and mistaken for the returning god, Kukulcan.

The Feathered Serpent (1981)
Driven to restore the decaying Mayan civilization, Julian travels to the Aztec and is caught up in Montezuma's tragic encounter with Cortes, the conquistador.

The Amethyst Ring (1983)
Escaping Cortes, Escobar returns to the Maya to find they are holding captive a bishop who wears an amethyst ring.

FICTION FOR YOUNGER READERS

Journey to Jericho (1969)

The Treasure of Topo-el-Bampo (1972)

Venus Among the Fishes (1995) with Elizabeth Hall

ADULT FICTION

Hill of the Hawk (1947)

The Sea Is Red: A Novel (1958)

ADAPTATIONS IN OTHER MEDIA

Island of the Blue Dolphins (1964)
Film starring Celia Kaye and George Kennedy.

The Black Pearl (1977)
Film starring Gilbert Roland.

Mysterious Cities of Gold (1982)
Animated television version of *The King's Fifth*.

FOR FURTHER READING

Fuller, Muriel, ed. *More Junior Authors*. New York: H. W. Wilson, 1963.

Higgins, James E. "Scott O'Dell." In *Twentieth-Century Children's Writers*, edited by Tracy Chevalier. 3d ed. Chicago: St. James Press, 1989.

Hopkins, Lee Bennett. *Pauses: Autobiographical Reflections of 101 Creators of Children's Books*. New York: HarperCollins, 1995.

Roop, Peter. "Profile: Scott O'Dell." *Language Arts*, November 1984.

Seiter, Ellen E. "Survival Tale and Feminist Parable." In *Children's Novels and the Movies*, edited by Douglas Street. New York: Frederick Ungar, 1983.

Thompson, Sally Anne M. "Scott O'Dell—Weaver of Stories." *Catholic Library World*, March 1978.

Townsend, John Rowe. *A Sense of Story: Essays on Contemporary Writers for Children*. Philadelphia: J. B. Lippincott, 1971.

Janette Oke

Inspirational fiction

Champion, Alberta, Canada
February 18, 1935
Women of the West Series

Janette Oke writes inspirational romantic and historical fiction, often in a western Canadian setting. Her books are issued by a Christian publishing house.

The daughter of U.S. citizens, a farmer and his wife, Oke received a diploma from Mountain View Bible College, Alberta, in 1957. The same year, she married Edward L. Oke, a professor. They raised four children. The Okes pastored at churches in Indiana and Alberta. Her husband died in 1984.

Oke worked as a proofreader, bookkeeper, and mail clerk. She was treasurer for Mountain View Bible College and a loan officer and teller at the Royal Bank of Canada in Alberta.

"My interest in writing the type of material that I have comes from a personal interest in that era of our history, and a feeling that little had been written with a Christian slant on the time period. I also have the feeling that society is searching for a deeper, more committed type of lasting love. Letters from readers have confirmed this," she told *Contemporary Authors*.

Oke said that she believes strongly in family values and opposes the depiction of sex in romantic novels. She said she writes for young adult readers because, "We must give them moral values."

"Even as a child Janette had enjoyed putting words together," Laurel Oke Logan stated in a biography of her mother, "but she had always promised herself that she would not attempt to write for publication until she received special training. Occasionally she chaffed against her self-imposed restriction. She wanted to get to writing, but certainly the training had not happened, and it was beginning to look as though it never would. There had just never been the time nor the money for it."

"In the beginning, her idea was simply to provide a clean, entertaining piece of fiction to fill a void in the market," continued Logan. "She loved to read fiction, but there was so little Christian fiction available, and what she found on the secular shelves was not what she wanted or enjoyed, particularly if she was looking for a short work that could be read in a few hours."

Yet thinking about writing, and actually writing, were two different things. In the summer of 1977, Oke wrote a draft of a novel. "She wrote in little snatches. The story had been in her mind and heart for a long time, so she had little work to do except to put it on the empty pages before her," Logan said. The first two publishers she sent it to returned the manuscript. The third, Bethany Fellowship, agreed to publish *Love Comes Softly* in 1979. She quickly wrote a sequel, and her career was under way.

"As her writing career blossomed," her daughter said, "she tried to picture each one of her books as a little 'paper missionary.' It had the potential, through the Spirit's working, to reach a heart crying out for truth, for answers somewhere, and she prayed often as she wrote that this would be so. Then, she prayed again after the books were completed."

When Calls the Heart, the first book in Oke's Canadian West series, is about pretty, cultured, and educated Elizabeth Thatcher. Raised in eastern Canada, she is not prepared for a teaching position on the frontier, but she meets her task with love, humor, and determination. She meets Wynn, a Royal Canadian Mounted Policeman, who is determined never to marry. Can she change his mind?

Heart of the Wilderness tells the story of trapper George McMannus, who travels night and day from his wilderness cabin when he learns that his daughter and son-in-law have died in a river accident. His only granddaughter, Kendra Marty, is not quite four years old, and he must provide for her, but is his backwoods life proper for the little girl?

Oke also wrote a series of three devotional books: *The Father Who Calls* (1988), *The Father of Love* (1989), and *Father of My Heart* (1990).

YOUNG ADULT FICTION

Hey, Teacher! (1981)

Quiet Places, Warm Thoughts (1983)

Too Long a Stranger (1994)
The sudden death of her husband leaves Sarah Perry and her baby alone in a small frontier town.

Canadian West Series

When Calls the Heart (1983)
Reared in the East, Elizabeth is not prepared for a teaching position in the Canadian frontier. She meets Wynn, a Royal Canadian Mounted Policeman.

When Comes the Spring (1985)
After a year at the one-room schoolhouse, Elizabeth and Wynn are planning a wedding and a future at a northern outpost.

When Breaks the Dawn (1986)
Surviving a harsh winter, Elizabeth and Wynn take on new challenges.

When Hope Springs New (1986)
Elizabeth and Wynn take over a more primitive outpost in the Canadian Northwest.

Seasons of the Heart Series

Once upon a Summer (1981)
An orphaned boy goes to live with his grandfather, uncle, and eighteen-year-old Aunt Lou at the turn of the century.

The Winds of Autumn (1987)
Joshua Chadwick Jones is on the brink of manhood.

Winter Is Not Forever (1988)
Joshua's life seems to have come to a standstill.

Spring's Gentle Promise (1989)
Joshua's grandfather and Uncle Charlie sign the farm over to him.

Love Comes Softly Series

Love Comes Softly (1979)
Marty, nineteen, vibrant and independent, travels west with her new husband, seeking adventure and fortune. Instead they meet tragedy and persevere through a love of God.

Love's Enduring Promise (1980)
Marty and her new love, Clark, have a growing brood of children at their prairie homestead.

Love's Long Journey (1982)
Missie and Willie take a covered wagon trip west.

Love's Abiding Joy (1983)
Grandparents Marty and Clark meet Missie and Willie's two sons.

Love's Unending Legacy (1984)
Missie and Clark are home again after Clark's unfortunate accident.

Love's Unfolding Dream (1987)
Belinda, Marty and Clark's "surprise child," becomes a nurse.

Love Takes Wing (1988)
Belinda is restless and looks for new opportunities.

Love Finds a Home (1989)
Belinda leaves the prairie town for excitement in Boston.

Women of the West Series

The Calling of Emily Evans (1990)
After Bible school, Emily is called to Christian service.

Julia's Last Hope (1990)
Without warning, the mill closes and ruins John and Julia Harrigan's life.

Roses for Mama (1991)
The Petersons move west for Mother's health, but when both her parents die, Angela, seventeen, must reshape her life to care for the other children in the family.

A Woman Named Damaris (1991)
Her pa is a drunk. Damaris, fifteen, is eager to go off on her own.

They Called Her Mrs. Doc (1992)
Cassandra Dell Winston falls in love with a young doctor but wonders at his plan to provide medical care on the western frontier.

The Measure of a Heart (1992)
Anna, sixteen, just out of school, is taken with Austin Barker, the church's fill-in pastor for the summer. Will she ever see him again?

A Bride for Donnigan (1993)
Kathleen O'Maley crosses the ocean and travels cross-country to a prairie farm to answer an advertisement.

Heart of the Wilderness (1993)
George McMannus's daughter and son-in-law die in a wilderness river accident, and he must make a home for young granddaughter Kendra.

The Bluebird and the Sparrow (1995)
Berta forever hears people exclaim over her little sister, Glenna. So she decides to become an opposite.

A Gown of Spanish Lace (1995)
Ariana, a rural schoolteacher, is abducted and held in an outlaw camp.

FICTION FOR YOUNGER READERS

Spunky's Diary (1982)

New Kid in Town (1983)

The Prodigal Cat (1984)

Ducktails (1985)

The Impatient Turtle (1986)

A Cote of Many Colors (1987)

Prairie Dog Town (1988)

Maury Had a Little Lamb (1989)

Trouble in a Fur Coat (1990)

This Little Pig (1991)

Pordy's Prickly Problem (1993)

FOR FURTHER READING

Drew, Bernard A. *Lawmen in Scarlet: An Annotated Guide to Royal Canadian Mounted Police in Print and Performance*. Metuchen, NJ: Scarecrow Press, 1990.

Logan, Laurel Oke. *Janette Oke: A Heart for the Prairie: The Untold Story of One of the Most Beloved Novelists of Our Time*. Minneapolis, MN.: Bethany House, 1993.

May, Hal, ed. "Janette Oke." In *Contemporary Authors*. Vol. 111. Detroit: Gale Research, 1984.

Francine Pascal

Romance

Family drama

New York City
May 13, 1938

Sweet Valley High Series

A book written specifically for teenage readers startled the publishing world in 1985. Francine Pascal's *Perfect Summer* appeared on *The New York Times* best-seller list—the first time a young adult novel had appeared on the list. The book was one from Pascal's Sweet Valley High series, which has become phenomenally successful.

Francine Rubin earned a bachelor of arts degree from New York University in 1958. She married John Robert Pascal, a newspaperman, in 1965. They had three daughters, Laurie, Susan, and Jamie. John Robert Pascal died in 1981. Francine Pascal enjoys traveling and reading. She has lectured widely.

Pascal's early writings were articles for magazines such as *True Confessions* and *Modern Screen*, then *Ladies' Home Journal* and *Cosmopolitan*. With her husband, she wrote scripts for the television soap opera *The Young Marrieds* in 1965. The two took the head writer's basic plots and fleshed them out with dialogue. They also created stage dramas. Pascal and her brother, theatrical writer Michael Stewart, wrote the words for the musical *George M.*, which was produced on Broadway in 1968. Also with her husband, Pascal wrote a television special for ABC-TV in 1970, based on the musical. The Pascals' nonfiction book *The Strange Case of Patty Hearst* (1974) was based on the sensational California trial, which John Pascal covered.

Three years later, Francine Pascal wrote the first of three young adult novels featuring Victoria Martin, a girl itching to grow up. The first, *Hangin' Out with Cici,* found a publisher two weeks after it was completed. Its sequel, *My First Love and Other Disasters,* which looks at issues such as responsibilities and teenage sex, was named a Best Book for Young Adults by the American Library Association in 1979.

Another Pascal book, *The Hand-Me-Down Kid,* is about a girl's dilemma: Should she confess that she borrowed her sister's prize bicycle and lost it to a thief, thus risking being in trouble for the rest of her life?

When Pascal's idea for a teenage soap opera did not win favor with the networks, she transformed it into the Sweet Valley High series of novels. The first book, *Double Love,* appeared in 1983. The main characters are identical twins, sixteen-year-olds Elizabeth and Jessica Wakefield. Elizabeth is studious, conscientious, thoughtful, and wants to be a writer. Jessica is active, fashion-conscious, and impulsive.

"These books are romances in the classic sense," Pascal told interviewer Marguerite Feitlowitz. "They deal with the ideals of love, honor, friendship, sacrifice, which account for their popularity. Adolescents are at a unique stage in their lives. They're terribly idealistic and on the brink of the adult world where they will be confronted with the trendiness, consumerism, and other pressures that impinge on idealism."

"Sweet Valley High is the essence of high school," Pascal explained to Steve Dougherty. "The world outside is just an adult shadow going by. The parents barely exist. Action takes place in bedrooms, cars, and schools. It's that moment before reality hits, when you really do believe in the romantic values—sacrifice, love, loyalty, friendship—before you get jaded and slip off into adulthood."

Pascal said that she originally presented the Sweet Valley characters in an idealized, almost fantasy world, but she received so many pleas from readers who were caught up in the twins and their friends, however, that she decided to add more realistic elements such as racial issues.

The books have come under criticism. For example, Judy Mitchell, reviewing the early Sweet Valley novel *Power Play,* said, "This is formula fiction in its darkest hour, folks. The characters are both unbelievable and one-dimensional; the plot depends upon a legion of clichés; and it is probably kinder to skip over conflict and theme."

Commenting on another book, *Dangerous Love*, Sarah Simpson said, "The characters are poorly developed. The work fails to address the pressures and problems today's young adults have in their relationships with members of the opposite sex."

Sweet Valley stories range from mysteries (the twins overhear a murder plot in *Murder on the Line*) to family turmoil (the girls' parents separate in *Who's to Blame?*). They look at fads (friend Robin diets too much in *The Perfect Girl*) and emotions (Jessica relentlessly gets her way to find a summer boyfriend in *Malibu Summer*).

In some books, both girls are prominently featured. In others, they alternate center stage, or even step to the background so that one of their California friends' stories can be told.

What worked for one age group of readers should also work for others, Pascal and her publisher reasoned. They now offer books for readers both younger and older than Sweet Valley High's regular audience of teenagers. Sweet Valley Twins books describe Elizabeth and Jessica's adventures in sixth grade. Unicorn Club books follow the girls and their friends through grade seven. Sweet Valley Kids books go back even further, to when the two are in elementary school. The Sweet Valley University series sends the look-alikes to college and independence from their family. There is a Sweet Valley saga, a longer book that traces the twins' family back through five generations to Alice Larson, who emigrated from Sweden, and frontier tomboy Jessamyn Johnson, who ran off to join a circus.

More than 300 Sweet Valley books have been published, all bearing Pascal's name, but she does not write them. She creates the characters and outlines the plots. The outlines are then turned into full-length manuscripts by contract writers. Kate William, "author" of the Sweet Valley High books, is a house name used by more than one writer. (Kate William was taken from the first names of Pascal's parents.) The Sweet Valley Twins books are published under the pseudonym Jamie Suzanne; the Kids books under Molly Mia Stewart; and the University titles under Laurie John. All the pseudonyms are taken from Pascal family members. Pascal created another series, Caitlin, which was written by others—real writers Joanna Campbell and Diana Gregory, whose names appeared on the books.

In September 1994, Pascal's original vision for Sweet Valley High came true. It began to air as a syndicated television series starring Cynthia Daniel and Brittany Daniel.

"It deals with real issues," Cynthia (who plays Elizabeth) told Linda Matchan. "Like, on one show, I'm on a motorcycle with my boyfriend and we get into an accident, and I'm in a coma."

"It was so cool," said her sister Brittany (who plays Jessica). "They used a stunt person for it."

"Like it was so cool," Cynthia said.

"Like it was really cool," Brittany agreed.

"I almost died," Cynthia added.

YOUNG ADULT FICTION

Hangin' Out with Cici (1977)
Victoria Martin, thirteen, chafes at her mother's constant directives and is nearly expelled from school, when an accident on the train zaps her into a time warp.

My First Love and Other Disasters (1979)
Victoria, now fifteen, persuades her mother to let her take a summer job on Fire Island so she can be near the boy she hopes will become her first boyfriend.

The Hand-Me-Down Kid (1980)
Ari Jacobs, eleven, can stick up for others but not herself.

Love and Betrayal and Hold the Mayo! (1985)
Victoria, sixteen, and best pal Steffi waitress at Camp Mohaph.

Caitlin: The Love Trilogy by Joanna Campbell

Loving (1985)
Beautiful, charming, rich, clever Caitlin needs one thing: love.

Love Lost (1986)
Jed uncovers Caitlin's darkest secret.

True Love (1986)
Caitlin and Jed face deadly danger.

Caitlin: The Promise Trilogy by Diana Gregory

Tender Promises (1986)
When they graduate from high school, Caitlin and Jed find friendship graduating into love.

Promises Broken (1986)
Caitlin gets caught up in the excitement of college sorority rush, football games, and parties. She still loves Jed, but then she meets Julian.

A New Promise (1987)
Caitlin, attending Carleton Hill University, breaks up with Jed, her loyal boyfriend from high school, but her new boyfriend, Julian, is only after revenge.

Caitlin: The Forever Trilogy

Dreams of Forever (1988)

Forever and Always (1988)

Together Forever (1988)

Sweet Valley High Series by Kate William

1. *Double Love* (1983)
   Jessica and Elizabeth Wakefield, popular twins at Sweet Valley High, vie for the same boyfriend, basketball player Todd Wilkins.
2. *Secrets* (1983)
   Jessica is determined to be crowned queen of the fall dance.
3. *Playing with Fire* (1984)
   Jessica goes after rich Bruce Patman.
4. *Power Play* (1984)
   Jessica is furious when Elizabeth nominates chubby Robin Wilson for Sweet Valley High's snobby sorority.
5. *All Night Long* (1984)
   Jessica sneaks off to a college beach party.
6. *Dangerous Love* (1984)
   Forbidden to ride on Todd's new motorcycle, Elizabeth does it anyway and is injured in an accident.
7. *Dear Sister* (1984)
   Elizabeth lies in a coma after the motorcycle accident.

8. *Heartbreaker* (1984)
Jessica makes a splash with surfer Bill Chase.

9. *Racing Hearts* (1984)
Roger Barrett has a crush on Lila Fowler.

10. *Wrong Kind of Girl* (1984)
Jessica vows never to allow Annie Whitman on the Sweet Valley High cheerleading squad.

11. *Too Good to Be True* (1984)
Jessica goes to New York; Elizabeth hosts snooty Suzanne Devlin.

12. *When Love Dies* (1984)
What terrible secret is Tricia keeping from Steven?

13. *Kidnapped!* (1984)
Volunteering at Sweet Valley's hospital, Elizabeth is kidnapped.

14. *Deceptions* (1984)
Elizabeth dates Nicholas Morrow then fears Jessica will find out.

15. *Promises* (1985)
Steven Wakefield is crushed when his girlfriend dies after a tragic illness.

16. *Rags to Riches* (1985)
No one has guessed that Roger Barrett, the poorest boy in Sweet Valley, is really one of the Patmans, the wealthiest family in town.

17. *Love Letters* (1985)
Caroline Pearce has always been one of the least popular girls at Sweet Valley High.

18. *Head over Heels* (1985)
Bruce Patman and Regina Morrow in love? Jessica bets Lila they will break up in two weeks.

19. *Showdown* (1985)
Jessica and Lila vie for the attention of Jack, but why is his past such a mystery?

20. *Crash Landing!* (1985)
George Warren looks forward to taking his girlfriend, Enid Rollins, along on his first licensed airplane flight.

21. *Runaway* (1985)
Jessica is fed up with her goody-goody sister and decides to run away.

22. *Too Much Love* (1985)
Bill Chase feels that longtime girlfriend, Deedee Gordon, has become too dependent.

23. *Say Goodbye* (1985)
Elizabeth's longtime boyfriend, Todd, is leaving Sweet Valley.

24. *Memories* (1985)
Steven Wakefield has not dated since his girlfriend died of leukemia.

25. *Nowhere to Run* (1985)
Will the school band lose Emily Mayer to the school newspaper?

26. *Hostage!* (1985)
Elizabeth discovers that Regina Morrow and her family are being held captive.

27. *Lovestruck* (1986)
Football star Kim Matthews falls in love with sophisticated Suzanne Henlon.

28. *Alone in the Crowd* (1986)
Lynne Henry is tall, awkward, and painfully shy.

29. *Bitter Rivals* (1986)
Elizabeth's childhood friend, Amy Sutton, is moving back to Sweet Valley.

30. *Jealous Lies* (1986)
Will Sandra nominate Jean for Pi Beta Alpha—and will their friendship last if she does not?

31. *Taking Sides* (1986)
Enid Rollins and Lila Fowler are fighting over a new boy at Sweet Valley High, Jeffrey French.

32. *New Jessica* (1986)
Jessica is sick of being an identical twin and creates a new image for herself.

33. *Starting Over* (1987)
After years in foster homes, Sally Larson moves in with her cousin Dawn's family.

34. *Forbidden Love* (1987)
Maria Santelli is engaged to Michael Harris, but they have not told their parents.

35. *Out of Control* (1987)
Will Aaron Dallas come between Elizabeth and Jeffrey?

36. *Last Chance* (1987)
Will Peter choose Amy or Johanna?

37. *Rumors* (1987)
Lila Fowler spreads vicious rumors about Susan Stewart's mother.

38. *Leaving Home* (1987)
Can Jessica find a way to keep Elizabeth from leaving Sweet Valley?

39. *Secret Admirer* (1987)
Penny Ayala advertises for a boyfriend and falls for a cruel hoax.

40. *On the Edge* (1987)
Amy Sutton schemes to take Bruce Patman away from Regina Morrow.

41. *Outcast* (1987)
Ever since Regina Morrow's tragic death at Molly Hecht's party, everyone has been treating Molly as if she had the plague.

42. *Caught in the Middle* (1988)
Is love enough to keep Sondra and Manuel together?

43. *Hard Choices* (1988)
Cara Walker does not think Steven Wakefield is paying her enough attention.

44. *Pretenses* (1988)
At Jessica's suggestion, Cara Walker adds some mystery to her relationship with Steven Wakefield.

45. *Family Secrets* (1988)
The twins' cousin, Kelly Bates, has a blind spot when it comes to her father and to her boyfriend.

46. *Decisions* (1988)
An offer from her rich aunt may ruin Robin Wilson's year.

47. *Troublemaker* (1988)
Shy, sensitive Julie Porter is attracted to conceited Bruce Patman.

48. *Slam Book* (1988)
"Slam books" are all the rage at Sweet Valley High—and soon start a lot of trouble.

49. *Playing for Keeps* (1988)
Jessica falls head over heels in love with A. J. Morgan and wants to compete in a fashion contest.

50. *Out of Reach* (1988)
Jade Wu may have to defy her father to get what she wants.

51. *Against the Odds* (1989)
Ronnie Edwards cannot keep up with payments to his bookie.

52. *White Lies* (1989)
John Pfeifer worries that Jennifer Mitchell is becoming too involved with dropout Rich Andrews.

53. *Second Chance* (1989)
Quiet, determined Kristin Thompson knows exactly what she wants from life.

54. *Two-Boy Weekend* (1989)
Facing a weekend without steady A. J. Morgan, Jessica meets Christopher.

55. *Perfect Shot* (1989)
Will Shelley Novak have a perfect date for the big dance?

56. *Lost at Sea* (1989)
When the boat capsizes, Jessica and Winston Egbert disappear into the fog.

57. *Teacher Crush* (1989)
Talented Olivia Davidson confides that she is lonely.

58. *Brokenhearted* (1989)
Elizabeth's heart is broken when Todd moves to Vermont; then she begins dating Jeffrey.

59. *In Love Again* (1989)
Todd moves back from Vermont, but with his new friends and lifestyle, can Elizabeth still be his girlfriend?

60. *That Fatal Night* (1989)
Terri is there for him when Ken loses his eyesight in a car crash.

61. *Boy Trouble* (1990)
Patty, a popular black student, is sure her boyfriend is seeing someone else.

62. *Who's Who?* (1990)
Jessica signs up with a computer dating service under two new identities.

63. *New Elizabeth* (1990)
Tired of being considered steady and dependable, Elizabeth takes up surfing.

64. *The Ghost of Tricia Martin* (1990)
Steven meets Andrea—the spitting image of Tricia, his longtime girlfriend who died.

65. *Trouble at Home* (1990)
The twins are caught in the middle as Ned Wakefield runs for mayor and his wife, Alice, wins an interior design contest and is busy away from home.

66. *Who's to Blame?* (1990)
The twins are miserable when their parents separate.

67. *The Parent Plot* (1990)
The twins plot to bring their parents back together.

68. *The Love Bet* (1990)
Dana would rather sing with her band; Aaron would rather play soccer; but Elizabeth wants them to fall in love.

69. *Friend Against Friend* (1990)
Friendships are strained when Neil sticks up for his black friend, Andy.

70. *Ms. Quarterback* (1990)
Ken plans to play quarterback for the Gladiators—but so does Claire.

71. *Starring Jessica* (1991)
Will Jessica or Lila be named the perfect American teen by a television talk show host?

72. *Rock Star's Girl* (1991)
Jessica is thrilled when rock star Jamie Peters moves to town.

73. *Regina's Legacy* (1991)
Elizabeth takes a picture of three suspicious men.

74. *The Perfect Girl* (1991)
Robin is obsessed with losing weight to keep her boyfriend, George.

75. *Amy's True Love* (1991)
Amy loves Tom, but Barry falls for Amy.

76. *Miss Teen Sweet Valley* (1991)
Jessica is confident she will win a beauty contest, but Elizabeth thinks it is sexist and wants to shut it down.

77. *Cheating to Win* (1991)
Annie must stop track star Tony from using "magic vitamins" to win a chance at the Olympics.

78. *The Dating Game* (1991)
Jean and Claire plot revenge when they both receive passionate love letters from the same guy.

79. *The Long-Lost Brother* (1991)
Sara Eastborne has not told anyone that her twin brother, Tim, is in reform school.

80. *The Girl They Both Loved* (1991)
April loves dirt bike racing—but it has become an obsession for her boyfriend, Michael.

81. *Rosa's Lie* (1992)
A teen must come to terms with her Mexican heritage.

82. *Kidnapped by the Cult!* (1992)
Jessica is mesmerized by magnetic Adam Marvel, leader of the Good Friends.

83. *Steven's Bride* (1992)
Will Steven marry Cara—or will she move with her family to London?

84. *The Stolen Diary* (1992)
Jessica must investigate the rumors about Elizabeth and Kris Lynch, if she is to get back together with Todd.

85. *Soap Star* (1992)
Will newfound fame ruin Jessica's relationship with a television star?

86. *Jessica Against Bruce* (1992)
Bruce dares Jessica to perform dangerous stunts and practical jokes.

87. *My Best Friend's Boyfriend* (1992)
Shy Ginny may lose a boyfriend when she sends a friend to answer a teen hotline call.

88. *Love Letters for Sale* (1992)
The twins start a letter-writing service.

89. *Elizabeth Betrayed* (1993)
Elizabeth has to clear her name of a charge of plagiarism at the Sweet Valley High newspaper.

90. *Don't Go Home with John* (1993)
John Pfeifer is showing a lot of interest in Lila Fowler.

91. *In Love with a Prince* (1993)
Elizabeth's longtime pen pal, Prince Arthur of Santa Dora, comes to visit.

92. *She's Not What She Seems* (1993)
Paula, a new transfer student, adores Jessica.

93. *Stepsisters* (1993)
Elizabeth and Jessica have a new neighbor, sorority sister Annie Whitman.

94. *Are We in Love?* (1993)
Everyone assumes Steven Wakefield and Anie Whitman's new stepsister, Cheryl, are a couple. So they give it a try.

95. *The Morning After* (1993)
This book and the next five form a "terror" sequence. Will Jessica ever come to grips with a sudden tragedy?

96. *The Arrest* (1993)
Elizabeth is arrested, and Jessica steals her boyfriend, Todd.

97. *The Verdict* (1993)
Jessica believes Elizabeth is guilty and will not talk to her.

98. *The Wedding* (1993)
Lila is thrilled that her parents are together again.

99. *Beware the Baby-Sitter* (1993)
Margo is insinuating herself into Sweet Valley, bringing together an evil scheme.

100. *The Evil Twin* (1993)
Margo hopes to dispose of the twins and take their place in the Wakefield home.

101. *The Boyfriend War* (1994)
This is the first of three books forming a "passion" trilogy. Jessica and best friend, Lila, are at war.

102. *Almost Married* (1994)
Elizabeth and Todd are living together!

103. *Operation Love Match* (1994)
Elizabeth and Jessica are determined to prevent Bruce's parents from divorcing.

104. *Love and Death in London* (1994)
The twins, in London as summer interns, are assigned by the *London Journal* to the Scotland Yard beat.

105. *A Date with a Werewolf* (1994)
Jessica's new friend, Lord Robert Pembroke, is not what he seems.

106. *Beware the Wolfman* (Super Thriller) (1994)
A werewolf is on the loose in London, and Jessica and Elizabeth could be its next victims.

107. *Jessica's Secret Love* (1994)
Jessica falls for Jeremy Randall—who is supposed to be engaged to the Wakefields' houseguest.

108. *Left at the Altar* (1994)
While Jessica helps Sue Gibbons plan her wedding, she is meeting secretly with Sue's fiancé.

109. *Double-Crossed* (1994)
Now that she has stopped Jeremy and Sue's wedding, Jessica is engaged—and immediately suspicious of Jeremy.

110. *Death Threat* (1994)
Sue Gibbons has been kidnapped.

111. *A Deadly Christmas* (1994)
Is Jeremy the man of Jessica's dreams—or is he a nightmare?

112. *Jessica Quits the Squad* (1995)
Heather Mallone is Jessica's match on the cheerleading squad—and with the boys.

113. *Pom Pom Wars* (1995)
Jessica starts her own cheerleading team.

114. *"V" for Victory* (1995)
The cheerleaders head for the nationals.

115. *The Treasure of Death Valley* (1995)
On a desert survival course, Elizabeth discovers gold.

116. *Nightmare in Death Valley* (1995)
The Sweet Valley gang faces hunger, thirst, and three escaped convicts.

117. *Jessica and the Genius* (1995)
How did Jessica manage an almost perfect SAT score? Why is Todd driving Elizabeth crazy?

118. *College Weekend* (1995), sequel to *Jessica and the Genius*
When Jessica falls for an older guy, will she keep him?

119. *Jessica's Older Guy* (1995), sequel to *College Weekend* and *Jessica and the Genius*
Jessica must make a decision, in this final book in a trilogy.

Sweet Valley Fear Thrillers

A Stranger in the House (1995)
John Marin, the man whom Ned Wakefield sent to prison for murder, is out and looking for revenge.

A Killer on Board (1995), sequel to *A Stranger in the House*
Marin is now after the twins, Jessica and Elizabeth.

Sweet Valley High Magna Editions Series by Kate William

The Wakefields of Sweet Valley (1991)
This saga follows five generations of Sweet Valley women.

The Wakefield Legacy: The Untold Story (1992)
At the turn of the century, Sarah Wakefield marries against her father's wishes.

A Night to Remember (1993)
This novel involves a person with evil, dangerous power.

Jessica's Secret Diary (1994)
This book incorporates scenes from early novels.

Elizabeth's Secret Diary (1994)
This book incorporates scenes from early novels.

Murder in Paradise (1995)
Jessica discovers a body at Paradise Spa, and Alice Wakefield disappears.

Sweet Valley High Super Editions Series by Kate William

Perfect Summer (1985)
The Wakefield twins and friends plan a biking trip up the California coast—but Liz is about to break up with Todd; Jessica is chasing sexy Robbie October, who ignores her; Bruce Patman is mean to his cousin, Roger; and Lila Fowler holds a grudge against Ms. Dalton.

Spring Break (1986)
The twins are off to the glamorous south of France.

Malibu Summer (1986)
The twins go to Malibu to take summer baby-sitting jobs and meet boys.

Winter Carnival (1986)
Elizabeth has midwinter blues, and Jessica has been avoiding her responsibilities.

Special Christmas (1987)
Jessica is determined to be Miss Christmastime, and Elizabeth is counting the days until she sees Todd again.

Spring Fever (1988)
Sleepy Walkersville, Kansas, is twice as exciting as the twins' hometown.

Sweet Valley High Super Stars Series by Kate William

Lila's Story (1989)
Lila's life is jostled when her father decides to remarry.

Bruce's Story (1990)
Bruce, handsome and arrogant, gets everything he wants.

Enid's Story (1990)
Enid gave up the wild crowd once; can she resist temptation again?

Olivia's Story (1991)
Olivia's mother reveals a startling secret and forces her to make an important decision.

Todd's Story (1992)
Todd and Elizabeth land jobs as camp counselors.

Sweet Valley High Super Thrillers Series by Kate William

Double Jeopardy (1987)
The twins intern at the *Sweet Valley News*, and Jessica is eyewitness to murder.

On the Run (1988)
Jessica is not convinced that writer Eric Hankman is as perfect as he seems.

No Place to Hide (1988)
The twins help two people in love and are threatened by an anonymous phone caller.

Deadly Summer (1989)
A patient escapes from a nearby psychiatric hospital.

Murder on the Line (1992)
Working again as summer interns at the *Sweet Valley News*, the twins overhear plans for a murder.

Sweet Valley High Slam Book by Laurie Pascal Wenk (1988)

Sweet Valley High TV Edition Series by the Editors of Sweet Valley High

1. *California Love* (1995)
Novelization of four episodes from the syndicated television series.
2. *Twin Hearts* (1995)

Sweet Valley University Series by Laurie John

1. *College Girls* (1993)
The twins and their friends are in college. Jessica has everything she wants—except one guy on campus. Elizabeth's longtime relationship with Todd is strained.

2. *Love, Lies and Jessica Wakefield* (1993)
   How far will Jessica go to keep wealthy, thrilling Mike McAllery?

3. *What Your Parents Don't Know . . .* (1994)
   Jessica has moved in with a boyfriend, Steven is furious, and Elizabeth is investigating a campus scandal.

4. *Anything for Love* (1994)
   Jessica thinks living with Mike will be perfect—but now he does not come home nights.

5. *A Married Woman* (1994)
   Jessica, now Mrs. Mike, still does not like his habits. Elizabeth is looking for the leader of an evil society.

6. *The Love of Her Life* (1994)
   Todd begs Elizabeth to come back. Steven is on trial for manslaughter.

7. *Goodbye to Love* (1994)
   Jessica's disastrous marriage is over. Elizabeth has a new love.

8. *Home for Christmas* (1994)
   Elizabeth brings new boyfriend Tom home. Old boyfriend Todd tries to get over her.

9. *Sorority Scandal* (1995)
   Jessica gets back at the exclusive Theta sorority.

10. *No Means No* (1995)
    Can Jessica's new boyfriend, James Montgomery, take no for an answer? Does Elizabeth tell her sister what she knows about him?

11. *Take Back the Night* (1995)
    James assaults Jessica on a date. Elizabeth crusades to help her sister.

12. *College Cruise* (1995)
    Jessica and Elizabeth go on the biggest spring break party ever.

13. *S.S. Heartbreak* (1995)
    Elizabeth catches Tom Watts kissing another woman. Jessica is anxious to find the stranger who saved her life.

14. *Shipboard Wedding* (1995)
    Jessica throws herself overboard for her dream man.

15. *Behind Closed Doors* (1995)
    Jessica falls for Louis Miles, but he is a college professor. Is she in over her head?

16. *Deadly Attraction* (1995)

Sweet Valley University Thriller Edition Series by Laurie John

Wanted for Murder (1995)
The FBI is after the young men Jessica and Elizabeth pick up on a Colorado skiing trip.

He's Watching You (1995)
Elizabeth and her dangerous enemy, William White, meet face to face.

Kissing of the Vampire (1995)
Elizabeth's new love Nicholas des Perdu is hiding a dark secret.

FICTION FOR YOUNGER READERS

Sweet Valley Twins Series by Jamie Suzanne

1. *Best Friends* (1986)
2. *Teacher's Pet* (1986)
3. *Haunted House* (1986)
4. *Choosing Sides* (1986)
5. *Sneaking Out* (1987)
6. *The New Girl* (1987)
7. *Three's a Crowd* (1987)
8. *First Place* (1987)
9. *Against the Rules* (1987)
10. *One of the Gang* (1987)
11. *Buried Treasure* (1987)
12. *Keeping Secrets* (1987)
13. *Stretching the Truth* (1987)
14. *Tug of War* (1987)
15. *The Older Boy* (1988)
16. *Second Best* (1988)
17. *Boys Against Girls* (1988)
18. *Center of Attention* (1988)
19. *The Bully* (1988)
20. *Playing Hooky* (1988)
21. *Left Behind* (1988)
22. *Out of Place* (1988)

23. *Claim to Fame* (1988)
24. *Jumping to Conclusions* (1988)
25. *Standing Out* (1989)
26. *Taking Charge* (1989)
27. *Teamwork* (1989)
28. *April Fool!* (1989)
29. *Jessica and the Brat Attack* (1989)
30. *Princess Elizabeth* (1989)
31. *Jessica's Bad Idea* (1989)
32. *Jessica on Stage* (1989)
33. *Elizabeth's New Hero* (1989)
34. *Jessica, the Rock Star* (1989)
35. *Amy's Pen Pal* (1989)
36. *Mary Is Missing* (1990)
37. *The War Between the Twins* (1990)
38. *Lois Strikes Back* (1990)
39. *Jessica and the Money Mix-Up* (1990)
40. *Danny Means Trouble* (1990)
41. *The Twins Get Caught* (1990)
42. *Jessica's Secret* (1990)
43. *Elizabeth's First Kiss* (1990)
44. *Amy Moves In* (1990)
45. *Lucy Takes the Reins* (1991)
46. *Mademoiselle Jessica* (1991)
47. *Jessica's New Look* (1991)
48. *Mandy Miller Fights Back* (1991)
49. *The Twins' Little Sister* (1991)
50. *Jessica and the Secret Star* (1991)
51. *Elizabeth the Impossible* (1991)

Sweet Valley Twins and Their Friends Series by Jamie Suzanne

Continuation of the Sweet Valley Twins series.

52. *Booster Boycott* (1991)
53. *The Slime That Ate Sweet Valley* (1991)
54. *The Big Party Weekend* (1991)
55. *Brooke and Her Rock-Star Mom* (1992)
56. *The Wakefields Strike It Rich* (1992)
57. *Big Brother's in Love!* (1992)
58. *Elizabeth and the Orphans* (1992)
59. *Barnyard Battle* (1992)
60. *Ciao, Sweet Valley!* (1992)
61. *Jessica the Nerd* (1992)
62. *Sarah's Dad and Sophia's Mom* (1992)
63. *Poor Lila!* (1992)
64. *The Charm School Mystery* (1992)
65. *Patty's Last Dance* (1993)
66. *The Great Boyfriend Switch* (1993)
67. *Jessica the Thief* (1993)
68. *The Middle School Gets Married* (1993)
69. *Won't Someone Help Anna?* (1993)
70. *Psychic Sisters* (1993)
71. *Jessica Saves the Trees* (1993)
72. *The Love Potion* (1993)
73. *Lila's Music Video* (1993)
74. *Elizabeth the Hero* (1993)
75. *Jessica and the Earthquake* (1994)
76. *Yours for a Day* (1994)
77. *Todd Runs Away* (1994)
78. *Steven the Zombie* (1994)
79. *Jessica's Blind Date* (1994)
80. *The Gossip War* (1994)
81. *Robbery at the Mall* (1994)
82. *Steven's Enemy* (1994)
83. *Amy's Secret Sister* (1994)
84. *Romeo and 2 Juliets* (1995)
85. *Elizabeth and the Seventh Graders* (1995)
86. *It Can't Happen Here* (1995)
87. *The Mother-Daughter Switch* (1995)
88. *Steven Gets Even* (1995)
89. *Jessica's Cookie Disaster* (1995)
90. *The Cousin War* (1995)

Sweet Valley Twins and Their Friends Super Editions Series by Jamie Suzanne

1. *The Class Trip* (1988)
2. *Holiday Mischief* (1988)
3. *The Big Camp Secret* (1989)
4. *The Unicorns Go Hawaiian* (1991)
5. *Lila's Secret Valentine* (1995)

Sweet Valley Twins and Their Friends Super Chiller Editions Series by Jamie Suzanne

1. *The Christmas Ghost* (1990)
2. *Ghosts in the Graveyard* (1990)
3. *The Carnival Ghost* (1990)
4. *The Ghost in the Bell Tower* (1992)
5. *The Curse of the Ruby Necklace* (1993)
6. *The Curse of the Golden Heart* (1994)

Sweet Valley Twins and Their Friends Magna Editions Series by Jamie Suzanne

The Magic Christmas (1992)
A Christmas Without Elizabeth (1993)
BIG for Christmas (1994)

The Unicorn Club by Alice Nicole Johansson

1. *Save the Unicorns!* (1994)
2. *Maria's Movie Comeback* (1994)
3. *The Best Friend Game* (1994)
4. *Lila's Little Sister* (1994)
5. *Unicorns in Love* (1995)

Sweet Valley Kids Series by Molly Mia Stewart

1. *Surprise! Surprise!* (1989)
2. *Runaway Hamster* (1989)
3. *The Twins' Mystery Teacher* (1990)
4. *Elizabeth's Valentine* (1990)
5. *Jessica's Cat Trick* (1990)
6. *Lila's Secret* (1990)
7. *Jessica's Big Mistake* (1990)
8. *Jessica's Zoo Adventure* (1990)
9. *Elizabeth's Super-Selling Lemonade* (1990)
10. *The Twins and the Wild West* (1990)
11. *Crybaby Lois* (1990)
12. *Sweet Valley Trick or Treat* (1990)
13. *Starring Winston Egbert* (1990)
14. *Jessica the Baby-Sitter* (1991)
15. *Fearless Elizabeth* (1991)
16. *Jessica the TV Star* (1991)
17. *Caroline's Mystery Dolls* (1991)
18. *Bossy Steven* (1991)
19. *Jessica and the Jumbo Fish* (1991)
20. *The Twins Go to the Hospital* (1991)
21. *Jessica and the Spelling-Bee Surprise* (1991)
22. *Sweet Valley Slumber Party* (1991)
23. *Lila's Haunted House Party* (1991)
24. *Cousin Kelly's Family Secret* (1991)
25. *Left-Out Elizabeth* (1992)
26. *Jessica's Snobby Club* (1992)
27. *The Sweet Valley Cleanup Team* (1992)
28. *Elizabeth Meets Her Hero* (1992)
29. *Andy and the Alien* (1992)
30. *Jessica's Unburied Treasure* (1992)
31. *Elizabeth and Jessica Run Away* (1992)
32. *Left Back!* (1992)
33. *Caroline's Halloween Spell* (1992)
34. *The Best Thanksgiving Ever* (1992)
35. *Elizabeth's Broken Arm* (1993)
36. *Elizabeth's Video Fever* (1993)
37. *The Big Race* (1993)
38. *Good-Bye, Eva?* (1993)
39. *Ellen Is Home Alone* (1993)
40. *Robin in the Middle* (1993)
41. *The Missing Tea Set* (1993)

42. *Jessica's Monster Nightmare* (1993)
43. *Jessica Gets Spooked* (1993)
44. *The Twins' Big Pow-Wow* (1993)
45. *Elizabeth's Piano Lessons* (1993)
46. *Get the Teacher!* (1994)
47. *Elizabeth the Tattletale* (1994)
48. *Lila's April Fool* (1994)
49. *Jessica's Mermaid* (1994)
50. *Steven's Twin* (1994)
51. *Lois and the Sleepover* (1994)
52. *Julie the Karate Kid* (1994)
53. *The Magic Puppets* (1994)
54. *Star of the Parade* (1994)
55. *The Jessica and Elizabeth Show* (1995)
56. *Jessica Plays Cupid* (1995)
57. *No Girls Allowed* (1995)
58. *Lila's Birthday Bash* (1995)
59. *Jessica + Jessica = Trouble* (1995)
60. *The Amazing Jessica* (1995)
61. *Scaredy-Cat Elizabeth* (1995)

Sweet Valley Kids Hairraiser

A Curse on Elizabeth (1995)

Sweet Valley Kids Super Special Series by Molly Mia Stewart

Trapped in Toyland (1994)

Sweet Valley Kids Super Snooper Editions Series by Molly Mia Stewart

1. *The Case of the Secret Santa* (1990)
2. *The Case of the Magic Christmas Bell* (1991)
3. *The Case of the Haunted Camp* (1992)
4. *The Case of the Christmas Thief* (1992)
5. *The Case of the Hidden Treasure* (1993)
6. *The Case of the Million-Dollar Diamonds* (1993)
7. *The Case of the Alien Princess* (1994)

ADULT FICTION

Save Johanna! (1981)

If Wishes Were Horses (1995)

ADAPTATIONS IN OTHER MEDIA

My Mother Was Never a Kid (1981)
Television special based on *Hangin' Out with Cici*.

The Hand-Me-Down Kid (1983)
Television special.

Sweet Valley High (1994–95)
Syndicated television series featuring Cynthia and Brittany Daniel.

FOR FURTHER READING

Dougherty, Steve. "Heroines of 40 Million Books, Francine Pascal's *Sweet Valley* Twins Are Perfection in Duplicate." *People Weekly*, 11 July 1988.

Feitlowitz, Marguerite. "Francine Pascal." In *Authors & Artists for Young Adults*, edited by Agnes Garrett and Helga P. McCue. Vol. 1. Detroit: Gale Research, 1989.

Huntwork, Mary M. "Why Girls Flock to Sweet Valley High." *School Library Journal*, March 1990.

Matchan, Linda. " 'Sweet Valley High': Cool Success." *The Boston Globe*, 14 October 1994.

Meet the Stars of Sweet Valley High. An authorized biography by the editors of Sweet Valley High. New York: Bantam Books, 1995.

Mitchell, Judy. Review of *Power Play. Voice of Youth Advocates*, August 1984.

Simpson, Sarah. Review of *Dangerous Love. ALAN Review*, spring 1984.

Katherine Paterson

Family drama

Inspirational drama

Qing Jiang, Jiangsu, China
October 31, 1932

Bridge to Terabithia

"I never wanted to be a writer, at least not when I was a child, or even a young woman," Katherine Paterson said in a promotional flyer from her publisher. "Today I want very much to be a writer. But when I was ten, I wanted to be either a movie star or a missionary. When I was twenty, I wanted to get married and have lots of children."

Katherine Womeldorf was the daughter of missionary parents. She attended King College, the Presbyterian School of Christian Education, the Naganuma School of the Japanese Language, and the Union Theological Seminary. In 1962, she married John Barstow Paterson, a Presbyterian clergyman. They have four children.

Her upbringing in Asia gave Paterson a long-lasting appreciation of its cultures, history, and languages. Her family moved frequently, living in fifteen homes in thirteen years when Katherine was growing up. One year was spent in the family's ancestral Richmond, Virginia, area. Katherine came home from first grade on February 14 without having received a single Valentine. Her mother later urged her to write about it. Many years later, the author told an interviewer that all her stories were about the time she did not get any valentines.

Paterson learned to read before she began school. Works of A. A. Milne and Kenneth Grahame's *The Wind in the Willows* were early favorites. Her first published work was a verse that appeared in the

Shanghai American, a school paper, when she was seven. She devoured the Elsie Dinsmore books by Martha Finley—Elsie was a rather humorless, pious Victorian child—and wrote imitative stories of her own. In college, an instructor noticed her ability to absorb and adopt the style of whatever literary figure she happened to be researching and writing a paper on. He encouraged her, therefore, to read only the best. She read Shakespeare, Sophocles, and *The Lion, the Witch and the Wardrobe* by C. S. Lewis in college. After college, Paterson taught school, then went to Japan as a missionary.

In a promotional flyer for Lodestar Books, Paterson said, "If you've read my early books, you must know that I came to love Japan and feel very much at home there. I went to language school and lived and worked in that country for four years. I had every intention of spending the rest of my life among the Japanese. But when I returned to the States for a year of study in New York, I met a young Presbyterian pastor who changed the direction of my life once again. We were married in 1962."

Paterson had returned to the United States with a keen awareness of language as a means of shaping ideas and feelings. After her marriage, she continued her writing. In 1973, her first novel, *The Sign of the Chrysanthemum*, was published. Japan was the setting for this book and for her next two books as well. She won the National Book Award for *The Master Puppeteer* in 1977, and for *The Great Gilly Hopkins* in 1979. She won the Newbery Medal for *Bridge to Terabithia* in 1978 and for *Jacob Have I Loved* in 1981.

Critic Anthea Bell remarked on the theology evident in Paterson's books: "Her Christianity is not that of the more recent born-again or charismatic movements; hers is the traditional Presbyterian variety, and has been with her from childhood. . . . I do admire Katherine Paterson's ability—increasingly sure from *Bridge to Terabithia* onwards—to make her own Christian convictions evident while not letting them become obtrusive: that is an achievement to impress the least religious of serious readers."

"Jess' ambition is to be 'the fastest runner in the fifth grade,' " reviewer Jack Forman said of *Terabithia*. A new girl, Leslie, beats him in a race. "The two quickly find they have much in common—and each has something to give the other.... The two friends build a secret hideout and invent an imaginary kingdom they call Terabithia, but soon torrential rains make it risky for them to get there. When Jess gets back from a day trip to nearby Washington, D.C., with a teacher, he learns that Leslie drowned trying to reach their meeting place and reacts first with shock, then selfishness, and finally grief. Jess struggles to memorialize Leslie and the meaning of their friendship. Jess and Leslie are so effectively developed as characters that young readers might well feel that they were their classmates."

"Their relationship is beautifully developed and shows young readers that girls and boys can indeed be real friends," Sharon Wigutoff said. "However, at the end of the story, the author surprises us by having Leslie die accidentally. This leaves the disturbing suggestion that perhaps such a friendship was, after all, too unreal to sustain. We realize, too, after the tears dry, that this is ultimately not a story about friendship at all, but about a young boy whose limited world is opened up by a temporary visit from an almost mystical character—this is a contemporary fairy tale. Leslie serves, in fact, less as a friend than as an enabler, and Jess clearly realizes this at the end of the story."

Paterson said of *The Great Gilly Hopkins* when accepting the National Book Award, "I wrote this book because, by chance rather than by design, I was for two months a foster mother. Now, as a mother, I am not a finalist for any prizes, but on the whole I'm serviceable. I was not serviceable as a foster mother, and this is why: I knew from the beginning that the children were going to be with us only a short time, so when a problem arose as problems will, I'd say to myself, 'I can't really deal with that. They'll be here only a few weeks.' Suddenly and too late, I heard what I had been saying. . . .

"A teacher had read aloud *The Great Gilly Hopkins* to her class, and Eddie, another foster child, hearing in the story of Gilly his own story, did something that apparently flabbergasted everyone who knew him. He fell in love with a book. Can you imagine how that made me feel? Here was a twelve-year-old who knew far better than I what my story was about, and he did me the honor of claiming it for himself."

"The book is outstanding in characterization, theme, and style," Marilyn Leathers Solt said. "The character of Gilly is believable and consistent and will remain in a reader's mind long after details of plot are forgotten."

The book was challenged in North Carolina, Texas, and Connecticut for what parents said was profanity and blasphemy, Herbert N. Foerstel stated.

Paterson has written several nonfiction works, such as *Consider the Lilies: Plants of the Bible* (1986) with John Paterson, and has translated two works, *The Crane Wife* by Sumiko Yagawa (1981) and *The Tongue-Cut Sparrow*, retold by Momoko Ishii (1987).

YOUNG ADULT FICTION

The Sign of the Chrysanthemum (1973)
An orphan, Muna, searches for his samurai father.

Of Nightingales That Weep (1974)
Takiko, the daughter of a samurai, finds her life disrupted by her mother's remarriage.

The Master Puppeteer (1975)
Jiro becomes a puppeteer's apprentice both to survive and to attain honor.

Bridge to Terabithia (1977)
Outsiders Jess and Leslie are true friends. When there is a tragedy, Jess is able to cope thanks to the independence he gained from her friendship.

The Great Gilly Hopkins (1978)
A girl abandoned by her flower-child mother, eleven-year-old Galadriel "Gilly" Hopkins eventually realizes that the foster home she has rejected is really a loving place.

Angels and Other Strangers: Family Christmas Stories (1979); British title: *Star of Night* (1980)

Jacob Have I Loved (1980)
Her pretty and talented twin sister, Caroline, has always been the favored one—until Louise learns to fight for love.

Rebels of the Heavenly Kingdom (1983)
Wang Lee and Mei Lin are caught up in clashes between Chinese warlords in the mid-nineteenth century.

Come Sing, Jimmy Jo (1985)
James Johnson joins his family's country music act. But why do his mother and uncle resent his success?

Park's Quest (1988)
Parkington Waddell Broughton V wants to learn about his father, a pilot killed during the Vietnam War.

Lyddie (1991)
Lyddie Worthen hopes to earn enough working in the textile mills in Lowell, Massachusetts, to reunite her family.

FICTION FOR YOUNGER READERS

The Tale of the Mandarin Ducks (1990)

The Smallest Cow in the World (1991)

The King's Equal (1992)

Who Am I? (1992)

Flip-Flop Girl (1994)

A Midnight Clear: Stories for the Christmas Season (1995)

FOR FURTHER READING

Bell, Anthea. "A Case of Commitment." *Signal*, May 1982.

Foerstel, Herbert N. *Banned in the USA: A Reference Guide to Book Censorship in Schools and Public Libraries*. Westport, CT: Greenwood, 1994.

Forman, Jack. Review of *Bridge to Terabithia. School Library Journal*, November 1977.

Paterson, Katherine. *Gates of Excellence: On Reading and Writing Books for Children*. New York: Elsevier Nelson, 1981.

———. *Katherine Paterson: Why I Became a Writer . . . .* New York: Lodestar Books, circa 1992.

———. "National Book Award Acceptance." *Horn Book Magazine*, August 1979.

———. *On Reading and Writing Books for Children*. New York: E. P. Dutton, 1988.

———. *The Spying Heart: More Thoughts on Reading and Writing Books for Children*. New York: E. P. Dutton, 1989.

Solt, Marilyn Leathers, and Linda Kauffman Peterson. *Newbery and Caldecott Medal and Honor Books: An Annotated Bibliography*. Boston: G. K. Hall, 1982.

Wigutoff, Sharon. "An Antidote to Series Romances: Books About Friendship." *Interracial Books for Children Bulletin*, May–August 1981.

Gary Paulsen

Outdoor drama

Minneapolis, Minnesota
May 17, 1939

The Hatchet

As an army veteran, self-educated, working at a deep-space tracking station in California, Gary Paulsen told *Publishers Weekly* that he "just kind of freaked. I thought, 'God, what am I doing?' I just hated it. I decided to be a writer, pretty much that night. I drove to Hollywood. If I'd been in the East I would have gone to New York. I needed to find writers." Paulsen did indeed become a writer. He is best known for his tales of adventure and endurance.

The son of an officer on General George Patton's staff, Paulsen did not meet his father until World War II had ended. His mother lived in Chicago and worked in a munitions factory, as Paulsen relates in his autobiography, *Eastern Sun, Winter Moon*. A recurring theme throughout Paulsen's books is that of a boy being raised by a mother and sent to stay with relatives in the country. It shows up in *A Christmas Sonata*, for example, when a boy and his mother spend Yule 1943 with relatives in Minnesota while his father is off fighting. It shows up in *Popcorn Days and Buttermilk Nights* when city-smart David comes under the spell of his hardworking Uncle David. It also shows up in *The Cookcamp* and *Harris and Me*.

Paulsen also relates in his autobiography that his mother led a rather promiscuous life while her husband was away. In *The Hatchet*, the character Brian struggles with a guilty secret: He has seen his mother with another man.

Toward the war's end, Paulsen's father sent for the family, and they went by ship to the Philippines. Along the way, they witnessed an airplane crash. Sailors on the ship were unable to rescue the victims. In the Philippines, Paulsen lived in a hut with servants. He became a wanderer and an adventurer and survived a typhoon. Both his parents were alcoholics.

Of these early years, he said, "I hesitated to write it. These were places too raw to pick at, I thought—wounds, scars, things to damage me—and I could hide them in fiction still or not speak of the rough parts." A friend advised him to write his story as truth, though, and he did.

Returning stateside, Paulsen and his family moved frequently. He developed a dual love for reading and for the outdoors. Paulsen attended Bemidji College and the University of Colorado, and he married twice. His second wife is Ruth Ellen Wright, an artist.

Paulsen's first book was a novel, *Some Birds Don't Fly*, followed by a young adult story, *Mr. Tucket*, which tells of a wagon train. "They both sold right away," the writer told *Publishers Weekly*, "and I thought, 'Christ, I'll have the Nobel in a week.' I didn't sell another word for seven years."

Paulsen fumbled through those seven years, drank heavily, took day jobs, swore off alcohol, then began to sell again—Westerns, mysteries, how-to books, plays, and hunting, trapping, and outdoor stories. He said in *Publisher's Weekly*, "Everybody thinks he can write a novel and nobody likes to write nonfiction, but there's an enormous demand for it. I kind of foundered along, in a good year making two or three thousand. One of the worst years I had, I made $683 writing."

After a drawn-out libel suit following publication of his novel *Winterkill*, Paulsen went from flying success as a prolific writer to quitting entirely. He took to the Minnesota big woods and trapped coyotes and beavers. When someone gave him four dogs, he had enough for an Iditarod team—and ran seventeen days in the 1,200-mile dogsled sprint. He returned to writing.

Paulsen's *Dogsong* is about an Eskimo boy in a village along the Iditarod route. It earned a Newbery Honor in 1986. The popular young adult novel *The Hatchet* is about a boy who struggles through the wilderness using his new hatchet. It, too, won a Newbery Honor in 1988.

"Plausible, taut, this is a spellbinding account," *Kirkus Reviews* said of *The Hatchet*. "Paulsen's staccato, repetitive style conveys Brian's stress; his combination of third-person narrative with Brian's interior monologue pulls the reader into the story."

Paulsen told *Writer's Digest* that he strives for a certain rhythm in his prose. "It changes with the subject," he said. "*Dogsong* is about a primitive thing, so it's written in a primitive way. It's more of a concept-driven book, so that the rhythms, the essences, are more important than they would be in *Hatchet*, which is more of a standard story. *Hatchet* is a story-driven book (to use a Hollywood term, which I hate to do), in which the story is as important as the concept. *Hatchet* is action and more action, and lots of things going on. It requires a more technical form of writing, whereas *Dogsong* is the smell of the wind. It's a different feel that I was after, so the two books are written differently."

A nonfiction counterpart is *Winterdance* (1994), in which he describes running sled dogs in the 1983 Iditarod race in Alaska.

The Monument takes place in Kansas grain country. Rachael Ellen Turner, known as Rocky, is curious when the town commissions an artist, Mick Strum, to create a memorial to the war dead. As she follows him around town, Rocky comes to see things—through Strum's drawings—that she did not know were there and that people do not want to see. The book makes fascinating statements about art, as Strum leads the diverse townspeople to accept an idea for a monument.

The Island is a reflective story of a fourteen-year-old boy, Wil Neuton, who moves with his parents to an isolated Wisconsin setting and discovers a small island drifting in a lake.

Paulsen has two ongoing series for middle readers, including one about young friends Amos and Dunc, the Culpepper Adventure series, whose humorous adventures range from coaching a local T-ball team to hang-gliding into the wilderness. (Amos, fortunately, has read a book about a boy who survived in the wilderness for fifty-four days; too bad he does not have a hatchet with him.)

Nightjohn, which Paulsen said is based on real events, is a stark yet inspiring story of a young girl slave, Sarny, on a southern plantation about a decade before the Civil War. She is fascinated by the scarred slave Nightjohn, who offers to trade alphabet letters for tobacco. She learns from him the rudiments of reading and writing—and the fearsome penalty that comes with it from the harsh slave master, Waller. *Nightjohn* is compellingly written, grim in history, rich in character.

Harris and Me is related by an unnamed boy, the son of alcoholic parents. Sent to spend the summer on his aunt and uncle's farm, the narrator meets an assortment of bizarre individuals, such as his cousin Glinnis, a teenager who is always slapping her brother, Harris, to keep him in line; dirty Louie, the hired man who carves little figures as a hobby; Ernie, the attack rooster; and Buzzer, the territorial barn cat.

Living at the farm means hard work and endless adventure. Harris, a latter-day Huck Finn, leads his cousin on military assaults on hogs, on gun-shooting horseback raids. It is hard to say no to Harris's schemes, but when his cousin breaks up the narrator's budding romance with a village girl, the narrator gets revenge in a wild wager: Will Harris pee on the live electric fence and risk getting zapped in a delicate place, in exchange for two dirty pictures?

"The farm life here is cruel, crude, and harsh with no nuances," said Carol Fox. "But there is also hilarity, untamed confidence, genuine concern for others, and a belief in goodness—one of the most optimistic fictional worlds to invite young visitors in a long while."

The book is written in economical, picaresque, and hilarious style, and the narrator is reminiscent of Paulsen.

Paulsen told *Writer's Digest* that his characters come from real people and from himself: "Yes, and people you meet, and people you know, and things you see and understand."

YOUNG ADULT FICTION

Some Birds Don't Fly (1968)

Mr. Tucket (1969, 1993)
Francis Alphonse Tucket, kidnapped from his Oregon Trail wagon train by Pawnees, is later taken in by a trapper, Jason Grimes.

Winterkill (1976)
In 1954 in a small Minnesota town, a thirteen-year-old boy is taken under the wing of an amoral, hard-bitten cop named Duda.

The Night the White Deer Died (1978)
In New Mexico, Janet, fifteen, lives a lonely life with her mother, a sculptor recently divorced. Then she meets an Indian, Peter Honcho, a wino who poses for tourist photos. They become close friends.

The Spitball Gang (1980)
Stu and Greg, cops who patrol a Denver ghetto, crack a series of bank robberies by a juvenile gang.

Dancing Carl (1983)
That winter in 1958, some said he was a bum and a drunk; some said he had escaped from an asylum; but none could deny Dancing Carl's power on the ice.

Popcorn Days and Buttermilk Nights (1983)
Carley, fourteen, a streetwise kid from Minneapolis, learns a new purpose in life while working with his Uncle David in a blacksmith shop in the country.

Tracker (1984)
John Borne, thirteen, looked forward to deer hunting with his grandfather, but this year, with his grandfather dying of cancer, he must hunt alone.

Dogsong (1985)
Russel Susskit took the old man Oogruk's dogs and sled and began a journey to the sea.

Sentries (1986)
Short stories.

The Crossing (1987)
In a Mexican border town, Manny is an orphan desperate to cross to the other side. He meets Robert, a sergeant who has found escape in a bottle.

The Hatchet (1987)
Traveling to visit his father in a remote part of Canada, Brian Robeson survives a plane crash and must make his way out of the wilderness using his brand-new hatchet.

The Island (1988)
Wil Neuton, fourteen, moves with his parents to Wisconsin's north woods. He discovers a small island adrift on a lake.

The Voyage of the Frog (1989)
David, fourteen, carries out his Uncle Owen's last wish and takes the twenty-two-foot boat *Frog* to sea to scatter his ashes.

The Winter Room (1989)
On a chilly winter night, Eldon and his brother, Wayne, listen to Uncle David's marvelous tale of the woodcutter.

Canyons (1990)
Coyote Runs, an Apache boy, takes part in his first raid, his first step into manhood. A hundred years later, Brennan Cole finds a skull and races through the canyon to return it to its sacred place.

The Boy Who Owned the School: A Comedy of Love (1991)
Jacob Freisten does not want to be noticed at school. Well, except maybe by Maria Tressor.

The Cookcamp (1991)
In 1944, Casey is sent to live with his grandmother, a cook for the men who are building a road from Minnesota into Canada.

The River (1991), sequel to *The Hatchet*
Brian is asked to teach his wilderness survival techniques to astronauts and the military. On a return trip, a freak storm hits, and he must carry a companion back to civilization.

The Haymeadow (1992)
John Barron, fourteen, must spend the summer with two horses and four dogs, tending 6,000 sheep.

The Car (1993)
Terry Anders, fourteen, assembles his own car from a kit and sets off from Cleveland to Portland to search for an uncle he barely remembers.

Harris and Me: A Summer Remembered (1993)
A boy participates in an escalating series of wild adventures on his cousin's farm one summer in the 1940s.

The Monument (1993)
Rocky follows the hired artist around town as he plans a memorial to the town's war dead.

Nightjohn (1993)
Sarny, a girl slave on the Waller plantation, learns the forbidden from Nightjohn—how to read and write.

Sisters Hermanas (1993)
Told in Spanish and English. Traci, fourteen, lives in an American suburb and, under her mother's pressure, tries out as a cheerleader. Rosa, fourteen, lives in Mexico City and yearns to emigrate out of her poverty.

Call Me Francis Tucket (1995), sequel to *Mr. Tucket*
More adventures on the Oregon Trail in the 1840s.

The Rifle (1995)
A flintlock rifle made two centuries earlier passes from owner to owner.

The Tent: A Parable in One Sitting (1995)
A Texas teenager and his father, desperately poor, steal a Bible, set up a tent, and become preachers.

FICTION FOR YOUNGER READERS

The CB Radio Caper (1977)

The Curse of the Cobra (1977)

The Foxman (1977)

The Golden Stick (1977)

Tiltawhirl John (1977)

The Green Recruit (1978) with Ray Peekner

Hope and a Hatchet (1978)

A Christmas Sonata (1992)

Dogteam (1993)

The Tortilla Factory (1995)

Culpepper Adventure Series

The Case of the Dirty Bird (1992)

Dunc's Doll (1992)

Culpepper's Cannon (1992)

Dunc Gets Tweaked (1992)

Dunc's Halloween (1992)

Dunc Breaks the Record (1992)

Dunc and the Flaming Ghost (1992)

Amos Gets Famous (1993)

Dunc and Amos Hit the Big Top (1993)

Dunc's Dump (1993)

Dunc and the Scam Artists (1993)

Dunc and Amos and the Red Tattoos (1993)

Dunc's Undercover Christmas (1993)

The Wild Culpepper Cruise (1993)

Dunc and the Haunted Castle (1993)

Cowpokes and Desperadoes (1994)

Prince Amos (1994)

Coach Amos (1994)

Amos and the Alien (1994)

Dunc and Amos Meet the Slasher (1994)

Dunc and the Greased Sticks of Doom (1994)

Amos's Killer Concert Caper (1995)

Amos Gets Married (1995)

Amos Goes Bananas (1995)

World of Adventure Series

Rodomonte's Revenge (1994)

Legend of Red Horse Cavern (1994)

Hook 'Em, Snotty (1994)

Danger on Midnight River (1994)

Gordon Slayer (1994)

Escape from Fire Mountain (1995)

Rock Jockeys (1995)

Danger on Midnight River (1995)

The Gorgon Slayer (1995)

Captive! (1995)

ADULT FICTION

The Death Specialists (1976)

The Implosion Effect (1976)

C. B. Jockey (1977)

The Sweeper (1980)

Compkill (1981)

Meteorite-Track 291 (1981)

Survival Guide (1981)

Clutterkill (1982)

The Meatgrinder (1984)

The Madonna Stories (1989)
Short stories.

Night Rituals: A Novel (1989)

Kill Fee: A Novel (1990)

Murphy Western Series

Murphy (1987)

Murphy's Gold (1988)

Murphy's Herd (1989)

Murphy's Ambush (1995) with Brian Burks

DRAMA

Communications (1974)
One-act play.

Together-Apart (1976)
One-act play.

FOR FURTHER READING

Bartky, Cheryl. "Write What You Are." *Writer's Digest*, July 1994.

Devereaux, Elizabeth. "Gary Paulsen." *Publishers Weekly*, 28 March 1994.

Fox, Carol. Review of *Harris and Me: A Summer Remembered. Bulletin of the Center for Children's Literature*, January 1994.

Kenney, Edwin J., Jr. Review of *The Island*. In *The New York Times Book Review*, 22 May 1988.

Paulsen, Gary. *Eastern Sun, Winter Moon: An Autobiographical Odyssey*. New York: Harcourt Brace Jovanovich, 1993.

———. *Father Water, Mother Woods: Essays on Fishing and Hunting in the North Woods*. New York: Delacorte Press, 1994.

Review of *The Hatchet*. *Kirkus Reviews*, 1 August 1987.

Richard Peck

Family drama

Decatur, Illinois
April 5, 1934
Blossom Culp Series

"I can only assume that the enduring [themes of young adult literature] will have nothing to do with the sexual revolution, the drug culture, and racial politics. The young now and in the future are not going to be able to solve these problems. It's a sickness from the '60s that we ever expected them to," Richard Peck said in *Literature for Today's Young Adults*.

"I imagine that the most acceptable new titles of the 1990s will be books about the sorrows of friendship and the painful necessity of growing up in a world new to no one but yourself. Books that include a little cautious nudge of optimism to offset what is blaring from a TV without an off knob. Books that invite the young to think for themselves instead of for each other."

Peck, the son of a merchant and a dietician, attended the University of Exeter in England, DePauw University, and Southern Illinois University. He did graduate work at Washington University in 1960–61. After his discharge from the U.S. Army, Peck taught college and high school English from 1958 to 1971. Then he began writing, with a ready supply of material from his teaching days.

Peck has received numerous awards for his works: the Edgar Allan Poe Award for best juvenile mystery, in 1976, for *Are You in the House Alone?*; the New York Times Outstanding Book of the Year, in 1977, for *Ghosts I Have Been*; the American Library Association Best Book for Young Adults, in 1981, for *Close Enough to Touch*; in 1985, for *Remembering the Good Times*; and in 1987, for *Princess Ashley*. He credits his storytelling ability to hearing old truck drivers, railroad workers, and farmers relating tales at his father's gas station.

"The old-timers had honed their stories with years of retelling and flavored them with tobacco juice," he told *Authors & Artists for Young Adults*. "The newspaper boys worked hard on their macho vocabulary and hoped to be believed. I was bombarded from both sides by the language of other generations, and from these rough tale-tellers I began to learn *style*."

Peck also found inspiration in Mark Twain. He wrote in *Horn Book Magazine*: "Huckleberry Finn never dies, and our books feature Hucks of both sexes, and often suburban. Sharing traits with the readers, they have to be imperfect enough for improvement and willing to stand up for who they are. They have to take one step nearer maturity in an age when maturing has become an elective, and show readers the way, give them the word."

"We never write about ordinary people," he continued. "Oh, there are inconvertible conformists and people running to type at the edges of our stories as a sort of Greek chorus, and all the peer-group leaders are hauntingly alike. But we celebrate rebels and rebels-to-be, Huck Finns looking for themselves and the way out of town. Young people who are beginning to run for their lives."

In his young adult fiction, Peck has written about such teenage issues as suicide, unwanted pregnancy, rape, and death. "As I'm typing I'm trying to look out over the typewriter and see faces," he told Roger Sutton. "I don't certainly want to 'write for myself' because I'm trying to write across a generation gap."

On the issue of censorship, Peck said in *Arkansas Libraries*: "A young adult book, in the minds of those who have never read many, is almost by definition a single-problem shocker on some harsh issue such as racial conflict, the drug culture, suicide, insanity, obesity, running away, or some other psychological, sociological, or sexual issue. Most of our books are neither that simple nor that easy. Growing up is not just one problem at a time. It is a great many, often quiet problems. Our books are mainly about human relationships, friendships, family life, and trying to grow up the best way you know how."

Peck's first young adult novel, *Don't Look and It Won't Hurt*, is about a girl who assumes the responsibility of visiting her pregnant sister in the hospital and persuading her to give up her illegitimate child. The story was based on the experiences of close friends of Peck, who took girls from a local facility for unwed mothers into their own suburban Chicago home.

His book *Are You in the House Alone?* was controversial. The story deals with a teenage girl who is raped and has to decide whether to face her attacker a second time, in a courtroom. In Peck's story, the victim remains a victim, and there is no happy ending. Michele Landsberg criticized the book for "playing on the fears of all young girls who baby-sit alone in other people's houses or answer the telephone to hear hoarse breathing," but then, after the rape, ignoring heroine Gail Osburne's rage, humiliation, and sense of violation. Landsberg further suggested that, since 1976, when it was written, rape victims no longer face such hostile and skeptical authorities: "Peck's careful realism is already dated, because he did not explore in any depth the wellsprings of prejudice encountered by a sexual victim," Landsberg said.

The decision faced by the seventeen-year-old hero of *Father Figure* is no easier than that of Gail Osburne. After their mother dies, Jim Atwater and his eight-year-old brother move in with the father they have never known. Jim becomes jealous of his father's growing bond with young Byron. Yet only by letting go can Jim move on to adulthood.

"It's a touching and brave novel, with rounded characters who are capable of surprising you, and with Peck's special gift: a devastatingly accurate eye for class distinctions, social styles, and affectation of dress and speech," Landsberg said.

Peck also writes humorous and supernatural stories, such as the Blossom Culp series about a girl ghost. "Blossom is one of several strong, adolescent female characters in Peck's novels," Hilary S. Crew wrote in *Twentieth-Century Children's Writers*. "The author portrays intelligent, resourceful girls, who are willing and able to make their own decisions and take on responsibilities, sometimes for others."

"This multilevel adventure tale is a quixotic mix," Diana L. Spirt said of *The Ghost Belonged to Me*. "On the surface, it is an exciting ghost story. Fundamentally, however, it is about a youngster's growing sense of his own adequacy because of the increasing unity between his imagination and his perception of reality. . . . The vivid touches that describe a boy's and girl's awareness of each other are human."

Peck has also edited several volumes of poetry and essays. He wrote a column on the architecture of historic city neighborhoods for *The New York Times* and contributed poetry to several anthologies and periodicals.

YOUNG ADULT FICTION

Don't Look and It Won't Hurt (1972)
A girl is pregnant, and her sister struggles to keep the family together.

Dreamland Lake (1973)
Brian and Flip discover a dead man in the woods behind Dreamland Lake.

Through a Brief Darkness (1973)
Karen, sixteen, is sent to England and loses touch with her father.

Representing Super Doll (1974)
Indiana farm girl Verna Henderson goes from Miss Hybrid Seed Corn to big-time beauty pageant queen.

Are You in the House Alone? (1976)
Gail is raped by the son of a prominent family in town—and no one believes her story.

Father Figure: A Novel (1978)
Jim Atwater's mother has committed suicide, and he and his younger brother must go live with a father they have never known.

Something for Joey (1978), based on a screenplay by Jerry McNeely
In 1973, while John Cappelletti is winning the Heisman trophy as outstanding American football player, his younger brother, Joey, is suffering from leukemia.

Secrets of the Shopping Mall (1979)
Two pursued teens hide by living in a suburban shopping mall.

Close Enough to Touch (1981)
Matt Moran, grieving over the loss of his first love, meets older, captivating Margaret Chasen.

Remembering the Good Times (1985)
A boy threatens to commit suicide, and his classmates do not tell anyone.

Princess Ashley (1987)
A tragic accident makes Ashley appreciate her guidance counselor mother.

Those Summer Girls I Never Met (1988)
Drew Wingate, sixteen, stuck on a cruise for senior citizens with his grandmother, meets Holly, the dance instructor.

Voices After Midnight: A Novel (1990)
Chad reluctantly ventures back in time.

Anonymously Yours (1991)

Unfinished Portrait of Jessica (1991)
Jessica blames her mother for her parents' divorce—until she spends time with her "perfect" father.

Bel-Air Bambi & the Mall Rats (1993)
Dad, a television producer, has gone bankrupt, and the Babcock sisters, Buffie and Bambi, suddenly find themselves in Nowheresville—Hickory Fork.

The Last Safe Place on Earth (1995)
A parent organization tries to ban books at a library.

Blossom Culp Series

The Ghost Belonged to Me: A Novel (1975)
In 1913 in Bluff City, Alexander Armsworth, thirteen, falls in love with the ghost of a southern belle and solves a mystery with the help of tenacious Blossom Culp.

Ghosts I Have Been: A Novel (1977)
Blossom, fourteen, discovers she has psychic powers.

The Dreadful Future of Blossom Culp (1983)
Is Blossom, now a high school student in 1914, stuck in a time warp?

Blossom Culp and the Sleep of Death (1986)
Blossom is haunted by an impetuous Egyptian princess and, with Alexander's help, tries to restore her to the throne.

CONTRIBUTOR

Sixteen: Short Stories by Outstanding Young Adult Writers, edited by Donald R. Gallo (1984)

Visions: Nineteen Short Stories by Outstanding Writers for Young Adults, edited by Donald R. Gallo (1987)

Connections: Short Stories by Outstanding Writers for Young Adults, edited by Donald R. Gallo (1989)

FICTION FOR YOUNGER READERS

Monster Night at Grandma's House (1977)

Lost in Cyberspace (1995)

ADULT FICTION

Amanda/Miranda (1980)

New York Time (1981)

This Family of Women (1983)

POETRY

Mindscapes: Poems for the Real World (1971)

ADAPTATIONS IN OTHER MEDIA

Are You in the House Alone? (1977)
Television movie starring Kathleen Beller and Scott Colomby.

Child of Glass (1979)
Television movie based on *The Ghost Belonged to Me.*

Father Figure (1980)
Film.

FOR FURTHER READING

Crew, Hilary S. "Richard Peck." In *Twentieth-Century Children's Writers,* edited by Tracy Chevalier. 3d ed. Chicago: St. James Press, 1989.

Donelson, Kenneth L., and Alleen Pace Nilsen, eds. "The People Behind the Books: Richard Peck." In *Literature for Today's Young Adults*. Glenview, IL: Scott, Foresman, 1980.

Landsberg, Michele. *Reading for the Love of It.* New York: Prentice Hall Press, 1987.

Peck, Richard. "Huck Finns of Both Sexes: Protagonists and Peer Leaders in Young-Adult Books." *Horn Book Magazine,* September–October 1993.

———. *Love and Death at the Mall: Teaching and Writing for the Literate Young*. New York: Delacorte Press, 1994.

———. "People of the Word." *Arkansas Libraries,* December 1981.

"Richard Peck." In *Authors & Artists for Young Adults,* edited by Agnes Garrett and Helga P. McCue. Vol. 1. Detroit: Gale Research, 1989.

Spirt, Diana L. *Introducing More Books: A Guide for the Middle Grades*. New York: R. R. Bowker, 1978.

Sutton, Roger. Interview with Richard Peck. *School Library Journal,* June 1990.

Robert Newton Peck

Rural drama

Vermont
February 17, 1928
A Day No Pigs Would Die

Family hardship forces a Vermont boy in the 1930s to give up his pet pig for slaughter in Robert Newton Peck's debut young adult novel, *A Day No Pigs Would Die*. In this and later works, the writer presents a strong sense of character and place. The father in *Pigs*, Peck said, was influenced by his own father, an illiterate farmer who offered earthy wisdom on a wide range of subjects.

"I wrote *A Day No Pigs Would Die* in twenty-one days," Peck said in *Authors & Artists for Young Adults*. "I had always wanted to write about my father but needed a way to bring the story line into focus. I finally realized that 'the pig' was it; it allowed me to bring out his honor and decency and special kind of sophistication. He was so knowledgeable about relationships in the natural order, and he accepted life for what it is—understanding its violence and its beauty."

"This episodic, autobiographical novel of a crucial year in a Vermont farm boy's life is wrapped firmly around the central theme of the relationship between father and son," Anne Scott MacLeod observed. "The language of the book is colloquial, the tone is warm and often humorous, yet the story deals with the fundamentals of life and death, growth and change, love and loss."

More than twenty years later, Peck wrote a sequel, *A Part of the Sky*. "Now that Rob's father is dead, the 13-year-old boy must take on the working of the small farm and the protection of his mother and elderly aunt," reviewer Hazel Rochman said. "He must become 'a Man.' He says so often. And lots of people tell him so: 'To grow up is to stand up. Manly.' " She found the book sentimental and less satisfying than *Pigs*.

Peck's *Arly* is about Arly Poole, a boy who lives in poverty with his picker father in Jailtown, presided over by Captain Tant. No one ever makes enough money to leave. Arly is almost old enough to start picking cotton himself. When a teacher comes to town and starts a school, he is one of the first students. Another student is Essie May Cooter, whose best prospects are to go to work in the town brothel. Both would like to escape Jailtown, but only Arly, with the teacher's help, succeeds.

The book captures a southern rural dialect and personality. It is often blunt. Miss Hoe, the teacher, asks Arly if he would like to borrow a handkerchief.

" 'You don't have a handkerchief?'

"I give her a grin. 'No, not me. Papa says that a poor man blows his snot on the ground, but a rich man puts it all back in his pocket.' "

The teacher inspires in Arly the spirit of learning, and he vows not to stop once he leaves Jailtown.

The youngest of seven children of a Vermont farming couple, Peck was the first in his family to learn to read and write. He attended a one-room rural schoolhouse and went on to Rollins College and Cornell University as a law student. Peck served with the U.S. Army from 1945 to 1947 in Italy, Germany, and France. He married Dorothy Houston in 1958. (Fred Rogers of television's *Mr. Rogers* was his best man.) Peck and his wife have two children.

Besides a string of novels, Peck has written a comic series about a Vermont boy named Soup. "As a farmer turned author, what I miss most of my Vermont boyhood is my work . . . haying, chores, helping Mama and Papa, and strong, silent men doing heavy labor. Tending the green and the growing . . ." Peck said in *Literature for Today's Young Adults*. "Boyhood wasn't all work. My best pal, Soup, and I really tore up the pea patch, as rascals. Yet our fervent respect of Miss Kelly (our teacher) always kept us straight as a fence. We believed in her. More importantly, she believed in us."

"I make a dandy character in several of my books," Peck said in *Fiction Is Folks*. "I put myself in them all the time. . . . All the Soup books are written in the first person, strictly from little Rob's point of view. The readers see and hear Soup through only Rob's eyes and ears; a reader is never allowed to know what Soup is thinking, feeling, or scheming. That was, in real life, the way we horsed around.

"He started trouble. I took the rap. Rob Peck, in the books, is merely the fall-guy shadow, the drag rider behind the herd, a recording

Boswell to a dominating Johnson, a Watson for Holmes, a Laurel for Hardy.

"It's not great literature; but for kids, it works. And it's so much fun to write a Soup book, because all I have to do is remember the joy, and agony, of being the richest boy on Earth. . . . one who has a best pal."

Peck frequently includes music and song in his stories; he belongs to a barbershop quartet and plays ragtime piano, self-taught.

YOUNG ADULT FICTION

A Day No Pigs Would Die (1972)
Hardship forces a New England boy to give up his pet pig for slaughter.

Millie's Boy (1973)
Tit Smith, sixteen, searches for the one who killed his mother.

Fawn, A Novel (1975)
In 1758 at Fort Ticonderoga, Fawn, the son of a scholarly French Jesuit and grandson of a fierce Mohawk warrior, takes no sides.

Wild Cat (1975)

Hamilton (1976)

Hang for Treason (1976)
Vermont in the days of the American Revolution.

Last Sunday (1977)

Patooie (1977)

Mr. Little (1978)
Drag and Finley are the worst practical jokers in the town of Sikeria—and their latest target is the new teacher.

Basket Case (1979)

Clunie (1979)
Only one person is willing to stand up for a retarded girl.

Hub (1979)
"Hub" Hubert wants his teacher, Miss Guppy, to win the big bicycle race.

Justice Lion (1981)
In Vermont during Prohibition, Muncie Bolt is the son of a lawyer who defends Justice Lion's son against a murder charge.

Kirk's Law (1981)
Kicked out of prep school, Collin Pepper is sent to live with an old man in Vermont named Wishbone Kirk.

Dukes (1984)

Jo Silver (1985)

Spanish Hoof (1985)
The Beechers run a Florida cattle ranch. Dab is in love, Harry has a new pony, and Mama hopes to pay off the bank soon.

Arly (1989)
A teacher brings progressive ideas to Jailtown, ideas the plantation supervisor does not welcome. Young Arly Poole, through his learning, has a chance to escape.

A Part of the Sky (1994), sequel to *A Day No Pigs Would Die*
His father now dead, thirteen-year-old Rob heads the household during the Great Depression.

FICTION FOR YOUNGER READERS

Rabbits and Redcoats (1976)

Banjo (1982)

Higbee's Halloween (1990)

Soup Series

Soup (1974)

Soup and Me (1975)

Soup for President (1978)

Soup's Drum (1980)

Soup on Wheels (1981)

Soup in the Saddle (1983)

Soup's Goat (1984)

Soup on Ice (1985)

Soup on Fire (1987)

Soup's Uncle (1988)

Soup's Hoop (1989)

Soup in Love (1992)

Soup Ahoy (1994)

Soup 1776 (1995)

Little Soup Series

Little Soup's Birthday (1991)

Little Soup's Hayride (1991)

Little Soup's Turkey (1992)

Little Soup's Bunny (1993)

Trig Series

Trig (1977)

Trig Sees Red (1978)

Trig Goes Ape (1980)

Trig or Treat (1982)

POETRY

Bee Tree and Other Stuff (1975)

King of Kazoo (1976)
A musical.

ADULT FICTION

The Happy Sadist (1962)

The King's Iron (1977)

Eagle Fur (1978)

The Seminole Seed (1983)

Hallapoosa (1988)

The Horse Hunters (1988)

ADAPTATIONS IN OTHER MEDIA

Soup (1978)
Television movie.

Soup and Me (1978)
Television movie.

Soup for President (1978)
Television movie.

Mr. Little
Television movie.

FOR FURTHER READING

Donelson, Kenneth L., and Alleen Pace Nilsen, eds. "The People Behind the Books: Robert Newton Peck." *Literature for Today's Young Adults*. Glenview, IL: Scott, Foresman, 1980.

MacLeod, Anne Scott. "Robert Newton Peck." In *Twentieth-Century Children's Writers*, edited by Tracy Chevalier. 3d ed. Chicago: St. James Press, 1989.

Peck, Robert Newton. *Fiction Is Folks: How to Create Unforgettable Characters*. Cincinnati, OH: Writer's Digest Books, 1983.

———. *Secrets of Successful Fiction*. Cincinnati, OH: Writer's Digest Books, 1980.

"Robert Newton Peck." In *Authors & Artists for Young Adults*, edited by Agnes Garrett and Helga P. McCue. Vol. 3. Detroit: Gale Research, 1990.

Rochman, Hazel. "After Happily Ever After." *The New York Times Book Review*, 13 November 1994.

Susan Beth Pfeffer

Romance

Family drama

New York City
February 17, 1948
About David

Susan Beth Pfeffer writes about teenage girls struggling with problems ranging from leaving friends behind when the family moves to coping with a missing brother. Her Sebastian Sisters series looks at family ties and romance. Her Make Me a Star series follows the adventures of six young people appearing in a television series.

Most of the characters in Pfeffer's books are from the middle-class America of Queens and Long Island, New York, where she grew up. Her father was a constitutional lawyer and later a professor at Long Island University. Her mother was a secretary who frequently took Pfeffer and her older brother, Alan, to the city to visit the planetarium and museums. The family had a summer home in the Catskills.

Pfeffer received a bachelor of arts degree in 1969 from New York University. She wrote her first book at age twenty, during her final semester in college. At the time, she was taking seventeen credits, nearly failing one class, and having a lot of dental work done. Still, she wrote five pages a day, five days a week, until she had completed a manuscript.

Pfeffer's books have at times drawn opposite reactions from reviewers. *Rainbows and Fireworks*, for example, troubled Marianne Jacobbi, who was dismayed by an "attempt at non-conformism" through characters such as "artistic parents who write pornography, their children who are independent and free-thinking." Conversely, Marilyn R. Singer approved of "the freshness of the situation and characters in this light, fast-moving novel about a pleasantly Bohemian family."

Reviewers found a freshness of plot and sprightliness of writing in Pfeffer's *The Beauty Queen* and its sequel, *Marly the Kid*. Susan Zaretsky said that *The Beauty Queen* offers teenage readers "a fresh plot, for one thing, fast-moving, easy-to-read, well-written prose for another; and a character who is interesting throughout."

The Beauty Queen is about Katherine "Kit" Carson, who is pushed into beauty pageant competition by her divorced, overbearing mother. She wins the local contest but rebels and decides to leave home to pursue her own career interests.

In *Marly the Kid*, Kit's younger, overweight sister, Marly, also has had it with her mother's acid tongue and moves in with her father and stepmother. Her stepmother becomes very supportive as Marly adjusts to her new life and gets in trouble in school for speaking back to a sexist teacher.

About David is one of Pfeffer's more controversial works. The heroine, Lynn, is shocked to find the police surrounding the home of her close friend, David. He went into a rage and killed his adoptive parents and himself. Lynn, numb and greatly troubled, tries to figure out what it means to herself and others. With the help of a patient boyfriend and the school psychologist, she emerges from her shock. The book was used in a suicide prevention program in several school systems but was removed from school library shelves in another.

"A teenager would not be likely to want to read many books with *About David*'s theme or impact, but this volume serves well," John Lansingh Bennett said. "With luck it may add a measure of empathy, some slight understanding of grief and how it passes, a touch of humanity to its teen readers."

"I wrote *About David* because I wanted to portray an unimaginable disaster that was peculiarly teenage, and I wanted to concentrate on the reactions of the survivors. One way people react is to get angry and swear and to question the existence of God," Pfeffer stated in *Authors & Artists for Young Adults*. "But these censorship incidents happen in the strangest ways in school systems that you cannot predict in any way. It's just not something I can worry about."

YOUNG ADULT FICTION

Just Morgan (1970)
A newly orphaned girl spends her first summer in New York with her guardian.

Better Than All Right (1972)
Sophisticated Iris Levin is expected to take her fourteen-year-old cousin, Caryn, under her wing while they visit an upstate New York resort.

Rainbows and Fireworks (1973)
Betsy Reisman, sixteen, has to leave best friends behind when her family moves to rural Pennsylvania.

The Beauty Queen (1974)
"Kit" Carson's mother forces her to enter a beauty contest. When she wins, her boyfriend urges her to run away before the state contest and pursue an acting career.

Whatever Words You Want to Hear (1974)
The summer before starting Princeton, Paula meets Jonny Stapleton and his troubled brother, Jordan, with whom she has her first sexual experience.

Marly the Kid (1975), sequel to *The Beauty Queen*
Marly follows her older sister's lead and leaves their nagging mother to live with her more understanding father and stepmother. She then gets in trouble in school by challenging a sexist teacher.

Starring Peter and Leigh: A Novel (1978)
Leigh Thorpe, sixteen, looks forward to her new home in suburban Long Island after being a child actress in hectic Los Angeles.

About David (1980)
Seventeen-year-old Lynn is shocked when her friend, David, kills his parents and himself. She copes with her grief and anger.

Starting with Melodie (1982)
Elaine tells the story of her friend, Melodie, whose famous actress mother and big-director father are divorcing.

Courage, Dana (1983)
A twelve-year-old saves the life of a child in the path of a car.

Truth or Dare (1983)
Sixth-grader Cathy Wakefield tries to make sophisticated Jessica her friend.

Fantasy Summer (1984)
Four girls become interns at snazzy *Image* magazine: Robin from Ohio, Anne from Massachusetts, Ashley from Missouri, and Torey from the Catskills.

Paper Dolls (1984)
Bored with school and her suburban life, sixteen-year-old Laurie Caswell's fantasy comes true: She gets to try out as a teen model.

Getting Even (1987), sequel to *Fantasy Summer*
Anne Powell begins an awful senior year at a Boston high school.

The Year Without Michael (1987)
Fifteen-year-old Jody Chapman's younger brother, Michael, disappears.

Dear Dad, Love Laurie (1989)
Laurie lives with her mom, who is divorced from her dad, and she keeps him posted on her activities with weekly letters.

Head of the Class (1989), based on the television series
Honors Program students at Fillmore High get a substitute teacher who does not know what exceptions have been made for the gifted.

Most Precious Blood (1991)
Cousin Michelle tells Val a family secret: "You're adopted."

Family of Strangers (1992)
Abby Talbott is the youngest of three sisters in a dysfunctional family.

Make Believe (1993)

The Ring of Truth (1993)
Sloan Fredericks, sixteen, creates a stir when she accuses a politician of making a pass at her.

Twice Taken (1994)
A sixteen-year-old recognizes the face of her father on a call-in television program about missing children.

Nobody's Daughter (1995)
Eleven-year-old Emily Lathrop Hasbrouck is sent to an orphanage after her aunt dies.

Make Me a Star Series

Prime Time (1985)
Miranda, a student with no acting experience, and T. J., a former child star, are among six teenagers auditioning for a new television series.

Take Two and . . . Rolling (1985)
Molly is tough and lonely, a child star who has known little of normal life.

On the Move (1985)

Hard Times High (1986)

Love Scenes (1986)

Wanting It All (1986)

Sebastian Sisters Series

Evvie at Sixteen (1988)
Evvie spends the summer as companion to her rich great-aunt Grace.

Thea at Sixteen (1988)
Thanks to dad's wheeling and dealing, the Sebastian family is sometimes rich, sometimes poor.

Claire at Sixteen (1989)
An old photo reveals a dark family secret. Claire seeks the information that can help her sister, Sybil, walk again.

Sybil at Sixteen (1989)
Claire blackmails relatives into paying Sybil's medical bills.

Meg at Sixteen (1990)
The mother of the Sebastian girls tells of her young adulthood.

CONTRIBUTOR

Connections: Short Stories by Outstanding Writers for Young Adults, edited by Donald R. Gallo (1989)

FICTION FOR YOUNGER READERS

Kid Power (1977)

Awful Evelina (1979)

Just Between Us (1980)

What Do You Do When Your Mouth Won't Open? (1981)

A Matter of Principle: A Novel (1982)

Kid Power Strikes Back (1984), sequel to *Kid Power*

The Friendship Pact (1986)

Rewind to Yesterday (1988)

Turning Thirteen (1988)

Dear Dad, Love Laurie (1989)

Future Forward (1989)

April Upstairs (1990)

Darcy Downstairs (1990)

Twin Surprises (1991)

Twin Troubles (1992)

Make Believe (1993)

The Riddle Streak (1993)

Sara Kate SuperKid Series

Sara Kate, SuperKid (1994)

Sara Kate Saves the World (1995)

FOR FURTHER READING

Bennett, John Lansingh. Review of *About David*. *Best Sellers*, November 1980.

Jacobbi, Marianne. Review of *Rainbows and Fireworks*. *Children's Book Review Service*, July 1973.

Pendergast, Tom. "Susan Beth Pfeffer." In *Authors & Artists for Young Adults*, edited by Kevin S. Hile. Vol. 12. Detroit: Gale Research, 1994.

Singer, Marilyn R. Review of *Rainbows and Fireworks*. *School Library Journal*, September 1973.

Zaretsky, Susan. Review of *The Beauty Queen*. *Children's Book Review Service*, August 1974.

Christopher Pike

Suspense

Brooklyn, New York
?
Chain Letter

Christopher Pike has been hailed as the "junior Stephen King." He writes suspense and horror fiction with teenage heroes, on themes ranging from revenge killings to ghosts to vampires.

Pike is not the writer's real name but a pen name, taken from a character in the pilot movie for the *Star Trek* television series. (Pike was the captain later replaced by James Kirk.) Pike's publisher will not release his identity; however, *Children's Literature Review* has identified Pike as Kevin McFadden. The reference book does not offer any further biographical information.

If we are to believe the biographies printed in recent Pike paperback novels, Pike was born in Brooklyn, New York. He grew up and still lives in Los Angeles. His hobbies include astronomy, meditating, running, and playing with his nieces and nephews.

A college dropout, he was a factory worker, a house painter, and a computer programmer before taking up writing. He tried writing adult mystery and science fiction. A book editor suggested he instead tackle a teen thriller. His first young adult book was *Slumber Party*, which was so popular he quickly produced two more: *Chain Letter* and *Weekend*.

The popularity of Pike's young adult novels stems from his keen plot hooks. He likes violent themes and graphic descriptions. He is perceptive about such teen issues as alienation, humiliation, drug abuse, and dating. Although his characters' problems are average, often their solutions are not; they may go beyond what is socially acceptable, to violence.

"I did sort of fall into writing for teens," Pike told Sarah Verney, "but I think I've stayed with it, not just because of the money, but because I have a very romantic idea of high school. I guess I'm very nostalgic."

The author said in a teachers' guide by Claudia Keeton, "I enjoy writing young adult novels. Teenagers are the most flexible characters to work with. They can act like mature adults as readily as spoiled kids. Teenagers generally feel much more intensely: love and loyalty, hate and revenge. In the mystery thrillers I specialize in, this intensity of feeling is crucial.

"Too often, young adult books are written down to the kids. The authors seem to feel that teenagers are only worried about getting a date for the prom and wearing the latest fashion. These things are important to teenagers, sure, but so are a lot of other things."

Although recognizing Pike's "veneer of sophistication," critics such as Adrian Jackson found that *Chain Letter* and *Spellbound* make "a few demands on logic and thought." Linda Newbery found *Slumber Party* "crude, stilted, sexist, violent and unconvincing." "These books are not Newbery Award contenders," Amy Gamerman said, "but even librarians find them hard to dismiss."

Zeroing in on what makes the books so popular, Tom Engelhardt suggested, "In these books of muted torture, adults exist only as distant figures of desertion; ET—the extraterrestrial teenager—does not call home, and junior-grade psychos reign supreme. If sex never proceeds beyond The Kiss, no mutilation is too terrible for the human face."

Teenagers, often female, narrate the Pike thrillers. The writer told *Publishers Weekly*, "I romanticize a lot about females because they seem more complex, and because in horror novels, it's easier for the girl to seem scared." Some of Pike's books are straight suspense and crime; others contain elements of the supernatural or the occult. Although his prose is at times crude, his characterizations have sufficient depth to interest the reader.

Die Softly has a voyeuristic theme. Herb Trasker takes secret pictures of cheerleaders in their school locker room. One of the cheerleaders mocks the portfolio photos he takes for her and refuses to pay his costs. He shrugs it off, but his frumpy friend, Sammie, has her own reasons for not liking the cheerleaders. She suggests that Herb install a timer on his camera and take pictures of them coming out of the showers. He does, and ends up with photos of Lisa just hours before she dies in an accident when her car goes over a cliff. Developing his film, Herb is shocked to see Lisa—and a shadowy figure sneaking up on her with a baseball bat!

The Midnight Club is a book that cannot have a happy ending. All the characters live at Rotterham Home, a hospice for terminally ill young people. Five of the patients begin meeting late at night and form the Midnight Club. Ilonka has stomach tumors. Anya has bone cancer. Sandra has a serious disease. Kevin suffers from leukemia, and Spence has AIDS. They tell each other stories, of horror and intrigue, of life and death. The tales are made up but are populated with strikingly familiar characters. As the characters begin dying, one by one, they make a pact: They will try to communicate with the living.

Pike gives detailed descriptions of photography and darkroom work in *Die Softly*. In *The Midnight Club* he explains at length the various painkillers and medicines taken by the teens. In blunt language, he offers an unrelenting depiction of teens with no future. Yet, in the end, he finds rays of hope within their despair. The book, Pike told Verney, was inspired by a fan who was dying of cancer. Pike and his fan spoke on the phone and shared thoughts on death and dying.

Pike said in Keeton's teachers' guide that he has been influenced by several writers. "I very much follow S. E. Hinton's philosophy of creating a world where teenagers can act without the intrusion of adult authority. I read Agatha Christie throughout high school and still believe there is nothing like a good mystery with a major twist at the end. And my all-time favorite writer, Stephen King, has taught me that people love to read about scary things happening to people they strongly identify with."

Critics are not particularly fond of the Pike books. Amy Gamerman in the *Wall Street Journal* called his suspense novels "gorier than most." She admitted, though, that Pike yanks the reader into the story and gives each book its own identity. In *The New York Times Book Review*, James Hirsch credited Pike and others with addressing topics that interest young adult readers, such as adolescent suicide and mental illness.

YOUNG ADULT FICTION

Slumber Party (1985)
Six teenage girls strike off for a remote cabin adventure that ends in romantic rivalry, strange disappearances, and death.

Chain Letter (1986)
Six high school friends share a guilty secret involving a car accident—and now they are receiving mysterious and demanding letters.

Weekend (1986)
Months ago, Robin was poisoned at a drunken party. She suffered permanent kidney damage. Now every teen who attended the party has been invited to spend the weekend at Robin's family beach house in Mexico.

Gimme a Kiss (1989)
Jane Retton will not let anyone read her diary—then it shows up at school.

Last Act (1989)
Melanie, a new girl in town, tries out for a play—and discovers a body.

Scavenger Hunt (1989)
Senior class members search for artifacts that lead to a haunted past.

Spellbound (1989)
No one believes Jason Whitfield when he says a bear killed Karen Holly.

Fall into Darkness (1990)
Did Ann jump from the cliff, or was she pushed?

See You Later (1990)
Mark goes to extremes to make Becky break up with her boyfriend.

Witch (1990)
Julia uses her supernatural powers to prevent a vision from coming true.

Bury Me Deep (1991)
The boy sitting next to the heroine on an airplane chokes and dies, then returns to life in her dreams.

Die Softly (1991)
Herb's hidden camera in the cheerleaders' locker room reveals more than he bargains for.

Whisper of Death (1991)
Everyone in town has disappeared, except Roxanne and four others who were involved in Betty Sue's suicide.

Chain Letter 2: The Ancient Evil (1992), sequel
Fran refuses to follow instructions in a chain letter and dies.

Master of Murder (1992)
No one knows Marvin writes best-selling stories—until mysterious fan letters begin arriving.

Monster (1992)
Mary takes a shotgun to a party; is she crazy or is something else happening?

The Eternal Enemy (1993)
Rela learns tomorrow's news from her VCR.

The Immortal (1993)
Vacationing in Greece, Josie finds an old artifact that begins to haunt her.

Road to Nowhere (1993)
Runaway Teresa picks up two unusual hitchhikers.

The Wicked Heart (1993)
Dusty is a high school senior—and a serial killer.

The Midnight Club (1994)
Five teens at a hospice for the terminally ill make a pact.

The Lost Mind (1995)
She awoke in the woods beside a dead body.

The Visitor (1995)
A teenager is a nice guy—or is he?

Cheerleaders Series

Getting Even (1985)
Will jealousy tear apart members of the Tarenton cheerleading squad?

Final Friends Series

The Party (1989)
A get-to-know-you party has been arranged for two recently merged high schools. An uninvited guest turns up—and Alice McCoy, who arranged the party, is dead.

The Dance (1989)
Michael Olson is not convinced that Alice killed herself.

The Graduation (1989)
Six months after the homecoming dance, Olson must complete his investigation and let Jessica Hart know his feelings for her.

Last Vampire Series

The Last Vampire (1994)
A 5,000-year-old vampire poses as a high school student.

The Last Vampire 2: Black Blood (1994)
Alisa and her partner, Ray, think they are the last vampires. Then they hear reports of brutal killings that could only be the work of other vampires.

The Last Vampire 3: Red Dice (1995)
Someone has discovered the secret of Alisa and her partner, and they want blood samples to duplicate.

Remember Me Trilogy

Remember Me (1989)
Shari Cooper's ghost comes back to solve her murder.

Remember Me 2: The Return (1994)
Killed by an attacker, Shari Cooper gets an unusual opportunity to return to life in the body of a depressed teenage girl.

Remember Me 3: The Last Story (1995)
The ghost Shari, who has a gift for storytelling, crafts a mystical blueprint that warns of great danger to humanity.

FICTION FOR YOUNGER READERS

Spooksville Series

1. *The Secret Path* (1995)
2. *The Howling Ghost* (1995)

ADULT FICTION

The Tachyon Web (1986)

Sati (1991)
Claiming she is God, Sati changes the lives of those around her.

The Season of Passage (1993)

The Cold One (1994)
The Cold One is an ancient evil, existing only to destroy mankind. Los Angeles police investigate a string of gruesome deaths. Journalist Peter Jacobs checks out an anonymous tip. Student Julie Moore falls in love with Peter.

The Listeners (1995)
Suspecting a conspiracy, FBI agent David Conner investigates the Listeners, a group of channelers with access to highly classified information.

FOR FURTHER READING

Alderdice, Kit. "Archway Launches Christopher Pike Novels in Multi-Book Contract." *Publishers Weekly*, 29 April 1988.

Engelhardt, Tom. "Reading May Be Harmful to Your Kids: In the Nadirland of Today's Children's Books." *Harper's*, June 1991.

Gamerman, Amy. "Gnarlatious Novels: Lurid Thrillers for the Teen Set." *Wall Street Journal*, 28 May 1991.

Hirsch, James. "Nancy Drew Gets Real." *The New York Times Book Review*, 9 October 1988.

Jackson, Adrian. Review of *Spellbound* and *Chain Letter. Books for Keeps*, November 1989.

Keeton, Claudia. *Teacher's Guide to Young Adult Mystery/Horror Best-Sellers*. New York: Archway Paperbacks, 1991.

Newbery, Linda. Review of *Slumber Party* and *Remember Me. Books for Keeps*, November 1990.

Verney, Sarah. "Christopher Pike." In *Authors & Artists for Young Adults*, edited by Kevin S. Hile and E. A. DesChenes. Vol. 13. Detroit: Gale Research, 1994.

Janet Quin-Harkin

Romance

Family drama

Bath, England
September 24, 1941

Sugar and Spice Series

Janet Quin-Harkin's young adult novels are lighthearted depictions of friendships, romance, and growing up. The four Friends books, for example, follow young Tess and Ali over four summers. Will their friendship survive growing up?

"What's the matter with you this summer? You're no fun anymore," Tess tells Ali when a third acquaintance threatens their relationship in *Tess & Ali and the Teeny Bikini*. "You're either worrying or you're sulking." "Okay," Ali replies. "Maybe I'm just immature, but I don't want to hang around with Jasmine anymore. I guess you can't be friends with both of us."

Born Janet Newcombe, the daughter of an engineer and a teacher, the author received a bachelor of arts degree from the University of London in 1963. She did graduate studies at the University of Kiel and the University of Freiburg, in Germany.

She was a studio manager in the drama department for the British Broadcasting Corporation in London from 1963 to 1966. During this time she wrote radio and television plays such as *Dandelion Hours*, about a small boy who befriends a hobo on a bomb site.

In 1966, she immigrated to the United States. She married John Quin-Harkin, whom she had met while in Australia working for the Australian Broadcasting Company. They have four children. Quin-Harkin has been an instructor in dance and drama since 1971. She has taught an advanced writing seminar at Dominican College in San Rafael, California, where she lives.

Her first effort at writing for young readers was for a series of school texts, followed by stories for children. Her first, *Peter Penny's Dance*, received several awards, including *The New York Times* Outstanding Book of the Year in 1976. She hired a literary agent who recommended that she write for young adults. Her *California Girl* launched Bantam Books' Sweet Dreams series, which was very popular because of its depictions of everyday people and activities.

Quin-Harkin produces a book every two months, in series such as On Our Own. In an interview, the writer said she tired of doing the Sugar and Spice series after six books but was forced to continue by publisher demand. A typical story line for this particular series is *Two Girls, One Boy*, in which Caroline is thrilled that a long-lost cousin, Chrissy, is coming to spend a year with her family. Caroline is reserved and polite, an only child, and she finds it hard to suddenly share her life with a loud, unsophisticated farm girl—especially when Chrissy begins spending a lot of time with Caroline's boyfriend, Alex.

Each book in the Heartbreak Cafe series, the author said, focuses on different characters and their problems and was more enjoyable to write. The Heartbreak Cafe books were inspired by the years Quin-Harkin spent on the Australian beach with sunbathers and surfers. Other books have been thoroughly researched, she said, whether set in Iowa or Australia.

YOUNG ADULT FICTION

Write Every Day (1982)
Kim is the misfit in her athletic family when she meets Brian, but this summer's camping trip to the mountains may not be so bad.

The Truth About Me and Bobby V (1983) as Janetta Johns

Tommy Loves Tina (1984)

Winner Takes All (1984)

Wanted: Date for Saturday Night (1985)
Everyone expects Julie Klein to bring her dream date to the freshman formal. When her cousin, Danny, whom she plans to pass off as her college boyfriend, does not show up, she gets desperate.

Fool's Gold (1991)

Amazing Grace (1993)

The Apartment (1994)
Toya's boyfriend walks out, leaving her with an empty apartment and a mountain of bills. Moving in are Sharon, who has just lost her mother, and Dorothy, who has run away from home to pursue a career in dance.

The Sutcliffe Diamonds (1994)
In love with someone her family hates, Laura Sutcliffe is banished to England, where she begins a quest for a lost inheritance.

Boyfriend Club Series

Ginger's First Kiss (1994)
The first assignment for the Boyfriend Club at Alta Mesa High: Hold a blowout party at Justine's house and give Ginger a new image.

Roni's Dream Boy (1994)
Roni holds a sort of seance with her friends, and pictures a cute new boyfriend.

Karen's Perfect Match (1994)

Queen Justine (1994)

Ginger's New Crush (1994)

Roni's Two-Boy Trouble (1994)

Changes Romance Series

Numbers 2–9 were by different authors.

1. *My Phantom Love* (1992)
10. *On My Own* (1992)

Friends Series

Starring Tess & Ali (1991)
Tess Neville and Alison Hinkle are best friends.

Tess & Ali and the Teeny Bikini (1991)
All of a sudden, Tess acts like a big phony to impress boy-crazy Jasmine.

Boy Trouble for Tess & Ali (1991)
Tess finds herself falling in love with Ali's brother, Josh.

Tess & Ali, Going on Fifteen (1991)

Heartbreak Cafe Series

No Experience Required (1990)

The Main Attraction (1990)

At Your Service (1990)
When the boss hires his girlfriend as second waitress at the Heartbreak Cafe, it disrupts Debbie Lesley's routine.

Catch of the Day (1990)
The Mexican girl falls in love with the lifeguard who saved her life, but her strict family and his prejudiced friends make things difficult.

Love to Go (1990)
A mysterious runaway takes refuge at the Heartbreak Cafe, and waitress Debbie is sure she is up to no good.

Just Desserts (1990)
When Joe decides to sell the cafe to developers, Debbie is in shock.

On Our Own Series

The Graduates (1986)

The Trouble with Toni (1986)

Out of Love (1986)

Old Friends, New Friends (1986)

Growing Pains (1986)

Best Friends Forever (1986)

Portraits Series

Summer Heat (1990)

Senior Year Series

Homecoming Dance (1991)

New Year's Eve (1991)

Night of the Prom (1992)

Graduation Day (1992)
Becky cannot stand Kyle, who disrupts class with his pranks—but she is about to flunk shop class, and she must let him bail her out.

Sugar and Spice Series

Two Girls, One Boy (1987)
Caroline is thrilled to find she has a long-lost cousin exactly her age, but she is horrified when Chrissy comes to spend a year with her family.

Flip Side (1987)
Two friends really like each other's boyfriends better than their own.

Tug of War (1987)

Surf's Up (1987)

The Last Dance (1987)

Nothing in Common (1987)

Dear Cousin (1987)
Chrissy is the new lonely-hearts columnist for the school paper.

Trading Places (1987)
Chrissy tries to impress wealthy Hunter with her "sophistication."

Double Take (1988)

Make Me a Star (1988)

Big Sister (1988)
Chrissy tries to straighten out younger brother Will when he becomes involved with the wrong crowd.

Out in the Cold (1988)
Chrissy and her younger brother, Will, finally come to terms.

Blind Date (1988)

It's My Turn (1988)

Home Sweet Home (1988)

Dream Come True (1988)

Campus Cousins (1989)

Roadtrip (1989)

One Step Too Far (1989)
Volunteer tutoring at a prison, Caroline is attracted to one of the inmates.

Having a Ball (1989)

Sweet Dreams Series

California Girl (1981)
A girl training as an Olympics swimmer moves to Texas, but she does not fit in until she meets a boy whose football career is over because of an injury.

Love Match (1982)

Ten-Boy Summer (1982)

Daydreamer (1983)

The Two of Us (1984)

Exchange of Hearts (1984)

Ghost of a Chance (1984)

Lovebirds (1984)

101 Ways to Meet Mr. Right (1985)

The Great Boy Chase (1985)
In France, Jill meets attractive boys and gets into humorous situations.

Follow That Boy (1985)

My Secret Love (1986)

My Best Enemy (1987)

Never Say Goodbye (1987)

FICTION FOR YOUNGER READERS

Peter Penny's Dance (1976)

Benjamin's Balloon (1979)

Septimus Bean and His Amazing Machine (1980)

Magic Growing Powder (1981)

Helpful Hattie (1983)

Billy and Ben: The Terrible Two (1992)

TGIF Series

1. *Sleepover Madness* (1995)

CONTRIBUTOR

Chandler Reading Program, edited by Lawrence Carillo and Dorothy McKinley (5 vols., 1967–72)

ADULT FICTION

Madam Sarah (1990)

Fool's Gold (1991)

FOR FURTHER READING

Hunter, Chris. "Janet Quin-Harkin." In *Authors & Artists for Young Adults*, edited by Agnes Garrett and Helga P. McCue. Vol. 6. Detroit: Gale Research, 1991.

Ann Rinaldi

Historical drama

New York City
August 27, 1934

A Break with Charity: A Story About the Salem Witch Trials

Ann Rinaldi writes young adult novels with historical settings, including three that take place during the American Revolution.

A Break with Charity depicts the hysteria of the infamous witch trials in colonial Massachusetts. When her parents are imprisoned, accused of being witches, Susanna English struggles with guilt. She knows the real reason that several girls have made accusations about her folks.

"The story is threaded around Susanna's personal struggle with guilt as she discovers the deadly intent of the accusing girls and is made fearful when she attempts to reason with them," Margaret A. Bush said. "The author's skillful manipulation of conventions of the young-adult novel—particularly the rich exploration of being an outsider and going against the mainstream—makes this book a superb vehicle for examining the social dynamics of this legendary event."

Ann Feis, whose father was a newspaper manager, attended high school in New Brunswick, New Jersey. In 1960, she married Ronald P. Rinaldi, a chief lineman for Public Service Gas & Electric. They have two children.

Rinaldi worked for twenty-one years as a columnist, feature writer, and editorial writer for the Trenton, New Jersey, *Trentonian*. She has won numerous awards for her columns and her historical novels: the American Library Association Best Books for Young

Adults, in 1986, for *Time Enough for Drums*, and in 1991 for *Wolf by the Ears*. She also lectures.

In 1979, Rinaldi reworked a short story into her first young adult novel, *Term Paper*. It is about a teenager who is working on an English class assignment, a term paper about her feelings about her father's death. As she completes the paper, she comes to grips with her emotions and understands why other family members are reacting the way they are.

"I wrote [the novel] because the characters had been part of me for years," Rinaldi said in *Library Journal*. "Most of the motivation came from my own life. Family relationships, especially the tremendous influence older siblings have over younger ones, have always intrigued me. The overall theme of the novel is love and forgiveness. I think I have answered, for young Nicki in my book, some of the questions I have not been able to answer yet for myself in my own life."

The writer's interest in history grew out of her family's involvement in an organization that reenacts famous battles. *Time Enough for Drums* is about a New Jersey girl who sees the American Revolution divide her town and family. She falls in love with a Tory sympathizer.

YOUNG ADULT FICTION

Term Paper (1980)
Nicki, fourteen, puts into words her feelings about her father's death.

Promises Are for Keeping (1982), sequel to *Term Paper*
To make up for ill-considered pranks, Nicki does volunteer work at the hospital.

But in the Fall I'm Leaving (1985)
Sixteen-year-old Brie falls in love with a boy her parents forbid her to see.

Time Enough for Drums (1986)
Jemima Emerson, fifteen, loves a Tory sympathizer during the American Revolution.

The Good Side of My Heart (1987), sequel to *But in the Fall I'm Leaving*
Brie dates and falls in love with troubled Josh.

The Last Silk Dress (1988)
To help the Confederates, Susan Chilmark collects silk dresses in Richmond to build a hot-air balloon.

A Ride into Morning: The Story of Tempe Wick (1991)
Wick and her cousin Mary must run the farm in the midst of the American Revolution.

Wolf by the Ears (1991)
Harriet Hemings, rumored to be Thomas Jefferson's daughter, can pass for white or remain a slave at Monticello.

A Break with Charity: A Story About the Salem Witch Trials (1992)
In 1692, Susanna English's parents are accused of being witches in Salem.

The Fifth of March: The Story of the Boston Massacre (1993)
Rachel Marsh, fourteen, is an indentured servant to ambitious young lawyer John Adams.

In My Father's House (1993)
In Virginia after the Civil War, Oscie McLean resents her stepfather, who believes the South must change.

Finishing Becca: The Story of Peggy Shippen and Benedict Arnold (1994)
Fourteen-year-old Becca Synge goes to work as personal maid to spoiled Peggy Shippen in Philadelphia.

Quilt Trilogy

A Stitch in Time (1994)
In Salem after the American Revolution, Hanna Chelmsford finds shadows in her family. Her father, a merchant, does not approve of her suitor, Richard Lander.

Broken Days (1995)

FOR FURTHER READING

Bush, Margaret A. Review of *A Break with Charity. Horn Book Magazine*, November–December 1992.

Carter, Betty. *Best Books for Young Adults: The Selections, the History, the Romance.* Chicago: American Library Association, 1994.

Commine, Anne, ed. "Ann Rinaldi." In *Something About the Author.* Vol. 51. Detroit: Gale Research, 1988.

Hile, Kevin S., ed. "Ann Rinaldi." In *Something About the Author.* Vol. 78. Detroit: Gale Research, 1994.

Ratner, Megan. "Ann Rinaldi." In *Authors & Artists for Young Adults*, edited by E. A. Deschenes. Vol. 15. Detroit: Gale Research, 1995.

Rinaldi, Ann. Interview. *Library Journal*, 1 October 1980.

Cynthia Rylant

Rural drama

Hopewell, Virginia
June 6, 1954

A Blue-Eyed Daisy

Cynthia Rylant, an award-winning author of children's and young adult books, sets many of her stories in West Virginia coal country, where she grew up.

Rylant also writes poetry. Critic Jacqueline L. Gmuca noted her conscious use of words: "Because of Rylant's lyrical use of language, we come to know why the main character never dreamed of a world beyond the mountains when she was young. There, love, adventure, and security wrapped her close. Characters are just as strongly evoked by Rylant's use of dialect and figurative language."

Gmuca added, "Distinctive to Rylant's work are her depictions of adult characters. Ellie's father is prominent in *A Blue-Eyed Daisy*. Like other coal miners, Oakey Farley used to drink, 'to scare away the coming week,' but with his accident in a slate fall and his inability to work, he begins to drink through the week as well. The novel traces Oakey's healing process, furthered by Ellie's love and Bullet, the hunting beagle he brings home one day."

Cynthia Rylant Smith's father was an army sergeant and her mother was a nurse. Her parents separated when she was four, and she and her mother moved in with her grandparents in West Virginia. She had little contact with her father, and he died when she was thirteen. In 1975, she received a bachelor's degree from Morris Harvey College, now the University of Charleston. She received graduate degrees from Marshall University and Kent State University. She is divorced and has a son.

Rylant has worked as an English instructor and children's librarian and continues to lecture part-time. Her first book, of poetry, was *Waiting to Waltz: A Childhood*.

In a Newbery Medal acceptance speech in 1993, Rylant said: "I was raised in an atmosphere of forgiveness, and this may be the finest gift God has given me on this Earth. Knowing that I would be forgiven by my mother, my family, if I ever failed at anything I tried gave me the courage to be a writer, the courage to place my work in the world for judgment, and the courage to keep on trying to say something important in my books. . . .

"Having grown up reading comic books and the Nancy Drew books my mother bought for me at the dime store, I did not know there was any such thing as children's literature. I had majored in English in college, and still I did not know this."

Her friend Diane Ward describes Rylant as "a private person who needs space for herself. Even when we visit, we give each other time to go off and read or simply be alone and then come together for tea and conversation, shopping trips, and meals out. She loves animals, and when you're sitting down having that cup of tea, Martha, a two-year-old, seventy-pound Lab, is trying to climb in your lap, and Leia, a nine-year-old Welsh Corgi, is bringing you her rawhide bone and wagging every inch of her body. . . .

"She believes that people have a right to lead any lifestyle that suits them. The important thing is to live life and be kind in the process. She walks gently through life, sifting her experiences and creating stories from them."

"The more I write, it seems the more willing I am to get closer to my real life today, who I am today," Rylant told Sally Holmes Holtze. "I wrote a book called *A Kindness*, about people who are learning to let go of each other, learning not to try to control each other. That's something I have to work hard on in my own life because I can be very insecure sometimes."

YOUNG ADULT FICTION

A Blue-Eyed Daisy (1985); British title: *Some Year for Ellie* (1986)
Ellie Farley lives in the coal mining hills of West Virginia. Her father has been injured in an accident and is out of work.

Every Living Thing: Stories (1985)
Short stories about humans and endearing experiences with animals.

A Fine White Dust (1986)
Pete, thirteen, leaves the supper table and slips into another world when a traveling preacher comes to town.

A Kindness (1988)
Chip, a high school sophomore, enjoys taking charge around the house for his single mom, but he is crushed when he finds she is going to have a baby.

A Couple of Kooks: And Other Stories About Love (1990)
Short stories.

Missing May (1992)
Aunt May has died, and Summer fears the same for Uncle Ob, who is grieving.

I Had Seen Castles (1993)
After the attack on Pearl Harbor, John Dante, seventeen, is urged by girlfriend Ginnie to become a conscientious objector. He joins the service anyway and fights in Italy. Years later, he is unable to lead a normal life.

POETRY

Waiting to Waltz: A Childhood (1984)

Soda Jerk (1990)

But I'll Be Back Again (1993)

FICTION FOR YOUNGER READERS

When I Was Young in the Mountains (1982)

Miss Maggie (1983)

This Year's Garden (1984)

The Relatives Came (1985)

Night in the Country (1986)

Birthday Presents (1987)

Children of Christmas: Stories for the Season (1987); British title: *Silver Packages, and Other Stories* (1987)

All I See (1988)

Mr. Griggs' Work (1989)

An Angel for Solomon Singer (1992)

The Dreamer (1993)

The Old Woman Who Named Things (1994)

Dog Heaven (1995)

The Van Gogh Cafe (1995)

Whales (1995)

Henry and Mudge Series

Henry and Mudge: The First Book of Their Adventures (1987)

Henry and Mudge in Puddle Trouble: The Second Book of Their Adventures (1987)

Henry and Mudge in the Green Time: The Third Book of Their Adventures (1987)

Henry and Mudge Under the Yellow Moon: The Fourth Book of Their Adventures (1987)

Henry and Mudge in the Sparkle Days: The Fifth Book of Their Adventures (1988)

Henry and Mudge and the Forever Sea: The Sixth Book of Their Adventures (1989)

Henry and Mudge Get the Cold Shivers: The Seventh Book of Their Adventures (1989)

Henry and Mudge and the Happy Cat: The Eighth Book of Their Adventures (1990)

Henry and Mudge and the Bedtime Thumps: The Ninth Book of Their Adventures (1991)

Henry and Mudge Take the Big Test: The Tenth Book of Their Adventures (1991)

Henry and Mudge and the Long Weekend: The Eleventh Book of Their Adventures (1992)

Henry and Mudge and the Wild Wind: The Twelfth Book of Their Adventures (1992)

Henry and Mudge and the Careful Cousin: The Thirteenth Book of Their Adventures (1994)

Henry and Mudge and the Best Day of All: The Fourteenth Book of Their Adventures (1995)

Mr. Putter and Tabby Series

Mr. Putter and Tabby Bake the Cake (1994)

Mr. Putter and Tabby Walk the Dog (1994)

Mr. Putter and Tabby Pick the Pears (1995)

FOR FURTHER READING

Gmuca, Jacqueline L. "Cynthia Rylant." In *Twentieth-Century Children's Writers*, edited by Tracy Chevalier. 3d ed. Chicago: St. James Press, 1989.

Holtze, Sally Holmes, ed. "Cynthia Rylant." In *Fifth Book of Junior Authors & Illustrators*. New York: H. W. Wilson, 1983.

Rylant, Cynthia. *But I'll Be Back Again: An Album*. New York: Orchard Books, 1989.

———. "Newbery Medal Acceptance." *Horn Book Magazine*, July–August 1993.

Ward, Diane. "Cynthia Rylant." *Horn Book Magazine, July–August 1993.*

Marilyn Sachs

Family drama

Bronx, New York
December 18, 1927

Veronica Ganz Series

One of Marilyn Sachs's best-known books is *Veronica Ganz*. "From Peter Wedemeyer's first taunting chant to Veronica Ganz's final (but the first of her life) girl-like giggle, this story of an 11-year-old bully has warmth and reality," reviewer Peggy Sullivan said. "Several subplots about Veronica's family and divorced parents are skillfully introduced but not resolved. . . . Marilyn Sachs has here fulfilled the promise of her earlier books."

Marilyn Stickle Sachs, the daughter of an insurance salesman, grew up in a neighborhood full of children. Sachs has described herself as a thin child, not particularly brave when it came to dealing with neighborhood bullies. She took refuge in the neighborhood library, where she particularly enjoyed the writers of heroic and fantastic tales. She decided at an early age to become a writer.

Sachs attended Hunter College and later Columbia University. She met her husband, Morris Sachs, a sculptor, while in college. They have two children.

"When I graduated from Hunter College in 1949," Sachs said in a promotional flyer, "I didn't know what to write about. Until I could make up my mind, I took a job as a children's librarian and worked for over ten happy years." She eventually realized that she wanted to write realistic books using her own childhood as inspiration. "Much of my own background is in all my books, and sometimes, when I write, I feel as if I am visiting old friends.

"One thing you learn as a writer is that you must distance yourself from your own life, or nobody will want to read what you write," she added. "It's necessary to start off with something that matters to you, but you must learn how to open it up for your readers as well."

Sachs wrote her first book, *Amy Moves In*, when she was twenty-five. She was surprised that publishers were not immediately receptive to a book about a poor Jewish family. Refusing to make changes, she shelved the manuscript. Years later, when her family lived in California, she heard from an editor who wanted to see the manuscript again. It was published in 1964.

Sachs said that she writes from a half to a full chapter each day. She sends drafts to her daughter, Anne, for comments.

"I am much harder on myself than I used to be," Sachs told Marguerite Feitlowitz, "and much more critical. My first books pretty much wrote themselves. I rarely stopped to rewrite a sentence. Now I am more aware and concerned with the craft of writing. Although I manage to keep up my momentum, I revise much more as I go along. I realize now that if I don't watch myself, I tend to use too many simple words and insipid, non-descriptive adjectives."

Her heroine Veronica Ganz, the author said, was modeled on childhood bullies who tormented her. She got her revenge on paper. "I never intended to like Veronica," the writer said in a publisher's pamphlet. "But I found I was growing fonder of the girl, beginning to understand through her all those childhood bullies. As it turns out, I like Veronica the best of all my make-believe kids. It's as if when you look at someone close enough, you find that there's good in just about everybody. I don't think I knew that when I wrote the book, but I do now."

Other books are based on events from history and from Sachs's family. She did research for *Call Me Ruth*, about factory workers and the International Ladies' Garment Workers Union. For *A Pocketful of Seeds*, she interviewed a woman she knew who had lived in Europe during the German occupation. Some of her books have drawn criticism: a picketer protested *Dorrie's Book* at one school because the fictional mother was pregnant.

YOUNG ADULT FICTION

Dorrie's Book (1975)
Dorrie O'Brien is an only child, until the triplets come.

A December Tale (1976)
Myra Fine and her brother are mistreated in a foster home.

A Secret Friend (1978)
Jessica Freeman and Wendy Cooper, once best friends, have split. Lonely Wendy begins receiving notes signed "A. S. F."

A Summer's Lease (1979)
In the 1940s, Gloria Reim is determined to become a writer.

Bus Ride (1980)
Judy figures Ernie will never take an interest in her—but there are those long rides on the bus.

Class Pictures (1980)
Shy, plump Lilly Schneiner and popular Pat Maddox, friends since kindergarten, switch roles by eighth grade.

Hello . . . Wrong Number (1981)

Beach Towels (1982)
Two teenage girls are friends.

Call Me Ruth (1982)
Young Jewish immigrants struggle in New York City at the turn of the century.

Class Pictures (1982)

Fourteen (1983)
It is not exactly a storybook romance for Rebecca.

The Fat Girl (1984)
Jeff despises the fat girl who keeps spying on him. When he plays a trick on her, his revulsion turns to guilt, then to fascination.

Thunderbird (1985)
It is an unlikely romance between a vegetarian animal lover (boy) and a Thunderbird-loving mechanic (girl).

Baby Sister (1986)
Penny wants to be like her older sister, Cass, who is smart and beautiful and full of life.

Almost Fifteen (1987)
Imogen Rogers fantasizes about handsome divorcé Adam Derman.

Just Like a Friend (1990)
Patti shares everything with her mother—until a family crisis changes everything.

Circles (1991)
Beebe Clark and Mark Driscoll would have a lot in common—if they could ever meet.

What My Sister Remembered (1992)
Separated after their parents died in a car crash, Molly cannot wait to be reunited with her sister, Beth.

Thirteen Going on Seven (1993)
Twins Dee and Dezzy have almost nothing in common.

FICTION FOR YOUNGER READERS

The Bears' House (1971)

A Pocketful of Seeds (1973)

Matt's Mitt (1975)

Fleet-Footed Florence (1981), sequel to *Matt's Mitt*

Underdog (1985)

Fran Ellen's House (1987), sequel to *The Bears' House*

At the Sound of the Beep (1990)

Amy and Laura Series

Amy Moves In (1964)

Laura's Luck (1965)

Amy and Laura (1966)

Veronica Ganz Series

Veronica Ganz (1968)

Peter and Veronica (1969)

Marv (1970)

The Truth About Mary Rose (1973)

DRAMA

Reading Between the Lines (1971)

FOR FURTHER READING

Feitlowitz, Marguerite. "Marilyn Sachs." In *Authors & Artists for Young Adults*, edited by Agnes Garrett and Helga P. McCue. Vol. 2. Detroit: Gale Research, 1989.

Marilyn Sachs. New York: E. P. Dutton, 1985.

Marilyn Sachs. New York: Scholastic, n.d.

Sullivan, Peggy. Review of *Veronica Ganz*. *School Library Journal*, April 1968.

J. D. Salinger

Coming-of-age stories

New York City
January 1, 1919
The Catcher in the Rye

"Still heading the list of favorite books to be censored . . . is the classic story of a teenager's quest for maturity, J. D. Salinger's *The Catcher in the Rye*," June Edwards said. " 'Obscene' is the usual cry, based on the four-letter words. 'Blasphemous' claim the protestors over the boy's caustic comments about religious hypocrisy. *Catcher* has become a symbol for critics of what they perceive to be a vile, ungodly plot on the part of schools to undermine the morals of American schoolchildren."

In beginning his own writing career, young adult author Paul Zindel surveyed what young people were reading. "I discovered that there weren't many writers who were getting through to them," he told interviewer Sean Mitchell. "There was *Catcher in the Rye*, from which so much teen-age literature stems, but I discovered that many teen-agers didn't really understand what it was about."

"No teenager has known angst quite like Holden Caulfield knew it," writer Jessica Shaw said. "And no writer has inspired such mythic curiosity as Holden's creator, J. D. Salinger, who—after publishing his classic first novel, *The Catcher in the Rye*, on July 16, 1951—went into hiding and never came out."

"By 1981 the original edition of the book had been reprinted thirty-five times and the paperback edition fifty-two times, with a total number of copies in excess of 10 million," Herbert N. Foerstel said. "Indeed, during 1981, *The Catcher in the Rye* had the unusual distinction of being the nation's most frequently censored book and, at the same time, the second-most frequently taught novel in the public schools.

"What is it about *The Catcher in the Rye* that makes schools and libraries so ambivalent about it? Most of the objections to the book have centered on its profane or vulgar language. A complaining parent in California counted 295 occasions in which God's name was taken in vain, while another complainant in Kansas noted 860 obscenities. A parent in Washington counted 785 profanities, including 22 *hells*, 27 *Chrissakes*, 7 *horneys*, as well as numerous *bastards, damns, craps*, and so on. All of this language comes from the adolescent hero of the book, Holden Caulfield. Yet Holden spends much of his time at school trying to wash obscene graffiti off the walls, because he feels younger children should not be exposed to such language."

Jerome David Salinger, the son of an importer, has been twice married and twice divorced. He has two children by his second marriage. He graduated from Valley Forge Military Academy in 1936 and attended Columbia University. Salinger served in the U.S. Army from 1942 to 1946, and he took part in the Normandy invasion.

Salinger has kept mum about early details of his life or has made up stories about himself. As a kid he was known for being unconventional. Thus his father sent him to military school. He began writing stories at Columbia, where he belonged to a writing group conducted by Whit Burnett. Salinger's first story, "The Young Folks," appeared in Burnett's magazine *Story*. Later stories appeared in *The New Yorker*.

Holden Caulfield, hero of *The Catcher in the Rye*, is sixteen years old, desperate, and lonely in the postwar era. About to be kicked out of prep school for poor grades, he decides to run away just before Christmas. He wanders around New York City, finally coming to grips with his feelings and a new sense of the possibility of goodness. He decides to return home.

"I was much relieved when I finished [the book]," Salinger told Shirley Blaney. "My boyhood was very much the same as that of the boy in the book, and it was a great relief telling people about it."

Readers found a voice for their generation in the novel. "*Catcher* almost immediately became a dog-eared favorite," said Shaw, "climbing the heights of the best-seller list. But its now-mild swearing and rebelliousness were attacked. Some thought it was immoral. It was banned from many school curricula."

The book was reprinted three times within one month of issue. In ten years in paperback edition, it sold 3,364,000 copies and was translated into fourteen languages.

"Like most of his literary predecessors . . . Holden Caulfield is on the side of the angels," Virgilia Peterson noted. "Contaminated he is, of course, by vulgarity, lust, lies, temptations, recklessness, and cynicism. But these are merely the devils that try him externally; inside, his spirit is intact. Unlike so many of his literary predecessors, however, he does not oversimplify his troubles. He is not tilting against the whole adult world (there are some decent adults); nor does he altogether loathe his worst contemporaries (he hates to leave them). He sees the mixtures, the inextricably mingled good and bad, as it is, but the very knowledge of reality is what almost breaks his heart. For Holden Caulfield, despite all the realism with which he is supposedly depicted, is nevertheless a skinless perfectionist."

Young adult writer Paula Danziger said that she "so identified with Holden that I read the book every day for over two years during my adolescence. Now I see it from a totally different perspective. Holden is still vivid, alive. Now I can also see his confusion, where once I only felt a kindred spirit."

Zen Buddhism began to influence Salinger's life in the mid-1940s. He moved to Cornish, New Hampshire, in the early 1950s. In early years there, he met frequently with teenagers. Later, he became reclusive. Since 1953, he has refused to be interviewed or sign autographs. He built a fence around his home. In 1986, he sued to prevent biographer Ian Hamilton from including excerpts from personal letters in *J. D. Salinger: A Writing Life*. Two years later, Hamilton came out with a different version of the book, using his own words to describe Salinger's sentiments from the letters.

Salinger's most recent story, "Hapworth 16, 1924," appeared in *The New Yorker* in 1965.

FICTION

The Catcher in the Rye (1951)
Thrown out of prep school, Holden Caulfield decides to sow a few wild oats before heading home.

Nine Stories (1953); British title: *For Esme—With Love and Squalor, and Other Stories* (1953)

Franny and Zooey (1961)
Two stories.

Raise High the Roof Beam, Carpenters, and Seymour: An Introduction (1963)
Two stories.

FOR FURTHER READING

Blaney, Shirley. "Shirley Blaney Interviews Salinger." *Daily Eagle*, 13 November 1953.

Cullinan, Bernice, and M. Jerry Weiss, eds. *Books I Read When I Was Young: The Favorite Books of Famous People*. New York: Avon Books, 1980.

Edwards, June. "Censorship in the Schools: What's Moral About 'The Catcher in the Rye?' " *English Journal*, April 1983.

Foerstel, Herbert N. *Banned in the USA: A Reference Guide to Book Censorship in Schools and Public Libraries*. Westport, CT: Greenwood, 1994.

Hamilton, Ian. *In Search of J. D. Salinger*. New York: Random House, 1988.

Mitchell, Sean. "Grown-Up Author's Insight into Adolescent Struggles." *Dallas Times Herald*, 27 June 1979.

Peterson, Virgilia. "Three Days in the Bewildering World of an Adolescent." *New York Herald Tribune Book Review*, 15 July 1951.

Shaw, Jessica. "The Birth of Holden Caulfield." *Entertainment Weekly*, 15 July 1994.

Ouida Sebestyen

Family drama

Vernon, Texas
February 13, 1924
Words by Heart

"I'm only comfortable writing about what I know, or think I know, and I've spent my life being either a daughter or a mother, and nearly twenty years being both at once, hands-on," Ouida Sebestyen said in *ALAN Review.*

"Maybe, as an only child with an only child, I've been more aware of the parent-child ties and stresses than more thickly-branched, sibling-rich families are. While I was struggling with the technical aspects of plot, character, dialogue and all the rest, in those first books I may instinctively have chosen families as the subject matter I could feel—well, *familiar* with."

"Sebestyen's characters provide the vehicle for dramatizing the themes," Beverly Haley explained. "Family plays a central role in all three [of the writer's first] novels, but not family in the traditional sense. *Words by Heart* centers around a black family in an early 1900s all-white Western town. Lena, the protagonist, idolizes her father, Ben, and loves her young stepmother, Claudie, half brother Roy, half sister Armilla, and the baby. Ben Sills, who once studied to be a minister, forms the strength and the center of the family; and he demands of his family that each one be at once strong and gentle."

"The eloquent story, though circumscribed in time and setting, dramatizes the black people's long struggle for equal opportunity and freedom," Ethel L. Heins said. "The year is 1910: Ben Sills, ambitious for his children, has bravely moved his family from the comparative security of an all-black Southern town to take up life as

American citizens in a white community further west. Ben is hardworking and dependable and soon incurs the enmity of the Haneys, a family of shiftless, ignorant sharecroppers."

Ouida Dockery, the daughter of two teachers, attended the University of Colorado. She worked at a training school for military pilots and as a day-care worker. She was also a housekeeper, gardener, seamstress, mason, and carpenter. She married Adam Sebestyen in 1960 and has since divorced. She has one child.

"I was an only child and books were my best friends," Sebestyen said in a teachers' guide. As she began writing, she could not find long stretches of time, so she had to put words to paper in "terribly earnest spurts which resulted in discouraging rejections. Four unsold adult novels and 50 unsold adult stories later, I decided I was writing for the wrong-sized people. When *Words by Heart* came pouring out, I felt I had found my niche. . . .

"Sometimes I tell young readers that growing up is like writing a novel," she continued. "Both are a mixture of pressures and pleasures, honesty and pretending, setting fine goals and stumbling toward them. Both are hard work, and need a lot of love and acceptance to come out right."

"To read Ouida Sebestyen is to feel deeply the power of good," Lyn Littlefield Hoopes said. "Her prose holds us at the edge of our senses, where awareness is acute and meaning bursts forth from the most ordinary. In each of her four novels for young adults we see the chain of evil—of hatred, resentment, fear—being broken, and in the face of much hardship, rendered powerless by good."

"Sebestyen's novels are about family and love," M. Jean Greenlaw said, "but there is no easy love in any of her works. She writes of people struggling to understand and accept each other and about families trying to be. . . . Sebestyen's works are provocative and thoughtful. They eschew the typical plot of the young adult novel and probe the inner recesses of human emotion. It took time for Sebestyen to find her voice, but it rings clearly today."

YOUNG ADULT FICTION

Words by Heart (1979)
No black family had lived in Bethel Springs before. Now Lena finds a knife stabbed viciously through a loaf of bread on the table.

Far from Home (1980)
Salty promises to keep the family together after his mother dies.

IOU's (1982)
Steve Garrett, thirteen, and his mother make do after his grandfather disowns them and his father abandons them.

On Fire (1985), sequel to *Words by Heart*
Sammy feels lost without his older brother, Tater Haney, now that Pop is in jail.

The Girl in the Box (1988)
Left in an underground room by an unknown captor, Jackie has food and water but no light or human contact. She digs deep to discover her rich reserves of strength and courage.

Out of Nowhere: A Novel (1994)
Harley, thirteen, is abandoned in the Arizona desert with only a pit bull he names Ish. He meets up with newly divorced May, who is seventy.

CONTRIBUTOR

Connections: Short Stories by Outstanding Writers for Young Adults, edited by Donald R. Gallo (1989)

FOR FURTHER READING

Cline, Ruth. *A Teacher's Guide to Ouida Sebestyen's* Words by Heart *and* On Fire. New York: Bantam Books, n.d.

Greenlaw, M. Jean. "Ouida Sebestyen." In *Twentieth-Century Children's Writers*, edited by Tracy Chevalier. 3d ed. Chicago: St. James Press, 1989.

Haley, Beverly. "Words by Ouida Sebestyen." *ALAN Review*, spring 1983.

Heins, Ethel L. Review of *Words by Heart*. *Horn Book Magazine*, June 1979.

Hoopes, Lyn Littlefield. "Novels of Ouida Sebestyen Share Thread of Good." *Christian Science Monitor*, 3 May 1985.

Sebestyen, Ouida. "Family Matters." *ALAN Review*, spring 1984.

William Sleator

Science fiction

Havre de Grace, Maryland
February 13, 1945

Interstellar Pig

"I prefer science fiction that has some basis in reality: psychological stories, time-travel stories, but especially stories about people," William Sleator told Dieter Miller.

Sleator, who is a former company pianist for the Boston Ballet, lives in Boston. The son of a professor, he grew up in Maryland and St. Louis, Missouri.

Sleator studied piano for twelve years and cello for five. He received his bachelor of arts degree from Harvard University in 1967. He went to England to work on a graduate degree. Sleator worked as an accompanist for ballet classes. He spent a year at the Royal Ballet School in London. He composed scores for ballets and amateur films and plays. Sleator's work as assistant to an artist, Blair Lent, prompted him to begin to write for children.

His first book, *Blackbriar*, was inspired by a visit to an isolated cottage in England. The story, with a mystery setting, is about a boy's struggle for independence from his guardian.

"There are strange doings in the woods, and weird people come and go both in and around Danny and Philippa's house, but the mystery remains so unformulated that we never develop a feeling of what is at stake," complained Ashley Darlington Grayson, who concluded, "Danny fails to earn any reader respect because he is thick as a post."

Other of Sleator's books "are built on equally unnerving subjects [as Satanism], like the time travel in *The Green Futures of Tycho* and

Singularity, an intergalactic fight for survival in *Interstellar Pig*, environmental reconditioning in *House of Stairs*, and supernatural transference of talent in *Fingers*," Margaret L. Daggett said.

Kirkus Reviews found *House of Stairs* a "riveting suspense novel with an anti-behaviorist message that works, despite the lack of subtlety or originality, because it emerges only slowly from the chilling events."

"In Sleator's hands even a science-fiction formula can be regenerated," Suzanne Rahn said, citing *Interstellar Pig*. In the story, hostile aliens disguise themselves as humans. A boy, Barney, unknowingly meets the aliens while on vacation. He gradually learns that Joe, Manny, and Zena are not from this planet, and that a deadly game they are playing has his own planet at stake.

Recommending the book, reviewer Rosalie Byard said that it should especially satisfy readers who enjoy strategy games. "Eerie menace penetrates the humdrum normality of the summer holiday scene in a convincing evolution from unsettling situation to waking nightmare."

"Using his keen eye for family relations . . . Mr. Sleator has made *Others See Us* so lean and suspenseful its flaws are minor distractions," observed M. P. Dunleavey. "No one who has ever fantasized about what his or her relatives are really thinking will be able to put the novel down until it reaches its unsettling conclusion."

YOUNG ADULT FICTION

Blackbriar (1972)
Danny, fifteen, and his middle-aged guardian settle at Blackbriar. They are shunned by the locals because of apparent links with Satanists.

Run (1973)
Lillian, fifteen, is frightened at the thought of spending a few days alone in her family's isolated summer cottage. She persuades two cyclists, caught in a storm, to stay overnight.

House of Stairs (1974)
Five orphans, age sixteen, are locked in a maze and fed by a machine in this science fiction story.

The Green Futures of Tycho (1981)
Tycho thinks it is just a strange silver egg when he digs it up one spring morning in his backyard, but the egg has weird powers that fling him into the future or past.

Fingers (1983)
Is Humphrey a musical genius—or are his fingers possessed?

Interstellar Pig (1984)
Barney is suspicious of the board game his new neighbors play.

Singularity (1985)
Harry agrees to house-sit with his twin, Barry, hoping to restore some of their lost childhood closeness.

The Boy Who Reversed Himself (1990)
Laura is scared by the mysterious notes she keeps finding.

Strange Attractors (1990)
When Max wakes up one morning, he discovers that there is a day missing.

The Duplicate (1991)
David finds a mysterious machine that can duplicate living things.

The Spirit House (1991)
Julie becomes suspicious of Bia, a Thai exchange student, who has become manipulative and secretive—and frightened of the "spirit house."

Oddballs: Stories (1993)
Short stories.

Others See Us (1993)
Sixteen-year-old Jared accidentally acquires telepathic powers—just as he arrives at a family reunion.

The Night the Heads Came (1995)

CONTRIBUTOR

Am I Blue? Coming Out from the Silence, edited by Marion Dane Bauer (1994)

FICTION FOR YOUNGER READERS

The Angry Moon (1970)

Among the Dolls (1975)

Into the Dream (1979)

Once, Said Darlene (1979)

That's Silly (1981)

Dangerous Wishes (1995)

FOR FURTHER READING

Byard, Rosalie. Review of *Interstellar Pig. The New York Times Book Review*, 23 September 1984.

Daggett, Margaret L. "Recommended: William Sleator." *English Journal*, March 1987.

Dunleavey, M. P. Review of *Others See Us. The New York Times Book Review*, 24 April 1994.

Grayson, Ashley Darlington. "Two by Sleator." *Fantasy Review*, December 1986.

Lerner, Fred. *A Teacher's Guide to the Bantam Starfire Novels of William Sleator*. New York: Bantam Books, 1990.

Miller, Dieter. "William Sleator." In *Authors & Artists for Young Adults*, edited by Agnes Garrett and Helga P. McCue. Vol. 5. Detroit: Gale Research, 1990.

Rahn, Suzanne. "William Sleator." In *Twentieth-Century Children's Writers*, edited by Tracy Chevalier. 3d ed. Chicago: St. James Press, 1989.

Review of *House of Stairs. Kirkus Reviews*, 15 April 1974.

Gary Soto

Family drama

Fresno, California
April 12, 1952
Crazy Weekend

Gary Soto, the son of Chicano field workers, is a poet and fiction writer. *Baseball in April and Other Stories,* his first young adult book, was published in 1990. A publisher's pamphlet describes it as "a warm and wise collection of short stories for and about children. Mr. Soto draws on the everyday lives of Latino children and transforms their experiences into tender and realistic stories that appeal to all children: Jesse tries out for the Little League team but doesn't make it and instead joins a neighborhood team in a local park; Victor seeks to impress a girl in his seventh-grade French class; Manuel overcomes his nervousness to lip-sync 'La Bamba' at the school talent show and has astonishing success."

Soto grew up in industrial south Fresno, California, and received a bachelor of arts degree from California State University in Fresno in 1975. He received a master's degree from the University of California in 1976. He is married to Carolyn Sadako Oda, with whom he has one child.

Soto lectured in Chicano studies at the University of California–Berkeley from 1977 to 1981. He was an assistant professor of English and Chicano studies from 1981 to 1985. He later became associate professor and senior lecturer in English. He has been a writer-in-residence at San Diego State University.

Although his parents were U.S.-born, they held onto their Mexican heritage when Soto was growing up. Both his parents and grandparents worked as laborers in vineyards, orange groves, and cotton fields, and money was always short. Soto remembered these times in his autobiographical *Living up the Street: Narrative Recollections* (1985).

The Elements of San Joaquin (1977) was the first of several collections of Soto's verse published. Recent prose books have been for young adult readers.

In one of these novels, *Crazy Weekend*, Hector Beltran and his close friend, Mando Tafolla, seventh-graders from East Los Angeles, expect to spend a quiet three-day weekend in Fresno with Hector's Uncle Julio, a struggling photographer. Julio takes them for a ride in a Cessna airplane with rust holes and no parachutes. They are afraid they may fall out. Julio takes aerial shots of a farm, and then they observe an armored car heist in progress below. They fly low, and Julio takes several photos. He sells the pictures to the local newspaper, and the boys are interviewed about their experience for a youth-page story.

Uncle Julio's photos and the article about the boys come out the next day. The two thugs who robbed the armored car see the newspaper and decide to get even. The boys are forced to take defensive action.

Soto also writes for middle readers, as in *Too Many Tamales*, about Maria's frantic efforts to find her mother's missing ring at Christmastime. She and her cousins eat a whole batch of tamales looking for it (assuming it was inside one of them), only to find it was on the shelf all the time.

"Soto's ability to tell a story, to recreate moments of his own past in a manner that transcends the boundaries of race or age, to transport his reader to the world of his own childhood is felt within each of his written works," Pamela L. Sheldon said. The writer's "remembrances are as sharply defined and appealing as bright new coins," Alicia Fields said. "His language is spare and simple yet vivid."

In addition to *Living up the Street*, Soto has written two other volumes of prose memoirs and essays, *Small Faces* (1986) and *Lesser Evils: Ten Quartets* (1988).

YOUNG ADULT FICTION

Baseball in April, and Other Stories (1990)
Stories set in Latino neighborhoods of Fresno, California, including one about a young man who wants to become a karate expert like his favorite movie star.

Taking Sides (1991)
Lincoln Mendoza and his mother move from the Mission District barrio in San Francisco to an affluent, mostly white suburb of Sycamore. He feels culture shock.

Pacific Crossing (1992), sequel to *Taking Sides*
Lincoln and Tony go to Japan on a student exchange. Lincoln's Mexican American heritage clashes with the customs of his host family.

Local News (1993)
Short stories, including one about Angel, who does not expect to get in trouble by taking a shower, and another about Alma, who decides that this year will be her last trick-or-treat.

The Pool Party (1993)

Crazy Weekend (1994)
Hector takes his friend Mando on an airplane flight with Uncle Julio, not expecting to witness an armored car heist or to become involved with the thugs.

Jesse (1994)
To escape a drunken stepfather, seventeen-year-old Jesse leaves home to live with his brother, Abel.

Boys at Work (1995)
Two boys take jobs to pay for a CD player they broke.

The Pool Party (1995)

Summer on Wheels (1995), sequel to *Crazy Weekend*
The boys take a six-day bike trip.

FICTION FOR YOUNGER READERS

The Skirt (1992)

Too Many Tamales (1993)

Chato's Kitchen (1995)

The Mustache (1995)

The Old Man and His Door (1995)

POETRY

The Elements of San Joaquin (1977)

The Tale of Sunlight (1978)

Father Is a Pillow Tied to a Broom (1980)

Where Sparrows Work Hard (1981)

Black Hair (1985)

A Fire in My Hands: A Book of Poems (1991)

Neighborhood Odes (1993)

Canto Familiar (1995)

EDITOR

California Childhood: Recollections and Stories of the Golden State (1988)

Pieces of the Heart: New Chicano Fiction (1993)

FOR FURTHER READING

Author at a Glance: Gary Soto. New York: Harcourt Brace Jovanovich, n.d.

Fader, Ellen. Review of *Too Many Tamales*. *Horn Book Magazine*, November–December 1993.

Fields, Alicia. "Small but Telling Moments." *The Bloomsbury Review*, January 1987.

Sheldon, Pamela L. "Gary Soto." In *Authors & Artists for Young Adults*, edited by Kevin S. Hile. Vol. 10. Detroit: Gale Research, 1993.

Jerry Spinelli

Family drama

Norristown, Pennsylvania
February 1, 1940

Maniac Magee

Jerry Spinelli's young adult fiction looks at both the humor and the poignancy of growing up.

"Each of us, in our kidhood, was a Huckleberry Finn, drifting on a current that seemed tortuously slow at times, poling for the shore to check out every slightest glimmer in the trees . . . the taste of brussels sprouts . . . your first forward roll . . . cruising a mall without a parent . . . overnighting it . . . making your own grilled cheese sandwich . . . the weird way you felt when Sally Duffy scrunched next to you in the mob coming out of the movie . . . the thousand landfalls of our adolescence. And the current flows faster and faster, adulthood's delta looms, and one day we look to get our bearings and find that we are out to sea," Spinelli said in a publisher's pamphlet. "And now we know what we did not know then: What an adventure it was!"

Details such as Spinelli offered in this encapsulation of growing up are his greatest strength as a writer, in the view of John Keller. "He gets it right. He gets the details right. I had never heard of a butterscotch Krimpet before I read *Maniac Magee* . . . had you? He gets it right about the ways boys both look forward to growing into manhood and regret leaving childhood behind. He gets it right about the fury brothers and sisters can inspire in one another as they live within a family that truly wants to function well. He gets it right about girls like Marceline McAllister who from an early age refuse to conform to the stereotypes that boys want to believe about them. He gets it right about prejudice and unconditional love, and he gets it right about the magic every young person carries within him or her—a magic that shines forth if anyone takes the time to listen and observe."

Spinelli, the son of a printer, received a bachelor's degree from Gettysburg College in 1963 and a master's from Johns Hopkins University the next year. He also attended Temple University. He married writer Eileen Mesi in 1977, with whom he has six children. Spinelli served in the U.S. Naval Reserve from 1966 to 1972. He was a magazine editor with Chilton from 1966 to 1989.

Spinelli's *Space Station Seventh Grade* and its sequel, *Jason and Marceline*, were criticized for sensationalism and flatness of character. Jason "reveals every nuance of his personality, but the other characters are flat and shadowy figures who move in and out of his awareness. Only his arch-enemy, Marceline McAllister, and for one heart-rending moment, his friend Peter Kim, emerge from the background as real people," Marilyn H. Karrenbrock noted of *Space Station*. "Jason, as he alternately gropes and hurtles toward maturity, will both exasperate and exhilarate his readers."

Jason, in the sequel, dotes on Marceline's body. "But the point of his story is to show Jason's fumbling efforts to treat Marceline as a whole person," Denise M. Wilms said. "Jason manages this at last, and ends up a little more sensitive to what's wrong with treating girls as sex objects. The crudeness here grates but is true to life, and the message is worthwhile. This will probably be popular with its intended audience, who might take comfort in the social struggles that are meaningfully depicted."

Spinelli's *Night of the Whale*, about partying high school seniors saving beached whales, was too crude, reviewer David Gale said: "Many teens won't stay around until day five of this hedonistic week, when the revelers meet the whales and—flash!—grow up." Yet Brook Dillon found "the description of the rescue of the suicidal mammals in the darkness of night spellbindingly magical and written in a breezy, yet poetic, style."

Spinelli won a Boston Globe–Horn Book Award in 1990 for *Maniac Magee*. In his acceptance speech, he explained that the book "is about, among other things, the kid as legendary hero." Magee is a superior athlete who goes back and forth between segregated sections of town, making friends and enemies and easing racial tensions. The book also earned a Newbery Medal in 1991.

The book "is a mythical story about racism," cautioned Joel Shoemaker. "It should not be read as reality. Legend springs up about Jeffrey 'Maniac' Magee, a white boy who runs faster and hits balls farther than anyone, who lives on his own with amazing grace, and is innocent as to racial affairs."

Spinelli also contributed to *Our Roots Grow Deeper Than We Know: Pennsylvania Writers—Pennsylvania Life* (1985), edited by Lee Gutkind, and *Noble Pursuits* (1988), edited by Virginia A. Arnold and Carl B. Smith.

YOUNG ADULT FICTION

Space Station Seventh Grade (1982)
Jason Herkimer ruminates on ways to avoid ninth-graders, who will pee in your sneaker, and fantasizes about cheerleaders, including Marceline McAllister.

Who Put That Hair in My Toothbrush? (1984)
Fifteen-year-old Greg is forever tormenting his twelve-year-old sister, Megin.

Night of the Whale (1985)
High school seniors, in the midst of a year-end fling at a beach house, help a dozen stranded whales.

Jason and Marceline (1986), sequel to *Space Station Seventh Grade*
Jason and Marceline gradually become friends in ninth grade.

Dump Days (1988)
J. D. and Duke go through scheme after scheme to make money.

The Bathwater Gang (1990)
At her grandmother's suggestion, Bertie Kidd, bored with summer, starts a gang.

Maniac Magee: A Novel (1990)
Jeffrey Lionel "Maniac" Magee can run, can hit—and can work wonders with kids from the East and West Sides.

There's a Girl in My Hammerlock (1992)
A girl joins the wrestling team. A girl?!

CONTRIBUTOR

Connections: Short Stories by Outstanding Writers for Young Adults, edited by Donald R. Gallo (1989)

FICTION FOR YOUNGER READERS

Fourth Grade Rats (1991)

The Bathwater Gang Gets Down to Business (1992)

Picklemania (1993)

Crash (1995)

School Daze Series

Do the Funky Pickle (1992)

Report to the Principal's Office! (1992)

Who Put Underwear up the Flagpole? (1992)

FOR FURTHER READING

Dillon, Brook. Review of *Night of the Whale. Book Report*, March–April 1986.

Gale, David. Review of *Night of the Whale. School Library Journal*, January 1986.

Jerry Spinelli. Boston: Little, Brown, 1990.

Karrenbrock, Marilyn H. Review of *Space Station Seventh Grade. ALAN Review*, winter 1985.

Keller, John. "Jerry Spinelli." *Horn Book Magazine*, July–August 1991.

Shoemaker, Joel. Review of *Maniac Magee. School Library Journal*, June 1990.

Spinelli, Jerry. " 'Maniac Magee': Home on George Street." *Horn Book Magazine*, January–February 1991.

Wilms, Denise M. Review of *Jason and Marceline. Booklist*, 1 January 1987.

R. L. Stine

Suspense

Columbus, Ohio
October 8, 1943

Fear Street Series

"R. L. Stine is so popular, it's scary," Jacqueline Blais said, adding that in 1994 Stine sold more books than any author in America.

"When I was nine years old, I discovered a typewriter in our attic," Stine stated in a teacher's guide to his fiction. "I dragged it downstairs and started typing little joke magazines and books. That's what I've been doing ever since, probably using a lot of the same jokes."

R. L. Stine's jokes have taken a gruesome twist. Stine—along with Christopher Pike—heads a swarm of young adult writers offering the thrills and chills of Stephen King but with younger characters and age-appropriate topics. Stine has established a niche for himself with two popular series: Fear Street, for teens, and Goosebumps, for their younger brothers and sisters.

A typical Fear Street story is *The Wrong Number*. Deena Martinson and best friend Jade Smith think it is a harmless prank to make sexy phone calls to the boys from school, but Deena's half brother, Chuck, finds out what they are doing and threatens to tell their parents—unless they let him in on the fun. He begins making random calls and threatening whoever answers. He thinks it is dangerous and exciting. They are all a little bit thrilled when news of the calls gets into the papers. There is a public uproar. Crank calls and false bomb threats are no joke.

Then Chuck calls the number of a house on Fear Street and joshes about murder to the wrong person: a murderer who knows who the callers are. He knows where they live, too, and they have no one they can call for help.

The Thrill Club is about Talia Blanton, who weaves her friends into the horror stories she writes. Everyone thinks it is a lark. Then the stories eerily start coming true. One by one, Talia's friends become her victims. Is Talia making her stories come to life, or is someone else?

Robert Lawrence Stine, the son of a shipping manager, received a bachelor of arts degree in 1965 from Ohio State University. He did graduate work the next two years at New York University. In 1969, he married. He and his wife, Jane, have a son.

Stine worked as a junior high social studies teacher in Ohio. He was an editor with *Junior Scholastic, Search, Bananas,* and *Maniac* magazines through 1985. Recently, he has been head writer for the children's television show *Eureeka's Castle* on Nickelodeon.

His earliest books were humor titles such as *The Absurdly Silly Encyclopedia and Flyswatter* and *The Complete Book of Nerds*. He wrote several books with his wife, including *Everything You Need to Survive: First Dates*.

Stine began writing dark novels for young adults in 1990. The Fear Street series was created to fill a marketing niche with young adult readers seeking new titles. The books are packaged for the publisher by Parachute Press, which is run by Stine's wife, Jane.

The Fear Street books are connected by a geographical setting, where, according to the book covers, "your worst nightmares live."

" 'Fear Street' is a place where terrible things always happen to its residents," Mary Lois Sanders said. "There are dark and mysterious legends and ominous happenings, with one street in town linking the series."

Fear Street stories follow "a fairly consistent set of formulas," observed Paul Gray. A young boy or girl suddenly finds his or her life threatened, perhaps by a supernatural menace, perhaps by a real one. Rather than run to adults for help, the protagonists use their own resources.

In *The Stepsister*, Nancy and Emily Casey, whose father drowned a year ago, look forward to a new stepsister moving in, now that their mother has remarried. Then Emily finds herself sharing a room with Jessie, who plays irritating little tricks on her. Will Jessie try something worse on a family camping trip?

"I believe that kids as well as adults are entitled to books of no socially redeeming value," Stine told *Contemporary Authors*.

Where does Stine get his ideas? "I don't know where my ideas come from," he answered, in an end note to *The Thrill Club*. "But I do know that I have a lot more scary stories in my mind that I can't wait to write."

"I outline every book," Stine told Danielle Claro. "I think of three or four things that I can put in to keep the reader from guessing the ending. I figure out who I'm going to make the suspect, and how I'm going to throw the reader off the track, so that the reader is fooled at the end."

Stine said in *Authors & Artists for Young Adults* that he generally knows how a book will end, then works backward, putting together a clear outline before he begins writing. To budding writers, he encourages: "Read, read, read."

YOUNG ADULT FICTION

Everything You Need to Survive: First Dates, with Jane Stine (1983)
A guide to coping with first dates, including places to go, etiquette, conversation, and clothes.

Blind Date (1986)
Kerry's blind date is the girl of his dreams—or nightmares.

Twisted (1986)
Abby would do anything to be in the school's exclusive sorority, but the initiation this year is murder.

Beach Party (1990)
Karen has two guys to choose from, one so handsome, one so dangerous.

The Boyfriend (1990)
It is not Joanna's fault Dex died after they broke up—is it?

Curtains (1990)
Can Rena survive the backstage horror of Merritt Baxter Summer Theater Camp for teens?

How I Broke Up with Ernie (1990)
Amy finds it not just hard to break up with Ernie, but impossible.

Phone Calls (1990)
Five teenagers declare telephone war.

The Girlfriend (1991)
Scotty regrets straying from his girlfriend when his new acquaintance threatens to love him to death.

Snowman (1991)
Heather fears that her guardian wants her dead, so he can have her money.

Beach House (1992)
A silent killer stalks the kids at the shore.

Hit and Run (1992)
Eddie, Scott, Wink, and Cassie go for a little drive one night—and have a little accident.

Dead Girlfriend (1993)
Annie does not know that Jonathan's last girlfriend may be dead, but she is definitely not gone.

The Hitchhiker (1993)
He wants a ride. She wants a thrill. He turns out to be much more than she expected.

The Beast (1994)
A roller coaster is haunted.

Call Waiting (1994)
A mysterious caller wants to kill Karen.

I Saw You That Night! (1994)
Roxie breaks into a house just to win a stupid bet—and sees something she should not see.

The New Boy (1994)
All the girls at Shadyside High want to date the new boy, Ross Gabriel—but they may be flirting with death.

The Beast 2 (1995), sequel to *The Beast*
James and Ashley take another ride—and Ashley disappears.

Baby-Sitter Series

The Baby-Sitter (1989)
Jenny is terrorized by the caller: "Hi, Babes."

The Baby-Sitter II (1992)
The crazy guy who tried to kill Jenny at her last baby-sitting job is back.

The Baby-Sitter III (1993)
Jenny visits her cousin, Debra—and again the telephone calls begin.

The Baby-Sitter IV (1995)
Jenny, who should know better, takes a job at a strange house.

Crosswinds Series

Broken Date (1988)
Jamie and Tom seem the perfect teenage couple—until they break up.

Fear Street Series

Halloween Party (1990)
Terry and his girlfriend, Niki, attend a costume party where someone is dressed to kill.

Haunted (1990)
Melissa wakes up screaming and sees an intruder at her window.

Missing (1990)
Mark and Cara do not know what to do when their parents disappear without a trace.

The New Girl (1990)
A girl is murdered in the woods without birds.

The Overnight (1990)
The kids think it will be more fun to make a trip to Fear Island without an adviser along—until the dangerous stranger appears.

The Sleepwalker (1990)
Mayra is convinced her employer has cast a spell on her, causing her to sleepwalk.

The Stepsister (1990)
Emily learns a terrible secret about her overbearing new stepsister, Jessie.

The Surprise Party (1990)
Terror stalks Meg Dalton's plans for a reunion.

The Wrong Number (1990)
Prankish phone calls and sexy whispers turn into something else when one of the numbers is on Fear Street.

The Fire Game (1991)
When one of their prankish fires ends in murder, Jill and her friends know they have gone too far.

Lights Out (1991)
Junior counselor Holly Flynn is determined to find out who is causing all the vandalism at Camp Nightwing.

The Secret Bedroom (1991)
Lea Carson's family moves into a creepy old house on Fear Street. A murder was committed in the attic a hundred years earlier.

Ski Weekend (1991)
Ariel, Doug, and Shannon are stranded at a hilltop lodge during a blizzard.

The Best Friend (1992)
Honey Perkins claims to be Becka Norwood's best friend—but Becka has never met her before.

First Date (1992)
Chelsea Richards, shy and lonely, may be dating a crazed killer.

The Knife (1992)
At Shadyside Hospital, student volunteer Laurie Masters stumbles onto a sick secret.

The Prom Queen (1992)
Shadyside High's prom night is full of romance—and horror: Someone kills the candidates for queen, one by one.

The Cheater (1993)
Carter Philips asks Adam Messner to take her math achievement exam for her—then does not want to pay his price.

Halloween Night (1993)
Brenda and her friends plan the perfect "murder" joke at their Halloween party.

Bad Dreams (1994)
Maggie Travers is plagued by nightmares about a murder.

The Dare (1994)
Johanna Wise longs to be part of Dennis Arthur's rich, popular crowd—even if it means helping him get away with murder.

The Dead Lifeguard (1994)
Lindsay Beck, lifeguard at North Beach Country Club, has to figure out the evil secret that may make her the next victim of a gruesome killer.

Double Date (1994)
The Wade twins, who have never learned to share, both fall for Bobby Newkirk.

Halloween Night II (1994), sequel
Brenda was stabbed by Dina at a Halloween party last year. She hopes this Halloween will be different—but Dina has been released from the psychiatric hospital!

The Mind Reader (1994)
Only Ellie Anderson can see the skeleton's hand beckoning from a shallow grave.

One Evil Summer (1994)
Chrissy, baby-sitter for Amanda's little brother and sister, may have killing on her mind.

Sunburn (1994)
Claudia Walker does not anticipate the horrible accidents when she spends a weekend at the beach.

The Thrill Club (1994)
Talie Blanton writes horror stories that terrify her friends—especially when the stories begin coming true.

College Weekend (1995)
It is strangely convenient for Chris to show Tina around when her boyfriend Josh does not return from a camping trip.

Dead End (1995)
Natalie Erickson and her friends are in the car the foggy night someone dies at the dead end.

Final Grade (1995)
Lily Bancroft hates her teacher—but enough to murder him?

The New Year's Party (1995)

The Stepsister 2 (1995), sequel
Emily still harbors fears when her sister Nancy comes home from the mental hospital.

Switched (1995)
Nicole and Lucy switch minds, and now Lucy is getting away with murder—in Nicole's body.

Truth or Dare (1995)
Seven teens are stranded in Dara Harker's luxury ski condo during a blizzard.

What Holly Heard (1995)

Wrong Number Two (1995), sequel
Deena and Jade break their vow and return to old tricks. Then someone wants revenge.

Fear Street Cataluna Chronicles

1. *The Evil Moon* (1995)
   Brian wants the Cataluna more than anything.
2. *The Dark Secret* (1995)
   Stepsisters Regina and Lauren have a hot new car—the Cataluna—which is cursed with bad luck.
3. *The Deadly Fire* (1995)
   The Doom Car has already destroyed race-car driver Stan McCloy, but his brother Buddy won't stay away from it.

Fear Street Cheerleaders Series

The First Evil (1992)
Corky and Bobbi Corcoran make the squad, just as a series of murders begins.

The Second Evil (1992)
Corky, back on the squad after Bobbi's death, meets a new friend obsessed by the occult.

The Third Evil (1992)
Corky is tormented by dreams of her dead sister, Bobbi.

The New Evil (1994)
Cheerleaders are being horribly injured—and Corky fears that the Evil is back.

Fear Street Saga

The Betrayal (1993)
Nora knows why so many horrible things happen on Fear Street.

The Secret (1993)
Elizabeth and Kate love the same boy.

The Burning (1993)
After generations of unspeakable horror, Daniel and Nora must unite the feuding families.

Fear Street Super Chillers Series

Party Summer (1991)
Cari and her friends look forward to working at Howling Wolf Inn, but the party is over when the mysterious owner is murdered.

Silent Night (1992)
Reva Dalby ignores the warning. A stalker could kill her holiday.

Goodnight Kiss (1992)
Matt notices twin puncture wounds on April's neck and suspects her next goodnight kiss may be her last.

Broken Hearts (1993)
Josie and Melissa are scared of whoever is sending deadly Valentines.

Silent Night 2 (1993), sequel
Santa is bringing Reva a little unexpected retribution.

Bad Moonlight (1995)
When one of the band's musicians is ripped to shreds, Danielle Verona, new lead singer, fears whatever is lurking out there.

The Ghosts of Fear Street Series

1. *Hide and Shriek* (1995)
2. *Who's Been Sleeping in My Grave?* (1995)
3. *The Attack of the Aqua Apes* (1995)
4. *Nightmare in 3-D* (1996)

99 Fear Street Trilogy

99 Fear Street: The First Horror (1994)
Cally and Kody Frasier and their family move to 99 Fear Street—and they must learn its secret or become victims of the House of Evil.

99 Fear Street: The Second Horror (1994)
When he moves to 99 Fear Street, Brandt McCoy does not know that it is haunted by Cally Frasier.

99 Fear Street: The Third Horror (1994)
Kody Frasier has returned to play her sister, Cally, in a movie about the house of horrors—but Cally's ghost wants revenge.

FICTION FOR YOUNGER READERS

The Absurdly Silly Encyclopedia and Flyswatter (1978) as Jovial Bob Stine

How to Be Funny: An Extremely Silly Guidebook (1978) as Jovial Bob Stine

The Complete Book of Nerds (1979) as Jovial Bob Stine

The Dynamite Do-It-Yourself Pen Pal Kit (1980) as Jovial Bob Stine

Dynamite's Funny Book of the Sad Facts of Life (1980) as Jovial Bob Stine

Going Out! Going Steady! Going Bananas! (1980) as Jovial Bob Stine

The Pigs' Book of World Records (1980) as Jovial Bob Stine

The Sick of Being Sick Book (1980) as Jovial Bob Stine with Jane Stine

Bananas Looks at TV (1981) as Jovial Bob Stine

The Beast Handbook (1981) as Jovial Bob Stine

The Cook Kids' Guide to Summer Camp (1981) as Jovial Bob Stine with Jane Stine

Gnasty Gnomes (1981) as Jovial Bob Stine

Bored with Being Bored! How to Beat the Boredom Blahs (1982) as Jovial Bob Stine with Jane Stine

Don't Stand in the Soup (1982) as Jovial Bob Stine

The Time Raider (1982)

Blips! The First Book of Video Game Funnies (1983) as Jovial Bob Stine

Everything You Need to Survive: Brothers and Sisters (1983) as Jovial Bob Stine with Jane Stine

Everything You Need to Survive: Homework (1983) as Jovial Bob Stine with Jane Stine

Everything You Need to Survive: Money Problems (1983) as Jovial Bob Stine with Jane Stine

The Golden Sword of Dragonwalk (1983)

Horrors of the Haunted Museum (1984)

Instant Millionaire (1984)

Through the Forest of Twisted Dreams (1984)

Wizards, Warriors and You: The Siege of the Dragonriders (1984) as Eric Affabee

The Badlands of Hark (1985)

Challenge of the Wolf Knight (1985)

Conquest of the Time Master (1985)

Demons of the Deep (1985)

The Invaders of Hark (1985)

Jovial Bob's Computer Joke Book (1985) as Jovial Bob Stine

Attack on the King (1986) as Eric Affabee

Blind Date (1986) as Jovial Bob Stine

Cavern of the Phantoms (1986)

The Doggone Dog Joke Book (1986) as Jovial Bob Stine

Miami Mice (1986) as Jovial Bob Stine

Mystery of the Imposter (1986)

One Hundred and One Silly Monster Jokes (1986) as Jovial Bob Stine

Operation: Deadly Decoy (1986)

The Jet Fighter Trap (1987) as Zachary Blue

The Protectors: The Petrova Twist (1987) as Zachary Blue

Wizards, Warriors and You: The Dragon Queen's Revenge (1987) as Eric Affabee

Ghostbusters II Storybook (1989)

Pork & Beans: Play Date (1989)

One Hundred and One Vacation Jokes (1990)

The Amazing Adventures of Me, Myself, and I (1991)

G. I. Joe Series as Eric Affabee

G. I. Joe and the Everglades Swamp Terror (1986)

G. I. Joe: Operation: Star Raider (1986)

G. I. Joe: Jungle Raid (1988)

Give Yourself Goosebumps Series

Tales to Give You Goosebumps (1994)
Collection. One story, "The House of No Return," was issued separately as a give-away booklet.

Escape from the Carnival of Horrors (1995)

More Tales to Give You Goosebumps (1995)
Short stories.

Tick Tock, You're Dead! (1995)

Goosebumps Series

1. *Welcome to Dead House* (1992)
2. *Stay out of the Basement* (1992)
3. *Monster Blood* (1992)
4. *Say Cheese and Die* (1992)
5. *The Curse of the Mummy's Tomb* (1993)
6. *Let's Get Invisible!* (1993)
7. *Night of the Living Dummy* (1993)
8. *The Girl Who Cried Monster* (1993)
9. *Welcome to Camp Nightmare* (1993)
10. *The Ghost Next Door* (1993)
11. *The Haunted Mask* (1993)
12. *Be Careful What You Wish For . . .* (1993)
13. *Piano Lessons Can Be Murder* (1993)
14. *The Werewolf of Fever Swamp* (1993)
15. *You Can't Scare Me!* (1994)
16. *One Day at Horror Land* (1994)
17. *Why I'm Afraid of Bees* (1994)
18. *Monster Blood II* (1994), sequel
19. *Deep Trouble* (1994)
20. *The Scarecrow Walks at Midnight* (1994)
21. *Go Eat Worms* (1994)
22. *Ghost Beach* (1994)
23. *Return of the Mummy* (1994)
24. *Phantom of the Auditorium* (1994)
25. *Attack of the Mutant* (1994)

26. *My Hairiest Adventure* (1994)
27. *A Night in Terror Tower* (1995)
28. *The Cuckoo Clock of Doom* (1995)
29. *Monster Blood III* (1995), sequel
30. *It Came from Beneath the Sink* (1995)
31. *Night of the Living Dummy II* (1995), sequel
32. *The Barking Ghost* (1995)
33. *The Horror at Camp Jellyjam* (1995)
34. *Revenge of the Lawn Gnomes* (1995)
35. *A Shocker on Shock Street* (1995)
36. *The Haunted Mask II* (1995), sequel
37. *The Headless Ghost* (1995)

Goosebumps Collector's Caps Collecting Kit (1995)

Indiana Jones Series

Indiana Jones and the Curse of Horror Island (1984)

Indiana Jones and the Giants of the Silver Tower (1984)

Indiana Jones and the Cult of the Mummy's Crypt (1985)

Indiana Jones and the Ape of Howling Island (1985)

James Bond Series

James Bond in Win, Place or Die (1985)

Space Cadets Series

Jerks-in-Training (1991)

Losers in Space (1991)

Bozos on Patrol (1992)

ADULT FICTION

Superstitions (1995)
A string of brutal murders does not spoil graduate student Sara Morgan's happiness with her new lover.

ADAPTATIONS IN OTHER MEDIA

Goosebumps (1995)
Fox network children's television series based on Stine books.

Fear Street (1996)
Announced motion picture based on the Stine series.

FOR FURTHER READING

Alderdice, Kit. "R. L. Stine: 90 Million Spooky Adventures." *Publishers Weekly*, 17 July 1995.

Blais, Jacqueline. "Spooky Stine Tackles TV Next." *USA Today*, 6 April 1995.

Claro, Danielle. "The Goosebumps Guy." *Nickelodeon Magazine*, April–May 1995.

Gray, Paul. "Carnage: An Open Book." *Time*, 2 August 1992.

Keeton, Claudia. *A Teacher's Guide to Young Adult Mystery/Horror Bestsellers.* New York: Archway Paperbacks, 1991.

"Meet R. L. Stine." *Waldenbooks Kids' News*, spring 1995.

"R. L. Stine." In *Contemporary Authors New Revision Series*, edited by Deborah A. Straub. Vol. 22. Detroit: Gale Research, 1988.

Sanders, Mary Lois. "R. L. Stine." In *Something About the Author*, edited by Diane Telgen. Vol. 76. Detroit: Gale Research, 1994.

Verney, Sarah. "R. L. Stine." In *Authors & Artists for Young Adults*, edited by Kevin S. Hile and E. A. DesChenes. Vol. 13. Detroit: Gale Research, 1994.

Todd Strasser

Family drama

New York City
May 5, 1950

Angel Dust Blues: A Novel

"When I was a teenager in the 1960s, I faced a lot of difficult choices," Todd Strasser said in a publisher's pamphlet. "I was always asking myself, 'Should I or shouldn't I?' But compared to today's teens, my life was sheltered. Teens today have even more difficult decisions to make. I hope that each of my books shows an example of a young adult who learns good judgment. Good YA literature should help the reader make the right choices."

Strasser, the son of an executive and a legal assistant, graduated from Beloit College in 1974. He married Pamela Older, a production manager, in 1981. They have one child.

Strasser has worked as a newspaper reporter, freelance writer, advertising copywriter, researcher, and president of a fortune cookie company. He speaks at teacher and librarian conferences and conducts writing workshops.

"Most teens today want books with characters they can identify with," Strasser stated in the pamphlet. "They want to be entertained, not preached to. I try to make my books funny, but not frivolous; readable but not patronizing. There's always an important underlying message that I want to get across.

"By the time they reach thirteen, many boys have started to resist reading fiction. Part of the reason, I think, is that many books for thirteen-year-olds have female protagonists whom boys no longer want to identify with. By writing books with male protagonists, I hope to attract those boys who would otherwise stop reading. Fortunately for me, girls seem to enjoy my books too."

Strasser told interviewer Nina Piwoz how he gathers firsthand information about young adults: "I eavesdrop on teenagers whenever I have the opportunity. Also, I have a few nephews and nieces in the eleven- to thirteen-year-old range who supply me with information, whether they know it or not."

Strasser's first book, *Angel Dust Blues*, is about suburban teenagers who experiment with drugs. It was taken from his own life. "My first story was based on that experience . . . and watching it occur," he said. "My second book, *Friends Till the End*, is about a healthy teenager who has a friend who becomes extremely ill with leukemia. When I moved to New York, I got a roommate . . . an old friend of mine. Within a few weeks he became very ill. I spent a year visiting him in the hospital, not knowing whether he was going to live or die. I thought it was an experience that teenagers could relate to and one they *should* relate to," quoted Nina Piwoz in a *Media & Methods* interview.

"This is rough and tough, both in subject and language," Zena Sutherland said of *Angel Dust Blues*, "but it is not didactic, although Alex learns something from his bitter experience, and it's not overdone; Strasser's writing has a depth and candor that puts the book's focus on the intricate and at times compassionate development of the characters and their relationships."

Although finding *Friends Till the End* more conventional than *Angel Dust Blues*, *Kirkus Reviews* said the book "has a spark of particularity that sets it apart from many more maudlin casebook scenarios."

Strasser explained how his characters develop: They "grow out of the story. Each story requires a certain group of characters to make it progress from beginning to end, and I supply them based on the story. I very rarely will pick a character and create a story around that character," quoted Nina Piwoz in a *Media & Methods* interview.

YOUNG ADULT FICTION

Angel Dust Blues: A Novel (1979)
Tired of his parents' upper-class expectations, Alex experiments with drugs. When he meets Ellen, he realizes that drugs are not everything.

Friends Till the End: A Novel (1981)
David realizes his own self-centeredness when he begins visiting a casual friend with leukemia, Howie, in the hospital.

The Wave (1981) as Morton Rhue
Novelization of a television drama by Johnny Dawkins. Teacher Ben Ross uses shock methods to bring discipline to his class.

Workin' for Peanuts (1983)
Jeff Mead sells peanuts at the stadium concession. He is surprised when an owner's daughter takes an interest in him.

The Complete Computer Popularity Program (1984)
Tony's father is an engineer at the unpopular nuclear power plant, and his only friend is computer nerd Paul. He decides to use a computer to get to know the most popular girl in school.

A Very Touchy Subject (1985)
Scott Tauscher, seventeen, is always bickering with his pretty, rich girlfriend.

Ferris Bueller's Day Off (1986)
Novelization of the film by John Hughes. A teenage con artist gets away with hooky.

The Mall from Outer Space (1987)

The Accident (1988)
Everyone had been drinking the snowy night Chris's car plunged into the ravine. Four friends are now dead.

Beyond the Reef (1991)
It has been five years, but should Chris and his father make one last stab at finding a lost Spanish treasure galleon?

The Diving Bell (1992)

Freaked (1993)

The Good Son (1993)

Hocus Pocus: A Novel (1993)

How I Changed My Life (1995)
A knee injury keeps Kyle off the football team.

Coming Attractions Series

Rock 'n' Roll Nights: A Novel (1982)
Four New York City high schoolers try to make it as a rock and roll band.

Turn It Up! (1984), sequel to *Rock 'n' Roll Nights*
The three boys and one girl in the rock band hire a new manager.

Wildlife (1987)

Lifeguards Series

Summer's Promise (1993)
Jess, a lifeguard, loves to put preppie Reed in his place, but Reed is accustomed to getting what he wants.

Summer's End (1993)
Jess's romance with Reed is taking hold when a tragic accident drives them apart.

CONTRIBUTOR

Connections: Short Stories by Outstanding Writers for Young Adults, edited by Donald R. Gallo (1989)

FICTION FOR YOUNGER READERS

Home Alone (1991)
Based on the motion picture.

Home Alone Two: Lost in New York (1992), sequel to *Home Alone*
Based on the motion picture sequel.

Addams Family Values (1993)
Novelization of the motion picture based on Charles Addams's *New Yorker* cartoons.

Beverly Hillbillies (1993)
Novelization of the motion picture based on the television series.

Free Willy: A Novelization (1993)
Based on the motion picture.

Super Mario Brothers: A Novel (1993)
Based on the video game.

Help! I'm Trapped in My Teacher's Body (1994)

Help! I'm Trapped in the First Day of School . . . Forever! (1994)

Three Ninjas Kick Back (1994)
Based on the motion picture.

Walt Disney's Peter Pan (1994)
Based on the motion picture.

Little Panda (1995)

Man of the House (1995)

Please Don't *Be Mine, Julie Valentine!* (1995)

Tall Tale: The Unbelievable Adventures of Pecos Bill (1995)

ADULT FICTION

The Family Man (1987)

ADAPTATIONS IN OTHER MEDIA

Can a Guy Say No? (1986)
Television movie based on *A Very Touchy Subject.*

FOR FURTHER READING

Piwoz, Nina. "I Was a Teenage Boy." *Media & Methods,* February 1983.

Review of *Friends Till the End. Kirkus Reviews,* 1 April 1981.

Sutherland, Zena. Review of *Angel Dust Blues. Bulletin of the Center for Children's Books,* February 1980.

Todd Strasser. New York: Delacorte Press, 1988.

Mildred D. Taylor

Family drama

Jackson, Mississippi
September 13, 1943

Roll of Thunder, Hear My Cry

Mildred D. Taylor's novels depict black family life in the rural South in the 1930s.

"I grew to know the South—to feel the South—through the yearly trips we took there and through the stories told," Taylor said in accepting the Boston Globe–Horn Book Award in 1988 for *The Friendship*. "In those days, before the civil rights movement, I remember the South and how it was. I remember the racism, the segregation. . . . But I also remember the other South—the South of family and community."

Taylor's family moved to a newly integrated town in Ohio when she was ten. She was the only black child in her class. She received degrees from the University of Toledo and the University of Colorado. She also joined the Peace Corps and spent two years in Ethiopia. Taylor has taught English and history and worked as a recruiter, a study skills coordinator, a proofreader, and an editor.

Taylor's *Roll of Thunder, Hear My Cry*, Emily R. Moore said, "describes a year during which Cassie Logan learns to handle the indignities inflicted upon herself, her family and neighbors. She also learns the importance of her family's struggle to keep their land and their economic independence. . . . Throughout the book, the reader is moved to tears by Ms. Taylor's vibrant, exquisite, and simple style. The dialogue is lightly seasoned with Southern colloquialisms."

Most of Taylor's young adult prose has been about the Logan family. In her Newbery Award acceptance speech for *Roll of Thunder, Hear My Cry*, Taylor stated: "Cassie was a spunky eight-year-old [in the first book], innocent, untouched by discrimination, full of pride, and greatly loved, and through her I discovered I now could tell one of the stories I had heard so often as a child. From that meeting came *Song of the Trees*.

"If you have met Cassie and her brothers—Stacey, the staunch, thoughtful leader; Christopher-John, the happy, sensitive mediator; and Little Man, the shiny clean, prideful, manly six-year-old—then perhaps you can understand why, when I sent that final manuscript off to Dial, I did not want to give them up. Those four children made me laugh; they also made me cry, and I had to find a way of keeping them from fading into oblivion. In August 1974 came the answer: I would write another book about the Logans, one in which I could detail the teachings of my own childhood as well as incorporate many of the stories I had heard about my family and others."

" 'A natural writer' is an overused expression I don't particularly like," said Phyllis J. Fogelman, "but in speaking of Mildred Taylor it seems absolutely appropriate. Mildred's words flow smoothly, effortlessly, it seems, and they abound in richness, harmony, and rhythm. Her stories unfold in a full, leisurely way, well suited to and evocative of her Southern settings. Her ability to bring her characters to life and to involve her readers is remarkable."

YOUNG ADULT FICTION

The Friendship (1987)
Tom Bee, a black man, saves the life of John Wallace, a white storekeeper. Years later, John forgets his debt.

The Gold Cadillac (1987)
In the 1950s, a black family travels to the South, not expecting the racism they face.

Logan Family Series

Song of the Trees (1975)
Cassie Logan, eight, tells of the conflict between her father and white men over trees on Logan land.

Roll of Thunder, Hear My Cry (1976)
Papa Logan is away, working on the railroad, and the rest of the family struggles with bigotry at home.

Let the Circle Be Unbroken (1981)
The Depression hurts rural southern sharecroppers, but whites and blacks support each other.

Mississippi Bridge (1990)
Jeremy Simms, ten, a white boy, reacts when Grandma Logan and other black passengers are put off a bus during a storm so that whites can ride in comfort.

The Road to Memphis (1990)
Cassie, now a senior in high school, dreams of becoming a lawyer. She is not prepared for a friend's rage at his white tormentors.

The Well: David's Story (1995)
A story about the generation before *Roll of Thunder, Hear My Cry*.

ADAPTATIONS IN OTHER MEDIA

Roll of Thunder, Hear My Cry (1978) Television miniseries.

FOR FURTHER READING

Fogelman, Phyllis J. "Mildred D. Taylor." *Horn Book Magazine,* August 1977.

Greenlaw, M. Jean. *A Teacher's Guide to* Song of the Trees, The Friendship, *and* The Gold Cadillac *by Mildred D. Taylor*. New York: Bantam Doubleday Dell, n.d.

Moore, Emily R. Review of *Roll of Thunder, Hear My Cry. Interracial Books for Children Bulletin* 7, no. 7 (1976).

Taylor, Mildred D. Newbery Award acceptance speech. *Horn Book Magazine,* August 1977.

Theodore Taylor

Outdoor drama

Statesville, North Carolina
June 23, 1921
The Cay

One of writer Theodore Taylor's best-known books, *The Cay*, has been highly controversial for its depiction of an interracial friendship.

The story, he told Norma Bagnall, "is fiction but based partially on fact, and the characters are drawn from real life. In 1955–56, I was researching an adult book on submarine warfare, and I came across an incident involving a small Dutch vessel. I had sailed those waters during the war, and I had also lived in the Caribbean for almost two years after the war. So I knew something about the people. For the character of Phillip, I used a boyhood friend whose mother hated blacks, any blacks. In turn, she tragically transferred that hatred to my friend. I'd known a number of West Indian sailors, one in particular, and they collectively became my Timothy. I combined the incident with the characters and out of that came *The Cay*. Even the cat had a true-life counterpart. It is a fictional story against a true background."

The story, which takes place during World War II, is "both a war survival story and one of overcoming prejudice," Charlotte S. Huck and Doris Young Kuhn said. "After the Germans torpedoed the freighter on which Phillip and his mother were traveling from wartime Curacao to the U.S., Phillip finds himself cast up on a barren little Caribbean island with an old black man named Timothy. A blow on the head during the wreck had left Phillip blind and completely dependent upon Timothy. Born in Virginia of Southern parents, Phillip was prejudiced toward blacks. Timothy, who has been criticized for being an 'Uncle Tom,' probably really was one. . . .

"Both Phillip and Timothy are products and prisoners of their backgrounds. Gradually, Phillip begins to understand and trust the wisdom and selflessness of Timothy. His way of overcoming his prejudice is to make Timothy white in his mind. . . . [The story presents] a realistic account of a survival story in the Caribbean in 1942. . . . [It] suggests human interdependence in time of crisis. It is one of the few stories that details the gradual loss of prejudice."

The story was criticized as racist by Albert V. Schwartz. He described it as "the initiation of a white upper-middle-class boy into his superior role in a colonialist, sexist, racist society."

"The black male character, called Timothy (no last name), conforms to the traditional stereotype of the faithful slave or retainer who is happy to serve and even sacrifice his life for his 'young bahss'—a term which establishes, at the outset, the man's implied inferiority," the Council on Interracial Books for Children stated.

Taylor told Bagnall that he refused "to be intimidated by any organization, because I cannot write with somebody sitting there behind my back." Taylor returned the 1970 Jane Addams Children's Book Award in a disagreement over the book's intent.

"Since 1970," Taylor wrote in *Top of the News*, "*The Cay* has been under varied attack as 'racist,' mainly from the [Council on Interracial Books for Children], but also from some black organizations; some individual librarians and teachers, white and black. . . . Needless to say, passages in any book can be underlined and utilized for whatever purpose the reader chooses. That purpose does not always coincide with what the writer had in mind; nor always with the total meaning; nor always with the majority of the readers. . . .

"In my own mind, I did not set out to write a 'racist' novel, vintage 1942; harm any human being, black or white; damage the black struggle for human equality. Further, I am not at all convinced that I did write a 'racist' novel. The goal was to the contrary. Directed primarily toward the white child (thinking that the black child did not need to be told much about prejudice), I hoped to achieve a subtle plea for better race relations and more understanding. I have reason to believe that I partially achieved that goal, despite acknowledged omissions and commissions; flaws."

Taylor, the son of a metal and plastics molder, attended Fork Union Military Academy in Virginia and the U.S. Merchant Marine Academy in New York. He also studied at Columbia University and the American Theatre Wing. He served in the U.S. Merchant Marines from 1942 to 1944 and was in the U.S. Naval Reserve. He has twice been married, to Gweneth Goodwin in 1946 and to Flora Gray Schoenleber in 1981. He has three children by his first marriage.

Taylor has worked for a number of newspapers in positions ranging from copyboy to sports editor. He has been a public relations director for a university and for Paramount Pictures. He has been a motion picture story editor, writer, and associate producer. He has produced and directed documentary films.

Taylor wrote a trio of stories, Cape Hatteras, set at the turn of the century on the Outer Banks of North Carolina. Ben O'Neal, age eleven in the opening book, helps rescue a girl, Teetoncey, from a shipwreck. She has lost her memory. Hoping to spark its return, Ben takes her to the stormy shore one night. Ben yearns to go to sea, and once Tee recovers her memory, she tells of treasure aboard the ship that sank. Ben and his friends seek the treasure, but there is tragedy. In the final book, his mother having died, Ben goes looking for his brother, and Tee leaves for her home in England. Their paths surprisingly cross again.

"Filled with local color and laced with regional expressions, homespun humor, and superstitions, the story evokes the chancy existence at the turn of the century of the sturdy, weather-tuned residents of the Carolina Shoals," Mary M. Burns said.

Taylor wrote a number of nonfiction books, including *People Who Make Movies* (1967), *Air Raid—Pearl Harbor! The Story of December 7, 1941* (1971), and *H.M.S. Hood vs. Bismarck: The Battleship Battle* (1982). He has written for a variety of magazines and has written books under the pen name T. T. Lang.

YOUNG ADULT FICTION

The Cay (1969)
An eleven-year-old white boy, Phillip, and a seventy-year-old black seaman, Timothy, survive when their boat is torpedoed by Nazis during World War II.

The Children's War (1971)
Twelve-year-old Alaskan Dory, whose father is a navy radioman, befriends a mysterious old hunter and hermit.

The Maldonado Miracle (1973)
Jose Maldonado, twelve, a Mexican boy, yearns to follow his father to the United States.

The Trouble with Tuck (1981)
Helen's golden Labrador dog goes blind.

Sweet Friday Island (1984)
A fifteen-year-old girl and her father vacation on a remote island off the Baja Peninsula.

Walking up a Rainbow: Being the True Version of the Long and Hazardous Journey of Susan D. Carlisle, Mrs. Myrtle Dessery, Drover Bert Pettit, and Cowboy Clay Carmer and Others (1986)
It is 1851. Susan Carlisle, thirteen, fights to save her property from the saloon owner who claims her father owed him $15,000.

The Hostage (1987)
A struggling salmon fisherman and his family hope to sell a killer whale to a marine park.

Sniper (1989)
Ben Jepson, fifteen, is left in charge of his parents' wild animal preserve while they travel to Africa.

Tuck Triumphant (1991), sequel to *The Trouble with Tuck*
Helen must convince her family to keep an adopted six-year-old Korean boy who, they have just discovered, is deaf.

The Weirdo (1991)
Chip Clewt lives in the swamp. People do not talk to him. They think he is deformed or something.

Maria, A Christmas Story (1992)
Maria Gonzaga is jealous to hear her friends describe the fun they have in San Lazaro's annual holiday parade.

Timothy of the Cay (1993)
Timothy has adventures before the events in *The Cay*.

To Kill the Leopard (1993)

The Bomb (1995)
Atomic weapon testing at Bikini Atoll provides the backdrop to this novel.

Cape Hatteras Trilogy

Teetoncey (1974)
Ben O'Neal wants to show the men of the rough Outer Banks of North Carolina in 1898 that he is as courageous as his father was. He rescues a young girl from a shipwreck.

Teetoncey and Ben O'Neal (1975)
Ben hopes to go to sea. Young Teetoncey remembers there was treasure aboard the ship that wrecked.

The Odyssey of Ben O'Neal (1977)
Ben heads off to find his brother; Teetoncey reluctantly returns to England—but their paths cross.

Outer Banks Trilogy

Stranger from the Sea (1995)

Box of Treasures (1995)

Into the Wind (1995)

ADULT FICTION

The Stalker (1987)

Monocolo: A Novel (1989)

TELEPLAYS

Tom Threepersons (1964)

Sunshine, the Whale (1974)

The Girl Who Whistled the River Kwai (1980)

SCREENPLAYS

Night Without End (1959)

Showdown (1973)

The Hold-Up (1974)

ADAPTATIONS IN OTHER MEDIA

The Cay (1974)
Television movie.

FOR FURTHER READING

Bagnall, Norma. "Theodore Taylor: His Models of Self-Reliance." *Language Arts*, January 1980.

Burns, Mary M. Review of *Teetoncey and Ben O'Neal. Horn Book Magazine*, December 1975.

Council on Interracial Books for Children. Letter to the Editor. *Top of the News*, April 1975.

Huck, Charlotte S., and Doris Young Kuhn, eds. *Children's Literature in the Elementary School*. 3d ed. New York: Holt, Rinehart & Winston, 1979.

Schwartz, Albert V. " 'The Cay': Racism Still Rewarded." *Interracial Books for Children* 3, no. 4 (1971).

Taylor, Theodore. Letter to the Editor. *Top of the News*, April 1975.

Joyce Carol Thomas

Family drama

Ponca City, Oklahoma
May 25, 1938

Marked by Fire

Marked by Fire, Joyce Carol Thomas's first novel, is about a girl who is struck mute after being raped.

"This is a powerful representative of a black rural Oklahoma community," Hazel Rochman said. "The story—told in a series of brief concentrated vignettes—is mainly about the women, and it focuses on one special child among them, Abyssinia (Abby) Jackson: the ritual of her birth in the cotton fields with the women all participating in the pain and the joy; her growth as the gifted beautiful darling of the community; the horror of her rape at age 10; her recovery and subsequent maturing. As she grows up, Abby learns—through her experiences with near drowning and with fire; through her dreams; and through her struggles with her alter ego, the mad Trembling Sally—that violence can lead to rebirth and to revelation."

"Thomas's poetic tone gives this work what scents give the roses already so pleasing in color," Dorothy Randall-Tsuruta observed. "In fact, often as not the lyrical here carries the reader beyond concern for fast action. Then, too, Thomas's short-lived interest in playwrighting figures in her fine regard for and control of dialogue."

Born Joyce Carol Haynes, the writer grew up in a migrant farming family in Oklahoma and California. Her father later became a bricklayer, her mother a hair stylist. Thomas attended San Francisco City College, the University of San Francisco, the College of San Mateo, San Jose State College, and Stanford University. She married

Gettis L. Withers in 1959; they divorced in 1968. She married Roy T. Thomas, Jr., a professor, in 1968. They divorced in 1979. She has four children.

Thomas has worked as a telephone operator, a language teacher, an assistant professor of black studies, and a teacher of drama and English. She has been a professor of English since 1983 at the University of Tennessee and a visiting associate professor of English at Purdue University. She has been a writer, poet, and playwright since 1982.

The writer has chronicled the black American experience in her young adult novels. She wrote a sequel to *Marked by Fire, Bright Shadow*, which *Publishers Weekly* said "reverberates with the lyricism that evoked unanimous critical praise [for the earlier work]. But readers need steely nerves to stick with the story of horrors visited upon young Abyssinia Jackson and her friends. [Aunt] Serena's appalling death at the hands of a mad man and the tragedy affecting Abby's lover, Carl Lee Jefferson, are crises the girl must surmount if she is to remain sane and hopeful."

In *Bright Shadow*, Abby "is attending college and falling in love with Carl Lee, though the latter displeases her father. Her quiet romance is interrupted by the psychotic murder of her Aunt Serena. Abyssinia, who has had some forebodings about Serena's new husband, is traumatized by her discovery of the mangled body. Her own faith, her parents' and Carl Lee's love, and a mysterious cat sustain her through her grief, while her parents come to appreciate Carl Lee's support and concern," Carolyn Caywood explained.

Thomas explored the stories of other family members in two later books, *Water Girl* and *The Golden Pasture*. Her own past has inspired her writing, Thomas said in *Something About the Author.* "I work for authenticity of voice, fidelity to detail, and naturalness of developments."

YOUNG ADULT FICTION

Journey (1990)
Meggie sets out to find why her young friends are disappearing.

When the Nightingale Sings (1992)
Marigold, fourteen, lives with an abusive foster mother and yearns to become a gospel singer.

Jackson Family Series

Marked by Fire (1982)
In rural Oklahoma, Abby Jackson, ten, is raped but recovers and grows beyond the experience.

Bright Shadow (1983)
Abby's aunt Serena is killed by a mad man, and she experiences a crisis with her own lover.

Water Girl (1986)
Amber Westbrook, fifteen, discovers she is adopted. Her real mother is Abyssinia Jackson.

The Golden Pasture (1986)
Carlton Lee Jefferson, the son of a Cherokee mother and a black father, feels closest to Gray Jefferson, his grandfather, who is an ex-rodeo star.

POETRY

Bittersweet: Poems (1973)

Crystal Breezes (1974)

Blessing: Poems (1975)

Black Child (1981)

Inside the Rainbow (1982)

Brown Honey in Broomwheat Tea: Poems (1993)

DRAMA

Look! What a Wonder! (first produced in 1976)

A Song in the Sky (first produced in 1976)

Magnolia (first produced in 1977)

Ambrosia (first produced in 1978)

Gospel Roots (first produced in 1981)

When the Nightingale Sings (first produced in 1991)
Musical based on the novel.

EDITOR

A Gathering of Flowers: Stories About Being Young in America (1990)

ADAPTATIONS IN OTHER MEDIA

Marked by Fire (1987)
Adapted by James Racheff and Ted Kociolek for the stage musical *Abyssinia.*

FOR FURTHER READING

Caywood, Carolyn. Review of *Bright Shadow. School Library Journal,* January 1984.

Commire, Anne, ed. "Joyce Carol Thomas." In *Something About the Author.* Vol. 40 and Biography Series no. 7. Detroit: Gale Research, 1985.

Randall-Tsuruta, Dorothy. Review of *Marked by Fire. Black Scholar,* summer 1982.

Review of *Bright Shadow. Publishers Weekly,* 28 October 1983.

Rochman, Hazel. Review of *Marked by Fire. School Library Journal,* March 1982.

Julian F. Thompson

Social drama

New York City
November 16, 1927

The Grounding of Group 6

Julian F. Thompson's first young adult novel, *The Grounding of Group 6,* has an unusual premise. Coldbrook Country in Vermont appears to be the perfect boarding school. Five incoming students go on a hike deep into the woods, thinking it is part of their orientation. Instead, they face a killer hired by their parents to bump them off. However, the hired gun, Nat Rittenhouse, has a change of heart. The whole group then has to confront the murderous parents.

Publishers Weekly hailed the writer as having "a remarkable literary style and frightening inventiveness."

"Obviously conversant with teenagers' attitudes and language," Nancy C. Hammond said, "the author develops his premise convincingly. Writing fluently about adolescents in one key (romantic realism) and about adults in another (surrealistic black comedy), he doesn't even pretend to play fair. The adolescents, once away from their parents, are all remarkably responsible, good citizens; the lunatic adults are all ridiculous, discordant, and heinously wicked."

Thompson, whose father was a playwright and businessman, graduated from Princeton and Columbia Universities. He has worked as a coach, a teacher at Lawrenceville School, and a high school director. He married artist Polly Nichy in 1978. He has been a writer since 1979.

"My writing style is based on a lot of years of really intimate involvement with kids like the ones I write about," Thompson said in a publisher's pamphlet. "In that time, and especially in the seven years I spent as director of an alternative school, I wasn't getting kids' views that they'd specially packaged for adult consumption, but their 'real-est' feelings, ideas and attitudes. I wasn't an adversary there, but an ally, and some of those people are still among my closest friends.

"Kids are sometimes a lot closer to the basic importances than their adult mentors. The kids in my books tend to be idealized, romanticized. That isn't so by reason of some accident, or because I'm trying to curry favor with my readers. I'm writing about *that* part of kids—that part of all of us, in fact; though some of us, as adults, learn to choke it back and forget about it."

"The author's advocacy of young adults is well known," noted Pam Spencer in describing *The Taking of Mariasburg*. Maria, seventeen, inherits money from a father she never knew and buys a small town to turn over to teenagers.

"He allows his characters to do 'grown-up' tasks, accepting and expecting that they can; certainly his plot of a town for teens reinforces his belief in them," Spencer said.

"Thompson is one of the most original and humorous of today's YA writers," said Stephanie Zvirin. "While his books will either enchant you or make you furious with their sexism, wholesale stereotyping, and smart-aleck characters, you shouldn't ignore him. . . .

"Certainly Thompson's way with words and his bizarre sense of humor are not to everyone's taste. But he is an innovative stylist: He has an ear fine-tuned to words and what they'll do; and he loves to turn reality on its head and challenge readers with his complicated visions."

YOUNG ADULT FICTION

The Grounding of Group 6 (1983)
Parents pay a private school "adviser" to kill their loser children.

Facing It (1983)
An injury ends his pro-ball chances, so Jonathan becomes a boys' camp counselor and baseball coach.

A Question of Survival (1984)
At a survival camp, Toby and Zack are at the mercy of their sadistic mates.

Discontinued (1985)
Dunc Banigan, seventeen, searches for a clue to the murder of his mother and older brother.

A Band of Angels (1986)
When his guardian is killed by a hit-and-run driver, Jordan is alone with a station wagon and a satchel full of money.

Simon Pure (1987)
Simon Storm, fifteen, attending Riddle University in Vermont, reveals the plans of a secret campus society.

The Taking of Mariasburg (1988)
Maria uses her inheritance to buy a whole town.

Goofbang Value Daze (1989)
Moral extremists take charge in a small Texas town.

Herb Seasoning (1990)
Herbie Hertzman tries out a variety of career options, including crime.

Gypsyworld (1993)
Five teens are transported to a parallel Earth—Gypsyworld—to see if they can adapt its harmonious ways to take back to save their planet's environment.

The Trials of Molly Sheldon (1995)
A girl awakens in the midst of a modern-day witch trial.

FOR FURTHER READING

Hammond, Nancy C. Review of *The Grounding of Group 6. Horn Book Magazine,* October 1983.

Julian F. Thompson. New York: Scholastic, 1988.

Review of *The Grounding of Group 6. Publishers Weekly,* 28 January 1983.

Spencer, Pam. Review of *The Taking of Mariasburg. Voice of Youth Advocates,* April 1988.

Zvirin, Stephanie. Review of *Herb Seasoning. Booklist,* 15 May 1990.

J. R. R. Tolkien

Fantasy

Bloemfontein, South Africa
January 3, 1892–September 2, 1973

The Hobbit and
The Lord of the Rings Trilogy

J. R. R. Tolkien had a profound influence on readers and other writers of fantasy literature.

He "seemed to have drawn his material from the medieval sagas, with their noisy battles between men and monsters and their simple social and moral structure," observed Alison Lurie. "But the message of *The Hobbit* (1937) was new. It presented a world in which the forces of evil might at times overcome the forces of good, and the true hero was no longer strong, handsome, aristocratic, and victorious in combat."

Noting Tolkien's attention to detail, including the use of long appendixes, Lin Carter said, "The end result of all this is simply that Middle-Earth is ever so much more real than [C. S. Lewis's] Narnia, [Clark Ashton Smith's] Zothique, [David Lindsay's] Tormance, or [Edgar Rice Burroughs's] Barsoom. No author in the history of fantasy has created so convincingly detailed and overwhelmingly realistic an imaginary world, and few have ever created so colorful a story."

"With appeal for all ages, the stories are filled with myth and legend; interesting characters with remarkable names; humor; warmth; and daring," said Susan Roman.

James Cawthorn and Michael Moorcock included Tolkien's The Lord of the Rings trilogy among their 100 best fantasy books, remarking on its impact: "Once upon a time there was a Hobbit. . . .

"Now there are millions of them. Or so, sometimes, it seems. For *The Hobbit* spawned a sequel [The Lord of the Rings: *The Fellowship of the Ring, The Two Towers*, and *The Return of the King*] so massive as to dwarf its parent. And the sequel generated theses, quiz-books, pseudo-scholarly studies of its pseudo-history, an incomplete animated film, and more bad artwork than any book since The Book. And a flood of heroic fantasy novels followed. . . .

"There are no irresistible warriors, male or female, in Tolkien's saga. Its strength lies in its embracing sweep, a combination of the panoramic view with a wealth of homely detail. Power, wisdom and authority rest largely in the hands of the older generations, and in Middle-Earth 'older' can be old indeed, for the Elves are virtually immortal."

John Ronald Reuel Tolkien, the son of a bank manager, was born in South Africa. When he was three, his mother brought Tolkien and his brother back to England for health reasons. His father, who stayed in South Africa, died of rheumatic fever a short time later. Tolkien's mother scratched out a living. She introduced her son to Andrew Lang's fairy books and George MacDonald's Curdie stories.

Tolkien grew to love the English countryside. His mother died in 1904, after the family had moved to the village of Birmingham. The boys were entrusted to a Roman Catholic priest. Religion would become a dominant force in Tolkien's creative output.

Tolkien began to study the classics at Exeter College in Oxford but switched to English and literature. He wrote poetry. He continued an interest in languages and in making up his own, supposedly those spoken by elves.

Tolkien served as a signal officer during World War I. He married Edith Mary Bratt, a pianist, in 1916. The loss of two close friends in the war inspired him to start writing *The Silmarillion,* an epic work. After the war, he taught. At age thirty-three he became one of Oxford's youngest professors. Instead of trying to find a publisher for *The Silmarillion,* he wrote bedtime stories for his four children.

One of Tolkien's children's stories was *Mr. Bliss,* published years after his success with the Rings trilogy. In 1930, he began writing *The Hobbit,* completing it seven years later. Pressed to pen a sequel, he came up with The Lord of the Rings. Fellow writer C. S. Lewis, a colleague at Oxford, encouraged Tolkien. Completed in 1949, the trilogy was not published until 1954–55. It was enormously popular.

"All historians of children's literature . . . agree in placing that book among the very highest achievements of children's authors during the twentieth century," Humphrey Carpenter and Mari

Prichard stated in *The Oxford Companion to Children's Literature.* "Tolkien himself came to believe that no author could write especially 'for' children—the first edition of *The Hobbit* contains a number of patronizing 'asides' to the child-audience, but many of these were removed later, when its author's views on the subject changed."

Tolkien held up publication of the Rings trilogy because he hoped to have the even longer but still not completed *Silmarillion* come out at the same time. *The Fellowship of the Ring* and *The Two Towers* eventually were published in 1954, *The Return of the King* the next year. By 1965, international copyright on the books lapsed. An American paperback publisher, Ace, brought the trilogy out in softcover but without paying royalties. Tolkien revised the work slightly for a new, "authorized" edition from his own publisher. The notoriety of the royalties dispute brought wide attention to the book, which was very popular with college students. Ace later paid royalties to Tolkien and withdrew its edition. By the end of 1968, about 3 million copies of The Lord of the Rings had sold worldwide. Tolkien's son Christopher completed *The Silmarillion*, and it was published in 1977.

Tolkien wrote many nonfiction works on topics of English literature, among them *A Middle English Vocabulary* (1922), *Beowulf: The Monsters and the Critics* (1937), and *Chaucer as a Philologist* (1943).

FICTION

Farmer Giles of Ham (1949; revisions 1950, 1975, and 1978), included in *The Tolkien Reader* (1966); included in *Farmer Giles of Ham; The Adventures of Tom Bombadil* (1975)

The Adventures of Tom Bombadil, and Other Verses from the Red Book (1962), included in *The Tolkien Reader* (1966); included in *Farmer Giles of Ham* (1949); *The Adventures of Tom Bombadil* (1975)

Tree and Leaf (1964), included in *The Tolkien Reader* (1966); included in *Smith of Wootton Major; The Homecoming of Beorhtnoth* (1975)

The Tolkien Reader (1966)
Besides the above-indicated works, this includes "The Homecoming of Beorhtnoth"

The Road Goes Ever On: A Song Cycle (1967)

Smith of Wootton Major (1967, 1975, and 1978), included in *Tree and Leaf* (1964); and *The Homecoming of Beorhtnoth* (1975)

The Father Christmas Letters, edited by Baillie Tolkien (1976)

Pictures by J. R. R. Tolkien (1979)

Poems and Stories (1980)

Unfinished Tales of Numenor and Middle-Earth, edited by Christopher Tolkien (1980)

Finn and Hengest: The Fragment and the Episode (1982)

Mr. Bliss (1982)

Middle-Earth Series

The Hobbit; or, There and Back Again (1937; revisions 1951, 1966, and 1978)
Bilbo Baggins, smaller than a dwarf but larger than a Lilliputian, is persuaded to accompany the wizard Gandalf on a quest for an ancestral treasure being held by a dragon.

The Fellowship of the Ring (1954), a sequel to *The Hobbit* and the first book of The Lord of the Rings trilogy
Frodo Baggins becomes heir to his cousin Bilbo's One Ring, ruler of all the Rings of Power. But Orc soldiers are after the One Ring, and the council rules that it must be destroyed to keep peace. Frodo and his companions venture to enemy territory. The soldiers harass them as they travel, and the fellowship is scattered.

The Two Towers (1954)
Second book of The Lord of the Rings trilogy. Frodo, separated from his mates, travels on with his servant. After Frodo tames Gollum, Gollum guides them along a secret way into enemy country.

The Return of the King (1955)
Third book of The Lord of the Rings trilogy. As Sauron and Gandalf take different tacks, the fate of Middle-Earth depends on Frodo—he must destroy the Ring.

The Silmarillion, edited by Christopher Tolkien (1977)
More is told of the background of the characters and setting of The Lord of the Rings trilogy.

Bilbo's Last Song (1990)
Verse extracted from *The Hobbit.*

History of Middle-Earth Series edited by Christopher Tolkien

The Book of Lost Tales, part 1 (1983)

The Book of Lost Tales, part 2 (1984)

The Lays of Beleriand (1985)

The Shaping of Middle-Earth: The Quenta, the Ambarkanta, and the Annals (1986)

The Lost Road and Other Writings: Language and Legend Before the Lord of the Rings (1987)

The Return of the Shadow: The History of the Lord of the Rings, part 1 (1988)

The Treason of Isengard: The History of the Lord of the Rings, part 2 (1989)

The War of the Ring: The History of the Lord of the Rings, part 3 (1990)

Sauron Defeated: The End of the Third Age. The History of the Lord of the Rings, part 4 (1992)

Morgoth's Ring: The Later Silmarillion, part 1 (1993)

FOR FURTHER READING

Anderson, Douglas A. *The Annotated Hobbit.* Boston: Houghton Mifflin, 1988.

Beard, Henry N., and Douglas C. Kenney. *Bored of the Rings.* New York: New American Library, 1993 (reissue of 1969 Harvard Lampoon publication).

Carpenter, Humphrey. *J. R. R. Tolkien: A Biography.* New York: Houghton Mifflin, 1978.

Carpenter, Humphrey, and Mari Prichard, eds. *The Oxford Companion to Children's Literature.* New York: Oxford University Press, 1991.

Carter, Lin. *Imaginary Worlds: The Art of Fantasy.* New York: Ballantine Books, 1973.

———. *Tolkien: A Look Behind the Lord of the Rings.* New York: Houghton Mifflin, 1969.

Cawthorn, James, and Michael Moorcock. *Fantasy: The 100 Best Books.* New York: Carroll & Graf, 1988.

Foster, Robert. *A Guide to Middle-Earth.* Manchester, MD: Mirage Press, 1971. (Revised as *The Complete Guide to Middle-Earth.* New York: Del Rey, 1981.)

Johnson, Judith A. *J. R. R. Tolkien: Six Decades of Criticism.* Westport, CT: Greenwood, 1986.

Lurie, Alison. *Don't Tell the Grown-Ups: Why Kids Love the Books They Do.* New York: Avon Books, 1990.

Roman, Susan. *Sequences: Annotated Guide to Children's Fiction in Series.* Chicago: American Library Association, 1985.

Shippey, T. A. *The Road to Middle-Earth.* Boston: Houghton Mifflin, 1983.

Stimpson, Catherine R. *J. R. R. Tolkien.* New York: Columbia University Press, 1969.

Tolkien, John, and Priscilla Tolkien. *The Tolkien Family Album.* Boston: Houghton Mifflin, 1994.

Tolkien, J. R. R. *Letters of J. R. R. Tolkien*, selected by Humphrey Carpenter and Christopher Tolkien. Boston: Houghton Mifflin, 1988.

Mark Twain

Outdoor adventure

Humor

Florida, Missouri
November 30, 1835–April 21, 1910
The Adventures of Huckleberry Finn

A steamboatman turned writer, Missouri-born Samuel Langhorne Clemens, alias Mark Twain, worked as a printer's apprentice and typesetter before taking to the Mississippi River. He later worked for the government in Nevada, mined, and reported for a newspaper. Once established as a successful fiction writer and humorist, Twain traveled widely and lectured. He also wrote many volumes of travel books, essays, and correspondence, as well as journals, manuscripts, speeches, and autobiographical books.

Twain created two enduring, youthful, literary adventurers named Tom and Huck. *The Adventures of Tom Sawyer* is set in a small Mississippi River town before the Civil War. Playful Tom, who with his serious brother, Sid, lives with Aunt Polly, quarrels with his sweetheart, Becky Thatcher, then runs off with rascally Huckleberry Finn on a nighttime adventure. They watch Injun Joe stab the town doctor. More adventures ensue; Tom and Huck hide on an island. They watch the town hold a funeral for them. After the two wanderers return to town, Tom and Becky become lost in a cave and stumble upon Injun Joe's hiding place. It is great rough-and-tumble fun for young readers. James D. Hart said that *Tom Sawyer* "is on the whole a keener realistic portrayal of regional character and frontier experience on the Mississippi."

Twain took characters and situations from his own childhood. "Most of the adventures recorded in this book really occurred; one or two were experiences of my own, the rest those of boys who were schoolmates of mine. Huck Finn is drawn from life; Tom Sawyer also, but not from an individual—he is a combination of the characteristics of three boys whom I knew, and therefore belongs to the composite order of architecture," he said in his *Autobiography*.

Considered a picaresque classic is the companion *The Adventures of Huckleberry Finn*, which Humphrey Carpenter and Mari Prichard described as "brilliant." Pascal Covici, Jr., described the book as "the greatest work so far of the American comic imagination." Huck, displeased with life with the Widow Douglas, strikes off down the river on a raft with a runaway slave, Jim. They witness a murder, help settle a legal claim, and consort with a variety of odd characters.

Huckleberry Finn has been controversial since it first appeared. *Century Magazine*, when publishing the novel in 1884–85, excised parts it considered "too lurid for the refined readers of the times," according to Jerry Allen in *The Adventures of Mark Twain* (1954). "Huck was not allowed to be 'in a sweat,' or go naked on the raft; people could not blow their noses, chaw tobacco, or recognize 'the signs of a dead cat being around.' " The book was banned at libraries such as one in Concord, Massachusetts—purportedly because Huck used the curse word *hell*.

The writer took censorship in stride. In his *Autobiography*, Twain said the Concord library "flung him [Huck] out indignantly, partly because he was a liar and partly because after deep meditation and careful deliberation he made up his mind on a difficult point, and said that if he'd got to betray Jim or go to hell, he would go to hell—which was profanity, and those Concord purists couldn't stand it."

Twain added, with tongue in cheek, that he thoroughly agreed that "the mind that becomes soiled in youth can never again be washed clean; I know this by my own experience, and to this day I cherish an unappeasable bitterness against the unfaithful guardians of my young life, who not only permitted but compelled me to read an unexpurgated Bible through before I was 15 years old."

"Twain's problems with the censor are well known," Donelson and Nilsen remarked. "*Century* editor Richard Watson Gilder apparently found some material too harsh or too coarse and left out the preacher's harangue at the camp meeting and the lynching of Colonel Sherburn.

"After the publication of *Huck Finn*, the Concord (Massachusetts) Library banned the book as trashy, vicious, and unfit to be placed next to books by Emerson or Thoreau. Louisa May Alcott said, 'If Mr. Clemens cannot think of something better to tell our pure-minded lads and lasses, he had best stop writing for them,' a comment Twain felt would sell an additional 25,000 copies. The Concord Library was not alone in damning the book. *The Springfield Republican* wrote in 1885, 'They [Tom Sawyer and Huck Finn] are no better in tone than the dime novels which flood the blood-and-thunder reading population. . . . Their moral tone is low, and their perusal cannot be anything less than harmful.' "

A century later, the clamor to censor *Tom Sawyer* and *Huckleberry Finn* has not abated. Herbert N. Foerstel, in *Banned in the USA*, catalogs numerous attempts to have the books removed from school reading lists and libraries in Texas, Illinois, Oregon, Michigan, Pennsylvania, and other states in the 1990s.

Young adult author Harry Mazer stated, in *Books I Read When I Was Young*, "What I remember from *The Adventures of Huckleberry Finn* was Huck in his father's grip, Huck imprisoned in a shack in the woods. In *The Adventures of Tom Sawyer* I remember how he was found out when he was disguised as a girl. I could hardly breathe when he was trapped in the cave."

"Huckleberry Finn never dies, and our books feature Hucks of both sexes, and often suburban," said young adult author Richard Peck. "Sharing traits with the readers, they have to be imperfect enough for improvement and willing to stand up for who they are. They have to take one step nearer maturity in an age when maturing has become an elective, and show readers the way, give them the word."

FICTION

The Celebrated Jumping Frog of Calaveras County, and Other Sketches (1867)

Eye Openers: Good Things, Immensely Funny Sayings, and Stories (1871)

Screamers: A Gathering of Scraps of Humour, Delicious Bits, and Short Stories (1871)

A Curious Dream, and Other Sketches (1872)

The Gilded Age: A Tale of Today (1873) with Charles Dudley Warner

Mark Twain's Sketches (1874)

Mark Twain's Sketches: New and Old (1876)

The Prince and the Pauper (1881)
Edward, Prince of Wales, and commoner Tom Canty are young doubles. They switch places.

A Connecticut Yankee in King Arthur's Court (1889); British title: *A Yankee at the Court of King Arthur* (1889)
A factory foreman slips thirteen centuries into the past, bringing all sorts of technology with him to the Round Table.

The American Claimant (1892)
Adapted from a play by Mark Twain and William Dean Howells.

Merry Tales (1892)

The 1,000,000 Pound Bank-Note, and Other New Stories (1893)

Pudd'nhead Wilson: A Tale (1894, British title); expanded U.S. edition: *The Tragedy of Pudd'nhead Wilson, and the Comedy of Those Extraordinary Twins* (1894)
Wilson solves a crime using the new science of fingerprint analysis.

Personal Recollections of Joan of Arc (1896) as Sieur Louis de Conte

The Man That Corrupted Hadleyburg, and Other Stories and Essays (1900)

A Double Barrelled Detective Story (1902)

A Dog's Tale (1904)

Extracts from Adam's Diary (1904); portions included in *The Diaries of Adam and Eve* (1971)

Eve's Diary Translated from the Original Ms. (1906); portions included in *The Diaries of Adam and Eve* (1971)

The $30,000 Bequest, and Other Stories (1906)

A Horse's Tale (1907)

Extract from Captain Stormfield's Visit to Heaven (1909)

The Mysterious Stranger: A Romance, edited by Albert Bigelow Paine and Frederick A. Duneka (1916)

The Curious Republic of Gondour, and Other Whimsical Sketches (1919)

Sketches of the Sixties (1926) with Bret Harte

Simon Wheeler, Detective (1963), edited by Franklin R. Rogers
Uncompleted novel.

The Adventures of Colonel Sellers (1965); Twain's portion of *The Gilded Age*, edited by Charles Nelder
Sellers is full of impractical, strike-it-rich schemes.

Short Stories of Mark Twain (1967)

Early Tales and Sketches, vol. 1: 1851–64, edited by Edgar M. Branch and Robert H. Hirst (1979)

Tom Sawyer and Huck Finn Series

The Adventures of Tom Sawyer (1876)
In a Mississippi River town, mischievous Tom romances Becky Thatcher and avoids the dangerous Injun Joe.

The Adventures of Huckleberry Finn (1884)
Huck, chafing at having to lead a civilized life, heads down the river with a runaway slave, Jim.

Huck Finn and Tom Sawyer Among the Indians and Other Unfinished Stories, foreword and notes by Dahlia Armon and Walter Blair (1989)

Tom Sawyer Abroad, by Huck Finn (1894)
Huck and Tom take a trip in a balloon.

Tom Sawyer, Detective, As Told by Huck Finn, and Other Stories (1896)
The boys solve a murder and theft.

Tom Sawyer Grows Up (1939) by Clement Wood
Based on the Twain characters.

The True Adventures of Huckleberry Finn (1970) by John Seelye
Based on the Twain characters.

The Further Adventures of Huckleberry Finn (1983) by Greg Matthews
Based on the Twain characters.

Mister Grey; or, The Further Adventures of Huckleberry Finn (1992) by Richard White
Based on the Twain characters.

DRAMA

The Gilded Age (1873) with G. S. Densmore
Adapted from the novel.

Colonel Sellers (first produced in 1874)

Ah Sin (first produced in 1877) with Bret Harte

The American Claimant; or, Mulberry Sellers Ten Years Later (published in 1877) with William Dean Howells

ADAPTATIONS IN OTHER MEDIA

Tom Sawyer (1917)
Film.

Huck and Tom (1918)
Film.

Huckleberry Finn (1920)
Film.

Tom Sawyer (1930)
Film starring Jackie Coogan.

A Connecticut Yankee (1931)
Film based on *A Connecticut Yankee in King Arthur's Court.*

Huckleberry Finn (1931)
Film starring Jackie Coogan.

The Prince and the Pauper (1937)
Film.

The Adventures of Tom Sawyer (1938)
Film starring Tommy Kelly.

The Adventures of Huckleberry Finn (1939)
Film starring Mickey Rooney.

Tom Sawyer, Detective (1939)
Film starring Billy Cook.

The Adventures of Mark Twain (1944)
Biographical film starring Fredric March.

The Best Man Wins (1948)
Film based on the short story "The Celebrated Jumping Frog of Calaveras County."

A Connecticut Yankee in King Arthur's Court (1949)
Film starring Bing Crosby.

Man with a Million (1953)
Film starring Gregory Peck, based on "The 1,000,000 Pound Bank-Note."

The Adventures of Huckleberry Finn (1960)
Film starring Eddie Hodges.

The New Adventures of Huckleberry Finn (1968–69)
Animated NBC television series with voices of Michael Shea, Kevin Schultz, LuAnn Haslam, and Ted Cassidy.

Tom Sawyer (1973)
Television movie with Josh Albee.

Tom Sawyer (1973)
Film starring Johnnie Whitaker.

Huckleberry Finn (1974)
Film starring Jeff East.

Huckleberry Finn (1975)
Television movie with Ron Howard.

Crossed Swords (1978)
Film starring Oliver Reed, based on *The Prince and the Pauper.*

Unidentified Flying Oddball (1979)
Film starring Dennis Dugan, based on *A Connecticut Yankee in King Arthur's Court.*

The Adventures of Huckleberry Finn (1981)
Television movie with Kurt Ida.

Rascals and Robbers—The Secret Adventures of Tom Sawyer and Huck Finn (1982)
Television movie starring Patrick Creadon and Anthony Michael Hall.

The Adventures of Huckleberry Finn (1985)
Television movie with Patrick Day.

The Adventures of Mark Twain (1985)
Animated film.

Big River: The Adventures of Huckleberry Finn (1985)
Broadway musical adaptation based on the Twain novel. It ran 1,005 performances. Book by William Hauptman; music and lyrics by Roger Miller.

Tom Sawyer (1986)
Animated film.

A Connecticut Yankee in King Arthur's Court (1989)
Television movie starring Keshia Knight Pulliam.

Back to Hannibal: The Return of Tom Sawyer and Huckleberry Finn (1990)
Television movie with Raphael Sbarge and Mitchell Anderson.

The Adventures of Huckleberry Finn (1993)
Film starring Elijah Wood.

Tom Sawyer (1995)
Movie starring Jonathan Taylor Thomas, Rachael Leigh Cook, and Brad Renfro.

FOR FURTHER READING

Abbott, Sean. "I Been There Before: Revisiting Adventures of Huckleberry Finn." *At Random*, December 1995.

Allen, Jerry. *The Adventures of Mark Twain*. Boston: Little Brown, 1954.

Carpenter, Humphrey, and Mari Prichard. *Oxford Companion to Children's Literature.* New York: Oxford University Press, 1984.

Covici, Pascal, Jr. "Mark Twain (Samuel Langhorne Clemens)." In *Dictionary of Literary Biography, American Humorists, 1800–1950*, edited by Stanley Trachtenberg. Part 2, M–Z. Detroit: Gale Research, 1982.

Cox, Clinton. *Mark Twain America's Humorist, Dreamer, Prophet: A Biography*. New York: Scholastic, 1995.

Cullinan, Bernice, and M. Jerry Weiss, eds. *Books I Read When I Was Young: The Favorite Books of Famous People*. New York: Avon Books, 1980.

Donelson, Kenneth L., and Alleen Pace Nilsen, eds. Article in *Literature for Today's Young Adults*. Glenview, IL: Scott, Foresman, 1980.

Foerstel, Herbert N. *Banned in the USA: A Reference Guide to Book Censorship in Schools and Public Libraries*. Westport, CT: Greenwood, 1994.

Gates, David. "Same Twain, Different Time." *Newsweek*, 10 July 1992.

Gilman, Susan. "A Peek at Twain's Unpublished Works." *Christian Science Monitor*, 14 September 1981.

Hart, James D., ed. *Oxford Companion to American Literature*. 3d ed. New York: Oxford University Press, 1956.

Haupt, Clyde V. *Huckleberry Finn on Film: Film and Television Adaptations of Mark Twain's Novel, 1920–93*. Jefferson, NC: McFarland, 1994.

Kaplan, Justin. *Mr. Clemens and Mark Twain*. New York: Simon & Schuster, 1966.

Mason, Bobbie Ann, Roger Angell, E. L. Doctorow, William Styron, and David Bradley. "Commentaries on Twain and His Novel." *The New Yorker*, 26 June and 3 July 1995.

Paine, Albert Bigelow, ed. *Mark Twain's Autobiography*. 2 vols. New York: Harper & Brothers, 1924.

Peck, Richard. "Huck Finns of Both Sexes: Protagonists and Peer Leaders in Young-Adult Books." *Horn Book Magazine*, September–October 1993.

"Poor Huck; His Critics Just Won't Listen to Him." Unsigned editorial, with companion article "This Book Is Just Trash," by John Wallace. *USA Today*, 25 August 1995.

Reif, Rita. "First Half of 'Huck Finn,' in Twain's Hand, Is Found." *The New York Times*, 14 February 1991.

———. "How 'Huck Finn' Was Rescued." *The New York Times*, 17 March 1991.

———. "Twain Manuscript Resolves Huck Finn Mysteries." *The New York Times*, 26 February 1991.

Smiley, Jane. "Say It Ain't So, Huck: Second Thoughts on Mark Twain's 'Masterpiece.' " *Harper's*, January 1996.

Twain, Mark. "Jim and the Dead Man." *The New Yorker*, 26 June and 3 July 1995.
A newly discovered episode from Huck Finn.

———. *Old Times on the Mississippi*. Toronto: Belford, 1876.

Cynthia Voigt

Family drama

Boston, Massachusetts
February 25, 1942
Homecoming

Cynthia Voigt has written fantasy books, as well as historical stories, but Voigt returns most often to Dicey and the other Tillerman children introduced in her contemporary novel *Homecoming* in 1981.

Homecoming begins the story of the fatherless Tillermans: Dicey and her siblings, James, Sammy, and Maybeth. Their mother leaves them in the car in a shopping center parking lot and never comes back. The oldest, Dicey, thirteen, quickly takes charge. Their mother must have gone to a relative's in Connecticut, she reasons. The quartet strike off, quickly exhausting their finances, occasionally complaining, but resourcefully making their way. They find their Connecticut cousin, but she is greatly disrupted by their presence. So the four take to the road again, looking for a grandmother they never knew they had. When they locate her, they must persuade her to let them stay on her dilapidated Maryland farm.

"Voigt tells it the way it is—what it's like to live close to the bone," Joanna Shaw-Eagle observed. "She is a serious writer on serious themes. Her characterizations have dimension and depth. The reader really cares about the characters. Dicey is an example; her name is especially important, and it sums up the book: 'dicey' is the British slang expression for chancy, risky."

Homecoming was nominated for the American Book Award in 1982. The sequel, *Dicey's Song*, won Voigt a Newbery Medal in 1983.

In the story, Dicey struggles to let her siblings become more independent, and she learns to understand her grandmother. "Under it all there's a goal of harmony that's eventually realized as Dicey learns what to reach out for and what to give up," Marilyn Kaye stated in *The New York Times*.

"*Homecoming* and its sequel, *Dicey's Song* . . . feature a remarkable female adolescent with more courage and smarts than most adults," Ann Martin-Leff wrote.

A trio of companion books to the series features other characters, such as Mina Smiths in *Come a Stranger.* These were not as well received by some critics. "Ever since being the only black at an all-white ballet camp one summer in Connecticut, 13-year-old Mina has been questioning her blackness. . . . Mina's search for identity takes her to the young married minister, Tamer Shipp . . . with whom she falls in love," explained Roger Sutton. "Tamer and Mina played dramatic supporting roles in previous books, but here they are unable to sustain a dull story."

Conversely, Ethel R. Twichell liked the book, in which "Mina grows before our eyes, profiting from each experience, into an independent yet warmly loving young woman, deeply involved with her community."

Rounding out the family cycle is *Seventeen Against the Dealer*, in which Dicey is determined to succeed as a boatbuilder—but at the risk of losing time with her family and her boyfriend, Jeff.

Born Cynthia Irving, daughter of a corporate executive, Voigt grew up in southern Connecticut and attended a private preparatory school. Her childhood was described by Elise K. Irving: "She had two sisters, and then when she was thirteen, suddenly twin brothers. She was a straight-haired, plump little bookworm, who felt that she lived in the shadow of her slender, curly-haired older sister. She puts it most succinctly: 'In nursery school—she was Miss Muffet, and I was the Spider. When we got to dancing school—she was a Sweet Pea, and I was a Head of Cabbage.' "

After graduating from Smith College, she took a job with the J. Walter Thompson Advertising Agency. From 1965 to 1967, Voigt taught English at Glen Burnie (Maryland) High School. Then she joined the faculty at the Key School in Annapolis, Maryland. She served as English department chair from 1971 to 1979. Over the next decade, she slowly gave up her teaching chores in favor of administrative responsibilities. In 1974, divorced and with one child, she married Walter Voigt, a teacher. They had a second child.

Voigt once said that she enjoyed the Cherry Ames, Nancy Drew, and other series books as she grew up in the 1940s and 1950s. She also took great pleasure in reading *The Secret Garden*. Thus, she was attracted to young adult fiction when she began writing herself.

Voigt has featured the Tillermans or their relatives or friends in later books, including *Seventeen Against the Dealer* (1989). She traveled to historical settings to research novels such as *The Callender Papers*, and she created a medieval, fanciful world for *Jackaroo* and its sequel, *On Fortune's Wheel*.

"Regardless of the time period of the novels, a thread of women's liberation or independence unites them all," Sylvia Patterson Iskander summarized. "A skilled craftsman, Voigt excels in creating characters who resonate in the reader's mind; readers eagerly approach another Voigt novel, particularly those in the Tillerman series."

YOUNG ADULT FICTION

Tell Me If the Lovers Are Losers (1982)
Three teenage girls are roommates at a women's college in the early 1960s.

The Callender Papers (1983)
This Gothic mystery is set in 1894. Jean is thirteen the year mysterious Mr. Thiel comes to catalog the family papers—and reveal their unfolding nightmare.

Building Blocks (1984)
Brann Connell travels back in time to meet his father in 1939.

Jackaroo (1985)
In a fantasy medieval kingdom, Geyn rebels at the rules.

Izzy, Willy-Nilly (1986)
Isobel Lingard, fifteen, is a pretty and popular cheerleader. Then she loses a leg in a car accident. How does one adjust to being an amputee?

Tree by Leaf (1988)
Clothilde's father comes home from the Great War in Europe, disfigured and reclusive.

On Fortune's Wheel (1990)
Two generations after *Jackaroo*, an innkeeper's daughter, Birle, and a lord, Orien, set off on a journey.

The Vandemark Mummy (1991)
Living in a motherless home, Althea and Phineas Hall investigate a mummy newly arrived at their professor father's university.

David and Jonathan (1992)
Henry and Jonathan are best friends until Jonathan's cousin, David, a victim of the Holocaust, comes to stay with his family.

Orfe (1992)
Orfe tries to help a friend overcome his addiction.

The Wings of a Falcon (1993)
When two boys escape from Damall's Island, they take the Damall's greatest treasure, a gemstone carved into a falcon.

When She Hollers (1994)
Tish rebels against her adoptive father's sexual abuse.

Tillerman Series

Homecoming (1981)
Four Tillerman children, abandoned by their mentally ill mother, strike off to find their never-seen grandmother.

Dicey's Song (1982)
The Tillermans, especially Dicey, the oldest, realize new relationships and meaning in life after settling with their grandmother.

A Solitary Blue (1983), companion to the Tillerman series
Jeff Graves, a friend of Dicey, has a hard time reconciling with his mother, who left the family to establish her own life.

The Runner (1985), companion to the Tillerman series
"Bullet" Tillerman, seventeen, hides his fear and anger at his iron-handed, racist father by training as a cross-country athlete. He is asked to mentor a black student.

Come a Stranger (1986), companion to the Tillerman series
Dicey's friend Mina Smiths, an African American, has her heart set on becoming a dancer. After she meets a new minister, she begins to realize things about herself and her race.

Sons from Afar (1987)
James and Sammy Tillerman, Dicey's brothers, search for their father, who abandoned them years before.

Seventeen Against the Dealer (1989)
Dicey finds it hard to start her own boatbuilding business.

FICTION FOR YOUNGER READERS

Stories About Rosie (1986)

Bad Girls (1995)

ADULT FICTION

Glass Mountain: A Novel (1991)

FOR FURTHER READING

Immell, Myra, ed. *The Young Adult Reader's Advisory: The Best in Literature and Language Arts, Mathematics and Computer Science.* New Providence, NJ: R. R. Bowker, 1989.

Irving, Elise K. "Cynthia Voigt." *Horn Book Magazine*, August 1983.

Iskander, Sylvia Patterson. "Cynthia Voigt." In *Twentieth-Century Children's Writers*, edited by Tracy Chevalier. 3d ed. Chicago: St. James Press, 1989.

Kaye, Marilyn. *The New York Times*, 27 November 1983.

Martin-Leff, Ann. Review of *A Solitary Blue. New Directions for Women*, May–June 1985.

Shaw-Eagle, Joanna. "Cynthia Voigt: Family Comes First." *Christian Science Monitor*, 13 May 1983.

Sutton, Roger. Review of *Come a Stranger. Bulletin of the Center for Children's Books*, October 1986.

Twichell, Ethel R. Review of *Come a Stranger. Horn Book Magazine*, November–December 1986.

Jill Paton Walsh

Family drama

London, England
April 29, 1937
Fireweed

Jill Paton Walsh grew up in a suburb of London, England, during World War II. Her family lived in fear of devastation from German bombings. This experience provided a backdrop to her early fiction.

"The unwavering heroism of British civilians during 'their finest hour' is sensitively portrayed," *Booklist* said of *The Dolphin Crossing*, "as are the personal relationships of the main characters, and the suspense and danger of the Channel crossing and rescue operation are vividly conveyed."

"The story emphasizes, as any good war story must, that transcending patriotism, courage, and idealism, is the realization of the uselessness and the ultimate waste of war," added Ethel L. Heins.

Born Gillian Bliss, the daughter of an engineer, the author suffered from Erb's palsy as the result of a breech birth. Her parents' early fear that she might have sustained brain damage proved unfounded, and she was only limited in some arm movement.

During the war, the author lived with a grandmother until the elder died of a heart attack. She spent a lot of time reading, particularly enjoying the classics in her grandfather's library. She did well in school and was accepted at Oxford, where she attended lectures by C. S. Lewis and J. R. R. Tolkien.

The author also attended St. Anne's College, Oxford. In 1961, she married Antony Edmund Paton Walsh, a chartered secretary, whom she had met at Oxford. She taught at Enfield Girls Grammar School in Middlesex, England, from 1959 to 1962, then left to raise their three children and to write. She was a lecturer for the Library of Congress in Washington, D.C., in 1978, and a visiting faculty member at the Center for the Study of Children's Literature at Simmons College in Boston from 1978 to 1986. With John Rowe Townsend, she founded Green Bay Publishers in 1986.

Her second attempt at writing a children's book, *Hengest's Tale* (1966), was accepted for publication. With that book, the author began using the name Jill Paton Walsh. *The Dolphin Crossing*, her second novel published, drew upon her wartime experiences, as did her third, *Fireweed*. In the latter, a boy and girl leave their evacuation sites to return to the city, then have to work together to survive the blitz.

Fireweed, Loretta B. Jones said, "is tender, moving, painfully real. The values presented arise from the boy's and girl's sacrifices for each other and from the warmth and kindliness of the adults who befriend them; superbly captured are the familiar or humorous little things that endure even in the midst of horror. Young people always revel in stories of self-preservation by their contemporaries, and they will thoroughly enjoy this superior work."

Paton Walsh's childhood home in St. Ives provided the setting for *Goldengrove*. Madge, a teenager staying at her grandmother's seaside retreat, has a crush, copes with growing up, and deals with a family secret.

Reviewer Barbara Wersba saw brilliance in the book in that the author "has chosen a technique whereby her material is presented on several levels, and not only is this ingenious, but it serves her talents to perfection. Set in the present tense, the story weaves in and out of the thoughts of its characters, all the while holding a steady narrative line and creating vivid atmosphere."

"Paton Walsh has always been the despair of those who like to put their authors into tidy packages," said Marcus Crouch. "This is a writer who never wastes her rare talents, but who brings to each book the same professionalism, wisdom, and regard both for her craft and her public."

Paton Walsh also wrote two nonfiction books, *Wordhoard: Anglo-Saxon Stories* (1969), with Kevin Crossley Holland, and *The Island Sunrise: Prehistoric Britain* (1975). She also edited a version of *Beowulf* (1975).

YOUNG ADULT FICTION

Hengest's Tale (1966)
Hengest the Jute, an invader, settles in fifth-century Kent.

The Dolphin Crossing (1967)
Two boys of different social classes become friends and sail for Dunkirk during World War II.

Fireweed (1969)
A boy and girl must survive in war-ravaged London during World War II.

Goldengrove (1972)
A stranger's surprising revelation spoils Madge and her cousin Paul's magical vacation at the shore.

The Dawnstone (1973)

Toolmaker (1973)
An abandoned member of a Stone Age tribe struggles to survive.

The Emperor's Winding Sheet (1974)
Young Piers Barber becomes the protector of Emperor Constantine.

The Huffler (1975); British title: *The Butty Boy* (1975)
Young Creep works in the mines in Victorian England.

Unleaving (1976), sequel to *Goldengrove*
Madge Fielding inherits her grandmother's seaside home and rents it to a college "reading party." She meets Patrick, the son of a visiting professor.

A Chance Child (1978)
A young boy, imprisoned all his life, ventures back through time.

A Parcel of Patterns (1983)
Villagers quarantine themselves during the great plague in the mid-1600s.

Torch (1987)
Two teens must deliver the last Olympic torch to the games.

Grace (1991)
Based on a true story from 1838, Grace Darling and her father, a lighthouse keeper, rescue shipwreck victims.

Children of the Fox Trilogy

Crossing to Salamis (1977)

The Walls of Athens (1977)

Persian Gold (1978)

FICTION FOR YOUNGER READERS

The Green Book (1981)

Babylon (1982)

Gaffer Samson's Luck (1984)

Lost and Found (1984)

Birdy and the Ghosties (1989)

Matthew and the Sea-Singer (1992)

When Grandma Came (1992) with Sophie Williams

Pepi and the Secret Names (1995)

ADULT FICTION

Farewell, Great King (1972)

Five Tides (1986)
Short stories.

Lapsing (1986)

A School for Lovers (1989)

FOR FURTHER READING

Crouch, Marcus. "Jill Paton Walsh." In *Twentieth-Century Children's Writers*, edited by Tracy Chevalier. 3d ed. Chicago: St. James Press, 1989.

Heins, Ethel L. Review of *The Dolphin Crossing. Horn Book Magazine*, February 1968.

Jones, Loretta B. Review of *Fireweed. School Library Journal*, May 1970.

Review of *The Dolphin Crossing. Booklist and Subscription Books Bulletin*, 15 March 1968.

Wersba, Barbara. Review of *Goldengrove. The New York Times Book Review*, 5 November 1972.

Barbara Wersba

Family drama

Chicago, Illinois
August 19, 1932
The Dream Watcher

Writing is the process of "unlearning all of the prejudices and conventional ideas that we're taught when we're young," Barbara Wersba told Paul Janeczko. "To be a writer you have to see the world for the first time and pretend you know nothing about it. You have to stay very fresh and open, and you have to get rid of the preconceptions formed in childhood. Writing is a very primitive and simple thing. People tend to complicate it and intellectualize it, but it's mostly a sensuous response to nature rather than an intellectual one."

Wersba attended Bard College and studied at the Neighborhood Playhouse and the Paul Mann Actors Workshop. She has worked as an actress in radio and television, summer stock, off-Broadway, and touring companies. She also has taught writing. She has been an active writer since 1960.

"Writing is a process of self-discovery," Wersba continued. "Many writers, if you read what they say about themselves, say they write a book to find out what they think. I write a book to find out who I am. It's a process of awakening; one of the richest ways of finding out what you think and who you are. Every book is yourself. You may disguise the characters, but they're all you and it's a very exciting experience for those who can stick with it."

Her first young adult novel was *The Dream Watcher* (1968), which J. A. Morrison said "explores a fine relationship between a suicidal young dropout, son of a neurotic, thwarted 'House Beautiful' mother and an alcoholic father, and an octogenarian ex-actress recluse—or so we thought."

"*The Dream Watcher* is loaded with adult wisdom," said John Weston, "but Miss Wersba weaves it smoothly into her overall creation."

"With my sixth book, *The Dream Watcher*, I entered the world of adolescence," Wersba said in the *Third Book of Junior Authors*. "The hero of this story, a fourteen-year-old misfit, is more personal to me than any character I have created."

"All of Wersba's novels have as their protagonists young men or women who refuse to shape themselves to society's mold," Audrey Eaglen said. "They are often alienated from their families and loners among their peers; they face their problems alone until someone equally unconventional enters the picture, and together they learn to accept themselves and a world that will always have sharp corners. Critics have sometimes faulted her books for these 'unrealistic' characters and situations, but Wersba's sensitivity and honesty in dealing with her characters have made her a favorite with a whole generation of young readers."

"Barbara Wersba writes about teenagers who are growing up in ways painfully removed from situations their parents can cope with—boys who love Shakespeare or art; girls who dress like Steve McQueen and play the harmonica," reviewer Ellen Abby Lazar said regarding *Tunes for a Small Harmonica*. "Her books are about alienation, androgyny, the individual, love, identity, pain, growth: in fact, one begins to suspect a formula. What one finds is not a rote, mechanical algebra, but deep and often beautiful derivations of theorems, carried out with care and understanding."

YOUNG ADULT FICTION

The Dream Watcher (1968)
Albert Scully, a depressed loner, meets eccentric Orpha Woodfin, a former actress.

Run Softly, Go Fast (1970)
David Marks, nineteen, rails against his father.

The Country of the Heart (1975)
Steven Harper, eighteen, is in love with a woman old enough to be his mother.

Tunes for a Small Harmonica: A Novel (1976)
J. F. McAllister is a confirmed tomboy; then she falls in love with Harold Murth, a distracted poetry teacher.

The Carnival in My Mind (1982)
Harvey Beaumont, fourteen, falls for an aspiring actress who is six years older and one foot taller than he is.

Crazy Vanilla (1986)

Fat: A Love Story (1987)
Rita falls for super-athlete Robert and takes a crash course toward a slimmer image.

Love Is the Crooked Thing (1987), sequel to *Fat*
Rita Formica's love interest, Arnold Bromberg, has gone to Europe to study music. She wants to find him and persuade him to come back.

Beautiful Losers (1988)
Rita Formica, eighteen, fat person and writer, does not want to go to college. She is in love with Arnold Bromberg, a man twice her age. She moves in with him.

The Best Place to Live Is the Ceiling: A Novel (1990)
Sixteen-year-old Archie's father sends him to a therapist. This book is the notebook Dr. Gutman asks him to keep.

You'll Never Guess the End (1992)

Heidi Rosenbloom Series

Just Be Gorgeous: A Novel (1988)
Heidi Rosenbloom is a lonely teenager who falls in love with a streetwise boy who is gay.

Wonderful Me: A Novel (1989)
Heidi, who for sixteen years has thought herself weird and unattractive, begins receiving love letters.

The Farewell Kid: A Novel (1990)
Nonconformist Heidi is in love with Harvey Beaumont. She rents a former barber shop to begin a dog rescue operation.

FICTION FOR YOUNGER READERS

The Boy Who Loved the Sea (1961)

The Brave Balloon of Benjamin Buckley (1963)

The Land of Forgotten Beasts (1964)

A Song for Clowns (1965)

Do Tigers Ever Bite Kings? (1966)

Let Me Fall Before I Fly (1971)

Amanda, Dreaming (1973)

The Crystal Child (1982)

POETRY

Do Tigers Ever Bite Kings? (1966)

Twenty-Six Starlings Will Fly Through Your Mind (1980)

DRAMA

The Dream Watcher (first produced in 1975)

FOR FURTHER READING

DeMontreville, Doris, and Donna Hill, eds. "Barbara Wersba." *Third Book of Junior Authors*. New York: H. W. Wilson, 1972.

Eaglen, Audrey. "Barbara Wersba." In *Twentieth-Century Children's Writers*, edited by Tracy Chevalier. 3d ed. Chicago: St. James Press, 1989.

Janeczko, Paul. "An Interview with Barbara Wersba." *English Journal*, November 1976.

Lazar, Ellen Abby. "Chromatic Fantasies." *The Washington Post Book World*, 10 October 1976.

Morrison, J. A. Review of *The Dream Watcher. Children's Book News*, September–October 1969.

Weston, John. Review of *The Dream Watcher. The New York Times*, 3 November 1968.

Robert Westall

Historical drama

Tynemouth, England
October 7, 1929–April 5, 1993
The Machine-Gunners

Robert Westall wrote books for young adults that are charged with energy and offer sharp insights into the feelings of adolescent protagonists. War is a frequent setting for his stories. He was accused of being overly violent and pessimistic in his realistic depictions of sexuality, family tensions, teenage emotions, and the horrors of war. Westall wrote many ghost tales and short stories as well as occasional works of historical fantasy and science fiction.

"Ever since I wrote *The Machine-Gunners* (and in spite of the fact that my last three books have been fantasies) people keep consulting me about realism in children's books," Westall said in 1979. "Rather as if I'd been appointed high priest and was being asked to read the entrails." He went on to say of violence and death in fiction that, "to a child, death has no immediacy. Children think they will live forever; dying is for grandpa and grandma—one of *their* duties, like giving sweets on demand, going bald or wrinkled, smelling funny and wearing old-fashioned clothes. Duties which render them as comfortably alien a species as the giraffe. So a child can afford to be detached and fascinated by death."

Westall won two Carnegie Medals for his fiction: for *The Machine-Gunners* in 1976 and for *The Scarecrows* in 1982. Educated at the University of Durham and the University of London, he was married and had a son.

The Machine-Gunners, perhaps the best known of his books, is about young teenagers in England who find and hide a machine gun during World War II. John Rowe Townsend found it "a powerful story, crowded with character and incident; it also shows an interest in violence which many have found disconcerting. Violence—physical or psychological, overt or suppressed—is in fact a major ingredient of Westall's novels."

"The plot, in the last fifty pages, becomes increasingly improbable," David Rees complained. "Macho characteristics, guts rather than integrity, are extolled, and there is too much emphasis on incidents of unpleasant violence." Rees offered further general criticisms of Westall, mentioning "the unpleasant attitudes about class (later to surface in *Fathom Five*) are already present. . . . He shows no compassion for gay people. . . . Westall's portrayal of relationships between men and women is often without gentleness. To macho men, women are for sex or doing the domestic chores."

Westall vigorously defended *The Machine-Gunners*, which was attacked by several librarians. He said its language barely replicated the way youngsters really spoke during the time period, and that his "descriptions of violence were nothing like as nasty as those in *The Lord of the Flies*, which 14- and 15-year-olds are now studying. . . . Violence is one of adolescents' main interests today. Anybody who has tried a classroom debate on Northern Ireland will tell you that boys (at least) want to hang, shoot, or burn the lot. It is an interest that needs addressing, and, ironically enough, in *The Machine-Gunners* I tried to address it from the pacifist angle. If I have a voice in the book, it is that of the war-weary air-gunner Rudi, who is about as militaristic as the good soldier Schweik. The hero of the book, Chas, as a result of using violence loses his best friend, his gang, his most precious possession (the machine gun), and his good name. Was there anything else *for* him to lose? Surely my whole theme is violence does not pay."

Some reviewers were favorable, however. "I can think of few writers who have put on paper as successfully as Robert Westall has done in *The Machine-Gunners* the sheer muddle of [World War II] and the day-to-day difficulty, for civilians at least, of deciding what was important," Margery Fisher said. "This book has a remarkable authenticity of atmosphere. It would be wrong to recommend it as anything but a story, but if young people want to know what the war was really like, this book should go some way toward telling them."

Westall also delved into the theme of war and youth in *The Children of the Blitz: Memories of Wartime Childhood* (1985), a nonfiction work that he edited; *Blitzcat* (1989); and *The Kingdom by the Sea* (1991). Of the last book, reviewer Margaret A. Bush noted, "This time the protagonist is a boy, twelve-year-old Harry Baguely, and his journey is as much a pilgrimage of the spirit as it is a search for a new home after his own is destroyed in a bombing raid. Believing that his entire family has been killed, Harry, fearful of being sent to live with relatives whom he heartily dislikes, sets out to create his own destiny. He is joined in this endeavor by a stray dog, who, like himself, has been left homeless by the Blitz. Despite the companionship afforded by his canine friend, Harry soon learns that a boy of his age must constantly keep on the move if he is to remain safe."

YOUNG ADULT FICTION

The Machine-Gunners (1975)
In war-ravaged England, Chas McGill hides a machine gun he recovered from a downed Nazi airplane. With friends, he builds a secret bunker to prepare for German invasion.

The Wind Eye (1976)
A professor and his family, vacationing on the Northumbrian coast, encounter the legend of St. Cuthbert when they travel back in time in an old boat.

The Watch House (1977)
When her family breaks up, Anne is left with her mother's old nanny, Prudie. She becomes interested in the Watch House, where the Garmouth Volunteer Life Brigade trains, and she meets two unusual ghosts there.

The Devil on the Road (1978)
John Webster, odd-jobber at a Suffolk barn, meets a time cat and travels into the past to defend a white witch.

Fathom Five (1979), companion to *The Machine-Gunners*
Four British youths in Garmouth in 1943 track down an enemy spy. Chas McGill reappears.

The Scarecrows (1980)
Simon nearly kills the prep school bully, then turns his rage on his new stepfather.

Break of Dark (1981)
Short stories.

The Haunting of Chas McGill, and Other Stories (1983)
In one story, Chas McGill discovers the ghost of a World War I deserter in an old house.

Futuretrack 5 (1983)
A computer called Laura runs the country. Social standings are determined by tests. Henry Kitson and his friend, Keri, challenge a secret scheme to genetically control the population.

The Cats of Seroster (1984)
In a country reminiscent of medieval France, a duke's son avenges his father's murder with the help of the royal cat, Sehtek.

The Other: A Christmas Story (1985)

Urn Burial (1988)
A British teen disturbs a mysterious grave.

Blitzcat (1989)
Lord Gort, a lost cat trying to find her way home, does not understand the firebombing of Coventry, England, during World War II.

Ghost Abbey (1990)
Since her mother died, things are difficult for Maggi. She must look after her twin brothers and their father. The family is invited to renovate an old abbey.

Echoes of War (1991)
Short stories.

The Kingdom by the Sea (1991)
In 1942, war orphan Harry befriends a dog and looks for a new home.

If Cats Could Fly (1992)

Yaxley's Cat (1992)
A mother and two children rent the wrong summer cottage. A stray cat moves in and starts digging in the garden—a nearly fatal mistake.

The Call, and Other Stories (1993)

Demons and Shadows: The Ghostly Best Stories of Robert Westall (1993)

Gulf (1993)

In Camera, and Other Stories (1993)

The Promise (1993)
It was easy for Bob to make promises when Valerie was so sick. Now that she is dead, one of those promises must be fulfilled.

Christmas Spirit: Two Stories (1994)

A Place for Me (1994)

A Place to Hide (1994)
Lucy struggles to come to terms with her mother's death when her father hands her a suitcase full of money and orders her to run away and begin a new life.

Shades of Darkness: More of the Ghostly Best Stories of Robert Westall (1994)

The Witness (1994)
The birth of Jesus is told through the eyes of a homeless, pregnant Egyptian cat, who finds her way into a Bethlehem stable.

Falling into Glory (1995)
A seventeen-year-old takes a romantic interest in his teacher.

CONTRIBUTOR

Short Circuits: Thirteen Shocking Stories by Outstanding Writers for Young Adults, edited by Donald R. Gallo (1992)

FICTION FOR YOUNGER READERS

Storm Search (1992)

The Stones of Muncaster Cathedral (1993)

EDITOR

Ghost Stories (1993)

FOR FURTHER READING

Bush, Margaret A. Review of *The Kingdom by the Sea*. *Horn Book Magazine*, January–February 1992.

Fisher, Margery. Review of *The Machine-Gunners*. *Growing Point*, October 1975.

Rees, David. *Painted Desert, Green Shade: Essays on Contemporary Writers of Fiction for Children and Young Adults*. Boston: Horn Book Magazine, 1984.

Robert Westall obituary. *The New York Times*, 20 April 1993.

Townsend, John Rowe. *Written for Children: An Outline of English-Language Children's Literature*. 2d rev. ed. New York: J. B. Lippincott, 1983.

Westall, Robert. "Defence of—and by—Author Robert Westall." *Library Association Record*, January 1977.

———. "How Real Do You Want Your Realism?" *Signal*, January 1979.

Phyllis A. Whitney

Romantic suspense

Yokohama, Japan
September 9, 1903
Mystery of the Haunted Pool

Phyllis A. Whitney has written mystery and suspense fiction for adults and young adults for five decades. In 1988, she was named Grand Master by the Mystery Writers of America, capping a distinguished writing career full of awards. She won the Edgar Allan Poe Award, Mystery Writers of America best juvenile mystery—in 1961 for *Mystery of the Haunted Pool* and in 1964 for *Mystery of the Hidden Hand*.

William L. DeAndrea called her "the reigning doyenne of romantic suspense. . . . Still delivering a book annually into her ninetieth year."

Marcia Muller and Bill Pronzini said, "Whitney has the ability to make her reader see the scenery, feel the crispness of the air, taste the national foods."

Born of missionary parents, Whitney lived in Japan, China, and the Philippines until her father died when she was fifteen.

"Whitney was a world traveler at an early age, and this taste for unusual and interesting places makes a distinctive contribution to her work," Jean Swanson and Dean James said. "Her novels vary in setting from Turkey, South Africa, Greece, Japan, and various parts of the United States. Along with an expertly sketched setting, Whitney gives her readers entertaining stories with a masterful sense of pace and suspense."

Whitney attended public schools overseas and in Texas and Chicago, where she settled after her mother's death (Whitney was seventeen). As a girl, she enjoyed reading L. Frank Baum's Oz books and Frances Hodgson Burnett's *The Secret Garden*. "Then when I was in my teens and was haunting libraries wherever I lived, I discovered Mary Roberts Rinehart. She may seem old-fashioned today, but again, her mystery novels inspired me and made me wonder if someday I would write a mystery story of my own," Whitney said in *Books I Read When I Was Young*.

She had already started to write stories when she married George A. Garner in 1925. They had one child and were divorced twenty years later. In 1950, she married Lovell F. Jahnke. He died in 1973.

Whitney worked as a children's book editor with the *Chicago Sun* in the early 1940s, then moved to the *Philadelphia Inquirer*. She taught juvenile writing at Northwestern University in 1945–46 and at New York University from 1947 to 1958. She has written guides to fiction writing, such as *Writing Juvenile Stories and Novels: How to Write and Sell Fiction for Young People* (1976).

The writer is known for light romantic suspense, with an emphasis on unusual settings. Typically, in the young adult novel *Mystery on the Isle of Skye*, family circumstances force Cathy MacLeod to spend the summer with her Corbin cousins at their ancestral home in Scotland. Aunt Bertha sends along several not-to-be-opened-until letters with Cathy, and as she follows their directions and clues, she must solve a puzzle and perhaps find a lost treasure. The treasure is an unsuspected one to a girl struggling to fit in with her family.

Whitney has not shied from controversial topics. *Willow Hill* (1947) is about a young white girl and her high school friends and the integration of a housing project into their community.

"There have been enormous changes in the children's book field since 1942, when my first teen-age novel was published," Whitney wrote in the introduction to *Writing Juvenile Stories and Novels*. "How prim and proper we were! And how careful lest damage be done to tender young readers through the books we gave them. Though even then young readers were probably far ahead of us! It seems quaint now to remember that John Tunis caused a furor in library circles when a character in one of his books for boys used the word 'damn.' An old-fashioned word by this time. Wars intervened, a new kind of bomb fell on Hiroshima, mores changed, and taboos were lifted. There is no use regretting our lost innocence and the fact that our children grow up a lot faster these days than they used to. In recent parlance, we'd better go with the flow—while still recognizing our responsibility in writing honestly for young people."

Whitney related advice from an instructor at Northwestern University, after he read her manuscript for *Willow Hill*: "First you tell a story about characters the reader will care about. As these characters learn, perhaps your readers will learn too. But ONLY if you tell them a good story." She forced herself to follow that advice and extensively edited the manuscript. She said she has been forever pleased with the results.

The author "has a proclivity for sustaining romantic suspense in what could easily be prosaic locations—the Poconos and Catskills, the Hamptons, New Hampshire, even northern New Jersey, all resort areas for the middle class," Nancy Regan said of Whitney's adult fiction. "Whitney achieves this transformation of these otherwise humdrum locales by means of some standard Gothic devices: the heroine's seeming isolation amid a hostile household whose shifting moods she only dimly understands; the Gothic house itself, be it old hotel or mansion; the careful removal of dailiness. In a Whitney novel, as in other Gothics, characters gather for meals less to eat than to confront each other, dress not to keep warm but to show off the latest fashions, and go to bed mostly to be disturbed by ominous noises, bad dreams, and an occasional murderer."

Obviously, Whitney used some of the same techniques in her young adult books. This passage is from *Mystery of the Black Diamonds*: "Angie's blood congealed with fright and her throat choked closed so that she couldn't utter a sound. She lay tense beneath the covers, aware of moonlight in the doorway and that wild howling outside. Whether it was animal or human, she could not tell."

YOUNG ADULT FICTION

A Place for Ann (1941)
Young people have to find work for themselves.

A Star for Ginny (1942)

A Window for Julie (1943)

The Silver Inkwell (1945)

Willow Hill (1947)
Val Coleman wants to edit the school newspaper, but the job goes to a black girl who lives in the new housing project.

Ever After (1948)

Mystery of the Gulls (1949)
Taffy Saunders finds mystery and adventure on Mackinac Island on Lake Michigan. Her mother has unexpectedly inherited a hotel.

Linda's Homecoming (1950)
Linda Hollis's life is disrupted by her mother's remarriage and a new stepfamily. She soon finds romantic distraction.

The Island of Dark Woods (1951); alternate title: *Mystery of the Strange Traveller* (1967)

Step to the Music (1953)
On Staten Island during the Civil War, Abbie Garrett's father is a Northerner, her mother is from Charleston.

A Long Time Coming (1954)
Christie Allard is caught in social strife at her family's canning plant when Mexican Americans are subjected to prejudice by some family members.

Mystery on the Isle of Skye (1955)
Cathy MacLeod, twelve, takes a surprise trip to the Isle of Skye in Scotland and discovers a puzzle.

The Fire and the Gold (1956)
Melora Cranby's family home is destroyed by the 1906 earthquake in San Francisco, and they have to begin anew.

The Highest Dream (1956)

The Mystery of the Green Cat (1957)
Andy and his brother do not get along with two new stepsisters. All are distracted by a mystery next door.

Secret of the Samurai Sword (1958)
Visiting Japan with her brother and grandmother, Celia spots the ghost of an ancient samurai.

Creole Holiday (1959)
In New Orleans in the 1890s, Laura Beaudine arrives from New England with her Creole father.

Mystery of the Haunted Pool (1960)

Secret of the Tiger's Eye (1961)
Benita's aunt's house in South Africa, with its trap doors and castle turrets, leads her to a one-eyed tiger's ghost, and more.

Mystery of the Golden Horn (1962)
Vicki goes to Istanbul to spend the summer with her father. Strange things begin to happen when she loses a pin given her by a Gypsy.

Mystery of the Hidden Hand (1963)
On a trip to a Greek island, Gale Tyler, twelve, stumbles onto the marble hand of a famous statue—and an old family secret.

Secret of the Emerald Star (1964)
Robin, thirteen, finds mystery on Staten Island.

Mystery of the Angry Idol (1965)
In Mystic, Connecticut, with her grandmother, Jan Pendleton is homesick for her family in Vietnam.

Secret of the Spotted Shell (1967)
Wendy arrives in the Virgin Islands just after her cousin has drowned.

Secret of Goblin Glen (1968)
Trina thinks it is interesting to have a black sheep in the family: Great-Uncle Will Hurst once robbed a New Hampshire bank.

Mystery of the Crimson Ghost (1969)
Janey Oakes has "horse fever": She falls in love with Star, a horse belonging to eccentric Mrs. Barly.

Secret of the Missing Footprint (1970)

The Vanishing Scarecrow (1971)
Joan looks forward to living on Rainbow Island, the fantastic children's amusement park her uncle built, but danger threatens.

Nobody Like Trina (1972)

Mystery of the Scowling Boy (1973)

Mystery of the Black Diamonds (1974)
Angie and her brother, Mark, are given a curious map by an old prospector. They search a Colorado ghost town for treasure.

Secret of Haunted Mesa (1975)

Secret of the Stone Face (1977)
Jo tries to prevent her mother from marrying again—and she solves a mystery.

ADULT FICTION

Red Is for Murder (1943)

The Quicksilver Pool (1955)

The Trembling Hills (1956)

Skye Cameron (1957)

The Moonflower (1958); British title: *The Mask and the Moonflower* (1960)

Thunder Heights (1960)

Blue Fire (1961)

Window on the Square (1962)

Seven Tears for Apollo (1963)

Black Amber (1964)

The Red Carnelian (1965)

Sea Jade (1965)

Columbella (1966)

Silverhill (1967)

Hunter's Green (1968)

The Winter People (1969)

Lost Island (1970)

Listen for the Whisperer (1972)

Snowfire (1973)

The Turquoise Mask (1974)

Spindrift (1975)

The Golden Unicorn (1976)

The Stone Bull (1977)

The Glass Flame (1978)

Domino (1979)

Poinciana (1980)

Vermilion (1981)

Emerald (1982)

Rainsong (1984)

Dream of Orchids (1985)

Fire and Gold (1986)

Flaming Tree (1986)

Silversword (1987)

Feather on the Moon (1988)

Rainbow in the Mist (1989)

The Singing Stones (1990)

Thundering Heights (1991)

Trembling Hills (1991)

Woman Without a Past (1991)

The Ebony Swan (1992)

Daughter of the Stars (1994)

Star Flight (1994)

FOR FURTHER READING

Budd, Elaine. *Thirteen Mistresses of Murder.* New York: Frederick Ungar, 1986.

Cullinan, Bernice, and M. Jerry Weiss, eds. *Books I Read When I Was Young: The Favorite Books of Famous People*. New York: Avon Books, 1980.

DeAndrea, William L. *Encyclopedia Mysteriosa: A Comprehensive Guide to the Art of Detection in Print, Film, Radio, and Television.* New York: Prentice Hall Press, 1994.

Pronzini, Bill, and Marcia Muller. *1001 Midnights: The Aficionado's Guide to Mystery and Detective Fiction.* New York: Arbor House, 1986.

Regan, Nancy. "Phyllis A. Whitney." In *Twentieth-Century Romance and Historical Writers,* edited by Lesley Henderson. 2d ed. Chicago: St. James Press, 1990.

Swanson, Jean, and Dean James. *By a Woman's Hand: A Guide to Mystery Fiction by Women.* New York: Berkley, 1994.

Viguers, Ruth Hill. Review of *Secret of the Emerald Star. Horn Book Magazine,* February 1965.

Whitney, Phyllis A. *Guide to Fiction Writing.* 2d ed. Boston: Writer, 1988.

———. *Writing Juvenile Stories and Novels: How to Write and Sell Fiction for Young People.* Boston: Writer, 1976.

Patricia C. Wrede

Fantasy

Chicago, Illinois
March 27, 1953

Dealing with Dragons

"I started writing fiction in the seventh grade," Patricia C. Wrede told Kenneth R. Shepherd, "and never really stopped in spite of the fact that for many years I did not really expect writing to be more than a hobby."

Patricia Collins, the daughter of a mechanical engineer and an executive, was a voracious reader as a child. She still has her Oz books and her copies of Walter Farley horse stories and the Chronicles of Narnia.

In 1974, she received a degree in biology from Carleton College. She earned her master's degree from the University of Minnesota in 1977. She married a financial consultant, James M. Wrede, in 1976. They divorced in 1992.

Wrede worked as a rate-review analyst for a hospital association, a financial analyst with several companies, and a senior accountant. She has written full time since 1985.

Wrede is noted for breaking new ground in the fantasy genre. She offers modern variations on old fairy tales and comic fantasies.

It took Wrede five years to finish her first novel, *Shadow Magic*. It introduced the magical world of Lyra, an alternate Earth that would reappear in others of Wrede's books. She created a second fantasy world, the Enchanted Forest, for another sequence of books.

Denise Perry Donavin, in *Best of the Best for Children*, termed *Dealing with Dragons* a "spirited yarn that turns fairy tale convention on its head and is continued in a lively sequel, *Searching for Dragons*."

Searching "gives an amusing modern twist to fantasy with a magician who is highly technical in his speech, a giant who takes up consulting on how to prevent hamlets from being pillaged, and a Wicked Uncle who is not so wicked after all," said reviewer Ann A. Flowers.

"I like writing about strong female characters," Wrede told Shepherd, "possibly because there haven't been a lot of them that I could identify with. If my strong female characters come from anything, it's essentially from the women that I know: My mother, my aunts, my grandmothers, the bosses, the women that I have worked for, or professors that I had in college. They were all very determined, active women. I hadn't seen a whole lot of that particular type in fantasy."

YOUNG ADULT FICTION

Shadow Magic (1982)
On Lyra, Alethia, daughter of a magic-using Shee, is kidnapped from her home by agents of a rival country.

Daughter of Witches (1983)
Also set on Lyra, Ranira, a servant, is sentenced to death on suspicion that he is a sorcerer.

The Seven Towers (1984)
Carachel, the wizard-king of Tar-Alem, struggles against Matholych.

The Harp of Imach Thyssel (1985)

Caught in Crystal (1987)

Sorcery and Cecelia (1988) with Caroline Stevermer
Set in an alternate, magical England, two cousins become entangled in a power struggle between wizards.

Snow White and Rose Red (1989)
Set in an alternate Tudor England, this is a variation on the Brothers Grimm fairy tale.

Mairelon the Magician (1991)
In England in the early 1800s, Kim, a street waif, is caught trying to burgle the wagon of a magician.

The Raven Ring (1994)
On Lyra, a fiery young woman leaves a mountain stronghold to travel to the city where her mother died and retrieve her mother's ring, but dark forces also seek the ring.

Chronicles of the Enchanted Forest

Talking to Dragons (1985)
Daystar, sixteen, is sent into the Enchanted Forest on a wizard's quest. He takes with him his fire-witch friend, Shiara, and a magic sword.

Dealing with Dragons (1990), prequel to *Talking to Dragons*
Cimorene, Daystar's mother, forced into a fixed marriage, flees to the lair of the dragon Kazul and helps him defeat the Society of Wizards.

Searching for Dragons (1991)
The focus switches to Mendanbar, Daystar's father, who is surprised to find that pieces of his kingdom are moving around.

Calling on Dragons (1993)
Queen Cimorene, Kazul the dragon, and the rest go on a quest for a magic sword.

CONTRIBUTOR

Liavek, edited by Will Shetterly and Emma Bull (1985)

Liavek: The Players of Luck, edited by Will Shetterly and Emma Bull (1986)

Spaceships and Spells, edited by Jane Yolen (1987) Includes the story "The Improper Princess," about the mother of Daystar from *Talking to Dragons.*

Liavek: Spells of Binding, edited by Will Shetterly and Emma Bull (1988)

The Unicorn Treasury, edited by Bruce Coville (1988)

Liavek: Festival Week, edited by Will Shetterly and Emma Bull (1990)

Tales of the Witch World 3, edited by Andre Norton (1990)

FOR FURTHER READING

Donavin, Denise Perry, ed. *Best of the Best for Children.* New York: Random House, 1992.

Flowers, Ann A. Review of *Searching for Dragons. Horn Book Magazine,* January–February 1992.

Shepherd, Kenneth R. "Patricia Wrede." In *Authors & Artists for Young Adults,* edited by Laurie Collier. Vol. 8. Detroit: Gale Research, 1992.

Patricia Wrightson

Fantasy

Mythology

Lismore, New South Wales, Australia
June 19, 1921

The Book of Wirrun

"We didn't even much like the few [Australian books] we had; there weren't any smugglers' caves, or castles with hidden treasures, or boarding schools, or people who talked in a funny way," Patricia Wrightson told *Authors & Artists for Young Adults*. "There were no snowy Christmases, with Yule logs on the roaring fires and people making punch; no springtime rejoicing, and far too much heat in summer. In fact—very subtly, and without our even knowing it—our books were teaching us that it was not much fun, and not very important, to be Australian; that every other place in the world was more interesting, and books about every other place were better and more exciting."

Thus, Wrightson, an Australian, said that she felt like a pioneer when she began writing books for teen readers that were set in her native land.

Born Patricia Furlonger, the daughter of a solicitor (lawyer) and a homemaker, the author lived on a farm for several years before the family relocated to a city. As a youngster, she devoured a set of Charles Dickens books purchased by her father and then expanded her horizons to other writers. As much as she enjoyed these books, she eventually realized that none was set in Australia—something she considered a shortcoming.

Wrightson attended St. Catherine's College and the State Correspondence School. In 1943, she married; ten years later, she divorced. She has two children. She worked as a hospital secretary and administrator from 1946 to 1960. She held the same job for a nursing association from 1960 to 1964. From 1964 to 1975, she worked as assistant editor, then editor, of *School Magazine*. She has written fiction since 1953.

Wrightson said of her craft in *Top of the News*, "Is there a right way to tell a story? Surely there is: a different one for every writer. And just as surely, this is what gives life and strength to literature. The same stories are told and retold and told again, and still they're fresh and different and alive: as alive and different and fresh as their authors, who are as different, fresh and alive as other people. Every writer has to discover the inner vision, as well as the techniques, that are secretly and only his."

Wrightson's trilogy, the Book of Wirrun, features an Aboriginal hero. Wirrun "is the archetypal Boy-Saviour rather than a child, and his companions and helpers are the host of beings with which the Aboriginal imagination has peopled the harsh land," Donald A. Young said. "The schoolboy fun gives way to the seriousness of the Quest, and the school playground becomes an arena for the titanic struggle between the forces of good and evil."

The Book of Wirrun, Audrey Laski said, "draws on the myths and folktales of the Aboriginals to produce a fantasy of great freshness and distinction."

Susan Cooper called Wrightson's *The Nargun and the Stars* "a wonderful book, with a hypnotic sense of place. Patricia Wrightson is deeply Australian, and she makes her fantasies out of the relationships and conflicts between ordinary, everyday human beings and the folk-spirits of the first Australians, the Aborigines—'not the ritual figures of the creative myths but the gnomes and heroes and monsters of Australia.' The real and the magical are interwoven, in the powerful landscape of that astonishing continent; these are fantasies not of good and evil but of unjudging, unjudged creatures who are, above all, *old*."

YOUNG ADULT FICTION

The Crooked Snake (1955)
Six children organize a secret society and discover people working against the environment.

The Bunyip Hole (1957)
Rival gangs of children find a cave.

The Rocks of Honey (1960)

The Feather Star (1962)
On the coast of New South Wales, two girls and two boys spend a holiday together. They discover things they have in common.

Down to Earth (1965)
Beings from another planet visit Woolloomooloo.

A Racecourse for Andy (1968); British title: *I Own the Racecourse!* (1968)
Andy, twelve, naively pays three dollars to a tramp for a racecourse—and its owners play along with the joke.

An Older Kind of Magic (1972)
A group of children and the Net-Net battle to protect their environment from industrialists.

The Nargun and the Stars (1973)
The Nargun is a monstrous rock that creeps across the country at night and rests by day.

Night Outside (1979)
In a moment of rage, Anne and James's father throws their pet budgerigar (parrot) out the apartment window.

A Little Fear (1983)
A tough old woman refuses to give up her independence and go into an institution.

Moon-Dark (1988)
Blue, a dog, gives another view of human treatment of the environment.

Baylet (1989)
Jo, fourteen, means no harm when she stows away in old Mrs. Willet's car.

The Old, Old Ngrang (1989)

The Book of Wirrun

The Ice Is Coming (1977)
Wirrun is an Aboriginal boy who must go on a heroic quest to stave off a frozen future.

The Dark Bright Water (1978)
Wirrun's second task is to tame the wild water-spirits.

Journey Behind the Wind (1981); British title: *Behind the Wind* (1981)
Wirrun must face the greatest enemy: Death.

EDITOR

Beneath the Sun: An Australian Collection for Children (1972)

Emu Stew: An Illustrated Collection of Stories and Poems for Children (1976)

FICTION FOR YOUNGER READERS

The Sugar-Gum Tree (1992)

FOR FURTHER READING

Cooper, Susan. "A Second Look: *The Nargun and the Stars*." *Horn Book Magazine*, September–October 1986.

Garrett, Agnes, and Helga P. McCue, eds. "Patricia Wrightson." In *Authors & Artists for Young Adults*. Vol. 5. Detroit: Gale Research, 1990.

Heins, Ethel L. Review of *Moon-Dark*. *Horn Book Magazine*, September–October 1988.

Laski, Audrey. Review of The Book of Wirrun. *The Times Educational Supplement*, 23 December 1983.

Wrightson, Patricia. "Stones into Pools." *Top of the News*, spring 1985.

Young, Donald A. "Patricia Wrightson, O.B.E." *Junior Bookshelf*, December 1981.

Laurence Yep

Family drama

Fantasy

San Francisco, California
June 14, 1948
Dragonwings

Of Chinese American ancestry, Laurence Yep writes realistic fiction as well as science fiction and fantasy. He often portrays an outsider searching for identity and delves into themes of alienation, tolerance, and imagination.

Yep attended Marquette University and received a degree from the University of California–Santa Cruz in 1970. He earned a Ph.D. from the State University of New York–Buffalo in 1975. A writer since 1968, he has also lectured and been a writer in residence.

Yep's father was born in China and immigrated to the United States as a boy. His mother was born in Ohio and grew up in West Virginia, where his paternal grandfather ran a laundry. The family eventually moved to California, where his parents met and married.

"Growing up as a Chinese American in San Francisco, I found few books which dealt with my own experience," Yep said in *Books I Read When I Was Young*. "I lived in a predominantly black area but commuted by bus every day to a bilingual school in Chinatown. Stories set on farms or in suburbia or Midwestern small towns were less real to me than science fiction or fantasy. Science fiction and fantasy dealt with strategies of survival: people adapting to strange new lands and worlds, or some fantastic or alien creature adjusting to ours. Adapting to different environments and cultures happened each time I got on and off the bus." Early favorites were books by Andre Norton, Ray Bradbury, and Robert Heinlein, he said.

"I was the Chinese American raised in a black neighborhood," Yep explained in *The Lost Garden*, "a child who had been too American to fit into Chinatown and too Chinese to fit in elsewhere. I was the clumsy son of the athletic family, the grandson of a Chinese grandmother who spoke more of West Virginia than of China. . . . When I wrote . . . I could reach into the box of rags that was my soul and begin stitching them together."

He began writing science fiction when eighteen and sold his first story at that age. A friend who worked for a publisher suggested that he write a science fiction book for younger readers. *Sweetwater* resulted. It is about Tyree and his family, who subsist by scavenging in a partially submerged city on the planet Harmony. People half of the land, half of the sea, are Silkies; Yep based them on old Scottish folklore. Facing more fully his Chinese American identity was Yep's *Dragonwings*, about an early aviator. The book is based on a newspaper clipping Yep found that described a Chinese immigrant who developed a successful flying machine a few years after the Wright brothers did.

"While Yep first became known as a 'fantasy' author, his work today expresses an earth-bound longing for acceptance," Patrick Burnson said. "[A] recent effort for young adults, *Dragon's Gate* . . . is a story explaining the Chinese immigrant's crucial contribution to the building of America's first intercontinental railroad. Although many of the chapters describe racism and frontier hardship, it is hardly a didactic chronology of suffering and woe. The author explains that 'outsiders' eventually come to realize who they are, and such a message needn't be hammered home: 'I always regarded myself as a San Franciscan first, an American citizen second, and of Chinese ancestry further down the line.' "

In *Literature for Today's Young Adults*, Yep credited his popularity with young adult readers to his "always pursuing the theme of being an outsider—an alien—and many teenagers feel they're aliens. As a Chinese child growing up in a black neighborhood, I served as the all-purpose Asian. When we played war, I was the Japanese who got killed; then when the Korean War came along, I was a North Korean communist. This sense of being the odd-one-out is probably what made me relate to the Narnia and the Oz books. They were about loneliness and kids in alien societies learning to adjust to foreign cultures. I could understand these a lot better than the stories in our readers where every house had a front lawn and no one's front door was ever locked."

Yep's versatility is seen in his two books of humorous tales set during the Civil War and featuring Mark Twain, *The Mark Twain Murders* and *The Tom Sawyer Fires;* in *Dragon of the Lost Sea* and its sequels, fantasies about a dragon; in *The Serpent's Children* and its sequel, *Mountain Light* about a Chinese girl's struggles in her native land; and in *Shadow Lord,* an entry in the popular Star Trek series.

Yep "has deliberately and effectively sought to combat racial stereotyping, and these novels have been praised because they have repaired some of the harm inflicted by racist persistence in describing Chinese or Chinese Americans as characters resembling Charlie Chan or Fu Manchu, or playing the seemingly omnipresent houseboy, gardener, or launderer," Francis J. Molson said in *Twentieth-Century Science-Fiction Writers.*

Yep found inspiration for several books in old folktales. According to Burnson: "Yep now indulges in his taste for Chinese folktales for much of his inspiration. According to the author, these fables combine mystery with the macabre in a manner that transcends generational appeal. 'In any one of these tales, there's a 50-50 chance that when a Chinese man meets a new creature he will either marry it or eat it,' Yep says with a chuckle. 'My first instinct as a writer was to take these tales and expand them and add dialogue, but I realized that their power was actually based on their leanness. I liken them to muscle cars stripped of all ornament. What you have left is raw power.' "

YOUNG ADULT FICTION

Sweetwater (1973)
Tyree and his family are Silkies on the planet Harmony.

Dragonwings (1975)
Moon Shadow, eight years old, sails from China to join his kite-maker father, Windrider, in San Francisco's Chinatown at the turn of the century. He must endure mockery and poverty.

Child of the Owl (1977)
A young Chinese American girl, Casey, discovers her heritage when she goes to live with Paw Paw, her grandmother in Chinatown.

Sea Glass (1979)
Craig Chin does not fit in when he moves to Concepcion from San Francisco's Chinatown. To his classmates, he is the fat Chinese "Buddha man."

The Green Darkness (1980)

Kind Hearts and Gentle Monsters (1982)
A high school boy, Charley, develops an unusual romance with a difficult girl, Chris.

The Mark Twain Murders (1982)
Twain, a newspaper reporter, covers the murder of a disreputable soldier. He teams with the dead man's fifteen-year-old stepson, His Grace, to solve the crime and subvert a major plot to rob the Mint.

Liar, Liar (1983)
Sixteen-year-old Sean wonders if his friend Marsh was accidentally—or intentionally—killed.

The Serpent's Children (1984)
Cassia's story of Chinese peasant life is told against the backdrop of the nineteenth-century Taiping Rebellion.

The Tom Sawyer Fires (1984)
Twain and His Grace from *The Mark Twain Murders* return. With a San Francisco firefighter named Tom Sawyer, they investigate a series of arson blazes.

Mountain Light (1985), sequel to *The Serpent's Children*
Squeaky Lar meets the Gallant, a crippled old man who teaches him about courage; Tiny, the giant who becomes his first friend; and Cassia, who captures his heart.

Monster Makers Inc. (1986)
On a far planet in the future, a mysterious warlike race challenges human space and threatens invasion. Doc Sawyer and his teenage son, Rob, are caught in the crisis.

The Star Fisher (1992)
Joan Lee, fifteen, is on a train from Ohio to West Virginia in 1927. Her family hopes to begin a new business, but they meet with racial taunts.

Butterfly Boy (1993)

Dragon's Gate (1994)
Otter dreams of going to America—he plans to learn all he can from his adoptive father and hero, Uncle Foxfire.

Hiroshima: A Novella (1995)
Based on accounts written by survivors of the atomic bombing.

Thief of Hearts (1995)
Stacy never thought much of being Chinese American until pairing with a new girl at school.

Dragon Series

Dragon of the Lost Sea (1982)
Shimmer the dragon befriends a boy, Thorn, and sets out to destroy her archenemy, Civet.

Dragon Steel (1985)
Shimmer and Thorn continue the quest to restore the dragon's homeland.

Dragon Cauldron (1990)
With the help of a monkey wizard and a repentant Civet, the dragon princess Shimmer seeks to use the magic of the dragon's cauldron.

Dragon War (1992)
Shimmer and companions Monkey and Indigo attempt to rescue Thorn, whose soul has been imprisoned in the boneless king's cauldron.

FICTION FOR YOUNGER READERS

The Curse of the Squirrel (1987)

The Rainbow People (1989)
A retelling.

The Lost Garden (1991)

Tongues of Jade (1991)

The Ghost Fox (1993)

The Man Who Tricked a Ghost (1993)

The Shell Woman and the King: A Chinese Folk Tale (1993)
A retelling.

The Junior Thunder Lord (1994)

The City of Dragons (1995)

Later, Gator (1995)

Tiger Woman (1995)

Tree of Dreams: Ten Tales from the Garden of Night (1995)

DRAMA

Age of Wonders (first produced in 1987)

EDITOR

American Dragons: Twenty-Five Asian American Voices (1993)

CONTRIBUTOR

World's Best Science Fiction of 1969, edited by Donald A. Wollheim and Terry Carr (1969)

Protostars, edited by David Gerrold (1971)

Quark Number Two, edited by Samuel Delaney and Marilyn Hacker (1971)

The Demon Kind: Eleven New Stories of Children with Strange and Supernatural Powers (New York: Avon, 1973).

Strange Bedfellows: Sex and Science Fiction, edited by Thomas N. Scortia (1973)

Last Dangerous Visions, edited by Harlan Ellison (1975)

Between Worlds, edited by Misha Berson (1990)

The Boy Who Swallowed Snakes, edited by Laurence Yep, et al. (1994)

ADULT FICTION

Seademons (1977)
On the colony of Fancyfree, the Folk cannot get along with the native Seademons.

Star Trek Series

Shadow Lord (1985)
Mr. Spock and Lt. Sulu are pitted against political factions in a semibarbaric world.

FOR FURTHER READING

Burnson, Patrick. "In the Studio with Laurence Yep." *Publishers Weekly*, 16 May 1994.

Cullinan, Bernice, and M. Jerry Weiss, eds. *Books I Read When I Was Young: The Favorite Books of Famous People*. New York: Avon Books, 1980.

Donelson, Kenneth L., and Alleen Pace Nilsen, eds. Article in *Literature for Today's Young Adults*. Glenview, IL: Scott, Foresman, 1985.

Molson, Francis J. "Laurence Yep." In *Twentieth-Century Children's Writers*, edited by Tracy Chevalier. 3d ed. Chicago: St. James Press, 1989.

———. "Laurence Yep." In *Twentieth-Century Science-Fiction Writers*, edited by Noelle Watson and Paul E. Schellinger. 3d ed. Chicago: St. James Press, 1991.

Stanek, Lou Willett. *A Teacher's Resource to Laurence Yep*. New York: HarperCollins, 1991.

Jane Yolen

Fantasy

New York City
February 11, 1939

Dragon's Blood: A Fantasy

Jane Yolen is a prolific writer of fantasy, poetry, and plays for children. She also writes novels for adults, essays, and criticism. She has edited many fiction anthologies. She is best known for her folk stories and fairy tales, in which she retells familiar stories and gives them new twists. She also makes up new stories using familiar frameworks and settings.

She spoke about the diversity of her work with Phyllis E. Alsdurf: "As a grown-up human being, I'm interested in a lot of things. I'm interested in politics, ecology, the environment, history. I'm interested in poetry, fairy tales, music, travel. So why can't my books reflect all of those interests? I'm not narrow as a human being, so why should my writing be narrow? In fact, I always wonder how anyone who is a writer can enjoy writing the same thing over and over again. You might as well work in a factory if you're interested in doing the same thing over and over and over again. . . . Writing is not just a job for me. . . . This is my life. This is what I love. I am one of those very, very lucky few people who absolutely adores what she does. And there's nothing that I enjoy more than sitting down and writing. So why should I narrow myself?"

The daughter of two writers, Yolen lived in California, New York City, and Connecticut when she was growing up. She was an avid reader who also studied ballet at Balanchine's for eight years and liked to play fantasy games. In high school, Yolen played basketball, worked for the student newspaper, and sang in the choir. She took an interest in different religions. She fell in love with things medieval and Arthurian. She wrote a lot of poetry.

Yolen received a bachelor of arts degree from Smith College in 1960. From the University of Massachusetts, she earned her master's degree in education in 1976.

She worked briefly for *This Week* magazine, then for *Saturday Review*. She did freelance writing and helped her father with a book on kite flying. Eventually, she began to turn out her own books. In 1962, she married David W. Stemple, a computer science professor, with whom she has three children. Yolen taught children's literature at Smith College for six years.

"I have no idea where the first draft which comes pouring off my fingers comes from," she told *Authors & Artists for Young Adults*. "I'm often surprised during the first draft, and think, 'Oh! Is *that* how the story ends!' But in revision I know that I have a hand in it. I tidy it up and I look for the right word and I rephrase. I truly enjoy that part. On a book or a story I might do up to twenty revisions—sometimes simply going through and polishing, sometimes tearing apart and putting back together again. I would say that each book I ever worked on has had at least three or four major revisions. I take things out, throw them away, and reshape. That comes from being a poet. I read everything aloud and when you read aloud you hear it again, the way you would a poem. People are amazed that someone as prolific as I am would be able to do that many revisions, but when I'm writing I am totally involved. There are times when I don't even hear the phone ring."

"Do I believe in magic? Since many of my books deal with the fantastic—talking pig butlers, weasel poets, toads in space, great fighting dragons, girls who cry flowers—I suppose it is a good question to ask," Yolen stated in a publisher's pamphlet. "But the answer may surprise you and even disappoint you—make me seem something less than 'special.'

"I believe that everything around us is touched by magic if we just look long enough and deep enough. I never met an angel, but I believe in the angelic experience whenever I come upon someone who is incredibly loving and good. I never met a dragon, but I have met fire-breathing humans whose words seem to poison the very air. (And I didn't touch a snake until I was 47 years old and only the tail end at that.) I never met a unicorn but . . . I think you get the point."

One of her first books for young adults was *The Gift of Sarah Barker*, in which she depicts the Shaker religion through young characters. "While the personal dynamics of the story could have been more fully developed," reviewer Stephanie Zvirin said, "Yolen effectively individualizes her characters and evokes a vivid image, rich in fact-based detail, of a tightly structured Shaker haven. Into the fabric of a teenage romance she also weaves complicated and disturbing—at times violent—undercurrents that add a dimension both powerful and provocative."

Yolen has also written nonfiction books for younger readers, including *Simple Gifts: The Story of the Shakers* (1976). Yolen herself is a Quaker.

YOUNG ADULT FICTION

The Gift of Sarah Barker (1981)
In a Shaker setting, a boy and girl fall in love, though their religion forbids it.

Neptune Rising: Songs and Tales of the Undersea Folk (1982)

The Stone Silenus (1984)

Children of the Wolf: A Novel (1986)
Mohandus, fourteen, living in an Indian orphanage, hears stories of ghosts in the jungle—but they turn out to be two girls reared by wolves.

The Devil's Arithmetic (1988)
Hannah suddenly transports, during Passover Seder, to a Nazi-occupied Polish village in the 1940s.

The Faery Flag: Stories and Poems of Fantasy and the Supernatural (1989)

Storyteller (1992)

Weather Report (1993)

The Wild Hunt (1995)
Two boys and Death go on a hunt.

Dragon's Blood Trilogy

Dragon's Blood: A Fantasy (1982)
On the planet Austar IV, Jakkin Stewart decides to train his own dragon and break free.

Heart's Blood (1984)
Master Jakkin and his red dragon, Heart's Blood, receive a request from an off-worlder.

A Sending of Dragons (1987)
Jakkin finds it hard to raise five baby dragons, especially amidst a revolution.

Fairy Tale Series

Sleeping Beauty (1986)

Briar Rose (1992)
Only after her grandmother dies does a girl discover her stories of Briar Rose were about a real-life Sleeping Beauty—a survivor of the Holocaust.

CONTRIBUTOR

Am I Blue? Coming Out from the Silence, edited by Marion Dane Bauer (1994)

A Dragon-Lover's Treasury of the Fantastic, edited by Margaret Weis (1994)

FICTION FOR YOUNGER READERS

The Witch Who Wasn't (1964)

Gwinellen, the Princess Who Could Not Sleep (1965)

Trust a City Kid (1966) with Anne Huston

The Emperor and the Kite (1967)

Isabel's Noel (1967)

Greyling: A Picture Story from the Islands of Shetland (1968)

The Longest Name on the Block (1968)

The Minstrel and the Mountain: A Tale of Peace (1968)

The Inway Investigators; or, The Mystery at McCracken's Place (1969)

The Seventh Mandarin (1969)

The Wizard of Washington Square (1969)

Hobo Toad and the Motorcycle Gang (1970)

The Bird of Time (1971)

The Girl Who Loved the Wind (1972)

The Adventures of Eeka Mouse (1974)

The Boy Who Had Wings (1974)

The Girl Who Cried Flowers, and Other Tales (1974)
Short stories.

The Magic Three of Solatia (1974)

Rainbow Rider (1974)

The Little Spotted Fish (1975)

The Transfigured Hart (1975)

Milkweed Days (1976)

The Moon Ribbon, and Other Tales (1976)
Short stories.

The Giants' Farm (1977)

Hannah Dreaming (1977)

The Hundredth Dove, and Other Tales (1977)
Short stories.

The Lady and the Merman: A Tale (1977)

The Seeing Stick (1977)

The Sultan's Perfect Tree (1977)

The Mermaid's Three Wisdoms (1978)

No Bath Tonight (1978)

The Simple Prince (1978)

Spider Jane (1978)

Dream Weaver (1979)

The Giants Go Camping (1979)

Mice on Ice (1980)

The Robot and Rebecca: The Mystery of the Code-Carrying Kids (1980)

Spider Jane on the Move (1980), sequel to *Spider Jane*

The Acorn Quest (1981)

The Boy Who Spoke Chimp (1981)

Brothers of the Wind (1981)

The Robot and Rebecca and the Missing Owser (1981), sequel to *The Robot and Rebecca: The Mystery of the Code-Carrying Kids*

Shirlick Holmes and the Case of the Wandering Wardrobe (1981)

Sleeping Ugly (1981)

Uncle Lemon's Spring (1981)

Owl Moon (1987)

Dove Isabeau (1989)

Baby Bear's Bedtime Book (1990)

Dinosaur Dances (1990)

The Dragon's Boy (1990)

Elfabet: An ABC of Elves (1990)

Sky Dogs (1990)

Tam Lin: An Old Ballad (1990)

All Those Secrets of the World (1991)

Eeny, Meeny, Miney Mole (1992)

Encounter (1992)

Jane Yolen's Mother Goose Songbook (1992)

Letting Swift River Go (1992)

Wizard's Hall (1992)

Here There Be Dragons (1993)

Honkers (1993)

Jane Yolen's Songs of Summer (1993)

Mouse's Birthday (1993)

Raining Cats and Dogs (1993)

Welcome to the Greenhouse (1993)

Beneath the Ghost Moon (1994)

Fever Dream (1994)

The Girl in the Golden Bower (1994)

Good Griselle (1994)

Grandad Bill's Song (1994)

Here There Be Unicorns (1994)

Jane Yolen's Old MacDonald Songbook (1994)

Little Mouse and Elephant: A Tale from Turkey (1994)
A retelling.

Old Dame Counterpane (1994)

Sacred Places (1994)

Three Bears Holiday Book (1994)

And Twelve Chinese Acrobats (1995)

The Ballad of the Pirate Queens (1995)

Here There Be Witches (1995)

Merlin and the Dragons (1995)

The Musicians of Bremen: A Tale from Germany (1995)

A Sip of Aesop (1995)

Witches (1995)

Commander Toad Series

Commander Toad in Space (1980)

Commander Toad and the Planet of the Grapes (1982)

Commander Toad and the Big Black Hole (1983)

Commander Toad and the Dis-Asteroid (1985)

Commander Toad and the Intergalactic Spy (1986)

Commander Toad and the Space Pirates (1987)

Piggins Series

Piggins (1987)

Picnic with Piggins (1988)

Piggins and the Royal Wedding (1989)

POETRY

See This Little Line? (1963)

It All Depends (1969)

An Invitation to the Butterfly Ball: A Counting Rhyme (1976)

All in the Woodland Early: An ABC Book (1979)

Dragon Night, and Other Lullabies (1980)

How Beastly! A Menagerie of Nonsense Poems (1980)

Ring of Earth: A Child's Book of Seasons (1986)

The Three Bears Rhyme Book (1987)

Best Witches: Poems for Halloween (1989)

Bird Watch: A Book of Poetry (1990)

Street Rhymes Around the World (1992)

What Rhymes with Moon? (1993)

Animal Fare: Poems (1994)

O Jerusalem: Voices of a Sacred City (1995)

Welcome to the Sea of Sand (1995)

DRAMA

Robin Hood (first produced in 1967)

The Bird of Time (first produced in 1982)

ADULT FICTION

Tales of Wonder (1983)
Short stories.

Cards of Grief (1984)

Merlin's Booke (1984)

Dragonfield, and Other Stories (1985)
Short stories.

Sister Light, Sister Dark (1988)

White Jenna (1989), sequel to *Sister Light, Sister Dark*

EDITOR

The Fireside Song Book of Birds and Beasts (1972)

Zoo 2000: Twelve Stories of Science Fiction and Fantasy Beasts (1973)

Rounds About Rounds (1977)

Shape Shifters: Fantasy and Science Fiction Tales About Humans Who Can Change Their Shapes (1978)

Dragons and Dreams (1986) with Martin H. Greenberg and Charles G. Waugh

Favorite Folktales from Around the World (1986)

The Lullaby Songbook (1986)

Spaceships and Spells: A Collection of New Fantasy and Science Fiction Stories (1987) with Martin H. Greenberg and Charles G. Waugh

Werewolves: A Collection of Original Stories (1988) with Martin H. Greenberg

The Laptime Song and Play Book (1989)

Things That Go Bump in the Night (1989) with Martin H. Greenberg

2040 A.D. (1990)

Hark! A Christmas Sampler (1991)

Vampires (1993) with Martin H. Greenberg

2041 A.D.: Twelve Stories About the Future by Top Science Fiction Writers (1994)

Camelot (1994)

Xanadu (1994)

Xanadu 2 (1994) with Martin H. Greenberg

Camelot (1995)

The Haunted House (1995) with Martin H. Greenberg

Xanadu 3 (1995)

CONTRIBUTOR

Dragons of Light, edited by Orson Scott Card (1981)

Elsewhere, vol. I, edited by Terri Windling and Mark Alan Arnold (1981)

Elsewhere, vol. II, edited by Terri Windling and Mark Alan Arnold (1982)

Hecate's Cauldron, edited by Jessica Amanda Salmonson (1982)

Faery!, edited by Terri Windling (1983)

Imaginary Lands, edited by Robin McKinley (1985)

Liavek, edited by Will Shetterly and Emma Bull (1985)

Moonsinger's Friends, edited by Susan Schwartz (1985)

Liavek: The Players of Luck, edited by Will Shetterly and Emma Bull (1986)

Liavek: Wizard's Row, edited by Will Shetterly and Emma Bull (1987)

Visions, edited by Donald R. Gallo (1987)

Arabesques: More Tales of the Arabian Nights, edited by Susan Schwartz (1988)

Invitation to Camelot, edited by Parke Godwin (1988)

Liavek: Spells of Binding, edited by Will Shetterly and Emma Bull (1988)

The Unicorn Treasury, edited by Bruce Coville (1988)

The Outspoken Princess and the Gentle Knight, edited by Jack Zipes (1994)

FOR FURTHER READING

Alsdurf, Phyllis E. "An Imagination Feast: Phyllis E. Alsdurf Talks with Jane Yolen." *Children's Book Review Magazine*, spring 1995.

Godown, Jan Florence. "An Interview with Jane Yolen on Tales and Transformations." *Storytelling Magazine*, January 1996.

Jane Yolen. New York: Coward-McCann, 1990.

"Jane Yolen." In *Authors & Artists for Young Adults*, edited by Agnes Garrett and Helga P. McCue. Vol. 4. Detroit: Gale Research, 1990.

Jane Yolen: HBJ Profiles. San Diego, CA: Harcourt Brace Jovanovich, 1991.

Yolen, Jane. *Guide to Writing for Children*. Boston: Writer, 1989.

———. *Touch Magic: Fantasy, Faerie and Folklore in the Literature of Childhood*. New York: Philomel, 1981.

———. *Writing Books for Children*. Boston: Writer, 1973.

Zvirin, Stephanie. "Books for Young Adults: 'The Gift of Sarah Baker.' " *Booklist*, 15 May 1981.

Paul Zindel

Family drama

Staten Island, New York
May 15, 1936

The Pigman: A Novel

Nonna Frankie, Italian grandfather to the neighborhood kids, had a great influence on Paul Zindel as a youngster and inspired the character Angelo Pignati in Zindel's popular young adult novel *The Pigman*.

Zindel's father was a police officer who left the family to live with a girlfriend, Zindel wrote in *The Pigman & Me*, a memoir. Zindel's mother, a nurse, and his sister, Betty, frequently moved around—they could not always pay the rent. The biography describes four years they spent next door to a black family in a largely Polish working town called Travis, New York, where Paul's mother got a job with an animal inoculation service and tried to raise collies. With the help of a new friend named Jennifer, Paul created a backyard haven from the town bullies. Nonna Frankie, an elderly Italian man, planted vegetables, asked a running stream of riddles, explained self-defense, and otherwise helped young Paul cope with growing up.

Zindel's memoir is bittersweet. He has amusing recollections of school lunch: "The cafeteria was in the cellar, and you had to get a tray, get on line, and pass by a lot of steam tables where ladies who looked like escaped electric-shock nurses gave you plates of weird-looking food. The hamburgers tasted like filets of kangaroo meat. The spaghetti looked like skinny white worms in red mud. The beef stew was so congealed, you had to smack it with a soupspoon to get it to break up."

Nonna Frankie taught Paul, "*Io sono differente*," meaning, "I am different." It was a way to overcome depression from worrying about dead-end lives and dying. Nonna Frankie, in time, became a father figure to Zindel. "I was breathing and feeling and caring about things, and trusting about being alive," he wrote.

Zindel graduated from Wagner College with a degree in chemistry and went to work for Allied Chemical in New York as a technical writer in 1958. The next year, he became a chemistry teacher at Tottenville High School in Staten Island, leaving ten years later to become a full-time writer of plays and young adult books.

The Pigman (1968), his first book, has been credited with establishing the realistic teenage novel as a distinct genre. The book received a number of awards, including American Library Association Notable Book in 1975 and Horn Book Honor list in 1969.

The Pigman is about John Conlan, a compulsive exaggerator known as the Bathroom Bomber of Franklin High, and Lorraine Jensen, who becomes his friend one day when she gets caught up in his uncontrolled laughing fit on the bus. They become soulmates, both feeling trapped in their dysfunctional homes (his father is an alcoholic, her mother overly demanding). Among their many pranks are phone marathons, calling people at random and trying to see how long they can keep the person on the line. One day Lorraine calls Mr. Pignati, who seems sympathetic to her plea for a donation to a charity. They go to visit him and find the Pigman—so named because of his collection of porcelain pigs—an old and lonely man, fond of telling jokes, making excuses for his wife who is visiting in California (she is really dead), and visiting Bobo the gorilla at the zoo.

John and Lorraine begin visiting the Pigman regularly. He gives them wine and treats them like adults. He inspires them with his memory tricks and comments on life. Then he suffers a heart attack, and a planned welcome-back celebration goes awry. When the Pigman dies, the two blame themselves. Are they murderers? Or were they a last chance at youth for an old man? The loss of Mr. Pignati means a loss within themselves and also a recognition of something within themselves.

"Few books that have been written for young people are as cruelly truthful about the human condition," wrote reviewer Diane Farrell. "Fewer still accord the elderly such serious consideration or perceive that what we term senility may be a symbolic return to youthful honesty and idealism."

"John gains at least a partial understanding not only of his Mexican American neighbors but also of himself. Some people—mostly adults—were shocked by the language in this book," according to Donelson and Nilsen.

Zindel explores the theme further in a sequel, *The Pigman's Legacy*. The story picks up four months later, with the two kids discovering a desperate old man on the run from the tax collector, hiding at the Pigman's house. They decide they have been given a chance to make amends.

"I write for the people who don't like to read, as a rule," Zindel told interviewer Paul Janeczko. "I found that the academic students, the ones from better homes and gardens, so to speak, were able to enjoy a whole range of material. Some were even able to enjoy Shakespeare! But as a rule, that left out an enormous body of students. I found even the subject of chemistry becoming too sophisticated and leaving behind a whole lot of kids, and even those from better homes and gardens weren't able to catch on to the new chemistry. And they had no need for it. They had need for other, more immediate bodies of information."

Zindel's second young adult novel, *My Darling, My Hamburger*, about a high school girl seeking an abortion, was also widely praised for its realistic dialogue and descriptions of teens as misfits or outsiders. The book also was panned by some as failing to follow through on issues raised.

"Teenagers have to rebel," Zindel told interviewer Jean F. Mercier. "It's part of the growing process. In effect, I try to show them they aren't alone in condemning parents and teachers as enemies or ciphers. I believe I must convince my readers that I am on their side."

"Young adult books should be used to improve the lives of our youth," Zindel said in *Literature for Today's Young Adults*. "A book is created by a writer who observes life and then freezes it into words. I think here's where we really need the school experience and the inspired teacher and librarian [to help turn] the words of the book . . . back into life."

Although some have called Zindel's work shallow and simple-minded, others, such as Beverly A. Haley and Kenneth L. Donelson, praise the writer for looking "at the world through the eyes of adolescents, many kinds of adolescents, all trying to find some meaning in a world apparently gone mad, all concerned with man's cruelty and 'matters of consequence.' By selecting an adolescent point of view, Zindel forces the reader to look at the world as if he were awakening to it for the first time, a kind of rebirth."

Zindel has a second career as a dramatist. His first play was inspired by his time in a tuberculosis sanatorium when fifteen. He later took a creative writing course taught by Edward Albee, author of *Who's Afraid of Virginia Woolf?*, and he became a fan of the plays of Tennessee Williams.

While he was teaching school, Zindel wrote his first successful play, *The Effect of Gamma Rays on Man-in-the-Moon Marigolds*. It premiered in 1964 at Houston's Alley Theatre. It is the story of a young girl, Tillie, who lives with her epileptic sister and her abusive mother. She finds fulfillment at last with recognition of her science project at school. Zindel has told interviewers that the story just popped from his head, the mother character, Beatrice, an exaggeration of his own mother.

Two years after its premiere, *Marigolds* was produced for public television, and in 1970 it opened off-Broadway. The playwright received the Obie for Best American Play in 1970, the Drama Desk Award for most promising play in 1970, and the Drama Critic's Circle Award in 1971. *Marigolds* moved to Broadway to the New Theatre, and Zindel won the Pulitzer Prize for drama in 1971. Zindel followed up *Marigolds* with *And Miss Reardon Drinks a Little*, which opened on Broadway in 1971.

In 1973, Zindel married Bonnie Hildebrand, publicity director at the Cleveland Playhouse, where *Marigolds* was being staged. They have two children. They moved to California for Zindel to pursue a new venture in screenwriting for such films as *Mame* and *Runaway Train*.

YOUNG ADULT FICTION

The Pigman: A Novel (1968)
Two lonely high school students meet a strange old man, Mr. Pignati, who dreams and visits his friend the gorilla at the zoo.

My Darling, My Hamburger: A Novel (1969)
A high school girl with abusive parents becomes pregnant and turns to an illegal abortionist.

I Never Loved Your Mind: A Novel (1970)
Dewey Daniels, seventeen and a high school dropout, meets oddball Yvette Goethals when he goes to work as a hospital orderly.

Pardon Me, You're Stepping on My Eyeball: A Novel (1976)
Marsh Mellow writes hate letters, keeps a raccoon in his pocket, and goes nuts for Edna Shinglebox, who looks as freaky and depressed as he does.

Confessions of a Teenage Baboon (1977)
Chris Boyd, sixteen, takes control of his life after meeting an older misfit.

The Undertaker's Gone Bananas (1978)
Bobby Perkins and his only friend, Lauri Geddes, prove that peculiar Mr. Hulka, who lives in the apartment next door, is a murderer.

The Pigman's Legacy (1980), sequel to *The Pigman*
John and Lorraine discover that an old man on the run from the tax collector is hiding in Mr. Pignati's empty house.

A Star for the Latecomer (1980) with Bonnie Zindel
Brooke Hillary, sixteen, would rather attend a Normal School than a special school for actors and musicians.

The Girl Who Wanted a Boy (1981)
Sibella Cametta is a science whiz but feels like a clod around boys.

To Take a Dare (1982) with Crescent Dragonwagon

Harry and Hortense at Hormone High (1984)
The title characters are convinced they are the only enlightened people in their messed-up, miserable high school—until they meet the mysterious and mesmerizing Jason, who believes he is Icarus reincarnated.

The Amazing and Death-Defying Diary of Eugene Dingman (1987)
Eugene begins a personal diary during his summer at an Adirondack resort, where he has a crush on Della and is bothered by big Bunker.

A Begonia for Miss Applebaum (1989)
Henry and Zelda are stunned: Their favorite teacher will not be coming back to school—she has not long to live. They become her companions.

David and Della: A Novel (1993)
David Mahooley is a would-be playwright with writer's block since his girlfriend, Kim, tried to jump out a third-story window in Mrs. Midgeley's biology class.

Loch: A Novel (1994)
At a remote Vermont lake, Loch Perkins, fifteen, aboard a high-tech search yacht, finds a creature that almost eats his girlfriend, Sarah.

The Doom Stone (1995)
A deadly predator stalks Stonehenge.

FICTION FOR YOUNGER READERS

I Love My Mother (1975)

Wacky Facts Lunch Bunch Series

Attack of the Killer Fishsticks (1993)

Fright Party (1993)

The Fifth Grade Safari (1993)

One Hundred Percent Laugh Riot (1994)

ADULT FICTION

When a Darkness Falls (1984)

DRAMA

Dimensions of Peacocks (first produced in 1959)

Euthanasia and the Endless Hearts (first produced in 1960)

A Dream of Swallows (first produced in 1964)

The Effects of Gamma Rays on Man-in-the-Moon Marigolds: A Drama in Two Acts (first produced in 1964)

Let Me Hear You Whisper: A Play (produced as a television play in 1966)

And Miss Reardon Drinks a Little (first produced in 1967)

The Secret Affairs of Mildred Wild: A Comedy in Three Acts (first produced in 1972)

Ladies at the Alamo (first produced in 1975)

The Ladies Should Be in Bed (first produced in 1978)

A Destiny with Half Moon Street (first produced in 1983)

Amulets Against the Dragon Forces (first produced in 1989)

SCREENPLAYS AND TELEPLAYS

The Effect of Gamma Rays on Man-in-the-Moon Marigolds: A Drama in Two Acts (1966)

Let Me Hear You Whisper: A Play (1966)

Up the Sandbox (1972)
Adapted from the Annie Roiphe novel.

Mame (1973)
Adapted from Patrick Dennis's *Auntie Mame.*

Alice in Wonderland (1985)
Adapted from Lewis Carroll's books.

Maria's Lovers (1985) with Gerard Brach, Andrei Konchalovsky, and Marjorie David

Babes in Toyland (1986)
Based on Victor Herbert's operetta.

Runaway Train (1986) with Djordje Milicevic and Edward Bunker

A Connecticut Yankee in King Arthur's Court (1989)
Based on Mark Twain's novel.

FOR FURTHER READING

Angelotti, Michael. *A Teacher's Guide to* Harry and Hortense at Hormone High *by Paul Zindel*. New York: Bantam Books, 1984.

Donelson, Kenneth L., and Alleen Pace Nilsen, eds. "The People Behind the Books: Paul Zindel." In *Literature for Today's Young Adults*. Glenview, IL: Scott, Foresman, 1980.

Farrell, Diane. "The Pigman." *Horn Book Magazine*, February 1969.

Haley, Beverly A., and Kenneth L. Donelson. "Pigs and Hamburgers, Cadavers and Gamma Rays: Paul Zindel's Adolescents." *Elementary English*, October 1974.

Hipple, Theodore W. *A Teacher's Guide to the Novels of Paul Zindel*. New York: Bantam Books, 1988.

Janeczko, Paul. "In Their Own Words, an Interview with Paul Zindel." *English Journal*, October 1977.

Mercier, Jean F. "Paul Zindel." *Publishers Weekly*, 5 December 1977.

Zindel, Paul. *The Pigman & Me*. New York: HarperCollins, 1991.

Author/Title/Series Index

Genre Index